THE WINES OF FRANCE

THE WINES OF FRANCE

THE ESSENTIAL GUIDE FOR SAVVY SHOPPERS

JACQUELINE FRIEDRICH

This book would never have seen the light of day if not for my super (in every sense of the word) agent Jane Dystel and Lorena Jones, Meghan Keeffe, and Aaron Wehner at the fiercely (and blessedly) independent Ten Speed Press.

Many people helped in its realization, among them Christine Ontivero, Wink Lorch, Michel Piron Soulat, Jean-Louis Carbonnier, Kermit Lynch and his staff, Guy and Annie Bossard, Alain and Isabelle Hasard, Jean-Yves Bizot, Michel and Thérèse Riouspeyrous, François Laplace, Peter Vezan, Philippe Blanc, Rémy Gresser and the following Interprofessional Committees: Alsace, Champagne, Beaujolais (special thanks to Anne Masson and Ludovic), Burgundy (particularly the irrepressibly garrulous Herve Bianchi), Jura (and Laurent Courthial), Provence, Bergerac (especially Marie-Pierre Tamagnon), Languedoc (particularly Jean-Philippe Granier), InterRhône and, in Châteauneuf-du-Pape, Michel Blanc and Audrey Domenech.

Finally, I'll never be able to adequately thank Peter M. F. Sichel but I can keep trying whenever the opportunity presents itself.

Ten Speed Press
Box 7123
Berkeley, California 94707
www.tenspeed.com

Distributed in Australia by Simon and Schuster Australia, in Canada by Ten Speed Press Canada, in New Zealand by Southern Publishers Group, in South Africa by Real Books, and in the United Kingdom and Europe by Publishers Group UK.

Cover and text design by Ed Anderson
Production by Jeff Brandenburg

Library of Congress Cataloging-in-Publication Data
Friedrich, Jacqueline.
The wines of France : the essential guide for savvy shoppers / Jacqueline Friedrich.
p. cm.
Includes index.
ISBN-13: 978-1-58008-688-2 (pbk.)
ISBN-10: 1-58008-688-8 (pbk.)
1. Wine and wine making—France. I. Title.
TP553.F755 2006
641.2'20944—dc22
2006023746

Printed in the United States of America
First printing, 2006

1 2 3 4 5 6 7 8 9 10 — 10 09 08 07 06

CONTENTS

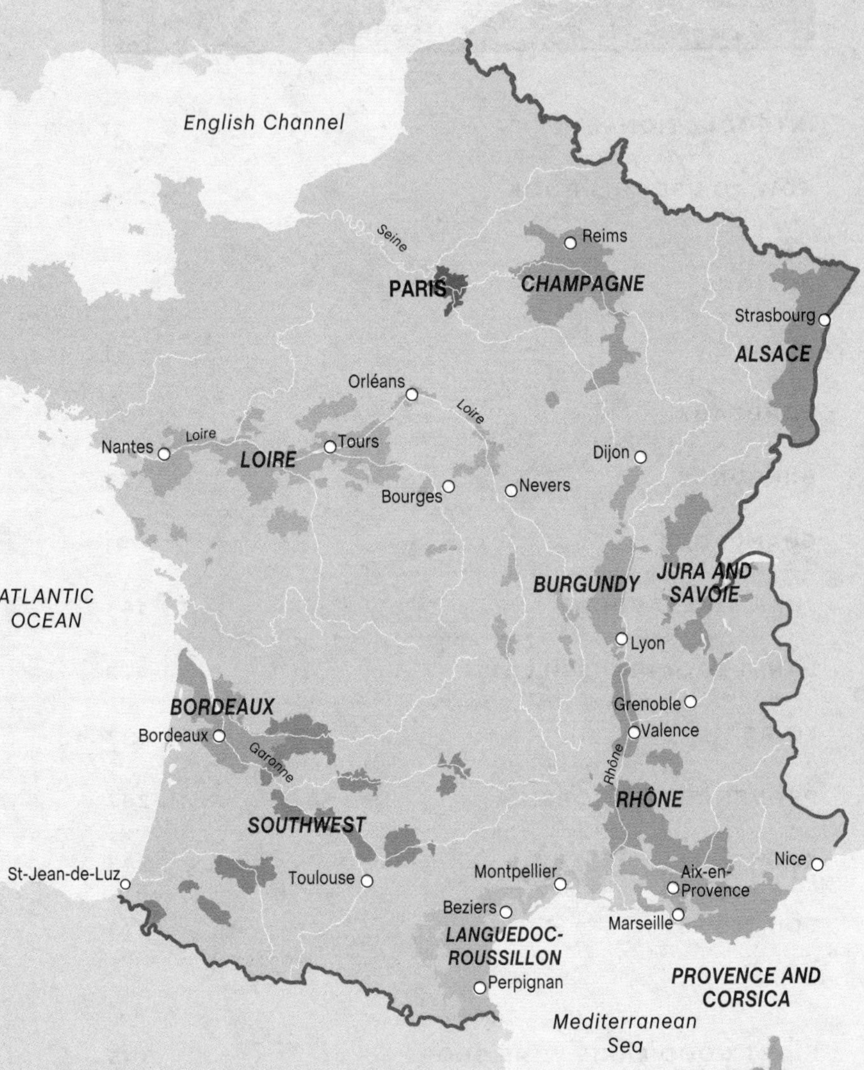
FRANCE
English Channel
Seine
PARIS
Reims
CHAMPAGNE
Strasbourg
ALSACE
Orléans
Loire
Nantes
Loire
LOIRE
Tours
Dijon
Bourges
Nevers
ATLANTIC
OCEAN
BURGUNDY
JURA AND
SAVOIE
Lyon
BORDEAUX
Grenoble
Bordeaux
Valence
Garonne
Rhône
RHÔNE
SOUTHWEST
Nice
St-Jean-de-Luz
Toulouse
Montpellier
Aix-en-
Provence
Beziers
Marseille
LANGUEDOC-
ROUSSILLON
PROVENCE AND
CORSICA
Perpignan
Mediterranean
Sea

INTRODUCTION

Recently I was dining in a nice little restaurant in an up-and-coming neighborhood in Paris. It was a casual storefront with ambitious food and a sensational wine list, featuring leading producers from emerging regions like Irancy, Collioure, Minervois, Cheverny, Faugères, and Pic St.-Loup.

Now, the waitress could not have been more accommodating, but she knew zilch about wine. A pretty, smiling slip of a girl, she asked, "Red or white?" when I ordered a bottle of Chablis. And she gamely attempted to speak English with a couple from Massachusetts, who in turn, gamely tried to speak French, resorting to their dictionary to find the word for glass.

Not an atypical state of affairs. But what would have happened had the New Englanders wanted more than just a glass each of the house red and had asked for suggestions on selecting a bottle? I can't imagine that that waitress, no matter how agreeable, could have intelligently advised the couple. What they needed, in addition to their dictionary, was a portable guide to the wines of France.

Proselytizer that I am, I probably would have leaned back in my chair and given them a rundown on all the wines being offered. And that, in essence, is what I'm doing here. This book is meant to be your very own personal shopper, the busybody leaning over your shoulder, giving you the guidance you need to buy a bottle of wine you'll find delicious—no matter what the price or when you want to serve it, whether it's for a cozy meal in front of the TV or a lavish dinner party for so-called connoisseurs—like me.

How did a middle-class girl from South Orange, New Jersey (that would be me) get to be such a maven? I was hardly to the manner born. My childhood home on your basic Norman Rockwell block was a wine-free zone. We drank milk, soda, fruit juice, coffee, and tap water (with ice made by the refrigerator). My first wine loves were Riunite Lambrusco, Lancers, and Mateus.

Fast-forward through years of wine clubs, informal tasting groups, wine-motivated travel, an expanding wine library, not to mention a bulging wine "cellar," a move to France to write a book on the wines of the Loire, followed by years of crisscrossing the French vineyards, serving on wine juries, meeting, talking, listening, and tasting, tasting, tasting. But enough about me.

My mission is to convince you that wine is not a closed, exclusive club. If I could learn, anyone can learn. And wine is actually an ordered universe. It's not random or chaotic, although, like art or music, it can be somewhat complicated. The world of wine is so interesting that the more you learn, the more you want to learn. Wine opens up all kinds of windows; it invites you into the culture and history of its place of origin. And it's just damned delicious.

Now, a couple of words—maybe fighting words—about French wine. Starting with this: France is the greatest winemaking country in the world. And it always will be, at least in our lifetimes.

France created the benchmarks for most, if not all, the classic wines in the world. That pinot noir they're freaking out about in the movie *Sideways*? Benchmark: Burgundy. That exciting sauvignon blanc from New Zealand? Benchmark: the Loire. That sensational shiraz from Australia? Benchmark: the Rhône. And so on.

Further, no one country can compete with France when it comes to diversity. I don't mean simple diversity. Many countries are capable of making an encyclopedic range of wines, but only France has proved that it can excel in every last one of the styles.

Wine is important to France. It's the country's primary agricultural export. And the history of wine in France is long and turbulent. Anything but calm, today's climate is best characterized by Dickens: it's the best of times and the worst of times.

You may have heard about a crisis in French wine. Well, it's real, it's many-tentacled, and it won't be solved overnight. For one, France took too long to recognize that it was no longer the only kid on the block, that it has significant competition, particularly from what's called the New World. Global politics, the strength of the dollar, and labor costs all play a part. Important châteaux—Montrose, for example, or Taittinger—are sold daily. Disgruntled growers in the Languedoc make headlines when they loot and riot, demanding additional state aid. And quite simply France is making too much wine.

That said, we are simultaneously living in a golden age of French wine. Many of the post–World War II practices that resulted in substandard wines are gradually but systematically being corrected. These practices included excessive grape yields (some as high as 150 hectoliters a hectare, which translates as close to eleven tons per acre), the harvesting of unripe grapes followed by the seemingly obligatory addition of industrial amounts of sugar to boost alcohol levels, and a general lack of hygiene. Further, "progress" came along in the form of mechanization (tractors, machine harvesters) and science (clones, aromatic yeasts, chemical fertilizers, and weed killers). Some of these were outright boons, making the vigneron's life easier; others would prove to be booby traps; and still others simply needed—and may still need—perfecting. Much of the worst wine was bottled and sold by *négociants,* who had come to be regarded as smirking, mustache-twirling villains.

Over the past fifteen years I've witnessed a dramatic evolution toward quality—a general lowering of yields, although many are still too high; a serious reduction of chaptalization (the addition of sugar); more enlightened use of machine harvesters; and a decisive move away from chemical vine treatments. Additionally, cooperative cellars have improved radically. There are more than a few that are downright enlightened when it comes to grape growing, winemaking, and wine marketing. There's a new generation of *négociants* who seem every bit as artistic as some of France's most idealistic and scrupulous vignerons. The Vin de Pays category has exploded in several very interesting directions. Along with little country wines (sometimes charming, sometimes not), there are now varietal wines—labeled chardonnay, merlot, sauvignon blanc, and so forth—that are fully competitive with their New World analogues. And there are the iconoclasts making wines that don't fit within the letter of the law so they turn their backs on the supposedly prestigious Appellation Contrôlée status to which their wines might have been entitled had they been willing to conform to the law's dictates—like using only the grape varieties permitted for their location. Instead, much like Italy's super Tuscans, they "demote" their wines to Vin de Pays—although they're usually a whole lot more expensive than their Appellation Contrôlée counterparts. Taking matters still further are the exponents of two more trends: "cult" or "garage" wine and what I call hypernatural wine. I think of these developments as some sort of atonement for "the sins of the fathers."

EXTREME WINES: THE WINES OF REDEMPTION

What are they? Cult wines might be considered the Pradas of the wine world. Initially, they were dubbed "garage" wines because they were made—literally—in a garage by someone with a couple of rows of vines but no winery. The *garagiste* tended his or her small parcel of vines as assiduously as a city dweller fusses over the basil and chives growing in pots on the windowsill. This level of diligence was maintained even after the vineyards expanded exponentially and the winemaking was transferred to state-of-the-art facilities. The *garagiste* kept yields extremely low—say, 20 hectoliters per hectare (or 1.42 tons an acre), or even lower. Then came tender loving vinification in the cleanest of cellars and the priciest of new oak barrels. No expense was spared, including the hiring such of high-profile wine consultants as Michel Rolland. And the resulting wines were plush, immediately seductive, awash in sumptuous ripe fruit and fine oak flavors, and low in acid; any abrasive tannins were absent. Made like haute couture, they were as expensive as haute couture. The movement started on the Right Bank of Bordeaux, primarily in St.-Émilion, but has since spread throughout France.

As for the hypernatural, you may have noticed that an increasing number of French wines are named after a specific soil type, like Didier Dagueneau's Silex. And that more and more winemakers put the humble tools of their trade, such as pruning shears, on the label. Here you have entered the world of the "Friends of the Earth." Ecologically friendly winemaking is one of the strongest trends in French viticulture. It takes a number of forms. The mildest is probably *lutte raisonnée* (literally, reasoned battle), a nondogmatic, basically undefined approach in which chemical treatments are used only when deemed absolutely necessary. Then there's organic winemaking. And there's the biodynamic method, a system whose principles were first spelled out by Rudolph Steiner, in which homeopathic vine treatments are used and vineyard operations are scheduled by the positions of the planets. Even more radical theories involve the influence of magnetic forces on wine.

Hypernaturalism goes further. *Hypernatural* is a word I've coined to cover wines made with the least intervention possible, using wild yeasts, no chaptalization, no acidification, no fining, no filtration, no added sulfur. Here, the resulting wines range from a fuzzy brew that might have been made by a caveman to something as polished and magnificent as one of the Prada-ish cult wines. One thing's for sure: purer wines you'll never taste.

Both cult-garage and hypernatural wines are controversial for reasons too numerous and contentious to discuss fully here. I would just like to point out that when you are shopping there are a couple of things to bear in mind. Where the cult wines are concerned, particularly the reds, the grapes are so ripe, sometimes overripe, that the wines may be overwhelmingly rich. They may take on a Port-like aspect and have sweet (or sweet-seeming) finishes. If you're having a dinner party, however, a glass or two per person will surely please the crowd.

Like the cult wines, hypernatural wines are also based on very low-yielding vines and very ripe grapes. By forgoing all the interventionist options, winemakers are, in effect, working without a net and exposing their wines to many risks that may result in off flavors and undesirable textures, some of which will disappear with aeration. When a wine has a prickly sensation for example, I simply pour it into a carafe and wait for it to settle down once it's had time to aerate.

Detractors have little patience with either style. A pity. I feel both schools are part of the same revolution. There's a common search for quality, for excellence, and/or "truth"—an attempt to make the best wine that can possibly be made—the definition of *best,* of course, depending on your philosophical or gustatory orientation. And both are motivated by a similar repudiation of past abuses. High yields? We'll get the lowest yields possible. Dead soils owing to chemical fertilizers and weed killers? We go organic or biodynamic or a variation thereon. Unripe grapes? We'll get that fruit to ripen to previously unimaginable levels, even if that results in heavy, cloying, or fragile wines. Each school has pushed its theories to the limit.

It is in the nature of revolutions to go too far. My hope is that with time (and luck) an equilibrium will be found. As vintners espousing either ideology feel less of a need to prove their point, when they realize they have essentially won the war, maybe they'll loosen up a bit and their wines will become less dogmatic. Or maybe I just want their Platonic idea of wine to correspond to my own.

That's another thing about French wine: never a dull moment.

HOW TO USE THIS BOOK

OVERVIEW

The book is divided into ten chapters, organized by region: Alsace, Bordeaux, Burgundy (including Beaujolais and Chablis), Champagne, Jura and Savoie, Languedoc-Roussillon, the Loire, Provence and Corsica, the Rhône, and the Southwest.

Each chapter starts with a broad overview of the region: where it is, what types of wine it makes (in terms of both appellations and wine styles), and the grape varieties it uses. Notes on vintages and prices follow.

The meat of each chapter is the following section. There are individual entries for both appellations and producers. Terminology specific to a given region is also explained.

The individual entries are organized alphabetically. Note, however, that producers whose wineries begin with the word *château* or *domaine* (followed or not by *de, du, de la,* and so on) are alphabetized according to the first identifying noun, adjective, verb, or adverb. Thus, Château des Jolies Filles would be listed under *J.* Also, where a producer uses his or her own name, the entry is alphabetized using the family name; thus, Domaine Henry Marionnet would be listed under the *M*s.

Appellations are distinguished in the book's layout by shaded boxes in which you'll find a description covering its defining factors. (Appellation Contrôlée is abbreviated as AC, Vin Délimité de Qualité Supérieure as VDQS.) This is followed by a list of all the recommended producers in that AC. Producers whose domaines are listed in small caps have individual entries; the others are described in a clause following the name of their property. (There is no profound distinction between producers who get their own entry and those who don't. In some cases, it's because I have more to say; in others, it's because I'm trying to save space, in still others, it's that I want to single someone out even though the entry is short enough to have kept the producer in the appellation box.)

At the end of each chapter is a crib sheet with listings of recommended producers in three categories: Must Trys, Smart Buys, and Safe Houses.

Wherever possible I tried not to use a producer in more than one category—despite the fact that they might qualify for two or even all three. Feel free, then, to scramble the listings, particularly those in Must Trys and Safe Houses.

THE BUCK STOPS HERE

I alone chose the wineries included in this guide. My criteria were very simple: if I liked a wine well enough to want to buy a bottle or if I found it interesting enough to want to taste it by the glass, the winery was included. I lowered the bar slightly in the case of very well known or widely distributed wines. But even those had to pass a "well, OK, I'll drink it" test.

RATINGS

There are no numerical ratings in this book. Inclusion in the guide is a recommendation in itself. A star (☆) appears by some producers, an up-arrow (↑) appears by others. Here is my rating system:

- No star or up-arrow: good to very good.
- Star: very good to sublime—breathtaking.
- Up-arrow: on the rise; worth following.

VINTAGES

I spend relatively little time discussing vintages. There are a number of reasons. My top three? First, the practical—when selecting wine, whether in a restaurant or a shop, the (or my, anyway) first consideration is the producer. If I see a winery I love on a list, I tend to buy whatever vintage is on hand. Next, there are fewer and fewer truly disastrous vintages, and short of a catastrophe (which occasionally happens even to the best vintners), the good producers usually manage to make something nice. Finally, unless we want computerized viticulture and winemaking, we ought to accept the vagaries of vintage as part of the miracle of wine—accepting (philosophically) the excesses of 2003, say, as we do the weaknesses of 2002 in the southern Rhône. I recommend recent vintages because that's what you're likely to encounter. When the vintage appears in parentheses it means that I have some reservations about the year, and I've probably discussed my concerns in the beginning of the chapter. These are vintages in which you should buy from tried-and-true producers. And, since some wines age fantastically well, I've included legendary vintages in these cases.

A TALE OF THREE VINTAGES

It's highly unusual to be able to make generalizations about a particular vintage for an entire country. Indeed, it's often difficult to generalize about any given vintage within a small region. Nevertheless, certain conclusions can be made about French wine in the 2005, 2004, and 2003 vintages.

The 2003 season broke every record with its high temperatures. Even the nights were intolerable. Grape vines shut down and their fruit stopped ripening. In some regions grapes burned on the vines. Yields were extremely low. Quality was uneven. Many of the wines turned out jammy, flabby, and tasting like cooked fruit; others pinch the palate with awkwardly added acid; still others have lots of natural alcohol but unripe, herbaceous flavors. There are, of course, lots of beauties. And northern regions—like the Loire and Chablis—may win over consumers with their atypically fat wines. But while some herald 2003 as a great year, I have serious doubts. Structurally, the wines seem fragile; I think most will evolve quickly. The two words that sum up the vintage are *extreme* and *unprecedented.* Buy accordingly.

In contrast, 2004 was a return to classicism throughout France. One caveat: yields. The vines responded to the conditions of 2003 with record crop potentials. The producers who thinned clusters and kept yields within reason made good, classic wine. Others produced dilute, watery wine.

As I write this, the first major tastings of the 2005 vintage have begun and the reactions have been ecstatic. It's a stellar year in just about every region in France. Even the appellations that fared less than brilliantly will have made good wine. So 2005 may be the first "vintage of the century" of the twenty-first century. Buy without fear.

PRICES

These are necessarily very approximate. While it would be feasible to cite you the exact price of a wine leaving its winery in France, it's nearly hopeless to try to tell you what a French wine is going to cost once it arrives on a shelf or wine list in the United States. Many factors come into play, including the state of the dollar, the retailer's markup, and the method chosen by the importer to transport the wines from one country to another. (Some just ship the stuff any old way; others give the wines tender loving care, starting with controlled temperatures. While that adds to the cost of the wine, it is obviously preferable.)

With this in mind the dollar signs you will see translate as follows:

- $ indicates that the wines cost up to $10
- $$ means the wines cost from $11 to $24
- $$$ means the wines cost from $25 to $55
- $$$$ indicates that the wines cost more than $55
  (note that these can cost significantly more than $55)

When a dollar sign appears in parentheses, for example $$($), it means that the wine is on the cusp of the two price ranges.

WHAT'S IN A NAME?

Winemaking goes back many centuries in France; relocating from one region to another is fairly recent. Thus, in any given wine region (or village) you'll find many people with the same name, such as Reverdy in Sancerre or Tissot in the Jura. Given names—Jean, for example, as opposed to Bernard, Christophe, or Eusèbe—count.

Producers have a perverse tendency to change the names of their domaines. One day it's Clos, the next it's Ferme, a week later it's the family name of the vintner in question. When you are looking for a particular producer, it's a good idea to scan the entire list of domaines recommended under a given appellation.

A FINAL PIECE OF ADVICE

This book is meant to help you in your hour(s) of vinous need—to ensure, as much as possible, that you never drink a bad and/or uninteresting bottle of French wine. Don't leave home without it!

ALSACE

BORDEAUX
BURGUNDY
CHAMPAGNE
JURA AND SAVOIE
LANGUEDOC-ROUSSILLON
LOIRE
PROVENCE AND CORSICA
RHÔNE
SOUTHWEST

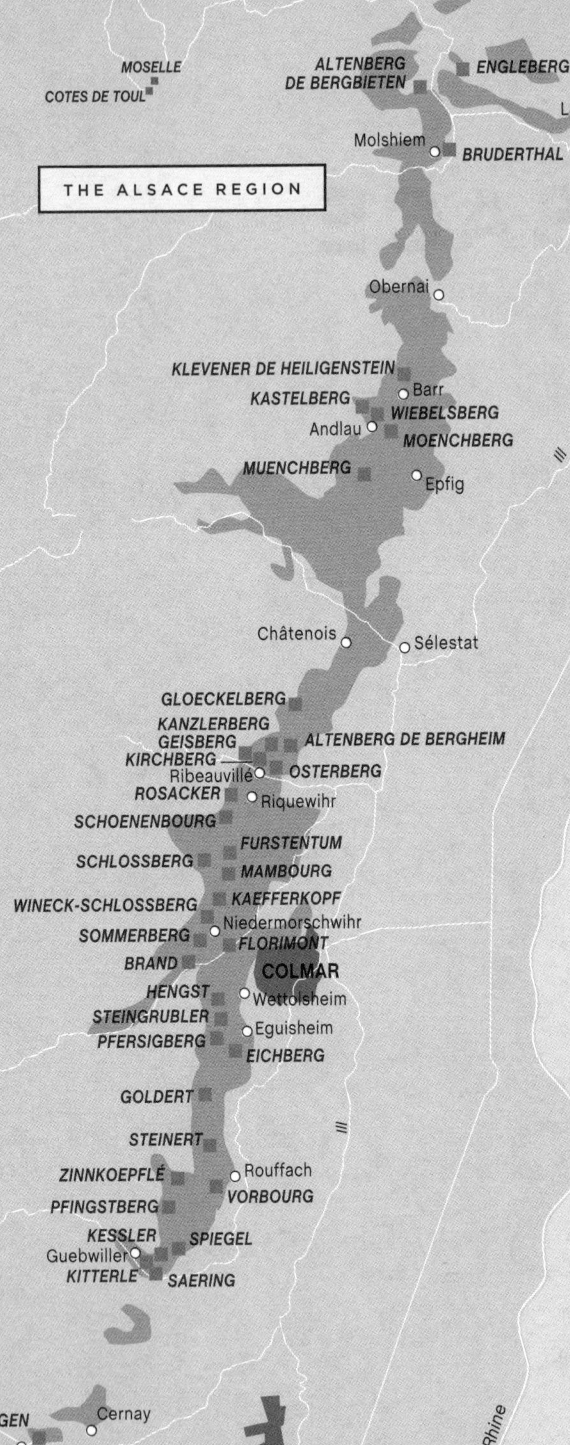
THE ALSACE REGION
MOSELLE
COTES DE TOUL
ALTENBERG DE BERGBIETEN
ENGLEBERG
STRASBOURG
Scheltigheim
Langolsheim
Ostwald
Illkirch-Graffenstaden
Molshiem
BRUDERTHAL
Obernai
Erstein
KLEVENER DE HEILIGENSTEIN
KASTELBERG
Barr
WIEBELSBERG
Andlau
MOENCHBERG
MUENCHBERG
Epfig
Ill
Châtenois
Sélestat
Rhine
GLOECKELBERG
KANZLERBERG
GEISBERG
ALTENBERG DE BERGHEIM
KIRCHBERG
Ribeauvillé
OSTERBERG
ROSACKER
Riquewihr
SCHOENENBOURG
FURSTENTUM
SCHLOSSBERG
MAMBOURG
WINECK-SCHLOSSBERG
KAEFFERKOPF
Niedermorschwihr
SOMMERBERG
FLORIMONT
BRAND
COLMAR
GERMANY
HENGST
Wettolsheim
STEINGRUBLER
Eguisheim
PFERSIGBERG
EICHBERG
GOLDERT
Ill
STEINERT
Rouffach
ZINNKOEPFLÉ
VORBOURG
PFINGSTBERG
KESSLER
SPIEGEL
Guebwiller
KITTERLE
SAERING
RANGEN
Cernay
Thann
Rhine
PARIS
MULHOUSE

Bordered by the Vosges mountains to the west and the Rhine River to the east, the region of Alsace snakes its way in a long, thin line from Marlenheim, due west of Strasbourg in the north, to Thann, due west of Mulhouse in the south. Its route encompasses the picturesque towns of Colmar, Ribeauvillé, and Riquewihr and scores of smaller villages where pots of flourishing geraniums decorate half-timbered houses. The region is dominated by white wines but is also the source of light, lean reds that are improving in quality.

The Alsace Appellation Contrôlée (AC) is unusual for France in that, with a few exceptions (which will be explained below), most of the wines are made from a single grape variety and the name of that grape is stated prominently on the label. Alsace Grand Cru, a superior appellation with stricter rules, shifts the emphasis to *terroir*. Fifty-one exceptional sites have been recognized and accorded *grand cru* status. Their names, such as Hengst or Furstentum, appear on labels accompanied, in most cases, by the name of a grape variety.

(Noteworthy Grand Crus are listed here alphabetically with an indication of their geographic location and a list of some of their best producers.) There are also many respected *lieux-dits*. These names also appear on labels although they are not independent ACs.

In general, wines labeled simply Alsace will be dry or off-dry. Grand Cru wines range from dry to decidedly sweet. When the AC on the label is accompanied by the designation Vendange Tardive (VT), indicating it was made from late-harvested, overripe grapes, or Sélection de Grains Nobles (SGN), made from botrytized grapes harvested by successive passes through the vineyard, the wine will be richer and, in most cases, sweet to intensely sweet. It is illegal to chaptalize either VTs or SGNs.

There are two additional ACs, Crémant d'Alsace, sparkling wines made by the *méthode traditionelle,* and Klevener de Heiligenstein, dry whites made from the klevener grape in and around Heiligenstein.

THE MAIN GRAPES: Riesling, gewürztraminer, muscat, sylvaner, pinot blanc, pinot noir, and pinot gris. (In Alsace, pinot gris is synonymous with tokay. Sometimes both names appear on the label. Because of possible confusion with Hungary's Tokaj, European law may eventually prohibit the use of the word *tokay,* but this has not yet come to pass.) The grapes for Grand Cru, Vendange Tardive, and Sélection de Grains Nobles wines include riesling, pinot gris, gewürztraminer, and muscat. Additionally, wine made by "complantation"—a field selection of a variety of grapes within the vineyard—is now permitted in the Grand Cru Altenberg de Bergheim and Kaefferkopf. It is likely that, as of the 2005 harvest, sylvaner will be added to the list of grapes permitted in Grand Cru Schwartzenberg.

THE SECONDARY GRAPES: Klevener de Heiligenstein (not to be confused with klevner, a commonly used name for grapes in the pinot family, particularly pinot blanc), chasselas, pinot beurot (an ancestor of pinot gris), and auxerrois, a white grape often blended with and frequently mistaken for pinot blanc. A wine made from pure auxerrois is usually soft and spicy. (In the southwestern region of Cahors, auxerrois is an alternative name for malbec, a black grape.)

STYLES OF WINE: The simplest wines are emphatically fruit driven, with fresh, clear flavors and lively acidity. They are usually dry or off-dry and should be drunk "on the fruit," within three to five years of the harvest. Wines from *lieux-dits* and Grands Crus should be complex, structured, less "varietal," and more *terroir*-driven, often with backbones of steel and the appetizing flavors of such medicinal herbs as chamomile and verbena. When well made, these wines are majestic, complex, and long-lived. A number are breathtakingly beautiful. It's an aggravating problem that few Alsace wines in this category indicate their level of sweetness. Some enlightened winemakers now specify, at least on the back label, the amount of residual sugar or whether the wine is dry, *moelleux*, or *liquoreux*.

BEST VINTAGES: The 2005 vintage is expected to be great. Viewed as a return to classicism after the "Mediterranean" summer of 2003, 2004 is appreciated for its vivacity and balance. But as elsewhere, unless controlled by the vintner, yields were high. Most of the vintners recommended here did control yields. The year 2003 is exceptional. It's interesting to note that the robust health of the grapes greatly reduced the production of Sélection de Grains Nobles. There is, however, a good quantity of Vendange Tardive. The weather during the 2002 growing season was variable—as was the quality. The wines run the gamut from thin and bland to sumptuous. Stick to recommended producers. The 2001 growing season was saved by an Indian summer. The rieslings are particularly successful. Some have hailed 2000 as a great vintage; others say the wines are open, fruity, and pleasing but less complex than they might be. Past great vintages: 1990, 1989, 1976.

PRICES: $ to $$$$.

PRODUCERS: In this chapter, all the producers have separate entries. Most make many different wines each year, as many as thirty-five, usually starting with a line of simple wines and graduating to *lieux-dits*, Grand Cru, Vendange Tardive, and Sélection de Grains Nobles. Two things worth noting: Many producers represent the eleventh, twelfth, or thirteenth generation working the same vines. And Alsace is the region with the greatest percentage of vintners practicing organic or biodynamic viticulture.

IMPORTANT ADVICE: If you are not yet in love with Alsace wines, do yourself a favor and try at least three wines from producers on the crib sheet or any of the starred producers.

Domaine Jean-Baptiste Adam ☆

68770 Ammerschwihr; 03.89.78.23.21; www.jb-adam.com; $ to $$
An excellent address for wines that are smooth, soigné, and full of character. Riesling from Grand Cru Wineck-Schlossberg is fresh as a waterfall, with endless flavors of lemon, lime, steel, and medicinal herbs like chamomile, linden blossom, and verbena. The off-dry Kaefferkopf Cuvée Traditionnelle (no grape is specified) is focused, textured, fragrant, and mineral. The gewürztraminer VT is downright seductive (and went beautifully well with an apple-based dessert). And the oak-aged pinot noir was a refined, ambitious light red.

Domaine Lucien Albrecht ☆

68500 Orschwihr; 03.89.76.95.18; www.lucien-albrecht.com; $ to $$$$
In the process of converting to organic viticulture, this large family domaine produces excellent wine on every level, from the fragrant pinot gris Cuvée Romanus, with its gorgeous focus, to the pinot gris SGN, picked berry by botrytized berry, a voluptuous melding of honey, white-fleshed peaches, and dried fruit flavors. In between there is, perhaps, the best Alsace pinot noir I've tasted, the concentrated, Burgundian Amplus, based on low yields, long maceration, and aging in new French oak. And there are the gems from Grand Cru Pfingstberg, of which the Albrechts are the largest proprietors, as well as being the sole owners of the Clos Schild, a parcel in the heart of the *cru* from which they make a graceful, pure, almost creamy riesling. The Albrechts are also the sole owners of the Clos Himmelreich. The riesling from this vineyard is exquisitely *terroir*-driven, like lace tatted from steel wire. Not only does their gewürztraminer VT taste like a celestial honey made from chamomile and linden blossom, its back label also gives nice consumer-friendly information—like the amount of residual sugar (52 grams per liter in this case), useful for deciding when, and with what, to serve the wine.

Altenberg de Bergbieten

Grand Cru due west of Strasbourg. Producers: DOM MOCHEL ◆ ROLAND SCHMITT.

Altenberg de Bergheim

Grand Cru slightly northeast of Ribeauvillé. Notably permits wines made from a blend of grapes. Producers: DOM MARCEL DEISS ◆ GUSTAVE LORENTZ ◆ SYLVIE SPIELMANN.

Frédéric Arbogast

67310 Westhoffen; 03.88.50.30.51; fredarbogast@wanadoo.fr; $ to $$
This good family domaine makes lovely rieslings from both Grand Cru Bruderthal, which are serious and extremely mineral, and the old vines on the *lieu-dit* Geierstein, which are lightish and floral. The focused VT gewürztraminer is simultaneously lush and airy. Its pinot noir is an honest-to-god light red that bursts with character.

Barmès-Buecher ☆

68920 Wettolsheim; 03.89.80.62.92; barmesbuecher@terre-net.fr; $$ to $$$$
François Barmès and Genevieve Buecher, with 16 hectares spread out over ninety parcels, including three Grand Crus, converted their vines to biodynamics in 1998. I'm pretty much of a fan. The simplest wines, such as the *edelzwicker,* the riesling Tradition, and the pinot blanc Rosenberg de Wettolsheim, are delicious. My favorite wines, the rieslings and gewürztraminers from Grand Cru Hengst, are majestic, simultaneously potent and subtle. In addition, there are scores of delectable discoveries, such as the unfiltered old-vines pinot noir from Hengst; and both Calcarius and the sweeter Silicis in the pinot gris from Rosenberg de Wettolsheim, each of which is beautifully balanced and appetizingly racy. From Grand Cru Steingrubler

there's an excellent off-dry riesling and a thrilling waterfall of a gewürztraminer. A crystalline pinot gris SGN from Herrenweg de Turckheim has succulent flavors of melon and exotic fruit. A charming and fascinating blend of thirteen grape varieties called Sept Grains is made from the juice that flows freely from the harvest sorting table before the grapes have been pressed. And the muscat ottonel SGN is so thick with residual sugar it poured like maple syrup yet remained appetizing, with flavors of mint and herbal tea as well as ripe peaches and apricots.

Domaine Philippe & Jean-François Becker

BP 24, 68340 Zellenberg; 03.89.47.90.16; vinsbecker@aol.com; $ to $$($)

The thirteenth generation of Becker vignerons has converted the domaine to organic viticulture. Their wines, often austere when young, seem to blossom after five years of cellaring. Nevertheless, certain recent vintages offer very nice drinking right now, particularly the flint-and-steel 2002 riesling Vieilles Vignes Hagenschlau, which could cut through *choucroute* like a knife; a limpid and pedigreed 2001 riesling Lerchenberg; and a mellow, orange peel– and herbal tea–scented 2001 gewürztraminer Grand Cru Schoenenbourg, which would be magnificent with a ripe Muenster.

Domaine Léon Beyer

68420 Eguisheim; 03.89.21.62.30; www.leonbeyer.fr; $$ to $$$

The wines of this well-established grower-*négociant* are featured on the lists of many of the most famous brasseries and grand cafés of Paris. They are pleasant and professional and suited to the distractions of a bustling public space.

Joseph & Christian Binner ☆

68770 Ammerschwihr; 03.89.78.23.20; vinsbinner@aol.com; $ to $$$

Adhering to biodynamic viticulture, avoiding filtration, and minimizing sulfur, the Binners are hypernaturalists who succeed handily, whether in their entry-level wines, like their delectable generic riesling, or their more nuanced riesling Unterberg, or the exotic riesling Kieffelkopf, which benefits from a good eight years of cellaring. Their gewürztraminer from the Grand Cru Kaefferkopf is dry but as rich as a VT, and their VTs, such as the 2000 gewürztraminer from the same vineyard and the 1998 riesling, are racy, concentrated, and too delectable. Their pinot noir comes across like a strong, riveting rosé and their Cuvée du Marriage, a blend from all their best *terroirs,* is a veritable fruit salad of flavors—slightly wacko but tasty.

Domaine Paul Blanck ☆

68240 Kientzheim; 03.89.78.23.56; www.blanck.com; $ to $$$$

This large, important house steadily improves under the current generation, Philippe and Frédéric. Not only is it growing in size, the increasingly eco-friendly domaine produces better and better wines—at all price levels, offering a good ratio of quality to price at every level. Starting with a very respectable range of screw-cap varietals, of which my favorite is the pinot gris, the wines progress through some tasty old-vines cuvées, before getting to the Grand Crus and *lieux-dits.*

The Blancks have major holdings on the great Grand Cru Furstentum, and every wine I've tasted from there has been distinctive and delectable. To cite just three: a sweet, crystalline pinot gris with an undertow of chamomile and verbena; a luminous gold, ten-year-old pinot gris SGN tasting of figs, caramel, and dried apricot, a noble nectar, indeed; and a 1997 riesling SGN. Gracious and mouthwatering, it made me smile with pleasure. A dry riesling from Grand Cru Schlossberg was fresh, tender, complex, and great with food. From *lieux-dits* such as Altenbourg and Patergarten, Blanck turns out equally admirable wines. I can sum up by citing my final notes on an 1989 gewürztraminer Grand Cru Furstentum SGN: damned delicious.

Domaine Léon Boesch ☆

68250 Westhalten; 03.89.47.01.83; domaineboesch@wanadoo.fr; $ to $$$($)
Another excellent biodynamic family winery. The jewels in the crown come from Grand Cru Zinnkoepflé, but there are many other gems. Start with a lipsmackingly tasty pinot blanc, at once rich and light as air; or a mellow, apple-scented sylvaner; or a spicy, lean, oak-aged pinot noir Luss Vallée Noble. There are seductive, fresh, and aromatic gewürztraminers from Breitenberg and Zinnkoepflé, equally alluring tokay-pinot gris from Clos Zwingel, and a knockout from Zinnkoepflé, racy, and deep, yet still food friendly. But, finally, it's the rieslings, every single one of them: a lacy Tradition that's full of character; a pure, steely Luss Vallée Noble with the tensile strength of Baryshnikov; a succulent VT from Breitenberg; and a thrillingly focused, mouthwatering, captivating version from Zinnkoepflé. Again, excellent.

Domaine Albert Boxler ☆

68230 Niedeermorschwihr; 03.89.27.11.32; albert.boxler@9online.fr; $$ to $$$
Jean Boxler, Albert's grandson, is about as conscientious and principled as they come. The high quality of his wines is so reliable you could set your watch by it. And they are as delicious as they are consistent. The pearls here are the wines from Grand Crus Sommerberg and Brand. I think Boxler prefers Sommerberg, perhaps because of the Sisyphus-like labor involved in working this near-vertical vineyard. And those wines are, indeed, admirable. Riesling or tokay-pinot gris, old vines, young vines, or Vendange Tardive, they are limpid, rich, and tender but light as air, serious and specific enough that you realize you've forgotten entirely about the grape variety. Peace, Jean, I prefer the wines from Brand. They are alive, so mouth-filling, with such focus and thrilling flavors of honey, verbena, lime, and quinine. It's a flavor profile I love.

Brand

Grand Cru in Turckheim, west of Colmar. Producers: DOM ALBERT BOXLER ◆ JOSMEYER.

Bruderthal

Grand Cru overlooking the town of Molsheim. Producers: ARBOGAST ◆ NEUMAYER.

Cave de Kientzheim-Kaysersberg

68420 Kientzheim; 03.89.47.13.19; www.vinsalsace-kaysersberg.com; $ to $$
This small co-op vinifies a significant portion of Grand Cru Schlossberg. What I've tasted—both a riesling VT and a gewürztraminer—has been dilute but elegant. I much prefer its wines from Grand Cru Furstentum and the *lieu-dit* Altenberg, a handful of fragrant, personality-filled VT gewürztraminers. I also admire their generic SGN tokay-pinot gris.

Le Cave (Vinicole) de Pfaffenheim & Gueberschwihr

68250 Pfaffenheim; 03.89.78.08.08; cave@pfaffenheim.com; $ to $$($)
This huge cooperative keeps growing. It recently bought the *négociant* house DOPFF & IRION and it also makes the wines of the Château d'Isenbourg in Rouffach under the label "Châteaux et Terroirs." Its entry-level wines are perfect for local brasseries; its special cuvées are distinct steps up. Favorites include the riesling Cuvée Jupiter, an austere but specific wine with tart lime flavors; the gewürztraminer Grand Cru Steinert, fresh, discreet, and long; and the tokay-pinot gris Cuvée Ste.-Catherine VT, with fine texture, depth, and herbal tea flavors.

Cave de Ribeauvillé

68150 Ribeauvillé; 03.89.73.61.80; www.cave-ribeauville.com; $ to $$($)

This large, important cooperative possesses some of the best vineyard sites in Alsace, including pieces of at least four Grand Crus. Additionally, its members have signed a charter pledging to follow such noble practices as respecting nature, controlling yields, and harvesting by hand. Not all of the wines bear witness to these articles of faith, but it's a good start. And some of its wines might serve as models of quality, notably the age-worthy tokay-pinot gris from Grand Cru Gloeckelberg and the "complantation" blend of riesling, pinot gris, and gewürztraminer from the Clos du Zahnacker in the heart of Grand Cru Osterberg.

Cave du Roi Dagobert/Cave de Traenheim

67310 Traenheim; 03.88.50.69.00; fax: 03.88.50.69.09; $ to $$($)

The vines owned by the cooperative members once furnished wine to the palace of the Merovingian kings. And there is at least one regal bottling coming out of the co-op's cellars—a racy, refined gewürztraminer Clos Rothstein, bottled at the property of Jean-Luc Christ. More mundane offerings can also be good. These fall into one of two lines, the fruit-driven "Sélection" and the site-specific "Terroir" from holdings on prime vineyards such as Grand Cru Engleberg. Both are recommended.

Cave de Turckheim

68230 Turckheim; 03.89.30.23.60; www.cave-turckheim.com; $ to $$$

Sizable cooperative with a broad range of wines, encompassing five Grand Crus and four respected *lieux-dits*. These, in addition to the wines in the co-op's "specialty" range, are the ones to go for here, notably the reasonably priced gewürztraminer Réserve du Baron de Turckheim and the pinot gris from such Grand Crus as Brand.

Cave Viticole de Cléebourg & Environs

BP 77, 67160 Cléebourg; 03.88.94.50.33; www.cave-cleebourg.com; $ to $$

Located in the northern reaches of Alsace wine country, this co-op has no Grand Crus. Its wines are a bit of a mixed bag but worth exploring for little treasures like the gewürztraminer Reifenberg Cléebourg, a delicate but firmly structured wine with lovely balance and an engaging apricot-flavored finish.

Clos St.-Landelin/René Muré ☆

68250 Rouffach; 03.89.78.58.00; www.mure.com; $ to $$$

This long-respected domaine moves from strength to strength. The *négociant* line, René Muré, improves yearly. Since 1998, the domaine has cultivated its own vines, under the Clos St.-Landelin label, using organic methods. Representative of the Clos St.-Landelin line are the creamy sylvaner Cuvée Oscar, which is all too easy to drink; the ambitious pinot noir, a cool-climate red with lots of character; the airy riesling Grand Cru Vorbourg with its honeyed fruit and dry, citrus-mineral finish; and the burnished gold gewürztraminer Grand Cru Vorbourg SGN, succulent, deep, and aristocratic.

Côtes de Toul

Tiny AC in Lorraine, to the west of the city of Nancy, on the right bank of the Moselle. Whites are made chiefly from auxerrois and reds and rosé from pinot noir. Gamay is also used for rosé. Drink the youngest available. Prices: $. Producers: Vincent Laroppe ◆ André & Roland Lelièvre ◆ Dom Mangeot.

Crémant d'Alsace

These are sparkling wines made by the *méthode traditionelle* (though usually less fizzy) throughout the Alsace region. They may be *blanc de blancs*, rosé, or *blanc de noirs*. Many producers make Crémant d'Alsace, among them: LUCIEN ALBRECHT ◆ PAUL BLANCK ◆ CAVE DE PFAFFENHEIM ◆ CLOS ST.-LANDELIN/RENÉ MURÉ ◆ DOM DE LA SINNE ◆ DOM STOEFFLER.

Domaine Marcel Deiss ☆

68750 Bergheim; 03.89.73.63.37; www.marceldeiss.com; $$ to $$$$

Be still, my heart! Why not say it outright? I think Jean-Michel Deiss, who adheres to biodynamics, is one of the greatest winemakers in the world. Genius is too feeble a word. Deiss has done nothing less than bring about a change in the INAO laws governing certain Grand Crus. I'll get there in a moment, but I'm starting simple, with a pinot blanc from Bergheim. Neither fined nor filtered, it's incredibly focused and textured and you'd swear you were in the heart of Burgundy. His pure pinot gris is fresh as a waterfall, a magnificent, *terroir*-driven wine. In fact, if talk about *terroir* seems a lot of mumbo jumbo to you, treat yourself to a Deiss. In particular, opt for one of his wines based on "complantation"—a field selection of a number of different grape varieties grown on the same parcel, which Deiss harvests and vinifies together.

Blending was not permitted under the *grand cru* laws until April 2005, when the powers that be decided to allow the mixing of grapes in the Grand Cru Alteberg de Bergheim, where Deiss has some of his best vines. His 2001 was a *vin de méditation.* A blend of just about all the grapes that grow in Alsace—including chasselas and pinot noir—it was unique and so magnificent that as you tasted, the world fell away. Ditto for his field mixes in Grand Cru Schoenenbourg and Mambourg, the latter of which is a sublime blend of all the pinots. Gruenspiel, which is not yet a Grand Cru, is equally thrilling. A complantation of riesling, pinot noir, and gewürztraminer, it is simply exquisite, spirited, and aerodynamic, with finely chiseled fruit and a core of minerals and herbal teas like linden blossom and verbena. These are inspired and noble wines. They seem as if they could age forever but will give immense pleasure whenever they are drunk. Every sip is a discovery.

Claude Dietrich

68240 Kientzheim; 03.89.47.19.42; fax: 03.89.47.36.67; $$ to $$$

The best wines from this small domaine are those that come from Grand Cru Furstentum. The generic pinot noir would be fun to taste in a wine bar, as would the somewhat stiff riesling Patergarten.

Domaine Dirler-Cade ☆

68500 Bergholtz; 03.89.76.91.00; jpdirler@terre-net.fr; $ to $$$

Jean and Ludovine Dirler make between twenty and thirty-five different biodynamic wines a year, starting with a couple of toothsome sylvaners. The common thread linking their wines from various *lieux-dits* as well as from four Grand Crus—Kessler, Kitterlé, Saering, and Spiegel—are power and delicacy. Their muscats from Saering and Spiegel are the best dry versions of that grape I've ever tasted—steely, elegant, fresh as mountain air, and loaded with oomph. The gewürztraminers are top-notch, particularly the searing (16.5 percent alcohol) Saering Grand Cru, a stunning match for refined exotic foods like chicken with lemongrass or biryani. The clutch of magnificent rieslings shares a family style: tight focus, the invigorating freshness and limpidity of a cascade, and never-ending length, with engaging differences from *cru* to *cru*. There's the poise and airy austerity of *lieu-dit* Bellzbrunner; the devastating elegance of Grand Cru Speigel, its vivid acidity balanced by residual sugar; the lemon-curd mellowness of Kessler; and, my all-time favorite, a 1998 VT from Saering, a demi-sec so light it seemed to have wings.

Dopff & Irion

68340 Riquewihr; 03.89.47.92.51; www.dopff-irion.com; $ to $$

This well-known house was purchased by the Pfaffenheim cooperative. Its wines are pleasant and competently made. The best come from Grand Crus Schoenenbourg and Vorbourg.

Edelzwicker: A white wine made from a blend of grapes, usually chasselas, sylvaner, pinot blanc, and auxerrois. Most Alsace producers make *edelzwicker*, and it is usually their least expensive wine. Drink the youngest available. $

Eichberg

Grand Cru in Eguisheim. Producers: DOM PAUL GINGLINGER ◆ HAUSHERR ◆ KUENTZ-BAS ◆ BRUNO SORG ◆ PAUL ZINCK.

Engleberg

Grand Cru in Dahlenheim et Scharrachbergheim, between Marlenheim and Molsheim. Producer: CAVE DU ROI DAGOBERT.

Florimont

Grand Cru to the northwest of Colmar. Producer: BRUNO SORG.

Charles & Dominique Frey

67650 Dambach-la-Ville; 03.88.92.62.23; frey.dom.bio@wanadoo.fr; $ to $$
Appetizing, three-dimensional biodynamic wine from a small family domaine. Recommendations include the fragrant, sweet gewürztraminer from *lieu-dit* Frauenberg; the structured old-vines riesling; and the tender tokay-pinot gris Cuvée de l'Ours.

Domaine Pierre Frick

68250 Pfaffenheim; 03.89.49.62.99; pierre.frick@wanadoo.fr; $ to $$($)
No newcomers to natural winemaking, the Fricks began farming organically in 1970. Over the years they have converted to biodynamics, always with a well-articulated philosophy. They never add sugar, acid, or industrial yeasts, and they keep sulfur to a strict minimum. The Fricks produce three levels of wine: the early-drinking Cuvée Classique, the wines from Grands Crus, and Cuvées Précieuses. The last, based on their own criteria, may change from year to year. A 2000 pinot blanc Précieuse was mellow and mineral, with firm flesh on its bones. Like all the Frick wines, it was very pure and very much in the hypernatural style, though, in my experience, without the flaws sometimes present in this genre.

Frick also makes some riveting wine from Grand Cru Steinert. Mellow and intensely pure, its 2001 riesling is the wine you'd want in a *winstub*—the strictly Alsatian version of a bistro—that served ambitious organic versions of Alsace classics. And Frick's VT gewürztraminer from Steinert is unique in a number of ways, starting with a soda cap instead of a cork (for the half-bottle). And it's downright poetic, evoking thoughts of late spring or early summer evenings when flowers exhale their fragrances.

Furstentum

One of the most famous Grand Crus in Kientzheim and Sigolsheim, between the larger towns of Ribeauvillé and Colmar. Producers: DOM PAUL BLANCK ◆ DOM SEPPI LANDMANN ◆ DOM ALBERT MANN ◆ DOM WEINBACH.

Geisberg

Grand Cru in Ribeauvillé. Producer: DOM ANDRÉ KIENTZLER.

Gentil: The name given to a blend of superior white grapes, chiefly riesling, gewürztraminer, pinot gris, and/or muscat.

Domaine Paul Ginglinger

68420 Eguisheim; 03.89.41.44.25; ginglin@club-internet.fr; $ to $$($)
Stylish, food-friendly wines, including a well-made pinot noir and some lovely damsels from the Grand Crus Pfersigberg and Eichberg. Cases in point: a discreetly sweet and peach-scented tokay-pinot gris Grand Cru Eichberg, the depth and balance of which should tempt chefs to match it with a wide variety of dishes; and a fragrant, focused gewürztraminer Grand Cru Pfersigberg that graciously expresses the majesty of its site.

Gloeckelberg

Grand Cru slightly north of Ribeauvillé. Producer: CAVE DE RIBEAUVILLÉ.

Goldert

Grand Cru south of Colmar. Producer: DOM ZIND-HUMBRECHT.

Domaine Rémy Gresser

67140 Andlau; 03.88.08.95.88; remy.gresser@wanadoo.fr; $$ to $$$
Solid organically run family domaine with holdings in the best vineyards of the Andlau region, among them Grand Cru Kastelberg, the only schist-based slopes in Alsace. Gresser's riesling from Kastelberg is resolutely *terroir*-driven, a riveting and creamy weave of mineral, blossoms, and riesling's characteristic petrol scent. Gresser's lightly off-dry riesling from Grand Cru Wiebelsberg runs a close second in pedigree, complexity, and tastiness. Rieslings from Grand Cru Moenchberg, aged in large barrels, and those from Duttenberg are also recommended. Gresser aims for an aperitif-style wine with his muscat from Brandhof, and he succeeds, making a delicately perfumed wine. His tokay-pinot gris VT from Brandhof is big and flavorful.

Hausherr ↑

68420 Eguisheim; 03.89.23.40.67; hubert-et-heidi.hausherr@wanadoo.fr; $ to $$$
Since the Hausherrs stopped delivering their harvest to the local co-op in 2000 they do everything by hand in their small eco-friendly domaine. Some might find their wines severe. I love that particular style. Their riesling Sungass has a sure sense of place. The version from Altengarten is pure and fresh as a waterfall. The lilting gewürztraminer from Eichberg Grand Cru is one continuous weave of beautiful flavors. And their gewürztraminer SGN from Altengarten surprised me with a note of the *espelette* pepper, a lightly hot pepper from the Basque region of France, mixed in with the classic lychee and rose fragrances.

Hengst

One of the most famous Grand Crus, southwest of Colmar. Producers: BARMÈS-BUECHER ◆ DOM JOSMEYER ◆ DOM ALBERT MANN ◆ DOM ZIND-HUMBRECHT.

Domaine Hering

67140 Barr; 03.88.08.90.07; www.vins-hering.com; $ to $$($)
Pure, good, fresh wines from Grand Cru Kirchberg. Best is the gewürztraminer Clos Gaensbroennel, from a parcel on that Grand Cru. Sweet and gracious, it would make a fine aperitif.

Albert Hertz

68420 Eguisheim; 03.89.41.30.32; fax: 03.89.23.99.23; $$

What I love about Hertz's limpid, austere riesling Grand Cru Pfersigberg is that it's an exhilarating partner for good, briny oysters. The tokay-pinot gris Grand Cru Zinnkoepfle is steely, too, and that's what excites me about it.

Jean & Hubert Heywang

67140 Heiligenstein; 03.88.08.91.41; heywang.vins@wanadoo.fr; $ to $$

The specialty of this eco-friendly domaine is the rare Klevener de Heiligenstein, which accounts for a third of the production. It's a lovely little white, vinous and mineral, with good, tight structure, good balance, and quite a bit of personality (with age it becomes plump and mellow). The wines from Grand Cru Kirchberg are recommended too: the riesling is very pure, steely, and flinty; the gewürztraminer VT is mellow, with convincing depth and alluring notes of honey.

Hugel & Fils

68340 Riquewihr; 03.89.47.92.15; www.hugel.com; $$ to $$$$

A large, important grower-*négociant* house with worldwide distribution. The wines, always impeccably professional, tend to be fruit driven, making bold varietal statements. The top of the line is the Jubilée bottling. Hugel also resurrected an ancient Alsace tradition of blending the region's leading grape varieties—riesling, gewürztraminer, pinot gris, muscat, and sylvaner—and bottling them under the name Gentil. The resulting wine is fresh and delicate, and its success has led other vintners to follow suit.

Domaine Josmeyer ☆

68920 Wintzenheim, 03.89.27.91.90; josmeyer@wanadoo.fr; $$ to $$$

Everything made by this large, exemplary domaine, recently converted to biodynamics, is recommended. Highlights include the mineral, substantial pinot auxerrois H Vieilles Vignes from the Grand Cru Hengst, a lipsmackingly super food wine; the riesling Grand Cru Hengst, a lovable yet refined blend of exotic fruit, citronella, and minerals; a powerful riesling from the granitic soils of Grand Cru Brand, as precise as it is virile; a clutch of deliciously easy drinking pinot gris (Le Fromenteau and the more serious 1854 Foundation Vieilles Vignes); and a succulent, sweet gewürztraminer, Les Folastries.

Kaefferkopf

Lieu-dit upgraded to Grand Cru in 2006. Blended wines, based on riesling, gewürztraminer, and pinot gris, permitted. Producers: DOM JEAN-BAPTISTE ADAM ◆ JOSEPH AND CHRISTIAN BINNER ◆ DOM MARTIN SCHAETZEL.

Kanzlerberg

Grand Cru in Bergheim, northeast of Ribeauvillé. Producer: SYLVIE SPIELMANN.

Kastelberg

Grand Cru in Andlau, south of Barr. Producers: RÉMY GRESSER ◆ MARC KREYDENWEISS.

Kessler

Grand Cru in Guebwiller, south of Colmar. Producer: DIRLER-CADE.

Domaine André Kientzler ☆

68150 Ribeauvillé; 03.89.73.67.10; fax: 03.89.73.35.81; $ to $$$($)

An excellent family domaine with extremely good wines on every level, from the structured and focused pinot blanc, to a limpid, aristocratic riesling Réserve

Particulière, with a long lemon-lime finish, to a nuanced VT gewürztraminer that seemed to have the pedigree of a *grand cru* without actually being one.

Kirchberg
Grand Cru in Barr. Producers: DOM HERING ◆ HEYWANG ◆ KIENTZLER ◆ STOEFFLER.

Domaine Kirmann
67680 Epfig; 03.88.85.59.07; www.kirmann.com; $ to $$
This eco-friendly family domaine multitasks: it runs a restaurant and a bookshop, offers "folkloric evenings," and makes reasonably priced wine, particularly the range of varietals from the *lieu-dit* Fronholz ($) and the Vieilles Vignes cuvées of tokay-pinot gris and gewürztraminer.

Kitterlé
Grand Cru in Guebwiller, south of Colmar. Producer: DOM DIRLER-CADE.

Klevener de Heiligenstein
A tiny AC in the Bas-Rhin, a specialty of the region since the eighteenth century. The wines are made from the local grape klevener, which is believed to be related to traminer and Jura's savagnin rosé. Klevener de Heiligenstein produces crisp, pleasant whites which become mellow and aromatic with several years of aging. Vintages: 2005, (2004), and (2003). Prices: $($). Producers: JEAN & HUBERT HEYWANG ◆ CHARLES WANTZ.

Domaine Marc Kreydenweiss ☆
67140 Andlau; 03.88.08.95.83; www.kreydenweiss.com; $$ to $$$
In the forefront of biodynamics in Alsace, Marc Kreydenweiss sets a stellar example. Everything is worthy of recommendation: the vinous pinot blanc from the *lieu-dit* Kritt and the smoky pinot gris from Grand Cru Moenchberg, both of which are full of character; the Clos du Val d'Eléon, a fresh, tasty blend of riesling and pinot gris; and a passel of riveting rieslings. Four favorites among the rieslings: the Clos Rebberg (both the dulcet regular with its tart lemon finish and the clean, honey-saturated SGN); the excellent, petrol-scented Wiebelsberg; and the fragrant, complex Grand Cru Kastelberg Vieilles Vignes, which seems as if it could age forever.

Kuentz-Bas ☆
68420 Husseren-les-Châteaux; 03.89.49.30.24; www.kuentz-bas.fr; $$ to $$$$
This first-rate domaine was sold to Jean-Baptiste Adam in February 2004. Given Adam's work elsewhere, there's reason to believe that the quality of the wines will remain excellent—incisive, aristocratic, and in the case of VTs, SGNs, and Grand Crus such as Pfersigberg, Rangen, and Eichberg, age-worthy. I'll simply note that in 2006 the 1999s from these vineyards were wonderful to drink, with plenty of life in them, and the 1998 riesling Grand Cru Pfersigberg VT Cuvée Caroline seemed to need another five to ten years of tender, loving cellaring.

Domaine Seppi Landmann
68570 Soultzmatt; 03.89.47.09.33; www.seppi-landmann.fr; $ to $$$$
The best wines from this important, solid domaine come from the Grand Cru Zinnkoepflé with an honorable mention for those from Grand Cru Furstentum. All are flavorful and specific but could be more refined. The pinot gris Bollenberg has lovely herbal tea flavors and a long, long finish. It needs to be carafed about two hours before serving.

Gustave Lorentz

68750 Bergheim; 03.89.73.22.22; www.gustavelorentz.com; $ to $$$

A well-established *négociant* house with a range of good wines. The Cuvée Particulière line makes for pleasant drinking in animated brasseries; the limpid rieslings from Grand Cru Altenberg de Bergheim mark their superiority with good focus and long mineral and lime finishes; the gewürztraminer VT is a classic in its genre.

Jean-Luc Mader ☆

68150 Hunawihr; 03.89.73.80.32; vins.mader@laposte.net; $ to $$($)

Although Mader's wines from Grand Cru Rosacker steal the show, his entire lineup is recommended, starting with the easy-drinking, entry-level pinot blanc. The sweet pinot gris Cuvée Théophile is focused and fresh, mingling lovely flavors of candied fruit and, strangely, pineapple steeped in rum. His riesling Muhlforst is delicate and airy, with a steel backbone; multiply those qualities by ten for the riesling Grand Cru Rosacker. The gewürztraminer Grand Cru Rosacker, with its lush core supported by a steel frame, practically flies. It's a blissful aperitif.

Mambourg

Grand Cru in Sigolsheim, between Ribeauvillé and Colmar. Producer: DOM MARCEL DEISS.

Domaine Albert Mann ☆

68920 Wettolsheim; 03.89.80.62.00; www.albertmann.com; $ to $$$

As a gift to beachgoers and picnickers everywhere, Maurice and Jacky Barthelme bottle 80 percent of their very good biodynamic, never-chaptalized wine with screw caps. Real corks, however, close the Grand Crus and SGNs. They make some damned good, pretty serious pinot noir—particularly the unfiltered versions from Clos de la Faille, Pfersigberg (labeled Grand P), and Hengst (labeled Grand H). There are a bunch of extremely tasty pinot gris, especially from the Pfersigberg and Hengst Grand Crus, but even more tempting are the various rieslings and gewürztraminers from the Grand Crus Schlossberg, Furstentum, and Steingrubler. What characterizes the Grand Cru rieslings is a combination of steeliness, freshness, complexity, length, and delicious flavors of citrus fruit. (I particularly love the blood orange notes in Furstentum.) An entirely botrytized 1995 riesling Cuvée Antoine, tasted in 2005, was a gloriously fresh blend of honey, preserved lemon, a whiff of petrol, and truffles. And no matter how rich, luscious, or succulent, the Mann gewürztraminers from Steingrubler and Furstentum never come off as pornographic. They're floral, spicy, elegant, and complex. The super rich gewürztraminer Grand Cru Furstentum SGN, scented with raspberry and peach, is simply to die for.

Domaine Julien Meyer

67680 Nothalten; 03.88.92.60.15; fax: 03.88.92.47.75; $ to $$($)

Son Patrick, who took over in 1982, converted the domaine to biodynamics. A neighbor of André Ostertag's, he works many of the same vineyards. His wines are less accomplished but they're pure and have personality, even if some go off the deep end, like the old-vines sylvaner that spent two years in *barriques*. The best I've tasted are a mellow, mineral klevner–pinot blanc; a tart, pineapple-scented riesling from the *lieu-dit* Grittermatte; a lively, off-dry pinot gris Fanny Elizabeth; a flowery gewürztraminer Les Pucelles; a honey and mineral gewürztraminer VT; and a limpid, riveting riesling VT from Grand Cru Muenchberg.

Domaine Meyer-Fonné ☆

68230 Katzenthal; 03.89.27.16.50; felix.meyer-fonne@libertysurf.fr; $ to $$$
A disciple of Zind-Humbrecht, Felix Meyer-Fonné is a gifted winemaker with a clutch of prestigious vineyard plots. From the Grand Cru Wineck-Schlossberg he makes a racy, off-dry riesling with light honey, petrol, and lemon flavors. Tokay-pinot gris from Dorfburg is simply lovely, and the SGN version from Hinterburg de Katzenthal is sumptuous, balanced, regal, and long.

Domaine Frédéric Mochel

67310 Traenheim; 03.88.50.38.67; www.mochel.net; $ to $$($)
A good family domaine making fresh, expressive rieslings, muscats, and gewürztraminers from Grand Cru Altenberg de Bergbieten, including riesling Cuvée Henriette.

Moenchberg

Grand Cru in Andlau and Eichhoffen, south of Barr. Producers: GRESSER ◆ KREYDENWEISS.

Domaine Moltes ↑

68250 Pfaffenheim; 03.89.49.60.85; www.vin-moltes.com; $ to $$$
Very good and improving wines are produced by this eco-friendly domaine. The new generation has made substantial investments and seems still to be finding its voice—as in a riesling Gaentzbrunnen and a tokay-pinot gris from Grand Cru Steinert that were impressive and tasty but not all that they might be. A gewürztraminer from Grand Cru Steinert, however, shows what Stéphane and Mickael Moltes can do: the wine is sweet and rich but light as air, *terroir*-driven and oh, so drinkable. Ditto for an SGN tokay-pinot gris that was liquid gold with lively herbal tea, apple, and citrus flavors.

Moselle

Microscopic Lorraine VDQS (Vin Délimité de Qualité Supérieure) in the Moselle department, known for whites, reds, and rosés, made from a variety of Alsace grapes as well as gamay, pinot meunier, and Germany's Müller-Thurgau. Drink the youngest available. Prices: $ to $$. Producers: Michel Maurice ◆ Oury-Schreiber ◆ Ch de Vaux.

Muenchberg

Grand Cru in Nothalten, south of Barr. Producers: DOM OSTERTAG ◆ DOM JULIEN MEYER.

Domaine Gérard Neumeyer

67120 Molsheim; 03.88.38.12.45; domaine.neumeyer@wanadoo.fr; $$
A reliable small producer that makes very nice wines from Grand Cru Bruderthal—particularly the fresh, civilized tokay-pinot gris—as well as steely, adaptable riesling from *lieu-dit* Finkenberg and a lissome pinot blanc Vin de la Tulipe that seems perfect for a ladies' lunch or tealess tea with scones and cucumber sandwiches.

Osterberg

Grand Cru in Ribeauvillé. Producers: CAVE DE RIBEAUVILLÉ ◆ LOUIS SIPP ◆ SIPP-MACK.

Domaine Ostertag ☆

67680 Epfig; 03.88.85.51.34; fax: 03.88.85.58.95; $$ to $$$

The word *artist* is easy to throw around. But André Ostertag truly is one. He's a serious poet—but that's beside the point in a wine guide. He's also an artist in wine, faithful to a Platonic vision of excellence. He went to winemaking school in Burgundy, palled around with Dominique Lafon, and came away with an idea of Alsace wine other than acid and sugar. He wanted the mouthfeel of a Meursault. Aside from being biodynamic, Ostertag's wines are marked by a distinctive tenderness. He downplays the flamboyance of both muscat and gewürztraminer, making gently exotic, long, mineral beauties (particularly from the *lieu-dit* Fronholz). His sylvaner Vieilles Vignes is scrumptious and inexpensive—the bargain of any wine list on which it appears. Pinot gris, a Burgundian grape, ferments in barrel resulting in a Côte d'Or–esque mellowness. Whether from Fronholz, Zellberg, or Grand Cru Muenchberg, these are singular wines, deliciously buttery and mineral. And it's from Muenchberg that Ostertag makes his greatest rieslings: stunningly pure, with beautifully molded fruit, they are long, profound, and peaceable.

Pfersigberg

Grand Cru in Eguisheim and Wettolsheim. Producers: DOM PAUL GINGLINGER ◆ ALBERT HERTZ ◆ KUENTZ-BAS ◆ DOM ALBERT MANN ◆ BRUNO SORG ◆ PAUL ZINCK.

Pfingstberg

Grand Cru in Orschwihr, above Guebwiller. Producers: LUCIEN ALBRECHT ◆ ZUSSLIN.

Rangen

The southernmost Grand Cru, located in Thann and Vieux-Thann. Often written as Rangen de Thann. Producers: KUENTZ-BAS ◆ SCHOFFIT ◆ ZINCK ◆ ZIND-HUMBRECHT.

Domaine Rieffel

67140 Mittelbergheim; 03.88.08.95.48; fax: 03.88.08.28.94; $ to $$

Who could resist a wine that comes from La Colline aux Escargots? (Translation: snail hill.) Why even try? Lucas and André Rieffel's truly tasty tokay-pinot gris from that vineyard is creamy and toasty (lightly oaked) with a solid steel core. Their off-dry riesling from Grand Cru Wiebelsberg is fresh as a spring shower, at once lyrical and stony. Their lean, oak-aged pinot noir is both ambitious and admirable.

Domaine Rolly-Gassmann ☆

68590 Rorschwihr; 03.89.73.63.28; rollygassmann@wanadoo.fr; $ to $$$

This important, large house is popular with sommeliers across France—with good reason. I'll never forget the sheer sensual pleasure I got from a VT gewürztraminer drunk as an aperitif on a rainy Sunday at a small, mom-and-pop restaurant (that had one Michelin star, all the same) in Rouen. No *grands crus* here, though some of the wines seem to have pretty noble bloodlines. It would be hard to be more true to place than the riesling Pflaenzerreben de Rorschwihr. A focused mingling of petrol, steel, lace, and lime, it has such force and traction, it could out-drive a Bugatti. The auxerrois from Rotleibel de Rorschwihr holds the road too. The tokay-pinot gris Rolly-Gassmann is downright statuesque, and the gewürztraminer Hagueneau de Bergheim VT is so classic it could be an ambassador for the category.

Domaine Eric Rominger ↑

68250 Westhalten; 03.89.47.68.60; vins-rominger.eric@w.fr; $ to $$$

This eco-friendly domaine at the foot of Grand Cru Zinnkoepflé works with a light, precise hand. Its entry-level varietal wines are good and charitably priced

($) but its stars come, of course, from Zinnkoepflé, such as a tokay-pinot gris VT, simultaneously rich and airy, like whipped cream. The best of these are labeled Les Sinnèles after a section of Zinnkoepflé. They include a cloud-and-steel riesling and a mellow, nuanced gewürztraminer. My favorite here, however, comes from the *lieu-dit* Lutzelberg de Westhalten. A "complantation" of pinot gris and pinot auxerrois, it is truly lovely and cool as mountain air.

Rosacker

Grand Cru in Hunawihr, south of Ribeauvillé. Producer: JEAN-LUC MADER.

Saering

Grand Cru in Guebwiller. Producer: DOM DIRLER-CADE.

Domaine Martin Schaetzel

68770 Ammerschwihr; 03.89.47.11.39; fax: 03.89.78.29.77; $$ to $$$

Run according to biodynamic principles, this domaine makes a range of coherent, characterful wines. Favorites include the textured riesling Kaefferkopf Granit, a steel and herbal-tea wake-up call; the riesling Grand Cru Schlossberg, with its pure expression of *terroir;* and the very classic gewürztraminer Kaefferkopf Cuvée Catherine.

Schlossberg

Grand Cru in Kientzheim. Producers: DOM PAUL BLANCK ◆ DOM ALBERT MANN ◆ DOM MARTIN SCHAETZEL ◆ DOM WEINBACH.

Domaines Schlumberger

68500 Guebwiller Cedex; 03.89.74.27.00; www.domaines-schlumberger.com; $ to $$$

The largest domaine in Alsace, Schlumberger shows signs of renewal. It recently hired a new team. And with 140 hectares, half of that area in Grand Crus, Schlumberger certainly has the land it needs to produce outstanding wines. I've liked the wines I've sampled from the Grand Crus Saering, Kitterlé, and Kessler but, tasty and professional as they were, I felt they could be more concentrated and focused and should be more majestic. The gewürztraminer Christine VT, from one of their best parcels, was solidly on track—multilayered and racy. Les Princes Abbés is a line of fruit-driven wines suitable for brasseries.

Domaine Roland Schmitt ↑

67310 Bergbieten; 03.88.38.20.72; rschmitt@terre-net.fr; $ to $$

Anne-Marie Schmitt and sons Bruno and Julien are in the process of converting their domaine to organic viticulture. Although some wines are a bit rough-hewn—such as the riesling Grand Cru Altenberg de Bergbieten Vieilles Vignes—they are pure, powerful, *terroir*-driven, and promising. Others are fully realized, such as a light-as-air riesling Grand Cru Altenberg de Bergbieten Cuvée Roland, with its fine focus and lemon, lime, and quinine flavors (it would be great with subtly spiced Pan-Asian or fusion food); and a delicate riesling Glintzberg with force enough to cut through the fat of a *flammenkuchen*, Alsace's "pizza" topped with crème fraîche, onions, and bacon.

Schoenenbourg

Grand Cru in Riquewihr and Zellenberg. Producers: BECKER ◆ MARCEL DEISS.

Domaine Schoffit ☆

68000 Colmar; 03.89.24.41.14; fax: 03.89.41.40.52; $$ to $$$$

Some consider Grand Cru Rangen the Chambertin of Alsace. It's certainly true that the best wines from this fine domaine come from a small parcel—the Clos St.-Théobold—on Rangen and that these wines are excellent and downright aristocratic. They are gifts that keep on giving. An off-dry riesling was layered and stony, with a core of chamomile and verbena. A tokay-pinot gris was creamy, mellow, and resplendent. A gewürztraminer was a resonant *vin dc terroir*. And the pinot gris Larme de Lave, with 4.5 percent alcohol (there's so much natural sugar, the yeasts gave up a third of the way through fermentation) was, like Hungary's Eszencia, a celestial marmalade. Masterly work.

Domaine Gérard Schueller

68420 Husseren-les-Châteaux; 03.89.49.31.54.; fax: 03.89.49.36.63; $ to $$$

I've tasted only two wines from this domaine but was impressed enough to want to know more. The wines, a supple, discreet 2003 muscat and a structured, possibly oaked 2000 riesling Zero Defaut, were both mineral-driven and seemed to be in the hypernatural camp.

René Simonis

68770 Ammerschwihr; 03.89.47.30.79; fax: 03.89.78.24.10; $ to $$

There's the occasional rough edge in the wines from this eco-friendly family domaine, but most of what I've tasted has been delicious. The limpid, sweet riesling Cuvée Réserve is charitably priced, as are the Caprice de Sylvaner, a lush, late-harvest *moelleux* and the peach- and lychee-scented gewürztraminer Vogelgarten (all $). The mellow, syrupy tokay-pinot gris Vogelgarten VT would be lovely paired with fish in a mushroom cream sauce; the same in SGN is a nectar of crushed peaches and apricots steeped in honey. It has the texture of velour.

Domaine de la Sinne ↑

687770 Ammerschwihr; 03.89.47.12.54; $$

Interesting wines here. Frédéric Geschickt converted the family domaine to biodynamics in 1998. He's got a piece of Grand Cru Wineck-Schlossberg, from which he turns out an ample, pure, and somewhat rough-hewn riesling. His generic pinot noir comes on like a dark rose with flavors of tea and forest undergrowth. It would be fun to pair it with food. His gewürztraminer SGN from *lieu-dit* Kaefferkopf mingles flavors of lychee, peach, and apricot with an overriding scent of roses. It's long and lush and very good.

Louis Sipp

68150 Ribeauvillé; 03.89.73.60.01; www.sipp.com; $ to $$$

The finest wine I've tasted from this domaine was the 2000 gewürztraminer Grand Cru Osterberg SGN Coeur de Tri. I was told they work the vineyard with a horse—understandable, given the near-perpendicular grade of some Grand Crus. The wine was balanced, ripe, and racy. Gewürztraminer seems to be their strong suit. Whether generic SGN or a Grand Cru Osterberg, they are flavorful, albeit somewhat heavy-handed. Good for aperitifs or loud brasseries. The rieslings from Grand Cru Kirchberg de Ribeauvillé bordered on the watery but didn't lack specificity and had attractive mineral flavors. In other words, I wouldn't kick them out of bed. Ditto for the pinot gris from *lieu-dit* Trottacker. The SGNs based on pinot gris, curiously, lacked concentration but they had attractive honey flavors and spicy, gewürz-like notes.

Domaine Sipp-Mack

68150 Hunawihr; 03.89.73.61.88; www.sippmack.com; $ to $$

This good family domaine produces a line of inexpensive, tasty dry and off-dry whites. The stars, though, are the wines from Grand Cru Osterberg, such as the racy petrol- and honey-scented riesling, a bracing, food-friendly call to attention; and special cuvées, such as the burnished gold gewürztraminer VT Lucie-Marie, a luscious and structured blend of honey and roses.

Sommerberg

Grand Cru in Niedermorschwihr and Katzenthal, near Colmar. Producers: DOM PAUL BLANCK ◆ DOM ALBERT BOXLER.

Bruno Sorg

68420 Eguisheim; 03.89.41.80.85; fax: 03.89.41.22.64; $ to $$($)

Very nice rieslings and tokay-pinot gris from Grand Cru Florimont; riveting, mineral, *terroir*-driven wines from Grand Cru Pfersigberg (especially Vieilles Vignes) and Eichberg; and a limpid SGN gewürztraminer that is sheer honey and roses.

Pierre Sparr

68240 Sigolsheim; 03.89.78.24.22; www.alsace-wines.com; $ to $$

A widely known *négociant* house with decent wines. The best come from the Grand Crus Mambourg and Schoenenbourg.

Spiegel

Grand Cru in Bergholtz and Guebwiller. Producer: DOM DIRLER-CADE.

Domaine Sylvie Spielmann

68750 Bergheim; 03.89.73.35.95; www.sylviespielmann.com; $$

Passionate and dedicated, Sylvie Spielmann runs her domaine according to biodynamic principles. The wines are direct and calm, avoiding all flamboyance. At times the expression of *terroir* in the Grand Crus could be more resonant, but the wines are always honest, frank, and friendly, from the pinots Réserve Bergheim (blanc, gris, and noir) to the lush gewürztraminers from the Grand Crus Altenberg and Kanzlerberg. You're getting honest wine here.

Steinert

Grand Cru in Pfaffenheim and Westhalten, south of Colmar. Producers: LA CAVE DE PFAFFENHEIM ◆ DOM PIERRE FRICK ◆ DOM MOLTES.

Steingrubler

Grand Cru in Wettolsheim, south of Colmar. Producers: BARMÈS-BUECHER ◆ DOM ALBERT MANN ◆ STENTZ-BUECHER.

Stentz-Buecher

68920 Wettolsheim; 03.89.80.68.09; stentz-buecher@wanadoo.fr; $ to $$

A light, sure hand makes the wine here. No jagged edges, no vulgarity, just good texture and focus, backbones of steel, pure flavors of minerals, and the zests of lemon and lime. The domaine has holdings on Grand Cru Steingrubler as well as on the *lieux-dits* Ortel, Marken, and Tannenbuehl.

Domaine Vincent Stoeffler ☆

67140 Barr; 03.88.08.52.50; vins.stoeffler@wanadoo.fr; $ to $$

Martine and Vincent Stoeffler, both enologists, combined their vineyards in the Haut- and Bas-Rhin, converted to organic viticulture, and produce reasonably priced, beautiful wine. Their entry-level wines—generic sylvaner, muscat, and so on—are delights, as fresh and glancing as dappled sunlight on new grass and spring flowers. The pinot noir Rotenberg was a juicy pleasure of a light red. Riesling from Grand Cru Kirchberg de Barr presents a bottomless well of minerals, steel, white peaches, and blossoms. The 1998 riesling VT from Muhlforst was closed up (in January 2006) but you could sense the power underneath. The 2002, on the other hand, was open and gracious, as was an old-vines tokay-pinot gris, both excellent food wines. Their old-vines gewürztraminer, harvested overripe in the excessively hot 2003 vintage, was a model of discretion, an outstanding example of the taming of that often garish grape variety. It would be perfect for a three-star Michelin restaurant.

Trimbach

68150 Ribeauvillé; 03.89.73.60.30; www.maison-trimbach.fr; $$ to $$$

Venerable grower-*négociant* house whose wines seem to be on the list of every restaurant in the world. The bottlings to look for here are the two jewels in the Trimbach crown: the riesling Clos Ste.-Hune, from a parcel within Grand Cru Rosacker, and the riesling Frédéric-Émile, from the Grand Crus Geisberg and Osterberg.

Vorbourg

Grand Cru in Rouffach and Westhalten. Producer: CLOS ST.-LANDELIN.

Charles Wantz

67140 Barr; 03.88.08.90.44; charles.wantz@wanadoo.fr; $ to $$

A grower-*négociant* with some original offerings, starting with an oak-aged Klevener de Heiligenstein Cuvée E. Wantz bottled by the Hospices de Strasbourg. Vinous and mellow, it's a pleasant, characterful white. The Pinot R Auxerrois is a clear, pure, well-proportioned white; the Rouge d'Ottrott Cuvée à l'Ancienne is pale and tannic, an agreeable curiosity. The tokay-pinot gris VT is very pure and honeyed, with flavors of applesauce and mead.

Domaine Weinbach/Colette Faller & Ses Filles ☆

68240 Kaysersberg; 03.89.47.13.21; www.domaineweinbach.com; $$ to $$$$

You can't go wrong at this deservedly popular and highly regarded domaine famously run by Madame Colette Faller and her daughters, Laurence and Catherine. Highlights include the lyrical gewürztraminer Grand Cru Furstentum Cuvée Laurence, with its superb mineral core, and the handsome, textured riesling Schlossberg Grand Cru Cuvée Ste.-Catherine.

Wiebelsberg

Grand Cru in Andlau. Producers: DOM RÉMY GRESSER ◆ DOM RIEFFEL.

Wineck-Schlossberg

Grand Cru in Katzenthal and Ammerschwihr. Producers: DOM JEAN-BAPTISTE ADAM ◆ DOM PAUL BLANCK ◆ DOM MEYER-FONNÉ ◆ DOM DE LA SINNE.

Paul Zinck

68420 Eguisheim; 03.89.41.19.11; www.zinck.fr; $ to $$$

A good family domaine. Prestige (or Portrait) is its line for its basic varietal bottlings, which are well-made and pleasant. Then come discreet, focused versions from Grand Crus Pfersigberg, Rangen (the dry, fresh-as-a-waterfall riesling was my favorite in the lineup), and Eichberg (its racy gewürztraminer ran a close second).

Domaine Zind-Humbrecht ☆

68230 Turckheim; 03.89.27.02.05; o.humbrecht@wanadoo.fr; $$$ to $$$$

Can wine get better than this? Wine can be as sublime as Zind-Humbrecht's (Alsace can provide a case or three in point), but I sincerely doubt it can get better. Yes, it's biodynamic. Yes, the Humbrechts have a wealth of great vineyards. But no one was more deserving of such richness: Léonard Humbrecht sought out these vineyards when no one wanted them, and he was a modern-day crusader for the truth of *terroir*. Alsace ought to put a statue of him in Colmar. And, OK, his son Olivier Humbrecht *is* a Master of Wine. But just taste! Such mastery. Here you will find an articulation of that which we call *terroir* that will leave you shaking your head in awe.

Take a gewürztraminer Herrenweg de Turckheim. It's majestic—layered, complex, meaty yet gracious, big yet discreet. Or a riesling Clos Windsbuhl: so mellow, so beautifully constructed, long, and appetizing, it takes your breath away. An empty bottle of pinot gris Rangen de Thann Grand Cru Clos Saint-Urbain sits on the windowsill of my country kitchen. I can't bring myself to throw it away. What an exciting wine! Such fleeting, mingled flavors of dry honey, citrus zests, and chamomile, such exquisite texture—silky, tensile, and voluptuous all at once. And is it sweet or is it dry? Whatever. It's a joy.

Zinnkoepflé

Grand Cru north of Guebwiller. Producers: LÉON BOESCH ◆ SEPPI LANDMANN ◆ ROMINGER.

Domaine Valentin Zusslin ↑

68500 Orschwihr; 03.89.76.82.84; www.valentin-zusslin.com; $ to $$$

Such pure, biodynamic, hypernatural wines. For Marie and Jean-Paul Zusslin, who work the slopes of Bollenberg and Grand Cru Pfingstberg, vineyards come first. They describe themselves as minimalists in the cellar. It's true, sometimes the wines could use a more controlling hand, as in some otherwise admirable wines that lacked structure, but everything produced here is worth trying. Out-and-out successes include a vivid pinot auxerrois Vieilles Vignes; a textured gewürztraminer Bollenberg La Chapelle; a racy riesling Bollenberg with thrilling focus and freshness; and an intensely mineral riesling Grand Cru Pfingstberg, as deep as it was lipsmacking.

ALSACE CRIB SHEET

MUST TRYS

Dom Lucien Albrecht (especially Clos Schild and Clos Himmelreich)

Barmès-Buecher (especially rieslings and gewürztraminers from Grand Cru Hengst)

Dom Léon Boesch (especially Grand Cru Zinnkoepflé)

Dom Marcel Deiss

Dom Dirler-Cade (especially Grand Cru Saering, more particularly muscat and riesling VT)

Kuentz-Bas (especially Grand Crus from 1998 and 1999)

Dom Albert Mann (especially gewürztraminer Grand Cru Furstentum SGN)

Dom Ostertag

Dom Schoffit (especially Grand Cru Rangen Clos St.-Théobold)

Zind-Humbrecht

SMART BUYS

Smart buys here are not so much individual growers as they are specific wines from top growers. Grand Cru wines as well as VTs and SGNs will always be expensive because they are labor intensive as well as costly and risky to make. Look, instead, for the special cuvées of sylvaner, pinot blanc, and auxerrois, and entry-level wines from:

Dom Paul Blanck for sylvaner and auxerrois Vieilles Vignes

Dom Léon Boesch for sylvaner and pinot blanc

Dom Marcel Deiss for pinot blanc

Dom Dirler-Cade for sylvaner Vieilles Vignes

Dom Ostertag for sylvaner Vieilles Vignes

GENERAL GOOD VALUES

Dom Jean-Baptiste Adam

Dom Pierre Frick

Jean & Hubert Heywang for Klevner de Heiligenstein

René Simonis for the Cuvée Réservée line and wines from *lieu-dit* Vogelgarten

Dom Stoeffler

SAFE HOUSES

Dom Paul Blanck

Dom Albert Boxler

Clos St.-Landelin/René Muré

Dom Josmeyer

Dom André Kientzler

Marc Kreydenweiss

Jean-Luc Mader

Dom Rolly-Gassmann

Dom Vincent Stoeffler

Dom Weinbach/Colette Faller & Ses Filles

ALSACE

BORDEAUX

BURGUNDY

CHAMPAGNE

JURA AND SAVOIE

LANGUEDOC-ROUSSILLON

LOIRE

PROVENCE AND CORSICA

RHÔNE

SOUTHWEST

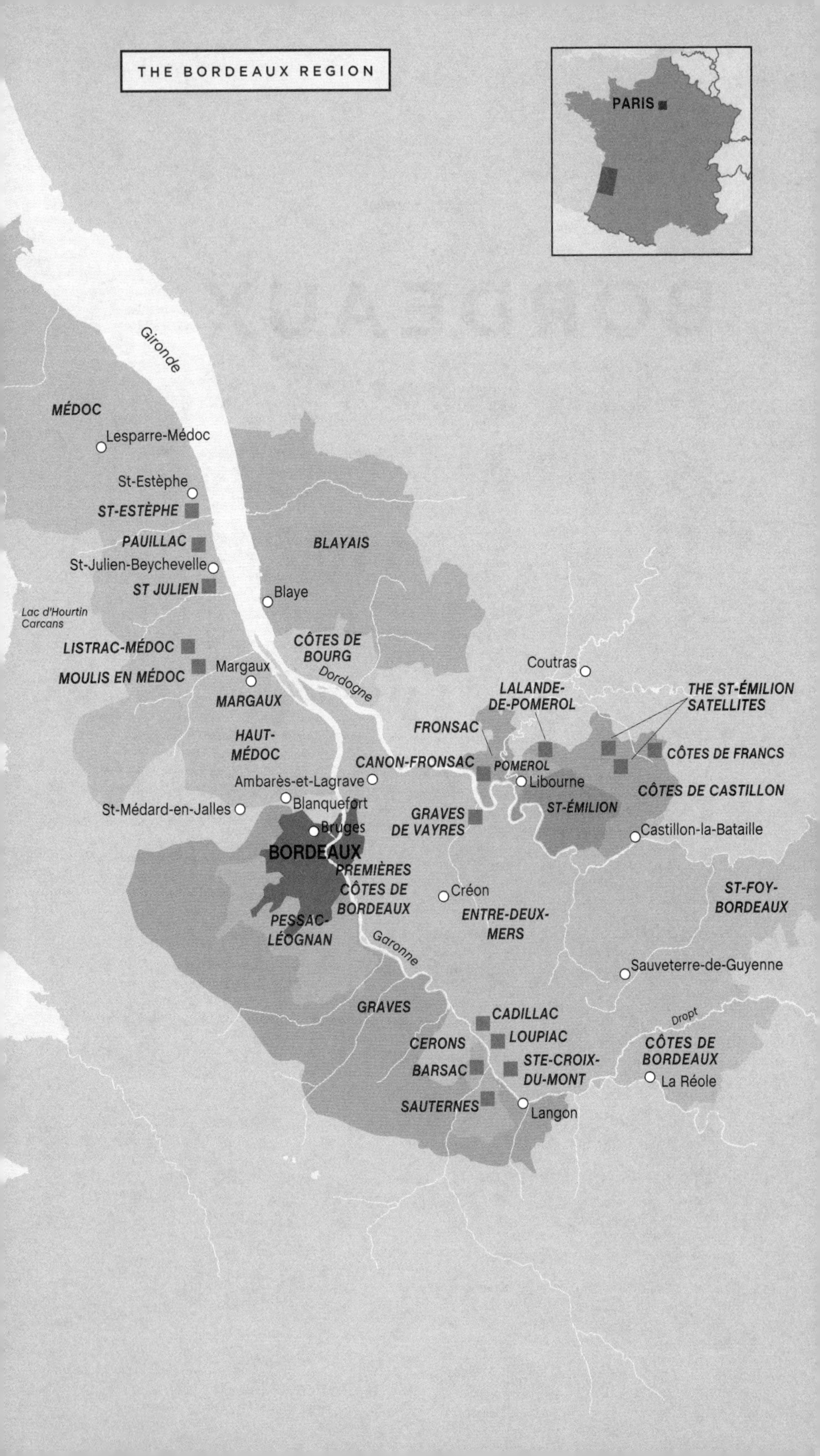

THE BORDEAUX REGION

Gironde
MÉDOC
Lesparre-Médoc
St-Estèphe
ST-ESTÈPHE
PAUILLAC
BLAYAIS
St-Julien-Beychevelle
ST JULIEN
Blaye
Lac d'Hourtin
Carcans
LISTRAC-MÉDOC
CÔTES DE BOURG
MOULIS EN MÉDOC
Margaux
Dordogne
Coutras
MARGAUX
LALANDE-DE-POMEROL
THE ST-ÉMILION SATELLITES
FRONSAC
HAUT-MÉDOC
CÔTES DE FRANCS
CANON-FRONSAC
POMEROL
Ambarès-et-Lagrave
Libourne
CÔTES DE CASTILLON
Blanquefort
St-Médard-en-Jalles
GRAVES DE VAYRES
ST-ÉMILION
Bruges
Castillon-la-Bataille
BORDEAUX
PREMIÈRES CÔTES DE BORDEAUX
Créon
ST-FOY-BORDEAUX
ENTRE-DEUX-MERS
PESSAC-LÉOGNAN
Garonne
Sauveterre-de-Guyenne
GRAVES
CADILLAC
Dropt
LOUPIAC
CERONS
CÔTES DE BORDEAUX
STE-CROIX-DU-MONT
BARSAC
La Réole
SAUTERNES
Langon

Despite the vagaries of the market, the name *Bordeaux* is still magic when it comes to wine, summoning reveries of the great châteaux that by now have become legendary—Pétrus, Lafite, Haut-Brion, Yquem, and so forth. Taking its name from the port city of Bordeaux, this sprawling region produces a vast variety of wines, from the inconsequential to the quintessential, and everything in between. It helps, therefore, to have a rough idea of the lay of the land. Imagine a wavy letter *V* embracing either side of the Gironde estuary. The city of Bordeaux lies slightly to the southwest of the base of the *V*. The region's best vines grow along either arm: to the northwest is a peninsula, known in the wine world as the Left Bank, where the wines of the Médoc are made; to the northeast is the Right Bank, the home of St.-Émilion and Pomerol and many other ACs; immediately to the south of the city of Bordeaux are the regions of Graves and Sauternes, which are commonly grouped along with the Left Bank wines. Farther south, southeast, and east are the stretches of vines that produce most of generic Bordeaux AC and Entre-Deux-Mers AC (the "deux mers" being the Dordogne and the Garonne Rivers, the confluence of which forms the Gironde estuary).

GRAPE VARIETIES: For reds, cabernet sauvignon, cabernet franc, and merlot are the most important. Ancillary grapes include petit verdot, malbec, and carmenère. There are essentially two whites: sémillon and sauvignon blanc.

STYLES OF WINE: There are fifty-seven individual ACs and, within each, there is a range of styles depending on the producer. Broadly, reds run the gamut from the cheap and very ordinary, to inexpensive and easy-drinking Bordeaux and Bordeaux Supérieur ACs, to medium-bodied, full-flavored bistro wines from ACs like Blaye, Côtes de Bourg, Canon-Fronsac, and Côtes de Castillon, to some of the most majestic, complex, long-lived wines in the world from ACs like Pauillac, St.-Julien, St.-Estèphe, Margaux, Pessac-Léognan, St.-Émilion, and Pomerol.

It is necessary to draw a distinction between the wines of the Left Bank, which include the wines of Graves and Pessac-Léognan, and those of the Right Bank. Not only does the *terroir* change but the grape mix varies as well. The Right Bank leans heavily on merlot, followed by cabernet franc, with cabernet sauvignon playing at best a cameo role. The Left Bank is the land of cabernet sauvignon. Here merlot and cabernet franc are handmaidens. Because grape varieties ripen differently, certain vintages are considered Left Bank vintages; others, Right Bank vintages. More important, the styles of the wines are different: Left Bank wines—we're still talking about reds—are authoritative. They have perfect posture and are capable of great elegance and longevity. Right Bank wines are cozier, spicier, more zaftig. Also capable of amazing elegance, they can be drunk somewhat sooner than those from the Left Bank.

Bordeaux's white wines can be dry or sweet. The most and best come from south and southeast of Bordeaux. The range of dry whites is the same as the reds, from quaffers meant to drink within the year, such as those from Entre-Deux-Mers, to age-worthy wines of some nobility—mostly from the Pessac-Léognan AC. The sweet wines also vary in intensity and seriousness. The best, like those from the Sauternes and Barsac ACs, are voluptuous, honeyed nectars made from botrytized grapes.

BORDEAUX VOCABULARY TO KNOW UP FRONT:

Classified Growths: Bordeaux contains a number of classified growths, each of which will be more fully explained in the text that follows. The most important of these is what is known as the 1855 Classification, after the year in which it was instituted, which categorizes what were then considered the top châteaux of the Médoc into five "growths," the topmost being the First Growth or Premier Cru Classé. At the same time, the châteaux of Sauternes and Barsac were also classified, but only three categories were designated—Premier Cru Supérieur Classé and Premier or Deuxième Cru Classé (see SAUTERNES). Subsequently, classifications were created for St.-Émilion (Premier Grand Cru Classé and Grand Cru Classé), for Pessac-Léognan, and for additional Médoc wines. In Médoc, the wine might qualify for Cru Artisan, Cru Bourgeois, Cru Bourgeois Supérieur, or Cru Bourgeois Exceptionnel. In lists of producers, when a château belongs within a classification, that classification appears in an abbreviated form as follows:

Cru Classé: CC
Grand Cru: GC
Grand Cru Classé: GCC
Cru Bourgeois: CB
Cru Bourgeois Supérieur: CBS
Cru Bourgeois Exceptionnel: CBE

There are two more terms of note in Bordeaux. A *grand vin* is a given property's top wine. Many châteaux ensure the high quality of their *grands vins* by making them with only their finest grapes. Grapes from young vines, or grapes otherwise deemed inferior, are used to make what are called second wines, or *deuxièmes vins.* These are often excellent and can be great values.

BEST RECENT VINTAGES: My initial impression of the 2005 vintage is that it's superb across the board—the vintage of a generation, it will be delicious both young and old. The year 2004 was mostly judged by the fact that it wasn't 2003 and has been widely hailed as a return to classicism. The crop was huge, but those who took the appropriate steps to control yields generally made very good, balanced wine, on both sides of the river. These appear to be evolving well, and 2004 will probably come to be considered a very good vintage—and good value.

Because of unprecedented heat, 2003 was perhaps one of the strangest years on record (it was so hot that some grapes burned on the vine). There is enormous variation in quality. The great wines may be very great, and these will surely include Sauternes, but they are likely to evolve more quickly than wines from more balanced years. The less-than-great wines range from bitter and astringent to jammy and heavy.

The underestimated vintages of 2002 and 2001 may offer good value. Of the two, I think 2001 is the better and more homogeneous, though the Right Bank does seem to have the upper hand here. The year 2001 is also acknowledged to be one of the great vintages for white wine, especially for sweet whites. The year 2000 is recognized as a great vintage for big, ripe, exciting reds. It was less favorable for Sauternes.

PRICES: With a vineyard area this vast, prices range from $ to $$$$ and then some. The top growths can cost several hundred dollars a bottle for a recent vintage.

SOME NAMES TO KNOW: Throughout this chapter the names of certain people, families, or businesses (insurance companies, banks, luxury goods manufacturers) will be mentioned repeatedly. Bordeaux is a land of dynasties, of multiple holdings. There's old money (the Rothschilds, the Merlauts, the Lurtons, the Delons, the Moueix clan, and so on) and new (Perse, Magrez, Cathiard, AXA Millésimes, Crédit Foncier-Caisse d'Epargne, Val d'Orbieu, LVMH…) and, more than in any other French region, even newer names are likely to appear over the next decade as properties change hands. (Indeed, as I write, I seem to read about an important new sale at least once a week.) Additionally, most châteaux rely on the advice of consultants. Bordeaux's three-star consultants are Michel Rolland, Stéphane Derenoncourt, and Denis Dubourdieu. All three have their own domaines as well. Dubourdieu is also professor of enology at the University of Bordeaux.

Domaine de l'A ☆

33330 St.-Émilion; 05.57.24.60.29; derenoncourt.stephan@free.fr
Wine: Côtes de Castillon. $$
Stéphane Derenoncourt, the rising star of wine consultation in France (but particularly in Bordeaux), shows what he can do on his own at this small, biodynamically run property. The wines, concentrated, succulent, and pure, give many a St.-Émilion a run for the money. The teacher shows how it's done. Don't think twice, these wines are much, much more than all right.

Château d'Aiguilhe ☆

33350 St.-Philippe-d'Aiguilhe; 05.57.40.60.10; www.neipperg.com
Wine: Côtes de Castillon. $$($)
Stephan von Neipperg, the owner of Canon la Gaffelière and La Mondotte, works with Stéphane Derenoncourt at all his properties. The wines he turns out here are as beautifully made as those from St.-Émilion, though the *terroir* statement is less pronounced. The 2005 is sensational.

Château Angélus ☆

33330 St.-Émilion; 05.57.24.71.39; www.chateau-angelus.com

Wine: St.-Émilion Premier Grand Cru Classé. $$$$

Emphatically stylish, plush St.-Émilions, the wines are racy and sweetly fragrant, with seductive flavors of oak, plump red fruit, and minerals. There's elegance and class here.

Château d'Angludet ☆

33460 Cantenac; 05.57.88.71.41; www.château-angludet.fr

Wine: Margaux Cru Bourgeois Supérieur. $$$

Reliably delicious, the Château d'Angludet Cru Bourgeois Supérieur is easily as good as many a classified growth. It's built to last but, when in a carafe, approachable by its fifth birthday.

Château Ausone ☆

33330 St.-Émilion; 05.57.24.68.88

Wine: St.-Émilion Premier Grand Cru Classé. $$$$

This is one of my desert island wines. (I should be so lucky!) With CHEVAL BLANC, it tops the Premiers Grands Crus Classés. The château's enviable site at the summit of St.-Émilion certainly goes a long way to explaining its preeminence, as does the work of Alain Vauthier, the excellent, affable, and wizardly proprietor. Still, I don't know how he does it, turning out wines this perfect, this breathtakingly detailed and elegant. And here comes one of those when-to-drink-it conundrums. The wines can certainly age with the best of them, but I recall, with thirst, drinking a 1998 in 2003. Surely too soon—yet the wine was glorious, so chiseled, such a nuanced weave of silk and velvet, of fragrant fruit and spices, and so forth and so on...

Barsac

A small but important AC for very sweet *(liquoreux)* whites based on grapes attacked by noble rot. Barsac producers may choose to use the AC Sauternes. Since the wines are so similar, the vintages, prices, and producers are described in the SAUTERNES listing, where you'll find these Barsac-area producers: Ch Broustet ◆ CH CLIMENS ☆ ◆ Ch Closiot ◆ Cru Barréjats ↑ ◆ CH DOISY-DAËNE ☆ ◆ Ch Doisy-Védrines ◆ Ch Massereau ◆ Ch Myrat ◆ Ch Nairac ◆ Ch de Rolland ◆ CH ROUMIEU-LACOSTE ☆.

Château Batailley

33250 Pauillac; 05.56.59.01.13; www.borie-manoux.fr

Wine: Pauillac, Cinquième Cru Classé. $$$

This Fifth Growth château recently hired Denis Dubourdieu as a consultant. New discipline has led to great improvement in the wines since 2002. And prices are reasonable.

Château Beau-Séjour-Bécot ☆

33330 St.-Émilion; 05.57.74.46.87; www.beausejour-becot.com

Wine: St.-Émilion Premier Grand Cru Classé. $$$ to $$$$

A top St.-Émilion property with deep, rich, fragrant wines. La Gomerie, from a small parcel, is the deluxe garage wine. It is intense and powerful but also elegant. It's twice as expensive as the normal bottling, however, and the straight Beau-Séjour-Bécot is mighty seductive, velvety, and at least as elegant as La Gomerie.

Château Belair ☆

33330 St.-Émilion; 05.57.24.70.94; www.chateaubelair.com

Wine: St.-Émilion Premier Grand Cru Classé. $$$ to $$$$

Pascal Delbeck, self-effacing and a purist's purist, converted this domaine to biodynamics. He believes in respecting the truth of the specific vintage. His wines are sometimes more austere or lighter than is currently fashionable, but they're excellent, fragrant, fresh, and delicious. A 2001, tasted in 2005, was silky, beautifully balanced, and as soft and inviting as a pillow.

Château Bel Air la Royère ☆

33390 Cars; 05.57.42.91.34; château.belair.la.royere@wanadoo.fr
Wines: Blaye and Premières Côtes de Blaye. $$ to $$$
Under the stewardship of Xavier Lauriaud this domaine has become one of the leading producers of the Blayais. The wines aren't cheap but they are stylish, specific, and delicious—in 2002 as well as in 2001 and 2003. A healthy dose of malbec may contribute to their particular succulence.

Château Bellefont-Belcier ↑

33330 Saint Laurent des Combes; 05 57 24 72 16; www.bellefont-belcier.fr
Wine: St.-Émilion Grand Cru. $$$
This once important St.-Émilion estate, which fell into disuse when its owners used it as a vacation home, was purchased about five years ago by partners Alain Laguillaumie and Jacques Berrebi. The domaine seems to have been returned to dedicated hands. With the Châteaux PAVIE, Larcis-Ducasse, and LE TERTRE-RÔTEBOEUF as neighbors, with new cellars, new consultants (including Michel Rolland), and enlightened vineyard practices such as cluster thinning and leaf removal, Bellefont-Belcier may well be on its way to Grand Cru Classé status in the 2006 reclassification. Thus far the wines are structured, specific, and promising.

Château Bellevue ☆

33330 St.-Émilion; 05.57. 24.74.23; pavie.macquin@wanadoo.fr
Wine: St.-Émilion Grand Cru Classé. $$$
For some years I've admired the work of Nicolas Thienpont at Pavie-Macquin. Since 2000 he has overseen the Château Bellevue property. Working with Stéphane Derenoncourt, he immediately lowered yields and harvested riper grapes. His 2002 (90 percent merlot) was so delicious I could have drunk several magnums of it on the spot—though it's built for the long haul—and the vintages that have followed are equally alluring.

Château Beychevelle ☆

33250 St.-Julien-Beychevelle; 05.56.73.20.70; www.beychevelle.com
Wine: St.-Julien Grand Cru Classé . $$$($)
I must confess to having a soft spot for the château that pushed me over the edge into wine geekdom. It wasn't even a good vintage, but I'd never tasted anything that layered, complex, or delicious in my life. I was dumbstruck. I still admire the wines for their indomitable character and fine focus but think that this Fourth Growth can do better in terms of ripening the fruit: I too often find the wines herbaceous and overoaked. Ditto for the second wine, Amiral de Beychevelle.

Blaye, Côtes de Blaye, and Premières Côtes de Blaye

Three distinct but related ACs, lying north of Bordeaux and across the Gironde estuary from the Haut-Médoc (the ferry ride is delightful). The Blaye AC produces a little bit of white but is largely devoted to red, which is made from the usual Bordeaux grapes in addition to some real oddities, beguignol and prelongeau (though it's unclear that anyone takes advantage of the opportunity thus offered). The AC Côtes de Blaye is solely for whites made chiefly from colombard, sémillon, and sauvignon. The Premières Côtes de Blaye AC, by far the largest of the three ACs, produces whites and reds based on the standard Bordeaux grapes. (This AC may be subsumed by the creation of the AC CÔTES DE BORDEAUX, as would Côtes de Blaye.) The wines are generally pleasant rather than grand—for drinking in the near term rather than for cellaring. They are priced accordingly, though some of the more ambitious producers, who do make more ambitious wines, post prices equal to those of the Médoc.

BEST RECENT VINTAGES: 2005, (2004), (2003), (2002), 2001, and 2000.
PRICES: $ to $$$

PRODUCERS: CH BEL AIR LA ROYÈRE ☆ ◆ Ch Charron (Premières Côtes de Blaye): look for the top cuvées, Acacia, a barrel-fermented white based on sémillon, and Les Gruppes in red ◆ Ch Gigault (Premières Côtes de Blaye): Stéphane Derenoncourt consults; the Cuvée Viva is rich and concentrated, with sweet fruit. The 2005 Cuvée Viva is deep and densely fruity, an overachiever. A producer to follow ◆ Les Grandes Maréchaux: from another Derenoncourt disciple, a very promising 2005 is fresh, with great succulence and a fine sense of place ◆ CH HAUT-BERTINERIE (Ch Bertinerie) ◆ Ch Petit Boyer: an eco-friendly domaine making several very worthwhile bottlings of both Blaye and Premières Côtes de Blaye ◆ Ch le Queyroux (Blaye): merely eight thousand bottles of hypernatural wine, separated into three fascinating bottlings—Le Joyau, the top cuvée, is silky with light oak accents. It seems exactly the kind of wine people want to drink now. Le Queyroux, the second wine, is direct, fruity, and very good. There's also a tasty and interesting pure petit verdot ↑ ◆ Ch Roland la Garde (Premières Côtes de Blaye): concentrated reds, not elegant but worthy, particularly for winter suppers by the fireplace.

Château le Bon-Pasteur ☆

33500 Pomerol; 05.57.51.23.05; fax: 05.57.51.66.08
Wine: Pomerol. $$$($) to $$$$
Star wine consultant Michel Rolland practices what he preaches at this property near Pomerol's border with St.-Émilion. Good vintage or bad, the wines are seductive, harmonious, ripe, and soigné, having been aged in the best of all possible oak barrels. Exuberantly perfumed, the plushness of the (perfectly) ripe fruit almost overwhelms the oak. Rolland succeeds very well with the Rolland style, though the pedigree evident in his Pomerols proves that the Rolland method allows the *terroir* to speak as well.

Bordeaux, Bordeaux Supérieur, Premières Côtes de Bordeaux, and Bordeaux Clairet and Rosé

Generic Bordeaux covers an immense region and, while most of the wine produced is red, the AC may apply to just about everything, from dry to off-dry whites, rosés, clairets, and sparkling wines. Bordeaux Supérieur, a more restricted appellation, applies chiefly to reds, which have a slightly higher alcohol content than simple Bordeaux. The Premières Côtes de Bordeaux, a still more limited region, applies to sweet whites and dry reds. There is a veritable ocean of mediocre wine in this category. However, there's dynamism too, and an increasing number of delectable wines—reds in particular—can be found. (Bordeaux Sec is the AC used for whites produced by châteaux in such prestigious red appellations as Margaux's Pavillon Blanc de Château Margaux.) In general, drink the youngest available. For the record, there is also a minuscule AC for dry and sweet whites called Bordeaux-Haut Benauge.

PRICES: Usually $, although some of the most ambitious wines will run to $$$.

PRODUCERS: Amavinum du Ch la Roche Beaulieu: Serge Tcheckov, a man of many vinous hats (he's a journalist and makes films for wine companies) makes a garage-style red. Based chiefly on merlot, it's plush, rich, oaky, and tannic ◆ Ch Beaulieu: working with Stéphane Derenoncourt, Vianney de Tastes is making rich, suave, new-oak-aged reds that are helping to raise the image of the generic Bordeaux AC ↑ ◆ Ch Bonnet: see ENTRE-DEUX-MERS ◆ Ch Carignan (Premières Côtes): look for the cuvée Prima, a cinnamon-scented, oaky, ambitious red ◆ Ch Clos de la Tour (Bordeaux and Bordeaux Supérieur): owned by the large merchant house Dourthe, this domaine turns out a respectable, commercial, if pricey Réserve bottling ◆ CH DUBOIS CHALLON ☆

◆ Ch Ducasse (Bordeaux): Hervé Dubourdieu makes a devastatingly delicious unfiltered white with accents of peach and minerals; see also Graville-Lacoste in the Graves listing and ROUMIEU-LACOSTE ☆ ◆ Ch Ducla (Bordeaux and Bordeaux Supérieur): the huge merchant Yvan Mau makes several worthwhile special bottlings, including Experience IX, a mellow white, and Permanence VI, a pungent, oaky red. Premius is a red bottling that would make a good airplane wine—no joke ◆ Ch Jean Faux: a barrel maker, Faux has been working with Stéphane Derenoncourt since 2003, Faux's first vintage. Both 2003 and 2004 are admirable—velvety, well-made, and nicely balanced (but expensive) ↑ ◆ GIROLATE ↑ ◆ Ch Grée Laroque (Bordeaux Supérieur): more very nice, expensive generic Bordeaux with the Derenoncourt touch; the reds are structured, lightly oaky, and fairly elegant ↑ ◆ Ch l'Isle (Bordeaux Supérieur): yet another Derenoncourt Pygmalion (first vintage, 2004), this one a creamy red with sweet, ripe fruit ◆ CH HAUT BERTINERIE ◆ Ch Jonqueyres (Bordeaux Supérieur): pleasant cuvées include the oaky Balthus and the focused Dorothée ◆ Ch Lagarette (Premières Côtes de Bordeaux): organic wine made by a Parisian turned vigneronne. The cuvée Renaissance recalls a nice Rioja ◆ Ch La Grave de Moustey (Bordeaux): suave, organic, beautifully balanced, "simple" Bordeaux, part of Pascal Delbeck's stable (see CH BELAIR) ☆ ◆ Ch Lavergne-Dulong (Bordeaux Supérieur): Sylvie Dulong, a trained enologist, is making balanced, focused, lightly oaked, and very noteworthy wines ↑ ◆ Ch Marjosse (Bordeaux): another Lurton property, this one run by Pierre. The wines are balanced, fairly elegant, if somewhat simple Bordeaux ◆ Ch Massereau (Bordeaux): see listings in GRAVES and SAUTERNES ↑ ◆ Ch Mont-Perat (Premières Côtes de Bordeaux): the Despagne family does a typically nice job here, with a lightly oaked, plummy red ◆ Ch Penin (Bordeaux Supérieur): look for the Les Cailloux bottling, a fragrant, stylish, user-friendly Bordeaux for near-term drinking ◆ Ch le Pin Beausoleil (Bordeaux Supérieur): the new owner, Michael Halleck, is working with Stéphane Derenoncourt—with predictably good results. The 2002 is drinking beautifully right now and the 2004 is a characterful red that goes down all too easily ↑ ◆ CH DE REIGNAC ☆ ◆ Ch Reynon (Premières Côtes de Bordeaux): see CLOS FLORIDÈNE ◆ Ch Ste.-Marie: see ENTRE-DEUX-MERS ◆ CH THIEULEY ◆ Ch Tour de Mirambeau (Bordeaux Supérieur): the Despagnes make a plush, seductive cuvée Passion from their best parcels of merlot and cabernet sauvignon.

Château Brane-Cantenac ☆

33460 Cantenac; 05.57.88.83.33; www.brane-cantenac.com
Wine: Margaux Deuxième Cru. $$$$
Since Henri Lurton took over the management of the property in 1996, quality has improved immensely at this Second Growth. Take the 1998 as an example: it's rich, ripe (with ripe tannins), supple, racy, and concentrated and textured. The 2000 seems as potent as a Pauillac, a young giant that will need a good ten years. The 2001 and 2002 can be drunk within five, if carafed and if you're willing to sacrifice some depth for beautiful fruit. Tasted blind, you might think 2003 had syrah in the blend. The second wine is Baron de Brane.

Cadillac

A tiny AC in the southern part of the Premières Côtes de Bordeaux, just north of the Loupiac AC. Cadillac produces sweet—demi-sec or *moelleux*—whites made from sémillon, sauvignon blanc, and muscadelle, hand-harvested overripe in successive passes through the vineyard. Producer: Ch Peyruchet: a good domaine, with a lovely, sémillon-dominated 2003—worth trying.

Château Calon-Ségur ☆
33180 St.-Estèphe; 05.56.59.30.08; fax: 05.56.59.71.51
Wine: St.-Estèphe Troisième Cru. $$$ to $$$$
A large Third Growth with potentially splendid wines. There's been some inconsistency in the recent past but the château seems on the path to recovering its former glory. To follow. Johnny Depp is an ardent and vocal fan.

Canon-Fronsac

A small AC west of Libourne, for potentially very good, reasonably priced reds made from the cabernets, malbec, and merlot. Producers also make wines under the AC Fronsac. The vintages are similar to ST.-ÉMILION.

PRICES: $$($)

PRODUCERS: Ch Barrabaque: the cuvée Prestige is a robust red, fine for wine bars and bistros ◆ Canon de Brem: respectable reds for casual drinking; see also Ch de la Dauphine in FRONSAC ◆ Ch Cassagne Haut-Canon: well-placed vineyards and careful vinification produce smooth, fresh reds with attractive fruit under the label La Truffière ◆ Ch du Gaby: Antoine Khayat bought this property in 1999 and has made substantial efforts in both vineyards and cellar. He seems to be aiming for a blockbuster style—concentrated, oaky reds. There's good, ambitious work here. To follow ↑ ◆ Ch Haut Ballet: owned by Olivier Decelle (see MAS AMIEL in the Languedoc-Roussillon), this property produces smooth, very professional, very nice midrange Bordeaux. The style is slightly New World; the prices are levelheaded. ◆ CH MOULIN PEY-LABRIE ↑.

Château Canon-la-Gaffelière ☆
33330 St.-Émilion; 05.57.24.71.33; www.neipperg.com
Wine: St.-Émilion Grand Cru Classé. $$$$
Over the past decade, Count Stephan von Neipperg has turned this property into one of the most exciting in St.-Émilion. Working with Stéphane Derenoncourt, he makes sumptuous, racy wines. The most famous and sought-after is his micro-cuvée La Mondotte. This is a heroic, lavish garage wine compared to the standard Canon-la-Gaffelière, which is pure elegance. Von Neippberg also owns the Clos de l'Oratoire, another Grand Cru Classé, where he makes similarly styled wines. And von Neippberg has become a shareholder in Château Guiraud in Sauternes following its sale in May 2006.

Château Carbonnieux ☆
33850 Léognan; 05.57.96.56.20; château.carbonnieux@wanadoo.fr
Wine: Pessac-Léognan (Cru Classé). $$$
Let the whites age three or four years and you'll be rewarded with statuesque wines, firm, mineral, with good grip; the reds, too, need a bit of time to flesh out but they're reliable, satisfying, and specific.

Cérons

A tiny AC forming an enclave within the Graves region, for sweet whites made from sémillon, sauvignon, and muscadelle, hand-harvested overripe in successive passes through the vineyard. See SAUTERNES for vintages and prices. Producer: Ch de Chantegrive: a very good domaine with satisfyingly nuanced wines accented by flavors of orange peel, honey, and herbal tea.

Château Chasse-Spleen ☆

33480 Moulis-en-Médoc; 05.56.58.02.37; cvillarsfoubet@chassespleen.com

Wine: Moulis-en-Médoc Cru Bourgeois Exceptionnel. $$$($)

Perhaps the quality leader in Moulis, this large domaine consistently produces full-bodied, well-structured, age-worthy reds. I think the smooth, fresh, and racy 1990 is ready to start drinking. (Why wait?) The seductive, meaty, black-olive–accented 1999 can wait a couple of years but the 1998 is already supple, well integrated, and bordering on elegant. All the wines from the twenty-first century are successes—fragrant, juicy, and harmonious.

Château Cheval-Blanc ☆

33330 St.-Émilion; 05.57.55.55.55; www.château-chevalblanc.com

Wine: St.-Émilion Premier Grand Cru Classé. $$$$

With CH AUSONE, the top Premier Grand Cru Classé. Reliably magnificent. What's unusual here is the reliance on cabernet franc. No expenses are spared to ensure that this ideally sited vineyard produces one of the greatest wines in the world. The effort bears fruit. The wine caresses the palate with silk and spices, the finest of tannins, and extreme elegance. A thoroughbred indeed. The second wine, Petit-Cheval, while smaller in every way, is still very good.

Domaine de Chevalier ☆

33850 Léognan; 05.56.64.16.16; www.domainedechevalier.com

Wine: Pessac-Léognan Cru Classé. $$$($)

Demand for the small amount of whites from this excellent property has long exceeded supply. The reds, while always very good and specific, are improving—with the help of Stéphane Derenoncourt. Both whites and reds exemplify the reserved elegance of the AC and seem effortlessly to combine authority and deliciousness. The 2005 red is racy and promises to be grandiose. Jump on it and try to make yourself wait to drink it.

Château Clauzet ↑

33180 St.-Estèphe; 05.56.59.34.16; château.clauzet@wanadoo.fr

Wine: St.-Estèphe (Cru Bourgeois). $$ to $$$

Beginning in 1997, Maurice Velge, a wine- and art-loving Belgian baron, began assembling acreage in St.-Estèphe, including the well-sited Château Clauzet. He spared no expense in renovating vineyards and cellars and putting together a top-notch team, determined to give his property the same TLC lavished on a classified growth. It appears to be working: Château Clauzet's wines are warm, supple, spicy, and harmonious.

Château Climens ☆

33720 Barsac; 05.56.27.15.33; www.chateau-climens.fr

Wine: Barsac Premier Cru Classé. $$$($) to $$$$

Owner Bérénice Lurton makes superb, finely tuned Barsacs (and therefore Sauternes). The wines are majestic and pure and have few rivals.

Château Clinet ☆

33000 Pomerol; 05.56.79.12.12; www.chateauclinet.com

Wine: Pomerol. $$$$

Jean-Louis Laborde, who bought this excellent property less than ten years ago, hired his friend Michel Rolland to help with the wines. Quality is constantly improving. The wines are velvety and sumptuous, with rich flavors of raspberry and black cherry, good freshness, and lovely integration of the oak. Behind all the lushness lurks pedigree—which I can only believe will take front stage after time in the bottle. The château's second wine is Fleur de Clinet.

Clos Floridène ☆

33210 Pujols sur Ciron; 05.56.62.96.51; reynon@gofornet.com

Wine: Graves. $$

Denis Dubourdieu is one of the leading enologists in France, particularly where white wines are concerned. A professor at the University of Bordeaux, he has influenced an entire generation of vintners. His own wines, not surprisingly, are textbook, always intelligent, balanced, and true to the vintage and the AC. They are also vibrant, flavorful, and focused. Reds and whites from another Dubourdieu property, Château Reynon (Premier Côtes de Bordeaux AC), are well structured and, obviously, well made. We're not talking complexity here; we're talking really nice, juicy, ample wines for bistro meals. See also DOISY-DAËNE, Dubourdieu's Barsac.

Clos Fourtet ☆

33330 St.-Émilion; 05.57.24.70.90; clostfourtet@wanadoo.fr
Wine: St.-Émilion Premier Grand Cru. $$$ to $$$$
Philippe Cuvelier took over this First Growth in 2001 and has been working with Stéphane Derenoncourt. The results are exciting and delicious. The 2004, in particular, looks exceptionally classic, racy, and structured, with lipsmacking flavors. The 2002 is also excellent—structured and velvety. And both the 2001 and 2003 are delectable successes as well.

Clos Puy Arnaud ☆

33350 Belves de Castillon; 05.57.47.90.53; clospuyarnaud@wanadoo.fr
Wine: Côtes de Castillon. $$
Thierry Valette, the owner, works with Stéphane Derenoncourt on this organically run domaine. The wines are fresh, elegant, and enticing; the oak enveloped in lovely fruit. Excellent even in 2002.

Château la Conseillante ☆

33500 Pomerol; 05.57.51.15.32; www.la-conseillante.com
Wine: Pomerol. $$$$
Not a bad vintage in sight here. Ideally located on a plateau between CHEVAL BLANC and PÉTRUS, la Conseillante produces majestic wines, as silky and noble as they are delicious. The 2001 (an underestimated vintage) was still closed in early 2006. The 1998, a great Right Bank year, was beginning to show its aristocratic lineage. A 1990, drunk at the same time, was still full of sap but seemed ready to drink—fresh, solid, long, with autumnal flavors and hints of sandalwood.

Château Cos d'Estournel ☆

33180 St.-Estèphe; 05.56.73.15.50; www.estournel.com
Wine: St.-Estèphe Grand Cru Classé. $$$$
One of the greats. A Second Growth that rivals First Growths. Concentrated, focused, and majestic. Les Pagodes de Cos is the second wine, a very worthy St.-Estèphe but a far cry from Cos.

Côtes de Blaye: See BLAYE.

Côtes de Bordeaux

Not yet an official AC, this appellation—if created—is intended to subsume five current ACs: Côtes de Bourg, Côtes de Blaye, Côtes de Castillon, Côtes de Francs, and Premières Côtes de Bordeaux. The new AC, which is intended to simplify life for the consumer, is expected to be created in time for the 2006 harvest. The Côtes de Bourg, which is opposed to the new AC, would not be included until later, if at all.

Côtes de Bourg

A dynamic, good-size AC about twenty miles north of Bordeaux and immediately south of the Blayais on the right bank of the Dordogne and the Gironde, the Côtes de Bourg is essentially a producer of red wines made from merlot, the cabernets, and malbec. The region also makes a minuscule amount of white (from sauvignon, colombard, sémillon, and muscadelle). The wines—with some notable exceptions—had typically been sturdy, bistro or hamburger Bordeaux, for near-term drinking. A new generation, however, has joined the early pioneers and is making more serious wine, easily on the level of some of the better Cru Bourgeois. Prices for special cuvées are climbing but you can still find some real values here. Drink the youngest available.

PRICES: $ to $$($)

PRODUCERS: Ch de Barbe: look for the cuvée Pourpre, a reasonably priced, plush and tasty red (80 percent merlot) that would be great with a grilled steak ◆ Ch Brulescaille: inexpensive, tasty versions of the AC ◆ Cave de Bourg-Tauriac: the merlot-based, new-oak-aged cuvée Évidence is pretty impressive, nicely structured, and fairly priced ◆ Clos Alphonse Dubreuil: Isabelle and Pascal Montaut, who own several properties, including Ch Les Jonqueyres in the Blayais, make a prestige bottling here. It's an elegant blend of ripe cabernet and merlot, with new oak and spice flavors ◆ Ch Croûte Charlus: part of the new generation in the AC, this domaine's wines reveal good, serious work but they're not yet ready for prime time ◆ COULÉE DE BAYON ↑ ◆ CH FALFAS ☆ ◆ Ch Fougas: the deluxe cuvée Maldoror merits a star for its easy elegance, its lovely concentrated fruit, and its fine balance. Very good work and very satisfying ◆ Ch Guionne: Michel Rolland brings his influence to bear on good wines from this property, particularly the succulent cuvée Renaissance ◆ Ch Haut Bajac: a promising domaine producing both whites and reds, run by an enologist ◆ Ch l'Hospital: part of the young generation, this eco-friendly domaine makes two cuvées, one in the old style, the other in the new. More alike than they are different, give or take some oakiness and heft, both are easy-drinking, intelligently made reds with attractive prices ◆ Ch Martinat: look for the fragrant, stylish cuvée Epicurea made from 90 percent merlot and 10 percent malbec and aged in new oak ◆ Ch Mercier: the bottling to look for here is the delicious Clos du Piat cuvée Jade, although the standard cuvée's not bad either ◆ Ch de Rivereau: cheap and cheerful reds with a hint of elegance ◆ CH ROC DES CAMBES ☆ ◆ Ch de Rousselet: a healthy percentage of malbec brings real juiciness to the charitably priced and lightly oaked wines of this promising domaine ↑ ◆ Ch le Sablard: 2001 was the first harvest for young, eco-friendly owners Catherine and Thomas Buratti-Berlinger. Their cuvée Prestige of that year was remarkable both for its price, $($), and for its tastiness ↑ ◆ Ch Tayac: the cuvée Prestige, based on old cabernet sauvignon vines, is chewy and good but, for a dollar or two more, you can get Les Terrasses, a sumptuous, star-worthy, serious red from old merlot vines ◆ Ch Tour de Guiet: another young, eco-friendly domaine very much worth following, its wines thus far are fragrant, structured, reasonably priced, and delicious ↑ ◆ Ch les Tours Séguy: cheap and cheerful wines, both oaked and nonoaked.

Côtes de Castillon

An AC to the east of St.-Émilion for very similar reds. (This AC may be subsumed by the creation of the AC CÔTES DE BORDEAUX.) The AC has attracted many Right Bank producers; its vintages correspond to those of St.-Émilion, as do the prices of its best wines.

PRODUCERS: ◆ DOM DE L'A ☆ ◆ CH D'AIGUILHE ☆ ◆ Ch Ampelia: another good Despagne property. At their best, as in 2001, these are mouthwatering wines with silky elegance, well worth a star ◆ Ch Cap de Faugères: see CH FAUGÈRES ☆ ◆ CLOS PUY ARNAUD ☆ ◆ Ch Joanin Becot: the proprietors of BEAU-SÉJOUR BÉCOT/LA GOMERIE produce an ambitious, fragrant, nicely structured red from this small domaine. Drink this before its tenth birthday ◆ Ch de Laussac: spicy, attractive reds with a whiff of the New World.

Côtes de Francs (Bordeaux-Côtes des Francs)

A small AC less than ten miles east of St.-Émilion on the northern border of the Côtes du Castillon. (This AC may be subsumed by the creation of the AC CÔTES DE BORDEAUX.) The AC principally produces reds made from merlot, cabernet franc, and malbec but a tiny quantity of whites made from muscadelle, sémillon, and sauvignon blanc is also produced. The region has attracted some dynamic producers from St.-Émilion. Vintages are similar and prices start lower but quickly climb to equal those of St.-Émilion.

PRODUCERS: Ch de Francs: Les Cerisiers is the name for the reasonably priced, well-upholstered, tasty cuvée of red made at a property created by two St.-Émilion producers, Hubert de Bouard (CH ANGELUS) and Dominique Hebrard (Trianon) ☆ ◆ Ch la Prade: Nicolas Thienpont (PAVIE-MACQUIN; PUYGUÉRAUD) has taken over this domaine and is making some typically impressive reds based chiefly on merlot ↑ ◆ CH PUYGUÉRAUD ☆

Coulée de Bayon ↑

33710 Bayon; 05.57.64.81.74

Wine: Côtes de Bourg. $($)

Is it cruel to recommend a domaine so small it doesn't even have a hectare of vines? That makes a paltry two thousand bottles a year? Particularly since the wines are super and cheap? Can't help it. Jean-Marc Delhaye came to wine late but with a passion. Everything is done by hand—even destemming—and with respect for nature. Mostly merlot and malbec, with yields kept to a mininum, the wines age in new and newish oak. They're fragrant, inviting, plush, and generous. Charming rather than majestic, they're wines you'd have to be really mean not to like.

Château Couspaude ☆

33330 St.-Émilion; 05.57.40.15.76; www.la-couspaude.com

Wine: St.-Émilion Grand Cru Classé. $$$ to $$$$

Modern, stylish, plush, oaky St.-Émilions—it would be easy to fault them for pandering to current tastes if they weren't so delicious. For Thanksgiving 2003, I opened a magnum of the 1996. It was inviting and mellow, wonderful to drink at the time and would surely have held, and perhaps deepened, over the next five years. Every bit the style of wine I've come to expect from this property, it was the star wine of the dinner for me as well as for invitees, who included two of my favorite vignerons. Jean-Claude Aubert also owns and make similarly styled wines at the Châteaux Messile Cassat (see the ST.-ÉMILION SATELLITE Montagne-St.-Émilion) and Jean de Gue in Lalande-de-Pomerol.

Château Coutet ☆

33720 Barsac; 05.56.27.15.46; 05.56.27.02.20

Wine: Barsac-Sauternes Premier Cru Classé. $$$($)

Look for wines that are clear and fresh as a waterfall, refined, lush, and simply magnificent—at prices that begin to be affordable.

Crémant de Bordeaux

An AC for sparkling wine made from Bordelais grapes according to the Champagne method (the *méthode traditionelle*).

Cru Artisan

A recent resuscitation of an old classification, Cru Artisan has been applied to forty-four small, hands-on domaines from the Médoc and Haut-Médoc as of the 2005 vintage.

Cru Barréjats ↑

33210 Pujols-sur-Ciron; tel/fax: 05.56.76.69.06

Wine: Sauternes. $$$($)

Mireille Daret, a charter member of the hypernatural club, produces singular organic Sauternes on her tiny domaine. The wines aren't perfect but they are always rich, pure, and tasty. And quality has clearly improved over the past decade. I'd also recommend the second wine, Accabailles de Barréjat. Daret occasionally makes a wacko wine, which she seems to view more as an amusement than as a statement of ideology. Case in point: a nameless dry white that fermented three times, reached 17 percent alcohol, and tastes like botrytized sherry.

Cru Bourgeois, Cru Bourgeois Supérieur, and Cru Bourgeois Exceptionnel

Just below the Fifth Growth rank, Cru Bourgeois status applies to 247 Médoc properties: 151 of these are Cru Bourgeois; 87 are Cru Bourgeois Supérieur; and 9 are Cru Bourgeois Exceptionnel. The nine, generally of Grand Cru Classé status, are Haut-Château Marbuzet, CHÂTEAU DE PEZ, CHÂTEAU LES ORMES DE PEZ, PHÉLAN SÉGUR, all in St.-Estèphe; in Margaux, CHÂTEAU SIRAN and Château Labégorce-Zédé (see MARGAUX); CHÂTEAU CHASSE-SPLEEN and CHÂTEAU POUJEAUX in Moulis; and CHÂTEAU POTENSAC in the Médoc.

Cru Classé

In 1855, sixty Médoc properties were classified into what were called five growths. Although there is much dispute over the current validity of the classifications, only one change has ever been made—in 1973 when Mouton-Rothschild was added to the First Growths. All, save Château Haut-Brion, are in the Médoc. Here they are.

First Growths (Premiers Crus): The Châteaux Haut-Brion, Lafite-Rothschild, Latour, Margaux, and Mouton-Rothschild.

Second Growths (Deuxièmes Crus): The Châteaux Brane-Cantenac, Cos d'Estournel, Ducru-Beaucaillou, Durfort-Vivens, Gruaud-Larose, Lascombes, Léoville-Barton, Léoville Las Cases, Léoville-Poyferré, Montrose, Pichon-Longueville-Baron, Pichon-Longueville Comtesse-de-Lalande, Rauzan-Ségla, and Rauzan-Gassies.

Third Growths (Troisièmes Crus): The Châteaux Boyd-Cantenac, Calon-Ségur, Cantenac Brown, Desmirail, Ferrière, Giscours, d'Issan, Kirwan, Lagrange, la Lagune, Langoa-Barton, Malescot-Saint-Exupéry, and Palmer.

Fourth Growths (Quatrièmes Crus): The Châteaux Beychevelle, Branaire-Ducru, Duhart-Milon-Rothschild, Lafon-Rochet, Marquis-de-Terme, Pouget, Prieuré-Lichine, Saint-Pierre, Talbot, and La Tour-Carnet.

Fifth Growths (Cinquièmes Crus): The Châteaux d'Armailhac, Batailley, Belgrave, Camensac, Cantemerle, Clerc-Milon, Cos-Labory, Croizet-Bages, Dauzac, Grand-Puy-Ducasse, Grand-Puy-Lacoste, Haut-Bages-Libéral, Haut-Batailley, Lynch-Bages, Lynch-Moussas, Pédesclaux, Pontet-Canet, and du Tertre.

(See also SAUTERNES for its 1855 classification.)

Château Doisy-Daëne ☆

33720 Barsac; 05.56.27.15.84; fax: 05.56.27.18.99

Wine: Barsac Deuxième Cru Classé. $$ to $$$($)

White wine wizard Denis Dubourdieu runs this domaine, which is situated in Barsac between the Châteaux CLIMENS and COUTET. His Barsacs are opulent and layered—and not unreasonably priced. In great years he produces a slightly richer cuvée Extravagant.

Château Dubois Challon ☆

33330 St.-Émilion; 05.57.24.70.94; www.chateaubelair.com

Wine: Bordeaux. $($)

Pascal Delbeck (see BELAIR) brings his considerable talent to this property. Fleur Amandine, a barrel-fermented blend of sauvignon, sémillon, and muscadelle, is truly excellent. It could easily compete with a good Pessac-Léognan.

Château Ducru-Beaucaillou ☆

33250 St.-Julien-Beychevelle; 05.56.73.16.73; fax: 05.56.59.27.37

Wine: St.-Julien Grand Cru Classé. $$$$

Classic in the best sense of the word, the wine of this Second Growth is reliably excellent, subtle, and fine. Advice: let it age a good ten years. (A 1970, tasted in 1999, was beautiful, with a marvelously hypnotizing finish.)

Château l'Église-Clinet ☆

33500 Pomerol; 05.57.25.96.59; www.eglise-clinet.com

Wine: Pomerol. $$$$

Superb but expensive. The basics are: old vines, pitiless selection (for perfect fruit), a healthy percentage of cabernet franc, and Denis Durantou, a proprietor who is an ambitious wine artist. The results: fresh, complex, complete, racy, vigorous wines, among the best in the AC. The second wine is La Petite Église.

Entre-Deux-Mers

A sizable AC between the Garonne and the Dordogne Rivers (the "deux mers"—two seas), for pleasant whites made from the usual Bordeaux grapes, particularly sauvignon blanc. Basically a large triangle, the AC is bounded by a cluster of smaller ACs such as Loupiac and Graves de Vayre. Drink the youngest available.

PRICES: $

PRODUCERS: Ch Bonnet: the seat of the dynamic André Lurton, this enormous property turns out well-made whites and, under the Bordeaux AC, reds including a garage-style wine called Divinus ◆ Ch Marjosse: see BORDEAUX ◆ Ch Ste.-Marie: this eco-friendly domaine makes two bottlings of the AC, a clean, tangy, bracing, nonoaked blend of sauvignon, sémillon, and muscadelle, and Madlys, a mineral, Graves-like, barrel-aged white. The best of the domaine's reds, AC Bordeaux Supérieur and Premières Côtes de Bordeaux, is the impressive Alios—to drink while the fruit and mineral flavors are still young and vibrant ↑ ◆ Ch la Tuilerie du Puy: in 2005 this domaine launched a limited edition of the deluxe model, 1616. Made from the old vines of sauvignon and sémillon, harvested at night, and fermented and aged in oak from Missouri, Slovakia, the Caucasus, and the Allier forest of France, it is very soigné, with lots of nice new oak (the kind of oak that even people who don't like oak will enjoy). There's also plenty of nice fruit and a bit of elegance. At $$($) it's expensive and should not be overchilled.

Château l'Évangile ☆

33500 Pomerol; 05.57.55.45.55; www.lafite.com

Wine: Pomerol. $$$$

Perfectly located between PÉTRUS and CHEVAL BLANC, this privileged domaine was purchased in the 1990s by the Domaines Baron de Rothschild, the owners of Château Lafite, who brought new funds to the winery and more consistency to the wines. Often said to smell of violets, these are perfumed Pomerols with superb potential. If only the tannins were a bit riper and the wines a bit less muscle-bound.

Château Falfas ☆

33710 Bayon; 05.57.64.80.41

Wine: Côtes de Bourg. $$($)

One of the quality pioneers of the AC, John and Véronique Cochran practice biodynamic viticulture—a no-brainer as Véronique's father, M. Boucher, is one of France's biodynamic gurus. There are two cuvées. The standard bottling, which leans heavily on merlot, is always very good, well balanced, and highly satisfying. Le Chevalier is made from old vines of chiefly cabernet sauvignon and aged in new oak. Suave and mellow after about five years' aging, it begins life rich, deep, and vivacious. It's always delicious.

Château de Fargues ☆
33210 Fargues-de-Langon; 05.57.98.04.20; www.chateau-de-fargues.com
Wine: Sauternes. $$$$
The former owner and director of Château d'Yquem, Alexandre de Lur Saluces brings the same exigence to this property. These are classic, ambassadorial Sauternes, with opulence, depth, and grace to spare. The 2003 is nothing less than a monument—a magnificent, complex wine for the ages, or for right now.

Château Faugères ☆
33330 St.-Étienne-de-Lisse; 05.57.40.34.99; www.chateau-faugeres.com
Wine: St.-Émilion Grand Cru. $$$ to $$$$
Silvio Denz, a Swiss businessman who made his fortune in the perfume industry, purchased this property from Corinne Guisez in 2005. Guisez had restored the domaine, building a winery worthy of *Architectural Digest* and bringing in Michel Rolland as consultant. The wines, including a Côtes de Castillon Cap de Faugères, were succulent, ripe, beautifully made, and deservedly popular. Peby Faugères, named after Guisez's late husband, was their voluptuous top of the line. Denz, who has been making wine in Spain, intends to keep the same winemaking team and to bring in Stephan von Neipperg (see CANON LA GAFFELIÈRE) as well.

Château de Fieuzal ☆
33850 Léognan; 05.56.64.77.86; fieuzal@terre-net.fr
Wine: Pessac-Léognan Cru Classé. $$$($)
The barrel-fermented whites of this house are reliably excellent—ample, mineral, and racy, all the while perfectly expressing the AC's characteristic stoicism. The reds are nuanced, reserved, and thoroughly pleasurable.

Château Figeac ☆
33330 St.-Émilion; 05.57.24.72.26; www.chateau-figeac.com
Wine: St.-Émilion Premier Grand Cru Classé. $$$$
An excellent property, although I often find vegetal notes in the wines, which I chalk up to the presence of near-equal parts cabernet franc, sauvignon, and merlot in the blend. That said, the wines are fresh, focused, and specific.

Château Fontenil ☆
33141 Saillans; 05.57.51.23.05; rolland.vignobles@wanadoo.fr
Wine: Fronsac. $$($)
Owned by the world's most famous wine consultant, Michel Rolland, and his wife, Dany, the wine of Château Fontenil is always plush and mouthwatering, with flavors of ripe, dark berries and good oak—no matter what the vintage. It would be an interesting exercise to taste Fontenil next to Rolland's Pomerol, Le Bon Pasteur. Both are delicious but the Fontenil, no matter how excellent it is, comes across as simpler, more "technical" than the more soulful, *terroir*-oriented Pomerol. It is, however, cheaper (though by no means inexpensive), and it gives you a chance to see the master at work.

Château de France ↑
33850 Léognan; 05.56.64.75.39; www.chateau-de-france.com
Wine: Pessac-Léognan. $$ to $$$
Since Arnaud Thomassin took the helm in 1996, bringing on Michel Rolland as consultant, the wines have steadily improved. Favorites include the suave, mellow 2001 and 2003 whites and the 2000 and 2002 reds, each of which combined succulence with Graves's characteristic austerity.

Fronsac

A small AC west of Libourne (and Pomerol) for pleasant, reasonably priced reds based on the cabernets, merlot, and malbec. Vintages will be the same as those for St.-Émilion. Prices: $$ to $$$

PRODUCERS: Ch Barrabaque: see CANON-FRONSAC ◆ Ch Bellevue: another Olivier Decelle property with very nice reds in the family style—intelligently priced, fragrant, easy-drinking, bistro ready. See also MAS AMIEL in the Languedoc-Roussillon ◆ Ch de la Dauphine: the same owners as Canon de Brem in Canon-Fronsac produce similarly discreet, supple reds for near-term drinking ◆ CH FONTENIL ☆ ◆ CH HAUT-CARLES ☆ ◆ Ch Haut Lariveau: see MOULIN PEY-LABRIE ◆ Ch Richelieu: following the advice of Stéphane Derenoncourt, the domaine makes ripe, concentrated reds that are worth following. The cuvée La Favorite de Richelieu is a big, oaky showstopper ↑ ◆ Ch de la Rivière: the owner, who makes machine harvesters, produces charming, small-scale reds. There's also a super-cuvée called Aria, pure merlot, oak aged, and priced like a classified growth ◆ Ch la Rousselle: the owners of this young domaine began working with Stéphane Derenoncourt in 2001. The wines—such as a discreet, elegant 2003—show real improvement ↑ ◆ Ch les Trois Croix: Patrick Léon worked at Mouton-Rothschild and manages to elicit elegance and a certain classicism even in difficult years like 2002 ◆ Ch la Vieille Cure: drink the pleasant cuvée Tradition "on the fruit"; the kirsch-scented, oaky cuvée DM needs a couple of years of cellaring ◆ Ch Villars: dynamic Jean-Claude Gaudrie makes mouthwatering, fragrant, unfiltered reds based on merlot (primarily) and the cabernets. Worth trying, even the 2002.

Château la Gaffelière ☆

33330 St.-Émilion; 05.57.24.72.15; www.chateau-la-gaffeliere.com
Wine: St.-Émilion Premier Grand Cru Classé. $$$ to $$$$
A first-rate property where the wines have greatly improved over the past decade, with a fresh, succulent 2000, for example, and a very promising 2004. Stéphane Derenoncourt's touch can be felt here too. The 2005 is elegant and pedigreed, and promises to be excellent.

Girolate ↑

33420 Naujan et Postiac; 05 57 84 55 08; contact@despagne.fr
Wine: Bordeaux. $($)
Talk about pushing the envelope. The Despagne family is surely going for broke with this blockbuster of a wine. My first encounter was with the 2001, the wine's debut vintage. Pure merlot, one ton an acre, fermented—yes, fermented—in barrel, it tasted like a liqueur. The 2002 was another monster, a silky, plush giant. Mighty impressive, but it seems that intensity is valued over elegance. Maybe that's the land, maybe that's the winemaker's intention. Still, a significant addition to the generic AC.

Château Giscours ☆

33460 Margaux; 05.57.97.09.09; www.chateau-giscours.fr
Wine: Margaux Grand Cru Classé. $$$ to $$$$
Following a change of ownership in 1995, this Third Growth has returned to its former glory. Though there's still room for progress, Giscours, at its best, billows with character, combining the elegance of Margaux with a bit of the power of Pauillac. The second wine is La Sirène de Giscours.

Château Grand Mayne ☆

33330 St.-Émilion; 05.57.74.42.50; www.grand-mayne.com
Wine: St.-Émilion Grand Cru Classé. $$$ to $$$$
Another Michel Rolland success story. Château Grand Mayne makes fragrant, rich, plummy, and amply oaked wines—very tasty and very much in the current

style. That said, they are not anonymous and technique does not obliterate *terroir:* St.-Émilion's presence is felt.

Château Grand-Puy-Lacoste ☆

33250 Pauillac; 05.56.73.16.73; fax: 05.56.59.27.37
Wine: Pauillac Grand Cru Classé. $$$ to $$$$
An excellent Fifth Growth owned by the Borie family, who also own DUCRU-BEAUCAILLOU, Château Grand-Puy-Lacoste produces classic Pauillacs that are spicy and robust.

Graves and Graves Supérieur

An important AC west and south of Bordeaux, starting near Mérignac, the Bordeaux airport, and stretching south along the Garonne to the outskirts of Langon. The AC Graves encompasses dry whites made from sauvignon, sémillon, and if producers so choose, muscadelle, and reds made from cabernet sauvignon, merlot, cabernet franc, petit verdot, and malbec. Graves Supérieur applies to sweet whites. Several independent ACs are carved into the Graves landscape. They are Sauternes, Barsac, Cérons, and most important, Pessac-Léognan. Until 1987 the PESSAC-LÉOGNAN AC was part of Graves AC. It is still permitted to refer to the Graves region on labels, although Pessac-Léognan is more prestigious. The word *Graves* refers to the region's distinctive, gravelly soils. While rarely as fine or complex as the wines from Pessac-Léognan, Graves dry whites are full-flavored and generous; the reds are firm but fleshy. Additionally, Graves should be drunk somewhat earlier than Pessac-Léognans: within six years of the vintage for whites; ten for reds. Graves Supérieur has not yet shown that it can compete with the wines from Sauternes, Barsac, and Cérons. Two domaines that make pleasant, three-dimensional versions are Château Chercy-Desqueyroux and Château de Rochefort.

BEST RECENT VINTAGES: The year 2005 is expected to be great. Where yields were controlled, 2004 represented a return to classicism following 2003: the reds are deeply colored, fresh, and ripe; the whites are very fruity but also mineral. The whites from 2003, as elsewhere, are high in alcohol and relatively low in acidity, which may make them appeal to a broader range of consumers; the reds are powerful and deeply colored but a heterogeneous lot. The 2002 vintage was was not an easy one; stick with highly recommended producers. For reds, 2001 was a very good year and for whites, a great one; 2000 was a great vintage for both. Best vintages of the recent past: For reds—1990, 1989, and 1986. For whites—1996 and 1989.
PRICES: $$

PRODUCERS: Alliage de Sichel: from the respected merchant Maison Sichel, clean, fresh, professional white wine, perfect for midrange restaurants of any type ◆ Ch Beauregard-Ducasse: look for the discreet, structured sémillon-dominated cuvée Albertine Peyri in white and the ambitious Albert Duran in red ◆ Ch le Bourdillot: sémillon dominated, the gently oaked white is appetizing and textured; the primarily merlot Tentation du Château le Bourdillot is a juicy red ◆ Ch Brondelle: with an even blend of sémillon and sauvignon, the white is mineral, discreet, and nicely oaked. The red cuvée Damien, a blend of merlot and cabernet, is stylish, textured, and very good ☆ ◆ Caprice de Bourgelat: a fresh, ripe, pure sémillon ◆ Ch de Chantegrive: an enormous domaine with reliable wines. Look for the ambitious cuvée Caroline in both white and red. The white, a blend of sauvignon and sémillon, ferments in oak and is quite successful. The red, a blend of merlot and cabernet sauvignon, is meaty and oak aged, with bright cherry fruit and good balance ◆ CLOS FLORIDÈNE ☆ ◆ Ch Crabitey: the cabernet sauvignon–dominated grand vin, with its cassis, cranberry, and oak flavors, seems like a New World wine made in an old land ◆ Ch de Fougères: primarily sauvignon blanc, Clos Montesquieu has a pungent presence—goat cheese wanted ◆ Grand Enclos du Ch de Cérons: ambitious work here. The partially oak-aged white, dominated by sémillon, includes sauvignon blanc and gris and is fresh, tangy, and textured. The structured red, an oak-aged blend of cabernet and merlot, is more imposing than most; it's juicy and three-dimensional ☆ ◆ Ch Graville-Lacoste: Hervé Dubourdieu makes an excellent, unfiltered white that is is beautifully textured and subtle. Rich, full, and ripe in 2003, it was Napa meets Graves ☆ ◆ Ch Haut Selve: pleasant, easy-drinking whites and reds ◆ Ch l'Hospital: see CH LOUDENNE ↑ ◆ Ch Magneau: they're not subtle, but the unfiltered, barrel-fermented whites from this domaine have depth and marrow and a real presence ◆ Ch Massereau: Jean-François Chaigneau, who started making wine in 2000, is in the hypernatural camp, using organic viticulture, no chaptalization, and so on. He harvests his Graves grape by grape and ferments the red in barrel. It's surprising, tasty, focused, and structured ↑ ◆ Ch du Mayne: careful winemaking, producing textured whites with tropical fruit accents and three-dimensional reds ◆ Ch Pont de Brion: mellow, mineral whites; reds with depth and elegance—good work ☆ ◆ Ch de Respide: look for the stylish, well-structured Callipyge bottling in both white and red ◆ Ch Saint Robert: the domaine belongs to the Crédit Foncier de France. Not surprisingly, the wines are commercial and flawless. Keep an eye out for the stylish, food-friendly Poncet Deville, whether white or red ◆ Ch du Seuil: its mineral, discreet white merits a mention ◆ Vieux Ch Gaubert: a reliable house with good barrel-fermented whites and juicy, structured reds ◆ Villa Bel Air: rich, pungent, barrel-fermented whites are the main attraction here, although the reds are pleasant and accessible.

Graves de Vayres

A small AC that, despite its name, has no relationship to Graves. Located on the left bank of the Dordogne, southwest of Libourne, the AC produces dry whites and reds from the basic Bordeaux grapes. Vintages: see BORDEAUX. Prices: $ to $$. Producers: Ch la Chapelle Bellevue ◆ Ch le Tertre.

Château Gruaud Larose ☆

33250 St.-Julien-Beychevelle; 05.56.73.15.20; fax: 05.56.59.64.72

Wine: St.-Julien Grand Cru Classé. $$$ to $$$$

This popular Second Growth joined the Merlaut family's stable in 1997 and has been on the rise ever since. The wines are fragrant, ripe, generous, and spicy. They well merit their classification. The good second wine is Sarget de Gruaud Larose.

Château Guiraud ☆

33210 Sauternes; 05.56.76.61.01; fax: 05.56.76.67.52

Wine: Sauternes Premier Cru. $$$ to $$$$

Xavier Planty runs Château Guiraud with idealism, respect for nature, and a refusal to chaptalize his wines. His Sauternes are reliably pure, honeyed, and mellow. In May 2006 the chateau was purchased by the FFP holding company, whose major shareholders are the Peugeot family. Xavier Planty owns a piece of the action, as does Stephan von Nieppberg of CANON LA GAFFELIÈRE.

Château Haut-Bailly ☆

33850 Léognan; 05.57.88.71.32; www.chateau-haut-bailly.com

Wine: Pessac-Léognan; $$$ to $$$$

Unlike most producers in the Pessac-Léognan AC, Haut-Bailly makes only red wines. But such nice reds they are! Like good old friends, they're personable, warm, and welcoming. Fragrant and spicy, these reds are simultaneously supple and austere (in the best Graves sense of the word), with specificity and a casual elegance. Always a pleasure.

Château Haut-Bertinerie

33620 Cubnezais; 05.57.68.70.74; www.chateaubertinerie.com

Wines: Première Côtes de Blaye, Côtes de Blaye, and Bordeaux Clairet. $ to $$

Eric and Frantz Bantegnies run an eco-friendly domaine. The label Château Haut-Bertinerie is applied to the prestige cuvées of Château Bertinerie. Generally ambitious, the reds are supple and appealing. The top cuvée, Le Landreau, comes from low-yielding old vines on a well-situated slope. The grapes are harvested by successive passes through the vineyard. The 2002, an iffy vintage, was a real success here: Le Landreau was smooth and beautifully knit. The domaine also makes pleasant whites and Bordeaux Clairet.

Château Haut-Brion ☆, Château la Mission Haut-Brion ☆, and Château Laville Haut-Brion ☆

33608 Pessac Cedex; 05.56.00.29.30; fax: 05.56.98.75.14

Wine: Pessac-Léognan Premier Cru Classé and Cru Classé. $$$$

Château Haut-Brion rouge is quite simply one of the best wines in the world. Always has been; with any luck, always will be. A monumental representative of its AC, it has a kingly authority, layer upon layer of flavor, and with a good decade of aging, a softness that caresses the palate. With even more age—say fifty years—it evolves into a truffley, dry liqueur and is absolutely fascinating. La Mission Haut-Brion, across the road from Haut-Brion and once its rival, is now under the same ownership and the wines are every bit as majestic. Haut-Brion produces a small amount of crystalline yet ample white. La Mission's whites, chiefly sémillon, are produced at Château Laville Haut-Brion. Haut-Brion also has an excellent second wine, Bahans Haut-Brion.

Château Haut-Carles ☆

33141 Saillans; 05.57.84.32.03; stephane_droulers@lazard.fr

Wine: Fronsac. $$($)

The top wine here, made from low-yielding vines (mostly merlot), is Haut-Carles. The owners receive the wise counsel of Robert Vifian, owner of the excellent Vietnamese restaurant Tan Dinh in Paris's 7ème arrondissement. Vifian is one of the world's experts on Pomerol. No surprise then that the wine is rich, succulent, deeply fruity, velvety, three-dimensional, and very stylish. Very much in the garage-cult wine style.

Château Haut-Marbuzet ☆

33180 St.-Estèphe; 05.56.59.30.54; henri.duboscq@haut-marbuzet.net

Wine: St.-Estèphe Cru Bourgeois Exceptionnel. $$$ to $$$$

A large percentage of merlot may account for the fragrance and succulence of Château Haut-Marbuzet's deservedly popular wines. Deep, silky, and spicy, they're very hard not to like.

Haut-Médoc

A relatively large AC that frames the prestigious communal ACs of the Médoc—Pauillac and company—like a lumpy, looping *W.* Devoted to red wines made from the usual Left Bank mix, the Haut-Médoc, which is situated beneath the Médoc AC, is home to five Grand Cru Classés and more than a hundred Cru Bourgeois. The general style is one of savory, medium-bodied Bordeaux, destined, for the most part, for near-term drinking. (The 1999s I tasted at the end of 2005 were perfect.)

BEST RECENT VINTAGES: 2005, (2004), (2003), 2001, 2000, and 1999.
PRICES: $ to $$$; this is a good AC in which to look for value.

PRODUCERS: There has been a large turnover in ownership within the past decade. Much of the change has been for the better, so this is also an AC to watch for important evolution in quality. In general, the new-generation wines are more polished and less rustic. ◆ Ch d'Agassac (CB): recent change of ownership is upgrading the wines of this well-established property ↑

◆ Ch Aney (CB): nicely satisfying Cru Bourgeois that goes down all too easily, perfect for a bistro meal ◆ Ch Belgrave (GCC): owned by the large wine company Dourthe, this Fifth Growth, in the backlands of St.-Julien, has made tangible improvements recently, producing stylish, ripe reds marked by toasty flavors of oak ◆ Ch Cambon la Pelouse (CBS): situated between Chx GISCOURS and Cantemerle (see below), this domaine produces well-crafted, full, stylish wines that are always user-friendly and usually very good value ◆ Ch Camensac (GCC): another domaine on the upswing with potentially gracious wines—when the oak has been digested ◆ Ch Cantemerle (GCC): a large, well-run Fifth Growth, reliably producing textbook Bordeaux ☆ ◆ Ch Cissac (CBS): steadfast, flavorful Médoc ◆ Ch Citran (CBS): since 1996 the property has returned to former owners and is once again in the Merlaut family portfolio. Its improving wines are fragrant, three-dimensional, and well balanced ↑ ◆ Ch Coufran: widely distributed, mostly merlot, foursquare Médocs ◆ CH LA LAGUNE ↑ ◆ Ch Malescasse (CBS): another domaine with improving, intelligently made, nicely balanced, flavorful wines ↑ ◆ Ch Maucamps (CB): good, easy-drinking, user-friendly Cru Bourgeois ◆ Ch Peyrabon (CB): improving, serious wines from a domaine also producing comparable Pauillac AC under the name La Fleur Peyrabon ◆ Ch Sénéjac (CBS): recently purchased by the family that owns CH TALBOT, the forthright traditional wines from this property have now been upstaged by an oaky, concentrated, pricey micro-cuvée, Karolus ◆ CH SOCIANDO-MALLET ☆ ◆ Ch la Tour-Carnet (GCC): Fourth Growth revitalized since 2000 when purchased by Bernard Magrez (see CH PAPE CLÉMENT); the wines are supple, polished, and well made.

Château Hostens-Picant ↑
33220 Les Lèves; 05.57.46.38.11; www.chateauhostens-picant.fr
Wine: St.-Foy-Bordeaux. $$ to $$$
Ambitious is the word for the domaine's top cuvée, Lucullus, a dense, plush, concentrated, red blanket of a wine. The whites, on the rise, are worth trying as well.

Château Lafaurie-Peyraguey ☆
33210 Bommes; 05.56.76.60.54; fax: 05.56.76.61.89
Wine: Sauternes Premier Cru Classé. $$$ to $$$$
Classic Sauternes in the best sense of the word: complex, long, and textured, they seduce with flavors of honey, oak, lime, and herbal tea.

Château Lafite-Rothschild ☆
33250 Pauillac; 05.56.73.18.18; www.lafite.com
Wine: Pauillac Premier Grand Cru Classé. $$$$
The graceful, feline face of Pauillac, more elegant than powerful, and always majestic, Lafite-Rothschild can age for decades. The excellent second wine is Carruades de Lafite. Other properties under the same ownership include Duhart-Milon (Pauillac), L'Évangile (Pomerol), and Rieussec (Sauternes).

Château Raymond-Lafon ☆
33210 Sauternes; 05.56.63.21.02; www.chateau-raymond-lafon.fr
Wine: Sauternes. $$$($)
This domaine, owned by the Meslier family (Pierre was Yquem's manager), defies the classification system. It is unrated yet its Sauternes are as refined, sumptuous, focused, racy, and complex as any of the classed châteaux. Excellent.

Château Lafon-Rochet ☆
33180 St.-Estèphe; 05.56.59.32.06; www.lafonrochet.com
Wine: St.-Estèphe Grand Cru Classé. $$$ to $$$$
This Fourth Growth has LAFITE-ROTHSCHILD and COS D'ESTOURNEL as its neighbors. While its wine displays none of their elegance, it is admirable for its imposing

muscularity and savoriness. To me, it's almost a caricature of St.-Estèphe brawn, but I certainly wouldn't kick it out of bed. Prices are reasonable, and it always impresses.

Château la Lagune ↑
33290 Ludon Médoc; 05.57.88.82.77; lalagune@club-internet.fr
Wine: Haut-Médoc Troisième Cru. $$$
Recently purchased by the Frey family, who owned Champagne Ayala (they sold the brand but kept the vines, go know?), this Third Growth in southern Médoc is making strides in the right direction. Not only has the new team invested in state-of-the-art equipment, they manifest a sincere concern for quality. Young Caroline Frey, who has taken charge of winemaking, studied and worked with Denis Dubourdieu, who consults. Early results show rich, ripe, well-balanced wines, with lots of promise. The Freys are also the new owners of JABOULET in the Rhône, where Caroline will also be in charge of winemaking.

Lalande-de-Pomerol
The satellite of Pomerol, Lalande-de-Pomerol produces the same type of wine from the same grapes. The best equal good Pomerols in quality. See POMEROL vintages.

PRICES: $$ to $$$

PRODUCERS: Ch Belles-Graves: a discreet, silky, satisfying Bordeaux with food-friendly balance ◆ Ch Grand Ormeau: Jean-Claude Beton, the creator of Orangina, owns this domaine. The wines, though not perfect and not inexpensive, do manifest some pedigree. The top cuvée is Madeleine ◆ Ch Jean de Gué: owned by Jean-Claude Aubert of St.-Émilion's CH LA COUSPAUDE, the unfiltered cuvée Prestige from this property is very much in the Aubert family style—well made, stylish, attractively juicy, with some depth. I inadvertently polished off an entire bottle while eating farmhouse chicken roasted with garlic and tarragon and watching Rick Stein's *Food Heroes* and *NYPD Blue*. Enjoyed every sip ◆ La Fleur de Bouard: Hubert de Boüard de Laforest, owner of St.-Émilion's CH ANGELUS, gets mixed results here. I was bothered by flavors of ivy in both the 2003 (marmalade of ivy) and the very different year of 2002 (crushed ivy). The 1999, which came across thick and somewhat cooked, seemed like the major wine in a minor wine region ◆ Ch Perron: La Fleur is the top cuvée. It's not always perfect but it manages to seduce nevertheless. Whether it's worth $$$ is another story ◆ CH LA SERGUE ◆ CH DE VIAUD.

Château Larcis Ducasse ↑
33330 St.-Émilion; 05.57.24.70.84; larcis-ducasse@wanadoo.fr
Wine: St.-Émilion Grand Cru Classé. $$$
Within the past five years owner Jacques-Olivier Gratiot has asked Nicolas Thienpont (see PAVIE-MACQUIN) and Stéphane Derenoncourt to manage this well-sited property. Recent vintages, 2003, 2004, and 2005 for example, show real elegance and pedigree allied with smooth black cherry fruit. Handsome wines, well worth following.

Château Lascombes ☆
33460 Margaux; 05.57.88.70.66; www.chateau-lascombes.com
Wine: Margaux Grand Cru Classé. $$$($)
The new investors who took over Lascombes in 2001 brought in both Michel Rolland and Alain Reynaud (see QUINAULT L'ENCLOS) as advisors as well as a new technical team eminently capable of turning out lovely Margaux on its own. Investments were made and yields lowered. The results put the château back on track as a solid Second Growth. The 2002 bears a Rolland-esque imprint of plush fruit and expensive oak. The charmingly evolving 2001 is fragrant,

inviting, and racy: very Margaux. Recent vintages of the second wine, Chevalier de Lascombes, have been silky, with rich berry fruit.

Château Lassègue ↑
33330 St.-Émilion; 05.57.24.19.49; www.chateau-lassegue.com
Wine: St.-Émilion Grand Cru. $$$($)
It was bound to happen: successful California vintners buying properties in prestigious French appellations. Enter Jess Jackson, of Kendall-Jackson. Since 2004 he's been producing two St.-Émilions: Château Vignot, a plushy, easy-drinking wine with a whiff of the New World, and Château Lassègue, chiefly merlot with some "very ripe" cabernet franc. It's the more serious of the two, more nuanced and age-worthy, but both are very promising.

Château Latour ☆
33250 Pauillac; 05.56.73.19.80; www.chateau-latour.fr
Wine: Pauillac Premier Grand Cru Classé. $$$$
Heroic and nearly immortal, Latour is the epic face of Pauillac. It doesn't get better than this—but you must let the wine age a minimum of ten years. (In a recent tasting of 1958 Premier Grand Cru Classé, Latour was the clear star of the lineup. It was virile, racy, complex, aristocratic, and still juicy, while the other wines had long since peaked, although they were riveting sips of history.) The second wine, Les Forts de Latour, is excellent.

Château Léoville-Barton ☆
33250 St.-Julien-Beychevelle; 05.56.59.06.05; www.leoville-barton.com
Wine: St.-Julien Grand Cru Classé. $$$ to $$$$
Here is another of my desert island Bordeaux. This Second Growth is all grace, discretion, balance, and elegance. Old vines help, as does the enlightened—and rather traditional—approach taken by Anthony Barton and his daughter Lillian. Never overoaked, never overly thick or jammy, the wines embody the poised lushness that is St.-Julien. Léoville-Barton is also one of the most reasonably priced great wines of Bordeaux.

Château Léoville-Las-Cases ☆
33250 St.-Julien-Beychevelle; 05.56.73.25.26; fax:05.56.59.18.33
Wine: St.-Julien Grand Cru Classé. $$$$
The Second Growth most likely to be promoted to First—should a reclassification ever take place—Léoville Las Cases has been run with a meticulousness bordering on the obsessional by the Delon family (the high percentage of wine allocated to the second wine, Clos du Marquis, illustrates the rigorous standards at work here). Las Cases is the most powerful and concentrated St.-Julien, not least because the vines are old and abut the vineyards of Latour. It's Pauillac meets St.-Julien and, in the Delon's hands, the marriage is awesome.

Château Léoville-Poyferré ☆
33250 St.-Julien-Beychevelle; 05.56.59.08.30; www.leoville-poyferre.fr
Wine: St.-Julien Grand Cru Classé. $$$ to $$$$
A sleeping beauty until awoken by AXA Millésimes, this Second Growth is currently a sure bet for reliably delicious, complex, structured, and racy St.-Juliens. The second wine, Château Moulin Riche, a Cru Bourgeois Supérieur, is smooth, layered, and suave and very reasonably priced. There's even a very good third wine, Pavillon des Connetables, made from young vines.

Listrac-Médoc
A small AC completely within the commune of Listrac producing sturdy reds made from the usual Bordelais suspects—often good value: $$. Producers: Ch Clarke: the property of Edmond de Rothschild, this is generally the most soigné and the most expensive of the Listracs ◆ The following four châteaux are more alike than they are different. Their wines are all solidly made and reliable, sharing a sporty character that has nothing to do with the rough-and-tumble of football,

more of a collegiate athleticism—tennis, say. All four are Cru Bourgeois: Ch Lestage ◆ Ch Fonréaud ◆ Ch Fourcas-Dupré ◆ Ch Fourcas-Hosten.

Château Loudenne ↑
33340 St.-Yzans de Médoc; 05.56.73.17.80; www.lafragette.com
Wines: Médoc, Pessac-Léognan, Graves, and Bordeaux. $ to $$$
The Lafragette family bought the large, popular Médoc Cru Bourgeois Supérieur La Loudenne in 2000. They hired Michel Rolland as consultant, harvest by hand, and raise their wines in *barriques* with a three-year rotation. The wines are nicely classic, with good freshness and flavor. They also make a white and rosé (both Bordeaux AC) from the same riverside property. In the late 1990s, the family purchased Château Rouillac in the Pessac-Léognan AC and Château l'Hospital in Graves. The latter, their first investment, seems the closest to hitting its stride: the white Graves, a 60/40 blend of sémillon and sauvignon, is mineral and three-dimensional; the red, chiefly merlot, is supple and specific. A family to watch.

Loupiac
Making sweet *(moelleux)* whites, Loupiac is a small AC north of Langon on the right bank of the Dordogne. Its wines, based on sémillon, sauvignon, and muscadelle, are very similar to those of the Ste.-Croix du Mont AC, which is directly to Loupiac's north. For vintages, see SAUTERNES. Prices: $$. Producers: Ch du Cros: very good versions of the wine, concentrated, structured, and well balanced ◆ Dom du Noble: stylish, oaky, limpid sweet whites with good structure; worth discovering ◆ Ch les Roques: fresh, juicy, floral Loupiac.

Château la Louvière ☆
33850 Léognan; 05.57.25.58.58; www.andrelurton.com
Wine: Pessac-Léognan. $$$
André Lurton's la Louvière is one of the most reliable and recognizable versions of the AC—a veritable goodwill ambassador. The whites, chiefly sauvignon, are racy, vibrant, and all of a piece; the reds are fragrant and svelte. Both age well.

Château Lynch-Bages ☆
33250 Pauillac; 05.56.73.24.00; www.lynchbages.com
Wine: Pauillac Grand Cru Classé. $$$ to $$$$
Owned by Bordeaux elder statesman Jean-Michel Cazes, this popular Fifth Growth regularly turns out meaty, generous, direct wines. No mystery, perhaps, but lots of oomph and character.

Château Malartic-Lagravière ↑
33850 Léognan; 05.56.64.75.08; www.malartic-lagraviere.com
Wine: Pessac-Léognan Cru Classé. $$$
Not leaving anything to chance, the new owners of this Cru Classé have hired both Michel Rolland and Denis Dubourdieu as consultants. The wines are modern and stylish yet remain faithful to their *terroir.* The whites, chiefly sauvignon, are vibrant and full. The reds are warm and spicy, with plump black cherry fruit flavors. Both have the wonderful austerity that's characteristic of the AC.

Château Malescot Saint-Exupéry ☆
33460 Margaux; 05.57.88.97.20; www.malescot.com
Wine: Margaux Grand Cru Classé. $$$ to $$$$
Recent improvements in this Third Growth have resulted in reliably fine wines. Since Michel Rolland has counseled harvesting the cabernet sauvignon when it's fully ripe, these always fragrant, racy wines have become more approachable in their youth.

Margaux

Roughly twenty miles north of Bordeaux, this is the first of the great Left Bank communes. The AC, which applies only to reds, encompasses twenty-one Grand Cru Classés including the eponymous Château Margaux, a First Growth, as well as twenty-five Cru Bourgeois. *Charm* is the byword here, which doesn't prevent the wines from being long-lived. These are the most feminine, the most seductive and sinuous of the great Médoc ACs.

BEST RECENT VINTAGES: 2005, (2004), (2003), (2002), 2001, 2000. 1999, and 1996. Best vintages of the recent past: 1990, 1989, 1982, 1961, and 1959.
PRICES: $$$ to $$$$

PRODUCERS: Owing to the many changes of ownership and management since the beginning of the 1990s, the word *improvement* will be seen in just about every entry here. ◆ CH D'ANGLUDET (CB) ☆ ◆ Ch Bel Air Marquis d'Aligre: organic Margaux, not always perfect but always captivating, pure, and simultaneously personal yet true to its *terroir* ◆ Ch Boyd-Cantenac (GCC): while they don't always live up to their Third Growth status, the wines from this property are often lovely, supple, and satisfying ◆ CH BRANE-CANTENAC (GCC) ☆ ◆ Ch Cantenac Brown (GCC): this tannic Third Growth seems more like a Pauillac than a come-hither Margaux, though recently the wines have seemed more balanced. Note, however, that the property, which had been owned by AXA Millésimes, was sold in 2006 to Simone Halabi a Syrian-born U.K. investor. José Sansfins, the director of the domaine since 1989, remains ☆ ◆ Clos des Quatre Vents: Luc Thienpont, formerly of Labégorce-Zédé, bought this 2-hectare property in 2000. Planted chiefly with very old, ungrafted vines, the Clos produces four hundred cases of wine a year. It is pure velvet ☆ ◆ Ch Dauzac (GCC): formerly disappointing, the wines from this Fifth Growth have gotten better over the past decade—since the property was bought by a French insurance company ☆ ◆ Ch Desmirail (GCC): Third Growth wines on the rise under the leadership of Lucien Lurton ◆ Ch Durfort-Vivens (GCC): a small, improving Fourth Growth, capably managed by the Lurton family ↑ ◆ Ch Ferrière (GCC): this Third Growth had been somewhat obscured by being taken over by CH LASCOMBES. In 1992 it became part of the Merlaut-Villars portfolio; investments were made and the pedigreed, cellar-worthy wines are now gaining recognition ☆ ◆ CH GISCOURS ☆ ◆ Ch d'Issan (GCC): known for light, elegant wines, this Third Growth has recently begun making wines with a bit more flesh on their bones ◆ Ch Kirwan (GCC): with the aid of Michel Rolland, the wines from this Third Growth have progressed enormously over the past five or six years ↑ ◆ Ch Labégorce: recent investments, after a change of ownership in 1989, should lead to higher quality at this sizable, well-situated property ◆ Ch Labégorce-Zédé (CBE): under the stewardship of Luc Thienpont, this CBE turned out racy, delectable wines, whether the vintages vintage was good or bad. The property was recently sold to the owner of Labegorce. Watch this spot ◆ CH LASCOMBES (GCC) ☆ ◆ CH MALESCOT SAINT-EXUPÉRY (GCC) ☆ ◆ CH MARGAUX ☆ ◆ Marojallia: See CH DE VALANDRAUD ☆ ◆ Ch Marquis-de-Terme (GCC): this Fourth Growth seems to be recovering from a lean patch in the 1990s ◆ Ch Monbrison (CBS): this light, fairly elegant Margaux could go further ◆ CH PALMER (GCC) ☆ ◆ CH PRIEURÉ-LICHINE (GCC) ☆ ◆ Ch Rauzan-Gassies (GCC): this underachieving Second Growth took a turn for the better in 1996; the wines are beginning to merit their privileged status ◆ CH RAUZAN-SÉGLA (GCC) ☆ ◆ CH SIRAN (CBE) ☆ ◆ Ch du Tertre (GCC): under the same ownership as CH GISCOURS, this domaine has been rejuvenated by recent investments; since the end of the 1990s, the wines have been riper, richer, and more concentrated as well as being reasonably priced.

Château Margaux ☆

33460 Margaux; 05.57.88.83.83; fax: 05.57.88.31.32
Wine: Margaux Grand Cru Classé. $$$$
Why dither? A very great property (First Growth), consistently making very great wine. A privilege to drink. As fragrant as the most recherché perfume, it caresses, it seduces, it convinces, and it demands that you pay attention. The

second wine, Pavillon Rouge, is excellent too, as is the white, Pavillon Blanc, sold as a Bordeaux AC.

Médoc

All red wines made in the Médoc can be labeled Médoc AC. In practice, however, the AC applies to red wines made in the northern section of the peninsula. That said, it is still the largest of the Left Bank ACs. The wines generally have a greater percentage of merlot in the blend than those made farther south. They tend to have good color, firm structure, and a fair amount of flesh on their bones. Most can be drunk before their tenth birthday.

BEST RECENT VINTAGES: 2005, (2004), (2003), 2001, 2000, and 1999.
PRICES: $ to $$$

PRODUCERS: ◆ Ch la Cardonne (CB): a large property with above-average wines that are moderately priced and widely distributed ◆ Ch les Grands Chênes (CB): in the Bernard Magrez portfolio since 1998, with a predictable change in style; see CH PAPE CLÉMENT ◆ Haut-Condissas: see Ch Rollan de By in this lisiting ◆ Ch Haut-Maurac (CB): owned by Olivier Decelle (see MAS AMIEL in the LANGUEDOC-ROUSSILLON chapter) the wines are well made and nicely structured, with attractive fruit and freshness. Nice prices, too ◆ CH LOUDENNE (CBS) ↑ ◆ Ch les Ormes Sorbet (CB): a deservedly popular, well-upholstered version of the AC with a bit of carmenère in the grape blend ◆ CH POTENSAC (CBE) ☆ ◆ Ch Preuillac (CB): full-flavored, chewy Médocs from a domaine that has recently benefited from the counseling of Stéphane Derenoncourt. The 2005 is polished, balanced, and utterly delicious ◆ Ch Rollan de By (CB): its stylish, merlot-leaning wines include a traditional bottling and a micro-cuvée based on grapes from selected parcels called Haut-Condissas ◆ Ch la Tour de By (CBS): since 2001 conscientious management has pulled through a weak period and is once again making tasty, site-specific wines ◆ Ch Vieux Robin (CB): good, meaty, easy-drinking Médocs.

Château Montrose ☆

33180 St.-Estèphe; 05.56.59.30.12; fax: 05.56.59.38.48
Wine: St.-Estèphe Grand Cru Classé. $$$$
In the spring of 2006 this great Second Growth, often called "the Latour of St.-Estèphe," was purchased by Martin and Olivier Bouygues, two French businessmen prominent in the fields of telecommunication and construction. I think we can expect that the wines will continue to be rich, lush, structured, and potent.

Château Moulin Pey-Labrie ↑

33126 Fronsac; 05.57.51.14.37; moulinpeylabrie@wanadoo.fr
Wines: Canon-Fronsac, Fronsac, and Bordeaux. $$ ($)
The Hubaus run an ambitious eco-friendly domaine, making attractive, promising reds based on pure merlot in both Fronsac (Château Haut Lariveau) and Canon-Fronsac, as well as agreeable whites under the Bordeaux AC. The reds from Haut-Lariveau are spicy and smooth. Those from Moulin Pey-Labrie are more structured, fragrant, and very easy to drink.

Moulis

Located about twenty miles northwest of Bordeaux, on the left bank of the Gironde, Moulis is a small AC producing fleshy, sappy, well-structured reds based on the traditional Médoc blend. The AC is home to a number of leading Cru Bourgeois. Best recent vintages: 2005, (2004), (2003), 2001, and 2000. Prices: $$ to $$$. Producers: Ch Biston-Brillette: pleasant, easy-drinking Moulis; a good restaurant wine ◆ CH CHASSE-SPLEEN ☆ ◆ Ch Maucaillou (CBS): a large property belonging to Dourthe, an important merchant house, its wines are reliable and attractive ◆ CH POUJEAUX ☆.

Château Mouton-Rothschild ☆
33250 Pauillac; 05.56.59.22.22; www.bpdr.com
Wine: Pauillac Premier Grand Cru Classé. $$$$
After a wobbly period in the 1980s, Mouton-Rothschild, perhaps the most openhearted of the First Growths, is back on track, making its inimitably opulent, deliciously plump, but still racy wines. I'd start drinking the seductively perfumed 1989, but there's no hurry. Château d'Armailhac, a Fifth Growth also owned by the Baroness Philippine de Rothschild, is less lavish than Mouton but textured and elegant and often good value; ditto for another Rothschild property, the Fifth Growth Clerc-Milon.

Château les Ormes-de-Pez ☆
33180 St.-Estèphe; 05.56.73.24.00; www.ormesdepez.com
Wine: St.-Estèphe Cru Bourgeois Exceptionnel. $$$
Owned by the Cazes family of Lynch-Bages, this solid property makes wines in the user-friendly family style. The 1997 might serve as a model of the anti-Rolland school of winemaking (whether or not that was intended), with its old-fashioned charm.

Château Palmer ☆
33460 Cantenac; 05.57.88.72.72; www.chateau-palmer.com
Wine: Margaux Grand Cru Classé. $$$ to $$$$
One of my desert island Bordeaux, this Third Growth often stands on equal footing with First Growths. There's quite a bit of merlot in the blend—which certainly contributes to a velvety mouthfeel. But what I love most is the discretion, the subtle sensuality of the wine. Always beautifully balanced, never overoaked, thick, or clumsy, it's really a *grande dame.* Alter Ego, another wine rather than a second wine, is more modern in style and made to be drunk in the near term. It's lovely, too, though it can seem somewhat New World in very rich years like 2000. I preferred the stunningly beautiful 2002 and 2001.

Château Pape-Clément ☆
33600 Pessac; 05.57.26.38.38; www.pape-clement.com
Wine: Pessac-Léognan Cru Classé. $$$$
This is a very great property, with a potential very close to that of Haut-Brion. It was purchased in the 1990s by Bernard Magrez, a businessman who made his fortune creating the wine and spirits company William Pitters and Malesan, a Bordeaux geared to supermarkets (now in the fold of the mammoth Castel wine company). Magrez hired Michel Rolland as consultant and has been turning out impressively stylish and tasty wines ever since. Pape-Clément produces a tiny amount of oaky, exotically scented white. Reds, however, are the focus. Also oaky, as well as ripe and soigné, they are geared to contemporary tastes and yet are undeniably racy.

Magrez also bought Château Fombrauge, one of the largest Grand Crus in St.-Émilion, where he is making similarly seductive wines, including a very plush, deluxe cuvée called Magrez-Fombrauge. Joint ventures with actor Gérard Depardieu result in oaky, ripe reds with names like Ma Vérité. Other Magrez properties include Château la Tour-Carnet and Château les Grands Chênes, both in the Médoc, and Château Poumey in Pessac-Léognan.

Pauillac
With its small harbor on Gironde estuary, this modest town has worldwide influence thanks to its 1,200 hectares of vines, which turn out some of the most legendary, majestic, and expensive red wines in the world. Pauillac AC is home to eighteen Grand Cru Classés, including three First Growths. Noble, profound, and ramrod straight, the wines are as true a representative of France as Charles de Gaulle.

BEST RECENT VINTAGES: 2005, (2004), (2003), (2002), 2001, 2000, 1999, and 1996. Best vintages of the recent past: 1990, 1989, 1982, 1961, and 1959.
PRICES: $$$ to $$$$

PRODUCERS: Ch d'Armailhac (GCC): very good, sizable Fifth Growth, owned by neighbor Mouton-Rothschild; the wine is potentially good value and some of the best in its class ☆ ◆ CH BATAILLEY ◆ Ch Clerc-Milon (GCC): sturdy, well-made, merlot-rich Fifth Growth, also owned by Mouton-Rothschild ☆ ◆ Ch Duhart-Milon-Rothschild (GCC): a substantial improving Fourth Growth, owned by Lafite-Rothschild ☆ ◆ Ch Fleur Peyrabon (CB): the name applies to that small parcel of Ch Peyrabon's vineyards entitled to the Pauillac AC (the greater part is Haut-Médoc AC); makes solid, sappy wines, reasonably priced ◆ Ch Fonbadet (CBS): domaine blessed with old vines; not always consistent but worth trying, good value ◆ Ch Grand-Puy-Ducasse (GCC): well-distributed Fifth Growth, not always up to its classification or AC ◆ CH GRAND-PUY-LACOSTE ☆ ◆ Ch Haut-Bages Liberal: well-run Fifth Growth, good expression of Pauillac, good prices ☆ ◆ Ch Haut-Batailley (GCC): once part of CH BATAILLEY, this property was created as a result of family inheritance laws. Still a Fifth Growth, its wines tend to be more tender than those from Batailley, potentially good value ◆ CH LAFITE-ROTHSCHILD ☆ ◆ CH LATOUR ☆ ◆ CH LYNCH-BAGES ☆ ◆ Ch Lynch-Moussas (GCC): under the same management as CH BATAILLEY, this Fifth Growth appears to be on the upswing; to follow ◆ CH MOUTON-ROTHSCHILD ☆ ◆ Ch Pibran (CBS): a small property in the AXA Millésimes family, making meaty, foursquare, near-term-drinking versions of the AC ◆ CH PICHON-LONGUEVILLE ☆ ◆ CH PICHON-LONGUEVILLE COMTESSE DE LALANDE ☆ ◆ CH PONTET-CANET ☆.

Château Pavie ☆

33330 St.-Émilion; 05.57.55.43.43; www.chateau-pavie.com
Wine: St.-Émilion Premier Grand Cru Classé. $$$$

French businessman Gérard Perse sold everything, he says, to buy himself this great property at the summit of St.-Émilion in 1997. He built new cellars, lowered yields, bought the finest new oak barrels, and so forth, to make deep, lavish St.-Émilions with relatively high proportions of the two cabernets. Fragrant, oaky, and extremely ripe, the wines sometimes have a sweet fruit quality (notably the 2003, which I found somewhat portlike), which has led to controversial disagreements among wine critics. Consumers able to afford the wines will probably love them. Perse also brings the same care to a neighboring property, Pavie-Decesse. Curiously, though this wine is chiefly merlot, it seems leaner, less of a blockbuster than the Pavie. Still, it's truly racy and delicious. Château Monbousquet, another Perse purchase, is well within the family style.

Château Pavie-Macquin ☆

33330 St.-Émilion; 05.57. 24.74.23; pavie.macquin@wanadoo.fr
Wine: St.-Émilion Grand Cru Classé. $$$ to $$$$

A personal favorite, this domaine is run with great exigence by Nicolas Thienpont in collaboration with Stéphane Derenoncourt. Farming is biodynamic. Though the wines need time to digest their oak, they are silky, focused, succulent, and racy—pure pleasures. And the 2005 tops everything: it's layered, textured, superb.

Pessac-Léognan

Situated on the outskirts of the city of Bordeaux, Pessac-Léognan is an important AC for reds (the cabernets, merlot, and petit verdot) and whites (sauvignon and sémillon, although muscadelle is permitted). It was carved out of the Graves AC because of the distinctive character of its soils. Its reds have a singular—and beautifully noble—austerity; its dry whites, often fermented and/or aged in oak, are the most nuanced and long-lived in the Bordelais. Since 1953, sixteen properties, all in Pessac-Léognan, have been recognized as Crus Classés de Graves. They are: Ch Bouscaut; Ch Carbonnieux; Dom de Chevalier; Ch Couhins; Ch Couhins-Lurton; Ch Fieuzal; Ch Haut-Bailly; Ch Haut-Brion; Ch Laville-Haut-Brion; Ch Malartic-Lagravière; Ch La Mission Haut-Brion;

Ch Olivier; Ch Pape-Clément; Ch Smith Haut-Lafitte; Ch La Tour-Haut-Brion; Ch Latour-Martillac.

BEST RECENT VINTAGES: 2005, (2004), (2003), 2001 (especially for whites), 2000, 1996, 1995, 1990, and 1989.
PRICES: $$ to $$$$

PRODUCERS: Ch Bouscaut: an improving Cru Classé, now under the Lurton banner; look for vintages post 1999 ↑ ◆ Ch Brown: one year with Stéphane Derenoncourt (but what a year!) gives terrific results: Graves austerity meets 2005 sumptuousness and the synthesis is extremely alluring, a scrumptious, *terroir*-driven wine ◆ CH CARBONNIEUX ☆ ◆ Ch les Carmes Haut-Brion: tiny neighbor of HAUT-BRION; location counts, pedigree is evident in the fragrant, detailed wines ☆ ◆ DOM DE CHEVALIER ☆ ◆ Ch Couhins-Lurton: fine sauvignon blancs from this small Lurton property; red is a recent addition ◆ CH DE FIEUZAL ☆ ◆ CH DE FRANCE ↑ ◆ CH HAUT-BAILLY ☆ ◆ Ch Haut-Bergey: improving domaine, look for red Branon ◆ CH HAUT-BRION ☆ ◆ CH LA LOUVIÈRE ☆ ◆ Ch Larrivet Haut-Brion: under the guidance of Michel Rolland, stylish versions of the AC ◆ Ch La Mission Haut-Brion: neighbor of HAUT-BRION, now under same ownership ☆ ◆ Ch Latour-Martillac: respected family domaine, though not my favorite ◆ Ch Laville Haut-Brion: see CH HAUT-BRION ☆ ◆ CH MALARTIC-LAGRAVIÈRE ↑ ◆ Ch Olivier: recent investments and new energy since 2002 should lead to much-improved wine from this historic property ↑ ◆ CH PAPE-CLÉMENT ☆ ◆ Ch de Rouillac: see CH LOUDENNE ↑ ◆ Ch Smith-Haut-Lafitte: a multitasking domaine—with a hotel, a spa offering vino-therapy, and a line of grape-based beauty products, this Cru Classé turns out respectable versions of the AC.

Château Petit-Village ☆
33500 Pomerol; 05.57.51.21.08; www.petit-village.com
Wine: Pomerol. $$$$
Nicely situated near CHÂTEAU L'ÉVANGILE and VIEUX CH CERTAN, this domaine has progressed enormously since it was purchased by AXA Millésimes. Deep, rich, racy, warm, savory, and tannic, the wine needs—and will reward—cellaring, though I confess, tasting the 2001 in 2004, I wanted to take it to bed immediately.

Château Pétrus ☆
33500 Pomerol; 05.57.51.17.96
Wine: Pomerol. $$$$
By now mythic, Pétrus is the ultimate expression of merlot when it is given the best land and the best care in vineyard and cellar. Horrifyingly expensive but as complex and detailed as it is dear.

Château de Pez ☆
33180 St.-Estèphe; 05.56.59.30.26; nicolasrouzaud@champagne-roederer.com
Wine: St.-Estèphe Cru Bourgeois Exceptionnel. $$$
Solid, meaty, and oaky, the wines from this very good property need long aging before they reveal the silkiness, elegance, and spice that lie beneath. Give recent vintages a good ten years, although I wouldn't mind seeing the solid, chewy 1997 on a restaurant list—to be carafed, of course.

Château Phélan Ségur ☆
33180 St.-Estèphe; 05.56.59.74.00; phelan.segur@wanadoo.fr
Wine: St.-Estèphe Cru Bourgeois Exceptionel. $$$
With the Châteaux MONTROSE and CALON-SÉGUR as its neighbors, Phélan-Ségur is virtually obliged to make very special, big, long-lived wines with lovely expressions of *terroir*. It doesn't shirk its duty. The wines are deep, firmly structured, limpid, and beautifully specific.

Château Pichon-Longueville ☆

33250 Pauillac; 05.56.73.17.17; www.chateaupichonlongueville.com

Wine: Pauillac Grand Cru Classé. $$$ to $$$$

Surprising to say, but this Second Growth situated across the road from PICHON LALANDE languished until it was taken over by the insurance company AXA Millésimes in the 1980s. Since then, the improvement has been more than dramatic. The wines exhibit professionalism at its best: they are profound, commanding, and delicious.

Château Pichon-Longueville, Comtesse de Lalande ☆

33250 Pauillac; 05.56.59.19.40; www.pichon-lalande.com

Wine: Pauillac Grand Cru Classé. $$$ to $$$$

Tough love from May-Eliane de Lenquesaing, the redoubtable matriarch of this excellent Second Growth, results in pedigreed, potently statuesque wines with fragrant black cherry fruit (when young). More "feminine" than most Pauillacs, the wines age as well as many and better than most. In the summer of 2006 Mme de Lenquesaing reportedly sold the château to the Hermès family but had been given a lifelong contract.

Château le Pin ☆

33500 Pomerol; 05.57.51.33.99

Wine: Pomerol. $$$$

A precursor garage wine, le Pin, owned by Jacques Thienpont, is produced in small quantities—eight thousand bottles yearly—and is all but entirely handcrafted. It's voluptuous, oaky, charming, and fearfully expensive (sometimes pricier than PÉTRUS). The ultimate trophy wine.

Pomerol

In size, one of the smaller ACs in the Bordelais; in quality (or potential quality), one of the grandest. Roughly twenty miles east of Bordeaux, on the right bank of the Dordogne next door to St.-Émilion, the AC is devoted to red wines made primarily from merlot, with the usual addition of a percentage of cabernet franc and sometimes cabernet sauvignon. The wines are plummy, ample, and sensual. They can be drunk young but also benefit from aging. Rule of thumb: a good Pomerol from a good vintage can be held for five to fifteen years (for an example, see the notes on LA CONSEILLANTE.)

BEST RECENT VINTAGES: 2005, (2004), (2003), 2001, 2000, and 1998. Best vintages of the recent past: 1995, 1990, 1989, and 1982.
PRICES: $$($) to $$$$+ (off any scale)

PRODUCERS: Ch Beauregard: owned by Crédit Foncier, this relatively large property makes stylish, well-balanced Pomerols ◆ Ch Beausoleil: this domaine produces reasonably priced, pretty Pomerols. Far from epic, the wines seem drawn on a smaller scale, but they are fragrant and nicely textured ◆ Ch Bellegrave: though it doesn't have the best vineyard site, this domaine produces reasonably priced Pomerols with juicy fruit and strong oak flavors. It needs a bit of time to digest the oak and flesh out ◆ CH LE BON-PASTEUR ☆ ◆ Ch Bonalgue: earthy, full-bodied, three-dimensional Pomerols ◆ Ch Certan de May: rich, tannic wines but, with this land, they could do better ◆ CH CLINET ☆ ◆ Clos du Clocher: The wines have gotten better since Michel Rolland came on as consultant. Proprietor Pierre Bourotte also owns Ch Bonalgue, another Pomerol where the quality has been enhanced by Rolland's guidance ◆ CH LA CONSEILLANTE ☆ ◆ Ch la Croix: one of a number of properties owned by Jean-François Janoueix, the wines are well-made, contemporary Pomerols on a smaller scale; they need time in a carafe for easy near-term drinking ◆ Ch la Croix du Casse: attractive and improving Pomerols from the same owner as CH CLINET ↑ ◆ Ch la Croix de Gay: lots of progress here since Alain Raynaud (CH QUINAULT L'ENCLOS) and his sister Chantal Lebreton took over the reins. The wines are fragrant, velvety, and plush—with abundant oak. The 2002 charmed with its discretion and elegance. A special cuvée Fleur de Gay is made only in the best vintages ◆ Ch du Domaine de l'Église: distributed by the big merchant house Borie-Manoux, which is directed by Philippe Casteja, the wines from this property have improved recently. They're richly fruity, sometimes pruney, and nicely structured. To follow ◆ CH L'ÉGLISE-CLINET ☆ ◆ CH L'ÉANGILE ☆ ◆ Ch Feytit-Clinet: Jeremy Chasseuil, the young, dedicated new owner, is determined to make this property live up to its stellar potential. The wines are already very good—and reasonably priced—and are bound to get better ↑ ◆ Ch la Fleur de Gay: see Ch la Croix de Gay in this listing ◆ Ch la Fleur Pétrus: located across the road from PÉTRUS, and under the same management, this domaine makes delicate, fine-quality, stylish Pomerols ◆ Ch le Gay: new ownership as of 2002 (Père-Vergé, who also owns Ch Montviel in Pomerol); the wines are full, tannic, and a bit rustic ◆ Ch Gazin: a large, well-positioned property (close to PÉTRUS) making high-quality, potent Pomerols that are full of character; its second wine is l'Hospitalet de Gazin ☆ ◆ Ch Gombaude-Guillot: reasonably priced, unfiltered Pomerol with gentle texture, some depth, and lovely aromas of sweet spices ◆ Ch la Grave à Pomerol: yet another Moueix property; the wines are suave and less expensive than others in the portfolio ◆ Ch Lafleur: a minuscule property making superb, near-mythic Pomerols (with a healthy proportion of cabernet franc); worth saving up for ☆ ◆ Ch Latour à Pomerol: this domaine was recently involved in a messy lawsuit between the owner and management. Keep an eye on it ◆ Ch Mazeyres: not the best land and not my favorite but several respected colleagues love it ◆ Ch Nenin: purchased by the Delons of LÉOVILLE-LAS-CASES, the wines from this property have steadily improved since the late 1990s; the second wine, Fugue de Nenin, is also very good ☆ ◆ CH PETIT-VILLAGE ☆ ◆ CH PÉTRUS ☆ ◆ CH LE PIN ☆ ◆ Ch la Pointe: small-scale Pomerol, pleasant and balanced but could try harder ◆ CH TROTANOY ☆ ◆ VIEUX CH CERTAN ☆ ◆ Ch Vieux Maillet: A small, low-profile domaine where lots of care is taken. The wines aren't perfect but they're specific, fragrant, and ambitious.

Château Pontet-Canet ☆

33250 Pauillac; 05.56.59.04.05; www.pontet-canet.com

Wine: Pauillac Grand Cru Classé. $$$ to $$$$

Next door to Mouton-Rothschild, this Fifth Growth produces powerful wines with a depth and elegance that can be entirely masked by tannins in their youth. The wines need a minimum of ten years of cellaring. Arguably the best Fifth Growth.

Château Potensac ☆

33340 Ordonnac; 05.56.73.25.26; dalton.borderac@wanadoo.fr

Wine: Médoc Cru Bourgeois Exceptionnel. $$$

Partly owned by the Delon family (see LÉOVILLE-LAS-CASES), this is the leading château in the Médoc AC, making its most structured, racy, and cellar-worthy wines. Although none of them had peaked, the 1989, 1995, 1997, 1998, and 1999 were all extremely rewarding and pleasant to drink in the fall of 2005. The meaty 1996, however, needed more time: you sensed that complexity would come with a couple of years' more age. Ditto for anything after 2000.

Château Poujeaux ☆

33480 Moulis en Médoc; 05.56.58.02.96; christophelabenne@wanadoo.fr

Wine: Moulis Cru Bourgeois Exceptionnel. $$($)

A large (60-hectare) family-owned property making reliably good, three-dimensional Bordeaux, even in disappointing vintages like 1998 and 1997. The latter should be ready to drink now and would be lovely to find on a restaurant list. I wouldn't wait long to drink the nicely made, very satisfying 2003, either.

Château Prieuré-Lichine ☆

33460 Cantenac; 05.57.88.36.28; www.prieure-lichine.fr

Wine: Margaux Cru Classé. $$$

Taking no chances, the new(ish) team at this popular Fourth Growth has brought in both Michel Rolland and Stéphane Derenoncourt as consultants. The 2003 was so charming, so Margaux, I could have drunk an entire bottle in the wine's infancy. In general, look for rich, savory, elegant wines.

Château Puyguéraud ☆

33570 St.-Cibard; 05.57.56.07.47; ch.puygueraud@wanadoo.fr

Wine: Côtes de Francs. $ to $$

Nicolas Thienpont, who directs CHÂTEAU PAVIE-MACQUIN in St.-Émilion, fashions fragrant, serious red with the counsel of Stéphane Derenoncourt. Using less merlot and a bit of malbec, Thienpont says he's aiming for "virility," but the wines, far from being powerhouses, are serious, velvety, and smooth, with no jagged edges. Cuvée George, 35 percent malbec, is not made every year but when it's produced, it's silky, sexy, and ravishing. In the same AC, Thienpont also runs Château La Prade.

Château Quinault l'Enclos ☆

33500 Libourne; 05.57.74.19.52; www.chateau-quinault.com

Wine: St.-Émilion Grand Cru. $$$$

Former doctor Alain Raynaud has turned this vineyard, literally in downtown Libourne, into one of the most forward-looking in the Bordelais. Yields are extremely low; vinification may take place in specially designed oak barrels. The style of the wines is very much in the Rolland camp—lush, velvety, and fruit- and oak-saturated, with appetizing freshness. They are stylish without losing their specificity.

Château Rauzan-Ségla ☆

33460 Margaux; 05.57.88.82.10; fax: 05.57.88.34.54

Wine: Margaux Cru Classé. $$$$

The Wertheimers, who own Chanel, bought this distinguished Second Growth in 1994. They've made substantial investments, which show in the finished wine. Here's one you must wait for, however. Rauzan-Ségla wants cellaring before it consents to reveal the finesse and subtlety that make it a potential rival for Château Margaux.

Château de Reignac ☆

33450 St.-Loubès; 05 56 20 41 05; château.reignac@wanadoo.fr

Wine: Bordeaux Supérieur. $$

Stephanie and Yves Vatelot make super, reasonably priced wine—fresh, balanced, with lots of delicious fruit backed up by a discreet amount of oak. Scrumptious. Multiply that by two or three for the Réserve bottling, which is neither fined nor filtered. Crowd-pleasers for sure here.

Château Rieussec ☆

33210 Fargues-de-Langon; 05.57.98.14.14; www.lafite.com

Wine: Sauternes Premier Cru Classé. $$$ to $$$$

Yquem's neighbor, owned by Domaines Barons de Rothschild, Rieussec produces gorgeous Sauternes—rich, layered, creamy, and specific, with mellow citrus zest accents.

Château Roc de Cambes ☆

33710 Bourg-sur-Gironde; 05.57.68.25.58; 05.57.74.42.11

Wine: Côtes de Bourg. $$$

François Mitjavile, who makes breathtakingly elegant St.-Émilion at CHÂTEAU LE TERTRE-RÔTEBOEUF, makes painfully elegant Côtes de Bourg here. Surely the most expensive bottle in the appellation, it is rich, concentrated, ample, and very convincing.

Château Roumieu-Lacoste ☆

33720 Barsac; 05.56.27.16.29; HerveDubourdieu@aol.com

Wines: Sauternes-Barsac. $$$$

This small domaine, owned by Hervé Dubourdieu, produces a number of riveting whites. The Sauternes are barrel-fermented, unfiltered, pure sémillon. The Sélection André Dubourdieu, which spends nearly three years in barrel, is a magnificent, lush wine with depth, freshness, and beautiful structure. From the same property, Dubourdieu produces a super Graves called Graville-Lacoste and a dry white Bordeaux called Ducasse, neither of them filtered. (Both are listed in their respective ACs.)

Ste.-Croix-du-Mont

A small AC on the steep slopes overlooking the Garonne, directly across the river from Sauternes and Barsac, known for sweet whites made from overripe sémillon, sauvignon, and muscadelle. Producer: Ch du Pavillon: the wines aren't perfect but, in good vintages, they're pretty convincing, with good flavors of honey and citrus zests.

St.-Émilion and St.-Émilion Grand Cru and Grand Cru Classé

A large, important AC roughly thirty miles east of Bordeaux, on the right bank of the Dordogne, known for high-quality red wines made chiefly from merlot and cabernet franc. Broadly, the style of the wines is cozier, spicier, and earlier-drinking than that of Médoc. There's a country cousin aspect, although the wines can be every bit as elegant and aristocratic as those from the Left Bank. St.-Émilion has its own classification system, reviewed every ten years. (The next reclassification will be 2006). At the very top are Premiers Grands Crus Classés (A): this elite category applies only to the Châteaux Ausone and Cheval Blanc. Next, there are the Premiers Grands Crus Classés (B), of which there are currently eleven; then come the Grands Crus Classés, which now number fifty-five. In order to qualify for the classification, a château must be certified Grand Cru. (An abbreviation—1er GCC, GCC, or CC—will appear next to the name of each château to which it applies.)

BEST RECENT VINTAGES: 2005, (2004), (2003), 2001, 2000, and 1998. Best vintages of the recent past: 1995, 1990, 1989, and 1982.
PRICES: $$$ to $$$$

PRODUCERS: CH ANGELUS ☆ ◆ CH AUSONE ☆ ◆ Ch Balestard la Tonnelle (GCC): tannic, spicy wine; carafe for drinking in the near term ◆ CH BEAU-SÉJOUR BÉCOT ☆ ◆ Ch Beausejour (Duffau-Lagarosse) (1er GCC): fragrant, fleshy, well-structured wines ☆ ◆ CH BELAIR ☆ ◆ CH BELLEFONT-BELCIER ↑ ◆ CH BELLEVUE ☆ ◆ Ch Berliquet (GCC): a small property with improving wines, worth trying if price is right ◆ Ch la Bienfaisance: see SANCTUS ☆ ◆ Ch Canon (1er GCC): excellent and improving property making fresh, fragrant wines with tannins cloaked in soft fruit ☆ ◆ CH CANON-LA-GAFFELIÈRE ☆ ◆ Ch Cap de Mourlin (GCC): fragrant, meaty wines to drink after their fifth birthday ◆ Ch le Castelot (GC): lightly vegetal but three-dimensional wines for near-term drinking ◆ CH CHEVAL BLANC ☆ ◆ CLOS FOURTET ☆ ◆ Clos de L'Oratoire (GCC): first-rate property, owned by Stephan von Neipperg, see CANON-LA-GAFFELIÈRE ☆ ◆ Ch Corbin (GCC): not massive but smooth, stylish, ripe wines with evident but unobtrusive oak; they go down easily ◆ Corbin Michotte (GCC): supple, velvety wines from a modernized, intelligently run property ◆ CH LA COUSPAUDE ☆ ◆ Ch Dassault (GCC): light, bright, meant for early drinking ◆ Ch Destieux (GC): improving, the wines are tasty, style-driven, potential crowd-pleasers, with thick fruit but attractive freshness ◆ Ch la Dominique (GCC): situated between CHEVAL BLANC and POMEROL AC, with Michel Rolland as consultant, the wines, based on very ripe merlot, are succulent and generous, worth trying ◆ CH FAUGÈRES ☆ ◆ Ch le Fer (GC): pure merlot, from 2 hectares of old vines on Ch Cheval Noir, this new-oak-aged micro-cuvée is ripe, rich, pedigreed, and merits following ↑ ◆ Ch Ferrand-Lartique (GC): Working with Stéphane Derenoncourt, Pierre Ferrand has been making fragrant, ripe wines that need more work but show promise. The seductive 2005 shows fine progress ◆ CH FIGEAC ☆ ◆ Ch la Fleur: a small property with engaging wines; until 2002 managed by J-P Moueix, now in the Dassault group; see Ch Dassault in this listing ◆ Ch Fleur Cardinale (GC): relatively light but inviting; good for near-term drinking ◆ Ch Fombrauge (GC): part of the Magrez stable, made in the family style; see CH PAPE-CLÉMENT ◆ Ch Fonroque (GCC): owned by eco-friendly Alain Moueix, who has made major investments, this is a domaine to watch; the wines are supple, with depth and pedigree ↑ ◆ Ch Franc-Mayne (GCC): this domaine has been getting better since the change of ownership in 1996; Rolland consults—a house to watch ◆ CH LA GAFFELIÈRE ☆ ◆ La Gomerie: see BEAU-SÉJOUR BÉCOT ☆ ◆ Gracia (GC): a *garagiste,* working with Jean-Luc Thunevin (see CH VALANDRAUD), wines the result of low yields, ultraripe fruit, new oak; quantity is limited and prices are high ◆ Ch Grand Corbin-Despagne (GC): a large property, owned by the Despagne family; well-made, structured wines ◆ CH GRAND MAYNE ☆ ◆ Ch Grand Pontet (GCC): improving wines with a touch of class ◆ Ch Haut-Sarpe (GCC): tasty, balanced, early-drinking; the wines have some sense of place, nice for an upscale bistro ◆ CH LARCIS-DUCASSE ↑ ◆ CH LASSÈGUE ↑ ◆ Ch Lucia (GC): the Derenoncourt touch is noticeable in the intense black cherry fruit, the succulence, the freshness, and the balanced use of oak. The 2005 is already complex and distinguished, a true delight. To follow ↑ ◆ Ch Magdelaine (1er GCC): the star of J-P Moueix's stable, this well-situated property turns out tender, elegant St.-Émilions ☆ ◆ Ch Monbousquet (GCC): see CH PAVIE ☆ ◆ La Mondotte: see CANON-LA-GAFFELIÈRE ☆ ◆ CH PAVIE ☆ ◆ Ch Pavie-Decesse (GCC): see PAVIE ◆ CH PAVIE-MACQUIN ☆ ◆ Ch Petit Faurie de Soutard (GCC): the wines can be astringent but they show some elegance and specificity ◆ QUINAULT L'ENCLOS ☆ ◆ Ch Rochebelle (GCC): recently promoted to GCC, this small (3-hectare) property is well situated near CH LE TERTRE-RÔTEBOEUF and turns out fragrant, plummy wines ◆ Rol Valentin (GC): owned by former soccer player Eric Prissette, this property is squarely in the *garagiste* camp. The wines are rich, dense, and concentrated but also fresh, textured, and fairly elegant; Stéphane Derenoncourt consults. The 2005 has great charm; it's delicious in every sense of the word ↑ ◆ SANCTUS DU CHÂTEAU LA BIENFAISANCE ☆ ◆ Ch Sansonnet (GC): purchased by the former owner of Champagne Piper-Heidsieck in 1999, this small property is well run and turns out fresh, tasty, balanced wines that lean toward elegance rather than power ↑ ◆ Ch de Sarpe: lithe, spicy, balanced, the wines may not be grandiose but they are respectable and specific ◆ Ch la Serre (GCC): fragrant, easy-drinking St.-Émilions ◆ CH SOUTARD ☆ ◆ Ch Tertre-Daugay (GCC): with the same ownership as LA GAFFELIÈRE and working with Stéphane Derenoncourt, the wines from this property have good fruit (and a large percentage of cabernet franc) and a classic feel, although they need two to three years to shed their baby fat ◆ CH LE TERTRE-RÔTEBOEUF ☆ ◆ Ch la Tour Figeac (GCC): new owners in 1994 converted the domaine (next door to FIGEAC) to biodynamics and have hired Stéphane Derenoncourt as consultant; the wines need work but there's lots of promise here. The 2005 is both alluring and pedigreed; it's yummy and built to last ◆ Ch Trianon (GC): purchased in 2001 by Dominique Hébrard, former owner of CHEVAL BLANC, this property is one to follow; the wines are fresh, pretty, and distinguished ↑ ◆ Trois Origines: a tiny, less-than-2-hectare property—formerly Ch Meylet—taken over by Stéphane Derenoncourt and his two assistants. Farming is biodynamic. The first vintage, 2005, is silky, aristocratic, and too delicious ◆ CH TROPLONG-MONDOT ☆ ◆ CH TROTTEVIEILLE ↑ ◆ CH DE VALANDRAUD ☆ ◆ Ch Vieux Sarpe (GC): not for the ages, but delicious, stylish wines for the near term.

The St.-Émilion Satellites

They are: Lussac-St.-Émilion, Montagne-St.-Émilion, Puisseguin-St.-Émilion, and St.-Georges-St.-Émilion. Immediately northeast of St.-Émilion, these four ACs are considered its satellites. They produce only red wine. Made in the style of St.-Émilion, but less majestic, these are usually less expensive. See ST.-ÉMILION vintages. Prices: $$($).

PRODUCERS: Ch de Barbe Blanche (Lussac-St.-Émilion): owned by André Lurton, the wines from this property are reliably sapid and well-made ◆ Ch Beauséjour (Montagne-St.-Émilion): Patricia and Pierre Bernault, working with Stéphane Derenoncourt, produce an exciting cuvée 1901 from vines planted in that year. The new-oak-aged cuvée, which accounts for 25 percent of the estate's production, is intense, deep, elegant, and impressive, with concentrated blackberry flavors ◆ Ch de Bellevue (Lussac-St.-Émilion): almost pure merlot, organic and unfiltered, these are fragrant, supple, well-balanced reds, lovely to drink in the near term ◆ Ch Calon (St.-Georges-St.-Émilion): attractive, food-friendly reds ◆ Ch Faizeau (Montagne-St.-Émilion): look for the full, rich, and fresh Vieilles Vignes from this trustworthy domaine ◆ Ch de Lussac (Lussac-St.-Émilion): lots of oak in these wines but they're also fluid and pleasant ◆ Ch Messille-Cassat (Montagne-St.-Émilion): owned by Jean-Claude Aubert (see Ch Couspaude in ST.-ÉMILION), the wine is similarly stylish, supple, and delicious. Also reasonably priced ◆ Ch des Rochers (Lussac-St.-Émilion): the unfiltered wines from this property are not perfect but they do have personality—making them worth following ◆ Ch Tour du Pas (St.-Georges-St.-Émilion): owned by the admirable Pascal Delbeck (see CH BELAIR), rich, firmly structured, and focused, the wines from this property seem more Médoc than they do St.-Émilion. That's OK. Biodynamic farming.

St.-Estèphe

The northernmost of the Médoc communal ACs, St.-Estèphe lies just above Pauillac. It includes five Grand Crus and more than forty Cru Bourgeois. Its wines—all red—are tannic and deeply colored. Brawny and vigorous, they need long aging. Ten years is a good start, though some of the weaker vintages, like that of 1997, can be drunk earlier, if carafed.

BEST RECENT VINTAGES: 2005, (2004), (2003), (2002), 2001, 2000. 1999, and 1996. Best vintages of the recent past: 1990, 1989, 1982, 1961, and 1959.
PRICES: $$$ to $$$$

PRODUCERS: CH CALON-SÉGUR ☆ ◆ CH CLAUZET ↑ ◆ CH COS D'ESTOURNEL ☆ ◆ Ch Cos Labory (GCC): next door to Cos d'Estournel, this Fifth Growth, now owned by an enologist who works at the lab in Pauillac, has improved dramatically since 1990 ↑ ◆ Ch le Crock (CBS): run by the same team as LÉOVILLE-POYFERRÉ, le Crock turns out suave, well-balanced wines ◆ Ch Haut-Beauséjour (CB): a good property, well run by Champagne Roederer ◆ CH HAUT-MARBUZET ☆ ◆ CH LAFON-ROCHET ☆ ◆ Ch Meyney (CB): a producer of potentially big and long-lived reds, Ch Meyney seems to be recovering from a disappointing patch—to follow ◆ CH MONTROSE ☆ ◆ CH LES ORMES-DE-PEZ ◆ CH DE PEZ ◆ CH PHÉLAN-SÉGUR ☆.

St.-Foy-Bordeaux

A small AC at the eastern end of Entre-Deux-Mers, St.-Foy-Bordeaux produces whites (dry and sweet) and reds made chiefly from the usual Bordeaux grapes. See BORDEAUX vintages and prices. Producers: Ch du Champ des Treilles ◆ CH HOSTENS-PICANT ↑.

St.-Julien

Roughly twenty-five miles northwest of Bordeaux, St.-Julien lies between Margaux and Pauillac and seems to marry the finesse of the former with the power of the latter. To speak in astrological terms, it's the Libra of the Médoc—harmonious, discreet, and always elegant. The AC is devoted to reds and there are eleven Grand Cru Classés.

BEST RECENT VINTAGES: 2005, (2004), (2003), (2002), 2001, 2000, 1999, and 1996. Best vintages of the recent past: 1990, 1989, 1982, 1961, and 1959.
PRICES: $$$ to $$$$

PRODUCERS: CH BEYCHEVELLE ☆ ◆ Ch Branaire (GCC): also known as Branaire-Ducru, this reliable Fourth Growth makes textbook St.-Julien, supple, elegant, and discreet; prices are reasonable too ☆ ◆ CH DUCRU-BEAUCAILLOU ☆ ◆ Ch Gloria: I confess I never was much of a fan of this popular château, now under the same ownership as Ch. St. Pierre, a Fourth Growth. Word has it that the wines are improving, making additional tastings an order of the day ◆ CH GRUAUD-LAROSE ☆ ◆ Ch Lagrange (GCC): bought by the Japanese company Suntory in 1983, this Third Growth is solid, oaky, and reasonably priced ◆ Ch Langoa-Barton: the baby brother of LÉOVILLE-BARTON, this reliable Third Growth is impeccably made, delicious, reasonably priced, and can be drunk sooner than Léoville; the good second wine is Réserve de Léoville-Barton ☆ ◆ CH LÉOVILLE-BARTON ☆ ◆ CH LÉOVILLE-LAS-CASES ☆ ◆ CH LÉOVILLE-POYFERRÉ ☆ ◆ Ch St. Pierre (GCC): improving Fourth Growth, now in the same family as Ch Gloria ◆ CH TALBOT ☆.

Sanctus du Château la Bienfaisance ☆

33330 St.-Christophe-des-Bardes; 05.57.24.65.83; www.labienfaisance.com
Wine: Saint-Émilion Grand Cru. $$$ to $$$$
Patrick Baseden, working with Stéphan Derenoncourt, produces a deluxe cuvée from this property. Very much in the current style, it's velvety, ripe, and oaky. It's also multidimensional, ambitious, and lipsmacking. A downside, however, is that the best grapes seem to go to this cuvée. No surprise there, but the standard Bienfaisance bottling seems to suffer for it.

Sauternes

The foremost AC for sweet white wines. Located on the left bank of the Garonne, north of Langon, Sauternes (and Barsac) is classically made from botrytized grapes harvested by successive passes through the vineyard. Sémillon and sauvignon are used, and muscadelle is also permitted. Aged, and often fermented, in oak barrels, the wines are shimmering nectars—honeyed, lush, opulent, deep, and long-lived. While some consider Sauternes dessert wines, I find they are best as an aperitif, with cheese, with foie gras, and certain other savory dishes—or all by themselves, as wines of meditation.

The chateaux of Sauternes-Barsac were classified in 1855 as follows (using their current names):

Premier Cru Supérieur: Château d'Yquem

Premiers Crus: Ch Climens, Ch Coutet, Ch Clos Haut-Peyraguey, Ch Guiraud, Ch Lafaurie-Peyraguey, Ch Rabaud-Promis, Ch Rayne-Vigneau, Ch Rieussec, Ch Sigalas-Rabaud, Ch Suduiraut, and Ch La Tour-Blanche.

Seconds Crus: Ch d'Arche, Ch Broustet, Ch Caillou, Ch Doisy-Daëne, Ch Doisy-Dubroca, Ch Doisy-Védrines, Ch Filhot, Ch Lamothe, Ch Lamothe-Guignard, Ch de Malle, Ch Myrat, Ch Nairac, Ch Romer-du-Hayot, and Ch Suau.

BEST RECENT VINTAGES: 2005, 2003, 2001, 1999, and 1997. Best vintages of the recent past: 1990, 1989, and 1988.
PRICES: $$ to $$$$

PRODUCERS: Barsac producers are also included here. ◆ D'Arche: recent change of ownership of this GCC gives cause for optimism. The wines always had breed and a certain classicism, now they may live up to the promise of their classification—with greater length and depth, among other things ◆ Ch Bastor-Lamontagne: another property in the portfolio of Crédit Foncier, this domaine is intelligently run, making tasty, relatively easy-drinking Sauternes that sell for reasonable prices. There is a more expensive, ambitious cuvée Cru Bordenave ◆ Ch Broustet: a CC, this domaine makes reasonably priced, foursquare Barsacs ◆ CH CLIMENS ☆ ◆ Ch Clos Haut-Peyraguey: excellent Sauternes at reasonable prices; the 2003, for example, was a luscious blend of honey, oak, and medicinal herb flavors ☆ ◆ Ch Closiot: an eco-friendly domaine making ample Barsacs; the 2003 was fragrant, racy, and appetizing ◆ Ch la Clotte-Cazalis: the idealistic, ambitious, eco-friendly owner works mostly with sémillon. The wines are still works in progress but promising ↑ ◆ CH COUTET ☆ ◆ CRU BARRÉJATS ↑ ◆ CH DOISY-DAËNE ☆ ◆ Ch Doisy-Védrines: very good, fragrant, nuanced, and reasonably priced Barsac ☆ ◆ CH DE FARGUES ☆ ◆ Ch Filhot: this large Sauternes property makes light use of oak. Its wines are appetizing and tasty, developing well over time. There may be an excess of sulfur, so get out a carafe ◆ Ch la Garenne: organic Sauternes, not perfect, but a good wine-bar discovery ◆ CH GUIRAUD ☆ ◆ CH LAFAURIE-PEYRAGUEY ☆ ◆ CH RAYMOND LAFON ☆ ◆ Ch Lamothe-Guignard: pleasant, if somewhat underachieving Sauternes from a CC ◆ Ch Massereau: Jean-François Chaigneau, who started making wine in 2000, is out to reinvent the wheel. His wines are organic, harvested grape by grape, with no added sugar, and fermented in barrel. He makes two cuvées of Barsac—La Pachère, which is pure, toasty, honeyed, and very tasty, and M, an impressive, structured wine. To follow. See also BORDEAUX and GRAVES ↑ ◆ Ch Myrat: extremely rich Barsacs, charitably priced ◆ Ch Nairac: quality varies but both 2001 and 2003 had all you could want, in abundance ◆ Ch Rayne-Vigneau: after a disappointing patch this property seems to be improving; a 1999 was textured and velvety and the 2003 bordered on the titanic ◆ CH RIEUSSEC ☆ ◆ Ch de Rolland: fluid Barsacs, less honeyed but attractively refreshing ◆ CH ROUMIEU-LACOSTE ☆ ◆ CH SIGALAS-RABAUD ☆ ◆ CH SUDUIRAUT ☆ ◆ CH LA TOUR-BLANCHE ☆ ◆ CH D'YQUEM ☆.

Château la Sergue

33500 Néac; 05.57.51.31.31; fax: 05.57.25.08.93
Wine: Lalande de Pomerol. $$($)
Fragrant, supple, discreet, and stylish reds—even in 2002—make this a house worth watching. The wines may come off oaky when young but they do balance out pretty quickly.

Château Sigalas-Rabaud ☆

33210 Bommes; 05.56.76.60.54; fax: 05.56.76.61.89
Wine: Sauternes Premier Cru Classé. $$$($)
Château Sigalas-Rabaud makes truly lovely Sauternes—mellow, honeyed, and beautifully balanced, with texture and depth. They're a pleasure.

Château Siran ☆

33460 Labarde-Margaux; 05.57.88.34.04; www.chateausiran.com
Wine: Margaux Cru Bourgeois Exceptionnel. $$$
Brigitte Miailhe takes pains to produce model Margaux, and her suave, caress-the-tongue 1989 and 1995 demonstrate that her efforts have, indeed, been fruitful. Almost ready to drink, the racy 1996 and the meaty 1999 are still austere, tannic, and reticent. There's good value here.

Château Sociando-Mallet ☆

33180 Saint-Seurin-de-Cadoune; 05.56.73.38.80; fax: 05.56.73.38.88
Wine: Pessac-Léognan. $$$ to $$$$
A great favorite among many wine professionals, this château, formerly a Cru Bourgeois, is considered worthy of classified growth status. It currently has no rating. Jean Gautreau, its talented but iconoclastic owner, declined to be considered for the latest Cru Bourgeois classification. In the meantime, he regularly turns out racy, intense, firmly structured reds that can take years of cellaring.

Château Soutard ☆

33330 St.-Émilion; 05.57.24.72.33; fax: 05.57.24.66.94
Wine: St.-Émilion Grand Cru Classé. $$$
François des Ligneris, a man who resolutely walks to the beat of his very own, handcrafted, idiosyncratic drum, makes organic (if not biodynamic) St.-Émilions. The wines are personalized, deep, and meaty. Des Ligneris also owns a very good wine bar in the center of St.-Émilion, l'Envers du Décor. The château is rumored to be for sale.

Château Suduiraut ☆

33210 Preignac; 05.56.63.61.92; www.suduiraut.com
Wine: Sauternes Premier Cru Classé. $$$ to $$$$
Now part of AXA Millésimes, Suduiraut has improved immensely. Opulent and age-worthy, its luscious, nuanced wines now fully merit their classification.

Château Talbot ☆

33250 St.-Julien-Beychevelle; 05.56.73.21.50; www.chateau-talbot.com
Wine: St.-Julien Grand Cru Classé. $$$ to $$$$
On the upswing, this reliable Fourth Growth is deservedly popular and always satisfying. Its generous, firmly structured, honest-to-god St.-Juliens age well. A 1945, tasted after its fiftieth birthday, was superb, with a devastatingly seductive bouquet.

Château le Tertre-Rôteboeuf ☆

33330 St.-Émilion; 05.57.24.75.46; fax: 05.57.74.42.11
Wine: St.-Émilion Grand Cru. $$$$
Another personal favorite. The Mitjavilles, as idealistic a couple as you'll find, have a beautifully sited vineyard that forms an amphitheater facing south-southeast. Over one hill lies TROPLONG-MONDOT, over another, BEAU-SÉJOUR BÉCOT. François Mitjaville doesn't believe that a vigneron can be an artist, but, he says, a wine can be art. He doesn't blend wines to achieve a style; he lets the ensemble of his *terroir* speak. He never makes a second wine. The wines are gorgeously inviting, silky, long, and elegant with the finest grain imaginable. They are pellucid, vivacious, majestic, and brilliant.

Château Thieuley

BP 8-33670 La Sauve; 05.56.23.00.01; thieuley@wanadoo.fr
Wines: Bordeaux and Bordeaux Supérieur. $ to $$
This large domaine turns out noteworthy wines at reasonable prices. Best are the Réserve Francis Courselle in both red and white. The red, chiefly merlot, is balanced, coherent, and very tasty; the white, barrel-fermented old-vines sauvignon and sémillon, borders on elegance, a lovely wine with appetizing citrus zest accents.

Château La Tour-Blanche ☆

33210 Bommes; 05.57.98.02.73; fax: 05.57.98.02.78
Wine: Sauternes Premier Cru Classé. $$$($)
Now the laboratory of a renowned school of viticulture, La Tour-Blanche turns out textbook Sauternes year after year. I find that they lack a bit of soul but compensate with rich and delicious flavors of honey, peach, and dried fruit.

Château Troplong-Mondot ☆

33330 St.-Émilion; 05.57.55.32.05; châteautroplongmondot@wanadoo.fr
Wine: St.-Émilion Grand Cru Classé. $$$$
An exceptionally situated property on a slope outside the town of St.-Émilion. The grapes are harvested at optimum ripeness. The wines are fleshy, deep, and fragrant. They can age for decades.

Château Trotanoy ☆

33500 Pomerol; 05.57.51.78.96; fax: 05.57.51.79.79

Wine: Pomerol. $$$$

Simultaneously earthy and aristocratic, Trotanoy (now under Moueix control) develops rich flavors of truffles and coffee, while remaining fresh and elegant.

Château Trottevieille ↑

33330 St.-Émilion; 05.56.00.00.70; domaines@borie-manoux.fr

Wine: St.-Émilion Grand Cru Classé. $$$$

A well-situated property, capable of making great St.-Émilions but, for many years, underachieving. Recent changes since 2000 are promising.

Château de Valandraud ☆

33330 St.-Émilion; 05.57.55.09.13; www.thunevin.com

Wine: St.-Émilion Grand Cru. $$$$

The garage wine phenomenon really started here, quite literally in the garage of Jean-Luc Thunevin and his wife, Muriel Andraud. Since that time (the early 1990s), their vineyard holdings have increased, they've built a state-of-the-art cellar, with easy-to-clean kitchen tiles lining the floors, and they've shaken up what was, at the time, the complacent Bordeaux landscape. Thunevin, a former bank clerk and restaurateur turned wine merchant, had plenty of good advice from both Michel Rolland and Alain Vauthier, his best friend, who happens to own CH AUSONE. Andraud, a former nurse's aide, comes from a horticultural family. She is in charge of viticulture—which is basically organic—and manages to treat acres upon acres of vines with the loving attention weekend gardeners lavish on their backyard plots of tomatoes, basil, and zucchini. You'd have to work very hard to make bad wines with the grapes she grows (this makes me think the movement should have been dubbed *vin de jardinière* and not *vin de garage.*) The leading wine, Château de Valandraud, is plush, velvety, and juicy, with mingled fruit and spice flavors. It's oaky, of course, but the oak is balanced by the richness and succulence of the fruit. The Thunevins make several other St.-Émilions, including Virginie de Valandraud and Clos Badon Thunevin (from a well-sited vineyard near PAVIE) and take charge of other vineyards as well, most notably Marojallia, in Margaux. The last produces a fragrant wine, as lush as it is complex and specific.

Château de Viaud

33500 Lalande-de-Pomerol; 05.57.51.17.86; fax: 05.57.51.79.77

Wine: Lalande-de-Pomerol. $$($)

A house worth watching, this property changed hands in 2002; it now belongs to Marjolaine, a Bordeaux *négociant.* The wines had been impressive in the past and, while the 2003 struck me as a bit peculiar, the 2002 was velvety, fragrant, and seductively fruity.

Château Vieux-Château-Certan ☆

33500 Pomerol; 05.57.51.17.33; www.vieux-château-certan.com

Wine: Pomerol. $$$$

Alexander Thienpont runs this excellent property. The wines, which flesh out with age, are racy, deep, and distinguished—good agers. Still vigorous, the 1990 was sheer pleasure to drink in the beginning of 2006. Fresh, solid, and long, it seduced with flavors of forest underbrush, sandalwood, and black olive.

Château d'Yquem ☆

33210 Sauternes; 05.57.98.07.07; fax: 05.57.98.07.08

Wine: Sauternes. $$$$

Purchased by the luxury goods company LVMH in the 1990s, this legendary domaine is now run by the very able Pierre Lurton, who seems to be following the perfectionist example set by former owner Alexandre de Lur Saluces. Yquem is one of *those* wines: everyone remembers the first time he or she tasted it, and many of today's top sweet-wine producers learned how to achieve great quality by working in its vineyards and cellars. The recipe is simple: take the greatest pains every step of the way. Yields, for example, are so low that a vine produces only a single glass of wine; the wine ages in new oak barrels for more than three years and is bottled unfiltered. It is an unbelievably beautiful wine; one taste and the world falls away. By the way, there is a superb dry white produced by Yquem called Y (Ygrec).

BORDEAUX CRIB SHEET

The Millionaire's Must Trys: The chateaux Ausone, Cheval Blanc, Haut-Brion, Lafite-Rothschild, Latour, Léoville-Las-Cases, Margaux, La Mondotte, Mouton-Rothschild, Pétrus, le Pin, Valandraud, and Yquem. However, before forking over a fortune on a single bottle, why not even the odds? Attend a sit-down tasting of a range of these wines. (Tastings where you stand are usually as crowded as the subway at rush hour—and about as pleasant. It's nearly impossible to concentrate on the wine you're tasting.)

MUST TRYS

I couldn't help but include some millionaire bottles.

Château Ausone: St.-Émilion (when you're feeling very rich) [$$$$]

Château Climens: Barsac (when you're not worried about the end of the month) [$$$($) to $$$$]

Clos des Quatre Vents: Margaux [$$$ to $$$$]

Château de Fargues: Sauternes [$$$$]

Château Haut-Brion: Pessac-Léognan (when you're feeling very rich) [$$$$]

Château Léoville-Barton: St.-Julien [$$$ to $$$$]

Château Léoville-Las-Cases: St.-Julien (when you're not worried about the end of the month) [$$$$]

Château Palmer: Margaux (when you're not worried about the end of the month) [$$$ to $$$$]

Château Rieussec: Sauternes [$$$ to $$$$]

Château le Tertre-Rôteboeuf: St.-Émilion [$$$$]

SMART BUYS

Seek out overlooked or underestimated vintages; 2001 is a prime and delicious example. You may be able to treat yourself to one of the blue-chip classified growths.

Domaine de l'A: St.-Émilion

Château Bellevue: St.-Émilion

Château Cambon la Pelouse: Haut-Médoc

Cap de Faugères: Côtes de Castillon

Château Clauzet: St.-Estèphe

Château Ducasse: St.-Émilion

Château Falfas: Côtes de Bourg

Château Fougas: Côtes de Bourg—especially the cuvée Maldoror

Château Puyguéraud: Côtes de Francs

Château Reignac: Bordeaux Supérieur

SAFE HOUSES

Château d'Aiguilhe: Côtes de Castillon

Château d'Angludet: Margaux

Château Chasse-Spleen: Moulis-en-Médoc

Château Doisy-Daëne: Barsac

Château Haut-Bailly: Pessac-Léognan [$$$ to $$$$]

Château Haut-Marbuzet: St.-Estèphe

Château Léoville-Poyferré: St.-Julien [$$$ to $$$$]

Château Pavie-Macquin: St.-Émilion [$$$ to $$$$]

Château Sociando-Mallet: Pessac-Léognan [$$$ to $$$$]

Château La Tour-Blanche: Sauternes

ALSACE
BORDEAUX
BURGUNDY
CHAMPAGNE
JURA AND SAVOIE
LANGUEDOC-ROUSSILLON
LOIRE
PROVENCE AND CORSICA
RHÔNE
SOUTHWEST

THE BURGUNDY REGION

CHABLIS
Chablis
Auxerre
ST-BRIS
IRANCY
Avallon
Vézelay
DIJON
MARSANNAY
Sombernon
Saulieu
FIXIN
GEVREY-CHAMBERTIN
MOREY-ST-DENIS
CHAMBOLLE-MUSIGNY
VOUGEOT
VOSNE-ROMANÉE
NUITS-ST-GEORGES
Nuits-St-George
BEAUNE
LADOIX
SAVIGNY-LÈS-BEAUNE
PERNAND-VERGELESSES
ALOXE-CORTON
CHOREY-LÈS-BEAUNE
MONTHÉLIE
VOLNAY
Beaune
ST-ROMAIN
POMMARD
AUXEY-DURESSES
MEURSAULT
PULIGNY-MONTRACHET
ST-AUBIN
Autun
CHASSAGNE-MONTRACHET
SANTENAY
Chagny
MARANGES
RULLY
MERCUREY
Chalon-sur-Saône
Le Creusot
GIVRY
CÔTE CHALONNAISE
MONTAGNY
Tournus
Loire
MÂCON
Saône
Charolles
POUILLY-LOCHÉ
ST-VÉRAN
Mâcon
POUILLY-FUISSÉ
JULIÉNAS
POUILLY-VINZELLES
Bourg-en-Bresse
MOULIN-À-VENT
ST-AMOUR
CHIROUBLES
RÉGNIÉ
BROUILLY
BEAUJOLAIS
Villefranche-sur-Saône
LYON
COTEAUX DU LYONNAIS

Located in central-eastern France, Burgundy stretches from Auxerre to Lyon. In its sweep it encompasses some one hundred distinct ACs, ranging from simple quaffers to the most expensive, exquisite wines in the world. The homeland for three major grapes—pinot noir, chardonnay, and gamay—it is the stamping ground in which each established its benchmark style.

BURGUNDY'S MAJOR SUBREGIONS AND THEIR WINE STYLES

Chablis: One of the most famous wines in the world, Chablis is situated in the northern reaches of Burgundy. The style of chardonnay produced here is unique: razor-sharp, flinty, mineral, bone-dry, and precise. But there's more to the northern limits of Burgundy than Chablis. There are charming, user-friendly wines such as the sauvignon blancs from St.-Bris, the pinot noirs from Irancy, and various reds and whites from many hyphenated Bourgognes, such as the firm, mineral chardonnays from Vézelay.

The Côte d'Or: The Golden Slope, as its name translates, stretches in a nearly unbroken line from just south of Dijon, past Beaune, to Chassagne-Montrachet, Santenay, and Maranges and traverses some of the most expensive, coveted vineyard land in the world. It is further divided into the northern Côte de Nuits and the southern Côte de Beaune. Each of these subdivisions is further delineated: there are numerous ACs, thirty-three Grand Crus, and hundreds of Premier Crus. A bird's-eye view of the Côte d'Or would look like cloisonné. Indeed, if there's anywhere the AC system could drive you stark raving mad, it's here. But if ever the AC system made brilliant sense, it's here, for there are real distinctions in all those obsessively demarcated parcels and plots.

Some of the more famous ACs in the Côte de Nuits include Gevrey-Chambertin, Chambolle-Musigny, and Vosne-Romanée. Some of its most famous Grand Crus—all ACs in their own right—are Chambertin, Clos de Vougeot, and Romanée-Conti.

Among the more famous ACs in the Côte de Beaune are Meursault, Pommard, Puligny, and Chassagne-Montrachet. And its most famous Grand Crus include Le Montrachet and Corton.

On the label, the Premier Crus will always name the AC first, followed by Premier Cru and the name of the *cru,* for example: Beaune Premier Cru Les Grèves. On the other hand, a Grand Cru, such as Montrachet, stands on its own, immediately followed by the designation Grand Cru and then the words *Appellation Contrôlée.*

It was common for villages in both the Côte de Nuits and the Côte de Beaune to attach the name of their most famous vineyard to their own; thus you have Gevrey-Chambertin and Puligny-Montrachet. Given this practice, it is easy more or less to identify the area in which a Grand Cru is located from its name. In most cases, therefore, I've detailed the Grand Crus within their respective ACs. For example, Latricières-Chambertin does not get an individual listing; it is included in the Gevrey-Chambertin entry. However, where the name of a Grand Cru gives no indication of its location—such as Échezeaux or Clos de Tart—it is individually listed. I have also given Grand Crus such as Le Montrachet that span more than one AC their own entries.

When Côte d'Or wines are good, they range from sheer pleasure to heart-stopping majesty. Don't look for blockbusters here. Nuance, grace, and detail are everything. They bring to mind the oft-quoted line from Baudelaire's poem "L'Invitation au Voyage," *"luxe, calme et volupté"* (luxury, calm, and voluptuousness).

The Côte Chalonnaise and the Mâconnais: South of the Côte d'Or, these two distinct but similar regions produce a wealth of reasonably priced, delicious reds and whites good for near-term drinking. The specific ACs in the Côte Chalonnaise are Givry, Mercurey, and Rully. In the Mâconnais you find Mâcon and all its hyphenates (Mâcon-Loché, for example), Pouilly-Fuissé, Pouilly-Loché, Pouilly-Vinzelles, and St.-Véran. Once written off as underachievers from which no one ever expected very much anyway, some of these ACs have become thrillingly dynamic. Young, impassioned vintners who can't afford land in the Côte d'Or are setting up in these regions and turning out wines that can compete with the top wines from the most prestigious ACs in the Côte de Beaune. There are no Grand Crus here but many Premier Crus.

Beaujolais: The kingdom of gamay, the font of the simple, knock-back, juicy red, as well as Beaujolais's ten *crus,* which are capable of producing wines that would grace the most elegant tables anywhere. The *crus,* each a distinct AC, are Brouilly, Côte de Brouilly, Chénas, Chiroubles, Fleurie, Juliénas, Morgon, Moulin-à-Vent, Régnié, and St.-Amour.

GRAPES: Burgundy's main white grape is chardonnay, followed (distantly) by aligoté. The main red grape is pinot noir, except in Beaujolais, where gamay reigns. Secondary grapes include sauvignon blanc and melon de bourgogne for whites and césar and tressot for reds.

PRICES: With wines that range all the way from a simple $5 Beaujolais to a more than $1,000 bottle of Domaine de la Romanée-Conti, giving a price range is not terribly helpful. Nevertheless: $ to $$$$

BEST RECENT VINTAGES: The year 2005 was very good to sublime. Considered a "winemaker's year" (in other words, only a really good, conscientious winemaker could make outstanding wine), 2004 presented many challenges—a very large crop, difficult weather (hail in some regions), and so forth—but where reasonable yields were maintained and grapes were carefully sorted, the wines will be very good. The reds are more heterogeneous than the whites, which are fruity and well defined. The heat wave of 2003 produced a small crop of very ripe grapes. There are some exceptional wines but also many atypically opulent ones. In general, these should be drunk in the near term. A very good to excellent vintage for both reds and whites, 2002 was a problematic year in Beaujolais. The year 2001 was good to very good for reds and very good to exceptional for whites. Bad weather during the harvest in the Côte d'Or made 2000 a generally disappointing year, particularly for reds; whites fared better. A very good year for reds, 1999 was a fair to good year for whites.

BEST VINTAGES OF THE RECENT PAST: 1996 (for reds), 1995, and 1990.
LEGENDARY YEARS: 1959, 1961, and 1969.

These vintage notes are primarily applicable to the Côte d'Or, the Mâconnais, and the Chalonnais. For additional information on Beaujolais and Chablis vintages, see those entries.

AGING THE WINES: It is a truth universally acknowledged that all good Burgundies taste good young. Some, however, improve—even dramatically—with age. Wines from Beaujolais, the Côte Chalonnaise, and Mâconnais will age more quickly than those from the Côte d'Or and Chablis. In the Côte d'Or and Chablis, "village" wines, such as Gevrey-Chambertin with no Grand Cru or Premier Cru designation, will age more quickly than Grand Crus or Premier Crus. Grand Cru and Premier Cru whites from a good vintage can (and some should) be cellared for five to ten years. Reds from the Côte de Beaune generally age more quickly than those from the Côte de Nuits. While I still drink some 1959s (bought at auction) with enormous pleasure, I'm not sure that today's red Burgundies will age in a similar manner. Discretion being the better part of valor, I'd drink—or at least try—the wines within ten years, although some will surely improve over a longer period.

Domaine de l'Abbaye du Petit Quincy

89700 Épineul; 03.86.55.32.51; gruhier@domaine-abbaye.com
Wine: Bourgogne Épineul. $ to $$
Expect excellent wine-bar Bourgognes—from the charming white, to the feisty rosé, to two really good cuvées of red: the juicy, fresh L'Âme des Dannots and the structured, nicely elegant Cuvée Juliette.

Domaine des Airelles

89800 Chichée; 03.86.42.49.60; didirobin@aol.com
Wine: Chablis. $$ to $$$
Sometimes verging on the bizarre—as in the 2002 Premier Cru Vaugiruat—these are quirky, *terroir*-driven Chablis that burst with character. The mouthfilling, deep Premier Crus Vaucoupin and Vosgros remind me of Sancerres from Cotat (which, after all, enjoy similar *terroir*). The 2003 Chablis Vieilles Vignes won a silver medal in the worldwide chardonnay competition. Rich but still steely and fresh, it deserves great credit for being more Chablis than 2003.

Domaine Stéphane Aladame ↑

71390 Montagny-les-Buxy; 03.85.92.06.01; aladame@wanadoo.fr

Wines: Montagny and Aligoté. $ to $$

This promising young, eco-friendly vigneron produces so-so aligoté but very good Montagny, including a focused, tight, and elegant Premier Cru and a deeper, more serious, oak-aged Premier Cru Cuvée Selection, a food-friendly white.

François d'Allaines ↑

71150 Demigny, 03.85.49.90.16; francois@dallaines.com

Wines: Givry, Rully, Beaune, St.-Aubin, Chassagne-Montrachet, and others. $$ to $$$

Young, very promising, this *négociant* house was created in 1990 and progresses steadily. There are several lovely cuvées of Rully blanc—including the Premier Cru Les St.-Jacques, with its fine integration of of oak and fruit, and the distinctive Premier Cru La Fosse. There's a plump white St.-Aubin Premier Cru En Remilly and a full-blown Chassagne-Montrachet Premier Cru Les Chaumées blanc, the richness of which is balanced by appetizing flavors of quinine and minerals. Its Beaune blanc Premier Cru Les Renversées seems to melt on the tongue.

Aloxe-Corton

A small Côte de Beaune AC, much of Aloxe-Corton is eaten up by the Grand Crus Corton and Corton-Charlemagne (which Aloxe-Corton shares with Ladoix and Pernand-Vergelesses). The wines are principally reds made from pinot noir; there's a small amount of chardonnay-based white. Many of Aloxe-Corton's thirteen Premier Crus are shared with Ladoix.

BEST RECENT VINTAGES: 2005, (2004), (2003), and 2002.
PRICES: $$$

PRODUCERS: DOM CHEVALIER PÈRE & FILS ◆ EDMOND CORNU ◆ Dom Follin-Arbalet: the domaine's pleasant ACs include two red Premier Crus, the smooth, pure Clos du Chapitre, and the meatier, more tannic Les Vercots ◆ DOM DE LA GALOPIÈRE ◆ DOM ANTONIN GUYON ◆ DOM ANDRÉ NUDANT ◆ Dom Michel Poulleau Père & Fils: very attractive wines with fine, focused fruit ◆ Dom Françoise Jeanniard: toasty reds with pleasant cherry flavors ◆ Dom Gaston & Pierre Ravault: a manly Aloxe-Corton, admirable in every respect, and two charming Ladoix ACs ◆ DOM TOLLOT-BEAUT ☆.

Domaine Guy Amiot & Fils ☆

21190 Chassagne-Montrachet; 03.80.21.38.62; domaine.amiotguyetfiles@wanadoo.fr

Wine: Chassagne-Montrachet. $$$

A very good family domaine with a reliably delicious range of Chassagne-Montrachets, starting with the racy, textured Village bottling. My favorite among Amiot's Premier Crus is the focused, aristocratic Les Caillerets, but the limpid Les Macherelles and the nuanced Les Champgains are also lipsmacking and serious. The mellow, oaky Les Vergers is a bit less majestic, but it's a great food wine: it even takes on—deliciously—smoked salmon. And the red La Maltroie, warm, delicate, and autumnal, had a savory-salty note that made it a suprisingly wonderful match with *brandade de morue,* the comforting mash of salt cod and potatoes.

Marquis d'Angerville ☆
21190 Volnay; 03.80.21.61.75; domaine.angerville@wanadoo.fr
Wines: Volnay, Pommard, and Meursault. $$$ to $$$$
Title or no title, the wines from this domaine are so aristocratic, they're prerevolutionary. All of the Volnays—Taillepieds, for example, or Clos des Ducs, or Champans—are thoroughly elegant, caressingly silky, and achingly fine-grained. The domaine's other wines are equally sumptuous, such as a refined, extremely mineral Meursault Premier Cru Santenots.

Domaine de l'Arlot
21700 Nuits-St.-Georges; 03.80.61.01.92; fax: 03.80.61.04.22
Wine: Nuits-St.-Georges. $$ to $$$$
The domaine has an exclusive on the Premier Cru Clos de l'Arlot, from which it makes an elegant white. Another exclusive, the Premier Cru Clos des Forêts St.-Georges, is an oaky, tasty red, although somewhat lighter-bodied than expected, despite coming from the very good 2002 vintage. And, while I liked the 2002 Clos du Chapeau, it seemed as lean as an Irancy, not really the style I associate with Nuits-St.-Georges.

J. Pierre & Michel Auvigue
71850 Charnay-les-Mâcon; 03.85.34.17.36; vins.auvigue@wanadoo.fr
Wine: Pouilly-Fuissé. $$
This very good *négociant* house offers three lovely cuvées of Pouilly-Fuissé, beginning with Les Chailloux, a racy, invigorating blend of grapefruit, lime, and mineral flavors. The old-vines bottling, from vines that are more than fifty years old at the foot of Pouilly's iconic Solutré rock, is deeper, oak-tinged, serious, and clear as a waterfall. The Hors Classe bottling comes from a late harvest in the best parcels. It's fermented in new barrels and, at least when young, is dominated by oak. I'll drink the others while waiting for this one to come around. The house also produces St.-Véran and Mâcon.

Auxey-Duresses
A small Côte de Beaune AC for medium-bodied reds from pinot noir and limpid, supple whites from chardonnay. The most famous of the Premier Crus is Les Duresses.

BEST RECENT VINTAGES: 2005, (2004), (2003), 2002, (2001), and 1999.
PRICES: $$ to $$$

PRODUCERS: Dom d'Auvenay: see DOM LEROY ☆ ◆ CHRISTOPHE BUISSON ↑ ◆ DOM DE CHASSORNEY ↑ ◆ DOM COCHE-BIZOUARD ☆ ◆ DOM CATHERINE & CLAUDE MARÉCHAL ◆ Maison Deux Montille: see DOM HUBERT DE MONTILLE ☆ ◆ Dom Michel Prunier: somewhat heavy, overripe whites, admirable for their creaminess, minerality, texture, and specificity ◆ Dom Vincent Prunier: above-average whites and good Premier Cru reds including Les Combes and Les Grands Champs ◆ Roblot-Monnot: truly lovely, mineral, pure, balanced unfiltered reds ◆ DOM ANNE-MARIE & JEAN-MARC VINCENT.

Ballot-Millot & Fils
21190 Meursault, 03.80.21.21.39; ballotmillotetfils@hotmail.com
Wines: Beaune, Chassagne-Montrachet, Pommard, Meursault, and Volnay. $$$($)
A very good family domaine with vineyards in a fair number of the best ACs. My favorites among the whites include the elegant and appetizing Meursault Premier Cru Genevrières, with its core of lime and herbal tea flavors, and the limpid, invigorating Chassagne Premier Cru le Morgeot. For reds, the textured, refined Volnay Taillepieds and the fresh, silky Pommard Premier Cru Pezerolles are pure, 100 percent charm, and the Beaune Premier Cru Épenottes is racy and nuanced.

Bâtard-Montrachet

An 11.11-hectare Grand Cru spreading between Chassagne and Puligny for full-bodied, long-lived, complex chardonnay. Bienvenues-Bâtard-Montrachet is a still smaller Grand Cru abutting Bâtard.

BEST RECENT VINTAGES: 2005, (2004), (2003), 2002, 2001, and 1999.
PRICES: $$$$

PRODUCERS: DOM JEAN-MARC BOILLOT ◆ BOUCHARD PÈRE & FILS ☆ ◆ Philippe Brenot: see CHASSAGNE-MONTRACHET ↑ ◆ JOSEPH DROUHIN ☆ ◆ DOM LOUIS JADOT ☆ ◆ DOM LEFLAIVE ☆ ◆ DOM PIERRE MOREY ☆.

Beaujolais

Beaujolais is a large, important viticultural region producing close to two hundred million bottles yearly. The three basic ACs, Beaujolais, Beaujolais-Villages (made in a slightly more restricted area), and Beaujolais Supérieur, are primarily light reds made from gamay. There is a minuscule amount of rosé, as well as a (relatively) small quanitity of white based on chardonnay. Beaujolais Supérieur refers only to red wines made from gamay. The AC Beaujolais Nouveau (or Primeur) applies to wines made and released on the market quickly, on the third Thursday of the November following the harvest. It amounts to 50 percent of Beaujolais production. Additionally, there are ten recognized *crus* of Beaujolais that, taken together, account for 25 percent of Beaujolais production. Each is listed separately. They are: Brouilly, Chénas, Chiroubles, Côte de Brouilly, Fleurie, Juliénas, Morgon, Moulin-à-Vent, Régnié, and St.-Amour.

STYLES OF WINE: Beaujolais is emphatically fruity and juicy, the quintessential light, quaffing red. Nouveau Beaujolais is even more exuberantly fruity. Meant to be drunk before the end of the year in which it was made, it's the ultimate "hi-good-bye" red. The *crus* are—or should be—much more ambitious, with more structure, character, and flavor. Some are magnificent. They can be placed, with pride, on any table. In general, Beaujolais should be served slightly chilled. The *crus* should be served cool but not cold.
BEST RECENT VINTAGES: The year 2005 is an excellent, very ripe vintage. In the variable year 2004 you'll find good wines from good vintners. An atypical heat wave year, 2003 produced extremely ripe, opulent wines. In 2002 rainy weather led to vine maladies that are more or less evident in the wines. The 2001 vintage was fair to good. And 2000 and 1999 were both excellent vintages.
PRICES: $ to $$($)

PRODUCERS: JEAN-PAUL BRUN ◆ Ch Cambon: a Lapierre family venture making fresh, discreet Beaujolais ◆ Cellier des Saint-Étienne: the Cuvée Prestige is an attractive light red ◆ Ch des Jacques: see DOM LOUIS JADOT ☆ ◆ Ch du Châtelard: Sylvain Rosier makes two Beaujolais blanc—a pleasant oak-aged version, and a Vieilles Vignes that is even nicer—as well as a fruity, well-balanced Beaujolais Villages Vieilles Vignes ◆ Dom de la Côte de Chevenal: see JULIÉNAS ◆ Philippe Deschamps: the Beaujolais Villages Cuvée Vieilles Vignes is fluid and all too gulpable ◆ GEORGES DUBOEUF ◆ Dom Dubost: see MORGON ◆ Dom Dupeuble: nicely structured, attractively fruity Beaujolais ◆ DOM LOUIS JADOT ☆ ◆ Dom du Grand Talence: the oak-aged Beaujolais blanc is mellow and pleasant, although it gives you no idea where it came from ◆ Dom Lapalu: see BROUILLY ◆ DOM DE LA MADONE ◆ DOMINIQUE PIRON ◆ Jean-Charles Pivot: easy-drinking Beaujolais-Villages and good Côte de Brouilly ◆ Dom de Pouilly le Chatel: focused, textured Beaujolais blanc ◆ Dom Romy: eco-friendly family domaine split between Dominique and Nicolas; Dominique's line includes good, mineral-accented Beaujolais—especially the barrel-aged L'Or des Treilles; chez Nicolas, look for the unfiltered Beaujolais blanc, a floral, fresh, barrel-aged chardonnay with a light metallic edge, worth discovering ◆ Dom de St.-Sorlin: Bernard and Eric

Jacquet hand-harvest the grapes for their very impressive, *terroir*-driven, *cru*-worthy Beaujolais-Villages, which, as it ages, takes on pinot noir–like flavors ☆ ◆ Dom des Terres Dorées: see JEAN-PAUL BRUN ◆ DOM DES TERRES VIVANTES ☆ ◆ Ch Thivin: see CÔTE DE BROUILLY ☆ ◆ Thorin: see MOULIN-À-VENT ◆ DOM DU VISSOUX ☆.

Beaujolais Primeur or Beaujolais Nouveau: See BEAUJOLAIS.

Beaune

Taking its name from the historic town at the center of the Côte d'Or, Côte de Beaune is an important AC for reds made from pinot noir and chardonnay-based whites, both of potentially very high quality. There are no Grand Crus but many Premier Crus, among the most famous of which are Clos des Ursules, Clos des Mouches, Les Épenotes, Grèves, and Teurons.

BEST RECENT VINTAGES: 2005, (2004), (2003), 2002, and 2001.
PRICES: $$ to $$$$

PRODUCERS: FRANÇOIS D'ALLAINES ↑ ◆ BALLOT-MILLOT & FILS ◆ Jean Boillot: look for the cool, elegant Premier Cru Clos du Roi ◆ BOUCHARD PÈRE & FILS ☆ ◆ Dom Cauvard: the nicely balanced white Clos de la Maladière and the delectable red Premier Cru Cent Vignes are worth trying ◆ MAISON CHAMPY ◆ Maison Chanson Père & Fils: an important grower-*négociant* now owned by Bollinger; expect improvements. My favorites in recent vintages include the red Beaune Premier Crus Clos des Fêves and Clos des Mouches ◆ DOM DU CHÂTEAU DE CHOREY ◆ Vincent Dancer: a rising Burgundian star whose appealing 2002 Beaune Premier Cru Les Montrevenots was undeniably tasty and well made but lacked the distinction expected of a Premier Cru. The Bourgogne blanc was also really very nice, another overachiever, very satisfying, and well-priced. ◆ DOM DOUDET-NAUDIN ◆ JOSEPH DROUHIN ☆ ◆ EMMANUEL GIBOULOT ↑ ◆ DOM A. F. GROS ☆ ◆ THIERRY GUYOT ◆ DOM LOUIS JADOT ☆ ◆ Dom Pierre Labet: see CH DE LA TOUR ☆ ◆ MACHARD DE GRAMONT ☆ ◆ DOM PARENT ◆ DOM JACQUES PRIEUR ☆ ◆ Dom Prieur-Brunet: see SANTENAY ◆ DOM ROSSIGNOL-TRAPET ◆ DOM TOLLOT-BEAUT ☆ ◆ DOM CHRISTOPHE VIOLOT-GUILLEMARD.

Domaine Bertagna ↑

21640 Vougeot; 03.80.62.86.04; fax: 03.80.62.82.58
Wines: Vougeot, Vosne, and Nuits-St.-Georges. $$$$
Seriously improving and increasingly reliable, this domaine has desirable holdings in top vineyards in Vougeot, Vosne, and Nuits-St.-Georges, including a monopoly on Vougeot Premier Cru Clos de la Perrière, a delicately fragrant red with fine tannins and sweet spice flavors. Another Vougeot Premier Cru, Les Petits Vougeots, is a leaner, elegant red, with focused fruit and well-integrated oak. The Vougeot Premier Cru blanc is a thoroughbred—complex, long, and classic. The Vosne-Romanée Premier Cru Les Beaux Monts is a svelte, racy, aerodynamic red. And the Nuits-St.-Georges Premier Cru Les Murgers is a deep, textured, tightly woven red that could not have been made anywhere but in Burgundy.

Domaine Bertheau ☆

21220 Chambolle-Musigny; 03.80.62.85.73; domaine.bertheau@libertysurf.fr
Wines: Chambolle-Musigny. $$$ to $$$$
If you want flash and sizzle in your Burgundy, skip this domaine. The Bertheau Burgundy is intimate and elegant, a silk and velvet weave, delicate as a poised iron butterfly. The Chambolle-Musigny Premier Cru is discreet and soft as a caress. The pellucid Chambolle Premier Cru les Amoureuses is as seductive as they come. Wonderfully complex, the Bonnes-Mares Grand Cru is detailed and fleshy, with notes of exotic spices.

Maison Albert Bichot

21200 Beaune, 03.80.24.37.37; www.albert-bichot.com

Wines: A complete range of Burgundies. $$ to $$$$

One of Beaune's largest grower-*négociant* houses, Albert Bichot has an encyclopedic range of Burgundies. Some are standard, others are truly admirable, particularly the wines in the Domaine du Clos Frantin line, such as a precise, delicious Vosne-Romanée. Bichot also owns Long-Depaquit in Chablis.

Domaine Simon Bize ☆

21420 Savigny-lès-Beaune; 03.80.21.50.57; fax: 03.80.21.58.17

Wines: Savigny-lès-Beaune and Pernand-Vergelesses. $$$ to $$$$

A highly respected Savigny-lès-Beaune grower producing balanced, rich whites, particularly the excellent layered and pedigreed Vergelesses, and exemplary reds, including the rectilinear Grands Liards and the silky, majestic Premier Cru Aux Vergelesses.

Jean-Yves Bizot ↑

21700 Vosne-Romanée; tel/fax:03.80.61.24.66; les.violettes@wanadoo.fr

Wines: Vosne-Romanée and Échezeaux. $$$ to $$$$

A University of Dijon–trained enologist, Jean-Yves Bizot practices extremely low yields, never adds sugar or acid to his wines, and never fines or filters them. The wines are pure, clear as a stream, and have a near thirst-quenching freshness; but, firmly in the hypernatural camp, they will not be to everyone's tastes. My favorites are the spicy, mineral Vosne-Romanée from the *lieu-dit* Les Jachées, which was planted between 1947 and 1951. Then there's the Grand Cru Échezeaux, discreetly authoritative, with a spot-on sense of place.

Blagny

A small Côte de Beaune AC for reds made from pinot noir, Blagny is named for a hamlet located between Meursault and Puligny-Montrachet. Blagny's white wines take the name of whichever of those two ACs in which that particular vineyard lies. If the vineyard in question is a Premier Cru and the wine is red, it will be called Blagny Premier Cru. Best recent vintages: see MEURSAULT. Prices: $$$. Producers: Dom Larue: the Premier Cru Sous le Puits is a tasty red, worth trying ◆ Matrot-Wittersheim: see MEURSAULT.

Guy Bocard

21190 Meursault; 03.80.21.26.06; fax: 03.80.21.64.92

Wine: Meursault. $$ to $$$

Bocard's Meursaults may not be ready for prime time—some have slightly weird flavors, others finish hot—but there's an authenticity about them. They are clearly the wines of one man working one plot of land. And the attributes are many—the limpidity and depth of the Meursault Limouzin; the layers and complexity of the Premier Cru Genevrières; and the extraordinary bloodlines of the Premier Cru Les Charmes.

Domaine Jean-Marc Boillot

21630 Pommard; 03.80.22.71.29; pommardiere@wanadoo.fr

Wines: Puligny-Montrachet and Pommard. $$$

He's located in Pommard, but Jean-Marc Boillot's best wines are whites. His excellent Pulignys, including Premier Cru Champ Canet, cascade over the palate with flavors of minerals, herbal tea, and quinine. Boillot also produces Vin de Pays d'Oc at the Domaine de la Truffière. The wines are pleasant but hardly as ambitious as his Burgundies.

Domaine Lucien Boillot ☆

21220 Gevrey-Chambertin; 03.80.51.85.61; fax: 03.80.58.51.23
Wines: Nuits-St.-Georges, Gevrey-Chambertin, and Volnay. $$$ to $$$$
A very good domaine making fine, self-effacing but delicious, site-specific, unfined and unfiltered wines in some of the best red ACs of the Côte d'Or. In the Côte de Nuits, for example, there's the deep, succulent Nuits-St.-Georges Premier Cru Les Pruliers; the limpid, juicy Gevrey-Chambertin Premier Cru Les Cherbaudes, and the extremely fresh, hauntingly nuanced Gevrey-Chambertin Premier Cru Les Corbeaux. In the Côte de Beaune, there are several Volnays, including a delicate, loosely woven Villages and a fragrant Premier Cru Les Angles that seems to wrap itself around you, a panorama of pleasure.

Maison Jean-Claude Boisset

21700 Nuits-St.-Georges, 03.80.62.61.61; www.jcboisset.fr
Wines: The entire range of Burgundies. $ to $$$$
Burgundy's largest grower-*négociant* house and the owner of such widely distributed labels as Bouchard Ainé (look for pleasant, above-average red Savigny-lès-Beaune Premier Crus), Pierre Ponnelle, and the Moreau Chablis, as well as part owner of Mommessin. While many of the wines are ordinary, the house is capable of more. Admirable bottles include a regal Puligny-Montrachet Les Champs Gains and some of the top-end ACs—for example Bonnes-Mares and Le Musigny—from the Domaine de la Vougeraie, which Boisset also owns.

Domaine de la Bongran ☆

71260 Clessé; 03.85.36.94.03; fax: 03.85.36.99.25
Wines: Mâcon and Viré-Clessé. $$ to $$$
Philosopher, historian, and above all brilliant, masterly vigneron, owner Jean Thévenet makes some of the most sumptuous, personalized chardonnay you're ever likely to taste. His standard bottling is fairly mainstream—at the very top end of that stream. The Cuvée Levroutée, made from overripe grapes, the skins of which have turned a shade of bronze, veers toward demi-sec, but it's so voluptuous and winds itself around your tongue in such an insinuating manner that you don't sense the sweetness. I once drank it with a Parmesan soup and the combo was brilliant—a scrumptious interplay of salt and sweet. Then there's Thévenet's most controversial wine—the Cuvée Botrytisée. Yes, 100 percent botrytized chardonnay. It's crystal clear, sapid, tangy, and devastatingly delicious. Thévenet is the only vintner I know who succeeds in making a superb, beautifully balanced chardonnay *liquoureux*. Thévenet's Émilian Gillet, a Mâcon-Viré, is a very good white for a meal. His son has another Mâcon property, Domaine Roally.

Bonneau de Martray ☆

21420 Pernand-Vergelesses: 03.80.21.50.64; fax: 03.80.21.57.19
Wine: Corton. $$$ to $$$$
A major vineyard owner in Grand Cru Corton-Charlemagne with a well-earned reputation for very high quality. The whites need cellaring—ten years at least. They are always imposing, majestic, grandly mineral, and extremely long. More recently, the house has been turning out refined, perfumed reds from Grand Cru Corton. They're very classy and you can drink them sooner than you can drink the whites.

Bonnes-Mares

A roughly 15-hectare Grand Cru located between Chambolle-Musigny and Morey-St.-Denis producing pinot noir–based reds. Their quality should be extremely high.

BEST RECENT VINTAGES: 2005, (2004), (2003), 2002, (2001), 1999, and 1996.
PRICES: $$$$

PRODUCERS: Dom d'Auvenay: see DOM LEROY ☆ ◆ DOM BERTHEAU ☆ ◆ JOSEPH DROUHIN ☆ ◆ DOM FOUGERAY DE BEAUCLAIR ◆ DOM LOUIS JADOT ☆ ◆ DOM DOMINIQUE LAURENT ☆ ◆ DOM JACQUES-FRÉDÉRIC MUGNIER ◆ DOM GEORGES ROUMIER ◆ Dom de la Vougeraie: see MAISON JEAN-CLAUDE BOISSET.

Bouchard Père & Fils ☆

21200 Beaune, 03.80.24.80.24; www.bouchard-pereetfils.com

Wines: Beaune, Corton, Meursault, Volnay, and others. $ to $$$$

A leading Burgundy grower-*négociant* with 130 hectares of vines. Since Joseph Henriot took over in the mid-1990s, Bouchard has evolved from a somnolent underachiever to one of the most dynamic, reliable, and quality-driven houses in the region. Bouchard's range is nearly encyclopedic. Its strength—in addition to the Chablis from William Fèvre—is in the Beaune area (that said, wines from the the Côte Chalonnaise and Mâconnais range from good to extremely good). Greatness, grandeur, and, dear reader, what will surely strike you as a superfluity of yet other superlatives are in store when we get to Corton, Meursault, Montrachet, Volnay, and Nuits-St.-Georges. Just a handful of examples: A subtle, detailed Meursault Premier Cru Genevrières that's as ample and textured as it is pure and racy. A savory, mineral Chevalier-Montrachet Grand Cru, simultaneously potent and delicate as lace. A monumental Montrachet Grand Cru, with amazing depth. A layered and lipsmacking white Beaune du Château Premier Cru, tightly focused and a torrent of freshness. A spicy, succulent Volnay Premier Cru Caillerets Ancienne Cuvée Carnot that has great promise but is so scrumptious it would be hard to keep from drinking it immediately. A deep and delicious Nuits-St.-Georges Premier Cru Les Cailles. The gaggle of sublime Beaunes includes the red Premier Cru Clos de la Mousse, a Bouchard exclusive; Beaune du Château Premier Cru, both red and white, blended from a number of estate-owned Premier Cru plots; and the house's signature Premier Cru Grèves Vigne de l'Enfant Jésus, the embodiment of the "iron fist in the velvet glove" analogy.

Jean-Marc Bouley

21290 Volnay; 03.80.21.62.33; jeanmarc.bouley@wanadoo.fr

Wines: Bourgogne-Hautes-Côtes de Beaune, Pommard, and Volnay. $ to $$$

Bouley makes expressive, fresh, and stylish reds in all three ACs. Look, in particular, for the pellucid, fine-grained Beaune Premier Cru Les Renversées.

Bourgogne

A regional AC producing whites, reds, and rosés. Its whites are made from chardonnay; the reds are primarily pinot noir. César and the near-extinct tressot are also permitted, and gamay is used in the ten *crus* of Beaujolais. Quality varies greatly—from watery and sharp to mind-blowing in the sense of that classic *New Yorker* cartoon in which a host pompously serves a wine saying something like, "It's a simple country wine but I think you'll be amused by its presumption." That's what you find yourself saying when you taste some of the "simple" Bourgognes from top producers in blue-chip ACs as well as from ambitious newcomers.

BEST RECENT VINTAGES: 2005, (2004), (2003), and 2002.
PRICES: $ to $$$ (often fine values)

PRODUCERS: DOM RÉGIS BOUVIER ◆ JEAN-MARC BROCARD ◆ La Buxynoise: see MONTAGNY ◆ MAISON CHAMPY ◆ PHILIPPE CHARLOPIN ☆ ◆ DOM DE CHASSORNEY ↑ ◆ DOM COCHE-BIZOUARD ☆ ◆ Vincent Dancer: see BEAUNE ◆ CATHERINE & DOMINIQUE DERAIN ↑ ◆ DOM RÉGIS DUBOIS & FILS ◆ ARNAUD & MARIE-ODILE ENTE ☆ ◆ DOM FICHET ↑ ◆ DOM FOUGERAY DE BEAUCLAIR ◆ DOM JÉRÔME GALEYRAND ↑ ◆ DOM DE LA GALOPIÈRE ◆ DOM ANNE GROS ☆ ◆ THIERRY GUYOT ◆ DOM PATRICK JAVILLIER ☆ ◆ DOM HUBERT LAMY ◆ DOM DOMINIQUE LAURENT ☆ ◆ DOM LEJEUNE ◆ MACHARD DE GRAMONT ☆ ◆ DOM CATHERINE & CLAUDE MARÉCHAL ◆ DOM MARÉCHAL-CAILLOT

◆ Ch de Marsannay: although this domaine has properties in a handful of prestigious ACs, the wine I like best is the Bourgogne blanc chardonnay Clos du Château, which comes on like a junior Meursault and costs $ to $$ ◆ Masse: see GIVRY ◆ DOM PIERRE MOREY ☆ ◆ Dom Noël Perrin: see MONTAGNY ◆ DOM ROULOT ☆ ◆ Dom St.-Denis/Hubert Laferrère: full, suave reds from Les Clos ◆ CÉLINE & LAURENT TRIPOZ ☆ ◆ DOM DU VIEUX COLLÈGE.

Bourgogne Aligoté

A regional AC for lean whites, made from aligoté, that are historically the base for Kir, a cocktail made with white wine and crème de cassis. Drink the youngest available. Prices: $ to $$.

PRODUCERS: Dom d'Auvenay: see DOM LEROY ☆ ◆ DOM COCHE-BIZOUARD ☆ ◆ DOM RÉGIS DUBOIS & FILS ◆ GHISLAINE & JEAN-HUGUES GOISOT ☆ ◆ DOM JAYER-GILLES ☆ ◆ DOM PIERRE MOREY ☆ ◆ DOM HENRI NAUDIN-FERRAND ↑ ◆ Noël Perrin: see MONTAGNY ◆ DOM MICHEL SARRAZIN ☆.

Bourgogne Chitry

A small AC in northern Burgundy, in the Auxerrois, for whites based on chardonnay and reds and rosés made from pinot noir, with the possible addition of césar and tressot. Drink the youngest available. Prices: $. Producers: Franck Chalmeau: juicy, perky reds, to drink chilled; and a nicely acidulated Bourgogne Grand Ordinaire based on sacy ◆ OLIVIER MORIN.

Bourgogne Côte Chalonnaise

A small AC in the Côte Chalonnaise (the region of Chalon-sur-Saône) for reds based on pinot noir and whites based on chardonnay. Best recent vintages: 2005, (2004), (2003), and 2002. Prices: $ to $$. Producer: DOM A. & P. DE VILLAINE ☆.

Bourgogne Côte St.-Jacques

A minuscule AC near the town of Joigny for pinot noir–based reds and chardonnay-based whites. Drink the youngest available. Prices: $ to $$.

Bourgogne Côtes-d'Auxerre

A small AC in the Auxerrois known for whites based on chardonnay and reds based on pinot noir, though césar is also used.

BEST RECENT VINTAGES: 2005, (2004), (2003), and 2002.
PRICES: $ to $$

PRODUCERS: Bailly-Lapierre: fresh, classic chardonnay ◆ Dom Pascal Bouchard: nice chardonnays from a young vigneron in Chablis ◆ Philippe Defrance: amiable light reds to chill and quaff ◆ GHISLAINE & JEAN-HUGUES GOISOT ☆ ◆ Sorin-Coquard: a good wine-bar Côte d'Auxerre that comes in two flavors—chardonnay and pinot noir.

Bourgogne Côtes du Couchois

A small AC at the southern limits of the Côte d'Or, in the Couchois, for reds based on pinot noir. Best recent vintages: 2005, 2004, 2003, and 2002. Prices: $$. Producer: DOM LES CHAMPS DE L'ABBAYE ↑.

Bourgogne Coulanges-la-Vineuse

A small AC in northern Burgundy, in the Auxerrois, Bourgogne Coulanges-la-Vineuse produces whites based on chardonnay and reds and rosés based on pinot noir, césar, and tressot. Drink the youngest available. Prices: $ to $$.

Producers: Dom Borgnat: a series of amiable, wine-bar-ready reds; look for the Tête de Cuvée and the Ch d'Escolives, a barrel-aged blend of pinot noir and césar ◆ Clos du Roi: Michel Bernard makes irresistibly gulpable, clear, juicy light reds ◆ Domaine Rigoutat: Pascale and Alain Rigoutat make serious, gutsy Bourgogne Coulanges-la-Vineuse, including a lime-tinged chardonnay, a textured rosé, and a very oaky red.

Bourgogne Épineuil

A small AC in the Tonnerrois for chardonnay-based whites and reds and rosés made from pinot noir, césar, and tressot. Drink the youngest available. Prices: $ to $$. Producers: DOM DE L'ABBAYE DU PETIT QUINCY ◆ JEAN-MARC BROCARD.

Bourgogne Grand Ordinaire (usually abbreviated as BGO) and Bourgogne Ordinaire

An AC applying to the entire vineyard area for reds and rosés based on gamay, pinot noir, césar, and tressot and whites of aligoté, chardonnay, melon de bourgogne, and sacy. Generally drink the youngest available, although certain producers are making astonishingly good wines. Prices: $ to $$. Producers: Franck Chalmeau: sassy little whites made with sacy ◆ ARNAUD & MARIE-ODILE ENTE ☆.

Bourgogne Hautes-Côtes de Beaune

An AC located in ninety-one communes in the Saône-et-Loire on land considered less desirable than that which qualifies for the more prestigious ACs. Reds are made from pinot noir, whites from chardonnay. Quality can be high.

BEST RECENT VINTAGES: 2005, (2004), (2003), and 2002.
PRICES: See Côtes de Beaune

PRODUCERS: Dom François Bergeret: dark, jammy wines to try by the glass ◆ JEAN-MARC BOULEY ◆ CHRISTOPHE BUISSON ↑ ◆ Henri Delagrange & Fils: engaging pinot noir ◆ Dom Rodolphe Demougeot: juicy, fleshy, easy wines ◆ DOM RÉGIS DUBOIS & FILS ◆ EMMANUEL GIBOULOT ↑ ◆ Dom Glantenet Père & Fils: a white with good focus and depth; a serious red worth following along with promising Bourgogne Hautes-Côtes de Nuits and a good Bourgogne Aligoté ◆ DOM HUBERT LAMY ◆ DOM HENRI NAUDIN-FERRAND ↑ ◆ Dom Claude Nouveau: good wines to drink by the glass, although you're even better off with the Santenay Premier Cru Grand Clos Rousseau, a lean but precise red ◆ Agnès & Sébastien Paquet: cool, fresh, alluring reds ◆ Jean-Claude Rateau: an ambitious domaine run biodynamically, but the wines need work ◆ DOM ANTONIN RODET ◆ Dom St.-Antoine des Échards: Marie-Christine and Franck Guérin produce very promising Bourgogne Hautes-Côtes de Beaune—a domaine to follow.

Bourgogne Hautes-Côtes de Nuits

An AC in sites considered less desirable than those qualifying for the Côte de Nuits ACs. Primarily for pinot noir–based reds although some chardonnay-based whites are also made. Quality can be very high.

BEST RECENT VINTAGES: 2005, (2004), (2003), and 2002.
PRICES: $$ to $$$

PRODUCERS: DOM RÉGIS DUBOIS & FILS ◆ Dom Maurice Garignet: see NUITS-ST.-GEORGES ◆ EMMANUEL GIBOULOT ↑ ◆ Dom Anne-Marie Gille: See NUITS-ST.-GEORGES ◆ Dom Glantenet Père & Fils: see BOURGOGNE HAUTES-CÔTES DE BEAUNE ◆ DOM A. F. GROS ☆ ◆ DOM ANNE GROS ☆ ◆ Dom Patrick Hudelot: a promising, organically farmed domaine with holdings in the Premier Crus Les Genevrières and Les Roncières ◆ DOM JAYER-GILLES ☆ ◆ DOM HENRI NAUDIN-FERRAND ↑ ◆ Dom Christian Perrin: an eco-friendly domaine with an exclusive on Clos des Fourches that's worth trying.

Bourgogne Passetoutgrains

An AC that covers the entire vineyard area; its reds and rosés must be made with a minimum of one third pinot noir and a maximum of two thirds gamay. In general, drink the youngest available. Prices: $ to $$. Producers: DOM LES CHAMPS DE L'ABBAYE ↑ ◆ DOM CHEVALIER PÈRE & FILS ◆ ARNAUD & MARIE-ODILE ENTE ☆ ◆ DOM MARÉCHAL-CAILLOT.

Bourgogne-Tonnerre

A new AC baptized in 2006 in the Yonne department, near Chablis, for white wines based on chardonnay. (Burgundy seems to have endless possibilities for hyphenation. Other subregions with the right to attach their place of origin to that of Bourgogne include Montrecul, La Chapelle Nôtre Dame, and Le Chapitre.)

Bourgogne-Vézelay

A small AC on the slopes of the historic town of Vézelay producing whites based on chardonnay. The wines are potentially complete and complex, with fine mineral flavors.

BEST RECENT VINTAGES: 2005, (2004), (2003), and 2002.
PRICES: $ to $$

PRODUCERS: Dom de la Cadette: a family winery created in 1988, farmed organically ◆ DOM MARIA CUNY ↑ ◆ Dom Henri de Vézelay: vivacious chardonnays with appetizing mineral and lime flavors ◆ Marc Meneau: the vinous venture of this Michelin three-star chef results in a mellow, structured, very tasty Les Chaumants ◆ Dom Elise Villiers: the mineral, quirky La Chevalière is worth trying by the glass.

Domaine Régis Bouvier

21160 Marsannay la Côte; 03.80.51.33.93; fax: 03.80.58.75.07
Wines: Marsannay and Bourgogne. $ to $$($)
This domaine's very good, stylish Marsannays include the fragrant, spicy Les Longeroies Cuvée Excellence and the deeper, more tannic Clos du Roy Tête de Cuvée. Bouvier also makes a lipsmacking red Bourgogne from the suggestively named *lieu-dit* Montre Cul (translation: shows ass).

Domaine René Bouvier ↑

21220 Gevrey-Chambertin; 03.80.52.21.37; rene-bouvier@wanadoo.fr
Wines: Fixin, Marsannay, Chambolle-Musigny, Clos Vougeot, Côte de Nuits, and Gevrey-Chambertin. $$ to $$$$
When René's son Bernard took over the domaine at the turn of this century, he gradually changed working methods. Now viticulture is eco-friendly and everything is done by hand. Bouvier's wines tend to be rich and to benefit from aeration: an hour or so in a carafe before drinking is recommended. It was from a carafe, in fact, that I first tasted his wine—a silky, fine-grained Fixin Crais de Chêne. Bouvier works five different *lieux-dits* in Marsannay AC, making a textured, fine En Ouzeloy; a deeper, tighter Clos du Roy; and a potent, clear, and a singular white from Le Clos, on which they have a monopoly. Bouvier makes a deeply fruity Côte de Nuits-Villages and a regal Chambolle-Musigny Premier Cru Noirots. There's a passel of riveting Gevrey-Chambertins, of which two are completely mouthwatering—the complex, lush, racy Jeunes Rois and Racines du Temps. Made from vines that are at least eighty years old, Racines du Temps is velvety and haunting.

Bouzeron

A tiny AC in the Côte Chalonnaise for bone-dry whites made from aligoté. The sharpness of these wines has made them the ideal basis for a Kir—in which they are blended with crème de cassis. Aligotés from this AC, however, have a bit more oomph and character. Drink the youngest available. Prices: $ to $$. Producers: Anne-Sophie Debavelaere: this wine makes top-notch Kirs; see also RULLY ◆ DOM A. & P. DE VILLAINE ☆.

Bret Brothers/La Soufrandière ↑

71680 Vinzelles; tel/fax: 03.85.35.67.72; lasoufrandiere@libertysurf.fr

Wines: Pouilly-Vinzelles, St.-Véran, and Mâcon. $$ to $$$

Another promising domaine. In 1998 La Soufrandière left the local cooperative. In 2000, after having worked in California as well as with Jean-Marie Guffens and Dominique Lafon, the young Bret brothers began bottling their own wine under La Soufrandière's label. Farming is now organic. Most cuvées ferment in Burgundy barrels. The wines are ambitious and all have something to say, although they don't seem quite ready for prime time. To date, my favorite is the Viré-Clessé Sous les Plantes Vieilles Vignes.

Jean-Marc Brocard

89800 Chablis; 03.86.41.49.00; www.brocard.fr

Wines: Chablis, St.-Bris, and Bourgogne. $ to $$$

This enterprising and substantial grower-*négociant* has a smart shop in town and a full and attractive range of all wines Auxerrois and Tonnerrois. His Chablis—from a solid Petit Chablis to a host of racy, textured Premier Crus including Montmains, Bougros, Vaucoupin, and Beauregard—are reliably well made. His St.-Bris is pungent and bracing, as is his Bourgogne Épineul, a tart, perky, light red. And he offers an ambitious line of geologically differentiated chardonnays—Portlandien, Jurassique, and my favorite, the creamy, pedigreed Kimmeridgian.

Brouilly

The largest *cru* of Beaujolais, Brouilly has the meatiest, most foursquare wines. See BEAUJOLAIS for vintages and prices.

PRODUCERS: Dom de Bel Air: see RÉGNIÉ ◆ Ch de la Chaize: the wines from this large property are well distributed, although quality is average ◆ Dom Chevalier-Metrat: see CÔTE DE BROUILLY ◆ DOM GEORGES DESCOMBES ◆ GEORGES DUBOEUF ◆ Dom Dubost: see MORGON ◆ Laurent Martray: an ambitious, idealistic vigneron whose concentrated cuvée Corentin beguiles with its exotic fruit flavors and lovely concentration ☆ ◆ Dom Lapalu: Brigitte and Jean-Claude Lapalu use Bordeaux bottles for their singular barrel-aged Brouilly made from a parcel of ninety-year-old vines, Cuvée des Fous. Their several bottlings of Beaujolais-Villages range from the thin but honest to the overripe but pleasantly quirky Rang du Merle ◆ MOMMESSIN ◆ Ch des Ravatys: see CÔTE DE BROUILLY ◆ Ch de Pierreux: see MOMMESSIN ◆ Dom de St.-Ennemond: an eco-friendly domaine producing attractive Brouillys, especially Dame de Briante ◆ Dom de Sancillon: see CÔTE DE BROUILLY ◆ Ch Thivin: see CÔTE DE BROUILLY ☆.

Jean-Paul Brun/Domaine des Terres Dorées

69380 Charnay; 04.78.47.93.45; fax: 04.78.47.93.38

Wines: Beaujolais, Côte de Brouilly, Moulin-à-Vent. $ to $$

Firmly in the hypernatural camp, Jean-Paul Brun makes two pellucid, mellow, very mineral Beaujolais blanc "chardonnays." There are also several cuvées of Beaujolais, including an extremely ripe, old-vines Beaujolais L'Ancien, a structured, singular Côte de Brouilly, and a resolutely pure Moulin-à-Vent. In addition, Brun has planted 2 hectares of pinot noir that will be aged in barrel and sold as Bourgogne AC.

Christophe Buisson ↑

21190 St.-Romain; 03.80.21.63.92; domainechristophebuisson@wanadoo.fr
Wines: St.-Romain, Savigny-lès-Beaune, Auxey-Duresses, and Bourgogne Hautes-Côtes de Beaune. $$ to $$$
A promising young vintner whose wines are not yet ready for the world stage—although they'd be quite welcome in a good wine bar, particularly one specializing in hypernatural wines. From the various St.-Romains (red and white) to the Bourgogne Hautes-Côtes de Beaune, all the wines are artisanal and authentic but not without a bit of overripeness here, or some unwanted fizz there. The most polished I've tasted have been a toothsome red Savigny-lès-Beaune Le Mouttier Amet and a rich, inviting, and lipsmacking Auxey-Duresses Les Grandes Vignes.

Domaine Alain Burguet ☆

21220 Gevrey-Chambertin; 03.80.34.36.55; domainealainburguet@wanadoo.fr
Wines: Gevrey-Chambertin and Chambolle-Musigny. $$$ to $$$$
Excellent organic Gevrey-Chambertin. Alain Burguet offers five different, generally unfiltered versions including the pungent, oaky En Billard and Mes Favorites Vieilles Vignes from sixty-year-old vines. The Mes Favorites is pure and racy but also strapping and hearty, perhaps something of a Prince Harry. Burguet recently acquired some vines in Chambolle-Musigny. Another pleasure to anticipate.

Benoît Cantin

89290 Irancy; 03.86.42.21.96. fax: 03.86.42.31.96
Wine: Irancy. $$
Charming, food-friendly light reds that are full of character. The barrel-aged Palotte bottling is focused and slender, with delicious plum flavors. It slips down the gullet with the greatest of ease.

Chablis

The northern outpost of Burgundy, the Chablis AC, which takes its name from a small town located between Paris and Beaune, is one of the most well-known and iconic wines in the world. Made solely from chardonnay, it has long been the quintessential bone-dry white. But it is much more than that. At its best, it is a riveting, indeed a breathtaking, wine of amazing purity, freshness, steeliness, and minerality; it is razor sharp without ever being severe. Even when atypically ripe and fat, as in 2003, it retains its cool and invigorating allure. There are four categories in the AC Chablis hierarchy, ascending from Petit Chablis, Chablis (which accounts for more than half the production), and Chablis Premier Cru to Chablis Grand Cru.

There are seven Grand Crus, all located on the right bank of the Serein River overlooking the town of Chablis. Unlike the Grand Crus in the Côte d'Or, the Grand Crus here always follow the name *Chablis* on the label. These are: Les Clos, Vaudesir, Valmur, Blanchot, Bougros, Les Preuses, and Grenouilles.

There are forty Premier Crus—actually seventy-nine, if you count the famous *lieux-dits* within the Premier Crus—some of the most famous being Fourchaume, Mont de Milieu, Montée de Tonnerre, and Vaillons.

A personal note on the wine style and *terroir* here: Chablis is in Burgundy, but its *terroir* is the same as that of the Sancerrois. When I taste really good, *terroir*-driven Chablis I can't help thinking of the very best Sancerres. The grapes—chardonnay and sauvignon blanc—truly take the back seat here. As far as I'm concerned, that's wonderful, a consummation devoutly to be wished.

BEST RECENT VINTAGES: The 2005 vintage shows all the signs of greatness. A winemaker's year, 2004 has lots of challenges; shop carefully. In 2003 there are some superb wines; some reveal the nature of the vintage and are atypically fat and low in acid. The years 2002 and 2000 are both excellent. And 1997, 1996, 1995, 1992, and 1990 were all very good to excellent vintages but should be drunk up.

PRICES: $$ to $$$$

PRODUCERS: DOM DES AIRELLES ◆ Dom Hervé Azo: makes invigorating Petit Chablis, equally bracing Chablis, and zingy Chablis Premier Cru Vau de Vey, as racy as it is piercing ◆ Dom Barat: above-average Chablis, particularly from the Premier Cru Les Fourneaux and Vaillons ◆ Jean-Claude Bessin: a domaine worth following; the Premier Crus Montmains and Fourchaume are particularly promising ◆ Dom Besson: the Premier Cru Montmains is fresh, serious, and well-made, a thoroughly admirable Chablis ◆ Dom de Bois d'Yver/Georges Pico: above-average Chablis, particularly the Premier Cru Beauregard ◆ Dom Boissoneuse: Julien Brocard's biodynamic Chablis are both mellow and steely; a domaine to follow ↑ ◆ JEAN-MARC BROCARD ◆ Dom Camu: if you're visiting Chablis, stop into Camu's shop and taste his good Premier Crus, which include Côte de Lechet and Beauroy ◆ LA CHABLISIENNE ☆ ◆ Madame Edmond Chalmeau: look for friendly little bistro Chablis, as well as a good Bourgogne-Chitry chardonnay and a Bourgogne Aligoté ◆ Dom des Chenevières: Frédéric Gueguen's entire range is worth trying, from the very good Petit Chablis, to a fresh, toothsome Premier Cru Côte de Lechet, to an impressive and delicious Fourchaume ↑ ◆ Dom Chevalier: although it's somewhat rustic, I recommend the Premier Cru Montmains for its sense of place ◆ Jean Dauvissat: there are numerous parcels and bottlings; it's the Premier Cru Vaillons Vieilles Vignes and Grand Cru Les Preuses that stand out ◆ DOM RENÉ & VINCENT DAUVISSAT ☆ ◆ DOM BERNARD DEFAIX ☆ ◆ JEAN-PAUL & BENOÎT DROIN ☆ ◆ JOSEPH DROUHIN ☆ ◆ Caves Duplessis/Gérard Duplessis: the Premier Cru Vaillons is worth trying ◆ JEAN DURUP PÈRE & FILS ◆ DOM WILLIAM FÈVRE ☆ ◆ Fourrey & Fils: two-dimensional Chablis, including Premier Crus Mont de Milieu and Côte de Lechet ◆ Dom Garnier: above-average Chablis, particularly the extremely ripe (perhaps overripe) cuvée Grains Dorés ◆ Dom Alain & Cyril Gautheron: try the Premier Cru Mont de Milieu ◆ Dom des Genèves: the Premier Cru Vaucoupin is certainly worth tasting ◆ Alain Geoffroy: superior AC wines; the Premier Crus are a clear step up, espcially the Beauroy and Fourchaume, which would make nice bistro Chablis ◆ Dom Jean Goulley & Fils: the Premier Crus Montmains and Mont de Milieu are recommended ◆ Dom Philippe Goulley: extremely fresh, organic Chablis and Petit Chablis; the Premier Crus Fourchaume and Montmains, with lemon-lime accents, are as clear and bracing as mountain streams ☆ ◆ CORINNE & JEAN-PIERRE GROSSOT ☆ ◆ DOM HAMELIN ◆ DOM LAROCHE ☆ ◆ ROLAND LAVANTUREUX ☆ ◆ Dom Long-Depaquit: owned by MAISON ALBERT BICHOT, this house possesses great vineyards in Premier Crus and Grand Crus. I don't think the wines live up to their potential—the disappointing quality of Moutonne, a Grand Cru of which they are the sole owners, is particularly dismaying. I feel compelled to note, however, that other wine critics disagree with me, responding much more favorably to the wines ◆ Ch de Maligny: see DURUP ◆ ALICE & OLIVIER DE MOOR ↑ ◆ DOM CHRISTIAN MOREAU ◆ Moreau-Naudet: reliably good Chablis, particularly the Grand Cru Valmur ◆ Dom de la Motte: the fresh, mineral Premier Cru Vauligneau Les Vieilles Vignes d'Henri is worth tasting ◆ DOMAINE OUDIN ◆ PHILIPPE PACALET ☆ ◆ Dom de Perdrycourt: there's promising work here, making this a domaine worth following ◆ DOM PINSON FRÈRES ◆ ISABELLE & DENIS POMMIER ◆ DOM RAVENEAU ☆ ◆ Jean Robin: characterful pedigreed Chablis, including a steely, intensely mineral Premier Cru Vosgros and a razor-sharp Premier Cru Montmains, fresh as a cascade and full of mineral and herbal tea flavors ☆ ◆ Louis Robin: makes a tight, steel-and-lemon Chablis, a deeper, more serious cuvée Vieilles Vignes, and an incisive Premier Cru Vaucoupin that could only be Chablis ◆ FRANCINE & OLIVIER SAVARY ☆ ◆ DOM SERVIN ◆ Verget: see GUFFENS-HEYNEN ☆ ◆ Dom Vrignaud: pleasant chardonnay-driven Chablis; the Mont de Milieu and Fourchaume Vieilles Vignes are racy and far superior.

La Chablisienne ☆

BP 14, 89800 Chablis; 03.86.42.89.89; www.chablisienne.com

Wine: Chablis. $ to $$$

This solid model cooperative accounts for one third of the production of Chablis, including significant shares of its Grand Crus and Premier Crus. The wines are well made, reliable, and user friendly, and each accurately reflects its standing within the Chablis hierarchy, starting with a sound, vivacious, very likable Petit Chablis. The Chablis Cuvée L.C. is lean and steely. The Premier Cru Grande Cuvée, a distinct step up, is textured and nuanced with rich lemon flavors supported by steel. The Premier Cru Mont de Milieu is exciting and perfectly lovely. The Grand Cru Grenouilles, tasted on its third birthday, was so rich it bordered on the viscous; young and tight, it wanted a couple of years to allow the compacted layers of flavor to relax and blossom.

Chambolle-Musigny

An important Côte de Nuits AC for fragrant, charming reds based on pinot noir. Of the numerous Premier Crus, the most evocatively named is Les Amoureuses. The Grand Cru Le Musigny consists almost entirely of red wine, although less than a hectare planted to chardonnay produces an infinitesimal amount of white. Part of the Grand Cru Bonnes-Mares also lies within Chambolle-Musigny's limits.

BEST RECENT VINTAGES: 2005, (2004), (2003), 2002, (2001), and 1999.
PRICES: $$$ to $$$$

PRODUCERS: DOM BERTHEAU ☆ ◆ DOM RENÉ BOUVIER ↑ ◆ DOM BRUNO CLAIR ☆ DOM CONFURON-COTETIDOT ☆ ◆ JOSEPH DROUHIN ☆ ◆ DOM RÉGIS DUBOIS & FILS ◆ MAISON ALEX GAMBAL ☆ ◆ Dom Maurice Garignet: see NUITS-ST.-GEORGES ◆ DOM ANNE GROS ☆ ◆ DOM A. F. GROS ☆ ◆ DOM ANTONIN GUYON ◆ DOM LOUIS JADOT ☆ ◆ DOM DOMINIQUE LAURENT ☆ ◆ DOM LEROY ☆ ◆ DOM JACQUES-FRÉDÉRIC MUGNIER ◆ PHILIPPE PACALET ☆ ◆ DOM JACQUES PRIEUR ☆ ◆ DOM DANIEL RION & FILS ◆ DOM GEORGES ROUMIER ◆ Dom Hervé Sigaut: the Premier Crus Les Chatelots and Les Sentiers (Vieilles Vignes) are worth trying ◆ COMTE DE VOGÜÉ ◆ Dom de la Vougeraie: see MAISON JEAN-CLAUDE BOISSET.

Domaine les Champs de l'Abbaye ↑

71510 Aluze, 03.85.45.59.32. alainhasard@wanadoo.fr

Wines: Bourgogne-Couchois, Rully, Mercurey, and Bourgogne Passetoutgrains. $$ to $$$

Take two disaffected, nature- and wine-loving psychology students, find them jobs in wine shops, and it's no surprise when they end up with their own vines—which they farm biodynamically—about the time that midlife changes are generally made. In the case of Alain and Isabelle Hasard, the Domaine les Champs de l'Abbaye was created in 1997 with 5 or 6 hectares of vines in the Couchois area of Burgundy. And the wines they made, and continue to make there, are sublime overachievers. Which just shows what passion, dedication, and talent can do. Neither fined nor filtered, all their wines age in barrel with a fair percentage of new oak. For the time being, we're talking about red wines, starting with a pure, succulent, barrel-aged Passetoutgrains, equal parts gamay and pinot noir, that bursts with vibrancy and joie de vivre, and a mineral, almost grandiose Les Vignes Martin. There's also an extremely serious, structured Les Rompeys and the fragrant, exotic Le Clos, which could be taken for a blue-chip Côte de Nuits.

It's hard to keep up with the Hasards, however. In 2006 this small domaine changed dramatically. They've added half a hectare in Rully and a hectare in Mercurey, and have relinquished most of their Couchois property, with the exception of Le Clos, Les Rompeys, Les Vignes Martin, and Passetoutgrains, so I'm not discussing the wines they no longer make. And they're keeping an eye out for other parcels. One thing's for sure: whatever they do, it will be excellent and delicious.

Maison Champy

21200 Beaune; 03.80.25.09.99; fax:03.80.25.09.95

Wines: Beaune, Corton, Savigny-lès-Beaune, and Pernand-Vergelesse, among others. $$ to $$$$

A first-rate *négociant* whose strength is in the Beaune area. The wines—from a red Beaune Premier Cru Champs Pimont, to mineral, balanced Pernand-Vergelesses (red), to a (white) Corton-Charlemagne Grand Cru—are well selected, very professional, and perfect for upscale French restaurants. Indeed, the Beaune Premier Cru Aux Cras, a big, healthy, pedigreed red with broad pinot noir, cherry, and strawberry aromas, is the type of Burgundy I imagine the late Princess Diana would have drunk.

Domaine de la Chapelle ☆

71960 Solutré; 03.85.35.81.51; fax: 03.85.35.86.43

Wine: Pouilly-Fuissé. $$

As layered and fresh as a mountain stream, la Chapelle's Pouilly-Fuissés include a Vieilles Vignes and the mellow and mineral Clos de la Chapelle, made from yet older vines (eighty and counting).

Philippe Charlopin ☆

21220 Gevrey-Chambertin, 03.80.51.81.18; charlopin.philippe@wanadoo.fr

Wines: Gevrey-Chambertin, Marsannay, Échezeaux, and others. $$$ to $$$$

Influenced by the great Henri Jayer, Philippe Charlopin makes mouthwatering, deeply fruity, succulent red Burgundies—in twenty-five different ACs. Always worth trying, his Marsannay En Montchenevoy, for example, is a fresh, lively weave of silk and velvet; his Gevrey-Chambertin Vieilles Vignes is more profound, pure velvet, with abundant ripe tannins.

Chassagne-Montrachet

An iconic Côte de Beaune AC for regal whites made from chardonnay and textured reds made from pinot noir. The sole Grand Cru located entirely within Chassagne is Criots-Bâtard-Montrachet; the commune shares the Grand Crus Montrachet and Bâtard-Montrachet with the commune of Puligny. Among its white Premier Crus are En Remilly, Morgeot, and Vide-Bourse (how did they know?). For reds there are Morgeot, Les Chenevottes, and Les Grandes Ruchottes.

BEST RECENT VINTAGES: 2005, (2004), (2003), 2002, (2001), and 1999.
PRICES: $$$ to $$$$

PRODUCERS: FRANÇOIS D'ALLAINES ↑ ◆ DOM GUY AMIOT & FILS ☆ ◆ BALLOT-MILLOT & FILS ◆ BOUCHARD PÈRE & FILS ☆ ◆ Philippe Brenot: an exciting young vigneron with a clutch of ambitious, captivating white Montrachets, including the racy, crystalline, new-oak-fermented Chassagne Premier Cru En Remilly; a fresh, pedigreed Puligny from the *lieu-dit* Les Enseignières; and a mellow, creamy, invigorating Bâtard Grand Cru ↑ ◆ Philippe Colin: good, tasty white Premier Cru Les Vergers Blanc and flavorful, nicely made red Les Chênes Rouges ◆ Michel Colin-Deléger & Fils: stylish, meal-friendly wines, both red and white, particularly the Premier Cru En Remilly and the Vieilles Vignes; the St.-Aubin Premier Cru Le Charmois is similarly appealing ◆ JOSEPH DROUHIN ☆ ◆ MAISON ALEX GAMBAL ☆ ◆ Marquis de la Guiche: see DROUHIN ◆ DOM HUBERT LAMY ◆ RENÉ LEQUIN-COLIN ◆ Dom Bernard Moreau & Fils: good, solid whites, from the simple Village AC to the Premier Crus Grandes Ruchottes, Maltroie, and Morgeot, each of which displays a true sense of place ◆ DOM PIERRE MOREY ☆ ◆ Dom Muzard: a promising young domaine with a racy, elegant red old-vines Chassagne-Montrachet, and in a couple of years they'll also have a white ↑ ◆ DOM FERNAND & LAURENT PILLOT ↑ ◆ PAUL PILLOT ↑ ◆ Dom Prieur-Brunet: see SANTENAY ◆ Ch de Puligny-Montrachet: see PULIGNY-MONTRACHET and DOM HUBERT DE MONTILLE ☆.

Domaine de Chassorney ↑

21190 St.-Romain; 03.80.21.65.55; chassorney@aol.com
Wines: Auxey-Duresses, Nuits-St.-Georges, St.-Romain, and Bourgogne.
$$ to $$$

A rising star, hypernaturalist Frédéric Cossard makes mouthwatering, unsulfured, unfiltered wines. His simple Bourgognes—the white Bigotes, the red Bedots—are pure and delicious. His St.-Romain blanc Combe Bazin is simultaneously ripe and mellow and as thrilling as white water. His red St.-Romain Sous Roche exudes crushed raspbarry flavors and is superb to drink when slightly chilled. His Nuits-St.-Georges Clos des Argillières is fresh and absolutely lovely.

Chénas

The smallest *cru* of Beaujolais, the wines of Chénas are fleshy and succulent. See BEAUJOLAIS for vintages and prices. Producers: Dom Pascal Aufranc: look for the oak-aged Vignes de 1939. Named for the year the vines were planted, the cuvée is suave and delicious ◆ Ch Bonnet: an eco-friendly domaine making fragrant, mineral Chénas as well as Beaujolais, Moulin-à-Vent, and Juliénas; look for the Vieilles Vignes ◆ Dom des Darroux: juicy, lipsmacking Chénas ◆ HUBERT LAPIERRE ☆ ◆ MARCEL LAPIERRE ☆ ◆ DOMINIQUE PIRON.

Domaine Chevalier Père & Fils

21550 Ladoix-Serrigny; 03.80.26.46.30; ladoixch@club-internet.fr
Wines: Corton, Ladoix, and Bourgogne. $$ to $$$$

A very good and improving family domaine, with appetizing wines that begin with a juicy Passetoutgrains and reach their pinnacle in a textured, oaky but fresh Corton-Charlemagne and a nuanced, unfiltered Corton rouge. In between, there's a range of attractive versions of Ladoix, of which my favorites are the Premier Cru Les Corvées, both red and white.

Chevalier-Montrachet

Grand Cru split almost evenly between Puligny and Chassagne-Montrachet, for very grand chardonnay-based whites. Best recent vintages: 2005, (2004), (2003), 2002, (2001), and 1999. Prices: $$$$. Producers: BOUCHARD PÈRE & FILS ☆ ◆ DOM LOUIS JADOT ☆ ◆ DOM LEFLAIVE ☆ ◆ JACQUES PRIEUR ☆.

Domaine Robert Chevillon

21700 Nuits-St.-Georges; 03.80.62.34.88; fax: 03.86.61.13.31
Wines: Nuits-St.-Georges. $$$ to $$$$

Look to Robert Chevillon for mellow, fleshy, plummy Nuits-St.-Georges, with several variations on the theme, for example the Premier Cru Les Bousselots, a potent red that, to me, got prettier with slight chilling, and a refined, balanced Premier Cru Les Vaucrains.

Chiroubles

In altitude the highest *cru* of Beaujolais, the wines of Chiroubles are fine, airborne, and flowery. See BEAUJOLAIS for vintages and prices. Producers: Cave des Producteurs des Grands Vins de Fleurie: curiously, all I've tasted is the co-op's very pretty, floral Chiroubles, although it also produces Régnié, Morgon, Moulin-à-Vent, and numerous cuvées of Fleurie—which are probably equally appealing ◆ Dom Cheysson: a good source for tasty Chiroubles ◆ GEORGES DUBOEUF ◆ Ch de Javernand: floral and supple, with pinot noir–like notes; the wines are also sold by DUBOEUF.

Domaine du Château de Chorey

21200 Chorey-lès-Beaune; 03.80.24.06.39; domaine-chateau-de-chorey@wanadoo.fr
Wines: Beaune, Chorey-lès-Beaune, Pernand Vergelesses, and others. $$$ to $$$$
A good source for lovely Beaune-centric Burgundies, including a textured Pernand-Vergelesses Les Combottes blanc; a jewel-like, rich, cool, and seductive Chorey-les-Beaune; and the newest cuvée: Tante Berthe, a Chorey-les-Beaune made from the old vines from several parcels, aged in new oak for two years, and bottled unfiltered. It's an oaky, stylish crowd pleaser.

Chorey-lès-Beaune

A small Côte de Beaune AC for reds based on pinot noir and chardonnay-based whites, which are relatively light in the Côte d'Or scheme of things.

BEST RECENT VINTAGES: 2005, (2004), (2003), and 2002.
PRICES: $$ to $$$

PRODUCERS: DOM DU CHÂTEAU DE CHOREY ◆ EDMOND CORNU ◆ JOSEPH DROUHIN ☆ ◆ Dom Jean-Pierre Dufour: pleasant, cherry-accented reds ◆ DOM DOMINIQUE LAURENT ☆ ◆ Dom Maratray-Dubreuil: meatier than the domaine's Ladoix, the Chorey-les-Bons Ores is inviting and appetizing ◆ DOM CATHERINE & CLAUDE MARÉCHAL ◆ DOM MARÉCHAL-CAILLOT ◆ DOM TOLLOT-BEAUT ☆.

Domaine Bruno Clair ☆

BP 22, 21160 Marsannay-la-Côte; 03.80.52.18.14; brunoclair@wanadoo.fr
Wines: Chambolle-Musigny, Gevrey-Chambertin, Marsannay, Morey-St.-Denis, Savigny-lès-Beaune, and Vosne-Romanée. $$ to $$$$
An exemplary family domaine making a broad range of very classic, cellar-worthy wines in manifold ACs as well as in numerous Premier Crus and Grand Crus. At the lighter end of the red-wine spectrum, there is the smooth and elegant Marsannay Les Longeroies, and a lithe, delicate Marsannay Les Grasses Têtes. The Savigny-lès-Beaune Premier Cru La Dominode is lean, pure, and singular. The domaine has a number of prime parcels in Gevrey-Chambertin, including a monopoly on Premier Cru Clos du Fontenay, an extremely refined, iron butterfly of a wine. The Premier Cru Cazetiers is richer, broader, and more concentrated but equally deep and fine.

Clos de la Roche

A tiny Côte de Nuits Grand Cru located in Morey-St.-Denis for reds made soley from pinot noir. Generally these are complex and potent. Best recent vintages: 2005, (2004), (2003), 2002, (2001), and 1999. Prices: $$$$. Producers: BOUCHARD PÈRE & FILS ☆ ◆ DOM DUJAC ☆ ◆ DOM LEROY ☆ ◆ DOM ARMAND ROUSSEAU ☆.

Clos des Lambrays

A small Côte de Nuits Grand Cru within Morey-St.-Denis, for potentially very fine reds made from pinot noir. Prices: $$$$. Producer: DOM DES LAMBRAYS ☆.

Clos de Tart

A tiny Côte de Nuits Grand Cru within Morey-St.-Denis for complex, rich reds made from pinot noir. The vineyared is exclusively owned by the Mommessin family at CLOS DE TART ☆.

Clos de Tart ☆

21220 Morey-St.-Denis; 03.80.34.30.91; contact@closdetart.fr
Wine: Clos de Tart. $$$$
Clos de Tart is owned by the Mommessin family, who do an exemplary job realizing the potential of this Grand Cru vineyard. The wines are fragrant, velvety, deep, and majestic.

Clos de Vougeot

A 47-hectare Côte de Nuits Grand Cru in Vougeot for reds made from pinot noir. When well made, these are graceful, racy, and elegant. Prices: $$$$.

PRODUCERS: MAISON ALBERT BICHOT ◆ DOM RENÉ BOUVIER ↑ ◆ DOM JEAN-JACQUES CONFURON ☆ ◆ DOM CONFURON-COTETIDOT ☆ ◆ MAISON FAIVELEY ☆ ◆ DOM JEAN GRIVOT ☆ ◆ DOM ANNE GROS ☆ ◆ DOM LOUIS JADOT ☆ ◆ DOM LEROY ☆ ◆ Dom Chantal Lescure: a promising domaine, which the current generation is converting to organic viticulture; the Clos de Vougeot is potentially rich and pedigreed ◆ DOM JACQUES PRIEUR ☆ ◆ CH DE LA TOUR ☆.

Clos St.-Denis

A small Côte de Nuits Grand Cru within Morey-St.-Denis for robust, compelling reds made from pinot noir. Producers: DOM BERTAGNA ↑ ◆ DOM DUJAC ☆ ◆ THIERRY GUYOT ◆ DOM LOUIS JADOT ☆.

BURGUNDY

Domaine Coche-Bizouard ☆

21190 Meursault; 03.80.21.28.41; coche-bizouard@terre-net.fr
Wines: Auxey-Duresses, Meursault, Monthélie, and Bourgogne. $$ to $$$($)
Everything here is absolutely delicious, 100 percent finesse, starting with a Bourgogne chardonnay that comes across like a junior Meursault. There are many Meursaults, and all are wonderful, from a simple Villages that is serious, long, and invigorating, to an appetizing, irresistible, *terroir*-driven Chevalières, to a savory, racy, ultrapure Premier Cru Charmes that is a meal in itself. The reds are equally fine. You can't go wrong with the seductive, precise Monthélie Premier Cru Les Duresses.

Domaine Jean-François Coche-Dury ☆

21190 Meursault; 03.80.21.24.12; fax: 03.80.21.67.65
Wines: Meursault, Corton-Charlemagne, and Puligny-Montrachet. $$$$
Something of a legend in his own time, Jean-François Coche makes heavily oaked whites of undeniable greatness. The majesty of the wines, when young, is often masked by aromas of charred wood. The solution? Let the wines age for at least ten years or put them in a carafe several hours before serving.

Anita, Jean-Pierre & Stephanie Colinot

89290 Irancy; 03.86.42.33.25; earlcolinot@aol.com
Wine: Irancy. $$
This leading Auxerrois winery blends 10 percent césar into its Irancy Vieilles Vignes. The wines are juicy and succulent. Special cuvées, such as the Côte de Moutier and Palotte, are equally delectable and more distinctive.

Domaine Jean-Jacques Confuron ☆

21700 Premeaux-Prissey; 03.80.62.31.08; fax: 03.80.61.34.21
Wines: Clos de Vougeot, Côte de Nuits, and Vosne-Romanée. $$$ to $$$$
Expect elegant, deep, rich red Burgundies with lovely drink-me-now balance, fruit, and freshness. Confuron has recently started a small *négociant* business called Féry-Meunier.

Domaine Confuron-Cotetidot ☆
21700 Vosne-Romanée; 03.80.61.03.39; fax: 03.80.61.17.85
Wines: Chambolle-Musigny, Clos de Vougeot, Échezeaux, Gevrey-Chambertin, Nuits-St.-Georges, and Vosne-Romanée. $$$ to $$$$
Ascetic in their youth, the very pure, unique wines from this domaine need to age a good ten years before they'll even consider revealing their fragrance, beauty, and majesty. Give them time and they won't let you down.

Yvan & Chantal Contat-Grange
71150 Dezize-les-Maranges; 03.85.91.15.87; contat-grange@wanadoo.fr
Wines: Marange, Santenay, and Bourgogne. $$ to $$$
Precise, full-flavored Maranges, both red and white; look, in particular, for the luscious Maranges Premier Cru Les Clos Roussots, with its fresh, seductive red fruit. Prices are reasonable.

Edmond Cornu
21550 Ladoix-Serrigny, 03.80.26.40.79; fax: 03.80.26.48.34
Wines: Aloxe-Corton, Ladoix, and Chorey-les-Beaune. $$$
A good family domaine with a smooth, cool Aloxe-Corton rouge; a fragrant, evocative Chorey-lès-Beaune Les Bons Ores that errs slightly on the side of tartness; and several inviting Ladoix rouges, particularly the focused, structured Vieilles Vignes.

Corton

The only red Grand Cru of the Côte de Beaune, Corton lies in three ACs—Aloxe-Corton, Ladoix-Serrigny, and Pernand-Vergelesses. The name of a specific *climat* (parcel) may be attached to that of Corton, as in the case of Corton-Bressandes or Corton-Les Renardes. The wines are potentially rich and powerful.

BEST RECENT VINTAGES: 2005, (2004), (2003), 2002, (2001), and 1999.
PRICES: $$$ to $$$$

PRODUCERS: BONNEAU DE MARTRAY ☆ ◆ BOUCHARD PÈRE & FILS ☆ ◆ MAISON CHAMPY ◆ DOM CHEVALIER PÈRE & FILS ◆ DOM ANTONIN GUYON ◆ DOM LOUIS JADOT ☆ ◆ DOM PATRICK JAVILLIER ☆ ◆ DOM MÉO-CAMUZET ◆ Dom Muzard: look for the Corton-Grèves, a gentle red ◆ DOM ANDRÉ NUDANT ◆ DOMAINE PARENT ◆ DOM DE LA POUSSE D'OR ↑ ◆ DOM JACQUES PRIEUR ☆ ◆ Dom du Comte Senard: after a slump, the domaine seems back in form with the 2002 and 2003 vintages, particularly with the Grand Crus Corton, a layered, rich white, and Clos des Meix, a full-flavored red exclusive to Senard ◆ DOM TOLLOT-BEAUT ☆.

Corton-Charlemagne

A Côte de Beaune Grand Cru for chardonnay-based whites, Corton-Charlemagne is located in the ACs Aloxe-Corton, Ladoix-Serrigny, and Pernand-Vergelesses. The wines are rich and powerful, often with exotic aromas.

BEST RECENT VINTAGES: 2005, (2004), (2003), 2002, 2001, and 1999.
PRICES: $$$$

PRODUCERS: BONNEAU DE MARTRAY ☆ ◆ BOUCHARD PÈRE & FILS ☆ ◆ MAISON CHAMPY ◆ DOM CHEVALIER PÈRE & FILS ◆ DOM LOUIS JADOT ☆ ◆ DOM MICHEL JUILLOT ◆ RENÉ LEQUIN-COLIN ◆ DOM ANDRÉ NUDANT ◆ Verget: see GUFFENS-HEYNEN ☆.

Coteaux du Lyonnais

A small AC mostly situated southwest of Lyon on the right bank of the Rhône. Sometimes called a junior Beaujolais, it has similar wines. Reds and rosés are made from gamay; whites from aligoté and chardonnay. Drink the youngest available. Prices: $. Producers: Louis Chambes: this is the agreeable house wine of my friends Agnès and Frédérique, who buy directly from the vigneron ◆ Étienne Descotes & Fils: one of the AC's leading producers, making fruity whites and reds meant for casual drinking.

Côte de Beaune

A tiny AC located on several *lieux-dits* on the Montagne de Beaune, for pinot noir–based reds and chardonnay-based whites: Prices: $$ to $$$. Producers: JOSEPH DROUHIN ☆ ◆ EMMANUEL GIBOULOT ↑ ◆ DOM JEAN PETITOT & FILS ↑.

Côte de Beaune-Villages

An alternate AC for the red wines from one of fourteen ACs: Auxey-Duresses, Blagny, Chassagne-Montrachet, Chorey-lès-Beaune, Ladoix, Maranges, Meursault, Monthélie, Pernand-Vergelesses, Puligny-Montrachet, St.-Aubin, St.-Romain, Santenay, and Savigny-lès-Beaune. Qualifying wines can be called Côtes de Beaune-Villages or may combine the two ACs, for instance, Chorey-Côte de Beaune.

Côte de Brouilly

The most centrally located *cru* of Beaujolais, this hilltop produces sleek, fine-grained Beaujolais, in contrast to Brouilly, which is generally beefier and broader. See BEAUJOLAIS for vintages and prices.

PRODUCERS: JEAN-PAUL BRUN ◆ Dom Chevalier-Metrat: two bottlings of rich, pure Côte de Brouilly, including an oak-aged, old-vines version and an equally engaging Brouilly ◆ Dom du Pavillon de Chavannes: fresh, lovely, well-balanced wines ◆ Jean-Charles Pivot: see BEAUJOLAIS ◆ Ch des Ravatys: mellow Côte de Brouilly, especially the Cuvée Mathilde Courbe, as well as the juicy, aromatic Brouilly Le Jardin des Ravatys ◆ Dom de Sancillon: vibrantly fruity Côte de Brouilly and supple Brouilly ◆ Dom des Terres Dorées: see JEAN-PAUL BRUN ◆ Ch Thivin: Claude Geoffray's substantial domaine makes admirably tasty Beaujolais Villages (Manoir du Pavé), as well as Brouilly, but his most alluring wines come from this AC; the pretty Cuvée de la Chapelle and the rich, lipsmacking Cuvée Zaccharie Geoffray are particularly worth looking for ☆ ◆ Dom de la Voûte des Crozes: Raymond and Nicole Chanrion make handsome, silky Côte de Brouilly.

Côte de Nuits-Villages

An AC dispersed over five communes, principally Premeaux (Prissey) and Comblanchien, primarily for structured, penetrating pinot noir–based reds; there's a tiny amount of powerful white.

BEST RECENT VINTAGES: 2005, (2004), (2003), 2002, 1999.
PRICES: $$$ to $$$$

PRODUCERS: BOUCHARD PÈRE & FILS ☆ ◆ DOM RENÉ BOUVIER ↑ ◆ DOM JEAN-JACQUES CONFURON ☆ ◆ DOM RÉGIS DUBOIS & FILS ◆ DOM FOUGERAY DE BEAUCLAIR ◆ DOM GACHOT-MONOT ◆ DOM JÉRÔME GALEYRAND ↑ ◆ Dom Glantenet Père & Fils: see BOURGOGNE HAUTES-CÔTES DE BEAUNE ◆ DOM HENRI NAUDIN-FERRAND ↑ ◆ DOM JEAN PETITOT & FILS ↑.

Crémant de Bourgogne

A regional AC encompassing the entire vineyard area of Burgundy. Crémant de Bourgognes are rosé and white sparkling wines made by the *méthode traditionelle*. The primary grapes are chardonnay and pinot noir. Gamay may be used as well, along with limited amounts of aligoté, melon de bourgogne, and sacy. Prices: $$. Producers: Maison André Delorme ◆ Dom Sophie & Gilles Guerrin ◆ CÉLINE & LAURENT TRIPOZ ↑.

Domaine Maria Cuny ↑

89450 St.-Père-sous-Vézelay; tel/fax: 03.86.33.27.95; maria@domaine-mariacuny.com
Wine: Bourgogne-Vézelay. $$
The mother of six children, Maria Cuny created her small domaine in 2000. She farms organically, maintains very low yields, and is in every other respect painstaking. The proof of the pudding: scintillating white Burgundy—taut, mineral, and lime-scented. These are serious whites from a humble AC that's on the rise.

Domaine René & Vincent Dauvissat ☆

89800 Chablis; 03.86.42.11.58; fax: 03.86.42.85.32
Wine: Chablis. $$$($)
Waiting list Chablis. The Dauvissats, considered artist-vintners, sell out their yearly production of roughly seventy thousand bottles—mostly Premier Cru and Grand Cru, (Les Clos, Les Preuses, and Les Forêts)—pretty much before the wine is bottled. Get whatever you can. The wines are majestic, ever so lightly oaked, immensely fresh and racy, and well worth the detour.

Domaine Bernard Defaix ☆

89800 Milly; 03.86.42.40.75; www.bernard-defaix.com
Wine: Chablis. $$($)
The pedigreed, *terroir*-driven Chablis from this domaine always remind me that great Chablis shares the same *terroir* as great Sancerre. The grape variety fades into the background. Cases in point: the fresh, textured Premier Cru Les Lys, with its flavors of herbal tea and quinine; the mouthfilling Premier Cru Côte de Lechet, all succulent lemon and lime; and the marvelous Premier Cru Côte de Lechet Réserve, made from the domaine's oldest vines. Racy, textured, and steely, with flavors of quinine and ginger, it's downright charismatic, a knockout.

Michel Delorme

71960 Vergisson; 03.85.35.84.50; micheldelorme@club-internet.fr
Wine: Pouilly-Fuissé. $$ to $$$
Interesting work with a scent of the hypernatural. The top bottling, La Maréchaude seems overripe and ample, with pineapple and mineral accents. At half the price, I prefer the Sur la Roche, which is equally pedigreed but more streamlined and elegant.

Catherine & Dominique Derain ↑

21190 St.-Aubin; 03.80.21.35.49; fax: 03.80.21.94.31
Wines: Mercurey, Pommard, St.-Aubin, and Bourgogne. $$ to $$$
Dominique Derain's wines are not for everyone. A former barrel maker who's not in favor of using new oak, Dominique Derain farms biodynamically, uses very little sulfur, and makes a range of wines that are sometimes delicious, sometimes not, but always intriguing. His Bourgogne rouge is pure, tart, lean, and yummy. His St.-Aubin Premier Cru En Remilly is a tight, racy white. The St.-Aubin Le Ban, based on old vines, was one of the few reds that prompted me to use one of my highest compliments—"waterfall." The *W* word came up again with another red, this one an airborne, raspberry-scented Mercurey from eighty-year-old vines that had been blended with 15 percent pinot gris. What a delicious discovery! By contrast, a Pommard Les Petits Noizons was simply delectable, a focused red with lovely berry fruit. As for forays into wackodom, Derain experiments to understand more about wine. In an attempt to comprehend how wine resists oxidation, for example, he produced Mur Mur, a white that fermented for two years and tasted like a cross between Jura's *vin de paille* and *vin jaune*. And it wasn't half bad.

Domaine Georges Descombes

69910 Villié-Morgon; 04.74.69.16.67; fax: 04.74.69.16.40

Wines: Brouilly and Morgon. $$

No fining, no filtration, no sulfur—Georges Descombes adheres to the hypernatural dogma, usually with delicious results. His wines are striking in their authenticity. The Brouilly Jeunes Vignes is firm, taut, and mineral. The Vieilles Vignes takes on the characteristics of pinot noir, as does the exotic, racy Morgon.

Eric Desvignes

Poncey 71640 Givry; 03.85.44.51.23; fax: 03.85.44.43.53

Wine: Givry. $$

Desvignes's wines—all red—aren't flashy, but they are delicious and would make lovely lunch Burgundies. These bottlings share an almost thirst-quenching fluidity. The appealing distinctions are in the details—the exotic, light cherry notes in the Meix au Roy; the mellow, spicy delicacy of Premier Cru La Grande Berge; and the deep, fragrant, and specific Premier Cru Clos Charlé.

Domaine Doudet-Naudin

21420 Savigny-lès-Beaune; 03.80.21.51.74; doudet-naudin@wanadoo.fr.

Wines: Aloxe-Corton, Beaune, St.-Aubin, and Savigny-lès-Beaune. $$ to $$$$

A serious, eco-friendly domaine run by three young vignerons and spanning numerous ACs. The very fine, fresh, mineral Savigny-lès-Beaune Premier Cru Redrescul is a standout. (The domaine has a monopoly on this vineyard, which they work by hand.) A red from the same AC, the Premier Cru Les Guettes, is soft and velvety. It is unfiltered, like all their reds, which include pleasures such as the Beaune Premier Cru Clos du Roy and Aloxe-Corton Premier Cru Les Maréchaudes.

Jean-Paul & Benoît Droin ☆

BP 19, 89800 Chablis; 03.86.42.16.78; www.jeanpaul-droin.fr

Wine: Chablis. $$ to $$$$

A well-established family domaine that's fortunate in its holdings—its 25 hectares include vineyards on seven Premier Crus and five Grand Crus. While the Petit Chablis and the Chablis Tête de Cuvée are just fine, the Premier Crus are excellent and the Grand Crus superb. The Fourchaume is fresh as a waterfall, while the Montée de Tonnerre is mineral, layered, and pedigreed. The oak-, citronella-, and lime-scented Valmur is so racy, so creamy and seductive, you'll want to bathe in it. And the smoky, flinty Les Clos, deep and invigorating as a mountain stream, is so nuanced that every sip brings a discovery.

Joseph Drouhin ☆

7 rue d'Enfer, 21200 Beaune; 03.80.24.68.88; www.drouhin.com

Wines: Burgundy, from Chablis to Beaujolais. $$ to $$$$

This leading Burgundy grower-*négociant* is eco-friendly and has high standards. The wines tend to share a family style of subtlety, finesse, and discretion. Drouhin's most iconic wine may well be Beaune Clos des Mouches Premier Cru. The red version is succulent, fleshy, and very elegant. The white is layered, deep, and regal. The Drouhin reach, however, starts up north in Chablis, where the firm owns some prime vineyards and produces a range of wines, including the pungent, lemon curd–flavored Vaudésir Grand Cru and the textbook classic Grand Cru Les Clos, in addition to a bright citrus-and-steel generic Chablis. And its realm continues to the southern borders of Burgundy with solid versions from just about every AC. In between there are suave, pedigreed Charmes-Chambertins; regal Nuits-St.-Georges Premier Cru Les Procès; delicate and refined Chambolle-Musigny Premier Cru; and many, many more, including another Drouhin icon, the Montrachet Marquis de Laguiche, a property the firm doesn't actually own but has managed for so long it ought to have squatter's rights.

Georges Duboeuf
71570 Romanèche-Thorins; 03.85.35.34.20; www.duboeuf.com
Wines: A complete range of Beaujolais and its *crus*. $ to $$
The name of the *négociant* Georges Duboeuf has become synonymous with that of Beaujolais—not surprising, as the firm markets some thirty million bottles a year. These range from technically perfect commercial beverages to fine representations of their respective ACs. Among the latter you'll find a sleek, focused Brouilly; a juicy, quaffable Chiroubles; an admirable and succulent St.-Amour Domaine du Paradis; and a surprisingly quirky Morgon Jean Descombes.

Domaine Régis Dubois & Fils
21700 Premeaux Prissey; 03.80.62.30.61; rdubois@wanadoo.fr
Wines: Côte de Nuits, Chambolle-Musigny, and seventeen other ACs. $$ to $$$($)
Béatrice, the winemaker, and Raphaël, in charge of sales, have taken over the eco-friendly family property from Régis. Their wines—from a fresh, mineral aligoté to an austere but aristocratic Nuits-St.-Georges Premier Cru Clos des Argillières—are not flashy; they're serious, honest, specific, and lean in the direction of delicacy. 2003 brought its heat to bear on the restrained style of the Dubois wines with delicious results: a Côte de Nuits-Villages blanc Les Monts de Boncourt was so fresh and lipsmacking, a bottle could disappear faster than you can say *terroir*.

Domaine Bernard Dugat-Py ☆
21220 Gevrey-Chambertin; 03.80.51.82.46; www.dugat-py.com
Wine: Gevrey-Chambertin. $$$ to $$$$
A masterly, painstaking vintner, Bernard Dugat turns out a range of deep, structured, succulent Gevrey-Chambertins from various *lieux-dits*, Premier Crus, and the Grand Cru Mazis-Chambertin. Try whatever you can find.

Domaine Dujac ☆
21220 Morey-St.-Denis; 03.80.34.01.00; www.dujac.com
Wine: Morey-St.-Denis. $$ to $$$$
Yes. Yes. Yes. Everything you want in a red Burgundy. I adore the entire range: The vibrant Morey-St.-Denis with its intriguing notes of exotic fruit and orange zests. The regal Clos de la Roche Grand Cru. And the vigorous, monumental Clos St.-Denis Grand Cru, which has the deep, seductive richness of a Côte-Rôtie. The whites include a racy, gorgeously balanced Morey-St.-Denis Premier Cru Les Monts Luisants. Owner Jacques Seysses and son Jerémy have recently extended their reach—branching out into Chambolle-Musigny and Gevrey-Chambertin with a small *négociant* business called Dujac Fils & Père. And the domaine, itself, continues to grow. In July 2005 the family, along with the Domaine de Montille, obtained 18 hectares of prime vineyard land, including pieces of Bonnes-Mares, Romanée-St.-Vivant, Chambertin, and Clos de Vougeot, that once belonged to the the Domaine Clos de Thorey. The land will be divided between de Montille and Dujac.

Domaine Dupont-Tisserandot
21220 Gevrey-Chambertin; 03.80.34.10.50; fax: 03.80.58.50.71
Wine: Gevrey-Chambertin. $$$ to $$$$
Dupont-Tisserandot produces a full range of stylish, alluring Gevrey-Chambertins, including a delectable Premier Cru Lavaux St.-Jacques and an irresistibly charming Charmes-Chambertin. Nuanced and feminine, this red has dark plum and black cherry fruit and great elegance.

Domaine Vincent Dureuil-Janthial ☆
71150 Rully; 03.85.87.26.32; vincent.dureuil@wanadoo.fr
Wines: Rully, Mercurey, and Nuits-St.-Georges. $$ to $$$
This brilliant young, eco-serious winemaker is a rising star. Based on extremely low yields and grapes harvested at precisely the right second, every single

one of his Rullys takes your breath away. The standard white, fermented in barrel, is superb—fresh, long, and headily aromatic. The vines in his Premier Cru Les Margottes were planted in 1947, and the wines from these grapes are sublime—racy, focused, and as voluminous as a white Hermitage. The vines in his Premier Cru Le Meix Cadot were planted in the 1920s. These wines are textured, richly layered, and grandiose. The basic red is cool, fresh, and structured; the old-vines version ups the ante. Dureuil-Janthial also makes a sensual red Mercurey that's so delicious you want to bite into it and an exquisite Nuits-St.-Georges Premier Cru Clos des Argillières.

Domaines Jean Durup Père & Fils/Château de Maligny

89800 Chablis; 03.86.47.44.49; www.durup.chablis.com

Wine: Chablis. $$ to $$$($)

With 170 hectares, Jean Durup has the most extensive holdings in Burgundy, is the largest producer of Chablis, and owns more vines of Premier Cru Fourchaume than any other grower, including parcels in some of its best *lieux-dits,* such as the sinisterly named L'Homme Mort. The 2004 of that *cru* was steely and razor sharp, well worth following. I was disappointed in the 2001 Fourchaume but admired the freshness, depth, and pedigree of both the 2003 (nicely balanced despite its heat-wave ripeness) and the 2004. While the Montée de Tonnerre Premier Cru came across soft in 2003, it was rich, mineral, and specific. The Vau de Vey Premier Cru is steely, concentrated, and firm, with strong mineral undertones. Durup also makes pleasant, fruit-driven Petit Chablis.

BURGUNDY

Échezeaux

A 36-hectare Grand Cru in the Côte de Nuits in Flagey-Échezeaux located between Vosne-Romanée and Clos de Vougeot, exclusively for reds based on pinot noir. The wines should be big-boned, structured, and racy.

BEST RECENT VINTAGES: 2005, (2004), (2003), 2002, (2001), 1999, and 1996.
PRICES: $$$$

PRODUCERS: JEAN-YVES BIZOT ↑ ♦ Jacques Cacheux & Fils: rough-hewn but tasty Échezeaux ♦ PHILIPPE CHARLOPIN ☆ ♦ DOM CONFURON-COTETIDOT ☆ ♦ DOM DUJAC ☆ ♦ MAISON FAIVELEY ☆ ♦ DOM A. F. GROS ☆ ♦ DOM JAYER-GILLES ☆ ♦ DOM LOUIS JADOT ☆ ♦ Dom des Perdrix: see NUITS-ST.-GEORGES ☆ ♦ DOM DE LA ROMANÉE-CONTI ☆ ♦ Dom Vigot: see VOSNE-ROMANÉE.

Arnaud & Marie-Odile Ente ☆

21190 Meursault; tel/fax: 03.80.21.66.12

Wines: Meursault, Volnay, Bourgogne, and Bourgogne Grand Ordinaire. $$$ to $$$$

This thirtysomething couple with a tiny (4.5-hectare), eco-serious domaine makes a small array of unfiltered, staggeringly magnificent wines. Their standard white Bourgogne, made from vines in the Meursault area but not within the AC, is finer, more elegant, and more textured than the Premier Crus from many Meursault houses. Their Bourgogne Grand Ordinaire—sixty-year-old gamay planted on Meursault land—is pellucid, gorgeous, and mind-blowing. By contrast, their sumptuous, finely tuned Volnay Santenots is what you should have every right to expect from one of the finest vineyards in that prestigious AC. Their Meursaults are among the best white Burgundies I've ever tasted. Two examples: The Premier Cru la Goutte d'Or, made from twelve-year-old vines, is wonderfully complex, mineral, and detailed, a great wine. The *terroir*-driven La Sève du Clos, from century-old vines, is so rich and layered it borders on syrup yet still remains ethereal. It's nothing less than a monument.

Maison Faiveley ☆

21700 Nuits-Saint-Georges; 03.80.61.04.55; www.bourgognes-faiveley.com
Wines: Mercurey, Nuits-St.-Georges, Gevrey-Chambertin, and others. $$ to $$$$
A large, venerable grower-*négociant* with a near-encyclopedic and realiably fine range of Burgundies. For reasonably priced, sleek, crisp chardonnays, their Montagnys—Les Joncs and Domaine de la Croix Jacquelet—are hard to beat. When it comes to reds, their deservedly popular Mercurey Premier Cru Clos des Myglands is joined by the fleshy, alluring La Framboisière. Faiveley followers will regret the loss of the superb *cru* Clos de la Maréchale (their lease expired after the 2003 vintage, and the property will now be managed by its owners, the Mugniers). Consolation may be at hand with a Gevrey-Chambertin Premier Cru Clos des Issarts, a delicate, rose- and spice-scented red, or the oakier, more succulent Beaune Premier Cru Clos de l'Écu, both Faiveley exclusives. The house has always been associated with Nuits-St.-Georges, and the unfiltered, aristocratic Premier Cru Aux Chaignots, more *terroir*- than fruit-driven, reveals an intimate understanding of that land. And their profound, racy Échezeaux Grand Cru is simply excellent.

Nadine Ferrand ☆

71960 Solutré-Pouilly; 06.09.05.19.74; ferrand.nadine@club-internet.fr
Wines: Pouilly-Fuissé and St.-Véran. $$
Look for textured St.-Véran; a structured, layered Pouilly-Fuissé Lise-Marie with rich oak and lemon-lime flavors; and a seductive Pouilly-Fuissé Prestige, a suave, worldly wine with the makings of greatness.

Domaine William Fèvre ☆

89800 Chablis; 03.86.98.98.98; www.williamfevre.com
Wine: Chablis. $$ to $$$$
Since this venerable Chablis house was purchased by Bouchard Père & Fils in 1998 the quality, already high, has gotten higher. Low yields, TLC in vineyard and cellar, intelligent use of newish oak, and a policy of doing everything possible to allow the wine to express its *terroir* result in a reliably stunning array of Chablis. The generic Chablis is better than many Premier Crus from other houses. And as the house has roughly half of its 47 hectares of Chablis in Premier Cru and Grand Cru vineyards, there are many gems. The chiseled, pellucid Premier Cru Fourchaume Vignoble de Vaulorent is a real favorite—it simply knocks me out. And I can drink it sooner than the magnificent Grand Crus such as Les Preuses and Bougros, which need cellaring for at least five years. A 1999 Grand Cru Les Clos tasted in 2005, for example, had come into its own. A wine of enormous elegance and freshness, it was authoritative and noble, an absolute beauty.

Domaine Fichet ↑

71960 Ige; 03.85.33.30.46; www.domaine-fichet.com
Wines: Mâcon Igé and Bourgogne. $ to $$
Olivier and Pierre-Yves Fichet produce several cuvées of ambitious Mâcon Igé that are full of character. La Crêpillione is fresh and vigorous. Château London is richer, more focused, and more specific. The best, however, is Terroir de la Cra Prestige, made from late-harvested, nearly overripe grapes, fermented in new Burgundy barrels. It's masterly and delicious. I also like their gamay-based Mâcon Igé rouge, but I preferred their reds based on pinot noir, particuarly the Bourgogne from the *lieu-dit* La Fraisière, a tasty, honest light red I'd love to find in a wine bar.

Fixin

A small Côte de Nuits AC about nine miles southwest of Dijon, principally for reds made from pinot noir and a small percentage of whites made from chardonnay. Technically there are eight Premier Crus—making both reds and whites—but only four or five are commonly used, chief among them Les Arvelets, Les Hervelets, and La Perrière.

BEST RECENT VINTAGES: 2005, 2004, 2003, and 2002.
PRICES: $$ to $$$($)

PRODUCERS: DOM RENÉ BOUVIER ↑ ◆ Dom Guy Dufouleur: look for the domaine's exclusive—the Premier Cru Clos du Chapitre ◆ DOM FOUGERAY DE BEAUCLAIR ◆ DOM JÉRÔME GALEYRAND ↑ ◆ DOM DU VIEUX COLLÈGE.

Fleurie

Called the most feminine *cru* of Beaujolais, the wines of Fleurie are known for their floral aromas and elegance. See BEAUJOLAIS for vintages and prices.

PRODUCERS: Dom Chamonard: hypernatural Fleurie and Morgon with clear mineral and fruit flavors ◆ Dom Chignard: look for the cuvées Vieilles Vignes and Les Moriers, both focused, seductive, and downright Burgundian with lovely flavors of blueberries and black cherries ◆ Dom de la Côte d'Adule: the Matray brothers, who took over the domaine in 2003, make fragrant, slightly exotic Fleurie ◆ Dom Jean-Marc Després/Dom de la Madone: Grillé Midi and La Madone Vieilles Vignes are suave, distinctive, structured, old-vines Fleurie ☆ ◆ Dom Lardy: perfect wine-bar Fleurie and Moulin-à-Vent ◆ Dom des Marrans: an old-vines Fleurie as pretty as the name of the AC itself ◆ Yvon Metras: its several cuvées of concentrated, pure, extremely mineral, hypernatural Fleurie include Le Printemps and the pricey Ultime Vieilles Vignes ◆ DOM DU VISSOUX ☆.

Domaine Jean Foillard ☆

60010 Villié-Morgon; 04.74.04.24.97; jean.foillard@wanadoo.fr
Wine: Morgon. $$
Foillard produces several cuvées of hypernatural, hyperdelicious Morgon. Do not miss the lipsmacking, barrel-aged Côte du Py. It's exotic; it's riveting; it's racy, suave, concentrated, and succulent; and it has the regal presence of a red from the Côte d'Or.

Domaine des Fossiles

71340 Mailly; tel/fax: 03.85.84.01.23
Wines: Vin de Pays de Saône et Loire. $
Jean-Claude Berthillot, Domaine des Fossiles' eco-friendly, overachieving owner, takes more care in the vineyards and cellars than many producers in more prestigious ACs. His wines, all oak aged, are very well made and include a clean, tasty chardonnay, a juicy old-vines gamay, and a sleek, cool pinot noir.

Domaine Fougeray de Beauclair

BP 36, 21160 Marsannay-la-Côte; 03.80.52.21.12; fougeraydebeauclair@wanadoo.fr
Wines: Marsannay, Bonnes-Mares, Côte de Nuits, Gevrey-Chambertin, and Fixin. $$ to $$$$
Look to Fougeray de Beauclair for a clutch of mellow whites and lean, precise reds from Marsannay; lithe and racy reds from Fixin's Clos Marion and Côte de Nuits; and nuanced, fine-grained Bonnes-Mares Grand Cru.

Domaine Gachot-Monot

21700 Nuits-St.-Georges; 03.80.62.50.95; gachot-monot@wanadoo.fr
Wines: Côte de Nuits, Nuits-St.-Georges, and Bourgogne. $$ to $$$$
A conscientious, eco-friendly family domaine, Gachot-Monot's reds, which are neither fined nor filtered, are pure, plummy, and need a little bit of time to shed their baby fat. If you come across a wine that prickles a bit, put it in a carafe and let it sit in a cool place until it calms down.

Domaine Jérôme Galeyrand ↑

21220 Saint-Philibert: 06.61.83.39.69; jerome.galeyrand@wanadoo.fr
Wines: Gevrey-Chambertin, Fixin, Côte de Nuits-Villages, and Bourgogne.
$$ to $$$

This promising young vigneron, whose first vintage was 2002, has wines that have been improving by leaps and bounds. Viticulture is organic, Galeyrand uses indigenous yeasts, and the wines are bottled according to the phases of the moon, without having been fined or filtered. Some of the 2002s were merely average but others were textured, and a Gevrey-Chambertin Les Crais was complex and racy. By 2003 the wines were all successful. Favorites: two Gevrey-Chambertins—a racy, full Vieilles Vignes and a subtle, fresh Villages—and two Fixins—a succulent, spicy Premier Cru Les Hervelets and a Vieilles Vignes that mingled flavors of plums, cherries, cherry pits, and citrus zests and that practically screamed "Drink me! I'm so delicious!"

Domaine de la Galopière

21200 Bligny-lès-Beaune; 03.80.21.46.50
Wines: Meursault, Ladoix, Pommard, Aloxe-Corton, Savigny-lès-Beaune, and Bourgogne. $$ to $$$

Looking for a truly hearty Burgundy? Wines from this family domaine are rugged and artisanal. While they may not be the most polished representatives of their respective ACs, they are the opposite of mass-produced, fruit-driven anonymity. The basic red and white Bourgognes are packed with flavor and vigor. The whites from Meursault (particularly Les Chevaliers) and Ladoix are big-boned, rustic, and savory with real depth and presence. The Pommard is a strapping lumberjack of a red with a stony, mineral, and very Burgundian core. Two 2003 reds leap out of the pack for their stylishness, nuance, and silky texture—an Aloxe-Corton and a Savigny-lès-Beaune.

Maison Alex Gambal ☆

4, rue Jacques Vincent, 21200 Beaune; 03.80.22.75.81; alexgambal@wanadoo.fr
Wines: Chambolle-Musigny, Chassagne-Montrachet, St.-Aubin, and Vosne-Romanée. $$ to $$$$

A Bostonian, Gambal took over an old Beaune merchant house and has created a small, high-quality *négociant* business for which he buys all the grapes and vinifies all the wines himself. The results are heartening. Examples include a creamy, smooth, and classic St.-Aubin Premier Cru, a finely focused white; a specific, layered Chassagne-Montrachet Premier Cru Les Morgeots; a gentle, pretty, pedigreed Chambolle-Musigny; and a flavorful, fresh Vosne-Romanée Vieilles Vignes of great subtlety. Definitely a house to follow.

Gevrey-Chambertin

An important Côte de Nuits AC known for powerful, long-lived, potentially majestic reds made from pinot noir. It has nine Grands Crus and twenty-six Premiers Crus.

The Grand Crus of Gevrey-Chambertin are: Chambertin, Chambertin-Clos-de-Bèze, Chapelle-Chambertin, Charmes-Chambertin, Griotte-Chambertin, Latricières-Chambertin, Mazis-Chambertin, Mazoyères-Chambertin, and Ruchottes-Chambertin. Among the Premiers Crus are Clos St.-Jacques, Les Cazetiers, and Clos des Varoilles.

BEST RECENT VINTAGES: 2005, 2004, 2003, 2002, 1999, and 1996.
PRICES: $$$ to $$$$

PRODUCERS: Dom d'Auvenay: see DOM LEROY ☆ ◆ DOM LUCIEN BOILLOT ☆ ◆ DOM RENÉ BOUVIER ↑ ◆ DOM ALAIN BURGUET ☆ ◆ PHILIPPE CHARLOPIN ☆ ◆ DOM BRUNO CLAIR ☆ ◆ DOM CONFURON-COTETIDOT ☆ ◆ JOSEPH DROUHIN ☆ ◆ DOM BERNARD DUGAT-PY ☆ ◆ DOM DUPONT-TISSERANDOT ◆ MAISON FAIVELEY ☆ ◆ DOM FOUGERAY DE BEAUCLAIR ◆ Dom Fourrier: a very good domaine with a lovely, mineral Premier Cru Cherbaudes ◆ DOM JÉRÔME GALEYRAND ↑ ◆ DOM OLIVIER GUYOT ↑ ◆ DOM HARMOND-GEOFFROY ◆ Dom Huguenot Père

& Fils: some enviable parcels, some admirable bottlings, including Grand Cru Charmes-Chambertin and Premier Cru Fontenay; see also MARSANNAY ◆ DOM LOUIS JADOT ☆ ◆ DOM DOMINIQUE LAURENT ☆ ◆ DOM LEROY ☆ ◆ PHILIPPE PACALET ☆ ◆ DOM ROSSIGNOL-TRAPET ◆ Joseph Roty: excellent, potent, singular reds ☆ ◆ DOM ARMAND ROUSSEAU ☆ ◆ DOM TRAPET ↑ ◆ Dom des Varoilles: pure, ambitious, unfiltered reds not yet ready for prime time but worth trying, particularly the Premier Crus Clos des Varoilles and La Romanée ◆ DOM DU VIEUX COLLÈGE ◆ Dom de la Vougeraie: see MAISON JEAN-CLAUDE BOISSET.

Emmanuel Giboulot ↑

21200 Beaune; 03.80.22.90.07

Wines: Côte de Beaune, Hautes-Côtes de Nuits, and St.-Romain. $$ to $$$($)

Thirtysomething Giboulot is another rising star on both the Burgundy and the biodynamic scenes. Aiming for "*terroir*" and not "making the wine," he says, he applies maximum gentleness to soil and grapes. His wines are characterized by definite stylistic threads: they are pure, mineral, beautifully balanced, specific, and multifaceted. Every one of those terms applies to the following whites: a creamy Hautes-Côte de Nuits with a stony finish; a cascading St.-Romain from sixty-year-old vines; a mouthfilling, extremely fine Côte de Beaune Les Pierres Blanches; and a pellucid—indeed, transparent—Côte de Beaune La Combe d'Ève. These traits are every bit as evident in the following reds: a beautifully restrained, racy Hautes-Côtes de Nuits Sous le Mont; a singular, steel-and-lace St.-Romain; a cool and succulent Bourgogne Hautes-Côtes de Nuits En Gregoire; and a beauteous, windswept Beaune Lulune.

Givry

A small Côte Chalonnaise AC several miles west of the town of Chalon-sur-Saône. Most Givry is medium-bodied, succulent red wine based on pinot noir, although about a quarter of the wines are whites made from chardonnay.

BEST RECENT VINTAGES: 2005, (2004), (2003), and 2002.
PRICES: $$($)

PRODUCERS: FRANÇOIS D'ALLAINES ↑ ◆ Michel Briday: see RULLY ◆ Dom Chofflet-Valdenaire: an eco-friendly domaine offering a clean, ample Givry blanc Les Galaffres and a lean though lively Givry rouge Premier Cru Clos Jus ◆ Clos Solomon: Ludovic du Gardin-Perrotto produces a mouthwatering, mineral Givry rouge Premier Cru from the Clos Solomon—with plenty of pretty fruit to balance the abundant oak flavors ◆ ERIC DESVIGNES ◆ Domaine Vincent & Baptiste Lumpp: improving family winery; try the Premier Crus Le Vigron and La Grande Berge ◆ Dom Masse: the Givrys—the red Champ Lalot, the white Clos de la Brûlée—aren't perfect but they're ambitious and worth trying; the domaine also produces a good Bourgogne aligoté for quality Kirs ◆ Dom Ragot: young Nicolas Ragot took over the reins of this family domaine in 2002, making it one to watch; the new-oak-aged Premier Cru Clos Jus is a pure and feisty red, and the Givry blanc Champ Pourot, pleasant now, will certainly improve ◆ DOM MICHEL SARRAZIN ☆.

Ghislaine & Jean-Hugues Goisot ☆

89530 St.-Bris-le-Vineux; 03.86.53.35.15; jhetg.goisot@cerb.cernet.fr

Wines: St.-Bris and Bourgogne-Côtes d'Auxerre. $$

An exciting, exemplary, eco-serious winery. The Bourgogne-Côtes d'Auxerre pinot noir Vieilles Vignes is cool, structured, and serious; from the same AC, the excellent barrel-fermented chardonnay from the *lieu-dit* Gondonné is creamy, layered, and lipsmacking. The St.-Bris is pungent, stony, and feisty, a great bistro white. The Goisots' top-of-the-line is called Corps de Garde. The

Bourgogne-Côtes d'Auxerre from old chardonnay vines is suave, pure and beautifully balanced. The Corps de Garde Gourmand St.-Bris is made from fié gris (or sauvignon rose). The super 2003 had the penetrating scent of ripe mirabelles; the textured and tightly focused 2002 had accents of pear and apple. Great wine-bar discoveries and great fun to drink.

Domaine Henri Gouges ☆

21700 Nuits-Saint-Georges; 03.80.61.04.40; www.gouges.com

Wine: Nuits-Saint-Georges. $$$ to $$$$

A blue-chip family domaine, Henri Gouges makes sleek, concentrated, masterly, and noble Nuits-Saint-Georges. My favorites include the Premier Crus Les St.-George, Les Pruliers, and Clos des Porrets.

La Grande Rue

Covering 1.65 hectares of Grand Cru vineyards in Vosne-Romanée in the Côte de Nuits, La Grande Rue is known for potentially exquisite reds made from pinot noir. Roughly 7,500 bottles are produced yearly. For vintages and prices, see the AC VOSNE-ROMANÉE.

Grands Échezeaux

A 9-hectare Côte de Nuits AC in Flagey-Échezeaux, located between Vosne-Romanée and Clos de Vougeot, exclusively for (potentially sublime) reds from pinot noir. Best Recent Vintages: 2005, (2004), (2003), 2002, 1999. Prices: $$$$. Producers: JOSEPH DROUHIN ☆ ◆ DOM A. F. GROS ◆ DOM LOUIS JADOT ☆ ◆ DOM DE LA ROMANÉE-CONTI ☆.

Pascal Granger ☆

69840 Juliénas; 04.74.04.44.79; fax: 04.74.04.41.24

Wines: Beaujolais, Juliénas, Chénas, and Moulin-à-Vent. $ to $$

I've only tasted the various cuvées of Juliénas from this family domaine. But what beautiful wines! The simplest cuvée is perfumed, succulent, and elegant. The Cuvée Grande Réserve, from very old vines, may be a bit too marked by oak, but it's lipsmacking. The Cuvée Spéciale, also from very old vines, is suave, with delicately mingled flavors—pure pleasure and simply gorgeous.

Domaine Albert Grivault ☆

21190 Meursault; 03.80.21.23.12; fax: 03.80.21.24.70

Wines: Meursault and Pommard. $$$ to $$$$

Excruciatingly delicious wines. First, the domaine holds the monopoly on the Clos des Perrières, widely acknowledged as the best of Meursault's Premier Crus. And the winemaking lives up to the potential of the *terroir*—with big, creamy, savory, regal wines. In Pommard, the domaine's Premier Cru Clos Blanc results in a scrumptious, racy Burgundy, a knockout.

Domaine Jean Grivot ☆

21700 Vosne-Romanée; 03.80.61.05.95; www.grivot.com

Wines: Vosne-Romanée, Nuits-St.-Georges, and Clos de Vougeot. $$$$

The studied, perfectionist winemaking of this domaine produces majestic, tightly focused, deeply fruity, profoundly succulent, and always profound red Burgundies. These come from some of the greatest vineyards in the Côte d'Or. There's freshness and elegance in all the 2002s, with a particularly firm statement of *terroir* in the Clos de Vougeot Grand Cru. The irresistible deliciousness of the 2003s makes it difficult not to polish off the Vosne-Romanée Bossières and the Nuits-St.-Georges Premier Cru Les Pruliers. And, oh, the silk and velvet weave of that 2003 Clos de Vougeot!

Domaine Anne Gros ☆

21700 Vosne-Romanée; 03.80.61.07.95; www.anne-gros.fr
Wines: Vosne-Romanée, Chambolle-Musigny, Clos Vougeot, and others.
$$ to $$$$

Direct, plain spoken, hardworking, Anne Gros inspires confidence. Add a hunk of talent to that blend—plus some prime Burgundy vineyards—and you get extremely fine, pure, delicious wines. A 2001 Clos de Vougeot Grand Cru Grand Maupertuis sums up the attributes: jewel-like fruit, firm but with a suggestion of femininity, structured but supple—asking you to cellar it but tempting you to drink it right away. Gros also makes some stellar, modestly priced, and quickly sold out Bourgognes, like a Hautes-Côtes de Nuits Cuvée Marine that is so impressive it could rival all but the highest *crus*.

Domaine A. F. Gros ☆

21630 Pommard; 03.80.22.61.85; www.af-gros.com
Wines: Bourgogne Hautes-Côtes de Nuits, Savigny-lès-Beaune, Vosne-Romanée, Chambolle-Musigny, Beaune, and Pommard. $$ to $$$$

Yes, this is a different Anne Gros. And the story's about to become slightly more confusing. This particular Anne (Françoise) inherited some property and bought additional property with her husband, François Parent. He, in turn, owns property inherited from his folks, the prominent Parents of Pommard, the wines from which he markets under the name Château des Guette. All the wines are described here and all have certain family traits. Gros and Parent do not make flashy, hit-'em-over-the-head-style wines. The words that come to mind again and again are *delicacy, restraint, finesse,* and *a true sense of place.* In the A. F. Gros line, all those descriptives fit the velvety Savigny-lès-Beaune Premier Cru Clos des Guettes; the alluring, structured Chambolle-Musigny; the long, mineral Vosne-Romanée Au Réas; the totally irresistible Vosne-Romanée Maizières; the compelling, deep Beaune Premier Cru Les Montrevenots; and the majestic, delicious Richebourg. The Pommards from Domaine François Parent—particularly the Premier Crus Les Épenots and Les Rugiens—merit the same accolades.

Corinne & Jean-Pierre Grossot ☆

Fleys 89800 Chablis; 03.86.42.44.64; fax: 03.86.42.13.31
Wine: Chablis. $$ to $$$

An excellent family domaine making overachieving generic Chablis, particularly the racy La Part des Anges cuvée; and a range of exciting Premier Crus, including a complex, pedigreed Les Fourneaux, thrillingly fresh even in the 2003 vintage; an ample, well-bred Vaucoupin, with lovely minerality and a long, long finish; and a majestic, mineral- and lemon-threaded Fourchaume.

Domaine Guffens-Heynen ☆

71960 Vergisson; 03.85.51.66.00; www.verget-sa.com
Wines: Mâcon, Pouilly-Fuissé, Chablis, Meursault, Puligny-Montrachet, and Corton-Charlemagne. $$ to $$$$

Once upon a time, in the mid-1980s, a crazy, *Big Chill*–generation Belgian who happened to be a quality-obsessed wine broker decided to put his money where his perfectionist palate was. And to do it in Burgundy. Soon were born two distinct but intimately related entities: Domaine Guffens-Heynen, making wine from its own grapes in the Côte Chalonnaise, and the *négociant* arm Verget, making wine from grapes purchased from across the Burgundy region. By 2004 Jean-Marie Guffens had extended his range to the Rhône and, in that vintage year, produced sixty-four different wines. Not one of them is less than excellent, even if some of them are named after Pink Floyd albums. The wines were and continue to be miraculous. Most are chardonnay. And those of you fortunate enough to taste one or more of them may well swear that you have never tasted a better chardonnay.

How to explain this prodigious ability? Guffens has great instincts, follows no recipe (especially where oak aging is concerned), and takes enormous pains at every single juncture. He makes Mâcon, St.-Véran, and Pouilly-Fuissé as if they were Le Montrachet. And they surely outclass many actual Chassagnes and Pulignys. I find there are two distinct styles: briefly, voluptuous or aerodynamic. I consistently prefer the aerodynamic but the voluptuous are gorgeous, too. A few highlights: a Chassagne-doppelgänger of a St.-Véran Terres Noires; a satiny, Mâcon-Charnay Le Clos St.-Pierre with flavors of pineapple and crème anglaise; an endless, magnificent, lacework, Puligny-like Mâcon-Vergisson La Roche; a limpid, majestic Pouilly-Fuissé Terroir de Vergisson; an enormously complex, *terroir*-driven, lightly salty, and extremely long Chablis Cuvée de la Butte; a regal, flinty, heart-stoppingly complex Chablis Premier Cru Vaillons; and the even more promising (if possible) Chablis Premier Cru Montée de Tonnerre. And, yes, there are mind-blowing post-2000 Meursaults, Corton-Charlemagnes, and Bâtard-Montrachets. But they will need to age for at least five more years. In the meantime, drink the wines from the Côte Chalonnaise.

Domaine Antonin Guyon

21420 Savigny-lès-Beaune; 03.80.67.13.24; www.guyon-bourgogne.com
Wines: Meursault, Corton, Chambolle-Musigny, and others. $$ to $$$$
Nice work but could do better is the most succinct way to describe the overall quality of the many different wines this domaine produces from numerous ACs. There's the well-behaved Meursault Premier Cru Les Charmes Dessus, which is very good but won't make you dream. The Corton Bressandes is a charming red that lacks depth. A smooth and delicate Chambolle-Musigny Clos du Village has flavor and class but is still an underachiever.

Domaine Olivier Guyot ↑

21160 Marsannay la Côte; 03.80.52.39.71; domaine.guyot@libertysurf.fr
Wines: Marsannay, Gevrey-Chambertin, and others. $$ to $$$$
An idealistic young vigneron who farms biodynamically and who was greatly influenced by his neighbor, the late Denis Mortet, Guyot is not entirely ready for prime time but is very promising. Reds account for most of his production, and they are bottled unfiltered. The most impressive wine I've tasted here is the full, deep, pedigreed Gevrey-Chambertin Premier Cru Les Champeaux, from vines planted in 1901—damned delicious.

Thierry Guyot

21290 St.-Romain; 03.80.212752; mplabrune@wanadoo.fr
Wines: Puligny-Montrachet, St.-Romain, Beaune, and Bourgogne. $ to $$$
One of Burgundy's first biodynamic practitioners, Guyot makes wines that are consistently pure and mineral. His Bourgogne rouge has more character than fruit—which I like. And his St.-Romain red is richer but similar. Never anonymous and sometimes imperfect, the wines reveal another aspect of Burgundy. A 2002 Beaune rouge, for example, came across like a supple, light, intensely mineral, and very dark rosé, and a Puligny-Montrachet was a real country wine, with tons of personality.

Domaine Hamelin

89800 Lignorelles; 03.86.47.54.60; domaine.hamelin@wanadoo.fr
Wine: Chablis. $$
Making distinctive Chablis at all levels. Even in 2003 Hamelin's generic Chablis was steely, taut, and rectilinear; the Vieilles Vignes was textured and *terroir*-driven; the Premier Cru Vau Ligneau was fresh as a waterfall; and the racy Premier Cru Beauroy was creamy, balanced, and mineral.

Domaine Harmand-Geoffroy

21220 Gevrey-Chambertin; 03.80.34.10.65; harmand-geoffroy@wanadoo.fr
Wine: Gevrey-Chambertin. $$ to $$$
A good family domaine, Harmand-Geoffroy has a range of robust, rich Gevrey-Chambertins, including a layered Vieilles Vignes, a velvet quilt of a Premier Cru

Lavaux St.-Jacques that you just want to sink into, and a monumental Grand Cru Mazis-Chambertin.

Irancy

A small AC about ten miles south of Auxerre, for light, lean reds with little or no body fat. Pinot noir is the grape, sometimes blended with the obscure local variety césar.

BEST RECENT VINTAGES: 2005 and 2004.
PRICES: $$

PRODUCERS: Bersan: look for the Cuvée Louis Bersan—to sample in a wine bar; see also ST.-BRIS ◆ BENOÎT CANTIN ◆ ANITA, JEAN-PIERRE & STEPHANIE COLINOT ◆ Dom Grand Roche: try the cool, lean Irancy from this house, along with its Bourgogne pinot noir Ma Préférence. The St.-Bris is also pleasant ◆ Dom St.-Germain: fresh, mineral, somewhat austere light red, to drink like a nice, serious rosé. A drop of césar adds an appetizing bitter note ◆ Dom Franck & François Givaudin: makes appealing versions of Irancy ◆ DOM VERRET.

Domaine Louis Jadot ☆

21 rue Eugène-Spuller, 21200 Beaune; 03.80.22.10.57; www.louisjadot.com
Wines: Beaune, Gevrey-Chambertin, Chassagne-Montrachet, Clos de Vougeot, Corton, and more. $$ to $$$$
I have nothing but praise for this vital grower-*négociant* house, which has a combined holding of nearly 150 hectares (including properties owned by Domaine Louis Jadot, Le Domaine des Héritiers Louis Jadot, Domaine Gagey, and Domaine Duc de Magenta, as well as vineyards in Beaujolais). Much of the credit is due to the brilliant, impassioned winemaker Jacques Lardière, who doesn't put a foot wrong. So how good are the wines? Let me tell you about a Domaine Gagey 2002 Beaune Grèves Le Clos Blanc, the breed of which hit me over the head—in the nicest possible way. There were notes of pineapple and the most crystalline expression of mineral and lemon with a subtle oak backdrop. But we're way beyond fruit here. Every sip was a discovery. Smacking my lips in kind of a blissful awe, I drank a third of a bottle without even realizing it, and once it was empty, I couldn't bring myself to throw the bottle away. There are many such Jadot-Lardière moments, including another Beaune, this one an exclusive, the Premier Cru Clos des Ursules Vignes Franches, an achingly nuanced and structured red with notes of cranberries, morello cherries, and licorice, and a nearly viscous, *terroir*-driven Bâtard-Montrachet of great freshness, elegance, and vigor. Beyond the Côte d'Or, Jadot makes appetizing whites in St.-Véran (Domaine de la Chapelle aux Loups) and in Pouilly-Fuissé.

It's in Beaujolais, however, that Louis Jadot produces wines to die for, starting in the modest Beaujolais-Villages AC with a barrel-fermented white Château des Jacques Grand Clos de Loyse, a lucid, mellow Burgundy, and the red Combe aux Jacques, which is so delicious and succulent you want to dive into it. The barrel-aged Morgons from Château des Lumières are spicy, fresh, serious reds, and the cuvée Côte du Py approaches the profound. My absolute soft spot here, though, is for the wines from Moulin-à-Vent, particularly the elegant, lipsmacking beauties from Château des Jacques, including its cuvées such as La Roche and Clos de Rochegrés, that you could easily take for, say, very, very good Volnays.

Domaine Patrick Javillier ☆

21190 Meursault; 03.80.21.27.87; fax: 03.80.21.29.39

Wines: Meursault, Pommard, Corton, and Bourgogne. $$ to $$$$

Here is a man to know in Meursault. Patrick Javillier's wines, often unfiltered, impress with their depth, the serious work that clearly went into making them, and their strong mineral (and light oak) flavors. The Meursault Cuvée Tête de Murger is lean, austere, and racy. Les Tillets Cuvée Spécial is lyrical, lime-scented, and very pretty. Les Clous is smooth, textured, and *terroir*-driven, with good acid support. I'd love to meet Javillier's majestic 2002 Meursault Charmes again in ten years though when tasting it in 2005, it was awfully hard not to finish the bottle. Javillier also makes excellent unfiltered white Bourgognes, including the tender Cuvée des Forgets and the inviting Cuvée Oligocène, both of them junior Meursaults.

Domaine Jayer-Gilles ☆

21700 Magny-les-Villers; 03.80.62.91.79; fax: 03.80.62.99.77

Wines: Nuits-St.-Georges, Côte de Nuits-Villages, Échezeaux, Bourgogne Hautes-Côtes de Nuits, Bourgogne Hautes-Côtes de Beaune, and Bourgogne Aligoté. $$ to $$$$

Gilles Jayer makes incisive, pure, powerful wines. His reliance on oak—100 percent new for the reds—is not to everyone's taste. I'm no fan of heavy oak flavors, but I have never been bothered by this in Jayer's wines. Indeed, I admire just about everything from this domaine, including his impressively rich aligoté and his forceful, mineral, citrus zest, and oak Haute-Côtes de Nuits blanc, a blend of chardonnay and a rare strain of pinot blanc obtained from a mutation of HENRI GOUGES's pinot noir. Jayer's reds are neither fined nor filtered. I find them uniformly marked by freshness, purity, succulence, and pedigree. My two favorites are the excellent, *terroir*-driven Nuits-St.-Georges Premier Cru La Damode, with its juicy, dark, blueberry fruit, and the authoritative, racy Grand Cru Échezeaux. The 2003s, tasted from barrel in the spring of 2005, were fresh, balanced, structured, and extremely promising, with the Nuits-St.-Georges Premier Cru Les Damodes and Échezeaux still my clear favorites.

Domaine Jeandeau ↑

71960 Fuissé; tel/fax: 03.85.29.20.46; www.domainejeandeau.com

Wine: Pouilly-Fuissé. $$ to $$$

Young, ambitious Denis Jeandeau has converted the family's small domaine to biodynamics and is turning out a number of impressive Pouilly-Fuissés, including a fresh, pure Tradition; a textured, buttery, barrel-fermented Les Prouges from the domaine's oldest vines; and a powerful, unfiltered Terres Jeanduc, made from sixty-year-old vines fermented in new-oak barrels.

François Jobard ☆

21190 Meursault; 03.80.21.21.26; fax: 03.80.21.26.44

Wines: Meursault and Bourgogne. $$$ to $$$$

Jobard's glorious, magisterial Meursaults are unfined and unfiltered, and need at least five years of tender, loving cellaring but can age longer than that. (A 1998 Genevrières was magnificent when drunk in 2003.) When young, they are tight and concentrated, with all the indications of flowering into noble, complex wines. This doesn't mean they're not delicious a bit earlier; a four-year-old 2001 En la Barre, a buttery, layered white, was as sensuous as velvet. And the Premier Cru Poruzots, still closed, had the muscularity of a ballet dancer. It was a big, broad wine with lots of grace, detailed, savory, and layered, with notes of lemon, salt, and butterscotch. It also had an appealing hand-hewn quality that gave it a coziness I feel Montrachet lacks. I happened to be listening to Nat King Cole at the time I was drinking it, and the wine was as mellow and caressing as his voice. And, forgive me but it's true, Cole was singing "Unforgettable." The timing couldn't have been better.

Alexandre Jouveaux ☆

71700 Uchizy; 03.85.40.58.15

Wine: Mâcon. $ to $$

With only 3 hectares, this painstaking producer sells his organic, barrel-aged Mâcons to top restaurants. The Mâcon-Villages is creamy, fresh, and tasty. The Mâcon Prety, from the "other" side of the Saône, is suave, mineral, original, and impressive.

Domaine Émile Juillot ☆

71640 Mercurey; 03.85.45.13.87; e.juillot.theulot@wanadoo.fr

Wine: Mercurey. $$ to $$$

This domaine produces exquisitely delicious red Burgundies from an often overlooked AC. The sirens include a nuanced, ample Villages; a coolly seductive, oak- and black cherry–scented Premier Cru Champs Martin; and a detailed, drop-dead beauty, Premier Cru La Cailloute, an Émile Juillot exclusive. The domaine is converting to organic viticulture.

Domaine Michel Juillot

71640 Mercurey; 03.85.98.99.89; infos@domaine-michel-juillot.fr

Wines: Aloxe-Corton and Mercurey. $$ to $$$$

The Mercurey blanc is just fine but I much prefer the reds from this house. These include a clutch of Mercureys—the fine-grained Premier Cru Clos des Barraults is a favorite, with its alluring raspberry, black cherry, and oak succulence—and a fresh and focused Aloxe-Corton.

Juliénas

The most "complete" *cru* of Beaujolais, in which the characteristics of the other nine seem to coalesce, Juliénas may be the Libra of the Beaujolais. See BEAUJOLAIS for vintages and prices.

PRODUCERS: Dom de Boischampt: smooth, appetizing Juliénas with an attractive mineral core ◆ Nadège & David Boulet: very good versions of Juliénas, especially the suave, oak-aged Vieilles Vignes ◆ Dom de la Côte de Chevenal: Jean-François and Pierre Bergeron produce truly pretty Beaujolais, whether it's the plummy, aromatic, and ample Juliénas or the Beaujolais Émeringes ◆ PASCAL GRANGER ☆ ◆ Dom Matray: Les Pacquelets is fluid and easy-drinking; the oak-aged Vieilles Vignes is more specific but maybe one cuvée would have sufficed ◆ LOUIS TÊTE ◆ Michel Tête/Dom du Clos du Fief: look for the black cherry–accented Clos du Fief and the Cuvée Prestige, as well as the St.-Amour and Beaujolais-Villages from this good vigneron.

Ladoix

A hamlet within the commune Ladoix-Serrigny gives its name to a small AC at the northern end of the Côte de Beaune. Primarily for pinot noir–based reds, Ladoix also applies to whites made from chardonnay and pinot blanc. There are seven Premier Crus, some of which overlap Aloxe-Corton AC, and part of Corton and Corton-Charlemagne also lie within its confines.

BEST RECENT VINTAGES: 2005, (2004), (2003), and 2002.
PRICES: $$ to $$$

PRODUCERS: DOM CHEVALIER PÈRE & FILS ◆ EDMOND CORNU ◆ DOM DE LA GALOPIÈRE ◆ Dom Maratray-Dubreuil: its light, zero-body-fat Ladoix reds include the sinewy, steely Les Nagets and Les Grechons ◆ DOM MARÉCHAL-CAILLOT ◆ DOM ANDRÉ NUDANT ◆ Dom Gaston & Pierre Ravault: two bright, cherry-flavored Ladoix—the Clos Royer and La Corvée; see also ALOXE-CORTON.

Domaine des Comtes Lafon ☆

21190 Meursault; 03.80.21.22.17; comtes.lafon@wanadoo.fr
Wines: Meursault and Volnay. $$$ to $$$$
How many winemakers have been influenced by the Meursaults of the Lafon family? And how many consumers could be excused for thinking that the Lafon family invented Meursault? The wines are just that grand, starting with an enormously nuanced, succulent but straight-as-an-arrow Clos de la Barre, moving along to a lipsmackingly profound, lime-, mineral-, and oak-flavored Premier Cru Charmes, and ending with a silky, mellow, bottomless Premier Cru Perrières. The reds are wonderful here, too. A fresh, young Volnay Premier Cru Santenots-du-Milieu, for example, seemed dusted with cinnamon, cumin, and caraway by a master from Guerlain.

Domaine des Héritiers du Comte Lafon ☆

71960 Milly-Lamartine, 03.80.21.22.17; comtes.lafon@wanadoo.fr
Wine: Mâcon. $$ to $$$
No surprise that the justly celebrated Lafon family would hit the ground running when they ventured into the Mâconnais. Even their simplest cuvée is ample and textured. The Clos de la Crochette is deeper still and more textured, and the Mâcon-Uchizy Les Maranches is rich and toothsome. Thus far, however, the finest cuvées seem to come from Mâcon Milly-Lamartine, and the finest of those is the Clos du Four, a lacy, elegant, nuanced, oak-tinged wine.

Domaine de Lalande ☆

71570 Chaintre; tel/fax: 03.85.37.43.58; www.cornin.net
Wine: Pouilly-Fuissé. $$
Fortysomething Dominique Cornin is converting the family domaine to biodynamics. He produces Beaujolais blanc, Mâcon, and St.-Véran, but his darlings are his barrel-fermented Pouilly-Fuissés. Of these, there are three: an intriguing, totally yummy, layered, lime-and-oak generic bottling; a nuanced and textured Les Chevrières; and a pellucid Clos Reyssie, fresh as a waterfall.

Domaine des Lambrays ☆

21220 Morey-St.-Denis; 03.80.51.84.33; fax:03.80.51.81.97
Wine: Clos des Lambrays. $$$$
Domaine des Lambrays makes finely tuned, elegant versions of the Grand Cru Clos des Lambrays. Grapes that don't qualify for the *clos* are made into a Morey-St.-Denis AC.

Domaine Hubert Lamy

21190 St.-Aubin; 03.80.21.32.55; domainehubertlamy@wanadoo.fr
Wines: Chassagne-Montrachet, St.-Aubin, and Bourgogne Hautes-Côtes de Beaune. $$ to $$$
Hubert and son Olivier are known for their excellent, reasonably priced St.-Aubins. The whites include a mellow, mineral Premier Cru Clos du Meix and a sterling, limpid, complex, cream-and-velvet Premier Cru En Remilly. Their reds are fine meal wines. The Chassagne-Montrachet La Goujonne is gentle but firm and has the structure to cut through the richness of dishes like *ris de veau*. The Bourgogne Hautes-Côtes de Beaune in opulent vintages like 2003 is practically a meal in itself. Duck with cherry sauce? I say, drink up and enjoy being in Burgundy.

Sylvain Langoureau

21190 St.-Aubin; tel/fax: 03.80.21.39.99
Wines: Meursault, St.-Aubin, and others. $$ to $$$
A serious young vigneron, Sylvain Langoureau makes ambitious, extremely ripe, handcrafted wines, including a structured, specific Meursault-Blagny Premier Cru La Pièce Sous le Bois, and a mineral, singular, quinine and citrus zest St.-Aubin Premier Cru En Remilly.

Hubert Lapierre ☆
71570 La Chapelle de Guinchay; 03.85.36.74.89; hubert.lapierre@terre-net.fr
Wines: Chénas and Moulin-à-Vent. $ to $$
Very low yields, very old vines, and a simple, light filtration before bottling partly explain the elegance and purity of Lapierre's wines. There are three excellent cuvées of Chénas—the fine-grained "traditional" bottling; the richer, more concentrated Vieilles Vignes, and a barrel-aged version—and two admirable cuvées of Moulin-à-Vent—the mineral and characterful "tradition" and the barrel-aged Vieilles Vignes, a discreet, specific red.

Marcel Lapierre ☆
69910 Villié-Morgon; 04.74.04.23.89; fax: 04.74.69.14.40
Wines: Beaujolais and Morgon. $$
A pioneer of hypernatural winemaking in the Beaujolais, Marcel Lapierre is, first and foremost, an exemplary grower. His barrel-aged Beaujolais and Morgon are pure, textured, and characterful. While not always perfect, they are usually delightful and always quirky, supple, and totally authentic. And, for the cautious, he offers the option of wine bottled filtered or nonfiltered, with sulfur or without.

Domaine Laroche ☆
89800 Chablis; 03.86.42.89.00; www.larochewines.com
Wine: Chablis. $$$ to $$$$
Dynamism, intelligence, and significant vineyard holdings (100 hectares) keep Laroche at the forefront of Chablis production. Quality is consistent and the wines range from very good (for example the invigorating, steely Chablis St.-Martin), to excellent (the powerful, textured Les Fourchaumes Vieilles Vignes), to superb (the unfiltered, succulent, and breathtakingly aristocratic Grand Crus Les Clos and Les Blanchots Réserve de l'Obedience). Most are available with a screw cap.

Domaine Fabrice Larochette ↑
71570 Chaintre; 03.85.32.90.78; fabrice.larochette@wanadoo.fr
Wines: Mâcon, Pouilly-Fuissé, and St.-Véran. $ to $$
This promising young winemaker is producing admirable, solid wines in Mâcon-Vinzelles and Mâcon-Chaintre (at the Château de Chaintre), as well as fresh, focused wines in St.-Véran, such as La Grande Vigne. For now, however, my favorites come from Pouilly-Fuissé—the fresh, savory, and mineral Les Robées and the textured, toothsome Le Clos de Monsieur Noly.

Maison Louis Latour
18, rue des Tonneliers, 21200 Beaune; 03.80.24.81.02; www.louislatour.com
Wines: The entire range of Burgundy. $ to $$$$
This large, high profile grower-*négociant*, marketing more than five million bottles annually, makes clean, commerical Burgundy wines.

Domaine Dominique Laurent ☆
21700 Nuits-St.-Georges; 03.80.61.49.94; dominiquelaurent@club-internet.fr
Wines: Gevrey-Chambertin, Nuits-St.-Georges, Morey-St.-Denis, and more. $$ to $$$$
An artisanal *négociant* and pinot noir devotee, Dominique Laurent has become a trendsetter in the matter of selecting and aging wines with maximum TLC. Most of the wines are ravishing, although some reveal the risks of working with very ripe grapes and very low sulfur. This drinker finds the risks well worth taking.

Roland Lavantureux ☆
89800 Lignorelles; 03.86.47.53.75; fax: 03.86.47.56.43
Wine: Chablis. $$ to $$$
No Premier Crus, no Grand Crus, just creamy, mineral, delicious Chablis and Petit Chablis, each of them overachievers in their respective categories. The

suave yet rectilinear 2002 Chablis was a like a razor couched in a kid glove. Excellent.

Domaine Leflaive ☆

21190 Puligny-Montrachet; 03.80.21.30.13; sce-domaine-leflaive@wanadoo.fr

Wine: Puligny-Montrachet. $$$ to $$$$

Anne-Claude Leflaive converted her enviable holdings in Puligny-Montrachet to biodynamics in 1990, and although she is thoroughly involved in the domaine, she has entrusted its direction to PIERRE MOREY. These whites need cellaring. If drunk before, say, their eighth birthday, they will benefit from being in a carafe several hours before drinking and kept in cool place. All of the Pulignys are rich, layered, savory, and *terroir*-driven. The richness and complexity escalate as you ascend the level of *crus,* starting with a precise, inviting standard Puligny, moving on to a butter-and-cream, extremely long Premier Cru Clavoillon or an oak-tinged Premier Cru Les Folatières, and ending with a grandiose and extremely fresh Bâtard-Montrachet Grand Cru.

Domaine Lejeune

21630 Pommard; tel/fax: 03.80.22.90.88; domaine-lejeune@wanadoo.fr

Wines: Pommard and Bourgogne. $$ to $$$($)

Painstakingly handcrafted, personalized, unfiltered reds that range from an intriguingly cumin-, caraway-, and white pepper–scented Bourgogne to two very different Pommard Premier Crus—a beefy, somewhat rugged Les Poutures and an elegant, layered Les Argillières that has some of the spice and pepper notes of the Bourgogne.

René Lequin-Colin

21590 Santenay; 03.80.20.66.71; renelequin@aol.com

Wines: Chassagne-Montrachet, Santenay, Corton, and others. $$ to $$$$

This well-established family domaine, with parcels in such prime Grand Crus as Bâtard-Montrachet, does a fine job with its less-vaunted vineyards as well, including a lyrical, herbal tea–scented Chassagne-Montrachet Clos Devant, an oak-tinged white, and a Santenay Premier Cru La Comme, which is a succulent, charming red.

Domaine Leroy ☆

21700 Vosne Romanée, 03.80.21.21.10; www.domaineleroy.com

Wines: Gevrey-Chambertin, Chambolle-Musigny, Clos de Vougeot, Corton, Nuits-St.-Georges, Richebourg, Romanée St.-Vivant, Savigny-lès-Beaune, and Vosne-Romanée. $$$$

Truly a legend in her own time, the redoubtable Lalou Bize-Leroy, the partial owner but the very soul of this domaine, is acknowledged to be one of the most exigent winemakers in the business. She is said to have a palate with perfect pitch. I also think of her as the conscience of Burgundy during the bad old days—as recently as the mid-80s—when finding a great bottle of Burgundy was as iffy as finding a menschy single guy on the streets of Manhattan. You could always count on a wine with her signature—even her *négociant* bottlings from Maison Leroy—to be breathtaking. Leroy was formerly the director of Domaine de la Romanée-Conti, which her ancestors were instrumental in creating. She applies even more rigorous standards at Maison Leroy and at the 4-hectare Domaine d'Auvenay, headquartered in St.-Romain, of which she is the sole owner. She has converted both domaines to biodynamics and realizes some of the lowest yields known to winedom. The direct rivals of those from Domaine de la Romanée-Conti, her wines are very great, very expensive, and always sold out. Look for a sit-down tasting in your area. The Domaine d'Auvenay produces wines in Auxey-Duresses, Bonnes-Mares, Puligny-Montrachet, Gevrey-Chambertin, and Meursault. Some of the wines from the less-vaunted ACs from both houses may actually approach affordability.

Machard de Gramont ☆

21700 Nuits-St.-Georges; tel/fax: 03.80.61.16.96

Wines: Nuits-St.-Georges, Savigny-lès-Beaune, and Bourgogne. $$$ to $$$$

A deservedly popular domaine with an enviable range of wines, particularly those from Nuits-St.-Georges, among which are a potent, succulent white Les Creux Fraîche-Eau and, in reds, the cool, patriarchal Les Hauts Poirets and a juicy, toothsome Les Hauts Pruliers. Apparently the domaine is scaling down and concentrating on its Nuits-St.-Georges properties. But I have tasted recent vintages from other ACs, and they're likely to be on the market—or on wine lists—and are well worth considering. They include a delectable red Bourgogne Le Chapitre with real depth; a plush, charming Pommard Premier Cru Clos Blanc; a seductive Savigny-lès-Beaunes Premier Cru Aux Guettes, a powerful red with seductive Morello cherry flavors; and an elegant, structured Beaune Les Épenottes.

Mâcon, Mâcon-Villages, and Viré-Clessé

A large AC in southern Burgundy, west and northwest of the town of Mâcon. While Mâcon-Villages is limited to whites made from chardonnay, Mâcon and Mâcons from one of twenty-odd villages may also be reds and rosés made from gamay and pinot noir (designated villages include Charnay, Fuissé, Igé, Lugny, Milly-Lamartine, Uchizy, and Vergisson). The AC Viré-Clessé, which applies only to whites made from chardonnay, was formed by combining Mâcon-Viré and Mâcon-Clessé.

BEST RECENT VINTAGES: 2005, (2004), (2003), and 2002.
PRICES: $ to $$$($)

PRODUCERS: Guy Blanchard: a promising producer of organic Mâcon-Villages; the 2003 was supple, creamy, and pure, with lots of character ↑ ◆ DOM DE LA BONGRAN ☆ ◆ BRET BROTHERS/LA SOUFRANDIÈRE ↑ ◆ Dom des Chazelles: makes two cuvées of ambitious Viré-Clessé, the oaky, ripe Le Creusseromme and the hefty Vieilles Vignes ◆ DOM FICHET ↑ ◆ Émilian Gillet: see DOM DE LA BONGRAN ◆ Ch de Chaintre: see DOM FABRICE LAROCHETTE ↑ ◆ DOM GUFFENS-HEYNEN ☆ ◆ Guillot-Broux: my favorite wine from this organic producer is the fresh, fruity red La Myotte; the white Mâcon and Mâcon-Cruzille are ambitious but not yet ready for prime time ◆ ALEXANDRE JOUVEAUX ☆ ◆ DOM DES HÉRITIERS DU COMTE LAFON ☆ ◆ DOM FABRICE LAROCHETTE ↑ ◆ MERLIN/DOMAINE DU VIEUX ST.-SORLIN ◆ Henri Perrusset: fresh, lemon-accented, and bistro-ready Mâcon-Farges Vieilles Vignes ◆ Dom des Pitoux: floral, ripe, focused wines ◆ Dom Rijckaert: the former partner of Jean-Marie Guffens, Jean Rijckaert produces exemplary wine in the JURA as well as in the Mâconnais; don't hesitate, the wines are full, balanced, mineral, and food friendly ☆ ◆ Dom St.-Denis: see BOURGOGNE ◆ DOMAINE SAINTE BARBE ☆ ◆ DOM JACQUES & NATHALIE SAUMAIZE ☆ ◆ Dom la Soufrandise: see POUILLY-FUISSÉ ◆ Éric Texier: this man's sui generis (see the Rhône chapter), so don't expect the usual from him. His riveting, concentrated, and refreshingly tart Mâcon Buissières Très Vieilles Vignes comes as close as wine can get to being chutney. Here's a chardonnay for Indian food! His botrytized Mâcon, while not in the class of DOM DE LA BONGRAN, is worth tasting, too ◆ CÉLINE & LAURENT TRIPOZ ☆ ◆ Valette: see POUILLY-FUISSÉ ◆ Vergé: Hypernatural (no chaptalization, wild yeasts, no sulfur), tank-fermented Mâcon-Villages and Viré-Clessé, with all risks involved therein. The various cuvées from Viré-Clessé, especially the Vieilles Vignes, made from century-old vines, and the mineral, flinty, Coteau des Quarts are the best ◆ Verget: see DOM GUFFENS-HEYNEN ☆ ◆ DOM DES VIGNES DU MAYNE.

Domaine de la Madone

69460 Le Perréon; 04.74.03.21.85; www.bererd-fils.com

Wines: Beaujolais. $ to $$

Jean Bererd's wines are eco-friendly and very ambitious, if not always perfect, and they give a different idea of Beaujolais from that of the mass-produced variety. His new-oak-aged Beaujolais Villages blanc is mellow and honest. His oak-aged Beaujolais Le Perréon is very ripe, pure, and succulent (the 2005 is a plush little velvet cushion). His barrel-aged, unfiltered Cuvée Jean Baptiste is a rich, soulful, kirsch-accented Beaujolais Villages made from fifty-year-old vines.

Maranges

A small Côte de Beaune AC, mostly for pinot noir–based reds, although a small amount of chardonnay-based white is also produced. There are six Premier Crus.

BEST RECENT VINTAGES: 2005, 2004, 2003, and 2002.
PRICES: $$ to $$$

PRODUCERS: YVAN AND CHANTAL CONTAT-GRANGE ◆ Dom Edmond Monnot & Fils: Stéphane Monnot took over the family property in 2000 and is turning out engaging Maranges, particularly the Premier Cru Clos des Loyères and the austere, aristocratic Premier Cru Clos de la Boutière Vieilles Vignes, from a vineyard of which they are the sole owners ◆ Dom Muzard: racy, mineral reds ◆ Dom Jean-Claude Regnaudot & Fils: mellow, smooth reds, particularly those from Premier Crus like Clos Roussot ◆ DOM MICHEL SARRAZIN ☆.

Domaine Catherine & Claude Maréchal

21200 Bligny-lès-Beaune; 03.80.21.44.37; marechalcc@wanadoo.fr

Wines: Bourgogne, Auxey-Duresses, Chorey-lès-Beaune, Ladoix, and Pommard. $$ to $$$

A serious domaine with a light touch. The Maréchals make lovely, reasonably priced restaurant Burgundies, ranging from a solid Bourgogne rouge Gravel, to a smooth, mineral Auxey-Duresses rouge, to a focused, medium-bodied red Savigny-lès-Beaune Vieilles Vignes and an expressive Pommard La Chanière.

Domaine Maréchal-Caillot

21200 Bligny-lès-Beaune, 03.80.21.44.55; marechalcaillot@aol.com

Wines: Ladoix, Savigny-lès-Beaune, Pommard, and Bourgogne. $$ to $$$

A small, serious domaine with tasty red Burgundies. Curiously, my favorite is the simple Burgundy Terroir les Lormes, which I would love to bring along on an ambitious picnic.

Marsannay

A small Côte de Nuits AC about eight miles southwest of Dijon, for reds and rosés made from pinot noir and a very small amount of white based on chardonnay. There are no Premiers Crus or Grands Crus in this AC.

BEST RECENT VINTAGES: 2005, 2004, 2003, and 2002.
PRICES: $$ to $$$

PRODUCERS: Dom Charles Audoin: look for the seductive, light Les Longeroies ◆ DOM RÉGIS BOUVIER ◆ DOM RENÉ BOUVIER ↑ ◆ Marc Brocot: nicely concentrated, well-balanced reds ◆ PHILIPPE CHARLOPIN ☆ ◆ DOM BRUNO CLAIR ☆ ◆ FOUGERAY DE BEAUCLAIR ◆ DOM OLIVIER GUYOT ↑ ◆ Dom Huguenot Père & Fils: one of Marsannay's rare chardonnay specialists, Philippe Huguenot also produces several cuvées of admirable pinot noirs, notably the Haute Expression bottling, made from a selection of the best grapes; see also GEVREY-CHAMBERTIN ◆ Dom Sylvain Pataille: enologist Sylvain took over the family property seven years ago and the prospects look fine—for textured, lemon-scented whites (particularly La Charme aux Prêtres), new-oak-aged rosé, and the oaky yet silky L'Ancestrale, an ambitious red ◆ DOM TRAPET ↑ ◆ DOM DU VIEUX COLLÈGE.

Domaine du Meix-Foulot

71640 Mercurey; 03. 85.45.13.92; fax: 03.85.45.28.10
Wine: Mercurey. $$
Paul de Launay, an eco-friendly producer, makes attractively layered, lightly oaked white Mercurey and a handful of lipsmacking red Mercureys, including a bright cherry Villages, a suave, silky, all-but-irresistible Premier Cru, and a deeper, more tannic, though still gracious, Premier Cru Clos du Château du Montaigu.

Domaine Menand

71640 Mercurey; 03.85.45.19.19; fax: 03.85.45.10.23
Wine: Mercurey. $$
Extremely alluring, intriguingly exotic red Mercureys. Les Vaux is silky and mouthwatering. Premier Cru Le Champs Martin is all seductive fragrances. The mingled aromas wafting up from the Premier Cru Vieilles Vignes des Combins Cuvée Prestige is so inviting you can't wait to taste the wine. And there's no disappointment—oriental spices blend with oak and pinot noir flavors. Absolutely delicious.

Domaine Méo-Camuzet

21700 Vosne-Romanée; 03.80.61.11.05; meo-camuzet@wanadoo.fr
Wines: Corton, Nuits-St.-Georges, and Vosne-Romanée. $$$$
Jean-Nicolas Méo had the great good fortune to take over vines that had been farmed by the legendary Henri Jayer, as well as to have benefited from time spent working with the master. Méo's wines are widely admired, but I haven't been that lucky. In several tastings, I've been underwhelmed, finding, for example, the unfiltered Nuits-St.-Georges Au Bas de Combes hard and unbalanced; a 2003 Hautes-Côtes de Nuits Clos St.-Philibert blanc lightly hot and vegetal; and the grand class lurking in the depths of a Vosne-Romanée Les Chaumes somewhat masked by youth (transitory) and turbidity (questionable).

Mercurey

The largest AC in the Côte Chalonnaise, Mercurey, which borders Rully and is about seven miles northwest of the town of Chalon-sur-Saône, produces medium-bodied, fragrant, juicy reds made from pinot noir and medium-bodied, all-purpose whites from chardonnay.

BEST RECENT VINTAGES: 2005, (2004), (2003), and 2002.
PRICES: $$ to $$$

PRODUCERS: BOUCHARD PÈRE & FILS ☆ ◆ Dom Michel Briday: see RULLY ◆ Ch de Chamirey: see DOM ANTONIN RODET ◆ DOM LES CHAMPS DE L'ABBAYE ↑ ◆ Paul de Couedic: suave, supple reds; ripe, creamy, lemon-accented whites ◆ CATHERINE & DOMINIQUE DERAIN ↑ ◆ DOM VINCENT DUREUIL-JANTHIAL ☆ ◆ Ch d'Étroye/Protheau & Fils: the barrel-fermented Les Ormeaux is a ripe, focused white with tropical fruit and citrus zest flavors; the pure, deep Clos des Corvées is a delicate, subtle, rose-accented red; Premier Cru Les Velley is fragrant, sinuous, and elegant despite the palpable oak presence ◆ MAISON FAIVELEY ☆ ◆ Dom Philippe Garrey: La Chagnée is a compact white; Premier Cru La Chassière is an oaky but nicely structured red ◆ DOM ÉMILE JUILLOT ☆ ◆ DOM MICHEL JUILLOT ◆ DOM DU MEIX-FOULOT ◆ DOM MENAND ◆ Ch de Mercey: see DOM ANTONIN RODET ◆ Ch de Santenay: owned by the bank Crédit Agricole, the domaine turns out several attractive cuvées of red, including Premier Cru Les Puillets, with its seductive notes of cherries and incense ◆ DOM TUPINIER BAUTISTA ↑ ◆ DOM A. & P. DE VILLAINE ☆.

Merlin/Domaine du Vieux St.-Sorlin

71960 La Roche Vineuse; 03.85.36.62.09; merlin.vins@wanadoo.fr
Wines: Mâcon, Viré-Clessé, St.-Véran, and Pouilly-Fuissé. $$ to $$$
One of the leaders of the Mâconnais renaissance, Olivier Merlin produces a number of admirable cuvées in the region's three main ACs, including a fresh, mineral Viré-Clessé Terroir de Clessé, a bracing, textured Mâcon La Roche Vineuse Vieilles Vignes, and a creamy, oak-accented Pouilly-Fuissé Terroir de Fuissé.

Meursault

An immensely important Côte de Beaune AC known for savory, complex, mouthfilling whites made from chardonnay and for a small amount of textured, fine reds made from pinot noir. There are no Grand Crus but there are seventeen Premier Crus. Les Charmes, Les Genevrières, and Les Perrières are among the most famous.

BEST RECENT VINTAGES: 2005, (2004), (2003), 2002, 2001, and (2000).
PRICES: $$$ to $$$$

PRODUCERS: MARQUIS D'ANGERVILLE ☆ ◆ Dom d'Auvenay: see DOM LEROY ☆ ◆ BALLOT-MILLOT & FILS ◆ Dom Buisson-Battault: while not ready for prime time, this domaine seems worth following. Overripeness and rough edges prevent the Premier Crus Goutte d'Or and Poruzots from displaying their creamy minerality and depth to the best advantage ◆ GUY BOCARD ◆ BOUCHARD PÈRE & FILS ☆ ◆ Dom Hubert Bouzereau-Gruère: look for the Meursault Charmes ◆ Dom Jean-Marie Bouzereau: smooth, creamy versions of the AC ◆ Philippe Bouzereau & Fils: also known as the Château de Cîteaux, look for the Premier Cru Perrières and the Vieux Clos du Château de Cîteaux, an exclusive ◆ DOM COCHE-BIZOUARD ☆ ◆ DOM JEAN-FRANÇOIS COCHE-DURY ☆ ◆ JOSEPH DROUHIN ☆ ◆ ARNAUD & MARIE-ODILE ENTE ☆ ◆ DOM DE LA GALOPIERE ◆ DOM ALBERT GRIVAULT ☆ ◆ DOM ANTONIN GUYON ◆ DOM PATRICK JAVILLIER ☆ ◆ FRANÇOIS JOBARD ☆ ◆ Labouré-Roi: this large *négociant* house produces a bit of everything, most of it ordinary, but the wines from its own vines—labeled Château Labouré-Roi—are a distinct step up, as is the mellow and savory Meursault Clos de la Baronne ◆ DOM DES COMTES LAFON ☆ ◆ SYLVAIN LANGOUREAU ◆ Maison Montagne Saint Nicolas: very good, *terroir*-driven, unfiltered, biodynamic Meursault Les Casses Têtes ◆ Matrot-Wittersheim: the Meursault-Blagny Premier Cru is a limpid white; focused, balanced, and discreet, it's not huge, it's a lovely cameo ◆ Maison Deux Montille: see DOM HUBERT DE MONTILLE ☆ ◆ DOM PIERRE MOREY ☆ ◆ DOM JACQUES PRIEUR ☆ ◆ DOM ROULOT ☆ ◆ Verget: see GUFFENS-HEYNEN ☆.

Domaine Michelot

21190 Meursault; 03.80.21.23.17; fax: 03.80.21.63.62
Wine: Meursault. $$$ to $$$$$
The serious, layered Meursaults from this domaine need aeration if drunk before their fifth birthday. After several hours in a carafe and kept cool, they reward with tingling flavors of lime and quinine. I'd recommend them all, but two favorites are the creamy Les Narvaux and the *terroir*-driven Premier Cru Les Charmes.

Domaine Moissenet-Bonnard

21630 Pommard; 03.80.24.61.34; fax: 03.80.22.3004
Wine: Pommard. $$$
Truly lovely, generally unfiltered Pommards. The star is the silky, sensual, deep Premier Cru Les Épenots, but I've also been seduced by the leaner Les Petits Noizons, the focused, pedigreed Les Charmots, and the succulent, racy Premier Cru Les Pézerolles.

Mommessin

69430 Quincie-en-Beaujolais; 04.74.69.09; fax: 04.74.69.09.28

Wines: Beaujolais, Brouilly, and Moulin-à-Vent. $$

Now owned by Boisset, this *négociant* house operates independently. It offers very good versions of six or seven of the *crus,* including a supple Brouilly Réserve du Château de Briante and the tasty Moulin-à-Vent Réserve du Domaine de Champ de Cour. The Château de Pierreux, which produces the firm's top-of-the-line wines, is an organically farmed property in Brouilly. Look for the robust Brouilly, and a particularly fine Réserve du Château.

Montagny

A small Côte Chalonnaise AC, for dry whites made from chardonnay. Potentially good value.

BEST RECENT VINTAGES: 2005, (2004), (2003), and 2002.
PRICES: $ to $$

PRODUCERS: DOM STÉPHANE ALADAME ↑ ◆ Dom Michel Andreotti: a respected local domaine with pleasant Montagny Premier Crus, including Les Guignottes ◆ BOUCHARD PÈRE & FILS ☆ ◆ La Buxynoise: the cave cooperative produces two cuvées of pungent Montagny Premier Cru, the oak-aged Fut de Chêne and the characterful Les Coères; there's also a Bourgogne Côte Chalonnaise rouge as fiery as salsa ◆ MAISON FAIVELEY ☆ ◆ Ch de la Guiche/André Goichot: mellow, succulent wines ◆ Jean Gagnerot: very good focused, mineral, svelte Montagny Premier Cru accented with lemon ◆ Dom Noël Perrin: pungent, pineapple- and citrus zest–accented Montagny Premier Cru Les Las, also fresh, vinous Bourgogne aligoté and Bourgogne blanc Clos de Chenoves, an appetizing wake-up call with flavors of preserved lemon and caramel.

Monthélie

A small Côte de Beaune AC for fragrant reds based on pinot noir and a small number of whites based on chardonnay. Potentially very good value.

BEST RECENT VINTAGES: 2005, (2004), (2003), and 2002.
PRICES: $$ to $$$

PRODUCERS: BOUCHARD PÈRE & FILS ☆ ◆ DOM COCHE-BIZOUARD ☆ ◆ JOSEPH DROUHIN ☆ ◆ Gilbert & Philippe Germain: light, pleasant reds at light, pleasant prices ◆ Ch de Monthélie: at this property Eric de Suremain (see RULLY) produces engaging, oomphy reds, particularly the structured, racy Premier Cru Sur la Velle ◆ DOM PIERRE MOREY ☆ ◆ DOM PARENT

Domaine Hubert de Montille ☆

21190 Volnay; 03.80.21.62.67; e-demontille@wanadoo.fr

Wines: Volnay, Pommard, Meursault, Beaune, Corton, and Puligny-Montrachet. $$$ to $$$$

One of the most colorful and articulate personalities of Burgundy, Hubert de Montille has long made some of its most poised, finely tuned, aristocratic reds. The torch having passed to his son Étienne, the quality of the wines remains irreproachable. Although everything is recommended, the domaine's most exciting reds are those from Volnay and Pommard. In Volnay, for example, there is the Premier Cru La Carelle sous la Chapelle, so ethereal yet resilient, it's like lace tatted from steel wire. The domaine's most iconic wine, the Premier Cru Taillepieds, is a regal, self-possessed beauty with a succulent, marrowy core. By contrast, the Pommard Pézerolles Premier Cru is fleshy and ample but equally pure, an exquisite, tender silk knit; and the pellucid Pommard Rougiens Premier Cru is simply grandiose, a fine distillate of cherries and rubies transformed into wine.

Étienne and his sister Alix have also created their own domaine, Maison Deux Montille, the first vintage of which was 2003. Whites account for 90 percent of production and their vinification falls to Alix, who does a stellar job, as evidenced by a layered, lipsmacking Puligny-Montrachet Premier Cru Le Champ-Gain, a racy, serious white Burgundy with a thrilling mineral and herbal tea core and an excellent, savory, chiseled Meursault Les Rougeots. And the de Montille holdings continue to grow. In July 2005 the family, along with the Seysses of Domaine Dujac, obtained 18 hectares of prime vineyard land—including an indecent percentage of Grand Crus—that once belonged to the the Domaine Clos de Thorey. The land will be divided between de Montille and Dujac.

Le Montrachet

A roughly 8-hectare Grand Cru split between Puligny and Chassagne-Montrachet, for what is, perhaps, the most famous white wine (chardonnay) in the world. Some 46,000 bottles are produced yearly. For vintages and prices see CHASSAGNE-MONTRACHET or PULIGNY-MONTRACHET. Producers: DOM JACQUES PRIEUR ☆ ◆ DOM DE LA ROMANÉE-CONTI ☆.

Alice & Olivier de Moor ↑

89800 Courgis; 03.86.41.47.94; alice.olivier-demoor@worldonline.fr

Wine: Chablis. $$

With pruning shears on the label there's a good chance that the wines from this young domaine are organic and maybe even hypernatural—which is more or less the case. Alice and Olivier de Moor, two enologists, farm organically, neither fine nor filter their wines, and use little or no sulfur. The wines aren't perfect but they're very promising, ultrapure, and anything but anonymous. The Chablis L'Humeur du Temps, designed to drink immediately, is bracing and thirst quenching. The barrel-fermented Bel Air wears its oak with dignity—the wine's as clear as a bell. The Rosette cuvée is vivid and pungent. The de Moors also make an old-vines aligoté and a St.-Bris that would be delightful to find in a wine bar.

Domaine Christian Moreau

89800 Chablis; 03.86.42.86.34; www.domainechristianmoreau.com

Wine: Chablis. $$ to $$$$

While most of the two-hundred-year old Moreau domaine was sold to MAISON JEAN-CLAUDE BOISSET, the current generation has been able to keep 12 hectares, much of that in Grand Cru and Premier Cru. Those are the wines to look for, particularly the racy bottlings from Les Clos, Blanchot, and Valmur. If I had a restaurant with three Michelin stars, I'd serve them by the glass.

Domaine Pierre Morey ☆

21190 Meursault; 03.80.21.21.03; morey-blanc@wanadoo.fr

Wines: Bourgogne, Aligoté, Meursault, and Monthélie. $$ to $$$$

In addition to running Domaine Leflaive, Pierre Morey makes his own wine on 9 hectares of vines, which he farms biodynamically. He makes a Bourgogne aligoté that's tart but much too good to mix with crème de cassis and a full-bodied, flavorful Bourgogne-Chardonnay. There are savory, long, appetizing white Meursaults, such as Les Tessons, that need a carafe and the pure, tannic Meursault Les Durots, an austere, young red presence, as well as a taut, pedigreed Monthélie rouge.

Morey-St.-Denis

A small AC in the Côte de Nuits primarily for potentially very fine reds made from pinot noir and a small amount of noteworthy white made from chardonnay. There are five Grand Crus: Clos St.-Denis, Clos de la Roche, Clos des Lambrays, Clos de Tart, and Bonnes-Mares. Among the numerous Premier Crus are Monts Luisants, Les Blanchards, Les Genevrières, and Aux Charmes.

BEST RECENT VINTAGES: 2005, 2004, 2003, 2002, 2001, 1999, and 1996.
PRICES: $$$ to $$$$

PRODUCERS: Dom Arlaud: meaty and spicy, with good fruit and balance, the Premier Cru Aux Cheseaux is worth trying ◆ DOM BRUNO CLAIR ☆ ◆ Maison Dufouleur Père & Fils: pleasant, reasonably priced Burgundies to drink young ◆ DOM DUJAC ☆ ◆ DOM DOMINIQUE LAURENT ☆ ◆ Dom des Monts Luisants: the Premier Crus Les Monts Luisants and Les Genevrières are fresh, racy and serious, and are well worth seeking out in every recent vintage ◆ DOM ROSSIGNOL-TRAPET ◆ DOM GEORGES ROUMIER.

Morgon

The most "virile" *cru* of Beaujolais, Morgon is potentially as distinguished as a Côte d'Or, particularly when vintners isolate the best *terroir,* as they have been doing on the Côte du Py. See BEAUJOLAIS for vintages and prices.

PRODUCERS: Guy Breton: richly fruity, silky, hypernatural Morgon; the Vieilles Vignes is particularly delicious and mineral ◆ Jean-Marc Burgaud: a very promising young producer whose wines from the Côte du Py and another privileged *climat,* Charmes, are suave, silky, concentrated, and just plain gorgeous, whether oaked or not; look, too, for Burgaud's Régnié and his Beaujolais Villages ↑ ◆ Dom Calot: the Calot brothers are reliable sources for seductive Morgon, particularly the Tradition, Cuvée Vieilles Vignes, and Tête de Cuvée ◆ Dom Chamonard: see FLEURIE ◆ Dom La Chaponne: tasty, often superb versions of the AC, especially the Côte du Py bottling ◆ Louis Claude Desvignes: two distinctive Côte du Py bottlings, the succulent generic version with its flavors of black cherry and blueberry, and the mineral, discreet Javenières ☆ ◆ DOM GEORGES DESCOMBES ◆ GEORGES DUBOEUF ◆ Dom Dubost: this energetic producer makes an excellent, barrel-aged Beaujolais Villages blanc, a downy Régnié Prieuré du Tracot, an admirable Brouilly Vieilles Vignes, and a silky, spicy Morgon Henri Dubost ◆ DOM JEAN FOILLARD ☆ ◆ DOM LOUIS JADOT ☆ ◆ MARCEL LAPIERRE ☆ ◆ Dom des Nugues: the Gelins produce several firm and seductive bottlings of Beaujolais Villages and an aromatic, tasty Morgon ◆ DOMINIQUE PIRON ◆ JP Thévenet: a fine producer in the hypernatural camp, Thévenet offers several cuvées of vibrant, pure, mineral Morgon, including a Vieilles Vignes that is fresh, complex, and just pure pleasure ☆ ◆ Dom du Tracot: see Dom Dubost above.

Olivier Morin

89530 Chitry; tel/fax: 03.86.41.47.20; morin.chitry@wanadoo.fr
Wine: Bourgogne-Chitry. $ to $$
The Bourgogne-Chitrys—red and white—from this ambitious little house take themselves quite seriously, and ambitious café owners might do well to use them as their house wines. The wines range from light, floral whites, to the focused, concentrated, oak-aged white Olympe, to the spicy, oak-aged red Vau du Puits.

Moulin-à-Vent

Potentially the most structured and elegant *cru* of Beaujolais. See BEAUJOLAIS for vintages and prices.

PRODUCERS: JEAN-PAUL BRUN ◆ Dom Desperrier: try the Clos de la Pierre, which comes from the sixty-year-old vines planted on a hillside *lieu-dit* entirely owned by the producer ◆ Dom Diochon: pleasant wine-bar wines, particularly the Vieilles Vignes ◆ Dom les Fines Graves: nice, compact Moulin-à-Vent ◆ Bernard Fumet: lovely, easy-drinking, eco-friendly versions of the AC ◆ Dom du Granit: characterful Moulin-à-Vent, especially the Vieilles Vignes, though all offer pretty fruit and an alluring streak of austerity ◆ DOM LOUIS JADOT ☆ ◆ HUBERT LAPIERRE ☆ ◆ MARCEL LAPIERRE ☆ ◆ Dom Lardy: see FLEURIE ◆ MOMMESSIN ◆ Dom des Terres

Dorées: see JEAN-PAUL BRUN ◆ Thorin: now owned by Boisset, Thorin produces a standard Beaujolais La Bareille, a decently structured Fleurie Terres de Granit Rosé, and a pleasant Moulin-à-Vent Terres de Silice ◆ DOM DU VISSOUX ☆

Domaine Jacques-Frédéric Mugnier

21220 Chambolle-Musigny; 03.80.62.85.39; info@mugnier.fr

Wine: Chambolle-Musigny. $$$ to $$$$

These refined, racy versions of Chambolle-Musigny include the Grand Crus Musigny and Bonnes-Mares. The Mugniers, owners of the Clos de la Maréchale, have reclaimed that prime parcel from MAISON FAIVELEY after its lease expired in 2003.

Domaine Henri Naudin-Ferrand ↑

21700 Nuits-St.-Georges; 03.80.62.91.50; dnaudin@ipac.fr

Wines: Côte de Nuits-Villages, Bougogne Hautes-Côtes de Beaune, and Hautes-Côtes de Nuits; Bourgogne aligoté. $ to $$$$

Claire Naudin, JEAN-YVES BIZOT's wife, runs this eco-serious, hypernatural-leaning domaine with an intelligence and skill evident immediately in a tangy Bourgogne aligoté. Her oak-aged Bourgogne Hautes-Côtes de Beaune is a straightforward pleasure, fresh, vinous, and nicely balanced. The Orchis Masculata bottling, an unsulfured red, is exotically scented with plush fruit, a delicious option for a swanky bistro. The red Bourgogne Hautes-Côtes de Nuits has vivid, succulent cherry fruit, a sure crowd-pleaser; and the Côte de Nuits-Village Vieilles Vignes is a serious red Burgundy at a very reasonable price.

Domaine André Nudant

21550 Ladoix-Serrigny; 03.80.26.40.48; domaine.nudant@wanadoo.fr

Wines: Ladoix, Aloxe-Corton, and Bourgogne Hautes-Côtes de Nuits. $$ to $$$

A good, eco-friendly domaine with numerous parcels spread out north of Beaune. The reds tend to be sinewy and steely, although the Aloxe-Corton Clos de la Boulotte, an exclusive, is warm and lipsmacking and both the Aloxe-Corton Premier Cru La Coutière and the Ladoix Premier Cru La Corvée show depth and an agreeable blending of fruit and oak.

Nuits-St.-Georges

An important Côte de Nuits AC centered around the small town of Nuits for important, structured reds made from pinot noir and a tiny amount of firm whites made from chardonnay. There are no Grand Crus but there are many Premier Crus, including Les Damodes, Les Murgers, and Aux Champs-Perdrix.

BEST RECENT VINTAGES: 2005, 2004, 2003, 2002, 2001, 1999, and 1996.
PRICES: $$$ to $$$$

PRODUCERS: DOM DE L'ARLOT ◆ DOM BERTAGNA ↑ ◆ DOM LUCIEN BOILLOT ☆ ◆ BOUCHARD PÈRE & FILS ☆ ◆ DOM DE CHASSORNEY ↑ ◆ DOM ROBERT CHEVILLON ◆ DOM CONFURON-COTETIDOT ☆ ◆ DOM RÉGIS DUBOIS & FILS ◆ DOM VINCENT DUREUIL-JANTHIAL ☆ ◆ MAISON FAIVELEY ☆ ◆ DOM GACHOT-MONOT ◆ Dom Maurice Garignet: irresistible, *terroir*-driven Nuits-St.-Georges Premier Cru Les Chaignots with mint and cherry accents; delightful, stylish Bourgogne Hautes-Côtes de Nuits Les Dames Huguette, a fresh, tasty red; and a chocolate- and kirsch-flavored Chambolle-Musigny Premier Cru Les Baudes ◆ Dom Anne-Marie Gille: there's sincere, good work here but the wines aren't perfect, except for the very delicious Premier Cru Les Cailles; a domaine worth following ◆ DOM HENRI GOUGES ☆ ◆ DOM JEAN GRIVOT ☆ ◆ DOM JAYER-GILLES ☆ ◆ DOM DOMINIQUE LAURENT ☆ ◆ Philippe and Vincent Lecheneaut: the wines aren't always perfect but there's purity, power, and specificity—all of which is very promising ◆ DOM LEROY ☆ ◆ Dom Chantal Lescure: a promising organic domaine; look for the juicy Premier Cru Les Vallerots ◆ MACHARD DE GRAMONT ☆ ◆ DOM MÉO-CAMUZET ◆ Dom des Perdrix: owned by Bertrand

Devillard, the director of RODET, this domaine produces dark, cool, focused, deep, and regal reds, including the Nuits-St.-Georges Premier Cru Aux Perdrix and the Grand Cru Échezeaux ☆ ◆ DOM JEAN PETITOT & FILS ↑ ◆ DOM PRIEURÉ-ROCH ☆ ◆ Dom Armelle & Bernard Rion: there's a lot to admire in this domaine's various Nuits-St.-Georges—particularly the Premier Crus Les Damodes and Les Murgers—but the wines still need work ◆ DOM DANIEL RION & FILS ◆ DOM ANTONIN RODET.

Domaine Oudin

89800 Chichée; 03.86.42.44.29; domaine.oudin@wanadoo.fr
Wine: Chablis. $$ to $$$
Ambitious, serious, *terroir*-driven Chablis. The generic Chablis Les Serres, from a rocky hillside, is focused, citrus-edged, and very mineral. The mouthfilling Premier Cru Vaucoupin is the most demanding—a steely, quinine-accented stream of fresh flavors. The steel- and lime-rich Premier Cru Vaugiraut makes me think of the greatest Sancerres of Chavignol. Abundantly acid, it's chiseled and nuanced, a real presence.

Philippe Pacalet ☆

21700 Nuits-St.-Georges; 03.80.62.31.05; fax: 03.80.61.34.69
Wines: Gevrey-Chambertin, Chambolle-Musigny, Pommard, St.-Aubin, and Chablis. $$ to $$$$
Energetic, to say the least, Philippe Pacalet makes very distinctive, organic, hypernatural wines from Chablis to St.-Aubin. If you like acidity, his 2004 barrel-fermented Chablis Premier Cru Beauroy is a must—exciting, rich, mineral, and fresh as a cascade. His St.-Aubin Premier Cru Les Murgers des Dents du Chien is even tarter but has plenty of minerals and lots of character. In reds, his Pommard is svelte, racy, and finely tuned—even in 2003. His Chambolle-Musigny is silky, pure, and succulent; and his Gevrey-Chambertin is bright and structured, with fine black cherry fruit and great finesse.

Domaine Parent

21360 Pommard; 03.80.22.15.08; parent.pommard@axnet.fr
Wines: Pommard, Corton, Monthélie, and Volnay. $$ to $$$$
The domaine makes some winsome wines in a number of the the Côte d'Or's major ACs—for example, a balanced, flavorful Corton Grand Cru blanc, a graceful Volnay Premier Cru Clos du Chênes, and a tasty Monthélie rouge. Their most impressive wines, however, are their reds from Pommard, particularly the nicely racy Premier Crus Les Chaponnières and Les Épenots.

Pernand-Vergelesses

A small Côte de Beaune AC several miles north of the city of Beaune, primarily for reds made from pinot noir although there is a small amount of white made from chardonnay. Sections of Grand Crus Corton and Corton-Charlemagne lie within its borders, and there are ten Premier Crus, the most famous being Île des Vergelesses.

BEST RECENT VINTAGES: 2005, (2004), (2003), and 2002.
PRICES: $$ to $$$($)

PRODUCERS: MAISON CHAMPY ◆ DOM DU CHÂTEAU DE CHOREY ◆ DOM BRUNO CLAIR ☆ ◆ DOM DOUDET-NAUDIN ◆ Dom Jean-Jacques Girard: look for the textured, elegant Premier Cru Les Belles Filles ◆ DOM LOUIS JADOT ☆ ◆ Dom Pavelot: the Premier Cru Sous Frétille is a fine, food-friendly white ◆ Dom Rapet Père & Fils: the Premier Cru Sous Frétille is a firm, lightly oaked white; the Île des Verglesses is a fragrant, focused, spicy red ◆ Dom Rollin Père & Fils: the Premier Cru Les Fichots is fragrant and sappy; the Sous Frétille is a ripe, floral white.

Domaine Jean Petitot & Fils ↑

21700 Corgolin; 03.80.62.98.21; domaine.petitot@wanadoo.fr
Wines: Nuits-St.-Georges, Côte de Beaune, and Côte de Nuits-Villages.
$$ to $$$
Hervé and his wife, Nathalie, an enologist, took over from Jean Petitot in 2002. I didn't know the domaine's wines before that time, but tasting the 2002s piqued my interest. This seems a domaine to follow. The wines aren't perfect but they have a lot to say. They impress me with their sincerity. Examples: the cool, minty Nuits-St.-Georges Les Poisets; the big, seductive and elegant Côte de Nuits-Villages Les Monts de Boncourt; and the dense, racy Côte de Nuits-Villages Les Vignottes Vieilles Vignes.

Domaine Fernand & Laurent Pillot ↑

21190 Chassagne-Montrachet; 03.80.21.99.83; fax: 03.80.21.92.60
Wines: Chassagne-Montrachet and Pommard. $$ to $$$($)
A domaine to follow—on the evidence of a limpid, racy Chassagne-Montrachet Premier Cru Vide Bourse and a fine, textured Premier Cru Morgeot as well as, in reds, a charming, spicy Pommard Premier Cru Les Charmots and an irresistibly delectable Rugiens.

Paul Pillot ↑

21190 Chassagne-Montrachet; 03.80.21.31.91; paul-pillot@wanadoo.fr
Wine: Chassagne-Montrachet. $$$
Chrystelle and her brother, Thierry, have succeeded their father, Paul, in running this extremely good family domaine, making many riveting variations on the theme of Chassagne-Montrachet. In whites, for example, there is the racy, preserved-lemon Premier Cru Cailleret and the powerful, elegant Premier Cru Les Grandes Ruchottes, which is as exhilarating as Champagne from Le Mesnil. The red Premier Cru Clos St.-Jean is so lipsmacking you can't stop drinking it.

Domaine Pinson Frères

89800 Chablis; 03.86.42.10.26; www.domaine-pinson.com
Wine: Chablis. $$ to $$$
A fine family domaine making fresh, generic Chablis and a range of very good Premier Cru—Montmains, La Forêt, Mont de Milieu—and Grand Cru Les Clos. The *cru* wines all receive some barrel age, generally discreet, except in a special cuvée of Les Clos called L'Authentique, which needs a couple of years to digest its oak. In general, the wines are racy and textured, with good depth and specificity.

Dominique Piron

69910 Villié-Morgon; 04.74.69.10.20; www.domaines-piron.fr
Wines: Beaujolais, Morgon, Moulin-à-Vent, and Chénas. $ to $$$
This sizable family domaine produces a broad range of the region's wines, from a silky, lipsmacking Beaujolais-Villages Les Vignes de Pierreux, to a focused and fresh Moulin-à-Vent Les Vignes du Vieux Bourg, to several noteworthy cuvées of Morgon, including the fine-grained Côte du Py and Grand Cras. In a partnership with Brouilly vintner Jean-Marc Lafont, Piron also produces Quartz, a vibrant, mineral Chénas.

Pommard

An important Côte de Beaune AC for firm, structured, and charming reds made from pinot noir. Among the numerous Premier Crus are Les Rugiens and Les Épenots.

BEST RECENT VINTAGES: 2005, (2004), (2003), 2002, 1999, and 1996.
PRICES: $$ to $$$$

PRODUCERS: MARQUIS D'ANGERVILLE ☆ ◆ BALLOT-MILLOT & FILS ◆ DOM JEAN-MARC BOILLOT ◆ JEAN-MARC BOULEY ◆ DOM COCHE-BIZOUARD ☆ ◆ CATHERINE & DOMINIQUE DERAIN ↑ ◆ DOM DE

LA GALOPIÉRE ◆ Dom Michel Gaunoux: lean but pedigreed Pommard, although the Premier Cru Grands Épenots has more flesh than the Premier Cru Rugiens ◆ DOM ALBERT GRIVAULT ☆ ◆ DOM LEJEUNE ◆ DOM LEROY ☆ ◆ Dom Chantal Lescure: pleasant, and improving, organic wines—look for the Premier Cru Les Bertins ◆ DOM CATHERINE & CLAUDE MARÉCHAL ◆ DOM MARÉCHAL-CAILLOT ◆ DOM MOISSENET-BONNARD ◆ DOM HUBERT DE MONTILLE ☆ ◆ Dom Muzard: try the discreet, racy, and fragrant Les Cras Vieilles Vignes; this is a domaine worth following ◆ PHILIPPE PACALET ☆ ◆ DOMAINE PARENT ◆ Dom François Parent: see DOM A. F. GROS ☆ ◆ DOM FERNAND & LAURENT PILLOT ↑ ◆ DOM DE LA POUSSE D'OR ↑ ◆ DOM ANTONIN RODET ◆ DOM CHRISTOPHE VIOLOT-GUILLEMARD.

Isabelle & Denis Pommier

89800 Chablis; 03.86.42.83.04; www.denis-pommier.com

Wine: Chablis. $$

Crowd-pleasing, ambitious, full-figured Chablis—even the Petit Chablis is pleasingly plump. The standard Chablis is fresh and specific. The Premier Cru Beauroy has agreeable traces of oak and lemon, while Premier Crus Côte de Lechet and Fourchaume place the accent on minerals, quinine, and citrus zests.

BURGUNDY

Pouilly-Fuissé, Pouilly-Loché, and Pouilly-Vinzelles

A relatively small AC southwest of Mâcon, Pouilly-Fuissé has a worldwide reputation for its full yet nervy whites made from chardonnay. The minuscule ACs Pouilly-Loché and Pouilly-Vinzelles are all but identical.

BEST RECENT VINTAGES: 2005, (2004), (2003), and 2002.
PRICES: $$ to $$$($)

PRODUCERS: J. PIERRE & MICHEL AUVIGUE ◆ Dom Daniel & Martine Barraud: a reliable house with several admirable, unfiltered bottlings, especially La Verchère, Les Crays, and En Buland ☆ ◆ BRET BROTHERS/LA SOUFRANDIÈRE ↑ ◆ DOM DE LA CHAPELLE ☆ ◆ Dom du Châlet Pouilly: structured, mineral, and appealing wines ◆ Dom Chataigneraie Laborier/Gilles Morat: La Roche and Belémnites, each eco-friendly and barrel fermented, are elegant, structured, lime-lemon-mineral Pouilly-Fuissés that I'd love to serve with delicately spiced exotic dishes ☆ ◆ Dom Alain Delaye: textbook, mouthfilling, tasty Pouilly-Loché ◆ MICHEL DELORME ◆ JOSEPH DROUHIN ☆ ◆ NADINE FERRAND ☆ ◆ Ch de Fuissé: the most famous property in the AC, this domaine produces a number of attractive barrel-fermented cuvées; look for the limpid Les Brûles and the layered Vieilles Vignes ◆ GUFFENS-HEYNEN ☆ ◆ DOM LOUIS JADOT ☆ ◆ DOM JEANDEAU ↑ ◆ DOM DE LALANDE ☆ ◆ DOM FABRICE LAROCHETTE ↑ ◆ MAISON LOUIS LATOUR ◆ MERLIN/DOMAINE DU VIEUX ST.-SORLIN ◆ Dom Romanin: although the wines need a bit of work, they're ambitious and worth following, particularly the unfiltered Vieilles Vignes bottling ◆ CH DES RONTETS ☆ ◆ DOM JACQUES & NATHALIE SAUMAIZE ☆ ◆ DOM SAUMAIZE-MICHELIN ☆ ◆ Dom Jean-Pierre Sève: there are three extremely fine cuvées of Pouilly-Fuissé—the expressive, fresh, and racy Terroir (the cheapest and my favorite), the ambitious, barrel-fermented Aux Chailloux, with its long finish and fine tropical fruit flavors, and the pedigreed, barrel-aged Sélection Vieilles Vignes, which ups the ante, as the most textured, layered, and lime-tinged of the three ☆ ◆ Dom Jacques Simonin: two cuvées of excellent Pouilly-Fuissé—the ample, invigorating and serious Vieilles Vignes and the fluid, pedigreed, oak-tinged Les Ammonites ☆ ◆ Dom La Soufrandière: see BRET BROTHERS ◆ Dom La Soufrandise: very good, ambitious producers of Mâcon-Fuissé and Pouilly-Fuissé, particularly the vivid, lime-accented Le Ronte Mâcon and the layered, intriguing, lightly exotic Pouilly ◆ CÉLINE & LAURENT TRIPOZ ☆ ◆ Frédéric Trouillet: the wines aren't perfect but Les Chailloux is specific and tasty, with its flavors of ripe tropical fruit ◆ Dom Valette: ambitious, handcrafted, risk-taking Mâcons and Pouillys, including a savory Viré-Clessé, a pungent, plump, and oaky Pouilly-Vinzelles, and a grapefruit-accented Pouilly-Fuissé ◆ Verget: see GUFFENS-HEYNEN ☆ ◆ DOM DES VIEILLES PIERRES ☆ ◆ Ch Vitalis: Denis Dutron's Pouilly-Fuissé Vieilles Vignes is sublime—perfumed, alluring, textured, fresh, mineral, and vibrant, and then some ☆.

Domaine de la Pousse d'Or ↑

21190 Volnay; 03.80.21.61.33; patrick@lapoussedor.fr

Wines: Corton, Pommard, Santenay, and Volnay. $$ to $$$$

Under the guidance of Patrick Landanger the domaine seems revitalized. Examples—all red—are a racy Corton Clos du Roi and a fine, ample thoroughbred, the Volnay Premier Cru En Caillerets.

Domaine Jacques Prieur ☆

21190 Meursault; 03.80.21.23.85; domainejprieur@wanadoo.fr

Wines: Beaune, Chambolle-Musigny Clos de Vougeot, Corton, Meursault, Puligny-Montrachet, and Volnay. $$$ to $$$$

The wines from this domaine, partly owned by RODET, make me swoon from pleasure, particularly the crystalline Pulignys, like the achingly elegant Premier Cru Les Combettes, a simply gorgeous, grandiose white. And the Meursaults are equally devastating—like the riveting Clos de Mazeray, a wonderful, mellow lemon and mineral presence. And then there's the patrician Beaune Premier Cru Champs-Pimont, a toothsome lemon-quinine-oak white. And the reds, such as the rich, focused Beaune Grèves Premier Cru, are every bit as regal and delicious.

Domaine Prieuré-Roch ☆

21700 Nuits-St.-Georges; 03.80.62.00.00; fax: 03.80.62.00.01

Wine: Nuits-St.-Georges. $$$ to $$$$

Owned by Henri Frédéric Roch, codirector (with Aubert de Villaine) of Domaine de la Romanée-Conti, this domaine makes wines with the same perfectionist philosophy. Their purity, majesty, and just plain deliciousness warrant their hefty price tags.

Puligny-Montrachet

An important AC, considered the center of gravity for Côte d'Or whites (chardonnay) of great finesse and complexity, although the AC also produces fine pinot noir–based reds. There are four Grand Crus: Le Montrachet, Bâtard-Montrachet, Bienvenues-Bâtard-Montrachet, and Chevalier-Montrachet. There are numerous Premier Crus, for reds as well as whites, among them Les Folatières, Clavoillon, Hameau de Blagny, and Les Pucelles.

BEST RECENT VINTAGES: 2005, (2004), (2003), and 2002.
PRICES: $$$ to $$$$

PRODUCERS: Dom d'Auvenay: see DOM LEROY ☆ ◆ Philippe Brenot: see CHASSAGNE-MONTRACHET ↑ ◆ DOM JEAN-MARC BOILLOT ◆ BOUCHARD PÈRE & FILS ☆ ◆ THIERRY GUYOT ◆ DOM LOUIS JADOT ☆ ◆ SYLVAIN LANGOUREAU ◆ DOM LEFLAIVE ☆ ◆ Maison Deux Montille: see DOM HUBERT DE MONTILLE ☆ ◆ DOM JACQUES PRIEUR ☆ ◆ Ch de Puligny: owned by the Crédit Foncier–Caisse d'Épargne, a savings and loan institution, management of the domaine has been put in the able hands of Étienne de Montille, who turns out some very appealing St.-Aubins (both red and white) and a handful of elegant white Pulignys, including a complex, ample, beautifully balanced Premier Cru Le Cailleret ◆ DOM ANTONIN RODET.

Domaine Raveneau ☆

89800 Chablis; 03.86.42.17.46; fax:03.86.42.45.55

Wine: Chablis. $$$ to $$$$

Exquisite, legend-in-its-own-time Chablis. The Raveneaus have only 7.5 hectares, but all their vines are Premier Cru (for example Montée de Tonnerre, La Forêt) or Grand Cru (Valmur, Les Clos). The forty thousand bottles they produce each year sell out immediately. Get what you can, although I have a very slight preference for Valmur. Neither oak, nor heat waves, nor rain can diminish the purity, majesty, and profundity of these wines.

Régnié

A *cru* of Beaujolais located between Morgon and Brouilly, its wines are characterized by cameo-like precision. See BEAUJOLAIS for vintages and prices. Producers: Dom de Bel Air: limpid, discreet Régnié and lovely, supple Brouilly ◆ Dom Dubost: see MORGON ◆ Dom Burnot-Latour: Christian Chambon makes pure, clear, serious Régnié with distinct pinot noir–like flavors.

Richebourg

An 8-hectare Grand Cru in Vosne-Romanée (in the Côte de Nuits), Richebourg is known for potentially exquisite, nuanced reds made from pinot noir. Roughly forty thousand bottles are produced yearly. For vintages and prices see VOSNE-ROMANÉE. Producers: DOM A. F. GROS ☆ ◆ DOM LEROY ☆ ◆ DOM DE LA ROMANÉE-CONTI ☆.

Domaine Daniel Rion & Fils

21700 Prémeaux-Prissey; 03.80.62.31.28; www.domaine-daniel-rion.com
Wines: Vosne-Romanée, Chambolle-Musigny, and Nuits-St.-Georges.
$$$ to $$$$
A serious family domaine. The viticulture is organic and the Rions seem willing to take risks to maximize the purity of their wines and to emphasize the *terroir*. The wines aren't always perfect, but they are never anonymous and are always worth your attention. Recent favorites among the reds—all 2002s—have included the specific Nuits-St.-Georges and the dense, textured Premier Cru Les Pruliers; as well as a racy, juicy, fresh Vosne-Romanée Premier Cru les Beaux Monts and another Premier Cru Les Chaumes that was clear, elegant, concentrated, and inviting.

Domaine Antonin Rodet

71640 Mercurey; 03.85.98.12.12; rodet@rodet.com
Wines: Meursault, Bourgogne Hautes-Côtes de Beaune, Nuits-St.-Georges, Mercurey, Puligny-Montrachet, and Pommard. $$ to $$$$
An important grower-*négociant* with a number of quality labels, including the Château de Chamirey and the Château de Mercey in Mercurey, as well as part ownership of the excellent house Jacques Prieur. The finest wines under Rodet's own label are those in the Cave Privée line, among them a lime-oak-mineral Meursault Premier Cru Perrières; a toasty, textured, pedigreed Puligny-Montrachet Premier Cru Hameau de Blagny; and, in reds, a vibrant Pommard Premier Cru Clos Blanc and a suave, racy Nuits-St.-Georges Premier Cru Les Porrets.

La Romanée

Only .85 of a hectare, La Romanée is a Grand Cru in Vosne-Romanée (the Côte de Nuits) for potentially sublime, complex reds made from pinot noir. Roughly five thousand bottles are produced yearly. For prices and vintages, see VOSNE-ROMANÉE.

Romanée-Conti

A 1.81-hectare Grand Cru in Vosne-Romanée (Côte de Nuits), for potentially awe-inspiring reds from pinot noir. Slightly more than seven thousand bottles are produced yearly. For prices and vintages, see VOSNE-ROMANÉE and DOM DE LA ROMANÉE-CONTI ☆.

Domaine de la Romanée-Conti ☆

21700 Vosne-Romanée; 03.80.62.48.80; fax: 03.80.61.05.72
Wines: Échezeaux, Grands Échezeaux, Montrachet, Richebourg, Romanée-Conti, Romanée-St.-Vivant, and La Tâche. $$$$
Deservedly the most prestigious label in the world, DRC (the common abbreviation) merits every accolade it receives. A bottle of wine that costs

more than my monthly mortgage payment is not something I'm likely to buy very often, if at all. Nevertheless, such is the importance of these wines that, for a wine lover, tasting at least one of them should be on the list of "Fifty Things to Do Before You Die." Price, particularly for the very rare Romanée-Conti, is based partly on simple lack of product: though DRC owns all of this Grand Cru vineyard, Romanée-Conti is less than 2 hectares in size. Given the low yields practiced by the domaine, this means that roughly five thousand bottles are made a year. But tasting it, or one of its siblings, is such an education in the infinite possibilities of pinot noir grown on *terroir* spectacularly adapted to coax out the maximum that earth and grape have to offer, that a wine lover really ought to try to find a sit-down tasting in which one or several of these treasures will be poured. Run by Aubert de Villaine and Henri-Frédéric Roch, DRC makes wines that are organic and that are based on exceedingly low yields and gazillions of details at each step of the grape growing and winemaking process. There is a hierarchy—although, to me, it's all a bit like asking how many angels can dance on the head of a pin—and here it is, in ascending order: Échezeaux, Grands Échezeaux, Richebourg, La Tâche, Romanée St.-Vivant, and Romanée-Conti. DRC also produces a small amount of Le Montrachet. It is exquisite. But if you can try only one DRC wine, let it be red.

Romanée St.-Vivant

An 8.7-hectare Grand Cru in Vosne-Romanée (Côte de Nuits) for potentially extraordinary reds made from pinot noir. For prices and vintages, see VOSNE-ROMANÉE: Producers: DOM LEROY ☆ ◆ DOM DE LA ROMANÉE-CONTI ☆.

Château des Rontets ☆

71960 Fuissé; 03.85.32.90.18; chateaurontets@compuserve.com

Wine: Pouilly-Fuissé. $$ to $$$

Former architects Claire and Fabio Gazeau-Montrasi run an ambitious domaine adhering to organic principles. Fortunate in their holdings, which include a high proportion of old vines, they produce three finely tuned cuvées, using wild yeasts and barrel fermentation. The "simplest" cuvée is Clos Varambon, a rich, tasty wine made from more than sixty-year-old vines. Next comes the unfiltered Pierrefolle. Vinified in newer barrels, it's creamy and savory and has the stuffing to support the oak. Les Birbettes, from vines planted in 1920, vinified in yet newer barrels, is also bottled unfiltered. Fresh and structured, it is the most aristocratic of the three. A ringer for a blue-chip AC in the Côte d'Or.

Domaine Rossignol-Trapet

21220 Gevrey-Chambertin; 03.80.51.87.26; info@rossignol-trapet.com

Wines: Gevrey-Chambertin, Beaune, and Morey-St.-Denis. $$ to $$$$

This youngish family domaine offers a fine array of harmonious, specific red Burgundies, from a pure, concentrated Beaune Les Mariages; to a structured, detailed, and regal Beaune Premier Cru Les Teurons; to a Morey-St.-Denis En la Rue de Vergy that you simply want to dive into; to a nuanced, limpid Gevrey-Chambertin Premier Cru Petite Chapelle.

Domaine Roulot ☆

21190 Meursault; 03.80.21.21.65; fax:03.80.21.64.36

Wines: Meursault and Bourgogne. $$$ to $$$$

Exquisite, chiseled Meursaults that range from an appetizing, lightly salty, and beautifully poised Les Luchets to a profound, monumental Premier Cru Charmes that borders on the viscous but balances its richness with the fresh, invigorating flavors of minerals, quinine, and lime. The plain Bourgogne blanc is better than top Meursaults from most other producers. Superbly textured, exciting, and mineral, it's a de facto Premier Cru.

Domaine Georges Roumier
21220 Chambolle-Musigny; 03.80.62.86.37; www.roumier.com
Wines: Chambolle-Musigny, Morey-St.-Denis, and Bonnes-Mares. $$$ to $$$$
Well represented on Michelin-starred wine lists, the classically made Burgundies from this domaine are structured, serious, and racy. Two favorites: the fleshy, specific Chambolle-Musigny Premier Cru Les Cras and the focused, meaty Morey-St.-Denis Premier Cru Clos de la Bussière.

Domaine Armand Rousseau ☆
21220 Gevrey-Chambertin; 03.80.34.30.55; www.domaine-rousseau.com
Wine: Gevrey-Chambertin. $$$ to $$$$
The current generation of Rousseau seems every bit as able as its predecessors to turn out discreet, finely tuned, aristocratic Gevreys that, at first blush, seem soft-spoken but carry mighty big *terroir*-talking sticks. Two examples from 2003—the subtly but seductively fragrant Premier Cru Clos St.-Jacques, quintessentially Burgundy, and the deep, secretive Chambertin.

Rully

A small AC about ten miles southwest of Beaune, at the southern tip of the Côte d'Or. Rully, the gateway to the Côte Chalonnaise, applies to whites and reds from chardonnay and pinot noir. As land is more affordable here than it is in the Côte d'Or, dynamic young vignerons are making this an exciting AC and a great place to find value for the dollar.

BEST RECENT VINTAGES: 2005, (2004), (2003), and 2002.
PRICES: $$

PRODUCERS: FRANÇOIS D'ALLAINES ↑ ◆ Dom Michel Briday: several admirable cuvées of white Rully, including a big and tasty Premier Cru La Pucelle and a plump, mineral Premier Cru Grésigny; there's also an appealing Mercurey Premier Cru Clos Marcilly ◆ DOM LES CHAMPS DE L'ABBAYE ↑ ◆ Anne-Sophie Debavelaere/Clos du Moulin-à-Vent: a promising vigneronne whose Rullys and Bouzerons show potential but aren't ready for prime time ◆ JOSEPH DROUHIN ☆ ◆ DOM VINCENT DUREUIL-JANTHIAL ☆ ◆ MAISON FAIVELEY ☆ ◆ P-M Ninot/Cellier Meix Guillaume: Pierre-Marie Ninot and his daughter Erell, who earned a degree in viticulture in Beaune and who joined her father in 2003, produce several tasty cuvées of Rully including a textured Premier Cru Grésigny (blanc) and a truly delectable Les Chaponnières (rouge) to drink "on the fruit" ◆ Eric de Suremain: pleasant Rully Premier Crus, both red and white, though Suremain makes more beguiling wines at the Ch de Monthélie ◆ DOM A. & P. DE VILLAINE ☆.

St.-Amour

The northernmost *cru* of Beaujolais, the wines of St.-Amour are characterized by their gracefulness and aromas of kirsch. See BEAUJOLAIS for vintages and prices.

PRODUCERS: Dom de l'Ancien Relais: very good family domaine with two alluring cuvées: Tradition is pretty, vibrant and succulent; Vieilles Vignes is more elegant and serious but equally delicious. They also produce Juliénas, Fleurie, and Beaujolais ☆ ◆ Dom de la Cave Lamartine: Paul Spay, the mayor of St.-Amour, makes a mellow, supple version of the AC from the *lieu-dit* Vers l'Église ◆ GEORGES DUBOEUF ◆ Christophe Terrier: floral, pinot-noir-like versions of the AC, especially Cuvée Angélique ◆ LOUIS TÊTE.

St.-Aubin

A small Côte de Beaune AC near Chassagne, Puligny, Meursault, and Blagny for good reds from pinot noir and even better whites from chardonnay. Among its

Premiers Crus are La Châtenière, Murgers des Dents de Chien, Les Castets, En Remilly, Les Cortons, and Les Frionnes.

BEST RECENT VINTAGES: 2005, (2004), (2003), and 2002.
PRICES: $$ to $$$$

PRODUCERS: FRANÇOIS D'ALLAINES ↑ ◆ Marc Colin: fresh, structured Premier Cru La Châtenière, perfect for a good bistro meal ◆ Michel Colin-Deléger & Fils: see CHASSAGNE-MONTRACHET ◆ Jean-Claude Fornerot: look for the white Premier Crus La Châtenière and Murgers des Dents de Chien ◆ MAISON ALEX GAMBAL ☆ ◆ DOM HUBERT LAMY ◆ SYLVAIN LANGOUREAU ◆ PHILIPPE PACALET ☆ ◆ PAUL PILLOT ↑ ◆ Ch de Puligny-Montrachet: see PULIGNY-MONTRACHET and DOM HUBERT DE MONTILLE ☆.

St.-Bris

A minuscule Auxerrois AC for brisk whites made from sauvignon blanc. (Sauvignon rosé—or fié gris is also used.)

BEST RECENT VINTAGES: 2005 and 2004.
PRICES: $ to $$

PRODUCERS: Dom Bersan & Fils: the partially barrel-aged Cuvée Louis Bersan is bracing and pungent with appetizing mineral undertones ◆ Dom Jean-Michel Daulne: a wake-up call of a sauvignon ◆ Jocelyne & Philippe Defrance: an exciting, *terroir*-driven sauvignon, limpid, elegant, and just plain excellent ☆ ◆ Dom Félix: look for the focused, ripe Cuvée Ste.-Claire ◆ GHISLAINE & JEAN-HUGUES GOISOT ☆ Dom Grand Roche: see IRANCY ◆ DOM VERRET.

Domaine Sainte-Barbe ☆

71260 Viré; 03.85.33.96.72; www.domaines-chaland.com
Wines: Mâcon and Viré-Clessé. $$
Jean-Marie Chaland's biodynamic Mâcons include a must-taste Viré-Clessé En Thurissey. Made from century-old vines, the wine approaches top Côte d'Or ACs in structure, richness, and complexity—superb. While not as mind-blowing, the Viré-Clessé L'Épinet and the Mâcon-Villages Les Tilles are rich, creamy, fresh, and tight. Delicious.

St.-Romain

A small Côte de Beaune AC, for firm whites based on chardonnay and supple reds based on pinot noir.

BEST RECENT VINTAGES: 2005, (2004), (2003), and 2002.
PRICES: $$ to $$$

PRODUCERS: CHRISTOPHE BUISSON ↑ ◆ Dom Henri & Gilles Buisson: delectable, mineral St.-Romain blanc Sous la Velle; delicate but persistent St.-Romain rouge Sous Roche—for drinkers more interested in charm than power ◆ DOM DE CHASSORNEY ↑ ◆ EMMANUEL GIBOULOT ↑ ◆ THIERRY GUYOT ◆ DOM CHRISTOPHE VIOLOT-GUILLEMARD.

St.-Véran

A small AC at the southern tip of the Mâconnais, for fresh, dry whites from chardonnay.

BEST RECENT VINTAGES: 2005, (2004), (2003), and 2002.
PRICES: $ to $$$

PRODUCERS: J. PIERRE & MICHEL AUVIGUE ◆ Barraud: see POUILLY-FUISSÉ ◆ JOSEPH DROUHIN ☆ ◆ NADINE FERRAND ☆ ◆ Dom de la Feuillarde: taut, textured, appetizing Vieilles Vignes ◆ DOM LOUIS JADOT ☆ ◆ DOM FABRICE LAROCHETTE ↑ ◆ MERLIN ◆ Rijckaert: see MÂCON ☆ ◆ DOM JACQUES & NATHALIE SAUMAIZE ☆ ◆ DOM SAUMAIZE-MICHELIN ☆ ◆ Dom Thomas: look for the fresh, citrus-accented, barrel-aged Prestige bottling, a good food wine ◆ Verget: see GUFFENS-HEYNEN ☆.

Santenay

An AC south of Chassagne-Montrachet in the Côte de Beaune, primarily for solid reds from pinot noir. It also produces a small amount of agreeable whites made from chardonnay. Its Premier Crus include La Maladière and Les Gravières.

BEST RECENT VINTAGES: 2005, (2004), (2003), and 2002.
PRICES: $$ to $$$

PRODUCERS: YVAN AND CHANTAL CONTAT-GRANGE ◆ RENÉ LEQUIN-COLIN ◆ Dom Mestre Père & Fils: a clutch of tasty wines, including an oak-aged white Champs Claude and, from red Premier Crus, a velvety Les Gravières-Clos de Tavannes, a distinctive, racy Maladière, and a lean but pedigreed Gravières ◆ Dom Lucien Muzard & Fils: the Premier Cru Maladière is tasty, admirable, and easy-drinking ◆ DOM DE LA POUSSE D'OR ↑ ◆ Dom Prieur-Brunet: a very good domaine with lovely, food-friendly Burgundies, including a structured white Chassagne-Montrachet Premier Cru Les Embazées, several stylish reds from Santenay including a very pretty Premier Cru Santenots, as well as a very admirable Beaune Premier Cru Clos du Roy ◆ Roux Père & Fils: satisfying, lunchtime Premier Cru Beauregard with attractive mineral and oak notes ◆ DOM ANNE-MARIE & JEAN-MARC VINCENT.

BURGUNDY

Domaine Michel Sarrazin ☆

71640 Jambles; 03.85.44.30.57; sarrazin2@wanadoo.fr
Wines: Givry, Maranges, and Bourgogne. $ to $$
Excellent wines, superb values. Sarrazin's red Givrys are so delicious, so succulent, they're almost impossible to resist. The nose of the Premier Cru Les Vieilles Vignes is so appealing you want to dive into the glass. On the palate, the wine is spicy and warmly fruity, with depth and lipsmacking savor. Toasty oak dominates the racy Premier Cru Les Grands Prétants but seductive flavors of black cherry and cherry pits suggest that a bit of age will resolve everything. The Givry blanc Les Grognots is layered, alcoholic, and oaky and the lean, tart Bourgogne Côte Chalonnaise Les Gorgères rouge has real wine-bar appeal.

Domaine Jacques & Nathalie Saumaize ☆

71960 Vergisson; 03.85.35.82.14; nathalie.saumaize@wanadoo.fr
Wines: Mâcon, Pouilly-Fuissé, and St.-Véran. $$
You'll find succulent, mineral wines from all three ACs, including a lemon- and herbal tea–flavored Mâcon Buissières; two lovely, textured, mountain-streamish St.-Vérans, En Crèches and Poncetys; and two mellow, classic Pouilly-Fuissés, Les Vieilles Vignes and Courtelong.

Domaine Saumaize-Michelin ☆

71960 Vergisson; 03.85.35.84.05; saumaize-michelin@wanadoo.fr
Wines: St.-Véran and Pouilly-Fuissé. $$
Roger and Christine Saumaize run their small domaine according to strict organic principles. Fermentation takes place in barrels, and there is little or no filtration. There are two cuvées of St.-Véran: Les Crèches is mineral and

textured; Vieilles Vignes is similar but more so. Vigne Blanche is the simplest of the four cuvées of Pouilly-Fuissé. It's tender, textured, and lovely. Clos sur la Roche, from a parcel with seventy-year-old vines, is deeper, mineral, and satisfying. The extremely pure Les Ronchevats comes from a very chalky parcel. It's ample and layered, a waterfall of a wine. Ampelopsis, a late harvest of very old vines from various parcels, fermented in new or nearly new oak, is potent and authoritative. It needs several years from the harvest to digest its oak, but it's a ringer for a good Côte d'Or.

Francine & Olivier Savary ☆

89800 Maligny; 03.86.47.42.09; f.o.savary@wanadoo.fr

Wine: Chablis. $$

A very good family domaine making forceful, serious Chablis. The Sélection Vieilles Vignes is fresh, steely, and profound. The discreet Premier Cru Fourchaume is a luscious blend of preserved lemon, peach, and blossoms. The Savarys also make a red wine, a pinot noir, under the AC Bourgogne Épineul.

Savigny-lès-Beaune

An important AC in the Côte de Beaune and just outside the town of Beaune for medium-bodied, alluring reds based on pinot noir and good whites made from chardonnay. Its Premiers Crus include Les Peuillets, Clos des Guettes, and Les Lavières.

BEST RECENT VINTAGES: 2005, (2004), (2003), and 2002.
PRICES: $$ to $$$

PRODUCERS: DOM SIMON BIZE ☆ ◆ Bouchard Ainé: see MAISON JEAN-CLAUDE BOISSET ◆ CHRISTOPHE BUISSON ↑ ◆ MAISON CHAMPY ◆ DOM BRUNO CLAIR ☆ ◆ DOM DOUDET-NAUDIN ◆ DOM RÉGIS DUBOIS & FILS ◆ DOM DE LA GALOPIÈRE ◆ Jean Michel Giboulot: I prefer the reds to the whites, particularly the cool Aux Grands Liards with its pretty cherry and cherry-pit fruit, and the succulent and stylish Premier Cru Aux Serpentières, which was yummy and had a real sense of place ◆ Dom Philippe Girard: look for the lean but elegant Premier Crus Les Lavières Vieilles Vignes and the pedigreed Les Peuillets Vieilles Vignes, which would be lovely paired with wild mushrooms ◆ DOM A. F. GROS ☆ ◆ Dom Pierre Guillemot: a zaftig, rough-hewn white with a real presence and three Premier Cru reds, all tasty—Les Grands Picotins, Serpentières, and Les Jarrons; also an ambitious little Bourgogne Pinot Noir ◆ Dom Pierre Labet: see CH DE LA TOUR ☆ ◆ DOM LEROY ☆ ◆ DOM CATHERINE & CLAUDE MARÉCHAL ◆ DOM MARÉCHAL-CAILLOT ◆ MACHARD DE GRAMONT ☆ ◆ DOM TOLLOT-BEAUT ☆.

Domaine Servin

BP 8, 89800 Chablis; 03.86.18.90.00; www.domaine-servin.fr

Wine: Chablis. $$ to $$$

A venerable family domaine with significant holdings in Premier Cru and Grand Cru vineyards. The wines are sometimes a bit rustic and slightly oxidized, but they're always pure, mellow, and sincere. A must taste is the Chablis Cuvée Massale made from the low-yielding, old vines from a single vineyard. What it lacks in elegance it makes up in character and flavor. Ditto for the racy, lime-tinged Premier Crus Vaillons, Les Fôrets, and Montée de Tonnerre. The Grand Crus Blanchot, Les Preuses, Bougros, and Les Clos all need time—or a carafe—to reveal the singularity that you perceive as through a glass darkly with a bottle less than five years old when it's freshly opened.

La Tâche

A nearly 6-hectare Grand Cru in Vosne-Romanée (Côte de Nuits) for potentially stunning reds made from pinot noir. Roughly 23,600 bottles are produced yearly. For prices and vintages, see VOSNE-ROMANÉE. Producer: DOM DE LA ROMANÉE-CONTI ☆.

Domaine des Terres Vivantes ☆

69460 Blace; 04.74.60.52.13; marie-ludovic.gros@wanadoo.fr

Wine: Beaujolais Villages. $

Ludovic Gros, the enologue for the Beaujolais Interprofessional Committee, makes two excellent cuvées of eco-serious Beaujolais on his vineyards. Both are delectable but the Vieilles Vignes, made from low-yielding seventy-five-year-old vines, harvested by three passes through the vineyard (to get grapes with the optimum ripeness), is particularly inviting and beautifully balanced, with exotic fruit flavors.

Louis Tête

69430 St-Didier-sur-Beaujeu; 04.74.04.82.27; louis.tete@gofornet.com

Wines: Beaujolais, Chiroubles, Moulin-à-Vent, and Juliénas. $ to $$

A solid, sizable producer of a full range of Beaujolais. Highlights include a fresh and reliable Chiroubles Cuvée Melinand and a discreet, balanced Juliénas Cuvée Tradition.

Domaine Tollot-Beaut ☆

21200 Chorey-lès-Beaune; 03.80.22.16.54; tollot.beaut@wanadoo.fr

Wines: Chorey-lès-Beaune, Corton, and Aloxe-Corton. $$ to $$$$

A classic house—in the best sense of the word—with a red Chorey-lès-Beaune that melts in the mouth, its jewel-like fruit blending with oak. The Aloxe-Corton Premier Cru Les Fournières is a fragrant, deep but feminine red, with a regal streak of austerity. The Corton-Bressandes Grand Cru has everything you want in a great red Burgundy.

Château de la Tour ☆

21640 Vougeot; 03.80.62.86.13; www.chateaudelatour.com

Wines: Clos de Vougeot, Beaune, and Savigny-lès-Beaune. $$$ to $$$$

Run by François Labet, this domaine, with 6 hectares, is the largest proprietor in the Clos de Vougeot. Farmed organically, its wines are bottled unfined and unfiltered. The silky cuvée Vieilles Vignes, from vines planted in 1910, is deep, juicy, and majestic. Labet also runs the Domaine Pierre Labet, the wines of which are also bottled unfined and unfiltered. There's an attractive array of Beaune ACs, including a fresh, tight white from the Clos du Dessus des Marconnets, a layered, textured red from the same vineyard, and a gentle Premier Cru Coucherais, a nicely nuanced red.

Domaine Trapet ↑

21220 Gevrey-Chambertin; 03.80.34.30.40; message@domaine-trapet.com

Wines: Gevrey-Chambertin and Marsannay. $$ to $$$$

Jean-Louis, the current generation of Trapet, has changed the direction of the domaine, converting the viticulture to biodynamics and, relying on hypernatural methods, aiming for pure, *terroir*-driven wines. There are risks involved in working this way and, at times, the wines reveal minor flaws, but they are always honest and noteworthy. The Premier Crus and Grand Crus fare the best, with a taut, riveting Clos Prieur; a fragrant, silky Latricières; and a velvety, racy Chambertin that caresses the palate.

Céline & Laurent Tripoz ☆

71000 Loché; tel/fax: 03.85.35.66.09; cltripoz@free.fr

Wines: Mâcon-Vinzelle, Pouilly-Loché, Crémant de Bourgogne, and Bourgogne. $$

Future wine stars here. Céline and Laurent Tripoz, who farm biodynamically, created their entire domaine. They make a number of different Crémant de Bourgognes, including a fresh, mineral, nondosed version that was the best I've ever tasted from that AC. Their Bourgogne rouge Chante de la Tour is so lipsmacking you could polish off a bottle without realizing it. Their Pouilly-Loché is elegant and crystalline—even in 2003; their structured, pure Mâcon-Vinzelles Les Morandes is like a mouthful of waterfall. And their Mâcon-Loché Les Chênes reiterates the waterfall freshness along with a light accent of oak.

Domaine Tupinier Bautista ↑
71640 Mercurey; 03.85.45.26.38; fax: 03.85.45.27.99
Wine: Mercurey. $$ to $$$
An up-and-coming star? Looks that way, from the high quality of the Mercurey Vieilles Vignes—the white is supple and mineral, the red is full of personality—and the even finer Premier Cru En Sazenay, a svelte, apple-and-oak white and the fresh, dark, classy red, which is delightful and specific.

Domaine Verret
BP 4, 89530 St.-Bris-le-Vineux; 03.86.53.89.61; www.domaineverret.com
Wines: St.-Bris, Irancy, and Bourgogne Côtes d'Auxerre. $ to $$
Paris wine baristas looking for engaging, flavorul country wines would do well to visit this Auxerrois domaine. The St.-Bris is a decisive, grapefruit- and lemon-accented sauvignon blanc. The rare grape césar adds a rugged note to the fragrant and characterful Irancy L'Âme du Domaine. As for the chardonnay and pinot noir, both AC Côtes d'Auxerre, they are well made, nicely balanced, and perfect for a light lunch.

Domaine des Vieilles Pierres ☆
71960 Vergisson; 03.85.35.85.69; fax: 03.85.35.86.26
Wine: Pouilly-Fuissé. $$
Jean-Jacques Litaud produces two cuvées of excellent Pouilly-Fuissé: the richly fruity, layered, nearly viscous, lightly oaked Les Crays Vieilles Vignes from a well-known *lieu-dit* and the tight, racy, and complex La Roche Vieilles Vignes.

Domaine du Vieux Collège
21160 Marsannay la Côte: 03.80.52.12.43; fax: 03.80.52.95.85
Wines: Marsannay, Gevrey-Chambertin, and Fixin. $$ to $$$($)
This domaine produces fresh, fragrant whites in both Fixin and Marsannay (particularly Les Vignes Mariés). Its focused red, perfect for special lunches, comes from the same ACs. In Fixin, look for the fine, lipsmacking Premier Cru Les Hervelets and the mouthwatering Les Champs de Charmes; in Marsannay, look for the lightly oaky, alluring Les Favières. The perfumed, textured Gevrey-Chambertin Premier Cru Les Champeaux is a step up and needs to age about three years longer than its stablemates.

Domaines des Vignes du Mayne
71260 Cruzille; 03.85.33.20.15; www.vignes-du-maynes.com
Wine: Mâcon-Cruzille. $$
Alain and Julien Guillot make a range of beguiling Mâcon-Cruzille, including an extremely ripe, rich, pear-scented Les Dardelles, made from vines planted in 1929; an elegant, rich, and chalky Aragonite; and a dense gamay-based red Manganite.

Domaine A. & P. de Villaine ☆
71150 Bouzeron; 03.85.91.20.50; www.de-villaine.com
Wines: Rully, Mercurey, Bourgogne, and Bouzeron. $$ to $$$
Aubert de Villaine runs this modest (everything's relative) domaine just as he does the Domaine de la Romanée-Conti. Viticulture is organic and winemaking as noninterventionist as possible. His Bouzeron is about as rich, mineral, and creamy as the aligoté grape ever gets. It's much too good for a Kir. The textured Bourgogne Côte Chalonnaise Les Clous reaches much higher than its AC—it could rival many whites from the Côte d'Or. And the complex Rully Les St.-Jacques is a focused white with a core of lime, minerals, stone, and quinine. Reds are bottled unfiltered. The Bourgogne Côte Chalonnaise rouge La Digoine is mineral, juicy, and pretty serious—in both 2002 and 2003. It's also a masterly example of what appears to be the hypernatural style. Not so the very ripe 2003 Mercurey Les Montots, which to me seemed uncomfortably gamey and prickly. So, if risks attach even to the wines of someone as meticulous and experienced as Aubert de Villaine, there are only two virtues I'd counsel—patience and tolerance.

Domaine Anne-Marie & Jean-Marc Vincent

21590 Santenay; 03.80.20.67.37; vincent.j-m@wanadoo.fr
Wines: Santenay and Auxey-Duresses. $$ to $$$
A good eco-serious family domaine with food-friendly Auxey-Duresses (particularly the bracing white Les Hautes) and both red and white Santenay, particularly the toasty, nicely balanced Les Gravières and the firm but delicate Premier Cru Beaurepaire.

Vin de Pays

Most of the Vin de Pays in Burgundy takes the name of the department in which it's made, for example Vin de Pays de Saône & Loire—in which I happen to have one good address, DOM DES FOSSILES. Drink the youngest available. Prices: $.

Domaine Christophe Violot-Guillemard

21630 Pommard; 03.80.22.49.98; thviolot@wanadoo.fr
Wines: Pommard, St.-Romain, and Beaune. $$$
My hunch is that the wines here are hypernatural—low yields, organic farming, natural yeasts, low (or no) sulfur. In any event, they—and their appealingly unusual labels—seem geared for the type of wine bar that specializes in the genre. And they're good examples. The St.-Romain blanc Clos des Ducs, for example, is ripe, ample, and ambitious. The Pommard La Vache is a very pure light red—despite its 13 percent alcohol. The similarly pure Beaune Premier Cru Clos des Mouches is piquant and spicy.

Viré-Clessé: See MÂCON.

Domaine du Vissoux ☆

69620 St.-Véran; 04.74.71.79.42; domaine.vissoux@wanadoo.fr
Wines: Beaujolais, Fleurie, Moulin-à-Vent. $ to $$
A personal favorite here. Pierre-Marie Chermette, an enologist, is meticulous and intelligent. Vines (farmed more or less organically) and wines get plenty of TLC. Even the Beaujolais Primeur is serious. His *crus* would be quite at home at a three-star restaurant. The Fleurie Poncie, with its achingly lovely fruit and mineral weave, is a wine of great balance and fluidity. The elegant Fleurie Les Garants could easily be mistaken for a Pommard, say, or a Volnay. The Moulin-à-Vent Rochegrés is dark and meaty but as elegant as the Fleuries. As if that weren't enough, Chermette also makes crème de cassis from his own fruit.

Comte de Vogüé

21220 Chambolle-Musigny; 03.80.62.86.25; fax: 03.80.62.82.38
Wines: Chambolle-Musigny and Bonnes-Mares. $$$ to $$$$
A classic domaine back in form after a slump in the '80s. Graceful renditions of Musigny, including a rare chardonnay-based white.

Volnay

An AC sandwiched between Pommard and Meursault for potentially perfumed, silky, suave yet structured reds made from pinot noir. Its Premier Crus include Taillepieds, Santenots, Caillerets, Clos des Ducs, and En Champans.

BEST RECENT VINTAGES: 2005, (2004), (2003), 2002, 2001, 1999, and 1996.
PRICES: $$$ to $$$$

PRODUCERS: MARQUIS D'ANGERVILLE ☆ ◆ BALLOT-MILLOT & FILS ◆ LUCIEN BOILLOT ☆ ◆ BOUCHARD PÈRE & FILS ☆ ◆ JEAN-MARC BOULEY ◆ JOSEPH DROUHIN ☆ ◆ ARNAUD & MARIE-ODILE ENTE ☆ ◆ MAISON ALEX GAMBAL ◆ Dom Michel Lafarge: ambitious, biodynamic Volnays, not always perfect, but original, satisfying, and authentic, particularly the Clos des Chênes and the Vendanges Sélectionnées ◆ DOM DES COMTES LAFON ☆ ◆ DOM LEROY ☆ ◆ DOM HUBERT DE MONTILLE ☆ ◆ DOMAINE PARENT ◆ DOM DE LA POUSSE D'OR ↑ ◆ Dom Prieur-Brunet: see SANTENAY.

Vosne-Romanée

A starry Côte de Nuits with an embarrassment of Grand Crus—Romanée-Conti, La Romanée, La Tâche, Romanée-St.-Vivant, Richebourg, and La Grande Rue—as well as a fair number of Premier Crus, including Aux Malconsorts, Les Suchots, and Les Beaux Monts. The grape is pinot noir and the wines should be majestic, complex, beautifully structured, fragrant, and fine of grain.

BEST RECENT VINTAGES: 2005, 2004, 2003, 2002, 2001, 1999, and 1996.
PRICES: $$$ to $$$$

PRODUCERS: DOM BERTAGNA ↑ ◆ MAISON ALBERT BICHOT ◆ PHILIPPE CHARLOPIN ☆ ◆ DOM BRUNO CLAIR ☆ ◆ Dom du Clos Frantin: see MAISON ALBERT BICHOT ◆ DOM JEAN-JACQUES CONFURON ☆ ◆ DOM CONFURON-COTETIDOT ☆ ◆ JOSEPH DROUHIN ☆ ◆ DOM RÉGIS DUBOIS & FILS ◆ MAISON ALEX GAMBAL ☆ ◆ DOM JEAN GRIVOT ☆ ◆ Dom Michel Gros: this domaine has an exclusive holding of the Premier Cru Clos des Réas and the wine is worth trying for its tastiness and true sense of place ◆ DOM ANNE GROS ☆ ◆ DOM A. F. GROS ☆ ◆ DOM DOMINIQUE LAURENT ☆ ◆ DOM LEROY ☆ ◆ DOM MÉO-CAMUZET ◆ Dom des Perdrix: see NUITS-ST.-GEORGES ☆ ◆ Dom Armelle & Bernard Rion: There's a lot to admire in the various Nuits St. Georges—particularly the Premier Crus Les Damodes and Les Murgers—but the wines still need work. The big-boned, racy Vosne-Romanée Premier Cru Les Chaumes, however, is so delicious you can't stop drinking it. ◆ DOM DANIEL RION & FILS ◆ Dom Fabrice Vigot: racy though somewhat lean Vosne-Romanée La Colombière and an ampler, tasty Échezeaux.

Vougeot

A small AC in the Côte de Nuits, Vougeot is dominated by its Grand Cru Clos de Vougeot. There are a handful of Premier Crus. While it's almost exclusively devoted to pinot noir-based reds, there are roughly 4 hectares of chardonnay producing the rare Vougeot white. The Premier Crus are generally a distinct step up from the Village wines, which nevertheless can be quite alluring. Best recent vintages: 2005, 2004, 2003, 2001, 1999, and 1996. Prices: $$$ to $$$$. Producers: DOM BERTAGNA ◆ Roux Père & Fils: pleasant Premier Cru Les Petits Vougeot ◆ Dom de la Vougeraie: see MAISON JEAN-CLAUDE BOISSET.

BURGUNDY CRIB SHEET

MUST TRYS

Unless you're a millionaire, try to find sit-down tastings that offer wines from the Domaine Leroy and Domaine de la Romanée-Conti.

Domaine Dujac
Arnaud & Marie-Odile Ente
Domaine Albert Grivault
Domaine Anne Gros
Domaine Guffens-Heynen
Domaine des Comtes Lafon
Domaine Hubert de Montille
Domaine Prieuré-Roch
Domaine Roulot
Domaine Armand Rousseau

SMART BUYS

Domaine de la Bongran
Domaine Alain Burguet
Domaine Les Champs de l'Abbaye
Domaine de Chassorney
Domaine Maria Cuny
Dom Vincent Dureuil-Janthial
Ghislaine & Jean-Hugues Goisot
Corinne & Jean-Pierre Grossot
Domaine Émile Juillot
Domaine Sainte-Barbe, especially the Viré-Clessé En Thurissey

SAFE HOUSES

Domaine Bertagna
Bouchard Père & Fils
La Chablisienne
Joseph Drouhin
Maison Faiveley
Domaine William Fèvre
Domaine Louis Jadot
Domaine Laroche
Domaine Jacques Prieur
Verget, the *négociant* of Domaine Guffens-Heynen

BEFORE YOU DISMISS BEAUJOLAIS, TRY

Jean-Marc Burgaud: Morgon
Domaine Jean-Marc Després/Domaine de la Madone: Fleurie
Domaine Jean Foillard: Morgon
Pascal Granger
Château des Jacques: see Beaujolais and JADOT
Domaine de St.-Sorlin: see BEAUJOLAIS
Domaine des Terres Vivantes
JP Thévenet: Morgon
Château Thivin: Côte de Brouilly
Domaine du Vissoux

ALSACE
BORDEAUX
BURGUNDY
CHAMPAGNE
JURA AND
SAVOIE
LANGUEDOC-
ROUSSILLON
LOIRE
PROVENCE
AND CORSICA
RHÔNE
SOUTHWEST

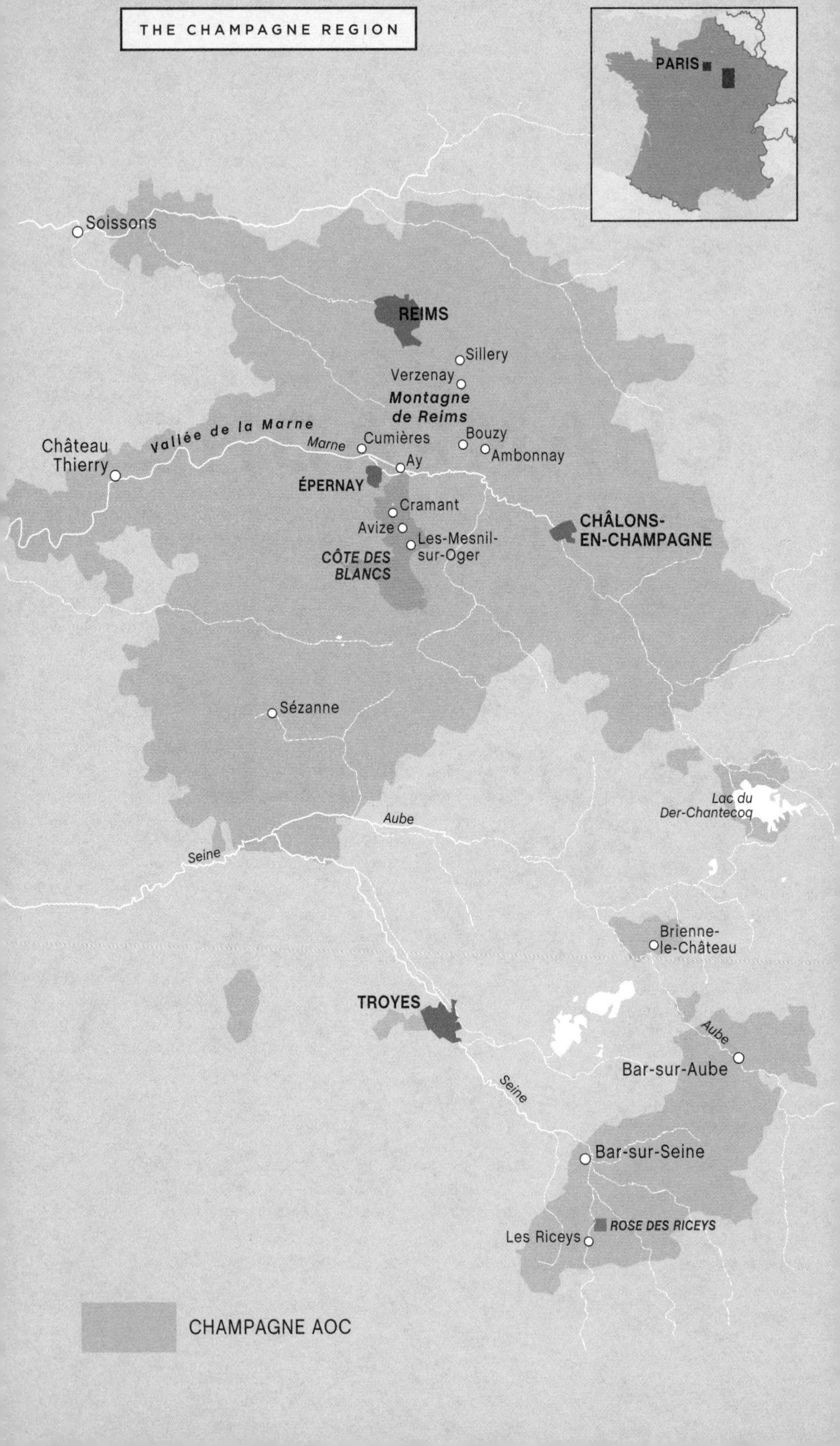

THE CHAMPAGNE REGION

PARIS

Soissons

REIMS

Sillery

Verzenay

Montagne de Reims

Vallée de la Marne

Marne

Cumières

Bouzy

Ambonnay

Château Thierry

Ay

ÉPERNAY

Cramant

Avize

Les-Mesnil-sur-Oger

CÔTE DES BLANCS

CHÂLONS-EN-CHAMPAGNE

Sézanne

Lac du Der-Chantecoq

Aube

Seine

Brienne-le-Château

TROYES

Aube

Bar-sur-Aube

Seine

Bar-sur-Seine

ROSE DES RICEYS

Les Riceys

CHAMPAGNE AOC

Less than 200 kilometers northeast of Paris, the singular appellation Champagne is the source of a unique sparkling wine, although two other ACs, Coteaux Champenois and Rosé des Riceys, produce infinitesimal quantities of still wines within the delimited area. The zone of production covers some 33,000 hectares, or 3.5 percent of the area devoted to winemaking in France. Most of Champagne's vineyards are concentrated around the provincial cities of Reims and Épernay but extend west to Château Thierry and, after crossing a landscape given over to cereal crops, to the southeast of the city of Troyes in the Aube.

Chalk, the principal constituent of the subsoils, is what makes Champagne so special and, to my mind, inimitable (though often imitated). There are, of course, distinctions within the soil types, expositions, and microclimates that influence not only the grape variety favored but also the style of the wine.

MAIN PRODUCTION AREAS: The Montagne de Reims, the Marne valley, the Côte des Blancs, and the Côte des Bar. Seventeen Grand Crus and forty-four Premier Crus have also been recognized, most of them in the Montagne de Reims and the Côte des Blancs. The four subregions are discussed in what follows.

GRAPES: Three—pinot noir, pinot meunier, and chardonnay, though a handful of vintners also use grapes that were once widely planted but have fallen out of fashion. For the most part, Champagne, whether white or rosé, is a blended wine, based on different quantities of two or all three grape varieties. Pinot noir contributes body, aroma, and power. Pinot meunier, another red grape, is supple and spicy, aging and expressing itself quickly. Chardonnay gives the wines finesse and definition. Some Champagnes are made from a single grape variety.

STYLES OF WINE: Most Champagne is nonvintage, a blend of the wines of several harvests. Vintage Champagnes, made from the grapes of a single harvest, are usually produced only in very good years. The possible variations on the theme mean that most producers make several different bottlings. Here are the basic styles and the abbreviations for them used in this chapter: Grand Cru (GC); nonvintage, a blend of a several vintages (NV); and Premier Cru (PC).

VINTAGES: Great years already on the market: 1982, 1988, 1989, 1990, 1995, 1996. Good years: 1997, 1998 (chardonnay-based wines are particularly fine), and 1999. In more recent vintages, the only clearly disappointing year was 2001. The 2004 vintage was very good in terms of both quality and quantity (a record harvest). And 2005 is still an unknown, as the wines are being blended as I write. The chardonnay, however, is exceptional.

PRICES: Most are $$$ to $$$$. Deluxe cuvées easily reach $100, with the most expensive cuvées scaling the $500 mark.

Champagne is the only wine region in France not currently in crisis. Its sales account for 25 percent of French exports in wine and spirits. The structure of production in Champagne is different from other wine regions. Its fifteen thousand growers own 90 percent of the vineyard land in Champagne (most of them hold fewer than 2 hectares) and most sell their harvest to big houses like Moët and Veuve-Clicquot. Only a third sell wine on their own or to a cooperative. Individual growers and cooperatives account for 30 percent of sales. Two thirds of Champagne production is sold by the big houses, or *grandes marques,* which roughly translates as "big-name brands." Moët & Chandon is by far the largest. It belongs to the luxury goods conglomerate LVMH (Louis Vuitton Moët Hennessey), the other assets of which include Veuve-Clicquot, Ruinart, and Krug. LVMH, alone, accounts for 20 percent of Champagne sales.

SOME ADVICE: The infrastructure has served Champagne well and most producers, including small growers, don't want to see it change, at least not in its essentials. I urge you, however, to try grower Champagnes. Not only are they cheaper—the price of a grower's top wine often compares favorably with the price of an entry-level wine of a big house—they are usually better. The entry-level wines of many of the growers recommended here can compete with deluxe cuvées from all but the best big houses. Further, while the big houses tend to blend for consistency, small growers are, after all, vignerons. Their Champagnes are never anonymous, never geared to please a common denominator. They are one of a kind. Whiskey lovers might compare them to single malts in a world of blended scotch. In the final analysis, however, these are wines from individual winemakers, just like Burgundy, Alsace, the Loire, and the Rhône.

As for the big houses, over the past few years the ownership of a number of them has changed. The most recent takeovers include Ayala, Besserat-Bellefon, Lanson, and Taittinger. Each house continues to make and sell wine (the wine currently being sold most likely comes from reserve stocks). All are listed here, but I have not described the wines as the future is so uncertain. Taittinger, for example, was sold again in June 2006.

CHAMPAGNE LABEL VOCABULARY: Champagnes range from bone-dry to sweet. Here are rough translations of the words used to indicate levels of sweetness:

- *Brut nature*, also *non-dosé*, or *dosage zéro:* bone-dry
- Extra brut: almost bone-dry
- Brut: dry, although a trace of sweetness is often perceptible
- Extra dry: slightly but perceptibly sweet
- Sec: "half-sweet"
- Demi-sec: fully sweet
- Doux: very sweet

ABBREVIATIONS USED IN THE CHAMPAGNE TRADE:

- NM—*négociant manipulant,* which refers to Champagne houses that buy grapes and/or wine that they then transform into Champagne
- RM—*récoltant manipulant,* which means a grower; however, if a grower buys more than a very small percentage of grapes, the category changes from RM to NM
- CM—*coopérative manipulant, a cooperative cellar producing champagne from the grapes of its members*
- MA—*marque d'acheteur* or "buyer's brand," for example Champagne sold by Fauchon under its own label

Agrapart & Fils

51190 Avize; 03.26.57.51.38; fax: 03.26.57.05.06; $$ to $$$

A very good grower with several reasonably priced, feisty cuvées of Grand Cru *blanc de blancs,* the best being the Cuvée l'Avizoise. Fermented in old oak barrels, this old-vines chardonnay entices with flavors of ripe fruit, ginger, hay, and somehow, aged honey.

Aubry

51390 Jouy-lès-Reims; 03.26.49.20.07; fax: 03.26.49.75.27; $$ to $$$

Twin brothers Philippe and Pierre Aubry run a fairly traditional, eco-friendly domaine on the outskirts of Reims and produce three provocative, unusual cuvées. All are vintage Champagnes but each is identified more by the peculiarities of its composition than by that fact that it comes from a particular growing season. The first is Cuvée Nicolas François Aubry Sable rosé, a quince-accented Champagne with about half the intensity of the typical fizz (in winespeak, this is referred to as "pressure"). Tasty, but La Nombre d'Or Sable *blanc de blancs* is more interesting. Nearly as mild as the rosé in terms of bubbles, it's a forceful blend of chardonnay, arbanne, and petit meslier. The last two grapes were once widely planted throughout Champagne. Now, with the exception of growers like Aubry and MOUTARD, they're on the verge of disappearing. Pinot gris, locally called fromenteau, is another vanishing Champagne grape. It brings its distinctive perfume and texture to La Nombre d'Or Campanae Veteres Vites, a cuvée that also includes arbanne, petit meslier, pinot meunier, chardonnay, and pinot noir in its blend. It's a fascinating wine and a delicious one, and it offers a taste of another facet of Champagne. Of the more traditional Aubry bottlings, the most toothsome is the vintage Aubry de Humbert.

Ayala

51160 Aÿ; 03.26.55.15.44; fax: 03.26.51.09.04; $$$

Watch this spot. In 2005 Ayala's name and facilities were sold to BOLLINGER and the vineyards were sold to Frey Financière, which always had an interest in the company, as it does in Billecart-Salmon. In May 2006 Bollinger put an Ayala line of Champagnes on the market—as yet untasted by me.

Paul Bara

51150 Bouzy; 03.26.57.00.50; fax: 03.26.57.81.24; $$ to $$$

The author of *Histoire de Bouzy,* Paul Bara is an ambassador for this pinot noir–dominated *cru.* His ample, reasonably priced Champagnes, all of them Grand Cru, make fine envoys as well—from the Grand Rosé de Bouzy, with its delicate strawberry notes underscored by stony minerality, to the elegant 1998 with its steel undergirding, to the fresh 1996 with its layered fruit flavors. Bara is also a good source for Coteaux Champenois Bouzy rouge.

Edmond Barnaut

51150 Bouzy; 03.26.57.01.54; www.champagne-barnaut.com; $$ to $$$($)

Enterprising and affable, Philippe Secondé, an enologist, is the sixth generation in charge of this fortunate domaine, which has most of its vines in Grand Cru Bouzy. Not surprisingly, he makes a Coteaux Champenois Bouzy rouge, a light, tart, refreshing red, and also produces ratafia, marc de Champagne, and *fine de la Marne,* all of which are sold in his attractive boutique in the village of Bouzy. Among the Champagnes, the Cuvée Edmond brut is a fruity, satisfying blend of chardonnay, pinot noir, and meunier. The Grand Réserve brut Grand Cru is graceful and nicely concentrated, with engaging flavors of brioche and strawberries. The Authentique rosé brut Grand Cru is an elegant weave of rhubarb, ginger, straw, and steel. These flavors are echoed in the elegant, full-bodied *blanc de noirs* brut Grand Cru. Savory and slightly salty, the Champagne went very well with a Sunday brunch featuring cold shrimp in a curry mayonnaise.

Françoise Bedel ↑

02310 Crouttes-sur-Marne; 03.23.82.15.80; www.champagne-francoise-bedel.fr; $$ to $$$

Françoise Bedel farms her 7 hectares in the Marne valley according to strict biodynamic principles. Given her location, her Champagnes are mainly based on pinot meunier. My favorite among her several cuvées was Comme Autrefois, a vibrant, steel, citrus, ginger, and rhubarb Champagne that was flavorful and specific. My guess is that it will go well with any top-quality "casual" food, as I was drinking it with a lunch of Corsican ham and avocado salad. The flavorful brut NV may not be deep but it's hardly anonymous, with its appetizing tartness and steel-edged fruit. The polychromatic label of Entre Ciel et Terre looks like a tarot card or an advent calendar for biodynamists. The Champagne inside is somewhat sudsy but pleasant. Like the label; prefer the other cuvées.

Besserat de Bellefon

51200 Épernay; 03.26.78.50.50; www.besseratdebellefon.com; $$$

Agreeable commercial Champagnes from this *négociant* house now part of Groupe Lanson International. The Cuvée des Moines bottlings are the pride of the firm.

Billecart-Salmon ☆

51160 Mareuil-sur-Aÿ; 03.26.52.60.22; www.champagne-billecart.fr; $$$ to $$$$

An excellent medium-size house. The bread-and-butter Champagnes—the brut NV and brut rosé NV—have had their ups and downs, but recent versions (tasted in June 2005) were very good. The brut NV, with at least 40 percent pinot meunier, was fruity and full-bodied; the rosé was delicate and fine, with accents of minerals and orange peel. The feisty NV *blanc de blancs* Grand Cru is a clear step up, crunchy and pedigreed with succulent fruit flavors. The elegant, rectilinear 1996 Nicolas-François Billecart is a ballerina—voluptuous but with zero body fat. The 1996 *blanc de blancs* Grand Cru is a superb expression of both chardonnay and the Côte des Blancs, a true presence and an exciting wine. The bubbles in the very feminine 1996 Elisabeth Salmon Grand Cru are so delicate they caress the palate, giving way to nuanced, extremely fine, long flavors. The Clos St. Hilaire is the deluxe cuvée, from a parcel of pinot noir behind the winery. The 1995 is structured, firm yet subtle, and thoroughly aristocratic, a wonderful Champagne but at four times the price of the *blanc de blancs* Grand Cru, I'd go for the latter.

Henri Billiot & Fils

51150 Ambonnay; 03.33.26.57.00.14; hbil@aol.com; $$$ to $$$$

Very good family domaine with 100 percent Grand Cru vineyards in the heart of pinot noir land. The carefully made wines are unfiltered, which may explain why, in every cuvée I've tasted, there's always been a lot of "there" there. The frisky Cuvée Julie Grand Cru was pedigreed but not intimidating, a friendly, specific Champagne with steel-framed fruit; the 1998 Grand Cru, distinctly *terroir*-driven, was simultaneously ample and bracing. It would make a fine dinner Champagne or a great accompaniment for ambitious hors d'oeuvres. Cautionary note: the brut Cuvée Tradition tasted sweet to me.

Boizel

51200 Épernay; 03.26.55.21.51; fax: 03.26.54.31.83

Part of the publicly quoted BCC group (Boizel Chanoine Champagne), this house makes pleasant, reasonably priced entry-level bottlings and admirable special cuvées. The firm is under the direction of Bruno Paillard, a major shareholder in the group, which also includes Alexandre Bonnet, Chanoine, Philipponat, and de Venoge. Boizel recently purchased Lanson, an acquisition that brought with it Besserat de Bellefond and Alfred Rothschild, among others.

Bollinger ☆

BP 4, 51160 Aÿ; 03.26.53.33.66; www.champagne-bollinger.fr; $$$ to $$$$

Breathes there a wine lover who doesn't have a soft spot for Bollinger? Consistently excellent, reliably unique, Bollinger owns 157 hectares of vines, which account for two thirds of its needs. (Historically, Bollinger sold two million bottles yearly. It plans to expand considerably over the next ten years, perhaps using the recently purchased Ayala name for a second range of wines, from grapes not up to house standard.) Bollinger Champagnes, based on pinot noir, always have a healthy percentage of Grand Cru and/or Premier Cru in the blend—usually half the pinot noir comes from Aÿ Grand Cru, for example—and age for a minimum of three years. Special Cuvée, the brut NV, is big and bready, a rich, lipsmacking, food-friendly Champagne. The barrel-fermented Grande Année 1997, with seven years' age, is vivacious, rich, and racy—truly superb. The lightly honeyed 1995 RD (recently disgorged) is creamy, mouthwatering, and full of sap and vigor. I have never tasted Bollinger's most legendary wine, Vignes à la Française, from ungrafted vines. I did see the vineyard; it's much more fascinating than a touristy toy train excursion through miles of underground cellars. And, after much pleading, I sampled a drop of base wine from the barrel. Where there's life, there's hope.

CHAMPAGNE

Cédric Bouchard ↑

10110 Celles-sur-Ource; 01.45.79.43.65; www.champagne-rosesdejeanne.com; $$ to $$$

This young Aube-area grower adheres to biodynamic principles as well as his own rule: one parcel, one grape, one vintage. Florescence Rosés de Jeanne, at seven thousand bottles, is his main bottling. A *blanc de noirs,* of pure, unfiltered pinot noir, it's a vinous, pure, gentle meal Champagne; Rosé de Jeanne, also *blanc de noirs,* from very low-yielding vines on a small parcel, is full bodied, with rich fig and honey notes. Very good and very much a wine.

Chartogne-Taillet

51220 Merfy; 03.26.03.10.17; fax: 03.26.03.19.15; $$ to $$$

Very good family domaine slightly northwest of Reims. My hands-down favorite cuvée here is the distinctive Fiacre bottling. Made only in the best years, it's 60/40 percent chardonnay/pinot noir. The latest version comes from the 1999 vintage blended with reserve wines from 1996. Quite ample—zaftig, even—it's mouthfilling and savory, with flavors of forest underbrush and dried fruit. The ginger-accented 1996 brut had a metallic backbone and the intriguing flavor of artichokes (faint but definite); the pungent Cuvée Sainte Anne brut is a flavorful wake-up call, a real presence, mingling flavors of apples, toast, and minerals.

Gaston Chiquet

51530 Dizy; 03.26.55.22.02; www.gastonchiquet.com; $$ to $$$

Model family domaine with uncommonly large vineyard holdings (22 hectares) and reliably good Champagne on every level. Recent favorite: the 1997 Or brut Premier Cru with flavors of brioche, apples, and fresh mushrooms. Specific, long, and flavorful, it went down all too easily with shellfish and fresh mayonnaise followed by salmon poached in Noilly Prat. Note, too, that Chiquet produces one of the only pure chardonnay *blanc de blancs* from the pinot noir–dominated Grand Cru vineyards of Aÿ.

Coteaux Champenois

The AC for still wines—red, white, and rosé—made within the Champagne zone. Production is infinitesimal, about 60 hectoliters a year, and prices are high, as the grapes could have been used for Champagne. Bouzy is the best-known commune.

PRICES: $$$

PRODUCERS: PAUL BARA ◆ EDMOND BARNAUT ◆ ROGER COULON ◆ DUVAL-LEROY ◆ EGLY-OURIET ◆ GATINOIS ◆ LARMANDIER-BERNIER ◆ DAVID LECLAPART ◆ MOËT & CHANDON ◆ JOSEPH PERRIER ◆ FRANÇOIS SECONDÉ ◆ ERICK DE SOUSA & FILS ◆ TARLANT.

Côte des Bar: The easternmost Champagne zone some 75 kilometers from the center of the region, southeast of Troyes, in the Aube department. Rosé des Riceys is also made here. Producers: DRAPPIER ◆ DOM JACQUES LASSAIGNE.

Côte des Blancs: Following the slopes on a north-south axis beneath Épernay, this Champagne zone is the kingdom of chardonnay. It's also home to many Grand Cru and Premier Cru villages, including Avize, Chouilly, Cramant, and Le Mesnil-sur-Oger. I often think that Côte des Blancs is the most exquisite expression of chardonnay—until certain Burgundian exceptions start tumbling in. So let's just say that you don't really know chardonnay until you've tasted a really good Côte des Blancs Champagne. Along with *elegant, patrician, razor-sharp, majestic,* and many other adjectives, there are a handful of seemingly wacky words that come to mind, such as *starchy, crunchy,* and *chalky.* I like to compare this exciting gustatory phenomenon to the crystallization that occurs in great, well-matured cheeses, like Parmesan.

PRODUCERS: AGRAPART & FILS ◆ PIERRE GIMMONET ◆ LARMANDIER-BERNIER ◆ LAUNOIS PÉRE & FILS ◆ DAVID LECLAPART ◆ LILBERT-FILS ◆ LE MESNIL ◆ JEAN MILAN ◆ PIERRE PETERS ◆ JACQUES SELOSSE ◆ VARNIER-FANNIÈRE.

Roger Coulon

51390 Vrigny; 03.26.03.61.65; www.champagne-coulon.com; $$ to $$$
This solid, eco-friendly grower from the Premier Cru village of Vrigny in the Montagne de Reims makes six different cuvées of Champagne, including one with a fair proportion of ungrafted pinot meunier. Coulon uses wild yeasts, and the vintage cuvées are neither filtered, fined, nor cold stabilized. The brut Tradition, 50 percent pinot meunier, is easy on the palate, pleasantly fresh, and fruity, a good aperitif Champagne. The vinous Grand Réserve, aged in used Burgundy barrels, is longer and more focused, with attractive pear, apple, and lemon zest flavors. The 1999, a blend of pinot noir and chardonnay, was a gentle, unpretentious, everyday, all-purpose Champagne. The 2000 had a bit more élan but was a tad too sweet for my palate. The barrel-aged brut Prestige les Champs de Vallier comes from a single parcel and is chiefly chardonnay. It's full and round, with flavors of ginger, crushed berries, and lemon curd. A meal Champagne. Coulon also makes an appealing new-oak-aged Coteaux Champenois rouge from 100 percent pinot meunier. It's fresh, balanced, and focused with good fruit and lots of oak flavors.

Delamotte ☆

51190 Le Mesnil-sur-Oger; 03.26.57.51.65; www.salondelamotte.com; $$$ to $$$$
The sister house to Salon (both are part of Laurent-Perrier), Delamotte benefits from its kinship: when Salon doesn't make a wine—which can be most years—Delamotte inherits the grapes. It does have its own vineyards in the Côte des Blancs (6 hectares) and its own contracts, however, and makes blended Champagnes as well as *blanc de blancs* from the Côte des Blancs. (Its pinot noir comes from Ambonnay and Bouzy; the pinot meunier from the Marne valley.) The brut NV, a blend of all three grapes, is airy and easy and displays

some of the richness of pinot noir; the *blanc de blancs* NV brut is vivacious and fine, with accents of mango and pineapple. The bracing but full 1997 *blanc de blancs* is almost Burgundian—Meursault in Le Mesnil.

Deutz ☆

51160 Aÿ; 03.26.56.94.00; fax: 03.26.56.94.13; $$$ to $$$$

An excellent small "big house," Deutz was purchased by Roederer in 1996 but operates independently, producing 1.3 million bottles a year. It owns 42 hectares in Premier Cru and Grand Cru villages, and its contracts with growers represent another 150 hectares. (Deutz also owns Delas in the Rhône). Deutz makes eight different cuvées of its own in addition to private-label Champagnes, for the Michelin three-star Taillevent, for example. The brut NV is always a good test of any Champagne house. Deutz comes out with flying colors. The combination of equal amounts of all three grapes, a fair percentage of which come from Grand Crus, and a minimum of three years' aging result in a round, fruity aperitif Champagne with appetizing ginger-lemon freshness. The fragrant and riveting 1998 *blanc de blancs* has lipsmacking lemon-lime overtones against a backdrop of minerals. The 1996 Cuvée William Deutz rosé, 80 percent pinot noir, all from Grand Crus, is virile and racy. The 1996 Cuvée William Deutz, chiefly Grand Cru pinot noir but with 35 percent chardonnay in the blend, is silky, elegant, round, and complex, with flavors of brioche and raspberry. The exquisite 1998 Amour de Deutz, pure chardonnay, primarily from Le Mesnil and Avize, with six years of aging, is mellow, pure, crunchy, and supremely aristocratic.

Drappier

10200 Urville; 03.25.27.40.15; www.champagne-drappier.com; $$$ to $$$$

This very good family domaine is run by Michel Drappier, who did a stint at Domaine Chandon in Napa. A third of Drappier's acreage is in the Reims area, the rest in the Aube. There are generally ten different cuvées, starting with a pleasant Carte d'Or brut based primarily on pinot noir and very reasonably priced. A number of my favorite Paris restaurants offer their Brut Nature (zero dosage) by the glass. Pure old-vines pinot noir, it's mineral, elegant, deliciously mellow, fresh, and long, with notes of orange peel and an exciting bite of acidity. I never miss the opportunity to order it. The refined Cuvée Anniversaire brut is based on a single vintage, a good year, though not one great enough to slap on the label. The deep, nuanced *blanc de blancs* Cuvée Signature is a vintage-dated Champagne of pure chardonnay, as is Grande Sendrée Cuvée Prestige brut, a creamy, full-bodied blend of pinot noir and chardonnay, with notes of lemon and eau-de-vie. Carte d'Or brut, also vintage-dated, is rich, long, and in the case of the 1992, tasted on its tenth birthday, both fresh and intriguingly evolved. Any of the last three would make fine dining Champagnes, which could carry you well into the wee hours of the morning.

Duval-Leroy ☆

51130 Vertus, 03.26.52.10.75; www.duval-leroy.com; $$$ to $$$$

Vegan Champagne? Yes. This family-owned small "big house" avoids the use of all animal products, for example gelatin, in its winemaking. Its roughly five million bottles of Champagne, therefore, qualify as vegan. Carol Duval-Leroy, the owner, has the great good sense to let winemaker Hervé Gestin have his way. Under his direction, farming is increasingly organic and the cellars, otherwise typically modern, show signs of feng shui influence or, as Gestin calls it, "geobiology," in the triangular yellow blocks placed here and there to reverse the magnetic effects of an underground river. So they mean it when they label their organic pinot noir Végétarien-Vegetatia brut. It's a pure, vinous, flavorful, deeply fruity Champagne. Duval-Leroy makes up to twenty different bottlings a year, including a pleasant Coteaux du Champenois rouge. The Fleur de Champagne line includes a singular, vibrant and crunchy chardonnay-based Premier Cru, and a racy, harmonious 1995 blend of chardonnay and pinot noir. There's an even racier vintage *blanc de blancs* Grand Cru—the 1998 was chalky, mineral, and pure—and the Cuvée Femme, a vintage Champagne, predominantly chardonnay, from five different Grand Crus. Aged for five years, it's a silky dazzler, with notes of honey and ginger—irresistible. Among Duval-

Leroy's latest creations is Lady Rose, a slightly sweet rosé, 100 percent pinot noir. Intended to be drunk with dessert, it is available only in half-bottles. It's very nice but much more intriguing is the Authentis line of three very distinctive vintage, barrel-aged Champagnes. The most unusual is made from 100 percent petit meslier, a once widely planted but now nearly extinct Champenois grape. Interesting and tasty but I prefer the organic pinot noir from Cumières, a big, round, racy Champagne. And my favorite is the biodynamic, 100 percent chardonnay Premier Cru—so pure, so majestic, with a light, honeyed grace note.

Egly-Ouriet ☆

51150 Ambonnay; 03.26.57.00.70; fax: 03.26.57.06.52; $$ to $$$$

A personal favorite, this meticulous, eco-friendly family domaine makes exceptional Champagne. Its fifty-odd parcels, all Premier Cru and Grand Cru, are scattered throughout the Ambonnay area, considered by some to be the equivalent of Vosne-Romanée for pinot noir in the Champenois. Grapes for the roughly half-dozen different cuvées ferment in Burgundy barrels. None of the wines is filtered. The most recent cuvée is Les Vignes de Vrigny, made solely from pinot meunier from a single Premier Cru vineyard. It's a mouthwatering Champagne, bracing and deep, with flavors of rhubarb and lemon zests. The brut Tradition Grand Cru, which accounts for half of the domaine's production, is 75 percent pinot noir and spends at least three years aging. It is absolutely yummy, very strong, very fine, full, complex, creamy, and toasty, with a steel and stone edge. The 1996 Grand Cru, made from old vines in Ambonnay, spent more than seven years aging. Pure and elegant, it's thrillingly alive and intensely chalky, with flavors of honey, citrus zests, apples, and more. Absolutely excellent. And along with several additional cuvées of superb Champagne, there's a remarkable Coteaux Champenois Ambonnay, a fragrant, silky red, as chiseled as a cameo.

Nicolas Feuillatte

BP 210, 51206 Chouilly-Épernay; 03.26.59.55.50; www.feuillatte.com; $$$ to $$$$

The prestige line of the largest cooperative cellars in the region, the Centre Viticole de la Champagne in Chouilly, Feuillatte produces well-made Champagnes at reasonable prices. Palme d'Or is their deluxe bottling. The 1996 is dry and elegant, with appetizing flavors of citrus zest and ginger. The 1998 *blanc de blancs* brut is a nice, crunchy Côte des Blancs; the basic Réserve Particulière, though a bit aggressive, is clean and invigorating; and the 1995 Cuvée Spéciale Premier Cru is full, mellow, and wheaty, with accents of preserved lemon and apple—first-rate.

Gatinois ☆

51160 Aÿ; 03.26.55.14.26. champ-gatinois@hexanet.fr.; $$ to $$$

Apropos of nothing, I always associate the extremely fine, devastatingly delicate Champagnes from this eco-friendly grower with the magical city of Venice. There's something dreamlike and glinting about both of them. Gatinois is located in one of the most prestigious Grand Cru areas for pinot noir; and the family's roots in Aÿ reach back to the beginning of the eighteenth century. Its ancestors were able to purchase the village's finest parcels, on its best-exposed slopes, which are planted 90 percent to pinot noir and to 10 percent to chardonnay. Even Bollinger buys from Gatinois. As Pierre Cheval-Gatinois says, Aÿ wines are sufficient unto themselves. They never need blending. Cheval-Gatinois describes his wines as full-bodied, meal wines, supple and amiable. I prefer to describe his very fine Grand Cru Tradition brut as pure, succulent, lipsmacking, and graceful; and his lacy, airborne 1999 Grand Cru brut, with its light mushroom notes, as one of the most elegant, harmonious pinot noir–based Champagnes I've tasted. Gatinois also makes a remarkable Coteaux Champenois Aÿ rouge from its oldest vines, treated to a bit of barrel age and a light egg-white fining.

René Geoffroy

51480 Cumières; 03.26.55.32.31; www.champagne-geoffroy.com; $$ to $$$

A serious family domaine. Viticulture is organic and the wines are based on a large proportion of red grapes—both pinot noir and meunier. The top-of-the-line is the barrel-fermented Cuvée R. Geoffroy, the 1996 of which had rich apple compote and autumn leaf flavors and a potent, moonshine-liquory core.

Pierre Gimmonet ☆

51530 Cuis; 03.26.59.78.70; champagne-gimonnet@wanadoo.fr; $$$ to $$$$
When you've got it, flaunt it. And the Champagnes from this excellent grower veritably trumpet the glories of their *terroir.* With 25 hectares of vines—mostly old vines, all in the Côte des Blancs Premier Cru or Grand Cru—Gimmonet makes all *blanc de blancs,* pure chardonnay. And every bottling says "I am a privileged Côte des Blancs *cru.*" The family style, from one cuvée to the next, is crunchy, pure, mineral, and decisive. To this profile, the current *blanc de blancs* Premier Cru Cuis adds notes of ginger and lemon. The discreet but patrician Cuvée Gastronome lays on ginger, lemon curd, and stone. The racy and yummy 1999 Fleuron hits high and low notes, a mezzo-soprano with a huge range. As for the achingly elegant, extra brut Oenophile, if platinum had a flavor, this would be it.

Henri Giraud

51160 Aÿ; 03.26.55.18.55; www.champagne-giraud.com; $$$ to $$$$
Here's an icebreaker: the corks in grower Henri Giraud's deluxe bottlings, the vintage-dated Cuvée Fût de Chêne, are kept in place with staples made of twenty-four carat gold. All of Giraud's bottlings are from Aÿ Grand Cru and all are flavorful—but in most cases the expression of the fine *terroir* of Aÿ is obscured by oak, which is used here in abundance.

CHAMPAGNE

Gosset ☆

BP 7, 51160 Aÿ; 03.26.56.99.56; www.champagne-gosset.com; $$$ to $$$$
A high-quality Champagne house run by the dynamic Béatrice Cointreau. The Grande Réserve brut, dominated by pinot noir, is suave and silky; the 1996 Grand Millésime is bracing and elegant; and the deluxe cuvées Celebris and Celebris Rosé are excellent, particularly the former, with its grand freshness and even grander finesse, its bready aromas, and its core of rich fruit.

Haton & Fils

51480 Damery; 03.26.58.41.11; www.champagne-haton.com; $$ to $$$
Jean-Noël Haton makes six cuvées of sound Champagne of which the best is the admirable Vintage Extra, a fresh, racy blend of chardonnay and pinot noir from Grand Cru and Premier Cru vineyards, aged for four years.

Charles Heidsieck ☆

51100 Reims; 03.26.84.43.50; fax: 03.26.84.43.86; $$$ to $$$$
Controlled by Rémy Martin (as is the less interesting Piper-Heidsieck), Charles Heidsieck has become one of the most reliable of the region's big houses. Champagne enthusiasts will find Heidsieck's labels admirably informative and the Champagnes, themselves, delicious at every level. The brut NV, equal parts chardonnay, pinot noir, and pinot meunier aged for four years, is full and flavorful, with lovely balance; the 1998 brut is vinous, elegant, and toasty; and the Blanc des Millénaires is downright patrician and pure pleasure.

Henriot

51100 Reims; 03.26.89.53.00; fax: 03.26.89.53.10; $$ to $$$$
This is a house to watch. It's to be hoped that Joseph Henriot, who has turned Bouchard Père & Fils and William Fèvre into leading lights of Burgundy, will work the same magic here. The brut NV is bracing and appetizing; the Blanc Souverain, 100 percent chardonnay from some of the best Côte des Blancs villages, is a bit aggressive but a full-throated soprano. The rosé brut NV is nicely done, if a bit too fizzy, as is the rich 1996 brut though the bubbles do settle down, letting the toasty, honey, citrus, and apple flavors come to the fore. The very good Cuvée des Enchanteleurs, a vintage Champagne, is fresh, textured, and toasty.

Jacquart

51100 Reims; 03.26.07.88.40; www.jacquart-champagne.fr; $$$

Improving cooperative. Look for Brut Mosaïque, vintage or nonvintage.

Jacquesson ☆

51530 Dizy; 03.26.55.68.11; champagne.jacquesson@wanadoo.fr; $$$ to $$$$

Another personal favorite, this small "big house" behaves like a grower. The eco-serious Chiquet family, the major shareholders, control roughly 30 hectares of vines, all in Premier Cru or Grand Cru, and supplement their holdings with purchased grapes to make 300,000 bottles a year. (This is why NM appears on the bottles rather than RM.) Since 1988 the Chiquets have been entirely revamping the Jacquesson line. There are currently two blends and five single-vineyard Champagnes, though not every cuvée is produced every year. Most of the wines ferment in big old barrels. They are not cold-stabilized or filtered. Significantly, this evolution has, as Jean-Hervé Chiquet noted, led to their being dissatisfied with the NV brut, which had been consistency-based from year to year. Now, to indicate the difference between one NV brut and another, the bottles are labeled in the following manner: #728 is based on the 2000 harvest; #729, on 2001; #730, on 2002, and so forth—all of which is explained on the back label. So #729, a blend of all three grapes, is based on 2001, the avowed worst vintage of the decade (though it's blended with two other vintages as well). It's exemplary, deeply vinous, suave, and beautifully balanced. The excellent and incredibly starchy 1995 Grand Cru Avize resonated with chardonnay, wheat, and brioche flavors. Ditto for the 1996, the mellowness of which recalled the Avize-based Champagnes of Anselme Selosse. The 2000 Premier Cru Dizy Le Clos is a *blanc de noirs* of pure pinot meunier from a parcel behind the cellars in which delicious wild strawberries grow along the borders of the vines. Immensely alluring, it's delicate, floral, lacy, and airborne but also firm and round. The racy 1996 Grand Cru Vauzelle Terme, a single-vineyard pinot noir, is smoky and seductive with penetrating notes of raspberry eau-de-vie. The 2000 Dizy Premier Cru Corne Bautray is pure old-vines chardonnay. A majestic presence, it's an iron fist in a silk glove. The 1995 Grand Vin Signature, a blend of pinot noir and chardonnay, all Premier Cru or Grand Cru, as grandiose as the Corne Bautray, was a tapestry of mineral and fruit flavors with the lingering freshness of lemon zests.

Krug ☆

51100 Reims; 03.26.84.44.20; www.krug.fr; $$$$

Now part of the LVMH portfolio—where it is the jewel in the crown—Krug is the ultimate deluxe Champagne. No expense is spared in the making, and no punches are pulled in the pricing. Grande Cuvée, its brut NV and roughly 80 percent of its production, costs more than $100. Like all of Krug's Champagnes, it ferments in small old wood barrels. Its blend contains as many as ten vintages from as many as twenty *crus*. When finally released, it is round, full, fine, greatly complex, and textured, a weave of many fleeting yet resonant flavors. This is the wine most people who taste Krug will sample. The vintage bottlings are exquisite, and alas, I've never had the good luck to taste its most precious wine, the Clos de Mesnil. But hope springs eternal.

Lanson: See BOIZEL.

Larmandier-Bernier ☆

51130 Vertus; 03.26.52.13.24; www.larmandier.com; $$$ to $$$$

I know you'll be surprised to hear this but there are actually wine lovers who don't like Champagne. When I meet them, I always want to whip out a bottle of Larmandier-Bernier to show them the error of their ways. On the other hand, I'd just as soon save the bottle for myself. These are extraordinary and drop-dead delicious Champagnes. Young, intelligent, and impassioned, Pierre Larmandier has converted his 15 hectares in the Côte des Blancs to biodynamics. He uses natural yeasts, very little sulfur, and a low dosage. Larmandier makes six different cuvées of Champagne a year as well as a Coteaux Champenois, the latter, out of respect for tradition. (Pray he'll continue: his 2002 Coteaux Champenois Vertus, pure, low-yielding, barrel-aged pinot noir, is one of the best I've ever tasted. Mineral, cool, firm, and flavorful, it's right up there with Egly-Ouriet.) And those Champagnes! The chalky, elegant brut Tradition Premier Cru, 80 percent chardonnay, is delicate, an extremely fine weave of citrus zests and minerals; the razor-sharp *blanc de blancs* NV is a vivid wake-up call, all pedigree with a twist of lemon peel. The tinglingly vivacious single-vineyard Terre de Vertus is an intense, chalky, pure Champagne with scrumptious citrus zest flavors. The gingery 1999 *blanc de blancs,* all Grand Cru and Premier Cru chardonnay, is deep and superb. Both this and the 2000 Grand Cru Extra Brut Vieilles Vignes de Cramant bowl me over with their succulent austerity. The latter cuts like a diamond, leaving a whisper of ginger on the tongue.

Domaine Jacques Lassaigne/Champagne Alexandre Montgueux ☆

10300 Montgueux; 03.25.74.84.83; www.montgueux.com; $$$ to $$$$

Future star here, behind the Alexandre L label. The patrician brut NV *blanc de blancs* Les Vignes de Montgueux, pure chardonnay, is chalky, with fine fruit, great freshness, and even greater elegance. The Rosé de Montgueux extra brut, though a tad aggressive, is a lovely blend of minerals and strawberry fruit. The dry, stony Cuvée Le Cotet, an old-vines *blanc de blancs,* has fig and apple accents; it's very beautiful and very special. When I tasted the 1999 *blanc de blancs* extra brut it had been carafed to show how it would evolve. It had lost almost all of its bubbles. What was left was an aristocratic, mineral chardonnay—fresh, structured, and extremely long. Superb.

J. Lassalle

51500 Chigny-les-Roses; 03.26.03.42.19; champagne.j.lassalle@wanadoo.fr; $$$ to $$$$

Fine family domaine with a half-dozen first-rate cuvées—every one of them Premier Cru and food friendly. For example, the characterful Préférence, a blend of all three grapes, with its mushroom, truffle, and forest underbrush flavors, might be paired with any dish featuring woodsy ingredients; the brut rosé, with its light strawberry and ginger notes, would be a fine pick-me-up with dessert. Delicate and lightly toasty, the 1999 *blanc de blancs* is an ideal aperitif. Angéline, a lacy, airborne blend of pinot noir and chardonnay, is rich yet so evanescent I simply want to put it with fresh raspberries. The 1997 Spécial Club, with its accents of ginger and flavors of rhubarb and red fruit, beautifully accompanied poached salmon.

Launois Père & Fils

51190 Le Mesnil-sur-Oger; 03.26.57.50.15; $$ to $$$

Smack in the center of Le Mesnil, this good family domaine produces an appetizing, biscuity *blanc de blancs* Cuvée Réserve Le Mesnil Grand Cru and a pleasant Veuve Clémence Chardonnay.

Laurent-Perrier

BP 3, 51150 Tours-sur-Marne; 03.26.58.91.22; www.laurent-perrier.fr; $$$ to $$$$

This reliable family domaine produces a good enough brut Laurent-Perrier, but its Ultra Brut is more interesting. Slightly sour, with light truffle notes, I'd pair it with oysters. It's a shellfish platter loaded with langoustines, crab, and shrimp for the 1996 brut, an elegant wine with flavors of minerals and preserved lemon. And I'd couple chicken or veal in a mushroom cream sauce with the Grand Siècle (vintage or non), a blend of pinot noir and chardonnay from roughly twelve different Grand Cru villages. With flavors of steel and lemon curd, it's a racy Champagne but could be more polished. My guess is that its innate elegance would be enhanced by longer aging—seven years, like the vintage *blanc de blancs,* instead of five.

David Leclapart ☆

51380 Trepail; 03.26.57.07.01; david.leclapart@wanadoo.fr; $$$$

Here's a rising star, both in Champagne and in biodynamics. David Leclapart has less than 5 hectares, all in the Premier Cru village of Trepail. His Champagnes are *blanc de blancs,* pure chardonnay, all Premier Cru. Destemming is done by hand, the punching down of the fermenting mass, by foot; Leclapart uses wild yeasts, eschews fining and filtering, and bottles his wines according to lunar cycles. The top two cuvées, L'Artiste and L'Apôtre, ferment in barrel. They are usually unblended, based on the wine of a single harvest. L'Artiste is elegant, gentle, and quite savory, with light almond notes and a mineral-citrus finish; L'Apôtre, made from vines planted in 1946, has a brawny majesty; it's vinous, very dry, rich, a strong, resolute presence. Racy and long, it can complete with the top Côte des Blancs. With the small amount of pinot noir Leclapart has, he makes rosé and a Coteaux Champenois rouge L'Éden.

R & L Legras

51530 Chouilly; 03.26.54.50.79; fax: 03.26.54.88.74; $$ to $$$

I've tasted only two bottles of this grower's Champagne—both in restaurants in Épernay—but I'm determined to taste more. The *blanc de blancs* NV brut was full and crunchy, with the elegance and specificity of a Grand Cru; the 1990 Cuvée St. Vincent was mouthwatering and pure, with finesse to spare. Total pleasures, each of them.

Lilbert-Fils ☆

BP 14, 51530 Cramant; 03.26.57.50.16; www.champagne-lilbert.com; $$ to $$$

This wonderful, eco-friendly family domaine has been located on a side street in the Grand Cru village of Cramant since 1746. Bertrand, who took over in 1999 after having gotten a degree in enology in Reims, worked at Piper-Sonoma and then in the enology lab in Épernay. He is sixth-generation vigneron. The Lilberts are *blanc de blancs* specialists, with less than 4 hectares spread out in three Grand Cru villages. They make 25,000 bottles of (unoaked) Champagne a year. The *blanc de blancs* brut NV is as special as a Grand Cru ought to be. It's vinous, racy, very pure, and totally appetizing. Its vintage Champagnes are entirely from Cramant and are aged for four to five years. When I visited in 2005, the Lilberts were selling the 1999. A *terroir*-driven *blanc de blancs,* it was racy and lipsmacking with flavors of lime, ginger, and apples. Brut Perle, made from seventy-year-old chardonnay vines, has about half the pressure (fizz) of traditional Champagne. My luck—it was completely sold out. So Lilbert *père* went off in search of what he considered his best vintage, 1982. A convincing argument for long lees aging, it had been disgorged less than three years earlier. Amazingly fresh and savory, it was racy, succulent, and powerful, simultaneously creamy and vivacious, a beauty.

Mailly Grand Cru ☆

51500 Mailly-Champagne; 03.26.49.41.10; www.champagne-mailly.com; $$ to $$$$

This admirable association of eighty-three growers with 70 hectares of vines in Mailly Grand Cru on the northernmost slopes of the Montagne de Reims makes ten different cuvées of Champagne, all Grand Cru, all dominated by pinot noir—and every one of them recommended. They include a very good, full but discreet brut réserve; an appetizing ginger- and brioche-scented extra brut; and a rather exotic 100 percent pinot noir *blanc de noirs.* A rosé made from a direct press of pinot noir following twenty hours of maceration actually tasted like roses—interwoven with strawberries, citrus zests, and minerals. There's a pellucid and mouthwatering brut L'Intemporelle, its rhubarb, strawberry, and mineral notes set against a backdrop of steel. There's also the newest entry, Le Feu 2000, both full and fleeting, and my favorite, the 1996 Les Échansons, a mellow, crunchy, elegant Champagne with flavors of lemon curd and ginger—the ginger ale of the gods.

Margaine ☆

51380 Villers-Marmery; 03.26.97.92.13; www.champagne-a-margaine.com; $$ to $$$

The Montagne de Reims is pinot noir country—except when you get to Villers-Marmery, an islet of chardonnay, the uniqueness of which is beautifully expressed by this conscientious grower. Every cuvée is recommended. My favorites are the sophisticated rosé with its whiff of strawberry and cotton candy; the racy 1996 Premier Cru Cuvée Angéline, a succulent compote of apple and rhubarb with a long mineral finish; and the ample yet aristocratic 1998 *blanc de blancs* Premier Cru Spécial Club, a pure chardonnay with flavors of ginger and lemon zest. Downright delicious and totally excellent.

Marne Valley

The westernmost Champagne zone, beginning at Château Thierry, these are the first vines you see if you take the train from Paris to Champagne. The principal grape is pinot meunier, though some of its best villages, Mareuil-sur-Aÿ, Dizy, and Cumières, for example, are known for their pinot noir or pinot noir and pinot meunier blends. Producers: FRANÇOISE BEDEL ◆ GASTON CHIQUET ◆ RENÉ GEOFFROY.

Le Mesnil

51190 Le Mesnil-sur-Oger; 03.26.57.53.23; upr-lemesnil@wanadoo.fr; $$($)

The Union des Propriétaires Récoltants-Manipulants of Le Mesnil is a small cooperative of growers who, as a group, control 150 hectares of vines. Their wines, all *blanc de blancs* from Le Mesnil, either nonvintage or vintage, are the real thing and offer high quality for the dollar. The 1998 Réserve Sélection brut is very dry, very crunchy, very Côte des Blancs, and very good.

José Michel & Fils ☆

51530 Moussy; 03.26.54.04.69; fax: 03.26.55.37.12; $$ to $$$

Four kilometers south of Épernay, with vineyards dominated by pinot meunier, José Michel makes excellent, underpriced Champagnes. His brut NV, a pinot meunier and chardonnay blend, could best the same cuvée in most, if not all, of the big houses. Fruity and lipsmacking, it's clean, firm, and fine from start to finish. The lacy extra brut *non dosé,* which ages for an additional year, is even better, adding notes of honey, citrus zests, and minerals. The 1999 *blanc de blancs,* with some new-oak age, is full, rich, and vinous, a firm but fine Champagne. The elegant and deep 1996 is an interlacing of honey, minerals, and succulent fruit. The 1997 Special Club brut, from very old chardonnay and pinot meunier vines, is extremely racy and razor sharp, with appetizing notes of citrus zests. Michel also sells older vintages, such as a very special 1992 *blanc de blancs,* a profoundly textured wine with notes of hay, honey, and minerals—tremendous.

Jean Milan

51190 Oger; 03.26.57.50.09; www.champagne-milan.com; $$ to $$$

I've tasted only one cuvée of the half-dozen or so bottlings made by this grower, but that cuvée—Terre de Noël—so impressed me the several times I drank it (in both the 2000 and 1998 vintages) that it is definitely worth mentioning. A Grand Cru Côte des Blancs from sixty-year-old chardonnay vines, it's very fine, very appetizing, and very mineral, with satisfying depth and length. And there's an unusual quality about it that I simply can't pin down.

Moët & Chandon

51000 Épernay; 03.26.51.20.00; www.moet.com; $$$ to $$$$

The largest Champagne house—it sells twenty-five million bottles yearly—Moët is part of LVMH, the luxury goods magnate with a portfolio that also includes Clicquot, Ruinart, Louis Vuitton, and Hennessey. The entry-level bottling, Brut Impérial, aims for consistency and is fair. The vintage bottlings are a step up.

Dom Pérignon is the deluxe bottling. Vinous and easy on the palate, it is never less than very good and is often excellent. (The base wine apparently comes from the Union Champagne/Cave Coopérative d'Avize.) There is also a Coteaux Champenois, Saran.

Pierre Moncuit ☆

51190 Le Mesnil-sur-Oger; 03.26.57.52.65; www.pierre-moncuit.fr; $$$
This superb artisanal family domaine has 19 hectares, almost all of them in Grand Cru Le Mesnil. All the Champagnes are *blanc de blancs* and all come from a single vintage, though only top years are so labeled. Cuvée Hugues de Coulmet Brut has a twinge of sweetness that would make it an excellent aperitif or dessert Champagne. The *terroir*-driven Pierre Montcuit-Delos Réserve is a real step up, vivacious and crunchy, with a long citrus zest finish; I'd love it with shellfish. The very fine 1999 *blanc de blancs* mellows the citrus notes with flavors of butter and brioche. The 1996, deep, layered, and long, is so good it gives me goose bumps.

Montagne de Reims

One of the most important Champagne-producing sectors, located between Épernay and Reims. Bordered by the Marne River to the south and the Vesle to the north, it is chiefly, but not exclusively, planted with pinot noir. Home to many Premier Cru and Grand Cru villages, among them: Ambonnay, Bouzy, Sillery, Verzenay. Producers: AUBRY ◆ HENRI BILLIOT & FILS ◆ CHARTOGNE-TAILLET ◆ ROGER COULON ◆ EGLY-OURIET ◆ MAILLY GRAND CRU ◆ MARGAINE ◆ PALMER & CO ◆ VILMART & CO.

Champagne Alexandre Montgueux: See DOM JACQUES LASSAIGNE.

Moutard Père & Fils

10110 Buxeuil; 03.25.38.50.73; champagne.moutard@wanadoo.fr; $$ to $$$
This eco-friendly family domaine is located in the Aube, at the southeastern limits of the Champagne AC. While all of Moutard's bottlings are recommended, the most interesting are those made from the obscure grapes arbane, petit meslier, and pinot blanc. Once widely planted in the region, each has all but disappeared from Champagne's vineyards. Moutard's arbane Vieilles Vignes is creamy and intriguing, with a light, pleasant note of oxidation; the Cuvée aux 6 Cépages blends the three untraditional grapes with the three conventional ones. With some barrel age, it's deeper, meatier, and more layered than the arbane. More mainstream is the appetizing brut Grande Cuvée, with its plump fruit and mineral flavors. Vintage Champagnes are disgorged on demand. The 1996 was a zaftig chardonnay; the 1990, an agreeably quirky mix of creamed corn and truffle flavors; and the 1985 was a lipsmacking weave of forest underbrush, honey, hay, and truffles. I could have polished off an entire bottle by myself.

Mumm

51100 Reims; 03.26.49.59.69; www.mumm.com; $$$
Another big house recovering from a slump, Mumm's most recognizable bottling is the pleasant (and improving) Cordon Rouge. The cuvée to look for, however, is still Mumm de Cramant Grand Cru brut chardonnay.

Bruno Paillard ☆

51100 Reims, 03.26.36.20.22; www.champagnebrunopaillard.com; $$$ to $$$$
This small, ambitious family firm makes admirable Champagnes. Both the brut Première Cuvée, a blend of all three grapes, and the rosé brut NV Première Cuvée, chiefly pinot noir, are punchy, bracing, and pleasant. Nec Plus Ultra, the deluxe bottling, is a blend of Grand Cru pinot noir and chardonnay. The latest vintage, 1990, had intriguingly autumnal flavors of dried leaves and forest underbrush.

Palmer & Co ☆

51100 Reims; 03.26.07.35.07; fax: 03.26.07.45.24; $$ to $$$

This noteworthy cooperative has three-hundred members and controls 400 hectares, half of them on the Montagne de Reims. Less than 10 percent of its yearly production of three million bottles is sold under the deluxe Palmer label. Much is buyer's own brand, as is the case with Sainsbury, an important client. Additionally, Palmer keeps a stock of old and very old vintages—undisgorged—which are usually sold to restaurants or at auction. The brut NV, with four years' age, is straightforward, with good citrus flavors; the toothsome 1995 brut *blanc de blancs* is deeper and more focused; and the very fine Amazone de Palmer, a blend of the best wines of 1992, 1993, and 1994 with nine years' age, was both fresh and tender, with appetizing notes of hay and honey. Perhaps to prove the availability of the old vintages, still gently aging in Palmer's cellars, a 1961 was disgorged in front of me. Still fresh, it was deeply mellow, with mouthwatering truffle accents.

Franck Pascal ↑

51700 Baslieux-sous-Châtillon; 03.26.51.89.80; franck.pascal@wanadoo.fr; $$$

What immediately strikes me about the Champagnes of this young Marne valley grower is that they are so personalized, so manifestly the work of a dedicated winemaker who farms biodynamically, maintaining extremely low yields and using lots of TLC. The Champagnes are still works in progress but they are always flavorful, with plenty of character. The vibrant 1999 brut Équilibre Cuvée Prestige was as hale and hearty as a high school athlete.

Joseph Perrier

51016 Châlons-en-Champagne; 03.26.68.29.51; josephperrier@wanadoo.fr; $$ to $$$

This small Champagne house relives the time when it furnished Queen Victoria and Edward VII with the name of its basic bottlings—Cuvée Royale—of which the brut NV, the easygoing entry-level bottling, makes up 75 percent of production. The *blanc de blancs* NV is mellow and tender, with pleasing flavors of apricots and minerals. The admirable rosé makes up in flavor what it lacks in elegance, and is a good dinner Champagne. Best are the vivacious and singular 1996 *blanc de noirs* and the airy 1995 Joséphine, a very feminine, tender wine with a long finish enlivened with citrus zest. Joseph Perrier also makes an interesting, barrel-aged Coteaux Champenois Cumières Rouge.

Perrier-Jouët

51200 Épernay; 03.26.53.38.00; www.perrier-jouet.com; $$$ to $$$$

This good-size Champagne house, famous for its Art Nouveau bottling Belle Époque, was in a slump during the end of the twentieth century. There are signs of a renaissance here, and the 1996 Belle Époque is nearly as pretty as the anemones painted on its distinctive bottle.

Pierre Peters ☆

51190 Le Mesnil-sur-Oger; 03.26.57.50.32; champagne-peters@wanadoo.fr; $$ to $$$

The wines from this sizable grower-producer embody that tooth-itching, exciting specialness of Côte des Blancs Champagnes. The starchy *blanc de blancs* extra brut Le Mesnil is all finesse, plumped up a bit with pineapple and ginger flavors. The Cuvée de Réserve brut NV, another Le Mesnil *blanc de blancs,* is starched lace and lemon curd. So fresh, so bracing. The 1998 Cuvée Spéciale brut is an extraordinary *blanc de blancs.* Made from seventy-year-old chardonnay vines in Grand Cru Le Mesnil, it's gingery and crunchy, with a long, long finish—the essence of elegance and very sexy. I love all three.

Pol Roger ☆

BP 199, 51206 Épernay Cedex; www.polroger.fr; $$$ to $$$$

First-rate, family-run house with nearly a hundred hectares of vines in both the Côte des Blancs and in some of pinot noir's preferred sites, Ambonnay and

Mareuil. The Brut Réserve is crunchy, elegant, and fresh; the *blanc de blancs* and the vintage (here 1996) are sapid, fine, and lipsmacking; the deluxe cuvée, Sir Winston Churchill, named after Pol Roger's most celebrated (and devoted) customer, is painfully elegant, a fine mesh of gold silk.

Pommery/Vranken

51100 Reims; 03.26.61.62.63; tgasco@vrankenpommery.fr; $$$ to $$$$
Purchased from LVMH in the 1990s by the lackluster Vranken Monopole, Pommery lost its vineyards. The Pommerys currently available are clearly superior to those from Vranken. Their "visiting card," the Brut Royale, is fresh, clean, and bracing; the 1996 brut Grand Cru displays some texture and elegance; and the deluxe Cuvée Louise is racy and refined. For the pierced-body-part generation there's Pop, in a soda bottle format, which can be drunk with a straw.

Jérôme Prévost

51390 Gueux; tel/fax: 03.26.03.48.60; $$$
A young vigneron to watch, Jérôme Prévost realized a long-held dream when, in 1996, he got hold of about 5 acres of vineyard land in the Côte des Blancs. He worked alongside ANSELME SELOSSE and has adopted many of that influential producer's ideas about viticulture, vinification, and the importance of *terroir.* He has gotten a lot of press and is a wine-bar favorite but his wines, for me, are still works in progress. La Closerie Les Béguines, pure pinot meunier, is fresh and crisp but can be dominated by such strong and varied apple flavors that it tastes like cider.

Alain Robert ☆

51190 Le Mesnil-sur-Oger; 03.26.57.52.94; fax: 03.26.57.59.22; $$$$
Enigmatic, elusive Alain Robert gets away with any and all eccentricities because his Champagne is stupendous. Taste whatever you can, wherever you can. Most of the Champagnes are vintage, all are *blanc de blancs* Le Mesnil Grand Cru, all age for ages and are unfiltered. The youngest of the wines he's currently selling are two 1986s. The first, Le Mesnil *blanc de blancs* Réserve, aged for nineteen years, is a diamond dazzler, very dry, very full, very gingery, with notes of green olive, flint, toast, and truffles. Breathtaking and perfect for drinking now. The barrel-fermented 1986 Tradition is twice the price of the former but, despite evolving flavors of forest underbrush, it doesn't seem at its apogee. Still, it's fleshy, creamy, and absolutely lipsmacking.

Louis Roederer ☆

51100 Reims, 03.26.40.42.11; www.champagne-roederer.com; $$$ to $$$$
This important family-owned house is much more than the purveyor of the very expensive, deluxe Cristal, the preferred swig of partying starlets and rappers. (What a shame that is—a Champagne so finely tuned and composed of such exquisite raw materials should be sipped reverentially. Humph!) With 200 hectares, mostly in Grand Cru and Premier Cru, and strict viticultural practices, Roederer turns out a range of superlative Champagnes, starting with an ample, vivacious brut Premier NV. Most of Roederer's Champagnes are vintage. The 1998 rosé is rich, fresh, and elegant with core of succulent fruit. The aristocratic 1998 *blanc de blancs* is crunchy, taut, fresh, and lilting as a lyric soprano, with a fine fruity finish. Even more elegant is the statuesque 1997 Cristal, an entrancing weave of flavors including ginger, citrus zests, wheat, and minerals.

Rosé des Riceys

A still rosé wine made in the commune of Riceys in the Aube. The wine, which is not produced every year, is made by a short maceration of pinot noir. There is very little of it and, because the grapes can also be used to make Champagne, it is necessarily expensive. Nevertheless, it is unique. Anyone who thinks rosé can't be serious should try it. Anyone who knows rosé can be serious will need little persuasion to try it. Prices: $$$. Producer: Alexandre Bonnet: the leading producer of Rosé des Riceys, its oak-aged wines are fresh, firm, and full of character, with flavors of dried and candied fruit.

Ruinart ☆

BP 85, 51053 Reims Cedex; 03.26.77.51.51; www.ruinart.com; $$$ to $$$$

Found mostly in fine restaurants and wine shops, Ruinart is the low-profile house in the LVMH brood. Its focus is on chardonnay and its Champagnes are reliably discreet and stylish. When tasted in June 2005, Ruinart *blanc de blancs* was full, tender, and easy on the palate. R de Ruinart, full without being fat, could have used a bit more focus but was very tasty. The recently disgorged R de Ruinart 1999 was a real step up—broader, deeper, more pedigreed, with inviting flavors of brioche. The appetizing 1996 Dom Ruinart was extremely fresh, round, and ample, with a delightful thread of vivacity. The 1990 Dom Ruinart rosé might seem over-the-hill and/or quirky for some, but I found it deliciously intriguing—with flavors of berries, forest underbrush, and tobacco converging in a long, long finish. If you visit Champagne, don't miss Ruinart's cellars with their Gallo-Roman *crayères,* cone-shaped shafts 34 meters high that have been classified as historic monuments.

De Saint Gall

51190 Avize; 03.26.57.94.22; fax: 03.26.57.57.98; $$$ to $$$$

This federation of a dozen cooperatives controls 1,200 hectares of vines, all Premier Cru or Grand Cru, with 900 hectares in the Côte des Blancs. They make the base wine for Dom Pérignon and supply wine to many other big houses, including Clicquot and Taittinger. They also make their own range of noteworthy Champagne under the de Saint Gall label. Their best wine, however, is called Orpale. It's always a safe bet. The 1995 is a vivacious, racy, and crunchy Champagne with flavors of lemon, lime, and Granny Smith apples.

CHAMPAGNE

Salon ☆

51190 Le Mesnil-sur-Oger; 03.26.57.51.65; www.salondelamotte.com; $$$$

Unique and luxurious, Salon is made from one grape (chardonnay), one *cru* (Le Mesnil Grand Cru), and one vintage (an exceptional one). It spends eight to ten years aging, so that the Champagnes Salon is selling now are from 1990, 1995, 1996, 1997, and 1999. (The 90s were unusually generous to Salon; the house generally makes wine only two or three years out of ten.) The Champagnes are, indeed, extraordinary. They have everything—great breadth, depth, and pedigree. They are creamy, with bubbles so gentle as to be almost imperceptible, with flavors of honey, brioche, hay, citrus zests, lime, and linden blossom. With a bit more age, notes of forest underbrush join the weave; the Champagne, though, maintains its vivacity.

François Secondé ☆

51500 Sillery; 03.26.49.16.67; fax: 03.26.49.11.55; $$ to $$$

This meticulous, eco-friendly family domaine is situated in the tiny Grand Cru Sillery on the Montagne de Reims. All the Champagnes are Grand Cru and all are very vivid and mighty delicious, starting with the ample, very toothsome brut NV. Clavier, two thirds chardonnay and one third pinot noir, is a big, burly, and starchy, a real presence. Champagne with fine fruit, accents of ginger, and more than a little elegance. The bone-dry Intégrale is satisfyingly rich and savory. Best of all is the vintage *blanc de blancs.* The unfiltered 1999, from chardonnay planted in 1962, is rich and meaty but also discreet; its fruit is extremely ripe, with flavors like preserved lemon, dried apples, and apricot, blended with hay and honey. Utterly delicious and amazingly inexpensive. Secondé also makes Coteaux du Champenois in red and white. They're quite good representatives of the genre, but I much prefer his lovely Champagnes.

Jacques (Anselme) Selosse ☆

51190 Avize; 03.26.57.53.56; a.selosse@wanadoo.fr; $$$ to $$$$

Someday there will be a statue of Anselme Selosse in the center of Avize. Perhaps the most influential Champagne producer of the baby boom generation, his obsessive research into *terroir* and his espousal of biodynamics made him an iconoclast, a pariah, at first. Now, many are following in his footsteps. Selosse studied enology at the Lycée Viticole de Beaune before taking over his father's 7 hectares of vines. Ask him about *terroir* and he pulls out charts and diagrams as well as a complete analysis of his soils performed by the incomparable "soil-ologist" Claude Bourgignon and draws all over them in different colored pens, explaining how the chalky soils of Avize came to exist. He prepares his own compost so that the soils of his own vineyards will be as rich with natural life as a virgin forest and basically practices noninterventionist winemaking—no chaptalization, no added yeasts, no decantation, no temperature controls, no fining, no filtration. It's hypernaturalism that works, and it's a philosophy that runs precisely contrary to that guiding the big Champagne houses: As Selosse says, "I want each wine to be totally original. I never want to feel that I've tasted this before." All the Champagnes are barrel fermented. Brut Initial is a vinous, berry- and apple-rich mouthful; extra brut is full and razor sharp. (Selosse describes it as "dignified, a bit stuffy, a bit British.") Substance *blanc de blancs* is a blend of more than ten vintages. Rich, mellow, fresh despite a whiff of oxidation, it's completely original, a personal search and a scrupulously honest winemaker's Champagne. Although Selosse downplays vintage in order to highlight *terroir,* his vintage *blanc de blancs* are magnificent. And, as someone who doesn't like so-called dessert wines (such as Sauternes or Banyuls) with dessert, I do have another proposition—Selosse's Exquise. With its 18 grams of sugar it qualifies as sec and it's exactly what I want with dessert.

Erick de Sousa & Fils ☆

51190 Avize; 03.26.57.53.29; www.champagnedesousa.com; $$ to $$$$

Breathtaking, must-try Champagnes. The basics: Erick de Sousa took over the family's 8.5 hectares of mostly old vines, planted in some of the best areas of the Côte des Blancs, in 1986. Since 1999 he has been converting the vineyards to biodynamics and does not filter his Champagnes. He also makes Coteaux Champenois and has created a *négociant* line called Âme de Terroir, which markets wines from selected vintners in other regions (Mas Karolina in the Roussillon, for example) and Champagnes under the Zoémie label. But it's de Sousa's Champagnes that are the irresistible draw here. The Brut Tradition is crunchy, airborne, and pure, as well as fruity and full—an excellent meal Champagne. The rosé brut NV is elegant, succulent, and lipsmacking. The brut réserve *blanc de blancs* Grand Cru is full, long, and pedigreed. The barrel-fermented Cuvée des Caudalies Grand Cru, from very old vines in one of the first parcels to be converted to biodynamics, is rich, savory, and aristocratic, with flavors of toast, brioche, and oak and a long, fine finish. The barrel-fermented 1999 Cuvée des Caudalies Grand Cru is extremely deep, fresh, and elegant. Its oak entirely melted into the wine, it's racy, mineral, and strikingly pure. It's one of those Champagnes that rise to the level of art.

Taittinger

51100 Reims; 03.26.85.45.35; www.taittinger.com; $$$ to $$$$

Taittinger Champagne was part of the package sold in September 2005 to Starwood Capital, a group of American investors. As Starwood was essentially interested in Taittinger's other holdings—notably the Hôtel Crillon in Paris—it resold the Champagne house in June 2006 to Crédit Agricole Nord-Est. The Taittinger family and the wine's U.S. importer are shareholders. With luck, we'll be able to continue drinking the top-of-the-line Comte de Champagne.

Tarlant ☆

51480 Oeuilly; 03.26.58.30.60; www.tarlant.com; $$$

Among the things I love about Jean-Mary Tarlant's handcrafted, organic Champagnes are the very explicit labels, disclosing the blend, the various vintages, the vineyards, and so forth—all the things I want to know. Then, I love the Champagnes themselves. The most basic is his brut *zéro,* a very dry blend of all three Champagne grapes, mostly from the 2000 harvest. A burnished gold, its bead was very fine and the flavor was full and fresh, with notes of apple, fig, and ginger, all of which lingered through the long, dry finish. Barrel-fermented Cuvée Louis NV brut is a chardonnay–pinot noir blend based on the 1995 vintage. Full and mellow, it had delicious accents of citrus zests and honey. It would make an excellent dinner Champagne.

Varnier-Fannière ☆

51190 Avize; 03.26.57.53.36; www.varnier-fanniere.com; $$$($)

Very good, small, family domaine with high-quality Champagnes, all Côte des Blancs Grand Cru. The Cuvée St.-Denis brut NV comes from a single parcel of old vines in Avize. Almost stingingly tart, it's an austere prince, vigorous, elegant, and chalky. The Grand Vintage 1999 is full, dry, and elegant, with tons of that crunchy Côte des Blancs character. Long and fine, it's super with shellfish. The brut NV is also highly recommended though not nearly as distinguished as its brothers.

Veuve-Clicquot-Ponsardin

51100 Reims; 03.26.89.54.40; www.veuve-clicquot.com; $$$ to $$$$

This immense Champagne firm is also part of the LVMH group. The house style is full-bodied with an emphasis on pinot noir. Its omnipresent entry-level bottling, the NV brut Carte Jaune has a hard-to-miss yellow-orange label, making it perfect for product placements. Grande Dame is the plump, savory deluxe cuvée.

Vilmart & Co ☆

51500 Rilly-la-Montagne; 03.26.03.40.01; www.champagnevilmart.fr; $$$

This very good family domaine has 11 hectares in and around the Premier Cru village of Rilly-la-Montagne, just south of Reims. All the Champagnes are Premier Cru, viticulture is organic, and the wines ferment in barrels of varying sizes and ages, though the oak presence is always discreet, sometimes barely noticeable. The nonvintage cuvées are quite fine all-purpose Champagnes. It's with the vintage bottlings, though, that the fun starts. The 1998 Grand Cellier Rubis is achingly elegant, light as a spring breeze, with just a whisper of rhubarb—a definite Valentine's Day bottle. The mouthwatering 1998 Premier Cru Grand Cellier d'Or is full and gingery, a real wine with ginger and caramel notes and a steel core; it's elegant despite its powerful presence. The invigorating 1996 Cuvée Création comes in a bottle with the decal of a stained glass window, and the wine does seem etched, crystalline. The 1997 Coeur de Cuvée, made from old vines, chiefly chardonnay, is discreet and polished, and excitingly crunchy.

CHAMPAGNE CRIB SHEET

MUST TRYS

Bollinger
Egly-Ouriet
Krug
Larmandier-Bernier
Jacques Lassaigne
David Leclapart
Pierre Moncuit
Alain Robert
Erick de Sousa & Fils

SAFE HOUSES

Billecart-Salmon
Delamotte
Deutz
Duval-Leroy
Pierre Gimmonet
Gosset
Jacquesson
Pol Roger
Louis Roederer
Vilmart & Co

SMART BUYS

Drappier—especially the Cuvée *non dosé*
Gatinois
Lilbert-Fils
Margaine
Le Mesnil
José Michel & Fils
Palmer & Co
Pierre Peters
François Secondé
Tarlant

ALSACE
BORDEAUX
BURGUNDY
CHAMPAGNE

JURA AND SAVOIE

LANGUEDOC-ROUSSILLON
LOIRE
PROVENCE AND CORSICA
RHÔNE
SOUTHWEST

THE JURA AND SAVOIE REGIONS

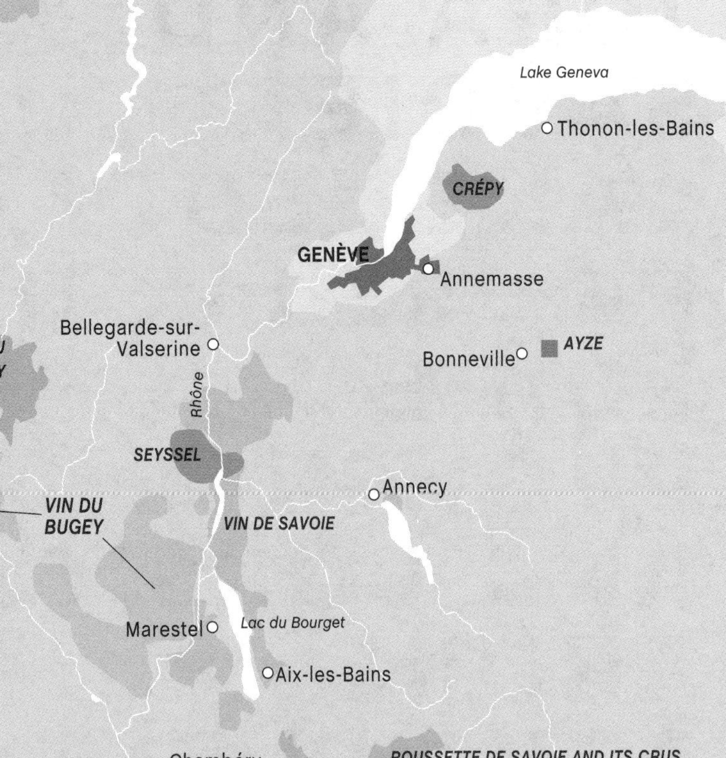

In the Alpine ski country, between Switzerland and Burgundy, you find two very special, nearly anecdotal, wine regions, Jura and Savoie. Each uses numerous varieties of grapes—some familiar, some obscure—to make an almost encyclopedic range of wines, including a few that are like nothing else in the world.

The wine appellations of Jura are easy to list: Arbois (including Arbois-Pupillon), Château-Chalon, Côtes du Jura, and l'Étoile. Then things get complicated. Both Arbois (and its Pupillon) and Côtes du Jura produce whites, reds, and rosés. All three, along with L'Étoile, make sinuous, sweet *vin de paille.* All make *vin jaune,* a searing, fino sherry–like wine that is aged for a minimum of six years. Indeed, Château-Chalon is devoted exclusively to the production of *vin jaune.* The best sparkling wines, made throughout the region, are Crémant du Jura. Macvin is a delectable *vin de liqueur* made from blending partially fermented grape juice with eau-de-vie.

In Savoie the ACs strike me as needlessly confusing. Most wines fall under the umbrella Vin de Savoie but tow along with them the name of a *cru,* such as Abymes, Apremont, Chignin, and so forth. Although the broad regional AC applies to reds, whites, and rosés, many of the hyphenated AC *crus* have their own rules. Roussette de Savoie, another important AC, is limited to whites made from the grape altesse (a.k.a. roussette). It, too, has its *crus,* as does the AC Bugey, of which the most interesting is Bugey-Cerdon, a low-alcohol, sweet, pink sparkling wine. Additionally, there are two minuscule ACs, Crépy, for whites made from chasselas, and Seyssel, for still and sparkling whites, based on altesse.

GRAPES: For whites: chardonnay, savagnin, altesse, mondeuse blanc, pinot gris, and local varietals like gringet (especially in Côtes du Jura-Ayze) and molette (chiefly used in sparkling wine). For reds and rosés: trousseau, poulsard, pinot noir, mondeuse, and gamay.

STYLES OF WINE: It would be simple to summarize the whites as lively and vinous. That, they are. Indeed, what I find thrilling in Savoie whites is their extreme freshness and crispness, which makes me think I'm drinking snow. In Jura, the subject is more complex. The traditional style, called *typé,* is perceptibly oxidized, having begun its life as a potential *vin jaune;* the modern style, called floral or *ouillé,* has the fresh flavors and aromas we more commonly find in young whites from, say, Mâcon, in nearby Burgundy. The reds, particularly the poulsards, are pale in color, almost as light as a rosé. More mineral and stony than fruity, they have zero body fat and plenty of personality.

BEST RECENT VINTAGES: At a minimum 2005 will be a very good (if not excellent) year globally. Jura fared better than Savoie in 2004. Benefiting from beautiful fall weather, those who controlled yields made very good wine. Incomparable here as elsewhere, 2003 resulted in exceptionally rich, ripe fruit that was handled more or less successfully depending upon the grape, the style of wine, and the work of the winemaker. Some whites seem clumsily acidified, and many chardonnays seem soft and heavy, but the reds are fuller and deeper. There may be excellent *vin de paille.* Both 2002 and 2000 were good but not great vintages, often lacking concentration. For *vin jaune,* the best years on the market are 1995 and 1996.

PRICES: $$ to $$$

Abymes

A VIN DE SAVOIE *cru* for whites, reds, and rosés. Producers: Marc & Roges Labbé: see VIN DE SAVOIE ◆ QUENARD ☆.

Apremont

A VIN DE SAVOIE *cru* for whites, reds, and rosés.

Arbin

A VIN DE SAVOIE *cru* for red wines made from mondeuse. Producers: DOM DE L'IDYLLE ◆ Dom Louis Magnin: see VIN DE SAVOIE.

Arbois and Arbois-Pupillon

Jura's most important ACs, centered around the charming town of Arbois (Louis Pasteur lived here). There's an extensive range of whites, reds, and rosés. The most typical are said to come from the environs of the village of Pupillon, but it's hard to taste the difference. The whites are made from savagnin and chardonnay. Reds and rosés are based on poulsard, trousseau, and pinot noir. The whites are either floral and fresh (*ouillé,* modern style) or partially oxidized (*typé*); reds and rosés are spare and mineral. *Crémants* are bright and brisk. See also VIN JAUNE and VIN DE PAILLE.

BEST RECENT VINTAGES: 2005, (2004), (2003), (2002), (2000). For *vin jaune:* 1995, 1996.
PRICES: $ to $$$.

PRODUCERS: Lucien Aviet/Caveau de Bacchus: interesting wines, including light, stony reds (especially the Cuvée des Géologues), smoky *vin jaune,* and a curious, intriguing chardonnay Cuvée des Docteurs ◆ CAVE DE LA REINE JEANNE ☆ ◆ Cellier Saint Benoît: The Arbois-Pupillin reds from this house, particularly the characterful Ploussard Feule, are captivating wines to discover in a wine bar ◆ E & P CLAIRET ◆ Daniel Dugois: the wines aren't perfect but they always have something to say, particularly the trousseau, the *vin jaune,* and best of all, the *vin de paille* ◆ Fruitière Vinicole d'Arbois: a good local cooperative; try the trousseau Château Béthanie and the limpid 2000 *vin de paille* ◆ Dom Martin Faudot: family domaine with above-average versions of the region's wines, particularly the 2001 *vin de paille* and a stiff but interesting poulsard ◆ DOM LIGIER PÈRE & FILS ↑ ◆ FRÉDÉRIC LORNET ☆ ◆ HENRI MAIRE ◆ Overnoy/Crinquand: personalized organic wines from a young domaine in Pupillon to follow ◆ Désiré Petit: family winery with pleasant Arbois-Pupillon; best is the flavorful, herby *vin de paille* ◆ DOM DE LA PINTE ☆ ◆ Auguste Pirou: there have been some missteps here, but the 2001 *vin de paille* was a tasty, orange-tinged nectar and the 1995 *vin jaune,* while a bit raw, had appealing nut and dried apricot flavors. The domaine also makes L'Étoile and a good *crémant* ◆ JACQUES PUFFENEY ☆ ◆ Dom Jean Rijckaert: the same man who makes delicious Mâcon produces structured, lipsmacking whites in both Arbois and the Côtes du Jura ☆ ◆ DOM ROLET ◆ DOM ANDRÉ & MIREILLE TISSOT ☆ ◆ Dom Jacques Tissot: the most interesting bets here are the chardonnay Grande Réserve, the pricey but ambitious pinot noir Vieilles Vignes

Grande Réserve, the concentrated but relatively dry *vin de paille,* and the aggressive *vin jaune.*

Ayze (also Ayse)

A VIN DE SAVOIE *cru* southeast of Geneva for still or sparkling white wines made from altesse, gringet, and mondeuse blanc. Producer: DOM BELLUARD.

Benoît Badoz

39800 Poligny; 03.84.37.11.85; www.badoz.fr

Wine: Côtes du Jura. $$ to $$$

Certainly not anonymous, Benoît Badoz's wines range from the austere, unfiltered reds, to the toast- and petrol-scented *vin jaune,* to the compact *vin de paille* with succulent flavors of candied orange peel. The *crémant* is good, too.

Domaine Belluard & Fils

74130 Ayze; 04.50.97.05.63; 04.50.25.79.66

Wine: Vin de Savoie. $$

The local grape gringet, which the Belluards say is a relative of savagnin, gets star billing here in very mineral still wines, particularly the Le Feu bottling, and in funky, stony sparkling wines.

Domaine Berthet-Bondet

39210 Château-Chalon; 03.84.44.60.48; www.berthet-bondet.net

Wines: Côtes du Jura and Château-Chalon. $ to $$$

An established, reliable domaine with important holdings in Château-Chalon. The 1996 Château-Chalon was a steely, nutty wake-up call. The brawny 1998 Château-Chalon *vin jaune* reminded me of the single malt whiskey Laphroaig in its smokiness. The simpler Côtes du Jura, both white and red, are authentic, if not stellar, but the 1999 *vin de paille* is delicious, creamy, and textured.

Bugey

A Savoie VDQS in the Ain department, spreading along the right bank of the Rhône from the outskirts of Bourg-en-Bresse to the borders of the Isère and Haute Saône departments. The appellation covers whites, reds, and rosés. Whites and rosés may be still or sparkling. The principal grape variety for whites is chardonnay, although other grapes, such as altesse and jacquère, are permitted. For reds and rosés, the main grape is gamay, along with pinot noir and mondeuse. Poulsard may also be used in the production of rosés. Bugey may be accompanied by the name of one of three communes: Bugey-Manicle for whites and reds; Bugey-Montagnieu for reds made from mondeuse as well as for sparkling wines from the same grapes as Bugey; and Bugey-Cerdon for sweet, pink sparkling wines made from gamay and poulsard.

Cerdon is the wine you are most likely to encounter. Light in alcohol (around 7 percent), with noticeable residual sugar, it is a popular aperitif in the Lyon area. The brilliant chef-restaurateur Yves Cambdeborde (of Le Comptoir du Relais in Paris) serves it, well iced, as a nightcap. This is perfect, as Cerdon has just the right amount of fizz, sweetness, and fruit to refresh the palate (and lift the spirit) at the end of a meal. Most Cerdon, like the two recommended here, is made by the *méthode ancestrale,* which means that it is bottled partway through its fermentation. Drink the youngest available. Prices: $. Producers: Catherine & Patrick Bottex: La Cueille ◆ Elie & Alain Renard-Fache ◆ Another Bugey producer, François Grimaud/Clos du Perron, makes a light red blend gamay-pinot noir that drinks like a sensational rosé.

Cave de la Reine Jeanne ☆

39600 Arbois; 03.84.66.08.27; fax: 0384.66.25.08

Wine: Arbois. $ to $$($)

Stéphane Tissot runs an exemplary small *négociant* house. Everything is recommended, starting with the delightful Arbois rosé made from poulsard. Les Rusards, an unfiltered pinot noir, has focus and depth. Also unfiltered, the old-vines chardonnay Grain de Pierre is delectably creamy with hints of complexity that argue in favor of cellaring it for a couple of years. Equally riveting is the Arbois traminer, with its lingering Alsace-like notes. The refreshing 2001 *vin de paille* is a celebration of honey and herbal tea flavors, rich, nuanced, endlessly interesting.

Les Chais du Vieux Bourg ↑

39140 Arlay; 06.14.36.25.26

Wine: Côtes du Jura. $$

The singular 2003 harvest was the first vintage for Ludwig Bindernagel and Nathalie Eigenschenck, and they met the challenge handily. Their poulsard was a serious "light" red with freshness and minerality; the white was equally appealing, with floral and nutlike aromas.

Château-Chalon

A small AC exclusively for *vin jaune* made from savagnin. Strict controls apply. See VIN JAUNE for style, serving suggestions, vintages, and prices. Producers: DOM BERTHET-BONDET ◆ Grand Frères: En Beaumont offers a glimpse of the AC's complexity ◆ JEAN MACLE ☆ ◆ DOM DE LA PINTE ☆.

Chignin

A *cru* of VIN DE SAVOIE for light white wines made from jacquère. When followed by the name of the grape, it can apply to reds, for example Chignin-Gamay, Chignin-Mondeuse, and Chignin-Pinot. Rosés are also made there.

Chignin-Bergeron

A *cru* of VIN DE SAVOIE for textured whites made from roussanne. Producers: Dom Louis Magnin: see VIN DE SAVOIE ◆ A & M QUENARD.

E & P Clairet/Domaine de la Tournelle

39600 Arbois; 03.84.66.25.76; domainedelatournelle@wanadoo.fr

Wine: Jura range. $$

The wines from this eco-friendly domaine are unusual and intriguing. The 2003 L'Uva Arbosiana, an unfiltered, zero-sulfur poulsard, was atypical in both the richness of its color and its fruitiness, which when combined with a stony mineral backbone resulted in a thoroughly engaging, lipsmacking wine. The nuanced Trousseau des Corvées was equally enchanting. And the Fleur de Savagnin, which spent two years in barrel on its fine lees, was a lovely marriage of oak and mineral flavors.

Côtes du Jura

A regional AC beginning north of Arbois and stretching along the Jura mountains to Burgundy. The AC covers a wide range of wines: whites (dry and sweet, still and sparkling), rosés (still and sparkling), and reds. Grapes: For whites, savagnin and chardonnay. For reds and rosés, poulsard, trousseau, and pinot noir. Styles of wine: The whites are fresh and floral (called *ouillé*), partially oxidized (called *typé*), or something in between, depending on the producer. Reds are pale, lean, and mineral but can be truly characterful and thirst quenching. The rosés are almost as dark as reds. See also VIN JAUNE and VIN DE PAILLE. The *crémants* are clean and invigorating.

BEST RECENT VINTAGES: 2005, (2004), (2003), (2002), (2000). For *vin jaune*: 1995, 1996.
PRICES: $ to $$$

PRODUCERS: Ch d'Arlay: important domaine with improving quality, as evidenced by the latest vintages of the Cuvée la Reine, a floral chardonnay, and a very good 1999 *vin de paille* ◆ BENOÎT BADOZ ◆ Cellier de Bellevue: the quality of Daniel Credoz's wines varies but the pure savagnin Clos Bacchus, fermented in new oak barrels, was appealing in its smooth creaminess; the domaine also makes lean, cool pinot noir and Château-Chalon ◆ Luc & Sylvie Boilley: ambitious work here but editing is needed—some wines are too oaky, others a bit heavy, still others, like the 2003 chardonnay Cuvée Prestige, are just right, both floral and mineral with some depth ↑ ◆ Peggy and Jean Pascal Buronfosse: there's promise in this young domaine, too, but the 2003s, while ambitious, didn't escape the pitfalls of this extraordinarily hot vintage ◆ LES CHAIS DU VIEUX BOURG ↑ ◆ Richard Delay: my favorite wine here is the 2000 *vin de paille* with its flavors of dried apricot and candied orange peel ◆ Fruitière Vinicole de Voiteur: respectable local cooperative with above-average wines, especially *crémant* ◆ DOM GANEVAT ↑ ◆ Domaine Grand Frères: in 2003, a source for attractive reds, particularly trousseau. The 2001 *vin de paille,* while drier than many, had intriguing flavors of thyme and herbal tea. The 1998 Château-Chalon En Beaumont was above average ◆ ALAIN LABET ☆ ◆ Julien Labet: ambitious work in progress here, especially the white blend La Reine and the red blend Les Varrons ↑ ◆ Dom Morel-Thibaut: lots of rough edges here but the wines are not anonymous ◆ DOM PIGNIER ↑ ◆ Xavier Reverchon: the *vin jaune* is worth trying—by the glass ◆ Dom Rijckaert: see ARBOIS ☆ ◆ DOM DE SAVAGNY ◆ Dom Jacques Tissot: see ARBOIS.

Crémant du Jura

An AC for a local sparkling wine made by Champagne methods (now called the *méthode traditionelle*). The primary grapes are chardonnay, poulsard, and pinot noir. A good Crémant du Jura offers great value for the dollar. The wines are extremely fresh and appetizing and generally cost around $10. Most are nonvintage brut. Producers: BENOÎT BADOZ ◆ CAVE DE LA REINE JEANNE ☆ ◆ ALAIN LABET ☆ ◆ DOM LIGIER ↑ ◆ HENRI MAIRE ◆ DOM DE MONTBOURGEAU ◆ DOM PIGNIER ↑ ◆ DOM DE LA PINTE ☆ ◆ Auguste Pirou: see ARBOIS ◆ DOM ROLET, especially Coeur de Chardonnay ◆ DOM ANDRÉ & MIREILLE TISSOT, particularly vintage-dated bottlings.

Crépy

A minuscule AC on the banks of Lake Geneva, the source of light, dry white wines made from chasselas. Drink the youngest available. Prices: $. Producer: Claude Mercier/La Goutte d'Or.

L'Étoile

A small Jura AC making white wines—both still and sparkling—based on chardonnay, savagnin, and poulsard. The range and style of wines is generally similar to the Côtes du Jura, although some find the wines more subtle. Vintages: See CÔTES DU JURA. Prices: $$.

PRODUCERS: Ch Étoile: somewhat *typé* (lightly oxidized) wines with a vegetal edge ◆ Dom Geneletti: above-average wines. The domaine also makes Château-Chalon and *crémant* ◆ DOM DE MONTBOURGEAU ◆ DOM ROLET ◆ Dom Philippe Vandelle: above-average versions of the AC and sapid, smoky, complex *vin jaune* L'Étoile.

Domaine Ganevat ↑
39190 Rotalier; tel/fax: 03.84.25.02.69
Wine: Côtes du Jura; $ to $$
This promising young domaine seems a good example of the new generation of Jura wine producers. Its focused, textured, barrel-aged savagnin reveals only the slightest hint of oxidation; Its old-vines chardonnay Les Grands Teppes is fairly complex and well-structured; its Cuvée Julien, pure pinot noir, is cool, stony, and specific. I love it but it's not for those who dislike austere wines. An abundance of oak deprives the *vin de paille* of a bit of succulence but it's still a serious, delectable wine.

Domaine de l'Idylle
73800 Cruet; 04.79.84.30.58; fax: 04.79.65.26.26
Wine: Vin de Savoie. $ to $$
Philippe and François Tiollier produce appealing wines with the savor of Savoie, notably a floral, fresh roussette, a full, oak-aged white from Cruet with a taste of snow, and a mondeuse from Arbin, a charming light red.

Alain Labet ☆
39190 Rotalier; 03.84.25.11.13; fax: 03.84.25.06.75
Wines: Jura range. $ to $$($)
A very good family domaine with ambitious, textured, oak- and mineral-flavored whites (Fleur de Marne en Chalosse and Fleur de Marne la Bardette), nicely structured poulsards, very good *crémants,* and truly lovely *vin de paille.*

Domaine Ligier Père & Fils ↑
39600 Arbois; 03.84.66.28.06; ligier@netcourrier.com
Wine: Arbois. $ to $$($)
A serious family domaine with noteworthy wines, particularly the fragrant trousseau, a light red that is fresh as a waterfall, and the excellent old-vines chardonnay, structured and beautifully *terroir*-driven. Pleasant *crémants,* too.

Frédéric Lornet ☆
39600 Montigny-les-Arsures; 03.84.37.45.10; frederic.lornet@club-internet.fr
Wine: Arbois. $$ to $$$
Lornet is one of those young artist-vignerons whose wines are always a discovery. His lees-aged savagnin is a vivid blend of minerals and ripe fruit. His mineral chardonnay Les Messagelins is deep and specific. His trousseau Des Dames is pellucid, with raspberry notes softening the mineral force. His attention-grabbing *vin de paille,* a blend of poulsard and savagnin, is a weave of honey and dried apricots. And his 1998 *vin jaune* is marvelously rich, nuanced, and complex.

Jean Macle ☆
39210 Château-Chalon; 03.84.85.21.85; fax: 03.84.85.27.38
Wines: Château-Chalon and Côtes du Jura. $ to $$($)
Regarded as a local sage, Jean Macle reclaimed and replanted one of the best slopes in Château-Chalon. A meticulous vintner, he ages the wines longer than the required six years. The resulting Château-Chalons, the 1997 for example, are streamlined and elegant, a thrilling blend of silk and steel. His Côtes du Jura, a blend of chardonnay and savagnin, are less emphatic but very much in the same style. With food? I loved the 1999 with the local Alpine pike.

Macvin du Jura
An AC for a liqueur made from unfermented grape juice blended with local *eau-de-vie de marc* and aged for a year in oak barrels. Generally between 16 and 20 percent alcohol, Macvin is strong and sweet. Best served chilled, as an aperitif. Prices: $$. Producers: Most Jura producers make Macvin. My favorites come from DOM DE LA PINTE ☆ ◆ DOM ROLET ◆ DOM ANDRÉ & MIREILLE TISSOT ☆.

Henri Maire
39600 Arbois; 03.84.66.42.75; www.henri-maire.fr
Wines: Jura range. $ to $$$
With nearly a thousand acres, Henri Maire is by far the largest producer in the Jura, marketing up to 50 percent of the region's wines. While some of the wines are ham-handed, others are simple beverage wines, and still others are tasty and admirable. My favorites include the 2001 *vin de paille* La Vignière, a toothsome wine with flavors of candied orange peel; the characterful, new-oak-aged Arbois chardonnay Collection Privée Henri Maire; and the mineral-driven Domaine Brégand pinot noir. Henri Maire converted this property to organic viticulture and the results are promising. The house is also known for its sparkling wines, particularly the Vin Fou (crazy wine). But I prefer its straightforward *crémant,* both stony and savory. I'd pair it with oysters.

Domaine de Montbourgeau
39570 L'Étoile; 03.84.47.32.96; domaine.montbourgeau@wanadoo.fr
Wines: L'Étoile, including *vins jaune* and *de paille*. $$($)
The Gros family domaine produces wines that are a bit rustic but bursting with personality. My favorite is L'Étoile *vin de paille,* which, like the standard white and the *vin jaune,* is heavy, steely, and full of character. It's also mighty tasty, with sweet spice flavors that remind me of Speculoo cookies, Belgium's gingerbread-type cookies. There's also a pleasant *crémant.*

Domaine Pignier ↑
39570 Montaigu; 03.84.24.24.30; www.domaine-pignier.com
Wine: Côtes du Jura. $ to $$$
The seventh generation of Pigniers converted their 15 hectares of vines to biodynamics in 2002. While some of the wines are works in progress, others are sheer delights. The Côtes du Jura trousseau was a lipsmacking model of purity and specificity. The 2000 *vin de paille,* fresh as a waterfall, was a succulent blend of dried fruit, marmalade, and oak flavors. The delightful Crémant du Jura Blanc, at less than $10, was a steal.

Domaine de la Pinte ☆
39600 Arbois; 03.84.66.06.47; www.lapinte.fr
Wines: Arbois range. $ to $$$($)
A favorite of mine, this winery (organic, by the way) is run with passion and intelligence by Philippe Chatillon. The Arbois savagnin has a whiff of oxidation but is extremely fresh, vigorous, and long. The creamy chardonnay has a stimulating lift. Terre Rouge, a blend of pinot noir, poulsard, and trousseau—like all the domaine's reds—is very dry, lean, and mineral with flavors of oak and dried fruit. The complex *vin jaune* falls somewhere between a manzanilla and a single malt whiskey with a touch of molasses. The *vin de paille* seems to melt in the mouth, spreading a wealth of flavors—honey, thyme, eau-de-vie, oak, and more. The marmalade-sweet, incredibly long 1997 Rêve d'Automne, a true *vin de méditation,* makes my mouth water just thinking of it. The Macvin is fresh, strong, and sapid. And, last but not least, the *crémant* is so full, dry, and elegant, I'd opt for it over many big-name Champagnes.

Jacques Puffeney ☆
39600 Montigny-par-Arbois; 03.84.66.10.89; fax: 03.84.66.08.36
Wine: Arbois. $ to $$$
Puffeney's chardonnay (neither fined nor filtered) is focused and deep, bordering on elegant; his savagnin is steely and firm. In the Cuvée Sacha he blends both grapes and lets a slight film form on the savagnin before adding the chardonnay. The result is very dry, very special, and very appetizing. Jura reds are not for everyone, but I adore Puffeney's austere Arbois trousseau Les Bérangères with its mineral and graphite edge. The poulsard, with dried fruit

and ash notes, is equally riveting. The 1996 *vin jaune,* pure savagnin, comes on like a great, dry oloroso with a tart, steely edge. It can age indefinitely.

André & Michel Quenard ☆

73800 Chignin; 04.79.28.12.75; am.quenard@cario.fr

Wines: Vin de Savoie range. $ to $$

The only mistake you can make here is to miss tasting at least two of the Quenards' wines. I can't imagine a better articulation of either the jacquère or the mondeuse grapes than their Chignin Vieilles Vignes. Their Les Abymes, with its whisper of fizz, is so fresh it's like drinking snow. The Chignin-Bergeron is a tightly focused delicacy, and the creamy, elegant Chignin-Bergeron Les Terrasses would marry beautifully with many dishes, starting with crab and lobster.

Domaine Rolet

39602 Arbois Cedex; 03.84.66.00.05; rolet@wanadoo.fr

Wines: Arbois, Côtes du Jura, and L'Étoile. $ to $$($)

Mixed but mostly positive reviews here, as for a very lightly oxidized 2001 L'Étoile chardonnay, very dry, precise, and fresh as mountain air; lean, mineral Arbois trousseaus; a delectable 2001 Arbois *vin de paille* with lovely structure and beguiling flavors of honey, herbal tea, and dried apricots; and a taut, steely 1997 Arbois *vin jaune.* Rolet makes several different *crémants.* The Coeur de Chardonnay could take on quite a few Champagnes—at half the price.

Roussette du Bugey

A VDQS designation near lake Bourget for whites made from altesse (a.k.a. roussette). It has two *crus*: Montagnien and Virien le Grand. Drink the youngest available. Prices: $ to $$.

Roussette de Savoie and Its *Crus*

A regional AC for dry white wines made from altesse (a.k.a. roussette). The name of one of four communes may be attached to that of the appellation: Marestel, Monterminod, Monthoux, and Frangy. In general, drink the youngest available, although some age well. Prices: $ to $$. Producers: Jean-Noël Blard ◆ Dom Dupasquier ◆ Dom Genoux ◆ Dom Jean-Pierre & Philippe Grisard ◆ Ch de Monterminod ◆ Dom Prieuré St. Christophe.

Domaine de Savagny

39570 Crancot; 03.84.87.61.30; fax: 03.84.48.21.36

Wine: Côtes du Jura. $ to $$($)

Some interesting wine here. The red, a blend of poulsard, trousseau, and pinot noir, is nicely balanced with good fruit. The 1999 *vin de paille,* curiously, seemed halfway between a sweet wine and an eau-de-vie but was fun to drink; and the admirable 1996 *vin jaune* was long, layered, and very specific.

Seyssel

A small Savoie AC for whites—both still and sparkling—made from altesse, although the local grape molette may be used in the sparkling wines. Vintages: See VIN DE SAVOIE. Prices: $$ to $$$.

Domaine André & Mireille Tissot ☆

39600 Montigny-les-Arsures; 03.84.66.08.27; fax: 03.84.66.25.08

Wines: Arbois and Côtes du Jura. $ to $$($)

Stéphane Tissot converted this leading domaine to organic viticulture and seems unafraid of taking risks in the winery. The results are always fascinating and usually delectable. An unfiltered, barrel-fermented 2003 Arbois chardonnay needed time to open up but an unfiltered trousseau, also a 2003, charmed me so completely that my tasting notes are covered with stars. The oaky, concentrated, very ambitious Côtes du Jura pinot noir En Barberon was, simply, excellent. Then there's an Arbois savagnin. Aged in barrel for three and a half years *sous voile,* it was well on its way to being a *vin jaune,* steely and nutty, with vivid acidity. The 1998 *vin jaune* was mild and nuanced; the 1995, cool and luminous. The various *vin de paille* are super, as are the *crémants,* particularly the vintage-dated versions.

Vin jaune: An exceptional dry white made from savagnin in the ACs Château-Chalon, Arbois, L'Étoile, and Côtes du Jura. After fermentation, the wine matures for six years and three months in oak barrels without being topped up. During this time a film of yeast forms over the wine protecting it from oxidation. The wine is thus said to be *sous voile* (under a veil). *Vin jaune* has its own bottle, the 62 centiliter *clavelin.* The wine is not for everyone. It most closely resembles a strong fino sherry, though it's steelier and much more acid. Typical flavors include walnuts and mushrooms. It's an assertive wine. You feel as if it focuses your taste buds and puts all those ducks in a row. It is served *chambré,* which means room temperature before radiators—or around 57 to 60 degrees Fahrenheit. *Vin jaune* can be enjoyed many ways—as an aperitif, with chicken with morels (a classic Jura recipe made with *vin jaune*), with strong cheeses, or on its own. It can age indefinitely. The best vintages currently available are 1995 and 1996. Prices: $$($). Most producers in the ACs listed above make *vin jaune.* My favorites are BERTHET-BONDET ◆ JEAN MACLE ☆ ◆ DOM DE LA PINTE ☆ ◆ JACQUES PUFFENEY ☆ ◆ DOM ROLET ◆ DOM ANDRÉ & MIREILLE TISSOT ☆.

Vin de paille: A very sweet, unctuous Jura white made with grapes that, after harvest, are left to shrivel and dry in an attic until they are pressed in the spring, thus concentrating the sugars. The wine ages for three years in oak barrels. It must have a minimum of 14.5 percent alcohol, with residual sugar ranging from 80 to 180 grams per liter. Good vintages now available: 2003, 2002, 2000, and 1999. Prices: $$($). Most Jura producers make a *vin de paille.* Some favorites: DOM BERTHET-BONDET ◆ CAVE DE LA REINE JEANNE ☆ ◆ DOM GANEVAT ↑ ◆ ALAIN LABET ☆ ◆ DOM DE LA PINTE ☆ ◆ DOM ROLET ◆ DOM ANDRÉ & MIREILLE TISSOT ☆.

Vin de Savoie

A regional AC for light to medium-bodied still whites, reds, and rosés and fresh sparkling whites and rosés. Produced in an area roughly bounded by Lake Geneva and Grenoble, most of the vineyards run in a north-south line along the right bank of the Rhône. With resorts such as Chambéry, Aix-les-Bains, and Lake Annecy, it is not surprising that most Savoie wine is consumed within the region.

GRAPES: For whites, the main grapes are altesse, chardonnay, jacquère, mondeuse blanc, chasselas, gringet, and molette (for sparkling wine only). For reds, the primary grapes are gamay, mondeuse, and pinot noir.

STYLES OF WINE: At their best, the reds are lean, juicy charmers to be drunk in the near term. I am particularly fond of the whites for the unique sensation they offer, that of drinking liquid snow.

BEST RECENT VINTAGES: 2005, 2004, (2003), 2000.
PRICES: $ to $$

PRODUCERS: Marc & Roger Labbé: a family domaine in the *cru* Abymes, making focused, "snowy," invigorating whites from jacquère ◆ Dom Louis Magnin: a leading grower, making excellent Arbin-Mondeuse, Chignin-Bergeron, and Roussette de Savoie ☆ ◆ DOM DE L'IDYLLE ◆ ANDRÉ & MICHEL QUENARD ☆ ◆ Dom Jean Vullien & Fils: good family domaine with pleasant reds and better whites, particularly those from the *cru* Montmélian.

JURA AND SAVOIE CRIB SHEET

Note that produces are listed more than once here because there are fewer really good producers. As they fit more than one category, I've mentioned the ones I really like.

MUST TRYS

- E & P Clairet: L'Uva Arbosiana
- Frédéric Lornet: *vin de paille* and *vin jaune*
- Jean Macle: Château-Chalon
- Domaine Pignier: 2000 *vin de paille*
- Domaine de la Pinte: Rêve d'Automne *vin de paille*
- Jacques Puffeney: Arbois trousseau Les Bérangères

BEST BUYS

- Cave de la Reine Jeanne: Arbois
- Domaine de l'Idylle: Vin de Savoie
- André & Michel Quenard: Vin de Savoie
- Domaine Rolet: Juras, especially the *crémant* Coeur de Chardonnay
- Domaine André & Mireille Tissot: Côtes du Jura

SAFE HOUSES

- Cave de la Reine Jeanne: Juras
- Alain Labet: Juras
- Frédéric Lornet: Arbois
- Domaine de la Pinte: Arbois
- Jacques Puffeney: Arbois
- André & Michel Quenard: Vin de Savoie
- Domaine André & Mireille Tissot: Côtes du Jura

ALSACE
BORDEAUX
BURGUNDY
CHAMPAGNE
JURA AND SAVOIE

LANGUEDOC-ROUSSILLON

LOIRE
PROVENCE AND CORSICA
RHÔNE
SOUTHWEST

THE LANGUEDOC-ROUSSILLON REGION
PARIS
Hérault
PIC ST-LOUP
NÎMES
COSTIÈRES DE NÎMES
MONTPEYROUX
Aniane
COTEAUX DU LANGUEDOC
MUSCAT DE LUNEL
Lunel
Arles
Clermont-l'Hérault
ST-GEORGES D'ORQUES
MONTPELLIER
FAUGÈRES
La Grande-Motte
Rhône
ST-CHINIAN
Pézenas
MUSCAT DE FRONTIGNAN
Mèze
PICPOUL DE PINET
Frontignan
MINERVOIS–LA–LIVINIÈRE
Sète
CABARDÈS
MINERVOIS
Béziers
Agde
Aude
Carcassonne
CÔTES DE LA MALPÈRE
Lézignan-Corbières
Narbonne
Limoux
LIMOUX
CORBIÈRES
FITOU
FITOU
Mediterranean Sea
St-Paul-de-Fenouillet
MAURY
Maury
Tautavel
CÔTES DU ROUSSILLON-VILLAGES
Rivesaltes
Caramany
St-Estève
PERPIGNAN
Prades
CÔTES DU ROUSSILLON
Elne
RIVESALTES
Céret
Collioure
Banyuls
BANYULS AND COLLIOURE
SPAIN

Administratively, the Languedoc-Roussillon is two regions. Wine-wise, however, it is one vast region, the history of which is long and complicated. Now recovering from its postwar reputation as a producer of plonk (wines used as the base of aperitifs and cheap blends), the Languedoc-Roussillon is the most dynamic region in France.

It is impossible to overestimate the progress being made here. New wine stars seem to be born on a daily basis. The wines have a distinctly New World feel. The best are perhaps the French wines most likely to please both New and Old World palates—naturally rich and ample but also very much the product of a specific place. Less ambitious wines, many of them sold as Vin de Pays d'Oc, are deliberately fashioned to appeal to New World palates, at competitive prices. Even jaded consumers will find there are endless discoveries to be made, in every price range.

THE MAJOR APPELLATIONS: In the Languedoc, Cabardès, Corbières, Costières de Nîmes, Coteaux du Languedoc (including Picpoul de Pinet), Faugères, Fitou, Côtes de la Malpère, St.-Chinian, and several types of fortified muscat. In the Roussillon, Collioure, Côtes du Roussillon, and Côtes du Roussillon-Villages, and the fortified wines Banyuls, Maury, Rivesaltes, and Muscat de Rivesaltes.

VIN DE PAYS: Many of the producers responsible for the creativity and the excellence in this vibrant region are mavericks. In order to do their own thing, they opt for the designation Vin de Pays or Vin de Table rather than conform to the regulations of the AC system. (As I write this, the AC laws are being redrafted. For an idea of what the changes may bring, see the box on page 178.)

GRAPES: Whites include grenache blanc and gris, bourboulenc, clairette, marsanne, muscat, roussanne, rolle (vermentino), picpoul (piquepoul), and viognier. For specific appellations and Vins de Pays: mauzac, chenin blanc, sauvignon blanc, and chardonnay may be used. Reds include grenache noir, carignan, syrah, mourvèdre, cinsault, and lladoner pelut. In Vin de Pays merlot, cabernet sauvignon, and others are permitted.

STYLES OF WINE: The variety is enormous. Whites can be fresh, relatively light wines, Picpoul de Pinet and Limoux, for example, or potent and layered, like those found in most of the other regions. Rosés range from inconsequential to surprisingly serious; reds, from generous quaffers, to powerhouses, to luscious, nuanced works of art.

BEST RECENT VINTAGES: It's difficult to find a truly miserable vintage, at least within the past decade. The 2005 vintage is shaping up to be exceptional, as was 2001. Very fine wines were made in 2004. Many 2003s are overripe, heavy, and jammy, thanks to the extraordinary heat. A number of 2002s may seem dilute because of the rain, although in general, they are much more successful than the 2002s of the southern Rhône. The 2003s should be drunk quickly; for the rest, there is no real track record. Most should probably be drunk by their eighth birthday.

PRICES: Prices can range widely from $4 to more than $100. Think $ to $$$$.

PROPOSED NEW AC REGULATIONS: The new regulations would create an appellation simply called Languedoc. This would cover the entire Languedoc-Roussillon area. It is intended to apply to light, fruity wines ready to drink in the near term. The AC Coteaux du Languedoc would be phased out as its subzones, such as Pic St.-Loup, Montpeyroux, and La Clape, are accorded AC or *cru* status.

Domaine de l'Aigle

11300 Roquetaillade; 04.68.31.56.72; www.rodet.com

Wine: Vin de Pays d'Oc. $$

Maison Antonin Rodet, an important Burgundy producer, took over this vineyard in the cooler reaches of the Limoux appellation. Here they produce convincing chardonnays and chenin blancs and blends of the two, as well as pinot noir. The wines are fresh, clean, and competitive.

Domaine l'Aiguelière

34150 Montpeyroux, 04.67.96.61.43; fax: 04.67.44.49.67

Wines: Montpeyroux, Coteaux du Languedoc. $$

The domaine's two red bottlings—Côte Dorée and Côte Rousse—are reliably rich, focused, and flavorful. Chewy and oaky in their youth, they benefit from a bit of aging or carafing. The domaine also produces very good whites.

Domaine des Aires Hautes ☆

34210 Siran; 04.68.91.54.40; gilles.chabbert@wanadoo.fr.

Wine: Minervois-la-Livinière. $ to $$

The "simple" Minervois is a cheap, cheerful, and bistro-ready red; the top-of-the-line Minervois-la-Livinière Clos de l'Escandil is lush, generous, and significant. The domaine also makes very tasty Vin de Pays d'Oc—a grapefruit-scented sauvignon blanc, for example, and a particular favorite, a smooth blueberry-blackberry charmer made from malbec.

Domaine d'Arfeuille ☆

66220 St.-Paul de Fenouillet; 05.57.51.49.89; domaine.darfeuille@laposte.net

Wines: Côtes du Roussillon and Vin de Pays des Côtes Catalanes. $$

Stéphane and Dominique d'Arfeuille, the owners of Château La Pointe in Pomerol, bought a 7.5-hectare parcel in St.-Paul in 2002. For now, all the wines are red and are aged in used Pomerol barrels. Ambitious and promising, they share a family style of freshness and elegantly mingled fruit. Les Gabax, a blend of carignan and grenache, and grenache Vieilles Vignes are both Vins de Pays. L'Originelle, a Côtes du Roussillon, is fine-grained, rich, and delectable.

Arnaud de Villeneuve/Les Vignobles du Rivesaltais

BP 56, 66600 Rivesaltes; 04.68.64.06.63; vignobles-rivesaltais@wanadoo.fr

Wines: Rivesaltes in all styles and Côtes du Roussillon. $ to $$

At this important cooperative cellar Vin Doux Naturel (fortified wine) accounts for 30 percent of production. There are numerous bottlings and a great stock of old vintages for sale at affordable prices (a 1982 Rivesaltes *ambré hors d'âge* for $$($) for example). Its creditable, sweet muscat Vin de Pays is overshadowed by its superior Muscat de Rivesaltes, which has more focus and punch.

Domaine d'Aupilhac ☆

34150 Montpeyroux; 04.67.96.61.19; www.aupilhac.net

Wines: Coteaux du Languedoc–Montpeyroux; Vin de Pays. $$

This domaine is an essential reference for Languedoc wine. Sylvain Fadat, in the vanguard of fine winemaking in the region, is a true role model. In an ongoing search for excellence, his work in the vineyards and cellars evolves constantly. Yields are low, indigenous yeasts are used, and vatting is long for the red wines, which are punched down regularly. The reds are neither fined nor filtered. There are numerous cuvées: Lou Maset is the seductive quaffer; then comes the Montpeyroux rouge, a cool, elegant blend of the region's five principal red grapes; then Le Clos, a serious Montpeyroux red, which needs cellaring, after which its formidable structure turns to velvet. Les Cocalières, another serious cuvée (in both red and white), comes from a single high-altitude parcel. Among Fadat's most enchanting wines are his Vins de Pays: Le Carignan Vin de Pays du Mont Baudile is a thoroughly fascinating and totally delectable expression of pure carignan; Les Servières reveals the best that cinsault can offer, particularly as it comes from century-old vines. Plos des Baumes rouge, from an old family parcel on a terraced hillside in Aniane, is a Bordeaux blend of cabernet sauvignon, cabernet franc, and merlot. It is a fine, *terroir*-driven red with loads of personality. Finally, there's a Vin de Pays de l'Hérault blanc, a creamy, mineral-rich white blend of barrel-fermented grenache blanc, ugni blanc, and chardonnay.

Domaine de Bachellery

34500 Béziers; 04.67.62.36.15; www.bachellery.com

Wines: Vin de Pays d'Oc and others. $

From their 100 hectares of vines in the Béziers area, Marina and Bernard Julien do an admirable job with an enormous range of unusual grapes. Their Ballade pour Mistral is a warm, Cotes-du-Rhône–like blend of six different red varieties. There's a sturdy rosé of pinot noir and a supple grenache. And there are offbeat sweethearts like a pure, easy-drinking tempranillo, with more than a whiff of Spain, and a sweet, fruit-driven Ballade en Straminer made from gewürztraminer (natch). I look forward to tasting their wines made from aubun, egiodola, and graciano.

Banyuls and Banyuls Grand Cru

Arguably France's most important Vin Doux Naturel (fortified wine), Banyuls is a Port-style wine; the best can easily compete with their Iberian counterparts. A small appellation of both red and white, Banyuls vines grow on the steep, terraced slopes along France's Mediterranean border with Spain, at the western edge of the Roussillon. Grenache is the principal grape variety. There are basically two styles of wine: The first, aged in barrel, tends to be amber-colored, with mellow flavors of nuts and toffee. The second, aged in bottle, generally comes from a very good vintage and, in its youth, has potent flavors of black cherry and cooked fruit. The local name for this version is Rimage or Rimatge. Banyuls Grand Cru must age for thirty months and contain a minimum of 75 percent grenache. All are best served slightly chilled—as an aperitif, with cheese (especially blues) or in a daring combination with such dishes as duck in cherry sauce. Some like them with chocolate desserts. Because the steepness of the slopes necessitates much manual labor, real Banyuls will never be cheap. Note that there is another, very singular wine—RANCIO—also made in this zone.

PRICES: $$ to $$$

PRODUCERS: La Cave de L'Abbé Rous: see Cellier des Templiers in this listing Les Clos des Paulilles: see CH DE JAU ◆ COUME DEL MAS ◆ L'Étoile: Banyuls specialist and a very good, reliable producer ☆ ◆ DOM MADELOC ☆ ◆ MAS AMIEL ☆ ◆ Dom du Mas Blanc: first-rate Banyuls. Look for the Vieilles Vignes ☆ ◆ DOM DE LA RECTORIE ☆ ◆ Cellier des Templiers: a grouping of eight cooperatives, offering nineteen different Banyuls. The Cave de L'Abbé Rous ☆ is the line of Banyuls sold only to wine shops, restaurants, and the export market. Look for Cuvée Helyos, an oaky, very concentrated, fleshy Banyuls made from very old grenache vines, and the vintage Castell des Hospices, a lovely Banyuls made only in great years and aged for a minimum of thirty months ◆ DOM DE LA TOUR VIEILLE ☆ ◆ DOM DE TRAGINER ☆ ◆ DOM VIAL MAGNÈRES ☆.

Léon Barral ☆

34480 Cabrerolles, 04.67.90.29.13; fax: 04.67.13.37

Wines: Faugères and Vin de Pays. $$

This producer is a personal favorite. Vines and grapes get maximum TLC—low yields, light plowing, homeopathic treatments, indigenous yeasts, no filtration—you get the picture. There's a white Vin de Pays made mostly from ninety-year-old terret, an increasingly rare local grape; Valinière, a velvety and serious Vin de Table made from 80 percent mourvèdre; and two types of Faugères. The first, basically an unoaked carignan-grenache blend, is lush and juicy and too delicious; the more serious, barrel-aged Jadis is mostly carignan and syrah. A sommelier friend and tasting companion called it the Chambertin of the south. It is a knockout, with majesty to spare.

La Baume

34290 Servian; 04.67.39.29.49; fax: 04.67.39.29.40

Wine: Vin de Pays d'Oc. $

Competitive, commercial wines are the focus here. Owned by the major group Grand Chais de France, La Baume got its impetus from its previous owner, the Australian group BRL Hardy. It has a vast selection of wines and, by and large, does a decent job with them. The range of screw-cap wines consists mostly of squeaky clean, hi-good-bye varietals—sauvignon blanc, cabernet sauvignon, merlot, viognier, for example—and includes a Summer Red that would be just fine chilled and drunk on the beach. The Domaine de la Baume Terroirs, and Sélection lines are cork-finished, professional, faultless, easily understood beverage wines.

Domaine de Bellevue

34400 Lunel; 04.67.83.24.83; muscatlacoste@wanadoo.fr

Wine: Muscat de Lunel. $ to $$

Francis Lacoste offers a dry muscat Vin de Pays d'Oc and the pleasant, nervy Mas de Bellevue, but the several cuvées of sweet muscat are the real attraction. Two favorites: the layered cuvée Vieilles Vignes Clos Bellevue, which has a surprising freshness for such a rich, fortified wine, and the deliberately oxidized Vendanges d'Octobre made from shriveled grapes. Either would make a lovely aperitif.

Blanquette de Limoux: See LIMOUX.

Château Bonhomme ☆

11800 Aigues-Vives. 04.68.79.28.47; 04.68.79.28.48. jpaimar@free.fr.

Wines: Minervois and Vin de Pays. $ to $$

This large domaine makes a number of different, equally succulent cuvées of Minervois. Les Amandiers is deliciously sapid, subtle, and appetizing. The oak-aged Les Alaternes, pure carignan, is denser, with rich flavors of minerals and cherries. The syrah-based Les Oliviers blends discreet oak flavors with luscious fruit. The domaine also produces a range of appealing Vins de Pays, among them a floral and mineral white based on grenache gris, an engaging pure cinsault, and a juicy red blend. All three would be delightful wine-bar discoveries.

Domaine Bordes ↑

34360 St.-Chinian; 04.67.38.26.37; p.bordes@wanadoo.fr
Wine: St.-Chinian. $ to $$
Emma and Philippe Bordes are a young, ambitious couple with a young, promising domaine. Their regular cuvée of St.-Chinian Les Narys would make a good wine-bar quaff. The more concentrated Cuvée Raicio is fresh, velvety, and very tasty. The Bordes also experiment, making a very sweet Vin de Table of late-harvested ugni blanc, Les Lutines. Neither fined nor filtered, it's very grapey and would make an interesting aperitif.

Borie la Vitarèle

34490 Causse et Veyran, 04.67.89.50.43; www.borielavitarele.fr
Wines: St.-Chinian, Coteaux du Languedoc, and Vin de Pays du Coteaux de Murviel. $ to $$
Jean François and Cathy Izarn-Planes are in the process of converting their 15 hectares to organic viticulture. In the winery, they avoid fining and filtering their reds. The results are reliably honest, tasty, and full of character. Their Coteaux du Languedoc includes a supple, easy-drinking ordinary cuvée and a muscular, stony Terres Blanches. In St.-Chinian, depending on the vintage, Les Schistes can be smooth and elegant or dense and oaky; Les Crès is tight, seductive, and generous. The refreshing rosé Cuvée des Cigales, a Vin de Pays Murviel, tastes like a juicy, very light red. And the Vin de Pays d'Oc La Combe combines cabernet sauvignon and syrah to make a supple, rich red loaded with dark fruit.

Domaine Brial/Cave des Vignerons de Baixas

66390 Baixas, 04.68.64.22.37; www.dom-brial.com
Wine: Rivesaltes. $$ to $$$ for old vintages
Fortified wines account for 40 percent of the production of this cooperative cellar. The Muscat de Rivesaltes is a vivid aperitif. The Muscat de Rivesaltes Château les Pins is voluptuous but well-balanced. A blend of white grapes fermented in new oak barrels, the Rivesaltes *ambrée* Château les Pins is almost too rich for anything but meditation. And the *hors d'âge* (a 1989 for example) is fresh with lingering flavors of dried apricots and currants.

Cabardès

A small Languedoc AC for reds and rosés. Located on hillsides in the westernmost reach of the Languedoc, overlooking Carcassonne, Cabardès unites the mild climate of the Atlantic with the heat of the Mediterranean. Both Bordelais grape varieties (merlot and cabernets sauvignon and franc) and those typical of the south (grenache noir and syrah) are cultivated there. The generous, structured reds offer a delicious melding of Bordeaux and southern France.

BEST RECENT VINTAGES: While 2001 stands out, there have been few truly bad recent vintages.
PRICES: $ to $$

PRODUCERS: Ch Jouclary: promising young domaine. The Cuvée Guilhaume de Jouclary, a blend of merlot and syrah aged in new oak, is tannic, dark, and potent. Cassoulet might make a good partner. Worth following ↑ ◆ Ch de Pennautier: See LORGERIL ☆.

Domaine Calvet-Thunevin ☆

33330 St.-Émilion; 05.57.55.09.13; www.thunevin.com

Wine: Côtes du Roussillon. $$ ($)

The original *garagiste* Jean-Luc Thunevin of St.-Émilion's Château Valandraud (see BORDEAUX) has teamed up with Jean-Roger Calvet to produce rich, cult-style wine in the Fenouillèdes. They have succeeded handily. Les Dentelles is a plush, deep red with mingled fruit flavors. Hugo is even more serious. This is Pomerol in Roussillon and it is mighty impressive.

Domaine Canet-Valette

34460 Cessenon-sur-Orb; 04.67.89.51.83; earl-canet-valette@wanadoo.fr

Wine: St.-Chinian. $ to $$

Sophie and Marc Valette practice organic viticulture and make two versions of St.-Chinian I'd love to meet in a wine bar. The first, Une et Mille Nuits, is pungent and deceptively potent, given its supple attack. Le Vin Maghani—the wine of the Magi—is the top cuvée. An intense, massive wine that seems to have swallowed the sun, it's best carafed and paired with a game stew. The Valettes also make a sweet red from shriveled grapes harvested in December. They'd pair this with chocolate; I'd pair it with blue cheese.

Carthagène: Based on unfermented grape juice and brandy, Carthagène is a local aperitif that's similar to Pineau des Charentes and Floc de Gascogne.

Château Cazal Viel

34460 Cessenon-sur-Orb; 04.67.89.63.15; info@cazal-viel.com

Wines: St.-Chinian and Vin de Pays. $ to $$

This large family domaine produces pleasant whites under the Vin de Pays d'Oc banner and a number of versions of St.-Chinian. The Vieilles Vignes cuvée is straightforward and nicely structured. The Cuvée Bardou, from a single vineyard, is aged in new oak and is rich enough to take it—an ambitious wine. Best of all is Larmes des Fées. Pure syrah, made only in fine vintages, it's a very good, serious, cult-style wine.

Domaine Cazes

66602 Rivesaltes; 04.68.64.08.26; info@cazes-rivesaltes.com

Wines: Rivesaltes, Côtes du Roussillon, and Vin de Pays. $ to $$

An important family domaine in the Roussillon, Cazes is the first name to remember when looking for a fine Rivesaltes (you can still buy the sublime 1976 for about $50). It makes every variation on the Rivesaltes theme and all are exemplary. The domaine has recently converted to biodynamics. Coincidence or not, the reds—Côtes du Roussillons—have shown marked improvement: cuvées include Alter, Ego, and my favorite, the ambitious Trilogy. Domaine Cazes also experiments, marketing the resulting wines as Vins de Table or de Pays. One example: an unusual late-harvest, barrel-aged maccabeu, which lovers of wine footnotes will enjoy tasting by the glass.

Domaine des Chandelles

11800 Barbaira; 04.68.79.00.10; fax: 04.68.79.21.92

Wine: Corbières. $ to $$

Susan and Peter Munday, an English couple, make a range of lovely bistro-worthy Corbières. Chais Suzanne is a vibrant quaffer. Le Luquet is a pampered new-oak-aged pure syrah, a fresh, intense but civilized wine. Syrah and grenache blend beautifully in the standard Domaine des Chandelles bottling, and there's a juicy, interesting pure carignan sold as Vin de Pays de l'Aude.

Clairette de Bellegarde

A minuscule Languedoc AC southeast of Costières de Nîmes, for white wines made from clairette. Drink the youngest available. Prices: Less than $. Producer: Mas Carlot.

Clairette de Languedoc

A tiny Languedoc AC for whites made from clairette. These may be dry, off-dry, or sweet. With age they develop nutty, oxidized flavors, which appeal to some consumers. When young, the wines have apple notes but are basically one-dimensional. Generally, drink the youngest available.

PRICES: Most cost about $, though the very sweet versions cost more.

PRODUCERS: Cave de Cabrières ◆ La Clairette d'Adisson ◆ Clos St. Pauline ◆ Domaine la Croix Chaptal ◆ Les Hauts de Saint-Rome ◆ Domaine Honoré Audran ◆ Domaine Mon Mourel.

Clamery/Les Vignerons de l'Occitane

BP 28, 34290 Servian; 04.67.39.07.39; www.vigneronsdeloccitane.com
Wines: Vin de Pays d'Oc, Côtes de Thongue, and others. $
Good producers of a range of fruit-driven wines well fashioned for the contemporary market. The punchy reds—with an emphasis on merlot, cabernet sauvignon, and syrah—give a bang for the buck.

La Clape

An important Coteaux du Languedoc subregion likely to become an independent AC. Located southeast of Narbonne, La Clape lies on the Mediterranean coast (it was once an island; its climate is decisively Mediterranean, with little rain but lots of sun and wind). The wines are powerful, age-worthy, and marked by flavors of eucalyptus and Provençal herbs. For vintages and prices, see COTEAUX DU LANGUEDOC.

PRODUCERS: DOM DE FIGUIÈRES ↑ ◆ CH DE LA NÉGLY ☆ ◆ Ch Pech-Redon ◆ Ch Rouquette-sur-Mer: see COTEAUX DE LANGUEDOC.

LANGUEDOC-ROUSSILLON

Clos de l'Anhel

11200 Lagrasse; tel/fax: 04.68.43.18.12; anhel@wanadoo.fr
Wine: Corbières. $ to $$
Sophie Guiraudon and Philippe Mathias produce a range of very tasty reds including Lolo, an easygoing quaffer; the fragrant Les Terrassettes, mostly carignan and grenache, perfect for a bistro lunch; and the more serious barrel-aged Les Dimanches, made from the domaine's oldest carignan together with syrah. Smooth, with well-defined fruit, it borders on elegant and is downright delicious.

Clos Bagatelle

34360 St.-Chinian; 04.67.93.61.63; closbagatelle@wanadoo.fr
Wines: St.-Chinian and St.-Jean-de-Minervois. $ to $$
Luc Simon and his sister Christine make a number of different St.-Chinians. My consistent favorite (and by far the most expensive) is the dark, structured, serious La Gloire de Mon Père. (The Cuvée Tradition, at about $, is a good value.) Within the same appellation, there is also the Donnadieu line, which includes the two cuvées Camille and Juliette and Matthieu and Marie. At less than $12, both are good values. There are several Vin de Pays and, finally, a fresh, perfumed Muscat de St.-Jean-de-Minervois.

Clos Centeilles

34210 Siran; 04.68.52.18; clos.centeilles@libertysurf.fr
Minervois-la-Livinière and Vin de Pays. $$
A reputable family domaine specializing in unoaked, or lightly oaked, reds. Favorites here include the pure cinsault Cuvée Capitelle des Centeilles, a pungent, cherry-scented Minervois; an interesting pure carignan called Cuvée Carignanissime de Centeilles; the Cuvée Clos Centeilles, smooth and rich at its best; and the food-friendly Campagne de Centeilles, a dark, rich Minervois with black olive notes.

Le Clos des Fées ☆

66600 Vingrau; 04.68.29.40.00; www.closdesfees.com
Côtes du Roussillon. $$ to $$$$
Hervé Bizeul is a man of many wine talents. A former Meilleur Sommelier de France, wine-bar owner, and journalist, he is now, first and foremost, a star on the French wine scene. He makes ultraconcentrated, very delicious cult-style wines based on viticulture as loving as a backyard garden hobbyist's, extremely low yields, and pampered, gentle vinification. His least expensive wine, Les Sorcières, is a juicy delight. His Vieilles Vignes cuvée, about twice the price, is elegant, with mingled aromas. Le Clos gets pretty massive. And the old-vines grenache Petite Sibérie is dense, packed with flavor, and often ends on a sweet note, which leads me to prefer the other bottlings. The last two cuvées are *vins d'auteur* (in the same sense as France's *cinéma d'auteur*), and they are very expensive. All except Les Sorcières are bottled unfiltered. Bizeul recently started his own small *négociant* line called, optimistically, Walden.

Clos Marie ↑

34270 l'Auret, 04.67.59.06.96; clos.marie@wanadoo.fr
Wine: Coteaux du Languedoc. $$ to $$$
Christophe Peyrus, a *terroir* fanatic, has a very promising young domaine. Everything is worth tasting. His simplest cuvée, L'Olivette, a blend of syrah and grenache, is fresh, juicy, and delicious. Simon is rich, vigorous, and oaky but still elegant—more refined than L'Olivette. A wine of structure and succulence, it's like biting into macerated Montmorency cherries—a juiciness that lightly masks a stony-mineral backbone. Glorieuses, destined to be a serious super wine, is fragrant, fine, structured, fresh, and very elegant. At another property he produces Metairie du Clos Vieilles Vignes, a suave, warm, and spicy red.

Clos del Rey ↑

66460 Maury; 04.68.59.15.08
Wines: Côtes du Roussillon-Villages and Vin de Pays. $$($)
At his young domaine, Jacques Montagne makes cult-style wines that, with a bit of age, recall the marvelous Priorats of Spain. There are several cuvées, the Clos del Rey being the signature wine. A blend of grenache and carignan, it's got wonderful fruit, balance, and freshness. Expect very fine things here.

Domaine du Clos Roca ↑

34320 Nizas; 04.67.25.19.43; www.closroca.com
Wines: Coteaux du Languedoc–Pézenas and Vin de Pays de l'Hérault. $$
Good on paper, good in reality, Jean-Christophe Michaux created his own domaine in 2003 after working for Domaine d'Aupilhac and Grange des Pères. His Vin du Pays sauvignon blanc À Propos may have been the best I've ever tasted from the Languedoc. His warm, unfiltered reds are equally appealing, including a tasty À Propos based on the maligned alicante grape; and Idée Reçue, a structured syrah-merlot-cabernet blend.

Clos du Rouge Gorge ☆

66720 Latour-de-France; tel/fax: 04.68.29.16.37
Wine: Vin de Pays in the Roussillon area. $ to $$
Cyril Fhal is a rapidly rising star on the French wine scene. And he's smart. He's experimenting with both organic and biodynamic viticulture; he practices

all the trendy, labor-intensive steps in the cellar. But he assiduously avoids exaggeration—be it overripeness, too much extraction, too much oak, or too little sulfur. The results, generally sold as Vin de Pays des Côtes Catalanes, are elegant, mineral, focused wines. There's a white based on old-vines maccabeu, tinged with flavors of oak and lime zest. His pure carignan, also old-vines, is fragrant and fresh as a waterfall.

Clot de l'Oum ↑

66720 Belesta de la Frontière; 06.60.57.69.62; emonne@web.de
Wine: Côtes du Roussillon. $$ to $$$
In Caramany, one of the winemaking villages of the Fenouillèdes, Leia and Eric Monne follow mostly organic, TLC principles in vineyard and cellar. They make three serious bottlings of red. The first, La Compagnie des Papillons, predominantly grenache with some old-vines cinsault, is exceptionally pure and smooth. The fragrant Saint Bart Vieilles Vignes is based on lladoner pelut and century-old carignan. The inky-dark Numero Uno, the domaine's finest syrah and carignan, is a complex weave of black cherry, prunes, and oak. The wines are bottled unfiltered.

Collioure

A small but important Roussillon AC for full-bodied reds, whites, and rosés. The zone, which takes its name from the charming Mediterranean seaport, covers the same area as Banyuls. Reds and rosés are based on grenache noir and may also include syrah, mourvèdre, carignan, and cinsault; whites are made from grenache blanc and gris. Red wines are by far the major part of the production. Quality varies, as does style. The wines range from pleasant quaffers to reds of real stature, both succulent and nuanced and completely satisfying at an early age.

BEST RECENT VINTAGES: 2005, 2004, 2001 (and there are good wines in both 2003 and 2002).
PRICES: $ to $$

PRODUCERS: Abbé Rous: very nice versions, for a hefty price, especially the soigné Cyrcée ◆ Dom Berta-Maillol: rich, cherry reds ◆ Bruno Duchêne: promising vintner quickly approaching readiness for prime time; look for Cuvée Corall (pure grenache), La Pascole, and La Luna ◆ Les Clos de Paulilles: see CH DE JAU ◆ COUME DEL MAS ◆ DOM MADELOC ☆ ◆ Dom du Mas Blanc: several distinctive, single-vineyard cuvées of Collioure and top-notch Banyuls ☆ ◆ DOM DE LA RECTORIE ☆ ◆ DOM LA TOUR VIEILLE ☆ ◆ DOM TRIBOULEY ↑ ◆ DOM VIAL MAGNÈRES ☆.

Domaine la Colombette

34000 Béziers, 04.67.31.05.53; lacolombette@freesurf.fr
Wine: Vin de Pays des Coteaux du Libron. $$
François Pugibet makes a broad range of varietal wines, including pleasant, clean muscat, chardonnay (both with and without oak), cabernet sauvignon, pinot noir (particularly nice when vinified as a white), and a charming grenache. The most interesting wine, however, is a red made from lladoner pelut, a Catalan grape (a.k.a. micocoulier). It would make a great wine-bar discovery.

Corbières

In volume the largest Languedoc AC, Corbières stretches from Carcassonne and Narbonne to the foothills of the Pyrenees, where it abuts the Roussillon. The AC covers reds and rosés made from carignan, grenache noir, syrah, cinsault, and mourvèdre, and whites made from grenache, bourboulenc, marsanne, maccabeu, and roussanne. In a region this vast, significant differences in quality—and price—are to be expected. In general, these are full, generous, user-friendly wines. The best are suave, elegant, and lipsmackingly delicious. The subregion Boutenac may be used on labels along with Corbières provided the wines have a minimum of 30 percent carignan and have been aged at least fifteen months in barrel and three months in bottle.

BEST RECENT VINTAGES: See COTEAUX DE LANGUEDOC.
PRICES: $ to $$$

PRODUCERS: Cave d'Embres-et-Castelmaure: excellent cooperative with wines ranging from the cheap and cheerful—Cuvées Vieille Jeep and La Chapelle—to the pricier, richer Cuvée #3 ☆ ◆ Ch Cascadais: for inexpensive, simple reds ◆ Le Champ des Murailles: François de Ligneris, the owner of St.-Émilion's Château Soutard, has purchased this Corbières-area property. The wines, generally sold as Vin de Pays, are called Arazim, a rich, oaky, structured red, and the easier-drinking Zinzolin, a blend of carignan and press wine ◆ DOM DES CHANDELLES ◆ CLOS DE L'ANHEL ◆ Ch Fabre-Gasparets: see CH VEREDUS ◆ Dom Faillenc Sainte Marie: nice work here in both the traditional Corbières and the cuvée syrah Conférence de Presse, made from the *vin de presse*, which I enjoy for its tastiness as well as for the pun in its name and its playful wink at journalists ◆ Dom de Fontsainte: warmhearted, easy-drinking reds and rosés ◆ Ch Gléon-Montanie: The domaine makes a fresh, nicely textured white, a pleasant rosé, and several cuvées of red. The Sélection Combe de Berre and the Cuvée Gaston Bonnes are chewy wines that give a bang for the buck ◆ DOM DU GRAND CRÈS ☆ ◆ CH HAUT-GLÉON ◆ Ch de Luc: see CH VEREDUS ◆ CH MEUNIER SAINT-LOUIS ◆ Ch de Lastours: reds loaded with Provençal flavor; the Cuvée La Grande Rompue is mellow and spicy ◆ Ch Prieuré Borde: Another domaine to follow. The cult-style Cuvée Ange is packed with flavors of oak and crushed berries; it's also alluringly fresh ◆ CH OLLIEUX ROMANIS ↑ ◆ Ch Pech-Latte: This is a large domaine owned by Maison Louis Max in Burgundy, producing interesting, tasty organic wines at sometimes puzzling prices—some unusually expensive, some (like the barbecue-friendly Tradition) good values ◆ Ch Sabaric: the world-spanning Lurton brothers are involved in this venture in which they satisfy contemporary preferences for fruit-packed wines ◆ DOM DE LA TREILLE MUSCATE ◆ Dom du Trillol: Bordeaux's Maison Sichel owns this property, turning out reds and whites that are competitive, professional, smooth, and tasty ◆ CH VEREDUS ◆ Ch Vieux Moulin: Alexander They produces some ambitious reds, including Vox Dei, chiefly syrah and mourvèdre, a mouthful of dark, rich fruit, and Les Ailes du Vieux Moulin, which ages on its lees in new oak barrels. It has real elegance and freshness. He also produces interesting Vin de Pays d'Aude at his Domaine St. Paul ◆ Ch la Voulte-Gasparets: a well-known domaine, its AC wines include the pricey, structured, but fruit-driven Cuvée Romain Pauc as well as an easy-drinking Cuvée Réservée.

Costières de Nîmes

Is it the Rhône or is it the Languedoc? Southeast of Nîmes, this AC might be considered a bridge between the two zones. It produces reds and whites, using the same grapes as both the Rhône and Languedoc, although its soils resemble those north of Avignon and its climate approaches that of Montpellier. For the moment, most of the wines are works in progress, best discovered by the glass.

BEST RECENT VINTAGES: 2005, (2004 where yields were controlled), 2003, 2001.
PRICES: $ to $$

PRODUCERS: Ch Amphoux: a domaine worth watching, particularly for its rich red Galion des Crêtes Vieilles Vignes ◆ Ch Beaubois: this domaine practices organic viticulture. Its perfumed syrah would be a lovely discovery in a forward-thinking wine bar ◆ Dom Cabanis: another organic practitioner, making supple, honest wines ◆ Cave de Vauvert: the *barrique*-aged cuvée Noble Gress, made from low-yielding old vines, is dark, chewy, and oaky ◆ Ch l'Ermitage: Cuvée

Ste.-Cécile is the top-of-the-line red here, oaky and stylish ◆ LES VIGNERONS D'ESTÉZARGUES: see the Rhône chapter ◆ PATRICK LESEC: see the Rhône chapter ◆ Dom des Perrières: Marc Kreydenweiss, a top winemaker in Alsace, owns this property on which he produces some of the AC's best wines as well as flavorful Vin de Pays. Look for Les Grimaudes, an appetizingly tart red, and for Ansata, a meaty syrah-mourvèdre blend ◆ Ch Mourgues du Grès: widely available wines, although I have found them thick and dark ◆ CH D'OR ET DE GUEULES ◆ Ch Saint Cyrgues: ambitious but not yet ready for prime time, this domaine's best bottling is the oak-aged, unfiltered Cuvée Amérique ◆ Ch de la Tuilerie: an important and well-known local domaine that makes above-average versions of the AC. The Cuvée Eole is the deluxe bottling in both red and white. Both are ambitious, good-tasting wines, but at $$ they've got competition.

Coteaux du Languedoc

A large regional AC for whites, rosés, and reds, the Coteaux du Languedoc stretches from Nîmes and the outskirts of Arles to Narbonne and Carcassonne, following the arc of France's Mediterranean coast. Modifications of the AC are expected (see the box on page 178) as recognition is given to distinct climatic regions and *terroirs*. Picpoul de Pinet, which produces only whites made from the picpoul grape, is expected to get AC status in 2006 and is so different from the rest of the Coteaux du Languedoc that it is discussed separately.

Other subzones of note, some of which are already highlighted on wine labels, include Pic St.-Loup, La Clape, Grès de Montpellier, Terrasses du Larzac, Pézenas, and Terre de Sommières. Montpeyroux, also featured on labels, is an exceptional growing area within the Terrasses du Larzac. St.-Georges d'Orques lies within the Grès de Montpellier. Other emerging place-names include Cabrières, La Méjanelle, St.-Christol, St.-Drézéry, and St.-Saturnin.

GRAPES: Reds and rosés are made principally from grenache, mourvèdre, syrah, carignan, and cinsault. Whites come from grenache blanc, bourboulenc, clairette, marsanne, roussanne, rolle (vermentino), and picpoul (piquepoul).

STYLES OF WINE: The Languedoc can easily make strong, generous rosés. It also produces both light, fresh whites (notably PICPOUL DE PINET) and strong, vinous, characterful ones with surprising freshness. The calling card here, though, is red wine. The range is endless; you'll find everything from charming quaffers, to blockbuster competition conquerors, to elegant, fine-grained works of art that would grace any table.

BEST RECENT VINTAGES: It's difficult to find a truly bad recent vintage in the Languedoc. Those of 2005, 2004, and 2001 were excellent. The year 2003 is as controversial here as it is elsewhere: there are beauties and there are heavy, jammy wines lacking freshness. It is likely they will age quickly. Thanks to heavy rain, 2002 was a lighter vintage. As a result, some of the wines have an appealing freshness.

As regards aging in general, the region hasn't had sufficient time to establish a track record, though some of the best wines indicate a strong potential. For now, enjoy them between their third and their eighth birthdays.
PRICES: Given the great diversity of quality, there is an equally great span of prices, going from $5 to more than $100. So, $ to $$$$.

PRODUCERS: This list includes producers that use the Vin de Pays and Vin de Table designations and are located within the Coteaux du Languedeoc. For producers of Picpoul de Pinet, see that listing. L'Abbaye de Valmagne: chewy, spicy reds from the Grès de Montpellier. La Cuvée de Turenne is the top bottling ◆ DOM DE L'AIGUELIÈRE ◆ DOM D'AUPILHAC ☆ ◆ Ch de Cazeneuve: This Pic St.-Loup domaine makes fresh southern whites based on barrel-fermented roussanne and several different reds, including a cool, structured Les Calcaires. Other bottlings include the equally recommended Roc des Mates and Le Sang du Calvaire ◆ Dom Alain Chabanon: see Dom Font Caude in this listing ◆ Dom Clavel: the wines are worth trying, particularly the top cuvée,

Copa Santa, although in rich vintages it can taste too thick ◆ CLOS MARIE ↑ ◆ DOM DU CLOS ROCA ↑ ◆ Ch la Clotte Fontane: ambitious, concentrated wines in a New World style, all up front ◆ Dom de la Coste: a very good domaine, the best in the St.-Christol area, making peppery, characterful reds from old mourvèdre ◆ Dom Cour St. Vincent: the warm, peppery Mille Pierres bottling has that fogged-in texture I often find in reds from the Grès de Montpellier area. Le Clos du Prieur is deeper, darker, more complex and less shut in ◆ DOM DES CRÈS RICARDS ◆ Dom Croix de Saint Privat: a young domaine on the Terrasses de Larzac making honest wines that are still a bit raw, such as the Cuvée Édouard, an oak-aged blend of syrah and grenache—good for a by-the-glass discovery, as is the Cuvée du Pastel, pure carignan, sold as a Vin de Pays de St.-Guilhem le Désert ◆ CH DE L'ENGARRAN ◆ ERMITAGE DE PIC ST.-LOUP ☆ ◆ Ch l'Euzière: The fragrant Les Escarboucles is a nicely structured red from Pic St.-Loup ◆ Ch d'Exindre: located in the Grès de Montpellier zone, this domaine makes a powerful red Amelius and very nice Muscat de Mireval ◆ DOM DE FIGUIÈRES ↑ ◆ Dom le Comte de Floris: smooth, refined red with lovely mingling of oak and fruit ◆ Dom Font Caude: in the heart of Montpeyroux, Alain Chabanon, a promising young vigneron, favors long, slow aging for his berry- and oak-packed reds, particularly L'Esprit de Font Caude and the pure, dulcet Les Boïssières, 90 percent grenache and generally unfiltered. Note that the property, as of 2006, is now called Dom Alain Chabanon ↑ ◆ DOM LES GRANDS COSTES ↑ ◆ LA GRANGE DE QUATRE SOUS ◆ GRANGE DES PÈRES ☆ ◆ DOM DE GRANOUPIAC ◆ CH GRÈS SAINT-PAUL ☆ ◆ Dom Haut Lirou: the Esprit du Haut Lirou is a serious, oaky red and relatively expensive at more than $25 ◆ Dom Henry: a domaine in the St.-Georges d'Orques region producing ambitious, interesting reds ◆ DOM DE L'HORTUS ☆ ◆ La Jasse Castel: a very promising domaine in the Montpeyroux area making nicely focused reds with good fruit and a bit too much oak—worth following ◆ Ch de Jonquières: another promising domaine, in their youth, its Terrasses de Larzac–based reds seem hefty and dense; with age, they become suppler and finer of grain ◆ Ch de Lancyre: the Grande Cuvée is a dense, robust red ◆ Dom Lacroix-Vanel: a Pézenas-area domaine worth following; try the softly perfumed Clos Melanie ◆ CH DE LASCAUX ☆ ◆ CH DE LA LIQUIÈRE ☆ ◆ DOM DE LA MARFÉE ↑ ◆ MAS DE LA BARBEN ☆ ◆ Mas des Brousses: the unfiltered reds from this domaine sometimes have an exceedingly dry finish, but they're spirited ◆ Mas Brugière: a reliably good Pic St.-Loup producer that makes rugged, invigorating wines with exuberant fruit ◆ Mas Brunet: a Terrasses de Larzac domaine making a silky, syrah-dominated Cuvée Prestige with spice and truffle notes ◆ Mas des Chimères: on the Terrasses de Larzac Guilhem Darde makes minty, thick reds, under either the Coteaux du Languedoc or the Vin de Pays des Coteaux du Salagou label. They're reasonably priced and fun to try ◆ MAS DAUMAS GASSAC ☆ ◆ Mas Foulaquier: another promising young domaine, its L'Orphée is a fresh, delectable red quaffer; Le Petit Duc Cuvée Exceptionelle is fragrant and serious—follow closely ↑ ◆ Mas Granier: Jean-Philippe Granier makes delicious, structured reds that are reasonably priced and pure pleasure ☆ ◆ Mas Haut Buis: Olivier Jeantet's cuvée Costa Caoude is a must taste for syrah lovers, even though there's grenache and carignan in the blend ◆ MAS JULLIEN ☆ ◆ Mas de Martin: Cuvée Ultreia has attractive baked red cherry and sweet spice flavors. It also has that confined texture I find in many reds from the Grès de Montpellier ◆ Mas de Mortiès: deservedly held in high regard, thanks to a very particular microclimate, the wines of this popular domaine are not typical of the Pic St.-Loup. Meaty, tarry, and minty, they perfectly reflect the domaine's *terroir* ◆ MAS DE LA SERRANNE ↑ ◆ Metairies du Clos: see CLOS MARIE ◆ CH DE LA NÉGLY ☆ ◆ Dom le Nouveau Monde: tannic, truffley, and warm, the Cuvée Brame-Reille is an ambitious and serious syrah-dominated red ◆ DOM PAS DE L'ESCALETTE ↑ ◆ Ch Pech Redon: This domaine in La Clape offers several cuvées named after plants or birds, signaling an eco-friendly orientation. The best are the easy-drinking Cades and the more serious, syrah-based Centaurée. The 2001 vintage was a generous black-red wine that went very well with lamprey cooked in red wine. See also VIN DE PAYS ◆ DOM PEYRE ROSE ☆ ◆ PLAN DE L'OM ☆ ◆ Dom du Poujol: Makes some interesting Vin de Pays. Podio Alto, its AC wine, a jammy, crushed berry red with New World flavors, is pretty good too, so this might be a domaine to watch ◆ PRIEURÉ DE SAINT-JEAN DE BÉBIAN ◆ DOM DE LA PROSE ☆ ◆ Ch Puech-Haut: a big, important St.-Drézéry-area domaine making big, showy whites and reds ◆ Ch Ricardelle: cheap and cheerful reds from La Clape ◆ Dom de Roucaillat: for a change of pace, consider Alain Rider's domaine. From vineyards located on the Hautes Terres de Camberousse, Rider makes only white wines and they are strong, fragrant, and creamy with oak and caramel notes ◆ CH LA ROQUE ☆ ◆ Ch Rouquette-sur-Mer: this La Clape–area domaine makes a very good white and several cuvées of red, including an expensive Clos de la Tour. The regular bottling has shown some ups and downs but the last vintage tasted, 2003, was smooth, with good cherry flavors and nice balance. And, at less than $10, the price is right ◆ CH ST. MARTIN DE LA GARRIGUE ◆ DOM DE LA SAUVAGEONNE ☆ ◆ Dom Serres Cabanis: vibrant, tobacco- and cherry-scented reds from the Terre de Sommière area, particularly the cuvée Cellier du Porche, a blend of syrah, grenache, and mourvèdre ◆ Dom du Silène des Peyrals: see ROBERT SKALLI ◆ DOM SINGLA ↑ ◆ Dom de Terre Mégère: the Cuvée Dolomies has the peppery quality typical of Grès de Montpellier reds; would go well with grilled foods that taste of fire ◆ Dom la Tour Penedesses: an interesting domaine making wine here, in Faugères as well as in the Vin de Pays category—Le Clos Magrignan, chiefly syrah, is lush, fresh, and promising ◆ CH DE VALFLAUNES ↑ ◆ Les Vignerons (or Cave) de St.-Saturnin: A good cooperative offering easy-drinking reds at reasonable prices ◆ Dom Zumbaum-Tomasi: an organic producer, its impressive Clos Maginiai is a dark, cult-style wine with superripe, sweet fruit.

Côtes de la Malpère: See MALPÈRE.

Côtes du Roussillon, Côtes du Roussillon-Villages, and Côtes du Roussillon Les Aspres

The Côtes du Roussillon is a large regional AC applying to whites, rosés, and reds of variable price and quality made throughout the Roussillon.

The ACs Côtes du Roussillon-Villages and Les Aspres apply to red wines only. The first come from the northern part of the zone, above Perpignan, notably in the Fenouillèdes, around the villages of Caramany, Lesquerde, Latour-de-France, and Tautavel, each of which may append its name to that of Roussillon-Villages. Les Aspres lies southeast of Perpignan. It, too, may join its name to that of Roussillon-Villages.

GRAPES: White wines are based on grenache blanc and gris, maccabeu, marsanne, and roussanne. Reds and rosés are generally blends based on grenache noir, carignan, syrah, mourvèdre, and lladoner pelut.

STYLES OF WINE: Roussillon wines are strong. The whites are vinous rather than varietal and often finish with an appetizing bitter-almond note. At their best, the reds are succulent, generous, and structured. Many recall the wines of Priorato in Spain. Some of the reds, particularly those from the Fenouillèdes, often seem to finish on a sweet note. These remind me of amarone or of 1970s late-harvest zinfandel. The best rosés are characterful—real wines.

BEST RECENT VINTAGES: 2005, 2004, 2001. There have been no truly bad recent vintages. Controversial here as elsewhere, 2003 produced highly alcoholic, extremely rich wines, to drink "on the fruit." And 2002 is a good year, but lighter than the best. As with the Coteaux du Languedoc, the Côtes du Roussillon hasn't had sufficient time to establish a track record with regard to aging, though some of the best indicate a strong potential. For now, enjoy the wines between their third and their eighth birthdays.
PRICES: $ to $$$$

PRODUCERS: (There has been a lot of recent investment here. Many domaines are no more than several years old, particularly in the Fenouillèdes. Most producers also make Vin de Pays; some of the noteworthy ones are listed here.) Dom Alary: located in the Fenouillèdes, this young producer is one to watch, as evidenced by its flavorful chardonnay Grain d'Orient, sold as a Vin de Pays ◆ Dom de l'Ausseil: another very good Fenouillèdes domaine the inviting Les Trois Pierres shows admirable elegance ◆ Ch la Bastide St. Roch: a mellow white Vin de Pays reveals the promise of this Fenouillèdes domaine ◆ Dom des Blanes: Marie-Pierre Bories took over part of the family domaine in 2000. Based on a tasting of several whites (pure grenache) and grenache-dominated reds, the future looks promising. Bories also makes Vin de Pays and Maury ◆ Dom Boudau: the cuvée Patrimoine, based on fifty-year-old grenache vines, is fragrant, ambitious, and packed with delicious fruit and the cuvée Le Clos is a generous charmer at $ ◆ Dom de la Capeillette: located in Latour-de-France in the Fenouillèdes, the domaine makes friendly reds, among them the fragrant cuvée Montredon and the ambitious Vieilles Vignes ◆ Ch de Caladroy: the large Fenouillèdes domaine recently hired a dynamic young winemaking team; the wines, particularly the reds, have improved ◆ DOM CALVET-THUNEVIN ☆ ◆ Ch la Cazenove: Étienne Montes makes intense Rivesaltes and several different Côtes du Roussillon, for example, the admirable cuvée Commandant Jaubert; pricier cuvées may be impressive but are too expensive ◆ DOM CAZES ◆ LE CLOS DES FÉES ☆ ◆ CLOS DEL REY ↑ ◆ CLOS DU ROUGE GORGE ☆ ◆ CLOT DE L'OUM ↑ ◆ LA COUME DU ROY ◆ DOM DES CRÈS RICARDS ◆ DOM FERRER-RIBIÈRE ◆ Dom Fontanel: a very good Fenouillèdes domaine, making fragrant whites and structured, often minty, reds like the cuvée Prieuré ◆ Dom Força Real: a good domaine for easy-drinking reds, particularly the more ambitious (and more expensive) Les Hauts de Forca Real ◆ Les Foulards Rouges: Jean-François Nicq's promising young domaine. He's getting his act together, reinventing the wheel—worth following. The wines are quite pure and in the hypernatural style ◆ DOM GARDIÈS ☆ ◆ DOM GAUBY ☆ ◆ CH DE JAU ◆ DOMAINE LAGUERRE ↑ ◆ DOM LAPORTE ◆ Dom Lhéritier: the kirsch-scented reds, based on grenache, go down very easily ◆ Dom Marcevol: a young, organic domaine, making pleasant, ambitious wines ◆ MAS AMIEL ☆ ◆ MAS BAUX ◆ Dom Mas Crémat: Cyril Fhal (see CLOS DU ROUGE GORGE) has been making the wines here since the death of the owner. I have only tasted an elegant, ample white, a grenache Vieilles Vignes, sold as a Vin de Pays Catalanes ◆ MAS DE LA DEVÈZE ↑ ◆ Mas Janeil: chewy reds from the globe-spanning winemakers Jacques and François Lurton ◆ MAS KAROLINA ↑ ◆ Mas de Lavail: a large domaine making good Maury, inviting Vin de Pays, and foursquare Côtes du Roussillon-Villages, especially the cuvée Désirade ◆ DOM DE MATASSA ↑ ◆ DOM PADIE ↑ ◆ Dom Piquemal: stylish barrel-fermented whites, along with pleasant Roussillon and dense, tannic Roussillon-Villages; see also RIVESALTES ◆ DOM OLIVIER PITHON ↑ ◆ CH PLANÈRES ☆ ◆ Dom Pouderoux: see MAURY ◆ Préceptorie de Centernach: see DOM DE LA RECTORIE ◆ LA ROC DES ANGES ↑ ◆ DOM SAINT ROCH ↑ ◆ Dom Salvat: pleasant reds and whites; look for Cuvée Taichac ◆ DOM SARDA-MALET ◆ DOM DES SCHISTES ◆ DOM SINGLA ↑ ◆ Domaine le Soula: a Fenouillèdes-area partnership led by Gerard Gauby and specializing in Vin de Pays; I haven't liked the white here, but the red is complex and serious ↑ ◆ La Tautevelloise: a good Fenouillèdes-area cooperative—try the cuvée Piedmont du Château ◆ DOM LA TOUR VIEILLE ☆ ◆ DOM TRIBOULEY ↑ ◆ Dom de Venus: Jean-Vincent Ridon worked in South Africa, drops "Davis" (as in University of California, Davis, the winemaking school) into conversations, and foot-stomps his red grapes. A recent arrival to the Fenouillèdes, he shows tremendous promise. I have only tasted his wines from barrel but, white and red alike, they are mouthfilling, mineral, and very much worth following ↑ ◆ Dom des Soulanes: the domaine's clutch of unfined, unfiltered reds include the succulent, crowd-pleasing Sarrat del Mas as well as a number of amiable Vin de Pays. This is also a good address for Maury ◆ DOM VIAL MAGNÈRES ☆.

Côtes de Thongue: See VIN DE PAYS.

Coume del Mas

66650 Banyuls-sur-Mer, tel/fax: 04.68.88.37.03; coumedelmas@tiscali.fr
Wines: Collioure and Banyuls. $ to $$

Philippe and Nathalie Gard make a good, barrel-fermented Collioure blanc, an even better rosé, and two worthwhile cuvées of red. The simpler cuvée Schistes is pure grenache with no wood age. It's charming. The spicy, oak-aged Quadratour needs food. The domaine also makes a barrel-fermented Banyuls blanc with rich apricot and pear flavors, and a chewy red Banyuls Quintessence.

La Coume du Roy

66460 Maury; tel/fax: 04.68.59.67.58

Wines: Côtes du Roussillon, Maury, and Muscat de Rivesaltes. $ to $$$

If you're looking for aged Maury, here's an excellent address, with vintages spanning the twentieth century. The 1977, for example, bottled in 2003, was a delectable mix of flavors—toffee, hay, and more—and costs about $$$. Younger vintages are also delicious, as is the Muscat de Rivesaltes. The Côtes du Roussillon are a mixed bag; the cheaper cuvées are a bit raw, the most expensive cuvée is a bit too expensive.

Domaine des Crès Ricards

34800 Ceyras, tel/fax: 04.67.44.67.63. foltran@cresricards.com.

Wines: Coteaux du Languedoc. $ to $$

The rosés here are tight, full, and powerful, and the reds are just about perfect for any bistro or wine bar. The cuvée Stecia is fragrant, balanced, and goes down easily. Les Hauts de Milesi ages in newish barrels and needs time to digest its oak, but it's elegant and promising. Ditto for Oenothera, the most serious of the three.

Domaine Pierre Cros

11800 Badens; 04.68.79.21.82; fax: 04.68.79.24.03

Wine: Minervois. $ to $$

A clutch of fascinating wines here, starting with the white blend of grenache and picpoul and an appetizing rosé. The real action starts with Les Mal Aimés, an old-vines red based on supposedly third-rate grape varieties like aramon, alicante, and picpoul noir. This is an herby, archetypal wine-bar wine. Vieilles Vignes Minervois, pure carignan, from vines planted in 1905, is characterful, mineral, and totally original. Finally there's the pure syrah Les Aspres, less rare but insanely rich.

Jean-Louis Denois

11300 Roquetaillade; 04.68.31.39.12; jl.denois@wanadoo.fr

Wine: Limoux. $$

This intelligently run domaine makes very good Crémant de Limoux and has particular success with chardonnay and chenin. The style is fresh, tender (there's usually a trace of residual sugar), and very professional. La Rivière is the svelte, easy-drinking chenin, Sainte Marie, the delightful barrel-aged chardonnay. In 2003, Denois blended the two to produce an ample yet vivacious Vieilles Vignes.

Domaine les Éminades ↑

34360 Cébazan; tel/fax: 04.67.36.14.38; les.eminades@wanadoo.fr

Wine: St.-Chinian. $$

Patricia and Luc Bettoni recently created this promising domaine. Their two cuvées of red Cebenna and Sortilège are big, meaty wines. I'd welcome more suppleness and elegance but the Bettonis are on the right track.

Château de l'Engarran

34880 Laverune: 04.67.47.00.02; lengarran@wanadoo.fr

Wines: Coteaux du Languedoc and Vin de Pays. $ to $$

This substantial domaine makes a range of worthwhile reds. Of particular interest are the velvety Quetton St.-Georges, chiefly syrah, and two pungent Vins de Pays, a red with 35 percent merlot and a sauvignon blanc.

Ermitage du Pic St.-Loup ☆

34750 St.-Mathieu-de-Treviers; 04.67.55.20.15; fax: 04.67.55.23.49

Wine: Coteaux du Languedoc Pic St.-Loup. $$ ($)

Jean-Marc Ravaille's wines would appeal to both Old and New World palates—without pandering to anyone. The standard bottling is buoyant, with intense black berry flavors and a long finish. The top-of-the-line Cuvée Guilhem Gaucelm is an ambitious, elegant red, worth cellaring. The Cuvée Sainte Agnès can be found in both white and red; the white is strong and characterful as well as crowd pleasing; the red is fragrant and serious and, at half the price of the Cuvée Guilhem, a good value.

Château des Estanilles

34480 Cabrerolles; 04.67.90.29.25; fax: 04.67.90.10.99
Wine: Faugères. $ to $$
By now the Louison family is part of the Faugères establishment, having paved the way for the generation now buying vineyards. Extended plantings, resulting in an increased percentage of young vines, have made recent vintages less exciting, but there is always a true taste of Faugères, from the drink-on-the-fruit standard bottling, to the oak-aged Cuvée Prestige, to the pure syrah Grande Cuvée. The domaine also produces a creamy white based on roussanne.

Faugères

Located north of Pézenas and Béziers, Faugères is a Languedoc AC that applies to reds and rosés made from grenache, syrah, mourvèdre, carignan, and cinsault. Since 2005 the AC can also be applied to white wines made from roussanne, marsanne, grenache blanc, and vermentino (rolle). Wines from Faugères tend to be big boned, rich, juicy, and aromatic. As quality progresses, the wines are also becoming more succulent and elegant. Watch this area!

BEST RECENT VINTAGES: Generally the same as the Coteaux du Languedoc: 2004 and 2001 were excellent. The year 2003 carries the usual caveats regarding potential overripeness caused by extraordinary heat, and 2002 was a good year despite heavy rain.
PRICES: $ to $$$

PRODUCERS: Abbaye Sylva Plana: good, solid reds, particularly the partially oak-aged Le Songe de l'Abbé, which is chiefly syrah ◆ Dom de l'Ancienne Mercerie: a young domaine with a range of nice wines, including the friendly red Les Petits Mains and the more serious, concentrated Couture ◆ LÉON BARRAL ☆ ◆ CH DES ESTANILLES ◆ Clos Fantine: biodynamics and an avoidance of sulfur are among the practices influencing this young domaine; its wines are very much works in progress ◆ CH DE LA LIQUIÈRE ☆ ◆ MOULIN DE CIFFRE ◆ Dom La Tour Penedesses: a young domaine worth following, the Montagne Noire rouge, largely mourvèdre, is rich and appealing. The domaine also produces Coteaux du Languedoc and Vin de Pays ↑ ◆ Dom Saint Antonin: another young domaine with promising wines, particularly the tasty Tradition and the more serious Magnoux ◆ Les Vins de Vienne: see the entry in the Rhône chapter. This dynamic group has just extended its reach to Faugères ↑.

Fenouillèdes

A Roussillon winemaking region north of Perpignan. Formerly devoted to Maury Vin Doux Naturel, it has become one of the most dynamic regions for red wine production—either as Côtes du Roussillon-Villages or as Vin de Pays. Caramany, Latour-de-France, Lesquerde, and Tautavel are all located here. The emergence of exciting red wines here has led a number of high-profile Bordelais (Jean-Luc Thunevin, for example) to invest in the area. And new domaines seem to be created on a daily basis, accounting for many of the ↑ icons in the producer lists. For vintages and prices see CÔTES DU ROUSSILLON.

Domaine Ferrer-Ribière

66300 Terrats; 04.68.53.24.45; domaineferrerribiere@aol.com
Wines: Côtes du Roussillon, Muscat de Rivesaltes, and Vin de Pays Catalan.
$ to $$$
There's a lot of winemaking going on here with, I find, mixed results. Denis Ferrer and Bruno Ribière have their hearts in the right place and when the wine works, it can be appealing and riveting, as in the Empreinte du Temps made from century-old carignan. Mémoire des Temps, chiefly syrah, is generally supple and pleasant. Cuvée Cana has seemed over-oaked with a glut of ripe, ripe fruit. The Muscat de Rivesaltes is rich, concentrated, and very good. The inexpensive red Tradition is raw but flavorful, good for a barbecue.

Domaine de Figuières ↑

La Clape 11100 Narbonne; 04.68.90.42.81; fax: 04.68.32.40.98
Wine: Coteaux du Languedoc–La Clape. $$
Stéphanie Dupressoir is making some very promising, impressive red wines at her young domaine, which at the time of this writing is in danger of closing. The Cuvée du Figuier, aged in newish oak, is elegant and concentrated. The carignan-rich Cuvée du Vitraille has flavors of kirsch and Provençal herbs. Cuvée Louis, chiefly late-harvest syrah, is a cult-style wine with elegance, concentration, and mingled flavors of black fruit, mint, and black olives.

Fitou

A western Languedoc AC devoted to red wine made from carignan and grenache noir, with the possible addition of syrah and mourvèdre. The appellation has the potential to produce distinctive and exciting reds—although, for the moment, this promise is seen only in the very best producers. Many also make Rivesaltes.

BEST RECENT VINTAGES: Similar to other Languedoc ACs; 2004 and 2001 are standouts.
PRICES: $ to $$

PRODUCERS: Dom Bertrand-Bergé: a popular producer, its top Fitou is Cuvée Jean Serven. The domaine also makes Rivesaltes ◆ Ch des Erles: consistent with their international style, the Lurton brothers produce crowd-pleasing wines—for example, the Cuvée des Ardoises, a tasty red ◆ MARIA FITA ↑ ◆ DOM LES MILLES VIGNES ↑ ◆ Ch de Nouvelles: good Rivesaltes and sturdy, stew-loving reds.

Domaine Gardiès ☆

66600 Vingrau; 04.68.64.61.16; domgardies@wanadoo.fr
Wines: Côtes du Roussillon, Rivesaltes, and Vin de Pays. $$ to $$$
An excellent family domaine. The old-vines grenache blanc, fermented in barrel, is a mellow, fragrant white. Reds are neither fined nor filtered. Les Millières, a luscious blend of syrah, grenache, and mourvèdre, should be drunk "on the fruit." The Vieilles Vignes Tautavel, chiefly grenache, is potent but remains fresh. Les Falaises Tautavel, mostly syrah, is rich but elegant and structured, a beauty. And La Torre, 90 percent mourvèdre, aged in new oak, is a powerhouse with fruit so sweet it recalls Amarone.

Domaine Gauby ☆

66370 Calce; 04.68.64.34.19; fax: 04.68.64.41.77
Wines: Côtes du Roussillon-Villages and Vin de Pays. $$ to $$$$
Gérard Gauby has become a cult figure—for young winemakers in the Roussillon as well as for many sommeliers and wine journalists. His domaine is run along biodynamic principles, yields are low, and wines are bottled without fining or filtration. Back in the twentieth century, Gauby endeavored to make superconcentrated wines. He has recently taken another course, aiming for

freshness and elegance. La Jasse, his least expensive white, is truly good and very food friendly. Of the several cuvées of red, there is an engaging grenache and the celebrated and very expensive La Muntada, which is chiefly syrah.

Domaine du Grand Crès ☆

11200 Ferrals-les-Corbières; 04.68.43.69.08; grand.cres@wanadoo.fr

Wine: Corbières. $ to $$

I love these wines so much that were I an importer, I'd have been bringing them into the United States since I first tasted them eight years ago. An agronomist, Hervé Leferrer has worked in different jobs in the wine world, most notably at the Domaine de la Romanée-Conti. Something rubbed off: his wines are Côte d'Or in the Languedoc. He makes an unoaked Corbières blanc that improbably reminds me of Didier Dagueneau's top cuvées of Pouilly-Fumé. At 95 percent roussanne and 5 percent muscat à petits grains for a whiff of exoticism, it's textured, fresh, and beautifully balanced. His viognier is equally delightful. He also makes lyrical sweet muscat *vin de liqueur* from shriveled grapes. His standard red Corbières, the cuvée Classique, is cool and elegant. I could drink it by the bucket. The cuvée Majeur, mostly syrah aged in newish oak, is a star. It deserves to be poured at the best tables the world over—superb.

Domaine les Grandes Costes ↑

34270 Vacquières; tel/fax: 04.67.59.27.42; www.grandes-costes.com

Wine: Coteaux du Languedoc. $ to $$

Jean-Christophe Granier, former Parisian and ex-journalist with *La Revue de Vin de France*, created his winery, just beyond Pic St.-Loup, in 2000. Influenced by Burgundy, Granier wants to make wines that are fresh and elegant. And the progress he has made indicates that he is on the right path. His big, tasty rosé could take on spicy food. His standard red bottling is pure pleasure. Grandes Costes, predominantly syrah, is velvety and long. And Sarabande, a blend of the usual red grapes, is fragrant, serious, and very promising.

La Grange de Quatre Sous

34360 Assignan; 04.67.38.06.41; hildegard.horat@wanadoo.fr

Wine: Vin de Pays d'Oc. $$

A very good address for fine-quality, tasty, reasonably priced reds, particularly the top cuvées Les Serrottes and Lo Molin. The Vin de Pays Le Jeu du Mail is a big, smooth white, perfect for sunny dishes.

Grange des Pères ☆

34150 Aniane; 04.67.57.70.55; 04.67.57.32.04

Wine: Vin de Table. $$$$

Serious, noble wine that makes you smile at how delicious it is. A blend of syrah, cabernet, and mourvèdre, it is silky, fine-grained, and elegant. Will it age beyond eight years? I don't know that anyone would be capable of keeping it around that long; it's completely satisfying in its youth. There is also a white, based on roussanne, that I have never tasted.

Domaine de Granoupiac

34725 St.-André de Sangonis; 04.67.57.58.28; cflavard@infonie.fr

Wines: Coteaux du Languedoc–Terrasses du Larzac and Vin de Pays. $ to $$

Marie-Claude and Claude Flavard run an admirable domaine. The white Chant des Cigales is focused, perfumed, and ample. The red Les Cresses, chiefly syrah, is dense with fruit flavors. It's fresh, structured, fairly serious wine; a good value, it needs carafing.

Les Grès de Montpellier

An important COTEAUX DU LANGUEDOC subzone southwest of Montpellier likely to get independent AC recognition. To make matters even more confusing, Grès de Montpellier has its own subzones, which may also, one day, get independent AC recognition: St.-Georges-d'Orques, St.-Christol, La Méjanelle, St.-Drézéry, and Vérargues. Though syrah must account for at least 20 percent of the wines, mourvèdre plays a particularly important role here. Intensely fruity, peppery, and jammy, the wines have aromas that recall the dry lavender-thyme scent of the *garrigues*. The zone is subject to night fogs, and I often find its wines have a fogged-in texture, particularly when compared to the airiness of wine from Pic St.-Loup. For vintages and prices, see COTEAUX DU LANGUEDOC.

PRODUCERS: Abbaye de Valmagne: see COTEAUX DE LANGUEDOC ◆ Dom Clavel: see COTEAUX DE LANGUEDOC ◆ Dom Cour St. Vincent: see COTEAUX DE LANGUEDOC ◆ CH DE L'ENGARRAN ◆ Ch d'Exindre: see COTEAUX DE LANGUEDOC ◆ CH GRÈS SAINT-PAUL ☆ ◆ Mas de Martin: see COTEAUX DE LANGUEDOC ◆ DOM PEYRE ROSE ☆ ◆ DOM DE LA PROSE ☆ ◆ CH ST. MARTIN DE LA GARRIGUE ◆ Dom de Terre Mégère: see COTEAUX DU LANGUEDOC.

Château Grès Saint-Paul ☆

34400 Lunel; 04.67.71.27.90; www.gres-saint-paul.com
Wines: Coteaux du Languedoc–Grès de Montpellier and Muscat de Lunel. $$
Sévillane is the name of Château Grès Saint-Paul's lovely Muscat de Lunel. There are two alluring reds: Antonin, chiefly syrah, is minty, berry-flavored, and dense. Syrhus (or Sirius) is even richer, a cult-style wine, ripe, fragrant, and elegant.

Château (and Domaine) Haut-Gléon

11360 Durban; 04.68.48.85.95; www.hautgleon.com
Wines: Corbières (the château) and Vin de Pays (the domaine). $ to $$$
Talk about a cottage industry. In addition to wine, the domaine produces olive oil, has a bed-and-breakfast, makes a range of curiosities such as the aperitif CARTHAGÈNE, and markets a *négociant* line, Léon Nicolas Duhamel. Care is taken and the domaine's own wines are generally good. G de Haut-Gléon is chiefly grenache blended with oak-aged syrah. It's suave and pleasant but a bit pricey at more than $30.

Domaine de l'Hortus ☆

34270 Valflaunes, 04.67.55.31.20; domaine.hortus@wanadoo.fr
Wines: Coteaux du Languedoc–Pic St.-Loup and Vin de Pays. $ to $$
Jean Orliac has a solid track record for producing fine, appetizing reds that are delicious within their first five years. The Grande Cuvée, a barrel-aged blend based on mourvèdre and syrah, has generous cherry and spice flavors and a gracious, self-assured feel. Tannins are there too, so carafe before drinking. The barrel-aged Clos du Prieur, chiefly grenache and syrah, is a mellow red with lots of stuffing. The less expensive Bergerie rouge is a nice lunch red, not too heavy, and reasonably priced. The whites, sold as Vin de Pays du Val de Montferrand, are chiefly chardonnay with some viognier and roussanne. Big, smooth, and easy to like, they should appeal to New World palates without offending traditionalists, like me, who regret the spread of chardonnay throughout the Languedoc.

Château de Jau

66600 Cases-de-Pêne; 04.68.38.90.10; daure@wanadoo.fr
Wines: Côtes du Roussillon, Muscat de Rivesaltes, and Vin de Pays d'Oc. $ to $$
The range of wines with the label Jaja de Jau, with its calculatedly casual packaging, appears in many wine shop windows. It's a smart marketing tool: the wines are cheap, well-made, pleasant picnic quaffs. The Daurés use their best red grapes for Talon Rouge—catchy packaging here, too—a blend of syrah and mourvèdre. Strong but not overdone, it would go well with grilled meats at a summer dinner. The domaine also makes a perfumed Muscat de Rivesaltes, and it has three other properties: Mas Cristine for Muscat de Rivesaltes, Viña las Niñas in Chile, and at the nearby Les Clos de Paulilles. There they produce a ripe, meaty Collioure red as well as extremely nice Banyuls, particularly the Cap Bear, which tastes like really good tawny port.

Domaine Laguerre ↑

66220 St.-Martin de Fenouillet; 04.68.59.26.92; domaine.laguerre@free.fr
Wines: Côtes du Roussillon and Vin de Pays. $$
Eric Laguerre, Gérard Gauby's partner at Le Soula, established his own Fenouillèdes domaine in 2002. Some five hundred meters high, they are the northernmost vineyards in the Roussillon, and Laguerre is in the process of converting them to biodynamics. There are two barrel-aged whites: the mellow, mineral Le Ciste and a fresh, lovely blend of marsanne and roussanne; and two reds, the inviting, elegant Le Ciste and a delectable Vin de Pays with cabernet sauvignon in its blend.

Domaine Luc Lapeyre

11160 Trausse-Minervois, 04.68.78.35.67; fax: 04.68.78.35.67
Wine: Minervois. $$
The Domaine Luc Lapeyre makes generous, nuanced reds. Its cuvée Les Clots is layered, lovely, and restaurant ready.

Domaine Laporte

Château Roussillon, 66000 Perpignan; 04.68.50.06.53; domaine-laporte@wanadoo.fr
Wine: Côtes du Roussillon. $ to $$
A source for three good AC reds, the top of the line being Sumeria, a thick, Port-like wine. Some love it; I find it a bit pricey, at more than $20.

Château de Lascaux ☆

34270 Vacquières; 04.67.59.00.08; jb.cavalier@wanadoo.fr
Wine: Coteaux du Languedoc–Pic St.-Loup. $$ to $$$
Jean-Benoît Cavalier is no newcomer, and his wines are self-assured and reliable. Thanks to Pic St.-Loup's cool microclimate, Cavalier can make very fresh whites. Les Pierres d'Argent, a barrel-fermented blend of roussanne, marsanne, and rolle, is toasty and generous. The simplest red has luscious fruit; the barrel-aged Les Nobles Pierres, chiefly syrah, is fine-grained and delightful; Les Secrets, a blend of grenache and syrah, is equally promising but needs time to digest its oak.

Limoux

Beginning southwest of Carcassonne, then stretching along the Aude valley to the foothills of the Pyrenees, Limoux encompasses four Languedoc ACs: three sparkling wines—Blanquette de Limoux, Crémant de Limoux, and Blanquette Méthode Ancestrale—and a still wine, Limoux. The region has been the source of sparkling wine since the sixteenth century, and this accounts for the most of the production. Owing to the influence of the Atlantic's maritime climate, the grapes used are not typical of the Languedoc. The chief grape is mauzac. Depending on the appellation, chardonnay and chenin may be added in limited quantities. Blanquette Méthode Ancestrale, which must be pure mauzac, is only partially fermented and remains slightly sweet and low in alcohol (less than 7 percent). The sparkling Limoux are light, vinous, and mild.

In still wines, Limoux blanc has no mandated minimum percentage of mauzac but the wine must be fermented and aged in barrel. They can be fresh, fragrant, and food friendly. The AC Limoux rouge was created in 2003. It may be made from carignan, syrah, grenache, malbec, merlot, and cabernets sauvignon and franc.

BEST RECENT VINTAGES: 2004, 2003, and 2001.
PRICES: $ to $$

PRODUCERS: These include some Vin de Pays producers within the region.
DOM DE L'AIGLE ◆ Antech: a quality producer and *négociant* with a variety of pleasant sparkling Limoux: the fresh Blanquette de Limoux Grande Réserve, the creamy, partially oak-aged Blanquette de Limoux brut Exception, and the

unusual, off-dry Blanquette de Limoux Doulce et Fruité, made from overripe grapes ◆ Alain Cavailles: a very good producer; try the vintage-dated wines ◆ JEAN-LOUIS DENOIS ◆ Dom de Pechugo: Sylvain Saux makes at least a half-dozen cuvées of Vin de Table in the Limoux area. In the hypernatural style, they are not yet ready for the world stage but Saux is interesting and worth following. My favorite is a red blend of carignan and alicante ◆ Dom Salasar: the Crémant de Limoux brut Légende, with a high percentage of chenin and chardonnay, is one of the best representatives of the appellation ◆ Sieur d'Arques: a major presence in the region, marketing numerous wines. Try the vintage Crémant de Limoux and the Toques & Clochers bottlings ◆ Dom Rosier: the quirky Blanquette, an ample wine with celery notes (of all things), is worth following ◆ Vignobles Vergnes: a good family domaine. Try Maistre Antoine.

Château de la Liquière ☆

34480 Cabrerolles; 04.67.90.29.20; fax: 04.67.90.10.00; www.chateaulaliquiere.com

Wine: Faugères. $ to $$

A very good family domaine with a broad range of wine, including the easy-drinking Les Amandiers (red, white, and rosé); the barrel-fermented Les Schistes, a blend of roussanne and grenache, an ample white with an admirably steely backbone; the Vieilles Vignes blend of extremely old grenache and carignan, a deep, textured red; and Cistus, a syrah-dominated red that's packed with fruit and oak flavors but remains tight and elegant. Food-friendly, it might marry well with Provençal-inspired dishes.

La Livinière: See MINERVOIS.

Lorgeril ☆

Château de Pennautier, B.P. 4 11610 Pennautier; 04.68.72.65.29; www.vignobles-lorgeril.com

Wine: Cabardès, Minervois-la-Livinière, and Vin de Pays d'Oc. $ to $$$

This is a dynamic and important grower-*négociant* house run with acumen by Miren and Nicolas de Lorgeril. The domaine produces two and a half million bottles yearly—90 percent of it red—at all price levels and always offering value for the dollar. At $ for a bottle, the Lorgeril wine sold in large grocery chains is practically a steal. The most interesting wines come from the vineyards the Lorgerils own: three in Cabardès (Château de Pennautier, Château la Bastide Rougepeyre, and Château de Caunettes) and one in Minervois-la-Livinière (Les Hauts de la Borie Blanche). There are several cuvées under each label. The Cabardès Collection Privée, in contrast to its exclusive-sounding name, is $, inviting you to its supple, generous fruit. Esprit de Pennautier is the top of the line here. Unfined and unfiltered, it is a luscious oaked blend of syrah and merlot, the Médoc meets the Midi. The Esprit de Bastide, a blend of côt and syrah, is equally delicious, a big, smooth red with notes of black pepper and mint. In Minervois, La Borie Blanche, chiefly syrah, is a succulent—and characterful—crowd pleaser.

Domaine Madeloc ☆

66650 Banyuls-sur-Mer; 04.68.88.38.29; domaine-madeloc@wanadoo.fr

Wines: Collioure and Banyuls. $$($)

With Rhône's PIERRE GAILLARD as part of the team, this is a domaine to watch. The barrel-fermented white is strong and flavorful. The rosé Foranell is delightful and serious. There are three reds, including the simplest, Serral, which is succulent and simply delicious, and the very pure Cuvée Magenca, somewhat in the hypernatural style. And the Banyuls—both Cirera and Robert Pagès—could induce Port houses to buy property in the Roussillon.

Domaine La Madura ☆

34360 St.-Chinian: tel/fax: 04.67.38.17.85; www.lamadura.com
Wines: St.-Chinian and Vin de Pays. $ to $$
Nadia and Cyril Bourgne—he's an enologist who formerly worked at Château Fieuzal in Bordeaux—pamper their 14 hectares of vines. Their wines are neither fined nor filtered. They produce a supple, discreet sauvignon blanc and two cuvées of red St.-Chinian. The first is gracious and silky with focused fruit, lighter-hearted than the Grande Cuvée, a blend of mourvèdre and syrah. Rich but buoyant, this is structured, seductive, and has a kind of gravitas.

Maxime Magnon ↑

11360 Villeneuve-les-Corbières; 04.68.45.84.71
Wine: Vin de Pays de la Vallée du Paradis. $ to $$
Here's a young man to watch. He's making riveting reds at MARIA FITA in Fitou. On his own he seems to be experimenting, very much into the hypernatural style—using eco-friendly viticulture, avoiding sulfur, and so forth. Different bottlings include Rozetta, a red that sometimes gives off nice syrahlike aromas and at others seems soft and gamy, and 1515 Carignan, a cinnamon-scented red. La Begou, a white, has a peachy tinge. It's mineral and interesting but, like most of Magnon's own wines, not yet for the world stage—unless you love oxidation. Try his wines by the glass. You won't be bored.

Malpère

The AC created from the VDQS Côtes de la Malpère, Malpère is located south of the Canal du Midi, in the western reaches of the Languedoc. The region is subject to the Atlantic's maritime influence, much like Cabardès and Limoux. Similarly, the reds and rosés it produces are made from both Atlantic (mostly Bordelais), and Midi grape varieties: merlot, cabernets franc and sauvignon, côt, grenache, lladoner pelut, and cinsault. Syrah is permitted for rosés. Medium-bodied and full-flavored, the red wines go well with the local specialty, cassoulet de Castelnaudary, and the best taste as if they come from the Gironde.

BEST RECENT VINTAGES: 2004 and 2001.
PRICES: $ to $$

PRODUCERS: Ch Hérail de Robert: Fleur de Girofle, with its black cherry and spice flavors, would be at home in a brasserie ◆ Dom de Matibat: two-dimensional, well-made wines ◆ Dom la Louvière: good wines, with a nice mingling of oak, dark fruit, and satisfying freshness ◆ Dom le Fort: a Bordeaux taste-alike with oak and cranberry flavors; it's a nice bistro red ◆ Ch Guilhem: the Cuvée Prestige, chiefly merlot, resembles a three-dimensional Bordeaux—a tasty red for a slightly upscale bistro ◆ Dom Girard: cheerful, meaty reds.

Domaine de la Marfée ↑

34570 Murviel-les-Montpellier; tel/fax: 04.67.47.29.37; thhasard@aol.com
Wine: Vin de Pays de l'Hérault. $$
The brother of Burgundy's Alain Hasard and the accountant for a celebrated neighbor, the GRANGE DES PÈRES, Thierry Hasard seems to come naturally by the quest for excellence and purity in his wines. A *terroir* fanatic whose vines are in the heart of St. Georges d'Orques, he produces a fresh, pear- and pineapple-scented white Les Gamines and, in reds, the tightly focused, spicy Les Vignes Qu'on Abat and Les Champs Murmures, a tannic, *terroir*-driven wine with a majestic basso presence.

Maria Fita ↑

11360 Villeneuve-les-Corbières; 04.68.45.86.12; earl.schmitt-magnon@wandoo.fr
Wines: Fitou and Vin du Pays. $$ to $$$
Jean-Michel Schmitt, a former restaurateur, is making some exciting, organic, unfiltered wine. Maxime Magnon is the winemaker, and one finds some of the same little flaws, such as oxidation in the whites, here that one finds with Magnon's own wines. The Maria Fita reds sold as Vin du Pays de la Vallée du Paradis are cheerful wine-bar wines. The two cuvées of Fitou are where the action is. The standard bottling is smooth, with depth and lovely black cherry flavors. MF du Dimanche, pure grenache, is rich, pure, and nuanced. It is made only in good vintages.

Mas Amiel ☆

66460 Maury; 04.68.29.01.02; lvod@wanadoo.fr
Wines: Banyuls, Maury, Côtes du Roussillon, and more. $$ to $$$
Olivier Decelle, who took over this important property in 1999, may be the right man at the right time. The former CEO of Picard, the superb (I weigh my words) frozen-food chain, he has his finger firmly on the consumer's pulse. The wines he makes demonstrate his lucid marriage of contemporary tastes and the imperatives of *terroir*. Everything can be recommended. The fortified wines—from the fresh Banyuls blanc to the mellow, velvety Maury, to the nectarlike Muscat de Rivesaltes—are all top-notch as are the Côtes du Roussillon. Altair, for example, is an oak-aged, focused blend of old-vines maccabeu and grenache. His Carérades, a Roussillon-Villages, is plush and deep, simultaneously specific and a crowd pleaser. Decelle is doing similar work in Bordeaux at the Châteaux Haut-Maurac (Médoc Cru Bourgeois), Haut-Ballet (Canon-Fronsac), and Bellevue (Fronsac).

Mas de la Barben ☆

30900 Nîmes; 04.66.81.15.88; fax: 04.66.63.80.43
Wines: Coteaux du Languedoc–Pic St.-Loup. $$ to $$$
From the vineyard closest to the Rhône come a number of rewarding reds. Les Lauzières, chiefly grenache, is elegant, juicy, characterful, and all too easy to drink. Les Sabines is deeper and oakier but also fresh and elegant. The pricey Calice, 90 percent grenache, is scented, serious, and delicious. It packs a lot of alcohol, so I prefer it slightly chilled.

Mas Baux

66140 Canet en Roussillon; tel/fax: 04.68.80.25.04; www.mas-baux.com
Wines: Côtes du Roussillon and Vin de Pays. $ to $$
There's a resolutely New World flavor to the wines from this ambitious domaine, and my nonwine friends—French or otherwise—love them. The packaging is clever and the wines are well made, user friendly, and blatantly fruity. Rouge Gorge, for example, is Napa meets Roussillon in its porty, blackberry-scented, barrel-aged blend of syrah, mourvèdre, and grenache. It's a Vin de Pays des Côtes Catalanes, as is the satisfying, velvety Rouge Baux, with its informative addition of cabernet sauvignon. The Côtes du Roussillon Soleil Rouge gives a good bang for the buck, as does the powerful, fruit-driven Baux Blond.

Mas Champart ☆

34360 St.-Chinian, 04.67.38.20.09; mas-champart@wanadoo.fr
Wines: St.-Chinian and Vin de Pays. $ to $$
Isabelle and Matthieu Champart and their wines could proselytize for the St.-Chinian appellation. Everything they do is based on reflection, good sense, and something pretty close to inspiration: they replant their vineyards with selected vines from some of the best producers in the Rhône and Provence, such as Beaucastel, Trevallon, and Tempier. Their St.-Chinian blanc is delightful, but the reds are the stars here. Most are neither fined nor filtered. Côte d'Arbo is a fragrant, appetite-whetting red. Causse du Bousquet, chiefly syrah, is robust, generous, and structured. My favorite is Clos de la Simonette. It's made with 70 percent mourvèdre and is one of the best expressions of that often tough

grape I've found. I'm also fond of Le Vin des Amis, a Vin de Pays d'Oc red based on cabernet franc. I have found that it goes quite well with take-out moussaka.

Mas la Chevalière
34215 Béziers; www.michellaroche.com
Wine: Vin de Pays d'Oc. $ to $$
Michel Laroche, an important Chablis producer and one of the first to put screw caps on Premier Crus from that appellation, is not someone who would fail to notice the potential of the Languedoc. All his wines are Vin de Pays. There are several different levels of quality—La Croix Chevalière is the prestige cuvée—but all are well-made beverage wines and great contenders for the international market.

Mas Daumas Gassac ☆
34150 Aniane; 04.67.57.71.28; www.daumas-gassac.com
Wine: Vin de Pays de l'Hérault. $$$ to $$$$
Here it is and here he is. There's the wine, principally the full, structured red that is regarded as one of the *grand crus* of the Languedoc; and there's the man, irascible, opinionated Aimé Guibert (of Mondovino and No-Mondavi-in-my-back-yard fame). The wine made from cabernet sauvignon and ten other red grapes (including merlot, malbec, tannat, nebbiolo, voskehat, and kontorni, the last two from Armenia) is, indeed, delicious—smooth, structured, berry-rich, and worthy of cellaring—although you may find the price excessive. There's also a big, powerful, lipsmacking white based on viognier, chardonnay, petit manseng, and chenin. It, too, can be cellared. The domaine markets a second line of wine, called Moulin de Gassac le Mazet (in the United States). Made by a local cooperative from the usual grape Languedoc grape varieties, both the red and the white are ordinary.

Mas de la Devèze ↑
66720 Tautavel; tel/fax: 04.68.29.42.47; vinum@wanadoo.fr
Wine: Côtes du Roussillon. $$
Yet another new, promising Fenouillèdes winery. Anne-Lise and Olivier Bernstein age their best reds in Burgundy barrels. The wines have lovely fruit, structure, and great freshness (the less ambitious reds could use more work). The white, Vin de Pays des Pyrénées Orientales, is a blend of maccabeu and grenache gris. It's well made, fruity, and food friendly.

Mas Jullien ☆
34725 Jonquières; 04.67.96.60.04; fax: 04.67.96.60.50
Wine: Coteaux du Languedoc–Terrasses du Larzac. $$
This very talented winemaker produces two reds, a white, and a rosé. Everything is worth trying, particularly the reds. The Mas Jullien, a traditional blend, is succulent, fine-grained, specific, and serious—excellent. État d'Âme is the red he calls his "*vin de liberté*." He does whatever he feels like with it. The wine is extremely tasty, but I prefer the Mas Jullien.

Mas Karolina ↑
66220 St.-Paul de Fenouillet; 05.57.40.53.21; mas.karolina@wanadoo.fr
Wines: Côtes du Roussillon, Maury, and Vin de Pays. $ to $$
Caroline Bonville, whose family makes wine in the Entre-Deux-Mers area of Bordeaux, created her 20-hectare Fenouillèdes domaine in 2003. Her barrel-aged white, a Vin de Pays blend of maccabeu and grenache, is mellow and ambitious. She makes an ingratiating red Vin de Pays, blending carignan and grenache, and a high-powered Côtes du Roussillon with rich fruit and new oak flavors. Her Maury is juicy and vigorous.

Mas de la Serranne ↑

34150 Aniane; tel/fax: 04.67.57.37.99

Wine: Coteaux du Languedoc–Terrasses de Larzac. $ to $$($)

Jean Pierre Venture produces a number of delectable cuvées at Mas de la Serrane. Clos de l'Immortelle is a syrah-scented red with lovely balance and silky texture. Cuvée Antonin et Louis, his top bottling, is a rich, cult-style wine with exotic fruit flavors—impressive. À l'Ombre du Figuier and Les Griottiers are both supple, mouthwatering reds. At $ the bottle, I'd buy a couple of cases.

Domaine de Matassa ↑

66600 Calce; 04.68.64.59.08; matassa@wanadoo.fr

Wines: Côtes du Roussillon, Vin de Pays des Côtes Catalanes, and Vin de Table. $$($)

Tom Lubbe (Gérard Gauby's son-in-law; see DOM GAUBY) and Sam Harrop MW created this promising domaine in 2002. At 600 meters, their 10 hectares of vines are among the highest in the region, accounting, surely, for the breezy freshness of their wines. Their structured, flavorful Vin de Pays is made from grenache gris and one-hundred-year-old maccabeu. The Vin de Table, pure old-vines carignan, "was hand-bottled with the ascending moon on the 24th December 2003." Neither fined nor filtered, it's silky, mineral, and captivating.

Maurel-Vedeau

34290 Servian; 04.67.39.21.20; fax: 04.67.39.22.13; www.maurel-vedeau.com

Wines: Vins de Pays d'Oc, Coteaux du Languedoc, and others. $ to $$

Philippe Maurel and Stéphane Vedeau are good examples of a new style of quality-conscious *négociant* with firm guidelines in both vineyards and cellars. Their wide range of wines, spanning the Languedoc, includes family domaines and the properties of about thirty carefully selected growers. They produce an unusually rich Picpoul de Pinet that, what with low yields, hand harvesting, and the like, is twice the price of other picpouls. And there's a clutch of Vins de Pays d'Oc—La Briffaude rouge, a pungent, chewy merlot; La Briffaude blanc, a rich, mineral sauvignon blanc; Terre d'Amandier blanc, an assertive, barrel-fermented chardonnay; and Terre d'Oliviers rouge, a generous Bordeaux blend.

Maury

A Roussillon Vin Doux Naturel (fortified wine) much like Banyuls, made from grenache on the foothills of the Pyrenees in the Fenouillèdes region behind Perpignan. At its best, Maury is fully as delicious as Banyuls and can be enjoyed as an aperitif, for example, or with cheese, particularly pungent blues.

PRICES: $$ to $$$

PRODUCERS: LA COUME DU ROY ◆ MAS AMIEL ☆ ◆ MAS KAROLINA ↑ ◆ Mas de Lavail: Expression is the name given to the attractively balanced vintage red Maury; there's also a nice, oaky white Maury ◆ Dom Pouderoux: bring on the blue cheese for the lovely, minty, and intense Maury and something smelly and runny for the mellow and complex Mise Tardive. The domaine also makes Muscat de Rivesaltes and Côtes du Roussillon-Villages ☆ ◆ Préceptorie de la Centernach: see DOM DE LA RECTORIE ◆ DOM DE SAINT ROCH ↑ ◆ Les Vignerons de Maury: has a stock of older vintages; advice to shoppers—the older the better.

Château Meunier Saint-Louis

11200 Boutenac; 04.68.27.09.69; info@pasquier-meunier.com

Wine: Corbières. $ to $$

Makes both a solid standard cuvée and A Capella. Chiefly syrah, it is, at first blush, the kind of up-front wine that wins competitions—fragrant, powerful, with lots of dark fruit, and oaky—but the suggestion of complexity makes you want to follow the wine's evolution.

Domaine Les Milles Vignes ↑

11480 La Palme; tel/fax: 04.68.48.57.14; les.mille.vignes@club-internet.fr

Wines: Fitou, Vin de Pays, and Rivesaltes. $ to $$$

Valerie Guérin is a young vigneronne to watch. Her handcrafted wines are based on very low yields and careful vinification. Her Fitous are as lovely and evocative as the names she gives to the individual cuvées, like Les Vendangeurs de la Violette (the violet harvesters), a strong, textured zinfandel-like red—it's chiefly mourvèdre and would go well with game dishes. Chasse-Filous is a pure grenache Vin de Pays, a delicious red. Her white Vins de Pays are even better. Le Pied des Nymphettes, a blend of a number of local grapes aged in used Meursault barrels on the lees of muscat, is a pure delight. I'd pair her Rivesaltes made from century-old grenache vines with aged sheep's milk cheese, and her fine Muscat de Rivesaltes, harvested grape by grape, would make a sterling aperitif.

Minervois and Minervois-la-Livinière

In the hillsides east of Carcassonne, the Languedoc AC Minervois produces some whites and rosés but mostly reds. The commune La Livinière, more or less in the center of the Minervois appellation, produces only reds. All of the reds are based on grenache and carignan with an increasing amount of syrah, particularly in La Livinière. There are a lot of new players here making exciting, full-throated wines that are progressing quickly in quality.

BEST RECENT VINTAGES: See COTEAUX DU LANGUEDOC.
PRICES: $ to $$

PRODUCERS: DOM DES AIRES HAUTES ☆ ◆ CH BONHOMME ☆ ◆ Dom Borie de Maurel: a rising star on the Minervois scene with a range of cuvées, peaking with Sylla ☆ ◆ CLOS CENTEILLES ◆ Clos du Gravillas: Nicole and John Bojanski are a young couple with a promising young domaine. Their ambitious wines are still works in progress and include L'Inattendu, a barrel-fermented white; Rendez-vous du Soleil, a fruity carignan; Lo Vièlh, a dense, rich, oak-aged carignan; and Vous en Voulez, en Voilà, an attractive red blend dominated by syrah and cabernet ◆ Dom Coupe-Roses: Françoise and Pascal Frissant make an engaging, food-friendly cuvée called Granaxa. It's 90 percent grenache from fifty-year-old vines. Decanted, it would be a nice choice in an upscale wine bar ◆ DOM PIERRE CROS ◆ Ch Faiteau: promising young vigneron with a very good syrah-based La Livinière ◆ LORGERIL ☆ ◆ CH D'OUPIA ◆ Dom Piccinini: a sincere family domaine making creamy whites, floral rosés, and a number of different cuvées of red, all pleasant and reasonably priced ◆ DOM JEAN-BAPTISTE SENAT ↑ ◆ Ch de Rieux: promising young domaine making Minervois and Vin de Pays. The wines are neither fined nor filtered. Results are mixed but always interesting ◆ Dom la Rouviole: up-and-coming domaine with showy, oaky Minervois-la-Livinière ◆ DOM LA TOUR BOISÉE ◆ Dom le Troubadour: Hervé Sénégasse is a promising young winemaker whose first vintage was 2001. His wines are neither fined nor filtered. Le Troubadour, lightly chilled, is a delicious juicy red; the barrel-aged Canto d'Amor is an intense red beautifully marked by syrah ↑ ◆ Ch Villerembert-Julien: a solid domaine producing well-made wines.

Domaine Monplézy ↑

34120 Pézenas; tel/fax: 04.67.98.27.81; www.domainemonplezy.fr

Wine: Vin de Pays Côtes de Thongue. $ to $$

Anna Sutra de Germa and Christian Gil exemplify the efforts young vintners are putting into Vin de Pays, starting with cluster thinning to keep yields very low. Their white, pure marsanne ages in new oak. It's fresh and is very, very good. The rosé is lovely. The cuvée Félicité, an oak-aged blend of carignan and grenache, is supple, suave, and somehow reassuring—wonderful for a wine bar.

Montpeyroux

An important growing area within the Terrasses de Larzac subzone of the COTEAUX DU LANGUEDOC. It is likely to get independent AC recognition or *cru* status in the near future. It is also considered the most typical of the Coteaux du Languedoc subregions because grenache and carignan blend exceptionally well here. The wines are more aggressive than those from Pic St.-Loup but can be elegant and marked by flavors of bay laurel, thyme, and black truffle. For vintages and prices, see COTEAUX DU LANGUEDOC.

PRODUCERS: DOM L'AIGUELIÈRE ◆ DOM D'AUPILHAC ☆ ◆ Dom Font Caude: see COTEAUX DU LANGUEDOC ◆ La Jasse Castel: see COTEAUX DU LANGUEDOC.

Moulin de Ciffre

34480 Autignac; 04.67.90.11.45; info@moulindeciffre.com
Wines: Faugères, St.-Chinian, and Vin de Pays. $$
This serious family domaine produces meaty Faugères and St.-Chinian. The top Faugères cuvée is Eole, a fragrant, oak-aged red with good balance. The rosé calls out for spicy food. The stylish viognier, a Vin de Pays des Coteaux de Murviel, would be a fine choice in an upscale bistro. Val Taurou, a red Vin de Pays, pleased me less as the cabernet sauvignon in the blend gave off a whiff of veggies, but the meaty, inexpensive St.-Chinian Tradition is good value for the dollar.

Domaine Moulinier

34360 St.-Chinian; 04.67.38.03.97; domaine-moulinier@wanadoo.fr
Wine: St.-Chinian. $ to $$
A good family domaine, making three solid reds. In ascending order: Tradition, a tasty, medium-bodied wine for casual meals; Sigillaires (fossils), a smooth, ample mourvèdre-syrah blend; and the potent, sensual Terrasses Grillées—basically pure syrah aged in new oak, it's a wine with a compelling presence.

Muscat

There are five fortified muscats (Vins Doux Naturels or VDN) in the Languedoc-Roussillon. Each will be discussed briefly below. As they are similar, it makes sense to describe their common characteristics collectively. Extremely sweet, dazzlingly perfumed, and with between 15 and 18 percent alcohol, they are nectarlike and almost viscous, with heady aromas and flavors of tropical fruit and lychee. They are best served chilled, as an aperitif, with cheese (particularly blue cheeses) or with fruit-based desserts.

BEST RECENT VINTAGES: Although vintages may be given, they are not really a concern here.
PRICES: Generally $ to $$

Muscat de Frontignan: A small coastal Languedoc AC near Sète. Producer: Ch de la Peyrade: for rich yet delicate wines with light peach notes; also an unsual, unfortified Vendange d'Automne, a lovely wine along the lines of Jurançon meets Languedoc ☆.

Muscat de Lunel: A small coastal Languedoc AC east of Montpellier. Producers: DOM DE BELLEVUE ☆ ◆ CH GRÈS SAINT-PAUL ☆.

Muscat de Mireval: Small coastal Languedoc AC between Sète and Montpellier. Producers: Dom de la Capelle: fresh, floral muscats ◆ Ch d'Exindre: expect extremely perfumed muscats.

Muscat de Rivesaltes: Roussillon's AC for Vin Doux Naturel (fortified wine) made from muscat à petits grains and muscat of Alexandria throughout the Rivesaltes, Banyuls, and Maury zones. See also entries under RIVESALTES, as most of those producers also make a Muscat de Rivesaltes. Producers: ARNAUD DE VILLENEUVE (cooperative) ◆ Dom Bertrand-Bergé: the domaine makes a range of above-average Rivesaltes, including muscat, but is more known for its Fitou ◆ DOM BRIAL ◆ DOM CAZES ◆ LA COUME DU ROY ◆ CH HAUT-GLÉON ◆ CH DE JAU ◆ Dom Jouret & Fils: source of well-made versions ◆ MAS AMIEL ☆ ◆ Dom Piquemal: see RIVESALTES ◆ VIGNERONS DE MONT TAUCH.

Muscat de St.-Jean-de-Minervois: A tiny Languedoc AC—it forms a pocket between Minervois and St.-Chinian—producing Vin Doux Naturel made solely from muscat à petits grains. These are the freshest and most elegant of Languedoc-area muscats, thanks to a high hillside location. Producers: Cave de St. Jean de Minervois: very good cooperative ◆ CLOS BAGATELLE ◆ Dom de Barroubio: well-regarded producer ☆.

Domaine Navarre ☆

34460 Roquebrun; 04.67.89.53.58; thierry.navarre@wanadoo.fr

Wines: St.-Chinian, Vin de Pays, and Vin de Table. $ to $$

Thierry Navarre aims to reinvent the wheel. He practices something between organic and biodynamic viticulture, conserves ancient grape varieties, develops his own yeasts, doesn't filter his wines, and in addition to his appellation wines, makes a handful of wacko wines. My favorite among the latter is his Vin d'Oeillades. Oeillade, he claims, is an ancient varietal, an ancestor of cinsault. To me, it's delightful with its orange blossom notes and seductive fruit. I'd love to meet it in a wine bar. Le Laouzil, his easiest-drinking St.-Chinian, is generous and full of character. The cuvée Olivier is made from old vines and barrel aged. Velvety, with exotic fruit flavors, it's sapid and mouthwatering.

Château de la Négly ☆

11560 Fleury d'Aude; 04.68.32.36.28; lanegly@wanadoo.fr

Wine: Coteaux du Languedoc–La Clape. $ to $$

Owner Jean Paul–Rosset's wines, whites, reds, and rosés, have a solid track record for being delicious and immediately satisfying. He produces fragrant, nicely structured whites, food-friendly rosés, and a range of reds, all delicious. In ascending order of consequence these are: La Côte, a scented charmer; Domaine de Boède Les Grès, aged in new oak and, like the succeeding reds, neither fined nor filtered, is Port-like and powerful; La Falaise is a big wine but silky and elegant and, surely, the most complex of the three. Then there's a range of micro-cuvées of about four thousand bottles each: L'Ancely, La Porte du Ciel, and Clos de Truffiers—each one of them important, lush, and riveting. Finally, there's a Vin de Pays des Côtes de Perpignan, Le Pavillon, a delectable red blend with the oxymoronic peculiarity of being a serious quaffer.

Château Ollieux Romanis ↑

11200 Montserrat; 04.68.43.35.20; ollieuxromanis@hotmail.com

Wines: Corbières and Vin de Pays. $$ to $$$

Pierre Bories took over the family property four years ago and converted it to organic viticulture. His white Corbières are smooth and juicy; his reds range from a picnic-friendly cuvée Alice, to the focused Prestige, to a pricey, very oaky, New World–influenced Cuvée d'Or. He ventures into hypernatural winemaking (wild yeasts, almost no sulfur) with his Vin de Pays Entramis. And that's how this pleasant light red should be drunk—among friends.

Château d'Or et de Gueules

30800 St.-Gilles; 04.66.87.32.86; chateaudoretdegueules@wanadoo.fr
Wine: Costières de Nîmes. $ to $$
Old carignan and mourvèdre vines blended with syrah and aged in oak produce what may be the best representative of the Costières de Nîmes appellation, the cuvée Trassegum, a succulent, scented, reasonably priced red.

Château d'Oupia

34210 Oupia; 04.68.91.20.86; fax: 04.68.91.18.23
Wines: Minervois, Vin de Table, and Vin de Pays. $ to $$
André Iché has a good track record but he's still experimenting and improving. He makes a pleasant summer white, a taut rosé and three red Minervois—the pungent Tradition; the ample old-vines Les Barons; and the oaky, nuanced Nobilis. Like many, he's got a couple of those endearing wacko wines: AR26 is pure grenache; fruity and vivid L'Émerantine is a late-harvested grenache blanc, a tender, floral white with the concentrated flavors of sultanas.

Domaine Padié ↑

66600 Calce; tel/fax: 04.68.64.29.85
Wines: Côtes du Roussillon and Vin de Pays. $ to $$
Another dynamic new Fenouillèdes domaine. Jean-Philippe Padié's vines are dispersed among twenty different parcels because Padié wanted all the different *terroirs* and expositions. The two grenache whites, one oaked, the other not, are both mellow and tasty. There's an easy-drinking red Petit Taureau with nice fruit and lovely balance and Ciel Liquide, made from Padié's oldest and best grenache and carignan. Aged in barrel, it blends oak, gorgeous fruit, and great freshness into a delectable whole.

Domaine Pas de l'Escalette ↑

34700 Pégairolles de l'Escalette; 04.67.96.13.42; fax: 02.48.64.62.87
Wines: Coteaux du Languedoc. $$ to $$$
A seriously promising new domaine owned by Julien Zernott, the winemaker at Henry Pellé in Menetou-Salon in the Loire, and his wife, Delphine Rousseau. Everything is recommended, from the creamy, oak-aged Les Clapas blanc, a Vin de Pays based on eighty-year-old carignan blanc and terret vines; to the rich Les Clapas red, a tasty Languedoc; to Le Premier Pas and Le Grand Pas, two red Languedocs, the first an easy though characterful quaffer, the second, the domaine's deluxe *barrique*-aged cuvée, an elegant wine, as generous as it is soigné.

Domaine Peyre Rose ☆

34230 St.-Pargoire; 04.67.98.75.50; fax: 04.67.98.71.88
Wine: Coteaux du Languedoc–Grès de Montpellier. $$$
Marlene Soria, now something of a local star (who "*vants* to be alone") makes blockbuster, highly concentrated reds that need several years of cellaring to soften. There are two cuvées, the redoubtable syrah Léone and, my preference, Clos des Cistes, which becomes fragrant, elegant, well-structured, and balanced with age.

Pézenas

A distinct Coteaux du Languedoc subzone below Faugères that's likely to get independent AC recognition. The wines have characteristic flavors of spices, like curry and cinnamon. The village, also named Pézenas, is the birthplace of Molière.

PRODUCERS: DOM DU CLOS ROCA ◆ Dom le Comte de Floris: see COTEAUX DU LANGUEDOC ◆ Dom Lacroix-Vanel: see COTEAUX DU LANGUEDOC ◆ PRIEURÉ DE SAINT JEAN DE BÉBIAN ◆ Dom de la Tour Penedesses: see FAUGÈRES.

Picpoul de Pinet

A small Languedoc AC on the Étang de Thau, Picpoul de Pinet is the source of light, fresh white made from picpoul (sometimes spelled piquepoul). The wine goes well with oysters from nearby Bouzigues and the local mussels. Drink the youngest available.

PRICES: $

PRODUCERS: Cave de l'Ormarine: the Cave produces 80 percent of the AC's wine and it's good, especially the cuvée Duc de Morny ◆ Dom la Grangette: look for the cuvée L'Enfant Terrible ◆ Mas St. Laurent: one of the best, if not the best, producers in the AC ◆ Cave les Costières de Pomerols: a good cooperative with a floral cuvée Hugues de Beauvignac ◆ MAUREL-VEDEAU ◆ Ch Pinet: a very good domaine run by a mother and daughter who make two cuvées, Jeunes Vignes and Vieilles Vignes ◆ CH ST. MARTIN DE LA GARRIGUE.

Pic St.-Loup

An important COTEAUX DU LANGUEDOC subregion likely to get independent AC recognition. The northernmost of the subregions, Pic St.-Loup wines are typically the freshest and most elegant, the wines with the most natural finesse in the Coteaux du Languedoc. In addition to impressive reds, the zone also produces strong, breezy whites. For vintages and prices, see COTEAUX DU LANGUEDOC.

PRODUCERS: Ch Cazeneuve: see COTEAUX DU LANGUEDOC ◆ CLOS MARIE ◆ ERMITAGE DU PIC ST.-LOUP ☆ ◆ Dom de l'Euzière: see COTEAUX DU LANGUEDOC ◆ Dom Haut Lirou: see COTEAUX DU LANGUEDOC ◆ DOM DE L'HORTUS ☆ ◆ CH DE LASCAUX ☆ ◆ Mas Brugière: see COTEAUX DU LANGUEDOC ◆ Mas Foulaquier: see COTEAUX DU LANGUEDOC ◆ Mas de Mortiès: see COTEAUX DU LANGUEDOC ◆ Ch la Roque: see COTEAUX DU LANGUEDOC ◆ CH DE VALFLAUNES ↑ ◆ Dom Zumbaum-Tomasi: see COTEAUX DU LANGUEDOC.

Domaine Olivier Pithon ↑

66600 Calce; 04.68.38.50.21
Wine: Côtes du Roussillon. $$
Olivier Pithon, the younger brother of Anjou's JO PITHON, has 9 hillside hectares in the heart of the Fenouillèdes. His winemaking has improved greatly over the past five years, indicating that he's someone to watch. His top cuvée Saturne, chiefly grenache and carignan, is oaky, characterful, and very tasty. The whites are promising, too.

Plan de l'Om ☆

34700 St.-Jean-de-la-Blaquière; tel/fax: 04.67.10.91.25; plan-de-lom@wanadoo.fr
Wine: Coteaux du Languedoc. $ to $$
Joël Foucou makes truly lovely, very perfumed wines. Feuillage, based on roussanne, is as highly scented as cologne, with pineapple accents and great freshness. Oeillade, starring cinsault, is silky with orange peel notes, a delicious "light" red. Miéjour, based on grenache, is denser and richer, and Roucan, chiefly barrel-aged syrah, is structured, discreet, and succulent.

Château Planères ☆

66300 St.-Jean-Lasseille; 04.68.21.74.50; www.chateauplaneres.com
Wines: Côtes du Roussillon and Côtes du Roussillon–Les Aspres. $ to $$
The operating principles of this admirable family domaine appear to be quality and intelligence. Pains are taken at every juncture in the vines and in the cellars, but there is no exaggeration anywhere. Prices are more than reasonable and the wines are fresh, balanced, and delicious, no matter how light or serious the cuvée. Chantail is the easy-drinking red charmer. The richer

La Romanie is a focused beauty from the new subappellation Les Aspres. Both La Romanie and the Cuvée Prestige age in oak barrels. The latter, a blend of syrah, mourvèdre, and grenache, is a lovely wine for a good meal. La Coume d'Ars, a blend of old-vines carignan, grenache, and syrah, is velvety and beautifully structured. It recalls some of the best Priorats of Spain.

Préceptorie de Centernach: See DOM DE LA RECTORIE.

Prieuré de Saint Jean de Bébian

34120 Pézenas, 04.67.98.13.60; www.bebian.com

Wine: Coteaux du Languedoc. $$ to $$$

Chantal Lecouty and Jean-Claude Le Brun, former owners of *La Revue du Vins de France,* are determined, ambitious, and high-profile producers. They have well-placed admirers of which I am not one. Their wines are often far from perfect (with occasional oxidation, horsiness, drying, or puckery finishes) but usually interesting. My notes on their 2003 Languedoc blanc—which I like a lot—sum up what I feel about their best wines, red and white: "oaky, quite full, creamy and somewhat viscous, decent balance, very good, but too expensive. The wine is serious but what's coming through is more technique and ripeness than *terroir.* That said, I think *terroir* is to be credited for the insinuating texture and the fine structure which, at least now, play second fiddle to dogmatic winemaking."

Domaine de la Prose ☆

BP-25-34570 Pignan; 04.67.03.08.30; www.domainedelaprose.com

Wine: Coteaux du Languedoc–St. Georges d'Orques. $$($)

There's some very nice, *terroir*-driven winemaking going on here. Cuvée Embruns Blanc is strong and focused; the red version, based on syrah, is rich and spicy. The Grande Cuvée, another syrah showcase, is even bigger, spicier, and more serious. It needs several years of tender loving cellaring. Cadières, a perfect little red, is, simply, a great value.

Domaine Puig-Parahy

66300 Passa; 06.14.55.71.71; fax: 04.68.38.88.77

Wines: Côtes du Roussillon and Vin de Pays. $ to $$

Georges Puig makes a pleasant barrel-fermented blend of grenache blanc and gris with the distressing name Miserys and three Côtes du Roussillon. As for their reds, Mes Amis is supple and easy-drinking; the Cuvée Georges is thickly concentrated; and the richly fruity La Fort St. Pierre is a bit too soft for me but others love it.

Rancio

The Spanish word for *rancid* is the name given to a category of wine made in the Banyuls area. A unique wine, it is generally made from grenache and aged for many years in barrels. As the barrels are not topped up, the percentage of alcohol increases as the percentage of water decreases by evaporation. Rancios usually range from 17 to 19.5 percent alcohol. They taste a lot like Oloroso sherry, with deep, tangy flavors of nuts, coffee, and toffee. Historically, rancios served as the wines used to celebrate mass. Today they have no legal definition through an application has been made for AC status. Most winemakers in the Roussillon area produce a bit of rancio and sell it as Vin de Pays de la Côte Vermeille. Price: $$ to $$$. Producers: Abbe Rous/Cellier des Templiers: see BANYULS ◆ DOM DE LA RECTORIE (Vin de Pierre) ◆ DOM DE LA TOUR VIELLE ☆.

Rimage: Also spelled Rimatge. The word is used to indicate vintage Banyuls.

Domaine de la Rectorie ☆

66700 Argèles-sur-Mer; 04.68.81.02.94; larectorie@wanadoo.fr
Wines: Collioure, Banyuls, and Vin de Pays. $$
I have long been an admirer of the Domaine de la Rectorie's wines, first having been impressed (at a wine bar in Strasbourg) by L'Argile, a fragrant, subtle food wine based on lightly oaked grenache blanc and gris. Then there was La Goudie, which may be the best rosé I have ever tasted. The three Collioures—Col del Bast, Le Séris, and the top, La Coume Pascole—are all deeply satisfying reds. Fragrant and supple yet structured, nuanced, and *terroir*-driven, with succulent fruit, they are reds you can drink young yet still sense the depth of the wine. Marc Parcé and Vincent Legrand, his son-in-law and the son of the great Paris *caviste* Yves Legrand, run La Rectorie, and it is worthwhile noting that they don't seek overripeness or hyperconcentration. The wines are always fresh and gracious. They also make lipsmackingly good Banyuls and experiment with various types of Vins de Table or *vins de liqueur.* They more recently entered into a collaboration with growers in the Fenouillèdes, the Préceptorie de Centernach, where they make good Maury, a very ripe and self-assured white Côtes de Roussillon Terres Nouvelles, and a very alcoholic red Vin de Table L'Oriental, which makes me think of Amarone.

Domaine Rimbert ☆

34360 Berlou; 04.67.89.74.66; www.domainerimbert.com
Wine: St.-Chinian. $$
Jean-Marie Rimbert is another of St.-Chinian's young movers and shakers. Les Travers de Marceau is light and mouthwatering. His more serious bottling, Mas au Schiste, is also mouthwatering but richer, with deep, succulent fruit. Carignator is the evocative name he's given to his pure carignan, a blend of two vintages, the unfermented juice of which was heated and then vinified in small oak barrels. Entirely original, it's intense and impressive, a Schwarzenegger of a red, mellowed by velvety fruit.

Rivesaltes

An AC for Vin Doux Naturel (fortified wine) made throughout the Roussillon and in Corbières and Fitou. The principal grapes are grenache and maccabeu. Young Rivesaltes, sold as rouge, is a deep red with flavors of cherries and blackberries; older Rivesaltes is either *ambré* or *tuilé,* both aged for at least two years in barrel. Still older Rivesaltes, those that have matured for at least five years, are labeled *hors d'âge.* Vintage Rivesaltes, like vintage Port, ages in bottle. Lightly chilled, Rivesaltes make fine aperitifs and marry well with cheese. They are also paired with dessert. See also MUSCAT DE RIVESALTES.

PRICES: $ to $$$

PRODUCERS: ARNAUD DE VILLENEUVE ◆ Dom Bertrand-Bergé: the domaine makes a range of above-average Rivesaltes, including muscat, but is more known for its Fitou. The charitably priced cuvée Mégalithes is savory, balanced, and a good partner for hearty dishes ◆ Dom Boudau: a range of good Rivesaltes from a young domaine that also makes very good Côtes du Roussillon ◆ DOM BRIAL ◆ Ch de Caladroy: large domaine with improving quality ◆ Ch la Casenove: see CÔTES DU ROUSSILLON ◆ DOM CAZES ◆ Mas Cristine: appealing, highly perfumed Rivesaltes with some complexity: see CH DE JAU ◆ Dom Piquemal: The most compelling wines here are the Muscat de Rivesaltes and the Rivesaltes with some real age on them, for example the 1982. The domaine also makes pleasant Côtes du Roussillon ◆ Dom Poujol: a domaine to watch, both for its good Rivesaltes as well as for its promising table wines ◆ Dom du Rancy: rightly known for its Rivesaltes, which offer value for money—you can buy a truly delicious vintage *ambré* for $$ ◆ DOM SARDA-MALET ◆ Dom Vacquer: Good Rivesaltes and Muscat de Rivesaltes. My favorite is the 1995 Post Scriptum *tuilé* with its cooked fig flavors. They also have a stock of terrific old Rivesaltes and make imaginative Vin de Pays ◆ Les Vignerons de Tautavel: look for the Rivesaltes *tuilé.*

La Roc des Anges ↑
66720 Montner, tel/fax: 04.68.29.16.62; rocdesanges@aol.com
Wines: Côtes du Roussillon, Vin de Pays, and Vin de Table. $ to $$$
Another domaine to watch. Young Marjorie Gallet began working her 20 hectares in 2001 with a passion for viticulture. This has resulted in some truly good wines, starting with a full, fragrant white based on old grenache gris. The Roussillon-Villages—particularly the Vieilles Vignes and Segna de Cor—are concentrated reds, quite delicious and very promising. There's also a fresh, interesting Vin de Table made from the sweet, shriveled grapes of maccabeu, and a Vin de Pays des Pyrénées Orientales made from carignan planted in 1903. Called Le Carignan de 1903, it's seductive, lush, and exotic.

Château La Roque ☆
34270 Fontanes; 04.67.55.34.47; fax: 04.67.55.10.18
Wines: Coteaux du Languedoc. $$ to $$$
Excellent Pic-St.-Loup–area producer with a vinous, focused normal cuvée of white and the unctuous, textured, fresh Cuvée Clos des Bénédictins, a blend of viognier, rolle, and marsanne. The delectable, structured, unfiltered reds include the barrel-aged Cupa Numismaë, predominantly syrah with some mourvèdre; and "les VV de Mourvèdre," a smoky, mourvèdre-dominated red with flavors of black berries, black olives, and Provençal herbs. Word has it that this domaine was sold in June 2006.

St.-Chinian

A good-size Languedoc AC northwest of Béziers for reds and rosés and, since 2005, whites. The red wines made in two zones within the AC have special recognition: St.-Chinian-Berlou and St.-Chinian-Roquebrun. The principal grapes for reds and rosés are grenache, syrah, and mourvèdre; whites must be a blend including at least 30 percent grenache blanc and may be completed with marsanne, roussanne, rolle, and others. A dynamic region with improving quality and very ambitious young vignerons.

BEST RECENT VINTAGES: See LANGUEDOC.
PRICES: $ to $$

PRODUCERS: DOM BORDES ↑ ◆ BORIE LA VITARÈLE ◆ CANET-VALETTE ◆ Cave de St.-Chinian: uncomplicated, two-dimensional wines, particularly special cuvées such as Renaud Valon and Berlou ◆ CH CAZAL VIEL ◆ CLOS BAGATELLE ◆ La Croix Ste. Eulalie: rich, oak-aged, old-vines whites that could charm New World palates ◆ DOM LES ÉMINADES ↑ ◆ DOM LA MADURA ☆ ◆ MAS CHAMPART ☆ ◆ Ch Maurel-Fonsalade: this family property makes three red St.-Chinians: a spicy, structured Vieilles Vignes; a warm, inviting Cuvée Frédéric; and the unusual Felix Culpa—chiefly syrah, the unfermented juice is heated during vinification. It's a good glass of red ◆ MOULIN DE CIFFRE ◆ DOM MOULINIER ◆ DOM NAVARRE ☆ ◆ DOM RIMBERT ☆ ◆ Dom de Souliés: organic viticulture is at the heart of this ambitious winery. Already good, the wines are getting better ↑ ◆ Dom de Tabatau: fresh, vinous whites and solid, tasty reds; Lo Tabataire is oak-aged ◆ Dom des Terres Falmet: there's high-quality fruit and freshness in the Vieilles Vignes cuvée.

St.-Georges d'Orques

An important growing area within the GRÈS DE MONTPELLIER subzone of COTEAUX DU LANGUEDOC. It is likely either to get an independent AC or to be recognized as a *cru*. For vintages and prices, see COTEAUX DU LANGUEDOC. Producers: CH DE L'ENGARRAN ◆ DOM DE LA PROSE ☆.

Château St. Martin de la Garrigue

34530 Montagnac; 04.67.24.00.40; www.stmartingarrigue.com

Wines: Coteaux du Languedoc–Grès de Montpellier and Picpoul de Pinet. $$

This domaine makes one of the best Picpoul de Pinets I've ever tasted, atypically rich (it was 2003) but very fresh. Their mellow chardonnay and their red Vins de Pays are all good beverage wines. I prefer, however, their more characterful Coteaux du Languedoc in both white and red. The Rouge Tradition is a suave red with black cherry and black olive flavors.

Domaine Saint Roch ↑

66460 Maury; 04.68.29.07.20; mbournazeau@aol.com

Wines: Côtes du Roussillon-Villages, Rivesaltes, Maury, and Vin de Pays. $$

Emma and Marc Bournazeau's first vintage was 2002. They produce three cuvées of Roussillon-Villages that are generally unfined and unfiltered. The barrel-aged Kerbuccio, a blend chiefly of mourvèdre and grenache, is a cult-style red, ambitious, elegant, and silky but also forceful. Saint Roch also produces a fresh, vinous white Vin de Pays based on grenache gris and some appealing Maury and Muscat de Rivesaltes.

Domaine Sarda-Malet

66000 Perpignan, 04.68.56.72.38. www.sarda-malet.com

Wines: Côtes de Roussillon, Rivesaltes, and Vin de Table. $ to $$($)

This well-established and well-regarded domaine is not satisfied to rest on its laurels. Jérôme Malet has become eco-friendly, starting with the vines he chooses to plant. He bottles most wines without fining or filtering them. There are two levels of wine in both white and red: Tradition, for both, is nicely priced and nicely made; Terroir Maillols is pricier and more ambitious and the wines are bigger and more complex, with increasing oakiness, minerality, and concentration. A very good address for Rivesaltes and other fortified wines, Sarda-Malet also ventures into the wacko-wine category with both red and white L'Insouciant. Sold as Vin de Table, the white, which tastes like oxidized apples, is made from overripe grenache gris which ferments in barrel where it stays, untouched, until bottling. The red, pure old-vines grenache, has both character and flavor.

Domaine de la Sauvageonne ☆

34700 St.-Jean-de-la-Blaquière; 04.67.44.71.74; la-sauvageonne@wanadoo.fr

Wines: Coteaux du Languedoc and Vin de Pays. $$ to $$$

Future wine star here? It's likely. After your first dazzling encounter with, say, Gavin Crisfield's Cuvée Pica Broca, a powerful, layered, pure and unfiltered blend of syrah, you may agree. Beyond that, there's Puech de Glen, almost pure syrah, grown on the highest slopes and aged in new oak. It's serious, rich, and fragrant, with the texture of velvet. Les Ruffes, the simplest red, is good and solid. Under the Vin de Pays du Mont Badille there's a peach-and-mineral blend of sauvignon blanc and La Sauvageonne herself, a plushly upholstered red, full of crushed berry and mineral flavors. It all but comes out to greet you.

Domaine des Schistes

66310 Estagel; 04.68.29.11.25; sire-schistes@wanadoo.fr

Wines: Côtes du Roussillon, Maury, Rivesaltes, and Vin de Pays. $ to $$

My favorites here fall smack in the middle of Jacques Sire's line, price-wise. They are Les Terrasses Blanches Vin de Pays des Côtes Catalanes, a barrel-fermented white made from grenache. It's ample, toasty, and fresh. Then there's the red Les Terrasses, a Côtes du Roussillon–Village Tautavel made from syrah and grenache. A tannic red, it tastes of mint and wild berries. Good Rivesaltes, in several styles.

Domaine Jean-Baptiste Senat ↑

11160 Trausse-Minervois; 04.68.78.38.17; jbsenat@terre-net.fr
Wines: Minervois and Vin de Table. $ to $$
Young, talented Jean-Baptiste Senat is one of the rising stars of this appellation. His Cuvée du Printemps is beautifully scented and full of charming fruit. Le Bois des Merveilles is more serious, smooth, well built, and extremely promising.

Domaine de la Serre ↑

66460 Maury; tel/fax: 04.68.59.18.36
Wine: Côtes du Roussillon-Villages. $$($)
Arnaud Véra began bottling his own wine at his Fenouillèdes-area domaine in 2002. The several cuvées he makes—the numbers seem to increase yearly—are all in the lush, concentrated style. Hypogée, based on old-vines carignan and syrah, is huge and saturated with color and flavor. Serre Longue, almost pure old-vines grenache, is lighter (everything's relative) with sweet, ultraripe fruit flavors of prunes and cherries. For those old enough to remember, it recalls a late-harvest zin.

Domaine Singla ↑

66250 St.-Laurent de la Salanque; tel/fax: 04.68.28.30.68; laurent.debesombes@free.fr
Wines: Côtes du Roussillon, Vin de Pays, and Vin de Table. $ to $$
Butch Cassidy might ask, "Who is this guy?" Damien de Besombes, the "guy" in question, is a young vigneron who has taken over a small part of his family's property, converted it to biodynamics, and joined the hypernatural club with a passion. His wines are very good, charitably priced, and sometimes even daring. What other modern, warm-climate vintner would age his old-vines carignan and grenache in tank and not in wood? Singla did, with his La Pinède, a very pure, tender, spirited red, not at all in the blockbuster style even though it's got 14.5 percent alcohol! All of his reds fit this profile (though some are barrel-aged). So, too, does his white Lacoste, pure old-vines maccabeu, which went beautifully with a Moroccan chicken recipe I happened to be cooking at the time I tasted it. Singla also makes very good Rivesaltes.

Robert Skalli

34204 Sète; 04.67.46.70.00; www.vinskalli.com
Wines: Vin de Pays d'Oc and Coteaux du Languedoc. $ to $$
A savvy businessman, Robert Skalli was one of the Languedoc's winemaking pioneers, producing consistently good, modern, varietal wines. There are different labels and wines for different markets but, within their respective price ranges, each meets consumer expectations of a well-made beverage wine (with increasing degrees of richness, barrel age, and so on). The top-of-the-line label is the Réserve F, the most successful being the merlot and the cabernet sauvignon. Skalli has also entered the AC field with the Domaine du Silène des Peyrals in the Coteaux du Languedoc. It fits the Skalli profile.

Terrasses de Larzac

A vast swath of hills at the western end of the Languedoc, Terrasses de Larzac has numerous soil types, expositions, and a great variety in styles of wine. MONTPEYROUX is considered the Larzac area's top *cru*. For vintages and prices, see COTEAUX DU LANGUEDOC.

PRODUCERS: DOM DES CRÈS RICARDS ◆ DOM DE GRANOUPIAC ◆ Ch de Jonquières: see COTEAUX DU LANGUEDOC ◆ Mas Brunet: see COTEAUX DU LANGUEDOC ◆ Mas des Chimères: see COTEAUX DU LANGUEDOC ◆ MAS JULLIEN ☆ ◆ MAS DE LA SERRANNE ↑ ◆ PLAN DE L'OM ☆ ◆ DOM LE PAS DE L'ESCALETTE ↑ ◆ DOM DE LA SAUVAGEONNE ☆ ◆ Producers recommended from Montpeyroux are found in that listing.

Terre de Sommières

A Coteaux du Languedoc subzone west of Nîmes that is like a hyphen linking the Rhône to the Languedoc. Its reds—based on syrah, grenache, and mourvèdre—tend to be medium-bodied, less tannic than those from other zones and marked by red fruit and Provençal herb flavors. For vintages and prices, see COTEAUX DU LANGUEDOC.

PRODUCERS: La Clotte-Fontane: see COTEAUX DU LANGUEDOC ◆ MAS DE LA BARBEN ☆ ◆ Mas Granier: see COTEAUX DU LANGUEDOC ◆ Dom Serres-Cabanis: see COTEAUX DU LANGUEDOC.

Domaine la Tour Boisée

11800 Laure-Minervois; 04.68.78.10.04; info@domainelatourboisee.com
Wines: Minervois and Vin de Pays. $ to $$($)
Marie-Claude and Jean-Louis Poudou produce a broad range of whites and reds, including a pure merlot Vin de Pays. Their wines are ambitious but sometimes a bit thick. The Minervois rouge À Marie-Claude has dark kirsch and oak flavors; the pricey À Marie-Claude Jardin Secret seduces with mingled fruit and mint flavors, but the searingly dry finish gives me the feeling that they have really nice raw material that they push too hard.

Domaine la Tour Vieille ☆

66190 Collioure; 04.68.82.44.82; fax: 04.68.82.38.42
Wines: Collioure, Vin de Pays, and Banyuls. $ to $$
Christine Campadieu and Vincent Cantié could be the poster couple for French family wineries: they're youngish, good-looking, and hard-working, and they make very good wine. I have a particular affection for their serious rosé and their white Les Canadells—saline, ample, and fresh. My favorites among their reds are the porty, cherry-pit-scented Puig Ambeille and Puig Oriol, a deliciously focused wine. Among their fortified wines, I can't resist the Banyuls Reserva, a mellow, subtle meditation wine with succulent flavors of coffee and a long and sapid finish.

Domaine du Traginer ☆

66650 Banyuls-sur-Mer; 04.68.88.15.11; fax: 04.68.88.31.48
Wines: Banyuls and Collioure. $$ ($)
Not only does Jean-François Deu adhere to the strictures of biodynamics, he is one of the last vintners to plough his vineyards with a mule. His Banyuls blanc is perfumed but not blowsy. His Rimage has an impressive mineral-slate backbone and good balance. The mellow Mise Tardive varies with the vintage—a 1995, for example, tasted of aged, crushed raspberries while a 1999 tasted of dried fruit. The *hors d'âge,* which spends ten years in small barrels, has tawny flavors of nuts and toffee. He also makes Collioure, but Banyuls is his forte.

Domaine de la Treille Muscate

11350 Padern; 04.68.45.07.67; catherine.marin-pestel@voila.fr
Wines: Corbières and Vin de Pays de Cucugnan. $
Young Catherine Marin-Pestel makes truly nice, very reasonably priced wines, particularly the silky red and firm white Corbières AC, both easy country wines with character.

Domaine Tribouley ↑

66720 Latour-de-France; 04.68.29.03.86; luisajeanlouis@aol.com
Wine: Côtes du Roussillon. $$
Another relatively new, extremely promising Fenouillèdes domaine. Among a number of attractive cuvées my clear favorite is Les 3 Lunes, a powerful, oaky red with lots of fascinating stuff hidden under the baby fat.

Val Donnadieu: See CLOS BAGATELLE.

Val d'Orbieu

11100 Narbonne; 04.68.42.75.36
Wines: Vin de Pays and various AC wines. $
A large association of growers and cooperatives throughout the Languedoc. The group produces a vast range of wines, both AC and Vin de Pays, the most famous being the expensively packaged Cuvée Mythique.

Château de Valflaunes ↑

34270 Valflaunes; tel/fax: 04.67.55.76.30
Wine: Coteaux du Languedoc–Pic St.-Loup. $$
Fabien Reboul is a young vigneron who mixes serious winemaking with a nice sense of playfulness. He seems to change his cuvées with regularity, and it's in their names that his whimsy expresses itself: Un Peu de Toi is a rich, oaky red based on carignan; Hardièsse, a superripe grenache aged in old barrels, is truly pretty and comes across like a very good Côtes du Rhône. T'em, T'em, based on young syrah vines, is as concentrated as a liqueur. Blue cheese, anyone?

Château Veredus (also Château Fabre-Gasparets and Château de Luc)

11200 Luc-sur-Orbieu; 04.68.27.10.80; fax: 04.67.39.27.69; masviel@aol.com
Wines: Corbières and Vin de Pays. $ to $$
Three domaines in one and I, for one, am lost in the maze of different bottlings. What I can tell you is this: the Château de Luc makes a really tasty organic red based on carignan at $! Château Veredus has a nice viognier sold as Vin de Pays d'Oc. And the red Corbières from Château Fabre-Gasparets vary in quality but would be good company for hamburgers or meat loaf.

Domaine Vial Magnères ☆

66650 Banyuls-sur-Mer; 04.68.88.31.04; al.tragou@wanadoo.fr
Wines: Banyuls, Collioure, Vin de Pays, and Vin de Table. $ to $$
Olivier Sapéras was one of the first to believe in grenache blanc, and his Armenn Le Petit Couscouril is so ample, fresh, saline, and characterful, it could be an ambassador for the grape, as well as for Collioure blanc. His Les Espérades is a delightful bistro red with dark cherry flavors. His 1993 Banyuls André Magnères, which spent five years in oak, could be a ringer for an oloroso sherry. And Rancio Cino, a name with which he avoids saying "fino," comes across like a slightly fatter, iodine-scented version of Andalusia's favorite quaff.

Vignerons de Mont Tauch

11350 Tauchan; 04.68.45.41.08; fax: 04.68.45.45.29
Wines: Fitou and Rivesaltes. $ to $$
This good cooperative makes several sturdy cuvées of Fitou, nice Rivesaltes, and even better Muscat de Rivesaltes.

Les Vignerons de l'Occitane: See CLAMERY.

Vin de Pays

The Languedoc-Roussillon, largely under the banner of Vin de Pays d'Oc, accounts for nearly half of French production of Vin de Pays, and leads in the export of French wine. Vin de Pays d'Oc covers the entire Languedoc-Roussillon. Expect anything and everything. There are, however, two strong styles. The first is a single-grape (varietal) style made to appeal to New World palates. These are usually competitively priced. This group is led by LA BAUME and ROBERT SKALLI. The second style applies to the mavericks, the liberty freaks, headed by MAS DE DAUMAS GASSAC and GRANGE DES PÈRES. These wines are more expensive (they make me think of the super Tuscans). And a large percentage of Languedoc-Roussillon producers who generally work within ACs also produce some Vin de Pays. Generally, price will tell you whether the wine is in the New World varietal or the maverick category.

Aside from the vast umbrella that is the Vin de Pays d'Oc, there are departmental Vins de Pays, for example the Vin de Pays de l'Aude, de l'Hérault, and so forth. And there are what seem to be hundreds of small to teeny Vins de Pays zones. Côtes de Thongue and Coteaux du Libron are two relatively important ones. But there are scores of others, though most of them are likely to disappear, as producers opt for more recognizable names. Here's a sampling of the wild bunch—all of whose names are preceded by Vin de Pays de(s): La Cité de Carcassonne; Coteaux de Bessilles; Coteaux de Font Caude; Coteaux de Miramont; Coteaux de Murviel; Coteaux de Narbonne; Côtes du Brian; Côtes Catalan; Côtes de Thau; La Côte Vermeille (see RANCIO); Cucugnan; St.-Guilhem le Désert; La Vallée du Paradis.

All of the Vin de Pays are subject to regulations. If producers want even more liberty, they can label their wines Vin de Table or, in the case of fortified wines, *vin de liqueur.*

BEST RECENT VINTAGES: See LANGUEDOC.
PRICES: $ to $$$$

PRODUCERS: The domaines listed here include major producers of Vin de Pays and Vin de Table as well as smaller producers not otherwise included with any of the ACs. Since so many of the producers listed in the various ACs also make Vin de Pays or Vin de Table, you might want to check the AC listings. Dom de l'Aube des Temps: the domaine makes a curious barrel-fermented, late-harvest chardonnay ◆ DOM DE BACHELLERY ◆ Dom de la Balmière: delicate dry muscat from the Fenouillèdes ◆ Baronnie de Bourgade (a.k.a. Les 3 Poules): hand-harvested grapes, cute labels, and a range of cute barbecue wines ◆ LA BAUME ◆ Dom de la Caumette: the domaine makes Faugères and Coteaux du Languedoc as well as a number of good beverage wines as Vin de Pays Coteaux du Libron ◆ CLAMERY/VIGNERONS DE L'OCCITANE ◆ DOM DE LA COLOMBETTE ◆ Domaine Deshenrys: In Faugères AC, they're known as Abbaye Sylva Plana. I prefer the Vin de Pays Côtes du Thongue they make under the Domaine Deshenrys label ◆ DOM LES ÉMINADES ↑ ◆ Dom Fabresse: from the Fenouillèdes, a fragrant, very good chardonnay ◆ Dom Faillenc Sainte Marie: this domaine primarily makes Corbières AC, but I was intrigued by Pas des Louves, a taut but off-dry white made from bourboulenc, maccabeu, clairette, and roussanne ◆ GRANGE DES PÈRES ☆ ◆ Mas d'Aimé: Burgundian-influenced Philippe Rustan is someone I'd like to know more about. His La Vieille Bataille, pure carignan, is fragrant, balanced, and lightly oaky ◆ MAS DE DAUMAS GASSAC ☆ ◆ Mas de Lavail: this Fenouillèdes family winery makes attractive Vins de Pays. Ego, pure grenache, is so dense and has such dark, thick fruit, it's best decanted before drinking. Le Sud, a barrel-aged white, is vinous, mineral, and textured ◆ MAUREL-VEDEAU ◆ Gabriel Meffre: an important Rhône *négociant* who has had great success with his recently launched Vin de Pays brands Fat Bastard and Wild Pig ◆ DOM MONPLÉZY ↑ ◆ Ch Pech Redon: this La Clape–area domaine makes Coteaux du Languedoc and a number of Vins de Pays, among them a pure Teinturier, an old varietal used to give color to wines—which explains the purple-black color. It's perfect for a good wine bar ◆ Dom du Possible: Loïc Roure makes Vin de Table and Vin de Pays in the Roussillon. His style is hypernatural and the wines are sui generis: Cours Toujours, a white pure maccabeu, which may have oxidized flavors, and La Fruit du Hasard, pure carignan, a kirschy and insistent little fellow, would both be fun to find in a wine bar. Roure's first vintage was 2003. I think he's worth following ◆ Dom du Poujol: the domaine is listed in Coteaux du Languedoc and in Rivesaltes, but its Vin de Pays is worth noting, particularly Pico, an exuberantly perfumed white ◆ ROBERT SKALLI ◆ Dom de la Truffière: the wines, sold by JEAN-MARC BOILLOT, a good Burgundy producer, are OK but nothing exceptional ◆ Dom Vacquer: although the wines are uneven and pricey, they can also be very good. L'Exception is fragrant and fresh, if sometimes a bit tannic, depending on the grape blend. Cuvée Bernard is smooth, easy, and pleasurable. The domaine also makes good Rivesaltes ◆ Les Vignes d'Élodie: a domaine with promise—try them by the glass.

Vin de Pays d'Oc: See VIN DE PAYS.

LANGUEDOC-ROUSSILLON CRIB SHEET

MUST TRYS

Léon Barral: Faugères, cuvée Jadis
Le Clos des Fées: Côtes du Roussillon-Villages
Clos Marie: Coteaux du Languedoc, cuvée Glorieuses
Clos du Rouge Gorge: Vin de Pays
Ermitage du Pic St.-Loup: Coteaux du Languedoc
Domaine du Grand Crès: Corbières, Cuvée Majeur
Grange des Pères: Vin de Pays de l'Hérault
Domaine Madeloc: Collioure and Banyuls
Mas Jullien: Coteaux du Languedoc
Domaine de la Sauvageonne: Coteaux du Languedoc

BEST BUYS

Domaine de Bachellery: Vin de Pays d'Oc
Cave d'Embres et Castelmaure: Corbières
Clos de l'Anhel: Corbières
Clos Bagatelle: St.-Chinian and St.-Jean-de-Minervois
Domaine Faillenc Sainte Marie: Corbières
La Grange de Quatre Sous: Vin de Pays d'Oc
Lorgeril: Minervois-la-Livinière, Cabardès, and Vin de Pays
Mas de la Serranne: Coteaux du Languedoc, Cuvées Ombre du Figuier and Les Griottiers
Mas Granier: Coteaux du Languedoc
Domaine Singla: Roussillon and Vin de Pays

SAFE HOUSES

Domaine des Aires Hautes: Minervois
Domaine d'Aupilhac: Coteaux du Languedoc
Domaine Gardiès: Roussillon and Rivesaltes
Domaine de l'Hortus: Coteaux du Languedoc
Château de Lascaux: Coteaux du Languedoc
Mas Amiel: Roussillon, Banyuls, and Maury
Mas Champart: St.-Chinian
Château de la Négly: Coteaux du Languedoc
Domaine de la Prose: Coteaux du Languedoc
Domaine de la Rectorie: Collioure and Banyuls

ALSACE
BORDEAUX
BURGUNDY
CHAMPAGNE
JURA AND SAVOIE
LANGUEDOC-ROUSSILLON
LOIRE
PROVENCE AND CORSICA
RHÔNE
SOUTHWEST

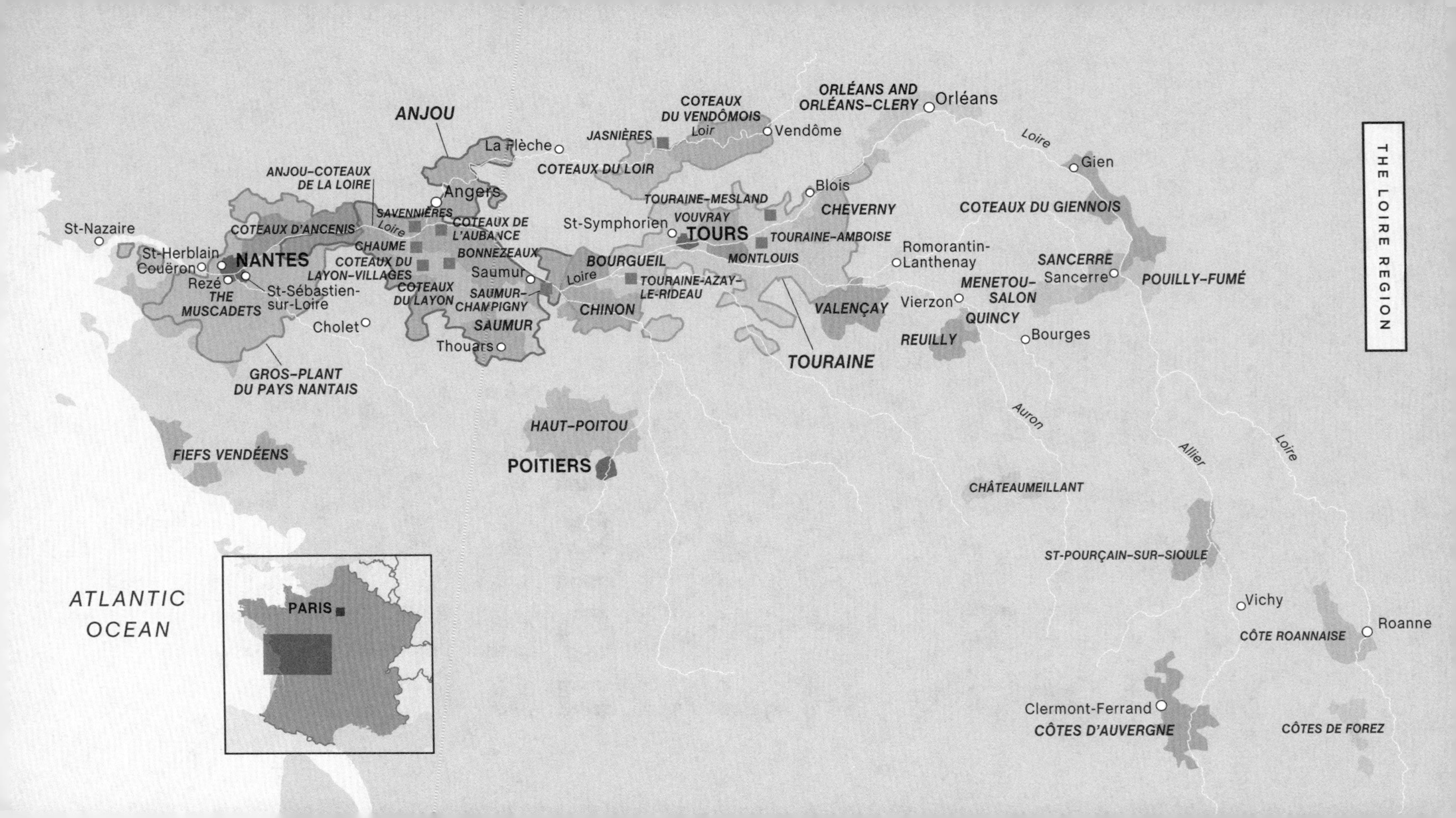
THE LOIRE REGION
ANJOU
COTEAUX
DU VENDÔMOIS
ORLÉANS AND
ORLÉANS-CLERY
Orléans
Vendôme
Loir
JASNIÈRES
La Flèche
Loire
Gien
COTEAUX DU LOIR
ANJOU-COTEAUX
DE LA LOIRE
Angers
Blois
TOURAINE-MESLAND
CHEVERNY
COTEAUX DU GIENNOIS
St-Nazaire
SAVENNIÈRES
COTEAUX DE
L'AUBANCE
St-Symphorien
VOUVRAY
TOURS
TOURAINE-AMBOISE
COTEAUX D'ANCENIS
Loire
CHAUME
BONNEZEAUX
Romorantin-
Lanthenay
SANCERRE
St-Herblain
Couëron
NANTES
COTEAUX DU
LAYON-VILLAGES
BOURGUEIL
MONTLOUIS
Sancerre
POUILLY-FUMÉ
Rezé
St-Sébastien-
sur-Loire
THE
MUSCADETS
COTEAUX
DU LAYON
Saumur
Loire
TOURAINE-AZAY-
LE-RIDEAU
MENETOU-
SALON
SAUMUR-
CHAMPIGNY
Vierzon
CHINON
VALENÇAY
Cholet
SAUMUR
QUINCY
Thouars
REUILLY
Bourges
TOURAINE
GROS-PLANT
DU PAYS NANTAIS
HAUT-POITOU
Auron
Allier
Loire
FIEFS VENDÉENS
POITIERS
CHÂTEAUMEILLANT
ST-POURÇAIN-SUR-SIOULE
ATLANTIC
OCEAN
PARIS
Vichy
Roanne
CÔTE ROANNAISE
Clermont-Ferrand
CÔTES D'AUVERGNE
CÔTES DE FOREZ

Known for its Renaissance châteaux, the Loire is also renowned as the garden of France. Everything grows here, not least of which, grapes. Sixty-eight different appellations are grouped along the banks of the Loire River and its tributaries. Most of the wine it produces is white, ranging from dry and off-dry to demi-sec, *moelleux*, and *doux*. Rosés may also be dry or sweet; reds, with the rare exception, are dry. The Loire is also an important producer of sparkling wine, including Crémant de Loire, as well as Vin de Pays, particularly Vin de Pays du Jardin de la France.

Winemaking in the Loire is separated into five distinct regions: the Nantais, Anjou-Saumur, Touraine, the Centre, and the Massif Central.

THE MAJOR APPELLATIONS, BY REGION: In the Nantais: Muscadet, Gros-Plant du Pays Nantais, Fiefs Vendéens ◆ Anjou and Saumur: Each of these is an umbrella AC. Its other ACs include Anjou-Villages, Bonnezeaux, Coteaux de l'Aubance, Coteaux du Loir, Coteaux du Layon, Coteaux de Saumur, Quarts-de-Chaume, Saumur-Champigny, and Savennières ◆ Touraine is an umbrella AC. Additionally there are Bourgueil, Cheverny, Chinon, Jasnières, Montlouis, Valençay, Vendômois, and Vouvray ◆ The Région de Centre : Sancerre, Pouilly-Fumé, Quincy, Reuilly, Coteaux du Giennois, Vin de l'Orléanais, and Châteaumeillant ◆ The Massif Central contains four small zones clumped in with the Loire, although arguably they'd be more appropriately aligned with Beaujolais. These are: Côtes d'Auvergne, Côtes de Forez, Côtes Roannaise, and St.-Pourçain.

GRAPES: The leading grape varieties for white wines are chenin blanc, sauvignon blanc, and melon de Bourgogne (muscadet). Reds and rosés are generally made from cabernet franc, côt (malbec), gamay, and pinot noir. Secondary grapes include cabernet sauvignon, grolleau, and pineau d'Aunis. There are also some obscure grapes like fié, romorantin, and tressallier.

STYLES OF WINE: These are northern-climate wines that, for all their diversity, share stylistic threads. Loire wines tend to be relatively low in alcohol and relatively high in acidity. They range from light to medium-bodied, with vividly etched fruit. Most of the reds can (and should) be served slightly chilled.

BEST VINTAGES: Vintages matter in the Loire. Although the harvest had barely ended at the time of this writing, 2005 promises to be a great vintage, on the order of 1989 or 1990 and, at least where reds are concerned, perhaps as great as 1947. The year 2004 was a mixed bag. Crop thinning was an absolute necessity. Where yields were controlled, the wines are very good, although the reds have an edge over the whites. It was not a great year for sweet chenins, however. Vouvray and Montlouis replenished their stocks of sparkling wine and dry whites; in

Anjou, a number of fastidious producers made no Layons as they refuse to chaptalize.

The record-setting heat wave of 2003 made that year as atypical in the Loire as it was elsewhere in France. To some, this is a blessing as the wines have more alcohol and less acidity than usual. There are, indeed, some very good wines from this vintage; however, they are uncharacteristically fat. I doubt their ageability. Many seem to be evolving quickly. The most classic, recent Loire vintage (in the positive sense) may be 2002. The wines are vibrant, well balanced, and ripe—with, of course, typical Loire acidity. Best vintages from the recent past: 1997, 1996, 1995, 1990, 1989, 1988.

PRICES: $ to $$$($)

Alliance Loire
49260 St.-Cyr-en-Bourg; 02.41.53.74.44; info@allianceloire.com
Wines: Numerous Loire appellations from Nantes to Vendôme. $ to $$
Created in 2002, this is a grouping of seven Loire valley cooperatives, comprising 700 vignerons and 3,600 hectares of vines, from the Nantais to Touraine and the Vendômois. The cooperatives are the Cave des Coteaux du Vendômois, Cave des Producteurs de Vouvray–Vallée Coquette, Cave des Grands Vins de Bourgueil, Vignobles du Paradis (Chinon), Caves des Vignerons de Saumur, Les Maîtres Vignerons Nantais, and Les Vignerons de la Noëlle. The alliance markets fifteen million bottles of Loire wine yearly. Of particular interest is the range of wines called Le Lieu-Dit. Each wine in this category comes from a single vineyard, the characteristics of which are noted on the label. Particularly good examples include the Saumur blanc *lieu-dit* Les Pouches, a white made from chenin blanc, and Saumur-Champigny *lieu-dit* Les Vignolles, a red made from cabernet franc.

Philippe Alliet ☆
37500 Cravant-les-Coteaux; 02.47.93.17.62; fax: 02.47.93.17.62
Wine: Chinon. $$($)
Good vintage or bad, Alliet succeeds in making benchmark Chinons. He has just begun bottling a little bit of white Chinon, but red Chinon, aged in barrels made to his specifications, is where his heart is. There are three different bottlings: a Chinon to drink young ("on the fruit"), an old-vines, and Coteau du Noiré, a wine produced from one of the best-situated slopes in the appellation. If you don't like this wine, you don't like Chinon.

Yannick Amirault ☆
37140 Bourgueil; 02.47.97.78.07; fax: 02.47.97.94.78
Wines: Bourgueil and St.-Nicolas de Bourgueil. $$($)
Honest, self-effacing, and painstaking Yannick Amirault turns out silky, delicious reds, especially his old-vines cuvées, in Bourgueil (Les Quartiers and La Petite Cave) and in St.-Nicolas de Bourgueil (Malgagnes and Graviers).

Ampelidae
86380 Marigny-Brizay; 05.49.88.18.18; ampelidae@ampelidae.com
Wines: Poitou and Vin de Pays (or de Table) de la Vienne. $ to $$
Frédéric Brochet, who holds a doctorate from the University of Bordeaux, produces thirteen ambitious wines on the family property outside of Poitiers. There are two series: Marigny-Neuf, VDQS Haut-Poitou, consists of fruity, easy-drinking wines made from young vines. The second series, Vin de Pays de Vienne, is made from older vines and costs three times as much as the first series. Brochet names these wines with single letters (to signify a specific

grape variety). Le K, for example, represents the lean, structured cabernet sauvignon; Le S is a meaty, fresh sauvignon blanc. Hand-harvested and nonchaptalized, all are surprising—and surprisingly good—particularly when compared to the norm in this region in the depths of Poitou.

(Les Vignes de l')Ange Vin ↑

72340 Chahaignes; 02.43.44.92.20; fax: 02.43.44.92.20

Wines: Jasnières and Coteaux du Loir. $$

Jean-Pierre Robinot is making the kind of wine he loved to sell when he owned a Parisian wine bar called l'Ange Vin. His mineral, structured Jasnières, fermented in barrel, struts its pedigree. His peppery pineau d'Aunis Coteaux du Loir is absolutely what I want to accompany Indian food. He also makes some attractive Vouvray from purchased grapes.

Anjou

Both a region and an umbrella AC, Anjou covers most of the western part of the Maine et Loire department and spills over into the northern tips of the Deux-Sèvres and the Vienne. Many types of wine are made here, including whites ranging from dry to sticky-sweet, dry and off-dry rosés, dry reds, and sparkling wines. A number of the Loire's most famous wines are Angevin, among them those of the COTEAUX DU LAYON, BONNEZEAUX, QUARTS-DE-CHAUME, and SAVENNIÈRES (including COULÉE DE SERRANT). The umbrella AC Anjou produces both dry whites and reds. Related appellations are Anjou-Villages, Anjou-Villages Brissac, and Anjou gamay.

GRAPES: Anjou blanc is generally pure chenin blanc, although limited amounts of chardonnay or sauvignon blanc are permitted. Cabernet franc and sauvignon are used for Anjou rouge, Anjou-Villages, and Anjou-Villages Brissac. Gamay is the base of Anjou-Gamay.

STYLES OF WINE: Anjou blanc is made in a number of styles: there are neutral quaffers; vivacious, fruity crowd-pleasers; and increasingly, fairly serious whites in the style of Savennières.

Anjou rouge is generally a user-friendly red made to be drunk within three years of the harvest and is at its best slightly chilled. Anjou-Villages, made within a more limited area and subject to stricter rules, is generally richer, more structured, more tannic, and more age-worthy. Anjou-Villages Brissac, a very recent AC, is identical to Anjou-Villages except that it is made within a still more limited zone, the same area as the sweet white COTEAUX DE L'AUBANCE. Anjou-Villages Brissac and Anjou-Villages are juicy, medium-bodied reds. Depending on the vigneron, they range from tannic and foursquare to lissome and elegant. Nearly all are best drunk within eight years of the vintage, though some can age a bit longer. They can be very good value.

BEST RECENT VINTAGES: 2005, (2004, where yields were controlled), 2003, 2002. Other top vintages: 1997, 1996, 1995, 1990, 1989, 1988, though all but the very best of those made earlier than 1997 will be on the decline by now.

PRICES: $ to $$

PRODUCERS: DOM DE BABLUT ☆ ◆ PATRICK BAUDOUIN ◆ Stéphane Bernaudeau: an interesting newcomer. Try the Anjou blanc Les Nourissons with 20 percent Verdelho ◆ DOM DE BRIZÉ ◆ PHILIPPE CADY ☆ ◆ Dom des Charbotières: the domaine seems to have adopted hypernatural methods, with some promising results, particularly in an ambitious Cabernet d'Anjou and very ripe Anjou blanc and Aubance ↑ ◆ Olivier Cousin: another promising newcomer, making rich Anjou-Gamay and a very good Anjou rouge Vieilles Vignes. No sulfur added here, so approach and handle with care ↑ ◆ DOM PHILIPPE DELESVAUX ☆ ◆ FERME DE LA SANSONNIÈRE ◆ DOM DES FORGES ☆ ◆ CH LA FRESNAYE ↑ ◆ JEAN-CHRISTOPHE GARNIER ↑ ◆ DOM LES GRANDES VIGNES ↑ ◆ Domaine de Haute Perche: Christian Papin is a reliably good producer of the Anjou range, particularly his Anjou-Villages Brissac ◆ DOM

DE JUCHEPIE ☆ ◆ DOM LAUREAU DU CLOS FRÉMUR ↑ ◆ Vincent Lecointre/Château la Tomaze: conscientious, good producer of Anjous, nice gamays ◆ RICHARD LEROY ☆ ◆ DOM DE MONTGILET ☆ ◆ MUSSET-ROULLIER ◆ VINCENT OGEREAU ☆ ◆ DOM DU PETIT VAL ◆ CH PIERRE-BISE ☆ ◆ DOM JO PITHON ☆ ◆ CH DE PUTILLE ◆ Dom de Putille: see ANJOU-COTEAUX DE LA LOIRE ◆ DOM DU REGAIN ↑ ◆ DOM RICHOU ☆ ◆ DOM DES ROCHELLES ☆ ◆ DOM DU ROY RENÉ ↑ ◆ DOM DES SABLONNETTES ↑ ◆ Dom du Salvert: the best wine at this newish domaine is the suave Anjou-Villages Les Demoiselles, not surprising, as one of the owners is the daughter of May de Lencquesaing of Pichon-Lalande in Pauillac ◆ FERME DE LA SANSONNIÈRE ◆ CH SOUCHERIE ☆ ◆ Ch de Tigné: Gérard Depardieu's Loire property, in case you were interested.

Anjou–Coteaux de la Loire

AC for semisweet to very sweet chenin blanc. Shaped by an arc in the Loire at the northwest limits of Anjou, this minuscule appellation may never produce wines as majestic or as deep as chenins from the Layon, but its wines can be quite fine and delicious.

BEST RECENT VINTAGES: 2005, 2003.
PRICES: $$

PRODUCERS: Dom du Fresche: AC stalwart, now organic, look for Cuvée Vieille Sève ◆ MUSSET-ROULLIER ◆ CH DE PUTILLE ◆ Dom de Putille: good small domaine with appealing versions of AC, especially Cuvée des Claveries.

(Vignoble de) l'Arbre Blanc

63450 St.-Sandoux; 04.73.39.40.91
Wines: Côtes d'Auvergne and Vin de Pays du Puy-de-Dôme. $
Young Frédéric Gounan makes light, mineral-driven wines that would be perfect wine-bar discoveries. My favorite is the super-specific La Caillasse, a blend of gamay and pinot noir that ages two years in barrel. It may be light but it's certainly not anonymous.

Domaine des Aubuisières ☆

37210 Vouvray; 02.47.52.61.55; info@vouvrayfouquet.com
Wine: Vouvray. $ to $$$
Bernard Fouquet makes superb, mineral-rich Vouvray in every style. (Depending on the vintage, the wines may or may not ferment in new and newish barrels but the oak, when used, is always a subtle presence.) Look, in particular, for Le Marigny, Les Girardières, Plan de Jean, Silex, and Cuvée Alexandre. And Fouquet is one of the few who make serious (and seriously delicious) Vouvray brut.

Domaine de Bablut ☆

49320 Brissac-Quince; 02.41.91.22.59; daviau.contact@wanadoo.fr
Wines: Anjou range, including Coteaux de l'Aubance. $ to $$
Christophe Daviau, an enologist who has worked both in Bordeaux and in Australia, converted this important family domaine to biodynamics. His Sélection de Grains Nobles wines are gorgeous, as are his Coteaux de l'Aubance (particularly such special bottlings as Unique, Grand Pierre, and Vin Noble). This is also the place to find good young as well as aged Cabernet d'Anjou and an ambitious, extremely ripe Anjou blanc called Ordovicien. The Daviaus also make the wines for the Château de Brissac. Not surprisingly, their own Anjou-Villages Brissac is rather nice, especially the Cuvée Petra Alba.

Domaine des Barres ↑

49190 St.-Aubin de Luigne; 02.41.78.98.24. fax: 02.41.78.68.37
Wines: Chaume, Savennières, and Coteaux du Layon. $$
Patrice Achard, a very promising producer who succeeded his father in the mid-90s, has 24 hectares of prime chenin vineyards, making Chaume (Les Pretises), Coteaux du Layon–St.-Aubin, and Savennières.

Patrick Baudouin

49290 Chaudefonds-sur-Layon, tel/fax 02.41.78.66.04; contact@patrick-baudouin-layon.com
Wines: Anjou range, including Coteaux du Layon. $$ to $$$
Impassioned and idealistic, Patrick Baudouin pushes his wines as far as they'll go, particularly in terms of ripeness. His syrupy Layon les Sens du Chenin took six years to ferment and has 690 grams of residual sugar. Cuvée Maria Juby must be sold as a Vin de Table because of its low alcohol level (8.5 percent). Such wines may not be to everybody's taste but they certainly are the true expression of one man and his *terroir*. His dry whites are more mainstream, though equally uncompromising: the Cuvée Effusion, my favorite in his entire lineup, is steely and razor-sharp; Le Cormaire is ampler, potent, and oaky. Baudouin's reds are also worth trying.

Domaine Bernard Baudry ☆

37500 Cravant-les-Coteaux; 02.47.93.15.79; bernard-baudry@chinon.com
Wine: Chinon. $$
An excellent family domaine making a range of fine-grained Chinons. In order of opulence (and price): Les Granges, Domaine, Grézeaux, Clos Guillot, a second Clos Guillot made from young, ungrafted vines, and Croix Boissée. Baudry and son Mathieu also make a tasty rosé and a fragrant and steely white Chinon. Baudry senior says that 2005 was the greatest vintage of his life.

Domaine des Baumard ☆

49190 Rochefort-sur-Loire; 02.41.78.70.73; www.baumard.fr
Wines: Anjou range, including Quarts-de-Chaume and Savennières. $ to $$$
Florent Baumard has taken over from his enologist father, Jean, in this important, indeed pioneering, domaine. You'll find the entire range of Anjou wines here, including top-notch Crémant de Loire. Baumard is particularly (and rightly) known, however, for exemplary Savennières (especially cuvées Clos du Papillon and, in great vintages, Trie Spéciale), Coteaux du Layon (cuvée Clos de Ste.-Catherine), and Quarts-de-Chaume. Also worth seeking out is the unusual and bracing Vin de Table, Vert de l'Or made from verdelho. Note that the screw-cap option is now available.

Domaine de Bellivière ☆

72340 Lhomme; 02.43.44.59.97; info@belliviere.com
Wines: Jasnières and Coteaux du Loir. $$($)
Éric Nicolas, an exciting producer of Jasnières and Coteaux du Loir, has put those two appellations on the map with his super-concentrated, extremely mineral wine from pampered, low-yielding vines. He makes a number of riveting cuvées in each appellation. All whites are barrel-fermented chenin blanc. Jasnières Calligramme is made from vines more than fifty years old; Les Rosiers is reserved for younger vines; and, in some years, Nicolas bottles the deeply complex Élixir de Tuf and Discours de Tuf. His white Coteaux du Loir—Vieilles Vignes Éparses, l'Effraie (young vines), and Haut-Rasné, a single vineyard—are better than most Jasnières. His red Coteaux du Loir, which mature for a year in barrel, are chiefly pineau d'Aunis. Hommage à Louis Derre, made from eighty- to one-hundred-year-old pineau d'Aunis vines, is remarkable. And the "lighter" cuvée, Le Rouge Gorge, is a serious light red made from this denigrated grape.

Domaine de la Bergerie ↑

49380 Champ-sur-Layon; 02.41.78.85.43; domaine.de.la.bergerie@wandoo.fr
Wines: Anjou range, including Savennières, Quarts-de-Chaume, and Chaume. $ to $$$
Yves Guegniard is another vigneron to watch. There's a lot of very noteworthy wine—in nearly every Anjou AC, including the rosés—coming from his property. He recently got a piece of Savennières, La Croix Picot. Fermented in barrel, the wine is oaky, rich, and mineral. His Anjou blanc, Les Pierres Girard, ages in oak and is both fresh and rich. La Cerisaie, his Anjou rouge, is fragrant and

LOIRE

discreet. Guegniard makes two Anjou-Villages based on cabernet sauvignon—Le Chant du Bois and the low-yield, oak-aged, tannic Evanescence—both of which would be fun to discover in a wine bar. There's a passel of Layons, all of them delicious and all accurately reflecting their respective *terroirs*. Not surprisingly, the most aristocratic and complex come from Chaume and Quarts-de-Chaume. Finally, there's a Vieilles Vignes Cuvée Fragrance in which the oak is completely digested by the richness of the succulent fruit.

Château de la Bonnelière ↑

54, Faubourg St.-Jacques, 37500 Chinon; 02.47.93.16.34; www.plouzeau.com

Wine: Chinon: $ to $$

Marc Plouzeau, like his older brother François (see GARRELIÈRE), has converted his domaine to biodynamics. His rosé is gulpable, as are his two cuvées of Chinon, particularly the La Chapelle bottling. Even in 2003 the wines were balanced, nicely structured, with no exaggeration—simply delicious.

Bonnezeaux

Small AC for sweet to extremely sweet, even syrupy, whites made from chenin blanc. One of the brightest jewels in Anjou's crown, this small appellation lies about fifteen miles south of Angers. It covers three southwest-facing hills overlooking the Layon on schist-rich soils streaked with quartz and silex. Made from overripe, botrytized, and/or shriveled chenin blanc grapes, Bonnezeaux, by law, must have a minimum of 230 grams of natural sugar, the highest in the Layon. While it can be drunk young, Bonnezeaux ages beautifully. If you are lucky enough to come across a 1959, a 1947, or a 1921, go for it!

BEST RECENT VINTAGES: 2005, 2003, 2002, 1997, 1996, 1995, 1990, 1989, 1988.

PRICES: $$ to $$$$ (often for a 50-centiliter bottle, which is a convenient size)

PRODUCERS: FERME DE LA SANSONNIÈRE ◆ CH DE FESLES ◆ DOM LES GRANDES VIGNES ↑ ◆ Godineau Père & Fils/Domaine des Petits Quarts: quality is variable but when it's good, it's very, very good; look for cuvées Les Melleresses, Beauregard, and Malabé ◆ DOM DU PETIT VAL.

Gérard & Thibaut Boulay ☆

18300 Chavignol; 02.48.54.36.37

Wine: Sancerre: $$

The Boulays are neighbors of the COTATS in Chavignol and work many of the same *lieux-dits* in much the same way. The wines bear a strong resemblance to those of the Cotats (including the occasional presence of residual sugar), and that's a good thing, as there is never enough to go around. Their simplest bottling is a great bistro sauvignon. The richer bottlings, like those from Cul de Beaujeu, are distinctly *terroir*-driven, ample, and mellow. Their red Sancerre is a characterful, light red, a delight.

Henri Bourgeois ☆

Chavignol 18300 Sancerre; 02.48.78.53.20; www.henribourgeois.com

Wines: Sancerre and Pouilly-Fumé. $ to $$$

An important house in terms of both quality and quantity, Henri Bourgeois is a grower and *négociant*. Now into its tenth generation in the charming wine village of Chavignol, it has 65 hectares of vines in Sancerre and Pouilly (Fumé) and a huge, new winery in New Zealand. Purchased grapes and juice account for about 40 percent of production and are used in such entry-level cuvées as Petit Bourgeois, a feisty sauvignon blanc. The top cuvées are among the best wines in their respective ACs. In Sancerre these include Les Baronnes (Grande Réserve in some markets), MD, Les Monts Damnés (full and layered in 2004), La Chapelle, La Bourgeoise (white and red), Jadis Sancerrois (fabulous in 2002),

D'Antan Sancerrois (which is neither fined nor filtered), Étienne Henri (aged in oak), and Le Chêne St.-Étienne (white, fermented in barrel, and red, aged in barrel). La Demoiselle (airy and elegant in 2004) is the winery's top Pouilly-Fumé. Bourgeois also markets the Sancerres of Domaine Laporte. These (La Cresle, for example) tend to be more austere than the ample Bourgeois line but are equally appealing in their lean, mineral style. Bourgeois also makes a steely little white in the Coteaux du Giennois.

Bourgueil

AC for reds and rosés made from cabernet franc, though cabernet sauvignon is permitted and sometimes used. The appellation spreads across the right bank of the Loire from the western edge of Touraine, on the border of Anjou-Saumur, and runs east to Ingrandes, at the outskirts of Langeais. The rosés are fragrant and easy-drinking; the reds come in two basic styles. Those from young vines and/or light, alluvial soils are vibrantly juicy and should be drunk on the fruit. Those from older vines and/or *tuffeau* soils can be equally succulent; depending on the vintner, these wines may be brawny and rather rustic, or suave and multidimensional.

BEST RECENT VINTAGES: 2005, (2004 where yields were kept low), 2003, 2002, 1997, 1996, 1995, 1990, 1989. Vintages prior to 1997 are recommended only for top producers.
PRICES: $ to $$$

PRODUCERS: YANNICK AMIRAULT ☆ ◆ Audebert & Fils: a reliable, quality-conscious grower-*négociant,* with good, reasonably priced wines both here and in St.-Nicolas de Bourgueil. Look for Les Marquises and Grand Clos ◆ CATHÉRINE & PIERRE BRETON ◆ Dom de la Butte (Jacky Blot): see DOM DE LA TAILLE AUX LOUPS ☆ ◆ Dom de la Chanteleuserie: the Boucards make pleasant bistro Bourgueils, particularly the Lys d'Or and the cuvées Beauvais and Vieilles Vignes. Their St.-Nicolas de Bourgueil is also worth sampling ◆ DOM DE LA CHEVALERIE ◆ Clos de l'Abbaye: pleasant, organic wines from the vineyards of the historic Abbaye de Bourgueil ◆ PIERRE-JACQUES DRUET ◆ Dom des Forges: Jean-Yves Billet makes gracious Bourgueils that often win local competitions. The two top cuvées are Les Bézards and Vieilles Vignes ◆ Dom de la Gaucherie: Régis Mureau's Bourgueils are faithful representations of their soil types: there's a tasty, drink-me-up version from sandy soils and a lusher, more mineral Bourgueil from a *tuffeau* slope ◆ DOM LAME-DELISLE-BOUCARD ◆ DOM DE LA LANDE ☆ ◆ Dom des Mailloches: Cuvée Sophie from the Demont family is a light, easy-drinking Bourgueil; the Vieilles Vignes is a bit more serious but just as tasty ◆ NAU FRÈRES ◆ THIERRY NÉRISSON ↑ ◆ DOM DES OUCHES ↑ ◆ Dom Pontonnier: look for the Vieilles Vignes cuvée from this family domaine.

LOIRE

Bouvet-Ladubay

49400 St.-Hilaire-St.-Florent; 02.41.83.83.83; www.bouvet-ladubay.fr
Wines: Saumur brut and others. $ to $$$
Bouvet-Ladubay is one of the best producers of Saumur brut. There is a wide range of bottlings, the best being the oak-fermented Cuvée Trésor (both *blanc de blancs* and rosé) and the Brut Zéro. The house also makes respectable still wines, Les Nonpareils and Extrême. Originally owned by Champagne Taittinger, the house was sold to the Indian beer company United Breweries in July 2006.

André-Michel Brégeon

44190 Gorges; 02.40.06.93.19; fax: 02.40.06.95.91
Wine: Muscadet de Sèvre et Maine. $
Brégeon's muscadets are full of character, all with strong backbones of mineral and flint, an attribute born of a very particular soil type called gabbro. And Brégeon's muscadets have that thrillingly fresh and marrowy texture of wines

that have spent a long, long time aging on their lees. His 1996 Gorgeois, tasted in 2005, was simultaneously bracing and mellow, with accents of lime, resin, and mushrooms and a long mineral finish. Older vintages are also available.

Cathérine & Pierre Breton

37140 Restigné, 02.47.97.30.41; catherineetpierre.breton@libertysurf.fr
Wine: Bourgueil. $ to $$($)
To say that this is an ambitious family winery adhering to organic viticulture is just the beginning. The Bretons have united like-minded vignerons throughout France; their traveling road shows draw every wine-bar owner in Paris. On his own domaine, Breton takes a lot of risks, notably eliminating sulfur in cuvées like Nuits d'Ivresse, which, as a result, is sometimes oxidized. Other cuvées include the young-vines Trinch! (this word comes from Rabelais; it's what you say when you clink glasses), Les Galichets, Clos Sénéchal, and Les Perrières, all in Bourgueil; and Les Picasses and Beaumont in Chinon. They are always worth trying.

Domaine le Briseau (Christian Chaussard) ↑

72340 Marcon; tel/fax: 02.43.44.58.53; nathalie.gaubicher@wanadoo.fr
Wines: Jasnières, Coteaux du Loir, and Vin de Table. $$
Christian Chaussard makes resolutely idiosyncratic hypernatural wines. My favorites are the characterful, peppery pineau d'Aunis–based reds and rosés, particularly Les Mortiers and Longue Vigne. His chenin blancs, such as the dry, creamy, oxidized Le Briseau that spent five years in barrel, are consistently original, and his Pet/Nat, a naturally sparkling chenin, is curiously appealing.

Domaine de Brizé

49540 Martigne-Briand; 02.41.59.43.35; delhumeau.scea@free.fr
Wines: Anjou range, including Coteaux du Layon. $ to $$($)
One of the best producers of Crémant de Loire, Luc and Line Delhumeau's substantial—and organically farmed—family domaine also makes very good Layon (the 2002 barrel-fermented cuvée Les Beausoleils is scrumptious), unusually rich and deep Anjou gamay, sturdy Anjou-Villages, and barrel-fermented Anjou blanc Loire Renaissance, so powerful it might stand up to ham roasted with pineapple.

Paul Buisse

69, Route de Vierzon, BP 112, 41402 Montrichard Cedex; 02.54.32.00.01; www.paul-buisse.com
Wines: Touraine range and more. $ to $$
Reputable *négociant* house with a full range of Loire wines. Top bottlings include Cristal Buisse, a sauvignon blanc; Tradition, a red blend; and L'Exceptionnel de Paul Buisse, a Saumur-Champigny.

Cabernet d'Anjou: See ROSÉS OF ANJOU.

Cabernet de Saumur: See SAUMUR.

Philippe Cady ☆

49190 St.-Aubin de Luigné; 02.41.78.33.69; cadyph@wanadoo.fr
Wines: Anjou range. $ to $$$($)
Cady doesn't make a lot of noise. He makes wonderful Anjou wine, particularly his sublime sweet chenins, which could be ambassadors for their respective appellations. In every vintage there's a Coteaux du Layon–St. Aubin and a Chaume and maybe a single-vineyard bottling like the excellent, windswept Les Varennes. When the vintage warrants, there's at least one gorgeous Sélection de Grains Nobles, Volupté, or Harmonie.

Domaine Cailbourdin ☆

Maltaverne, 58150 Tracy-sur-Loire; 03.86.26.17.73; fax: 03.86.26.14.73

Wine: Pouilly-Fumé. $ to $$

Alain Cailbourdin is a serious, reliable vintner who makes top-notch Pouilly-Fumé, particularly the elegant Les Cris.

Cailloux du Paradis

41230 Soings-en-Sologne; 02.54.98.71.97; fax: 02. 54.98.77.38

Wines: Vin de Pays and Vin de Table. $ to $$($)

Claude Courtois looks like R. Crumb's Mr. Natural, and his wines are just as ruggedly individualistic. Marginal, decidedly wacko, but possessed of a warts-and-all appeal, Courtois's wines—there are usually seven or eight cuvées, all fermented with wild yeasts and made with little or no sulfur—are sold as Vin de Table or Vin de Pays du Loir et Cher. Plume d'Ange, based on sauvignon blanc, is often lightly fizzy and oxidized but also mineral and concentrated. Racines, a blend of red grapes, is usually hyperconcentrated, warm, and rustic. It's Courtois's most reputed wine.

Caves de Pouilly-sur-Loire

58150 Pouilly-sur-Loire; 03.86.39.10.99; www.cavespouillysurloire.com

Wines: Pouilly-Fumé, Pouilly-sur-Loire, and Coteaux du Giennois. $ to $$

A solid cooperative making thoroughly respectable wines in all three appellations, with quite a few different bottlings in Pouilly-Fumé, the latest being Les Vieillottes, made from vines grown on silex-rich soils.

Catherine & Didier Champalou ☆

37210 Vouvray, 02.47.52.64.49; champalou@wanadoo.fr

Wine: Vouvray. $ to $$($)

Exemplary family domaine. Favorite wines include the mineral demi-sec Cuvée des Fondraux (beautifully balanced and exquisitely fresh in 2003) and anything *moelleux*, particularly the Cuvée CC. Their Vouvray brut is also worth trying.

Domaine des Champs Fleuris ↑

49730 Turquant; 02.41.38.10.92; www.champs-fleuris.com

Wines: Saumur range. $$($)

Patrice and Catherine Rétif and Denis Rétiveau, three enologists, are turning this into one of Saumur's leading domaines. They produce discreet, creamy Saumur blanc, an authoritative, crystalline, barrel-fermented late-harvest chenin Cuvée Les Demoiselles, and a Coteaux de Saumur, a velvety, quince-accented delicacy. Their reds are equally recommendable, from the easy-drinking Les Tufolies, to the richer, unoaked Vieilles Vignes, to the suave, barrel-aged, single-vineyard Les Roches.

Châteaumeillant

A minuscule VDQS in George-Sand country, near the source of the Indre, south of Bourges. Gamay and pinot noir make light reds and *vin gris*, a rosé made by the direct pressing of the red grapes. Drink the youngest available.

PRICES: $

PRODUCERS: Cave des Vins de Châteaumeillant (Cave de Tivoli): the local co-op does a decent job producing most of the wine in this tiny appellation. Look for special cuvées like the Vieilles Vignes ◆ Valerie & Frederic Dallot: this young couple, trained in viticulture and enology, created their domaine in the mid-90s; their work is serious, guided by good principles, and the results are well above average. To follow ◆ Dom Geoffrenet-Morval: this recently created domaine has quickly become one of the region's quality leaders, with several very good, wine-bar-ready cuvées of red (Version Originale and Jeanne Vieilles Vignes) and a cheerful, fresh rosé Comte de Barcelone ◆ Patrick Lanoix: a good, well-established family winery with some of the best reds in the zone ◆ Dom des Tanneries: the Raffinats, another established family in this region, produce pleasant light reds and rosés.

Laurent Chatenay ☆

37270 St.-Martin-le-Beau; 02.47.50.65.58; www.laurentchatenay.com

Wine: Montlouis. $ to $$($)

Lovely, *terroir*-driven Montlouis in every style, from Les Maisonettes, the nonfiltered dry version, with floral and mineral flavors; to the voluptuous La Vallée aux Prêtres, its honey balanced by herbal tea accents; to Le Clos Michet, sheer liquid gold.

Domaine de Chatenoy ☆

18510 Menetou-Salon; 02.48.66.68.70; fax: 02.48.66.68.71

Wine: Menetou-Salon. $ to $$

The domaine's benchmark Menetou-Salon is better than many Sancerres. The unoaked white is a lively, grapefruit-accented sauvignon. The barrel-fermented Cuvée Pierre Alexandre is rich and boldly flavored. La Dame de Chatenoy is mellow and creamy with attractive fig notes. Chatenoy's reds are accurate light pinot noirs with charm to spare.

Chaume

An enclave in the commune of Rochefort-sur-Loire, Chaume was, until 2003, a Coteaux du Layon-Villages. It has since been promoted but its official status is unclear because of a lawsuit. In actuality, its south-facing slopes overlooking the Layon on the southern bank of the Loire have long been known to have extraordinary potential, promise equal to that of Quarts-de-Chaume. The wines are made from chenin blanc, harvested by hand, and by *tri* (successive passes through the vineyard), and are *moelleux, liquoreux,* or *doux.* Vintages and prices correspond to those for Layon-Villages and Quarts-de-Chaume.

BEST VINTAGES: 2005, 2003, 2002, 1997, 1996, 1995, 1990, 1989, 1988.
PRICES: $$ to $$$$

PRODUCERS: DOM DES BARRES ↑ ◆ DOM DE LA BERGERIE ↑ ◆ PHILIPPE CADY ☆ ◆ Domaine des Deux Vallées: Philippe and René Socheleau took over this property in 2001. Their 2003 Chaume Privilège is delicious, indicating that this is a house worth following—all the more so as they bought Ch de Suronde in Quarts-de-Chaume in 2005 ↑ ◆ DOM DES FORGES ☆ ◆ Dom Grosset: see COTEAUX DU LAYON ◆ Château du Petit Métris: Joseph Renou is a reliable source for good Layon–St. Aubin and even better Chaume, especially Les Tetuères and Quarts-de-Chaume ◆ CH PIERRE-BISE ☆ ◆ Ch de Plaisance: rustic, unreconstructed but flavorful Chaume, Layon, and Quarts-de-Chaume ◆ Dom de la Roche Moreau: clean, applesauce- and honey-scented Chaume ◆ CH SOUCHERIE ☆.

Bernard Chéreau/Château de Chasseloir

44690 St.-Fiacre-sur-Maine; 02.40.54.81.15; bernard.chereau@wanadoo.fr

Wine: Muscadet de Sèvre et Maine. $($)

Formerly one of the most important grower-*négociants,* under the name Chéreau-Carré, the house has been divided between the two heirs, with each sibling receiving several prime vineyards. Château de Chasseloir, one of muscadet's finest vineyards, stays with Bernard, and he continues to make two cuvées, a very good basic bottling and the excellent Comte Leloup de Chasseloir from vines over a hundred years old. He has also kept the very good l'Oiselinière de la Ramée, a bracing, vivacious muscadet.

Véronique Chéreau-Günther

44690 St.-Fiacre-sur-Maine; 02.40.54.85.24; fax: 02.51.71.60.96

Wine: Muscadet de Sèvre et Maine. $($)

Véronique Chéreau-Günther, Bernard's sister, inherited another family jewel: the gorgeous Château de Coing de St.-Fiacre vineyard, fully the equal of Château de Chasseloir. From this vineyard she makes four muscadets—a basic bottling; a barrel-fermented cuvée; Comte de St. Hubert (from selected old vines); and Tradition Millénaire, made from vines over a hundred years old. It's nearly impossible to make bad muscadet from land this good, but I wonder if the wines wouldn't be more distinctive if there were merely two cuvées rather than four. Chéreau-Günther has also inherited two additional vineyards, Château de la Gravelle and Grand Fief de la Cormeraie, both very good.

Domaine de la Chevalerie

37140 Restigné; 02.47.97.37.18; fax: 02.47.97.45.87
Wine: Bourgueil. $ to $$
This family domaine, created in 1640, has magnificent troglodyte cellars. The Bourgueils, made by Pierre Caslot, are pretty good too, particularly the cuvées Busardières and Galichets. And the prices are reasonable.

Cheverny

Small central Loire AC in a town of the same name with a château of the same name. The light, simple whites are predominantly sauvignon blanc, blended or not with chardonnay, chenin blanc, and arbois. The light country reds and rosés are essentially gamay with or without the addition of cabernet franc, pinot noir, and côt. Rosés may also use pineau d'Aunis. In general, drink the youngest available, preferably in a funky bistro. Note that producers of Cheverny may also make wines under the TOURAINE AC, which Cheverny AC resembles, as well as the COUR-CHEVERNY AC, made only from the rare romorantin grape.

PRICES: $ to $$

PRODUCERS: Cave des Vignerons de Mont-Près-Chambord: a good local cooperative with reliably correct versions of both Cheverny and Cour-Cheverny ◆ François Cazin (Le Petit Chambord): a frequent presence on wine-bar blackboards, Cazin makes above-average Cour-Cheverny and light, fragrant Chevernys in both red and white ◆ CLOS DU TUE-BOEUF (PUZELAT BROTHERS) ◆ CONFRÉRIE DE VIGNERONS DE OISLY ET THÉSÉE ◆ Dom de la Désoucherie (Christian and Fabien Tessier): reliable family domaine, with pungent whites and reds as light and juicy as fruit punch (serve chilled). Look for the 2003 Solea, a rich expression of Cour-Cheverny ◆ DOM DES HUARDS ◆ Jérôme Marcadet: distinctive versions of the AC. Look for the Cuvée des Gourmets (red), Cuvée de l'Orme (white), and the refreshing rosé ◆ DOM DU MOULIN/HERVÉ VILLEMADE ◆ Dom Sauger: an eco-friendly domaine making personalized versions of the AC ◆ Philippe Tessier: a recent convert to organic viticulture, Tessier makes good Cour-Cheverny (Les Sables and Porte Dorée) as well as direct, ripe versions of Cheverny.

François Chidaine ☆

37270 Montlouis-sur-Loire; 02.47.45.19.14; francois.chidaine@wanadoo.fr
Wines: Montlouis and Vouvray. $ to $$$
This dedicated winemaker goes from strength to strength. After transforming his 17 hectares of Montlouis to biodynamics, he rented 10 hectares of prime vineyards in Vouvray from among Philippe Poniatowski's best sites. Chidaine's wines are characterized by their accuracy and limpidity. They are rectilinear, graceful, and mineral. Cuvées include Les Choisilles, Clos du Breuil (usually dry), Les Tuffeaux, Clos Habert (a single vineyard with old vines), and Le Lys (usually sweet) in Montlouis; and Clos Baudoin (dry), Les Argiles, and Le Bouchet in Vouvray.

Chinon

A central Loire AC for reds, whites, and rosés, Chinon takes its name from a small, historic town on the banks of the Vienne. There is an anecdotal (though growing) amount of white Chinon made from chenin blanc, but most of the wines are red, made from cabernet franc. Producers usually offer at least two different bottlings of red, a *vin de soif* (thirst-quenching wine) made from either young vines and/or wines from lighter, generally alluvial soils; and a more serious red from older vines and/or soils rich in clay and chalk. The first type of Chinon should be buoyant and juicy, with vivid fruit and lively acidity; it is best served slightly chilled. The second, often aged in barrel, offers the same characteristics on a more structured and serious level, and adds spices, sandalwood, and musk to the flavor spectrum. At best, these are silky, fine-grained, and elegant cabernet francs with finely etched fruit and soft tannins. Both styles of Chinon rouge, if underripe or machine harvested, can be herbaceous.

BEST RECENT VINTAGES: 2005, (2004, for those who kept yields low), 2003, 2002. Best vinatges of the recent past: 1997, 1996, 1995, 1990, 1989.
PRICES: $ to $$$

PRODUCERS: PHILIPPE ALLIET ☆ ◆ DOM BERNARD BAUDRY ☆ ◆ CH DE LA BONNELIÈRE ↑ ◆ CATHÉRINE & PIERRE BRETON ◆ Dom des Béguineries: Jean-Christophe Pelletier makes several tasty bottlings of Chinon, some oaked (the Vieilles Vignes and Cuvée Élise, for example), some not (Cuvée du Terroir) ◆ Dom de la Chapelle: Philippe Pichard has progressed significantly over the past five years, although the evidence of his growth is, for now, manifested solely in the cuvée L'Archestral. Based on low yields, it is aged in new oak and is neither fined nor filtered. At $$ to $$$, it's a bit steep but it's a very good, stylish Chinon ◆ CH DE COULAINE ↑ ◆ COULY-DUTHEIL ☆ ◆ PIERRE-JACQUES DRUET ◆ CH DE LA GRILLE ◆ DOM CHARLES JOGUET ◆ Patrick Lambert: a solid producer with a deliciously gulpable Chinon and a more serious, meaty, oak-aged Chinon ◆ Guy Lenoir: ultrahonest, handcrafted Chinons that can be mighty tasty—if they haven't stayed too long in barrel ◆ Le Moulin de Sablons: Stéphane Filliatreau doesn't seem ready for prime time but he's surely worth following, particularly for his Clos de la Ville au Maire Vieilles Vignes bottling, with its inborn elegance. Filliatreau also makes Touraine AC at the Ch du Petit Thouars ↑ ◆ Dom de la Noblaie (Manzagol-Billard): there has been dramatic improvement in the wines from this domaine with the advent of the current generation, Jérôme Billard, who did stints at Pétrus and in California and New Zealand. The (unfined and unfiltered) reds, particularly the age-worthy Pierre de Tuf, are full, ripe, and well-balanced; the white Chinons, which were always good, are now the best in the AC ↑ ◆ DOM DE NOIRÉ ☆ ◆ Jean-Louis Page: three cuvées of light, charming Chinon of which my favorite is the unoaked bottling ◆ Dom de la Perrière: Christophe Baudry is a dependable producer of above-average Chinons in both a drink-me-up style and a more serious version ◆ Dom Olga Raffault: a *must* for those who want to try a good, old-fashioned Chinon ◆ Dom du Raifault: Julien Raffault's cuvée Clos du Villy is a gracious version of Chinon. Other cuvées, as well as the white Chinon, are also worth trying, and the 2004 and 2005 are scrumptious ◆ Philippe Richard: formerly an address for locals who stopped by the cellars to stock up on easy-drinking Chinon, this domaine has begun to emerge on the market with several tasty cuvées of red: Vieilles Vignes and Tyfaine, and the oak-aged Tymothe ◆ Dom de la Roche Honneur: Diamont Prestige is the most powerful of Stéphane Mureau's potent, muscular Chinons ◆ Dom du Roncée: Christophe Baudry and Jean-Martin Dufour teamed up to take over this sizable domaine, where they make a range of good versions of Chinon. The cuvées Coteau des Chenanceaux and Clos des Marronniers are recommended ◆ Wilfrid Rousse: warm, supple Chinons from a conscientious vigneron ◆ Ch de Saint-Louand: tasty, no-nonsense Chinons.

Clau de Nell ↑
49700 Ambillou-Château; tel/fax: 02.41.59.35.29
Wines: Anjou range. $$($)
Talk about unique. Nelly and Claude Pichard can substantiate that claim many times over. Their small domaine, which they bought in 2000 and are converting to biodynamics, is devoted to dry and sweet reds and rosés made from grolleau and cabernet franc. The Pichards practice extremely low yields, harvesting grape by grape before hand-carrying the fruit to a gentle eighteenth-century wood press. Each cuvée is dedicated to a relative who influenced that particular wine: Thus for Marie-Louise, a barrel-fermented dry rosé of grolleau, a Vin de Table full of character; for Vincent, an unfined, unfiltered dry red from grolleau fermented in large oak barrels, which results in a superb Vin de Pays du Jardin de la France that comes across more like a Burgundy; for Norbert, a fragrant *barrique*-aged Anjou rouge, pure cabernet franc; for Paulette, an irrefutably sweet rosé of cabernet franc so tasty it could make converts to this style of wine; and for Albert, a sweet red from cabernet franc, admirable. OK. They're not cheap. But they are 100 percent handcrafted, and I wouldn't miss them for the world.

Domaine du Clos Naudin (Philippe Foreau) ☆
37210 Vouvray; 02.47.52.71.46; fax: 02.47.52.73.81
Wine: Vouvray. $$ to $$$
Vintage after vintage, Philippe Foreau turns out benchmark Vouvrays of great purity and elegance. Everything is fervently recommended, even the sparkling wines that Foreau ages for several years longer than the norm. There has been no chaptalization in this house since 1984. If you need to be converted to Vouvray, try here.

Clos du Papillon: Splendid vineyard in the Savennières AC, meriting *cru* status, alongside Coulée de Serrant and La Roche aux Moines. Producers: DOM DES BAUMARD ☆; DOM DU CLOSEL.

Clos Roche Blanche ☆
41110 Mareuil-sur-Cher; 02.54.75.17.03; fax: 02.54.75.17.02
Wine: Touraine. $ to $$
Didier Barrouillet and Catherine Roussel make succulent organic wine in the heart of the Cher, including lush sauvignon blanc, peppery pineau d'Aunis, and old-vines côt that could not be more delicious.

Clos Rougeard ☆
49400 Chacé; 02.41.52.92.65; fax: 02.41.52.98.34
Wines: Saumur-Champigny, Saumur blanc, Coteaux de Saumur. $$ to $$$
Charly and Nady Foucault, who make wine the way their granddaddy did, have a cult following. Their three Champignys, which include Les Poyeux and Le Bourg, age for up to two years in new or newish Bordeaux barrels. They are unfiltered, full of character, often controversial, and usually scrumptious. A recent, welcome addition is a Saumur blanc Brézé, a fine dry chenin. When the vintage permits, they also make delectable barrel-fermented sweet Chenin Coteaux de Saumur. All can age.

Clos du Tue-Boeuf (Puzelat Brothers)
41120 Les Montils; 02.54.44.05.16; fax 02.54.44.13.37
Wines: Touraine, Cheverny, and Vin de Pays. $ to $$
Darlings of the current generation of Paris wine bars and pioneers of hypernatural winemaking in France, Thierry and Jean-Marie Puzelat practice organic viticulture with low yields; they use indigenous yeasts and never filter wines that ferment in barrel. The results are light, true, mineral wines with seemingly fragile structures. Among roughly a dozen different bottlings, several are spicy versions of Cheverny rouge, either blends of gamay and pinot noir

or pure pinot noir; Le Frileuse, a Cheverny blanc (a blend of sauvignon and chardonnay); and several Touraine ACs, including Le Buisson Pouilleux Vieilles Vignes, a barrel-fermented old-vines sauvignon blanc. Thierry also acts as *négociant*, offering a range of Touraine wines made in the same style as Tue-Boeuf.

Domaine du Closel/Château des Vaults

49170 Savennières; 02.41.72.81.00; www.savennieres-closel.com
Wines: Savennières and Anjou-Villages. $$
Madame de Jessey, a grand local presence, has expanded the domaine she inherited from her great-grandfather, who was a chamberlain of Napoléon Bonaparte, and her wines have improved steadily over the past decade. She is fortunate to have a good chunk of the Clos du Papillon, and it is always her best wine.

Domaine Patrice Colin

41100 Thoré-la-Rochette; 02.54.72.80.73; patrice.colin1@tiscali.fr
Wine: Coteaux du Vendômois. $
A dedicated winemaker who produces some of the best versions of Vendômois wine, particularly his reds and rosés (*vins gris*) based on pineau d'Aunis (especially Les Vignes d'Émilien Colin) and his special cuvées of chenin blanc, such as the sweet La Pente des Coutis.

Domaine du Collier ↑

49400 Chacé; tel/fax: 02.41.52.69.22
Wines: Red and white Saumur. $$($)
Like father, like son. Antoine Foucault, the son of Charly Foucault (CLOS ROUGEARD), has been making wine on the well-positioned hillsides of Brézé since 1999. The results have been very promising, particularly the barrel-fermented white and the oak-aged La Ripaille, his most ambitious cabernet franc.

Confrérie des Vignerons de Oisly et Thésée

41700 Oisly; 02.54.79.75.20; oisly.thesee@wanadoo.fr
Wines: Touraine and Cheverny. $ to $$
A dynamic association of Cher valley growers. Applying ever more stringent standards, the *confrérie* makes a wide range of wines, all reliably good. Best are the estate bottlings, including Domaine du Bouc and Château de Vallagon. There is also a small percentage of organic wine.

Domaine des Corbillières

41700 Oisly, 02.54.79.52.75; dominique.barbou@wanadoo.fr
Wine: Touraine. $ to $$
A fine address for Touraines, particularly the Cuvée Justine Barbou, a delectable old-vines sauvignon blanc, and the Cuvée Angéline, a delicious Touraine red based on côt and cabernet.

Bruno Cormerais

44190 St.-Lumine de Clisson; 02.40.03.85.84; fax: 02.40.06.68.74
Wine: Muscadet de Sèvre et Maine. $($)
Truly fine muscadets in a range of styles, from light and sassy to ample and characterful, especially Cuvée Chambaudière, Cuvée Vieilles Vignes, Réserve Granit de Clisson, and a novel Vin de Pays, an oak-aged red blend made from cabernet franc, cabernet sauvignon, and abouriou.

Pascal Cotat

18300 Sancerre; tel/fax: 02.48.54.14.00
Wine: Sancerre. $$($)
Tiny production from the steep slopes of La Grande Côte and Les Monts Damnés. Yields are low, grapes are harvested when extremely ripe, and the resulting wines are often off-dry if not downright sweet. Among the few in this appellation that benefit from cellaring, these are big, cult Sancerres, full of minerals and character. Regrettably, Cotat is phasing out his extraordinary rosé.

Coteaux d'Ancenis

A small AC east of Nantes on essentially the same turf as Muscadet–Coteaux de la Loire. Source of pale, light, dry and off-dry whites made from chenin blanc and pinot gris (locally called malvoisie) and light reds and rosés made from gamay, cabernet franc, and sauvignon. Drink the youngest available.

PRICES: $

PRODUCERS: Athimon & Ses Enfants: steadfast family domaine, the wines of which should be sampled locally ◆ Dom Pierre Guindon: reliable family winery, particularly known for off-dry malvoisie ◆ Vignerons des Terroirs de la Noëlle: good cooperative with satisfactory renditions of the AC.

Coteaux de l'Aubance

A small AC south of Angers for off-dry to extremely sweet whites made from overripe, botrytized, and/or sun-shriveled chenin blanc. Generally more nervy than similar wines from the Layon. Since 2002 the wine label may state SGN (Sélection de Grains Nobles) for wines with a natural potential alcohol content of 17.5 percent. The number of excellent producers is relatively high.

BEST RECENT VINTAGES: 2003, 2002, 1997, 1996, 1995. Best vintages of the recent past: 1990, 1989, 1988.
PRICES: $$ to $$$

PRODUCERS: Dom des Charbotières: not quite ready for prime time, this domaine has taken the hypernatural route, with promising results. The Aubance is a bit heavy but ambitious and worth following ↑ ◆ DOMAINE DE BABLUT ☆ ◆ Dom de Haute Perche: Christian Papin makes reliably good Aubance, whether the traditional bottling or the oak-aged Les Fontenelles ◆ DOM DE MONTGILET ☆ ◆ DOM RICHOU ☆ ◆ DOM DES ROCHELLES ☆.

Coteaux du Giennois

A small AC spanning both banks of the Loire north of Sancerre and Pouilly. The whites, made from sauvignon blanc, are generally like Sancerre on a diet; reds and rosés, from a blend of gamay and pinot noir, can, in the right hands, be totally charming. Drink the youngest available.

PRICES: $($)

PRODUCERS: Balland-Chapuis: see DOM GUY SAGET ◆ HENRI BOURGEOIS ☆ ◆ Michel Langlois: the oak-aged red and the mineral-scented white are worth trying ◆ CAVES DE POUILLY-SUR-LOIRE ◆ GITTON PÈRE & FILS ◆ Lycée Agricole de Cosne-sur-Loire: respectable versions of the AC from the local school. Look for the Cuvée Prestige ◆ ALAIN PAULAT.

Coteaux du Layon and Coteaux du Layon-Villages

Key Anjou AC for sweet whites made from overripe, botrytized, and/or sun-shriveled chenin blanc grapes. Depending on the vintage and the vintner, the wines range from *moelleux,* to *doux,* to *liquoreux;* some are practically marmalade. The natural acidity of chenin blanc, however, keeps the wines fresh, balanced, and appetizing.

Six villages may attach their names to the AC. They are Faye-d'Anjou, St.-Lambert du Lattay, Rablay-sur-Layon, Beaulieu-sur-Layon, Rochefort-sur-Loire, and St.-Aubin-de-Luigné. The most complex examples seem to come from the last three, where the schist-based soils are striated with a variety of spilite, feldspar, quartz, phtanite, and much more. The wines can age almost indefinitely, when they can become heartstoppingly nuanced. See also BONNEZEAUX, CHAUME, and QUARTS-DE-CHAUME, which are considered *crus* of the Layon.

LOIRE

Since 2002 wine labels may state SGN (Sélection de Grains Nobles) for wines with a natural potential alcohol content of 17.5 percent.

BEST RECENT VINTAGES: 2005, 2003, (2002 despite occasional and very minor whiffs of geosmin), 1997, 1996, 1995. Best vintages of the recent past: 1990, 1989, 1988. Great older vintages include 1976, 1975, 1971, 1969, 1959, 1955, 1949, 1947.
PRICES: $$ to $$$$

PRODUCERS: DOM DES BARRES ↑ ◆ PATRICK BAUDOUIN ◆ DOM DES BAUMARD ☆ ◆ DOM DE LA BERGERIE ↑ ☆ ◆ DOM DE BRIZÉ ◆ PHILIPPE CADY ☆ ◆ Domaine des Closserons: consistently superior family domaine, particularly for Layon-Faye ◆ DOM PHILIPPE DELESVAUX ☆ ◆ Domaine des Deux Vallées: see CHAUME ↑ ◆ CH DE FESLES ◆ DOMAINE DES FORGES ☆ ◆ CH LA FRESNAYE ↑ ◆ JEAN-CHRISTOPHE GARNIER ↑ ◆ DOM LES GRANDES VIGNES ↑ ◆ Domaine des Griottes: a young, hypernatural domaine with wines that, while promising, are works in progress; for example, an extremely oaky, syrupy Layon La Navine ↑ ◆ Dom Grosset: rustic, unreconstructed versions of the entire range of Anjou wines; the Layons and the Chaume are not without a certain prehistoric charm ◆ DOM DE JUCHEPIE ☆ ◆ Vincent Lecointre/Ch la Tomaze: a good family domaine for the entire range of Anjous; Layons are lighter and less sweet than those from the Rochefort area but are very good ◆ RICHARD LEROY ☆ ◆ VINCENT OGEREAU ☆ ◆ Dom du Petit Metris: see CHAUME ◆ DOM DU PETIT VAL ◆ CH PIERRE-BISE ☆ ◆ DOM JO PITHON ☆ Ch de Plaisance: See CHAUME ◆ DOM DU REGAIN ↑ ◆ DOM DU ROY RENÉ ↑ ◆ DOM DES SABLONNETTES ↑ ◆ DOM GUY SAGET ◆ CH SOUCHERIE ☆.

Coteaux du Loir

Small AC in La Sarthe, north of Tours. With Jasnières and the Vendômois, the northernmost Loire AC. Whites are made from chenin blanc; reds and rosés from pineau d'Aunis, gamay, côt, and cabernet. Up to 25 percent grolleau may be used in the rosés. In general, drink the youngest available, though some age astonishingly well.

PRICES: $ to $$

PRODUCERS: (LES VIGNES DE) L'ANGE VIN ↑ ◆ Aubert la Chapelle: see JASNIÈRES ◆ DOM DE BELLIVIÈRE ☆ ◆ DOM LE BRISEAU (CHRISTIAN CHAUSSARD) ↑ ◆ Dom de Cézin (François Fresnau): see JASNIÈRES ◆ Dom de la Charrière (Joel Gigou): see JASNIÈRES.

Coteaux de Saumur

An AC for nervy off-dry to very sweet whites made from chenin blanc in a zone roughly the same as, though a bit more extensive than, Saumur-Champigny. The small (but growing) number of producers who make wine there generally do so only in good vintages. All the producers recommended here are described in the Saumur or Saumur-Champigny entries.

BEST RECENT VINTAGES: 2005, 2003. Best vintages of the recent past: 1997, 1996, 1990, 1989.
PRICES: $$

PRODUCERS: DOM DES CHAMPS FLEURIS ↑ ◆ CLOS ROUGEARD ☆ ◆ Yves Drouineau: see SAUMUR-CHAMPIGNY ◆ DOM LAVIGNE ◆ Dom de Nerleux: see SAUMUR-CHAMPIGNY ◆ ☆ CH DE VILLENEUVE ☆.

Coteaux du Vendômois

Outside the provincial town of Vendôme, the vineyards of this small AC are dispersed along patches of hillsides. Pleasant, light whites are made from chenin blanc with the possible addition of chardonnay. Slender, simple reds and rosés are made from pineau d'Aunis (minimum 40 percent) and limited amounts of gamay, cabernet, and pinot noir. *Vin gris* from pineau d'Aunis is the AC's most interesting and representative wine. Drink the youngest available.

PRICES: $

PRODUCERS: Dom du Carroir: Jean and Benoît Brazilier produce pleasant whites, appetizing rosés (or *vins gris*), and a good Tradition ◆ Cave des Vignerons du Vendômois: the cooperative accounts for more than half the production of the AC's wines. They do a respectable job. Part of ALLIANCE LOIRE, they make a line of wines in the *lieu-dit* program ◆ DOM PATRICE COLIN ◆ DOM DU FOUR À CHAUX ◆ Dom Minier: this small family domaine multitasks, making really tasty goat cheese and funky local wine ◆ DOM DE MONTRIEUX (ÉMILE HÉRÉDIA) ↑

Côte Roannaise

Small AC on the outskirts of Roanne, due west of Beaujolais. Based on gamay, the often beguiling reds and rosés from the Roannaise have more in common with their eastern neighbors than they do with wines from the heart of the Loire. The best, however, have a silky, mountain breeziness unique to this region. Generally drink the youngest available.

PRICES: $

PRODUCERS: Alain Baillon: the cuvée Montplaisir, based on very old gamay vines, is well worth trying ◆ Paul Lapandéry: a dauntingly steep slope, very low yields, long barrel age, and no filtration make the most ruggedly (and engagingly) individual wines from this AC. And don't miss the succulent, inexpensive Vin de Pays d'Urfé made from pinot noir, so good it merits a star ◆ Dom du Pavillon: a good family domaine with nice reds and even nicer rosés ◆ Jacques Plasse: tasty light reds include Boutheran and a cuvée Vieilles Vignes ◆ Robert Serol: well established in the region, the Serols make several commercial cuvées of Roannaise wine with the Troisgros family, of three-Michelin-star fame.

Côtes d'Auvergne

Loire VDQS on the steep slopes south of Clermont-Ferrand known for light whites, reds, and rosés. Five villages may include their names on labels: Boudes, Chanturgues, Châteaugay, Corent (particularly for rosés), and Madargue.

GRAPES: Whites are made from chardonnay; reds and rosés, from gamay and pinot noir. Drink the youngest available.

PRICES: $

PRODUCERS: (VIGNOBLE DE) L'ARBRE BLANC ◆ Yvan Bernard: the Corent reds and rosés from this young, ambitious domaine would make delightful wine-bar discoveries ◆ Cave St.-Verny: this good cooperative, owned by Limagrain, Europe's largest seed specialist, produces above-average versions of the region's wine. Look for the oak-aged Prestige bottlings, the cuvée Renaissance, a blend of gamay and pinot noir, and the Corent rosé ◆ Charmensat: a good family domaine, producing a pleasant range of wines from Boudes ◆ Pierre Goigoux: a passionate vigneron whose wines from Châteaugay are well above average ◆ DOM DE PEYRA ◆ Dom Sauvat: a solid family domaine with friendly, Auvergnat gamays, particularly Les Demoiselles Oubliées du Donazat and the oak-aged Prestige.

Côtes de Forez

A small (175-hectare) Loire AC producing drink-me-up reds and rosés from gamay. Drink the youngest available. Prices: $. Producers: Gilles Bonnefoy ◆ Clos de Chozieux ◆ Vignerons Foréziens ◆ Domaine du Poyet ◆ Odile Verdier.

Château de Coulaine ↑

37420 Beaumont-en-Veron; 02.47.98.44.51; chateaudecoulaine@club-internet.fr
Wine: Chinon. $ to $$
The wines have steadily improved here since Étienne and Pascale de Bonnaventure, who have converted the family domaine to organic viticulture, took over in 1999. The top cuvée is La Diablesse, but this drinker prefers the simpler bottlings, including Clos de Turpenay.

Coulée de Serrant (the vineyard)

A *cru* of Savennières, and thus of Anjou, this 7-hectare vineyard, shaped like an amphitheater overlooking the Loire, must have been ordained by the wine gods, so perfect is its exposure and so complex are its soils (schist striated with volcanic rock). Wines made from this slope ought to be as majestic as the best Montrachets. That's not always the case. But such is the grandeur of Coulée de Serrant that it is always riveting despite less-than-meticulous vinification.

Coulée de Serrant (the winery)

49170 Savennières; 02.41.72.22.32; coulee-de-serrant@wanadoo.fr
Wines: Savennières, Coulée de Serrant, and La Roche aux Moines. $$ to $$$
The Joly family is the sole owner of the great *cru* Coulée de Serrant. Nicolas Joly, the current director of the domaine, is France's spokesperson for biodynamics, the principles of which are practiced in his vineyards. He is a magnetic speaker and seemingly passionate about viticulture. Winemaking is another story. It could, and should, be better. (His daughter is taking over winemaking, so optimism is in order.) Such is the greatness of this vineyard, however, that the wine is always significant, and often majestic. Joly suggests carafing the wine two days before serving. I suggest carafing the wine several hours before serving and keeping the carafe in a cool place.

Couly-Dutheil ☆

12 rue Diderot, 37502 Chinon Cedex; 02.47.97.20.20; fax: 02.47.97.20.25
Wines: Chinon, Bourgueil, Saumur-Champigny, and Saumur. $ to $$$
Important changes—at least structurally—are underway as Chinon's leading domaine sorts out succession issues. For now, know that the Chinons from 2002 through 2005 were excellent. Though the firm has interests in vineyards in neighboring appellations (such as La Minière in Bourgueil and Les Moulins de Turquant in Saumur-Champigny), Couly's nerve center is Chinon, where it currently produces solid versions in all colors, including a fragrant white, Le Chanteaux, and multiple bottlings of red. The simplest are Les Gravières and La Diligence. Domaine René Couly and Baronnie Madeleine occupy a middle ground for near-term drinking. At the top, the Clos de l'Olive is the most elegant and specific; the Clos de l'Écho, the warmest and manliest; and Crescendo, a special cuvée of selected lots from Écho aged in new oak, the most powerful. All but Gravières and La Diligence reward cellaring.

Cour-Cheverny

A microscopic AC parceled out over several communes in the heart of Cheverny AC, it is unique in that its wines—all white—are made from the romorantin grape, which was introduced into the area by François I in 1519. High in acidity, lightly viscous, often with a light note of oxidation, they age well and can take a good five years of cellaring.

BEST RECENT VINTAGES: 2005, (2004, where yields were controlled), 2002, 2003.
PRICES: $ to $$

PRODUCERS: The producers recommended here are more fully described in the Cheverny listing: Cave des Vignerons de Mont-Près-Chambord; Cazin/Le Petit Chambord; Dom de la Desoucherie; Dom des Huards (Michel Gendrier); Philippe Tessier.

Crémant de Loire

An AC for sparkling wine made throughout Anjou, Saumur, Cheverny, and Touraine adhering to stricter principles of harvesting, vinifying, and aging than those applicable to wines made using the *méthode traditionelle.* The permitted grape varieties include chenin blanc, cabernet franc, pineau d'Aunis, pinot noir, chardonnay, arbois, and grolleau (maximum of 30 percent). Most wines are not vintage dated; those that are generally represent *réserve* or special bottlings.

PRICES: $ to $$

PRODUCERS: DOM DES BAUMARD ☆ ◆ DOM DE BRIZÉ ◆ LANGLOIS-CHÂTEAU ◆ Dom de Nerleux: see SAUMUR-CHAMPIGNY ◆ CH DE PUTILLE ◆ DOM RICHOU ☆.

François Crochet ↑

18300 Bué; 02.48.54.21.77; fax: 02.48.54.25.10

Wine: Sancerre. $ to $$($)

In 2002 François succeeded his father, Robert. He's a young vigneron to follow, making delicious wines in three colors. His rosé is creamy, rich, and dry; his two red bottlings—the mellow, fruity basic cuvée and the richer cuvée Réserve de Marcigoue, which gets some new-oak age—are both delicious; and his whites (none of them oaked) are even better, particularly the two nonfiltered special bottlings, the limpid, mineral Les Amoureuses and the *terroir*-driven Chêne-Marchand, as bracing as a waterfall.

Lucien Crochet ☆

18300 Bué; 02.48.54.08.10; fax: 02.48.54.27.66

Wine: Sancerre. $$($)

Excellent Sancerre house. The wines from the *négociant* arm of the firm are just fine but the domaine-bottled Sancerres are the ones to look for, starting with La Croix du Roy in both red and white. Cuvée Prestige, made from old vines, is the top wine in both colors and is often released several years after the harvest. It is first-rate. In great vintages Crochet also makes a powerful late-harvest white.

Didier Dagueneau ☆

58150 St.-Andelain; 03.86.39.15.62; silex@wanadoo.fr

Wine: Pouilly-Fumé. $$ to $$$$

Considered one of the best white-wine makers of his generation, the perpetually controversial Dagueneau launched the quality revolution (as yet incomplete) in the Sancerrois. He makes four cuvées of Pouilly-Fumé: En Chailloux is full and aromatic. Buisson Renard comes from a parcel making markedly pungent, even "foxy" wines. The barrel-fermented Pur-Sang lives up to its name, which translates as Thoroughbred. And Silex, also barrel-fermented, is as expensive and as majestic as a top Burgundy. Additionally, there's Astéroïde, made from late-harvested grapes grown on ungrafted vines. It is so rare one wonders if it actually exists. Dagueneau also acquired a property in Jurançon; 2003 was his first vintage.

Serge Dagueneau & Filles ☆

58150 Pouilly-sur-Loire; 03.86.39.11.18; www.s-dagueneau-filles.fr

Wines: Pouilly-Fumé and Pouilly-sur-Loire. $$

Didier's uncle and his cousins Valérie and Florence, both of whom have worked at the Peter Michel Winery in Calistoga, make brawny, forthright Pouillys. There's nothing subtle about the top cuvée, Clos des Chaudoux, but its freshness balances its power. Les Filles is an extremely rich, mouthfilling, late-harvest bottling. The Dagueneaus make the best Pouilly-sur-Loire (based on very old vines, it's a must-taste), as well as several Vins de Pays des Coteaux Charitois, including a light pinot noir that would be a charming discovery in a wine bar.

Domaine Philippe Delesvaux ☆

49190 St.-Aubin-de-Luigné; 02.41.78.18.71; dom.delesvaux.philippe@wanadoo.fr
Wines: Anjou range, especially Layon. $ to $$$
A serious winemaker with stellar Sélection de Grains Nobles wines. Layons from Delesvaux's St. Aubin-de-Luigné vineyards are also very good, sometimes excellent. Delesvaux makes an ambitious, late-harvested, barrel-fermented Anjou blanc sec Feuille d'Or and a couple of juicy reds—Anjou rouge (cabernet franc) and Anjou-Villages (cabernet sauvignon, aged in oak).

Deletang ☆

37270 Montlouis-sur-Loire; 02.47.50.67.25; deletang.olivier@wanadoo.fr
Wines: Montlouis and Touraine. $ to $$($)
Textbook Montlouis from a reliable family domaine. The range includes the mineral Les Petits Boulay and—a particular favorite for its concentration and character—Les Bâtisses. Both are made as sec and demi-sec, vintage permitting. Deletang also makes good Touraine reds and whites, notably a brisk sauvignon blanc.

Michel Delhommeau ↑

44690 Monnières; 02.40.54.60.37; michel.delhommeau@wanadoo.fr
Wine: Muscadet de Sèvre et Maine. $
A very promising newcomer making mineral-rich muscadets based on low yields and long aging on the lees, particularly the Cuvées Harmonie and Vieilles Vignes.

Pierre-Jacques Druet

37140 Benais; 02.47.97.37.34; pjdruet@wanadoo.fr
Wines: Bourgueil and Chinon. $ to $$$
A wizard in the cellar, Druet produces some fine-grained Chinon (especially Clos de Danzay) and a broad range of Bourgueils—a supple, barrel-aged rosé; a juicy, early-drinking Cent Boissellées (increasingly aimed at supermarkets); a medium-bodied Beauvais; and Grand Mont and Vaumoreau, both age- and noteworthy.

Domaine de l'Écu ☆

La Bretonnière, 44430 Le Landreau; 02.40.06.40.91; bossard.guy.muscadet@wanadoo.fr
Wines: Muscadet de Sèvre et Maine, Gros-Plant du Pays Nantais, Vins de Pays and de Table. $($)
Guy Bossard is, quite simply, one of the best, most honest, most self-effacing winemakers in France. Having practiced organic viticulture since 1972, he converted his estate to biodynamics in the early 90s. His gros-plant is better than most muscadets; his cabernet Vin de Pays rivals many Saumurs; his sparkling wine, sold as Vin de Table, outclasses top *crémants*; and his muscadet, of which there are three versions, is sensational. Named after their soils, the tenderest is labeled Expression de Gneiss, the ampler midrange is Expression de Orthogneiss, and the heavy hitter is Expression de Granite, a beautifully elegant, mineral white that ages with surprising grace and power. If you doubt muscadet can be serious, taste here.

Château d'Épiré

49170 Savennières; 02.41.77.15.01; luc.bizard@wanadoo.fr
Wines: Savennières and Anjou rouge. $$
A dreamily beautiful estate making very good (and steadily improving) Savennières, including a textured, generally unfiltered Cuvée Spéciale made

from the best grapes, the single-vineyard Le Hu-Boyau, and the sweet Cuvée Armand Bizard. There is also a fragrant Anjou rouge, Clos de la Cerisaie.

Ferme de la Sansonnière

49380 Thouarce; tel/fax: 02.41.54.08.08

Wines: Anjou, including Bonnezeaux. $$ to $$$

Mark Angeli could be the poster boy for biodynamics (in the nicest possible way, of course). Changing the name of the winery from *domaine* to *ferme* says it all. Angeli can make celestial Bonnezeaux, but perpetual iconoclast that he is, he has decided not to produce Bonnezeaux every year. Dry wines now fascinate him. And, though his ambitious experiments don't always work, even the less-than-successful cuvées of Anjou blanc sec, Anjou rouge, gamay, and the rosés are intriguing. When on target, they're also scrumptious, original, unique. (One favorite is the Anjou blanc Les Fouchardes.)

Château de Fesles

49380 Thouarce; 02.41.68.94.00; loire@vgas.com

Wines: Anjou range, especially Bonnezeaux and Coteaux du Layon. $$ to $$$

This historic château, which, under a previous owner, pioneered the production of top-quality sweet wines in Anjou, is now owned by Vignobles Germain and is part of a package that also includes the Château de Roulerie in the Layon, another venerable domaine, which had been known for its glorious Chaumes "les Aunis." Today, the wines are stylish and correct. Germain's range of wines also includes Anjou rouge and Savennières.

Le Fief Guérin/Domaine des Herbauges

44830 Bouaye; 02.40.65.44.92; j.choblet@wanadoo.fr

Wines: Muscadet Côtes de Grand Lieu, Gros-Plant, and Vin de Pays. $($)

Jérôme and Luc Choblet, the owners of this fine family domaine, are the leading producers of Muscadet Côtes de Grand Lieu, making wines every bit as good as those from Sèvre et Maine. Look for Domaine des Herbauges, Clos de la Fine, Clos de la Senaigerie, and Fief Guerin. They also produce pleasant Vin de Pays in all three colors.

Fiefs Vendéens

VDQS near the Atlantic coast beach resort Les Sables d'Olonnes consisting of four distinct enclaves: Pissotte, Vix, Brem-sur-Mer, and Mareuil-sur-Lay. The white wines are blends of chardonnay, chenin blanc, colombard, melon, and sauvignon blanc. Reds and rosés are made from cabernet franc and sauvignon, gamay, and pinot noir. Groslot gris and négrette also enter into the mix. Most are adequate beach wines; some are distinctly more. Drink the youngest available.

PRICES: $

PRODUCERS: Dom de la Barbinière: just beyond the limits of the appellation, Philippe Orion sells his very good wine as Vin de Pays de Vendée. A pity. They'd be among the best wines in the VDQS ◆ Xavier Coirier: located in Pissotte, this family winery is one of the best in the appellation ◆ Mourat Père & Fils/Ch Marie du Fou: based in Mareuil-sur-Lay, the domaine makes pleasant, easy-drinking reds ◆ DOM SAINT-NICOLAS ☆.

LOIRE

Paul Filliatreau ☆

49400 Dampierre-sur-Loire; 02.41.52.90.84; fax: 02.41.52.49.92

Wines: Saumur and Saumur-Champigny. $$

Paul Filliatreau put Saumur-Champigny on the map and on Paris wine lists with his reliable, user-friendly versions, of which there are a range of bottlings. There's the all-too-gulpable Jeunes Vignes; the more serious Vieilles Vignes and La Grande Vignole; Lena Filliatreau (made from purchased grapes); a *barrique*-aged, old-vines cuvée L'Affûtée; and both a white and a red Saumur AC, Cuvée Imago and Château Fouquet, respectively.

Domaine des Forges/Vignobles Branchereau ☆

49190 St.-Aubin-de-Luigné; 02.41.78.33.56; vitiforge@wanadoo.fr

Wines: Nearly the entire range of Anjous, including Savennières and Quarts-de-Chaume. $ to $$$

A solid family winery with vineyards in Quarts-de-Chaume, Chaume, Coteaux du Layon–St. Aubin, and Savennières Roche aux Moines. Wines from these appellations always do credit to Anjou, as do the dry whites, reds, and rosés from less prestigious ACs.

Domaine du Four à Chaux

41100 Thore la Rochette; 02.54.77.12.52; fax: 02.54.80.23.22

Wine: Coteaux du Vendômois. $ to $$

For the past twenty years, fortysomething Dominique Norguet, the owner of this domaine, has been one of the moving forces—as well as one of the best producers—of this small AC. Everything is recommended, but my favorite wines from Norguet are those he makes from pineau d'aunis, whether rosé or red, when it might be blended with gamay or pinot noir.

Château la Fresnaye ↑

49190 St.-Aubin-de-Luigné; tel/fax: 02.41.54.78.55; pbaudin@chateaulafresnaye.fr

Wines: Anjou range, including Coteaux du Layon and Anjou-Villages. $ to $$

A young domaine (first vintage 1999) with good land, good principles, and enormous promise. The chenins are particularly successful, from the barrel-fermented Anjou blanc sec—especially the concentrated, serious Cuvée l'Échalier—to a number of gorgeous cuvées of Layon, including La Dame Blanche; a beauty from vines just beyond the Bonnezeaux limits; and, in 2003, a velvety Cuvée L as rich and honeyed as a top Sauternes. But don't ignore the Anjou rouge. The grandfather of Julien Coutenceau, one of the young owners of Fresnaye, was Hubert Lebreton, the man who pioneered red wine production in Anjou. Fresnaye's barrel-aged Cuvée Festina Lente (two thirds cabernet sauvignon) is a finely tuned blend of spice, oak, and ripe fruit.

Domaine Gadais Père & Fils

44690 St.-Fiacre-sur-Maine; 02.40.54.81.23; musgadais@wanadoo.fr

Wine: Muscadet de Sèvre et Maine. $ to $$

Very good family winery with riveting, taut muscadets, particularly the cuvées La Grande Réserve du Moulin and aux Avineaux.

Château Gaillard ☆

41150 Monteaux; 02.54.70.28.89; biovidis@libertysurf.fr

Wine: Touraine-Mesland. $ to $$

Vincent Girault, an early convert to biodynamics, makes the best wines in this subappellation. Look for impressive country reds, blends of cabernet, côt, and gamay, particularly the Vieilles Vignes bottling. He has also taken over his father's vineyard, Clos de la Briderie, in the same appellation; the Vieilles Vignes is a delicious red blend. And he makes a fruity, simple Vin de Table from an ancient local grape, le Gascou. Girault doesn't think Gascou is about to replace cabernet, but he doesn't want to let it disappear. Amen.

Jean-Christophe Garnier ↑

49700 Ambillou-Château; 06.11.19.53.53

Wines: White and rosé Anjou. $ to $$

An extremely promising newcomer to Anjou, practicing organic viticulture and maintaining very, very low yields. A source of sapid, fresh, and mineral Anjou blancs, including the concentrated late-harvest Les Dreuilles, which ages in barrel; a surprisingly singular (and tasty) rosé d'Anjou made from late-harvested grolleau; a fresh, dry rosé de Loire, based on grolleau gris; and an evolving series of experiments in the Vin de Table category.

Domaine de la Garrelière ☆
37120 Razines; 02.47.95.62.84; francois.plouzeau@wanadoo.fr
Wine: Touraine. $ to $$
The scion of a well-known Chinon-based *négociant*, François Plouzeau created his own domaine, adhering to biodynamic principles, in the less-prestigious AC Touraine, in a landscape of cereal crops and melon fields. His success is well deserved, as evidenced by his excellent range of bottlings, from such entry-level varietals as sauvignon blanc and gamay to more elaborate cuvées such as Cendrillon (chenin and sauvignon partially vinified in barrel) and Cinabre, an oak-aged cabernet franc. Plouzeau's wines are always good value for the dollar and always rewarding.

Château Gaudrelle ☆
37210 Vouvray; 02.47.52.67.50; gaudrelle1@libertysurf.fr
Wine: Vouvray. $$
Alexander Monmousseau champions *sec-tendre* (slightly off-dry) as the most representative style of Vouvray. And, indeed, his wines could be ambassadors for the style. They are classic in the best sense of the word. When the vintage permits, he makes super *moelleux* and *liquoreux* as well.

Gitton Père & Fils
18300 Ménétreol Sancerre; 02.48.54.38.84; cavegitton@worldonline.fr
Wines: Sancerre, Pouilly-Fumě, and Coteaux du Giennois. $ to $$
A large domaine that bottles its wines by parcel. It's a good principle, though with more than fifteen different cuvées of Sancerre, Pouilly-Fumé, and Coteaux du Giennois, Gitton may be overextended. It's often hard to tell the difference between one bottling and another. Best are Le Galinot, Les Belles Dames, and Les Herses.

Domaine les Grandes Vignes ↑
49380 Thouarce; 02.41.54.05.06; www.domainelesgrandesvignes.com
Wines: Anjou range, including Bonnezeaux. $ to $$($)
The Vaillant family is rapidly making a name for itself—for the high quality of its comprehensive range of organic Anjou wines, including exemplary versions of the three types of rosés. There are numerous bottlings, all recommendable, some irresistible. All whites ferment in newish oak barrels. My favorite among the Anjou blancs is the structured, mineral, very ripe Varenne de Combre; in Anjou-Villages, it's the plush, oak-aged, unfiltered Les Cocainelles; and in Layon, it's a tie between the sumptuous, beautifully balanced Sélection de Grains Nobles and the limpid, aristocratic Bonnezeaux Noble Sélection.

Domaine la Grange Tiphaine ↑
37400 Amboise; 02.47.57.64.17; lagrangetiphaine@ifrance.com
Wines: Montlouis and Touraine-Amboise. $$
Ambitious and idealistic, Damien Delecheneau, who is under thirty but looks all of fourteen, is barely out of enology school but quickly making a name for himself. An eco-friendly trained enologist, he makes the full range of Touraine-Amboise and Montlouis (including the red blend François 1er) and both dry and off-dry rosés. Everything is worth sampling. Some favorites: the deeply fruity, structured Touraine-Amboise côt Vielles Vignes; and the Clef de Sol, old-vines, the top-of-the-line bottlings in both appellations. In Montlouis, it's focused, vibrant, and mineral (the 2005 is demi-sec). In Touraine-Amboise, it's a pert, juicy blend of côt and cabernet that goes down all too easily.

Château de la Grille
BP 205 37502 Chinon Cedex; 02.47.93.01.95; fax: 02.47.93.45.91
Wine: Chinon. $$
La Grille's Chinons are atypical for their long barrel age (sixteen months). And the domaine stocks its wines in bottle for two years before marketing them. Upon release, the reds are warm, tannic, and spicy. The rosés, which ferment in barrel, are terrific.

Gros-Plant du Pays Nantais

Thin, acid white wine made from gros-plant (also known as folle blanche) produced throughout and beyond the muscadet region. Doctors once prescribed the wine as a diuretic. Drink the youngest available.

PRICES: $

PRODUCERS: ANDRÉ-MICHEL BRÉGEON ◆ Ch de Briacé: textbook versions from the local school for enology ◆ BRUNO CORMERAIS ◆ Dom le Demi-Boeuf: Michel Malidain makes one of the better versions of the beast ◆ DOM DE L'ÉCU ☆ ◆ DOM LES HAUTES NOËLLES ◆ DOM LANDRON ☆ ◆ PIERRE LUNEAU-PAPIN ☆.

Domaine Guiberteau ↑

49260 St.-Just-sur-Dive; 02.41.38.78.94; domaine.guiberteau@wanadoo.fr
Wine: Saumur. $$
A welcome addition to the Saumurois, Guiberteau makes ambitious and very tasty Saumur blanc and rouge, two versions of each. The domaine's top Saumur blanc, Les Clos, is textured and mineral, with light oak accents. Les Motelles and Les Ardoises, both Saumur rouge, are equally delicious, but I find the latter has more breed.

Domaine de la Haute Borne ↑

37210 Vouvray; tel/fax: 02.47.52.71.28
Wine: Vouvray. $ to $$
Vincent Carême is a young vigneron with good land and good winemaking philosophy. Not all of his Vouvrays are ready for prime time but they're certainly on the right path, particularly the 2002 demi-sec, a wine that always captivates me.

Domaine la Haute Févrie ☆

44690 Maisdon-sur-Sèvre; 02.40.36.94.08; haute-fevrie@netcourier.com
Wine: Muscadet. $ to $$
Claude Branger produces superb Muscadets de Sèvre et Maine *sur lie,* particularly the bottlings Excellence–Clos des Maugeitonnières, Excellence–Quartier Brison, and Terroir-les-Gras-Moutons, with their strong mineral cores and their texture of raw silk.

Domaine les Hautes Noëlles

44710 St.-Léger-les-Vignes; 02.40.31.53.49; fax: 02.40.04.87.80
Wine: Muscadet. $
The most visionary producer in the Muscadet–Côtes de Grand Lieu appellation, Serge Bâtard is a former wine-shop owner who brings a bit of Burgundy to his top cuvée of muscadet, fermenting and aging it in oak barrels. He also makes a decent gros-plant and a range of quirky varietals, such as grolleau, as Vin de Pays.

Haut-Poitou

A small VDQS (Vin Délimité de Qualité Supérieure, but applying for promotion to AC) on the outskirts of the provincial town of Poitiers, producing easy-drinking reds, whites, and rosés from a number of grape varieties. Best are the sauvignon blanc and gamay. Drink the youngest available.

PRICES: $ to $$

PRODUCERS: AMPELIDAE ◆ Cave de Haut-Poitou: Beaujolais's Georges DuBoeuf holds a 40 percent share of what was formerly the local cooperative. The wines are well made. The best come from individual properties, such as Château de Brizay (sauvignon blanc) and Château la Fuye (cabernet) ◆ Dom des Lises: a promising new(ish) domaine, created by the enologist Pascale Bonneau.

Domaine des Herbauges: See LE FIEF GUÉRIN.

Domaine des Huards

Les Huards, 41700 Cour-Cheverny; 02.54.79.97.90; info@gendrier.com
Wines: Cheverny, Cour-Cheverny, and Touraine. $ to $$
Michel Gendrier converted this solid family domaine to biodynamics. He's a reliable source for good wine-bar reds, particularly Le Pressoir, made from 80 percent pinot noir and 20 percent gamay, and for his benchmark Cour-Cheverny, which benefits from a couple of years of cellaring.

Huet ☆

37210 Vouvray; 02.47.52.78.87; huet.echansonne@wanadoo.fr
Wine: Vouvray. $$ to $$$$$
This mythic Vouvray house, formerly owned by the legendary Gaston Huet, is the AC's benchmark. Recently Anthony Hwang, who owns an important winery in the Tokaj region of Hungary, purchased the majority share. Noël Pinguet, Huet's son-in-law, who has made the wines for the past twenty years and who converted the domaine to biodynamics, has a minority share and will continue at the helm. These are *terroir*-driven Vouvrays of great authority and power. They come from three prime vineyards overlooking the Loire: Le Haut Lieu, Le Mont, and Clos du Bourg.

Jardin de la France: See VIN DE PAYS DU JARDIN DE LA FRANCE.

Jasnières

AC for white wines made from chenin blanc grown on a four-kilometer-long vineyard in La Sarthe. The wine may be dry, off-dry, or fully sweet. Jasnières always has a strong mineral core and a scent of apples. Though it can be drunk earlier, it benefits from cellaring for up to ten years. Curnonsky, prince of gastronomes, famously said, "Three times a century, Jasnières makes the best wine in the world."

BEST RECENT VINTAGES: 2005, (2004, where yields were controlled), 2003, 2002. Best vintages from the recent past: 1997, 1996, 1995.
PRICES: $ to $$($)

PRODUCERS: (LES VIGNES DE) L'ANGE VIN ↑ ◆ DOM DE BELLIVIÈRE ☆ ◆ DOM LE BRISEAU (CHRISTIAN CHAUSSARD) ↑ ◆ Dom de Cézin (François Fresneau): makes charmingly rustic, doggedly honest wines in both Jasnières and Coteaux du Loir. Try a glass of the light red Janus ◆ Aubert la Chapelle: Jean-Michel Aubert is a talented, skilled, and conscientious winemaker. His Jasnières and Coteaux du Loir are textbook examples of their appellations. Favorites include the Jasnières Cuvée Anne-Mathilde and the dry, cinnamon-scented pineau d'Aunis–based rosés in Coteaux du Loir AC ◆ Dom de la Charrière (Joël Gigou): a reliably good producer in both Jasnières and Coteaux du Loir.

Domaine Charles Joguet

37220 Sazilly; 02.47.58.55.53; www.charlesjoguet.com
Wine: Chinon. $$ to $$$
Not quite the quality—not to mention the soul—as when Joguet, himself, was present, but still worthwhile, particularly the Clos de la Dioterie, Varennes du Grand Clos, and Clos du Chêne Vert bottlings. The domaine has also begun making a pleasant white Touraine La Plante Martin.

Pascal Jolivet

18300 Sancerre; 02.48,78.60.00; info@pascal-jolivet.com

Wines: Sancerre and Pouilly-Fumé. $$ to $$$

Although recent vintages proved disappointing, Jolivet is an intelligent and ambitious producer/*négociant* with a broad range of wines in Sancerre (red, white, and rosé) and Pouilly-Fumé. Top bottlings are La Grande Cuvée; there are also several *lieux-dits* in Sancerre (Le Chêne Marchand, Clos du Roy, and Château du Nozay are all white; Domaine du Colombier is red); and one, Les Griottes, in Pouilly-Fumé. A recent addition is a pricey, New World–style sauvignon blanc Vin de Pays called Attitude.

Domaine de Juchepie ☆

49380 Faye-d'Anjou; 02.41.54.33.47; www.juchepie.com

Wines: Coteaux du Layon and Anjou blanc. $$ to $$$

Eddy and Marie-Madeleine Oosterlinck left Belgium to make serious sweet wine in the Layon. Viticulture is organic, yields are low, and wines are fermented in barrel with indigenous yeasts. The Anjou blanc sec is superb; the Layons are heavenly, all of them, but the Cuvée Alexander, La Passion, Quintessence, and the Les Churelles bottlings are particularly gorgeous.

De Ladoucette

Château de Nozet, 58150 Pouilly-sur-Loire; tel/fax: 03.86.39.18.33

Wines: Pouilly-Fumé, Sancerre, and Vouvray. $$($)

Baron Philippe de Ladoucette put Pouilly-Fumé on the map. His wines are consistently of good commercial quality, but revelations are few. The top Pouilly-Fumé bottling is Baron de L. Sancerre, made from purchased grapes and juice, sold under the Comte Lafond label. Ladoucette also owns the Marc Brédif domaine in VOUVRAY.

Claude Lafond

36260 Reuilly; 02.54.49.22.17; claude.lafond@wanadoo.fr

Wine: Reuilly. $ to $$

Reuilly's leading producer makes a number of delectable bottlings. Favorites include Clos des Messieurs (single-vineyard sauvignon blanc), La Grande Pièce (pinot gris), and Les Grandes Vignes (pinot noir).

Domaine Lame-Delisle-Boucard

37140 Ingrandes-de-Touraine; 02.47.96.98.54; lame.delisle.boucard@wanadoo.fr

Wine: Bourgueil. $ to $$

Makes respectable old-fashioned Bourgueil as well as the slightly rebellious Cuvée René Boucard, a Touraine made from pure cabernet sauvignon.

Domaine de la Lande

37140 Bourgueil; 02.47.97.80.73; fax: 02.47.97.95.65

Wines: Bourgueil, St.-Nicolas de Bourgueil, and Chinon. $ to $$

The Delaunays, the owners of this fine family domaine, are trustworthy producers of medium-bodied cabernet francs (in all three appellations) that are purely and simply delicious.

Domaines Landron/Domaine de la Louvetrie ☆

44690 La Haye–Fouassières; 02.40.54.83.27; www.domaines-landron.com

Wine: Muscadet de Sèvre et Maine *sur lie*. $

Superb, ambassadorial muscadet. Also organic. Jo Landron offers a number of excellent bottlings, including the fresh, sassy, wine-bar-favorite Amphibolite (nonfiltered) and the more profound cuvée Fief du Breuil (I'm still drinking the 1986!).

Langlois-Château

49426 Saumur Cedex; 02.41.40.21.40; www.langlois-chateau.fr
Wines: Crémant de Loire and other Loire wines. $$ to $$$
Owned by Champagne Bollinger, Langlois-Château is one of the best sparkling wine producers in the Loire, specializing in *crémant*. The vintage versions, which age for three years, are particularly good, as is the deluxe bottling Quadrille, which ages for four years. The firm also produces good still wines in Loire Valley appellations from Muscadet (Dom de Grand Maison) to Sancerre (Ch de Fontaine-Audon), with two Saumur-Champignys (Ch de Varrains and La Bretonnière).

Domaine Laureau du Clos Frémur ↑

4900 Angers; 02.41.72.2554; laureau.fremur@wanadoo.fr
Wines: Savennières and Anjou. $ to $$
Damien Laureau took over this family domaine in 1999. It includes the Clos Frémur, a vineyard on the edge of the city of Angers that has been producing wine since the Middle Ages. The distinctive Anjou blanc Laureau makes here is particularly promising, as are his two bottlings of Savennières, the unoaked Cuvée Les Genêts and the extremely mineral, barrel-aged Cuvée du Bel Ouvrage.

Domaine Lavigne

49400 Varrains; 02.41.52.92.57; scea.lavigne-veron@wanadoo.fr
Wines: Saumur-Champigny, Coteaux de Saumur, and Saumur blanc. $ to $$
Sometimes ravishing, sometimes not, always better than average Champignys (especially the cuvée Les Aieules Vieilles Vignes), brawny Saumur blancs, and, vintage permitting, structured, floral Coteaux de Saumur.

René Noël Legrand

49400 Varrains; 02.41.52.94.11; renenoel.legrand@wanadoo.fr
Wines: Saumur-Champigny, Coteaux de Saumur, and Saumur blanc. $ to $$
Characterful, handcrafted wines in all three ACs. Legrand's wife says they're ripping up their chenin vines but then adds that they may replant them. My favorite bottling here is always Les Rogelins, a *terroir*-driven, powerful, and pure Saumur-Champigny, an excellent bistro red.

Lemaire-Fournier ↑

37210 Vernou-sur-Brenne; 02.47.52.12.46; marie-annick.lemaire@wanadoo.fr
Wine: Vouvray. $$
Envy! Marie-Annick Lemaire won the lottery, bought a beautiful vineyard in Vouvray, hired a talented, experienced winemaker, and her first vintage—2002—is so good it's already on top restaurant lists in Paris. The wines are concentrated, specific, and well balanced, particularly Les Morandières. Going organic is the next step.

Richard Leroy ☆

49750 Rablay-sur-Layon; tel/fax: 02.41.78.51.84
Wines: Coteaux du Layon and Anjou. $$ to $$$
Not so long ago Richard Leroy was a Paris banker taking wine appreciation classes. Now, with a small vineyard in the Layon, he's making truly fine Coteaux du Layon (always botrytized) and exemplary *terroir*-driven Anjou blanc sec, of which I particularly admire the appetizing, rich, and structured Clos des Rouliers, which in great vintages might not be dry at all but a glorious Sélection de Grains Nobles; and the svelte, mineral, fresh-as-a-waterfall Les Noëlles de Montbenault.

Loire Renaissance: An association of Anjou producers crusading for quality chenin blanc by adhering to rigorous practices in vineyard and cellar. The resulting wines are often named Loire Renaissance. Members include DOM DE LA BERGERIE ↑ ◆ DOM DE BRIZE ◆ DOM LES GRANDES VIGNES ↑ ◆ DOM LAUREAU DU CLOS FRÉMUR ◆ MUSSET-ROULLIER ◆ DOM JO PITHON ☆ ◆ DOM DES SABLONNETTES ↑.

Pierre Luneau-Papin ☆

44430 Le Landreau; 02.40.06.45.27; domaineluneaupapin@wanadoo.fr
Wine: Muscadet de Sèvre et Maine. $ to $$

Pierre Luneau makes a range of tender, feminine Muscadets of excellent quality, including the supple Clos des Allées, Les Pierres Blanches (old vines in the village of Chapelle Heulin), Le L d'Or (old vines from the village of Le Landreau), and Manoir Pierre Luneau-Papin (old vines from Le Landreau, fermented and aged in new oak barrels). The Luneau-Papins also make a point of cellaring and marketing older vintages of Muscadet and, with the 2002 harvest, participated in an official experiment by making a special cuvée called Excelsior/Clos des Noëlles that aged thirty months on its lees. It's extremely textured, and extremely good.

Domaine Henry Marionnet ☆

La Charmoise, 41230 Soings en Sologne; 02.54.98.70.73; henry@henry-marionnet.com
Wine: Touraine. $ to $$$

Indomitable and irrepressible, Marionnet never stops inventing tasty new bottlings. His entry-level sauvignon blanc and gamay are just fine, but his special cuvées are usually remarkable. There's the lush, late-harvested sauvignon blanc Le M; the Première Vendange, a gamay that's neither chaptalized nor sulfured (Marionnet succeeds here where many have failed); the inky, seductive Cépages Oubliés, made from the not entirely legal gamay de Bouze; and a clutch of luscious wines called Vinifera made from ungrafted vines—a chenin, a sauvignon, a gamay, a cabernet, and a côt. There's also a luminous romorantin, made from hundred-year-old vines, called Provinage, that is not to be missed.

Domaine Masson-Blondelet

58150 Pouilly-sur-Loire; 03.86.39.00.34; www.masson-blondelet.com
Wines: Pouilly-Fumé and Sancerre. $$($)

A reliable family domaine making a range of Pouilly-Fumé; Les Angelots and Villa Paulus are the two lightest. Tradition Cullus, the most serious and most expensive, is made from old vines and vinified in barrel. There's also a good Sancerre, Thauvenay.

Domaine Alex Mathur (formerly Levasseur) ↑

37270 Montlouis-sur-Loire; 02.47.50.97.06; fax: 02.47.50.96.80
Wine: Montlouis. $ to $$

Eric Gougeat has transformed a ho-hum domaine into an exciting new force in Montlouis. Grapes are hand-harvested and ferment in barrel. Les Lumens, the *sec* bottling, is an invigorating wake-up call, tinged with honey and lime. Dionys, a *sec-tendre,* is clear as a bell, with a strong mineral backbone. The luxuriously sweet 2003 *liquoreux* was a touch hot but otherwise delectable.

Alphonse Mellot ☆

18300 Sancerre; 02.48.54.07.41; www.mellot.com
Wine: Sancerre. $$ to $$$$

Over the past decade this house has become one of the best producers of Sancerre for both white and red. At the helm are Alphonse (eighteenth generation) and Alphonse (nineteenth generation). Together they have eliminated the firm's *négociant* business and have concentrated on quality, with exciting results for all cuvées: La Moussière (the entry-level red and white) and the more serious bottlings, based on old vines, Génération XIX (red and white), Cuvée Edmond (white), and En Grand Champs and La Demoiselle (both red). For the special cuvées the reds are unfiltered and the whites are barrel-fermented. Génération XIX comes from the oldest of the old vines and, in both colors, is ample, textured, and mellow. Good wines for haute cuisine. The characterful yet graceful En Grands Champs is a red I'd enjoy in an upscale bistro. The Mellots are also making very appealing chardonnay and pinot noir Vin de Pays des Coteaux Charitois called Les Pénitents.

Menetou-Salon

This AC begins where Sancerre ends, using the same grapes (sauvignon blanc and pinot noir) and making essentially the same style wines, albeit with a less pronounced expression of *terroir*.

BEST RECENT VINTAGES: 2005, (2004, for those who kept yields low), 2003, 2002.
PRICES: $ to $$($)

PRODUCERS: DOM DE CHATENOY ☆ ◆ Gilbert Chavet: quality is variable but the best wines from this domaine are clean and go down easily ◆ DOM HENRY PELLÉ ☆ ◆ Jean-Max Roger: good Sancerre-area *négociant* with reliable versions of Menetou-Salon ◆ LA TOUR SAINT MARTIN.

Louis Métaireau ☆

44690 Maisdon-sur-Sèvre; 02.40.54.81.92; marielucemetaireau@hotmail.com
Wine: Muscadet de Sèvre et Maine. $$
A revolutionary house under its founder, Louis Métaireau, the domaine has calmed down now that daughter Marie-Luce has taken over. The top bottlings are Number One, as razor sharp and exciting as ever, and Cuvée MLM, a riper, less wild version of the erstwhile Cuvée LM. Marie-Luce has also created Grand Mouton O'Féminin, generally a supple Muscadet selected by a group of female wine professionals.

Domaine de Montgilet/Victor & Vincent Lebreton ☆

49610 Juigne-sur-Loire; 02.41.91.90.48; montgilet@terre-net.fr
Wines: Coteaux de l'Aubance, Anjou-Villages Brissac, and the rest of the Anjous. $ to $$$
A key member of the generation that revolutionized winemaking in Anjou, eco-friendly Victor Lebreton, who runs this domaine with his brother, Vincent, makes lipsmackingly delicious barrel-aged Aubance. Depending on the vintage, Lebreton may bottle five different versions, including the cushy Les Trois Schistes and the more concentrated super cuvées Clos Prieur, Clos des Huttières, both from relatively young vines, and the old-vines nectar Tertereaux. Reds, like the Brissac Les Yvonnais, have historically been heavily extracted and often hard, but Lebreton recently assured me that he's now focusing on elegance. Watch this spot.

Montlouis

AC for whites—dry, demi-sec, *moelleux, liquoreux,* and sparkling—made from chenin blanc. Located just beyond the city of Tours, its wines are similar to those of VOUVRAY (which it faces across the river) though generally leaner, drier, and starker.

BEST RECENT VINTAGES: 2005, 2003, 2002. Best vintages from the recent past: 1997, 1996, 1995, 1990, 1989.
PRICES: $ to $$($)

PRODUCERS: Claude Boureau: sympathetic, faintly rustic, old-style Montlouis, from sparkling to *moelleux* ◆ LAURENT CHATENAY ☆ ◆ FRANÇOIS CHIDAINE ☆ ◆ Stéphane Cossais: another new eco-friendly face with a promising future, as evidenced by the 2003 Cloclôte, a succulent Montlouis *moelleux* with a lime–herbal tea undertow. Cossais also produces Touraine AC and Vin de Table, including a sweet gamay ↑ ◆ DELETANG ☆ ◆ DOM LA GRANGE TIPHAINE ↑ ◆ DOM ALEX MATHUR ↑ ◆ Dom Moyer: Dominique Moyer has just passed the flame to the next generation. Always a solid house, quality will surely continue. Look, in particular, for the Vieilles Vignes (sweet) and Les Croisés (dry) cuvées ◆ Le P'tit Caporal: Frantz Saumon, whose first vintage was 2002, is making extremely promising, new-oak-fermented Montlouis. The wines are cool, steely, focused, and characterful ↑ ◆ DOM DE LA TAILLE AUX LOUPS (JACKY BLOT) ☆.

Domaine de Montrieux (Émile Hérédia) ↑
41100 Naveil; tel/fax: 02.54.77.75.40; domaine.montrieux@tele2.fr
Wine: Coteaux du Vendômois. $ to $$
A dedicated young vintner making organic Coteaux du Vendômois, the best of which are the peppery reds and barrel-fermented rosés (or *vins gris*) made from pineau d'Aunis, which are great with spicy food.

Domaine Éric Morgat ↑
49170 Savennières; 02.41.72.22.51; eric.morgat@wanadoo.fr
Wine: Savennières. $$
The scion of an established Coteaux du Layon family, Éric Morgat crossed the river and invested in land in Savennières. The resulting eco-friendly wines, fermented in barrel, show a firm hand and an understanding of delicacy. The latest good news is that Morgat has planted a vineyard in Layon-Beaulieu and has taken over half a hectare of La Roche-aux-Moines.

Domaine du Moulin/Hervé Villemade
Le Moulin-Neuf, 41120 Cellettes; 02.54.70.41.76; herve.villemade@wanadoo.fr
Wines: Cheverny and Cour-Cheverny. $
A favorite in Paris wine bars, Villemade is one of the more promising producers in these ACs, with a *terroir*-driven Cour-Cheverny, a barrel-fermented Cheverny made from Sauvignon blanc called La Croppe, and a bunch of quirky country reds.

The Muscadets

AC for dry white wine made from melon de Bourgogne (muscadet) in a vast zone east, south, and southwest of Nantes. More mineral than fruit-driven, good muscadet is singularly fresh and vivacious, with a slight, appetizing prickle if and when aged *sur lie*. To qualify for the *sur lie* designation, the wine must be bottled directly from its lees no earlier than the March following the vintage. Qualifying wines have a raised Nike-like swoosh on their bottlenecks. There are three subregions and most producers use one of them. All, however, may use the broad Muscadet AC. Great with oysters, seafood, and assorted antipasti and mezes.

BEST RECENT VINTAGES: 2005, (2004, where yields were controlled), 2003, and 2002. (Note: very good muscadet ages well.)
PRICES: $ to $$

PRODUCER: Most are listed under subregions. Ch de la Preuille: ambitious, good producer in the simple Muscadet zone.

Muscadet–Coteaux de la Loire: Small AC due east of Nantes, essentially the same zone as Coteaux d'Ancenis. Producers: Athimon & Ses Enfants: try locally ◆ Dom Pierre Guindon: one of the more established and reliable domaines in this sub-AC ◆ PIERRE LUNEAU-PAPIN ☆ ◆ Vignerons des Terroirs de la Noëlle: good cooperative, part of ALLIANCE LOIRE. Look for Les Folies Siffait.

Muscadet–Côtes de Grand Lieu: Small muscadet zone southwest of Nantes, named after the Lac de Grand Lieu. Producers: Dom le Demi-Boeuf/Michel Malidain: satisfactory Muscadets; the quirkier Vin de Pays and gros-plant are more interesting here ◆ LE FIEF GUÉRIN ◆ DOM LES HAUTES NOËLLES.

Muscadet de Sèvre et Maine: The tail wags the dog—Muscadet de Sèvre et Maine, the most prestigious of the subzones, accounts for about 85 percent of all Muscadet production. Named after the two rivers running through, it begins just south of Nantes and runs to the Vendée border. Arguably the best, richest, most structured, and most mineral muscadets come from this subregion. The finest can age: the best recent older vintages are 1996, 1995, 1990, 1989, 1987, and 1985. Producers: ANDRÉ-MICHEL BRÉGEON ◆ Ch de Briacé: the local winemaking school produces respectable versions of the AC ◆ Ch du Cleray: a well-distributed brand with a wide offering; best is Cardinal Richard Haute Culture ◆ BRUNO CORMERAIS ◆ MICHEL DELHOMMEAU ↑ ◆ Donatien Bahuaud: a leading *négociant* with many bottlings, the most famous being the jury-selected Le Master ◆ DOM DE L'ÉCU ☆ ◆ Dom de la Fruitière: excellent family domaine; look, in particular, for Première and Baron Noury, the delicious top cuvées ☆ ◆ DOM DE LA HAUTE FÉVRIE ☆ ◆ DOM LANDRON ☆ ◆ PIERRE LUNEAU-PAPIN ☆ ◆ Dom la Quilla/Daniel and Gérard Vinet: first-rate producers. Look for Le Muscadet and Clos de la Houssaie ◆ CH DE LA RAGOTIÈRE ☆.

Gilles Musset–Serge Roullier

49620 La Pommeraye; 02.41.39.05.71; musset-roullier@wanadoo.fr
Wines: Anjou–Coteaux de la Loire and Anjous. $ to $$
A partnership of two hardworking vintners who turn out classic (in the best sense) Anjou–Coteaux de la Loire (in 2003 the cuvée Raisins Confits was sheer nectar), award-winning Anjou rouge and Anjou-Villages (Petit Clos), tasty Anjou gamay, and a beautifully mineral and concentrated Anjou blanc sec Tris Sélectionnés.

Domaine Henry Natter

18250 Montigny; 02.48.69.58.85; info@henrynatter.com
Wine: Sancerre. $$
There's good value for the dollar in the solid Sancerres from this family domaine at the outer limits of the appellation. The top cuvée is François La Grange de Montigny.

Nau Frères

37140 Ingrandes de Touraine; 02.47.96.98.57; naufreres@wanadoo.fr
Wine: Bourgueil. $
A sentimental favorite for reliably good, somewhat old-fashioned Bourgueils. The 2005s are irresistibly yummy.

Thierry Nérisson ↑

37210 Rochecorbon; 02.47.52.53.46; nerisson1@hotmail.com
Wines: Vouvray and Bourgueil. $$ to $$$
A former sommelier at the two-Michelin-star Jean Bardet in Tours, Thierry Nérisson has set up his own small *négociant* business, the name of which, Authenticité Terroir, gives a good idea of what he's after. Nérisson buys organically farmed grapes from selected vintners and, using his own barrels, makes the wine at each individual property. The 2003 Bourgueil, unfined, unfiltered, unsulfured, was rich and pure. There are numerous cuvées of Vouvray, all of them treated to more than two years of aging in used barrels. The best are the full, very mineral, and creamy cuvée L'Authentique and the bracing but creamy La Queue de Morue, a riveting single-vineyard bottling.

Domaine de Noiré ☆

37500 Chinon; 06.76.81.91.29; fax: 02.47.98.32.33
Wine: Chinon. $$
Jean-Max Manceau has long been recognized as one of the most talented winemakers in the AC. But the recognition was local as Manceau put his craft to work for the Château de la Grille. He still heads La Grille's cellars but has his own small domaine on one of the best hillsides in Chinon. There, he produces a top-notch rosé and two lipsmackingly delicious Chinons, the silky, early-drinking Élégance and the more structured and tannic—though still supple—Caractère.

Vincent Ogereau ☆

49750 St.-Lambert du Lattay, 02.41.78.30.53; fax 02.41.78.43.55

Wines: Coteaux du Layon and Anjous. $ to $$$

A reliably excellent producer of Coteaux du Layon (especially the cuvées Clos des Bonnes Blanches and Saint-Lambert Prestige) and Anjou-Villages (particularly the Côte de la Houssaye), Ogereau has recently gotten a piece of Savennières, Clos du Grand Beaupreau, and the results are extremely promising. He even makes good cabernet d'Anjou.

Orléans and Orléans-Clery

Two VDQS on the outskirts of Orléans. Just to complicate matters, what was once a single minuscule VDQS has become two even tinier ones. The first, Orléans, located on both banks of the Loire, south of the city, makes light whites from chardonnay (here called auvernat blanc) and light reds and rosés from pinot meunier (locally, gris meunier), and pinot noir (auvernat rouge). The reds, in particular, can be charming wine-bar quaffs. Orléans-Clery VDQS is reserved for reds made from cabernet franc, never a sure thing this far north and east: the wines are often vegetal. Drink the youngest available.

PRICES: $

PRODUCERS: Clos St. Fiacre: The Montigny-Piel family is one of the two best producers in both appellations ◆ Vignoble du Chant d'Oiseaux: Jacky Legroux is the other top producer in both VDQS ◆ Les Vignerons de la Grand'Maison: a good local cooperative.

Domaine des Ouches ↑

37140 Ingrandes de Touraine; 02.47.96.98.77; domaine.d.ouches@wanadoo.fr

Wine: Bourgueil. $ to $$

The latest generation of Gambiers has significantly improved the quality of the Bourgueils at this reliable address, making it one of the "go-to" domaines in the AC. Particularly rewarding are the Les Ouches and the Grande Réserve bottlings.

Alain Paulat

Villemoison, 58200 St.-Père; 03.86.26.75.57; fax: 03.86.28.06.78

Wine: Coteaux du Giennois. $($)

Alain Paulat, who marches to the beat of his own drum, makes the best wine in this appellation. All organic, all red or rosé, all barrel-fermented, and all delicious. Paulat releases the wines for sale when he thinks they're ready to drink. At the time of this writing, he's selling the 1998 red. I found it too evolved but, once chilled well, I discovered it married perfectly with a spicy guinea hen recipe from the Île de la Réunion.

Domaine Henry Pellé ☆

18220 Morogues; 02.48.64.42.48; henry.pelle@wanadoo.fr

Wines: Menetou-Salon and Sancerre. $$

Excellent Menetou-Salon (red and white). Best are the special bottlings. In whites, there's the charming bistro-ready Morogues; the tender, mouthfilling Clos des Blanchais, and the pedigreed, mineral, delightful Clos de Ratier, both from parcels within Morogues. In reds, it's the vibrant, juicy, specific Les Cris and, in special vintages, the silky, elegant Coeur de Cris. Pelle's Sancerre Croix du Garde (red and white) are also highly recommended.

Domaine du Petit Val
49380 Chavagnes; 02.41.54.31.14; denis-goizil@tiscali.fr
Wines: Anjou range, including Bonnezeaux. $ to $$
Self-effacing Denis Goizil doesn't make headlines but he does make seriously delicious Coteaux du Layon (especially the Vieilles Vignes and Cuvée Simon) and Bonnezeaux (including a ravishing cuvée La Montagne). The reds are also very nice.

Domaine de Peyra
63800 St.-Georges-sur-Allier; tel/fax: 04.73.77.31.84
Wines: Côtes d'Auvergne and Vin de Table. $
Three mavericks (Éric Garnier, Stéphane Majeune, and Jean Maupertuis) on the steep slopes of Auvergne make wine from gamay, pinot noir, and an obscure local grape called noirfleurien (also known as mirefleurien). Low yields, hand-harvesting, wild yeasts, and little or no filtration or sulfur result in a clutch of characterful cool mountain reds and rosés, notably a Corent rosé and a late-harvest rosé called Brumaire and the quirky Les Puys and Mauvaises Herbes, both Vins de Tables.

Château Pierre-Bise ☆
49750 Beaulieu-sur-Layon; 02.41.78.31.44; fax: 02.41.78.41.24
Wines: Anjou range, including Chaume, Quarts-de-Chaume, and Savennières. $ to $$$
Château Pierre-Bise's Claude and Joëlle Papin make some of the most ambitious, delicious, and riveting wine in Anjou. *Terroir* is the obsession here. There are roughly a half-dozen different sumptuous Layons, vinified and bottled by soil type, including L'Anclaie, Rouannières, Les Soucheries, and Tetuères, plus a gorgeous Chaume and a grandiose Quarts-de-Chaume. (I'm less enthusiastic about the recent vintages of their dry white Haute de la Garde.) In reds, the Anjou-Villages is lipsmackingly delicious, the potent, age-worthy Anjou gamay is a revelation, and their off-dry rosé d'Anjou could make converts to this style of wine. Crossing the river, the Papins have taken charge of the vines and the winemaking at Clos du Coulaine, with marvelous results in both white (Savennières) and red (Anjou-Villages). They recently took over several other parcels, one in La Roche aux Moines. The 2004 from that vineyard is limpid and extremely mineral, with wonderful flavors of pineapple, herbal tea, and quinine. It should be superb.

Domaine Vincent Pinard ☆
18300 Bué; 02.48.54.33.89; fax: 02.48.54.13.96
Wine: Sancerre. $$($)
Top-notch Sancerres from a leading family domaine. Every bottling is recommended though Harmonie (white) and Charlouise (red) deserve to singled out—they are excellent.

François Pinon ☆
37210 Vernou-sur-Brenne; 02.47.52.25.51; francois.pinon@wanadoo.fr
Wine: Vouvray. $ to $$
Flavorful organic Vouvrays with a pure sense of place, handcrafted by an intelligent, dedicated vintner. Everything is recommended, and the 2005s should be spectacular. One of the best price-to-quality ratios in this AC.

Domaine Jo Pithon ☆
49750 St.-Lambert du Lattay; 02.41.78.40.91; jopithon@jopithon.com
Wines: Coteaux du Layon, Quarts-de-Chaume, Savennières, and Anjou blanc. $$ to $$$$
Trendsetting, high-profile Anjou wines that usually merit the attention they get. The wines are organic, ultraripe, extremely concentrated, site-specific, and barrel-fermented chenin blancs. Particularly impressive: Les Bergères Anjou blanc sec (the 2002 was excellent and revealed a savvy change of direction in favor of freshness and elegance); Les Pepinières, a stylish and specific sec;

the fluid, long, and elegant Savennières La Croix Picot, and in the very sweet category, the always impressive Clos des Bonnes Blanches, Les 4 Villages, and Quarts-de-Chaume Les Varennes. All that said, their most thrilling wine may be another dry white, the Anjou blanc Les Treilles, from vines the Pithons planted on an abandoned hillside. Its first vintage was in 2004, and the wine was extremely long and extremely mineral, immediately impressing you with the power of its *terroir.*

Pouilly-Fumé

An important AC for full-flavored sauvignon blancs. These are somewhat broader than SANCERRE but otherwise almost indistinguishable, thanks to similar soils and climate.

BEST RECENT VINTAGES: 2005, (2004, for those who kept yields low), 2003, 2002.
PRICES: $$($)

PRODUCERS: Dom Michel Bailly: pungent, ample Pouillys ◆ Cedrick Bardin: interesting Pouillys to try by the glass ◆ François Blanchet: brisk, silex-driven Pouillys, particularly the bracing Vieilles Vignes and Silice, which cuts like a diamond ◆ Bouchie-Châtellier: more solid, silex-rich Pouillys ◆ HENRI BOURGEOIS ☆ ◆ DOM CAILBOURDIN ☆ ◆ Domaine Châtelain: reliably good domaine, especially Les Charmes and Prestige ◆ CAVES DE POUILLY-SUR-LOIRE ◆ DIDIER DAGUENEAU ☆ ◆ SERGE DAGUENEAU & FILLES ☆ ◆ André Dezat & Fils: see SANCERRE ◆ Ch de Favray: good family domaine with lively Pouillys ◆ Dom André and Edmond Figeat: a reliable family domaine, with flint-and-petrol Pouillys. Look for Côte de Nozet and Les Chaumiennes ◆ GITTON PÈRE & FILS ◆ DOM MASSON-BLONDELET ◆ CH DU NOZET: see DE LADOUCETTE ◆ Michel Redde: the top bottling, Cuvée Majorum, is worth trying ◆ DOM GUY SAGET ◆ CH DE TRACY ☆.

Pouilly-sur-Loire

Diminishing AC for vinous whites made from Chasselas. Drink the youngest available.

PRICES: $

PRODUCERS: CAVES DE POUILLY-SUR-LOIRE ◆ Dom Châtelain: see POUILLY-FUMÉ ◆ SERGE DAGUENEAU & FILLES ☆ ◆ Dom André & Edmond Figeat: see POUILLY-FUMÉ ◆ GITTON PÈRE & FILS.

Château de Putille

49620 La Pommeraye; 02.41.39.02.91; chateau.putille@wanadoo.fr
Wines: Anjou range, including Anjou–Coteaux de la Loire. $ to $$
Pascal Delaunay's entire range is highly recommended, including his Anjou-Villages Cuvée Prestige and his *crémant,* Les Schistes de Loire. Sweet chenin is still the star, however, particularly the appetizing, structured cuvées of Anjou–Coteaux de la Loire Pierre Carrée, Clos du Pirouet, and Clos du Salvert.

Quarts-de-Chaume

A tiny AC for super sweet (*moelleux* to *liquoreux* and *doux*) whites made from chenin blanc in the heart of the Coteaux du Layon. Exposure, complexity of schist-based soils, and harvest by a *tri* of shriveled and/or botrytized grapes conspire to bring forth all that is noble and delectable in chenin. As with Bonnezeaux, Quarts-de-Chaume can be drunk young or left to age almost indefinitely.

BEST RECENT VINTAGES: 2005, 2003, 2002, 1997, 1996, 1995, 1990, 1989, 1988. Legendary vintages include: 1959, 1947, and 1921.
PRICES: $$ to $$$$

PRODUCERS: DOM DES BAUMARD ☆ ◆ DOM DE LA BERGERIE ↑ ◆ DOM DES FORGES ☆ ◆ Domaine du Petit Metris: see CHAUME ◆ Château de Plaisance: see CHAUME ◆ CH PIERRE-BISE ☆ ◆ DOM JO PITHON ☆ ◆ Ch de Suronde: formerly owned by the dedicated François Poirel, the château was recently purchased by the owners of Dom des Deux Vallées: see CHAUME.

Quincy

A small AC near Bourges for medium-bodied white wines made from sauvignon blanc. Quality is variable.

BEST RECENT VINTAGES: 2005, (2004, for those who kept yields low), 2003, 2002.
PRICES: $ to $$$

PRODUCERS: Dom Mardon: very good family winery with steely, vivid versions of the AC ◆ SILICE DE QUINCY ☆ ◆ Adele Rouze: a promising young vigneronne ◆ Tatin-Wilk: very good producer with fresh, breezy wines from two domaines, Ballandors and Tremblay.

Château de la Ragotière ☆

44330 La Regrippière; 02.40.33.60.56; www.freres.couillaud.com
Wines: Muscadet de Sèvre et Maine, Vin de Pays, and Vin de Table. $ to $$
The Couillaud brothers make as much chardonnay as they do Muscadet and deservedly win awards for each. Their Les Zunics line consists of wines made from grape varieties not contemplated in Nantais legislation: viognier (only in sunny vintages, when the wine is perfumed and mineral), petit manseng (when vinified dry, my favorite), muscat, pinot gris, and sauvignon gris (fié; a wine to drink with asparagus), and a blend of the five that lacks definition but is nonetheless a good glass of white.

Domaine du Regain ↑

49540 Martigne-Briand; 02.41.40.28.20; domaine.regain@wanadoo.fr
Wines: Anjou, including Layon. $$
Take note—there are future Loire stars here. Frédéric and Fatima Étienne created their domaine in 2002. The wines are organic, the work behind every one of them is meticulous. The Anjou blanc secs are first-rate, particularly the cuvée Les Hauts du Regain, made from the best grapes and fermented in newish oak barrels. Corto is an elegant, mineral Anjou-Villages; double that acclaim for the Cuvée Vieilles Vignes. The Coteaux du Layon Les Paradis, fermented in Burgundy barrels, is fresh as a torrent, with sublime balance and finely etched yet luscious fruit.

Reuilly

A small AC west of Sancerre historically known for *vin gris* made from pinot gris. Now a good source for reasonably priced sauvignon blanc and pinot noir, as well as pinot gris.

BEST RECENT VINTAGES: 2005, (2004 for those who kept yields low), 2003, 2002.
PRICES: $($)

PRODUCERS: CLAUDE LAFOND ◆ Valéry Rénaudat: a promising young vigneronne who has recently succeeded her father in this respectable family domaine ◆ DOM DE REUILLY ◆ Jean-Michel Sorbe: quality is variable but the wines are always better than the average. Look for La Commanderie (red, preferably).

Domaine de Reuilly

36260 Reuilly; 02.38.66.16.74; denis-jamain@wanadoo.fr

Wine: Reuilly. $($)

Bring out the chèvre when you uncork a bottle of Denis Jamain's invigorating Les Pierres Plates, his white Reuilly, which is better than quite a few Sancerres. The taut, fragrant rosé is equally food-friendly and the firm red is a good, light pinot noir.

Domaine Ricard ↑

41140 Thésée; 02.54.71.00.17; domaine.ricard@wanadoo.fr

Wine: Touraine: $

Here's a jolly young vintner whose wines are now featured in lots of Paris wine bars. It's hard to find a more toothsome gamay; his Le Vilain P'tit Rouge, a blend of côt and cabernet, is a Loire fruit bomb; and the range of sauvignon blancs is compelling, including the easy-drinking Le Petiot, the deeper Les Trois Chênes Vieilles Vignes (made from very old vines, it was superb in 2003), and L'Effrontée. A late-harvest bottling the sweetness of which depends on the vintage, L'Effrontée can be serious, excellent, and a great aperitif—as it was in 2002—but it also takes us to the edge of the wacko-wine realm. We cross the border with Le Vinsans Ricard, a naturally sparkling blend of sauvignon blanc and chardonnay, fermented in barrel, that's a totally refreshing version of wine as soda pop. It's fun to drink.

Domaine Richou ☆

49610 Moze-sur-Louet; 02.41.78.72.13; domaine.richou@wanadoo.fr

Wines: Anjou range, including Coteaux de l'Aubance and Anjou-Villages Brissac. $$

Hard to go wrong here, though the stars are Richou's delectable cuvées of Aubance, including the elegant demi-sec Les Grandes Rogeries; the grandiose, sumptuous Le Pavillon; and Trois Demoiselles. Chauvigné is the very mineral Anjou sec. Les Châteliers, an Anjou gamay, would be perfect in a wine bar.

Roche-aux-Moines

A tiny *cru* of Savennières capable of producing distinctive chenin blanc. For vintages and prices see SAVENNIÈRES. Producers: COULÉE DE SERRANT (Clos de la Bergerie) ◆ Dom aux Moines: good, relatively straightforward versions ◆ DOM ÉRIC MORGAT ↑ ◆ CH PIERRE-BISE ☆.

Domaine des Rochelles ☆

49320 St.-Jean de Mauvrets; 02.41.91.92.07; jy.a.le.breton@wanadoo.fr

Wines: Anjou range, including Coteaux de l'Aubance and Anjou-Villages Brissac. $ to $$

Hubert Lebreton pioneered red-wine making in Anjou. Son Jean-Yves and his wife and kids continue the fine work. Cuvée La Croix de Mission, pure cabernet sauvignon, is as good as that grape gets in the Loire and it's delicious, as are the domaine's Coteaux de l'Aubance. A very reliable house.

Domaine des Roches Neuves

49400 Varrains; 02.41.52.94.02; thierry-germain@wanadoo.fr

Wines: Saumur-Champigny and Saumur blanc. $$ to $$$

Thierry Germain's wines are generally well made and popular. I find them too heavily oaked, particularly his top bottlings, the Saumur-Champigny Cuvée Marginale and the Saumur blanc L'Insolite.

Rosés of Anjou

There are three, each of which is discussed individually here, with producers for all listed at the end. There is a market (however limited) for aged Cabernet d'Anjou but, in general, drink the youngest available for all these rosés.

PRICES: $

Cabernet d'Anjou: An off-dry rosé, it would be easy to believe that this appellation existed solely to confuse consumers: Why isn't it red? Well, it's not. It's rosé, made from cabernet (essentially franc), and it ranges from off-dry to sweet. And it's often vegetal. In its favor, it's a good wine to pair with asparagus.

Rosé d'Anjou: A vinous off-dry or sweet rosé made in Anjou and Saumur from grolleau, cabernet, gamay, côt, and pineau d'Aunis.

Rosé de Loire: Dry rosés made throughout Anjou and Touraine from cabernet, gamay, grolleau, pineau d'Aunis, and pinot noir.

PRODUCERS: Many producers include at least one rosé as part of their range. It's a fair assumption that the better the producer, the better the rosé. DOM DE BABLUT has always given special care to Cabernet d'Anjou and has some quite old vintages. As Anjou continues to reinvent itself, its current young Turks are reinventing the rosés, with very interesting results. Examples include: DOM DE LA BERGERIE ↑ ◆ Dom des Charbottières: See ANJOU ◆ CLAU DE NELL ↑ ◆ JEAN-CHRISTOPHE GARNIER ↑ ◆ DOM LES GRANDES VIGNES ↑ ◆ DOM DES SABLONNETTES ↑.

Domaine du Roy René ↑

49750 Chanzeaux; 02.41.7832.32; domaine.roy.rene@wanadoo.fr
Wines: Anjou range, including Layon. $$
Antoine and Nicolas Chéreau took over this domaine at turn of this century. While the wines are works in progress, they are very promising, from the nicely oaked whites to the inky gamays, to pineapple-rich Layons.

Domaine des Sablonnettes ↑

49750 Rablay-sur-Layon; 02.41.78.40.49; domainedessablonnettes@wanadoo.fr
Wines: Layon and the entire range of Anjous. $ to $$$
From 1991 to 1996 Joël Ménard converted his domaine to biodynamics, stopped chaptalizing, and switched from industrial to indigenous yeasts. The resulting wines—all the Anjous, beginning with the rosés and gamays—are soft, pure, and mineral, and constantly improving. Of particular note are the Anjou blanc sec Les Genêts made from overripe grapes, the Anjou-Villages Les Grands Chênes, and the various cuvées of Layon, including the handsome and gracious Vieilles Vignes, the tender and expressive Noblesse, the honeyed and impressive Érables, and La Bohème and Quintessence, which border on the majestic. Le Villain Canard, a Vin de Table, is a tasty sweet chenin from declassified Layon vines. Ménard also makes a couple of knock-back wines with names inspired by a Georges Brassens song: Les Copains d'Abord and Les Copines Aussi.

Domaines Guy Saget

58150 Pouilly-sur-Loire; 03.86.39.57.75; www.guy-saget.com
Wines: Many Loire appellations. $ to $$
The largest proprietor in the Loire, either owning or controlling nine sizable estates (close to 400 hectares) from the Nantais to Pouilly: key estates are Guy Saget for Pouilly-Fumé and Pouilly-sur-Loire; Domaine Saget for Pouilly-Fumé; Domaine de la Perrière for Sancerre; Domaine Joseph Balland-Chapuis for Sancerre and Coteaux du Giennois; Domaine d'Artois for Touraine-Mesland, Touraine-Amboise, Crémant de Loire, and Touraine AC; and Domaines

Chupin and La Mulonnière for Coteaux du Layon and the Anjous, including Savennières. Best are wines from the firm's home base, the Pouillys, Sancerres (especially the Sélection Première from Guy Saget and Le Vallon from Balland-Chapuis), and pleasant, light Coteaux de Giennois. The Layon-Beaulieu from Château de la Mulonnière is admirable as well.

Domaine de Saint-Just

49260 St.-Just-sur-Dive; 02.41.51.62.01; www.st-just.net

Wines: Saumur-Champigny, Saumur blanc, Coteaux de Saumur, and Crémant de Loire. $$

Yves Lambert's 40 hectares are split evenly between Saumur and Saumur-Champigny. Viticulture is organic; harvest for the top cuvées—those based on *terroir*—is by hand. These include a first-rate, oak-aged Saumur blanc, La Coulée de St. Cyr, and three user-friendly Champignys: Terres Rouges, the lightest, is a good wine-bar red; La Montée des Roches is what the French would call *caressant;* and Le Clos Moleton is the most concentrated and "serious." Vintage permitting, there is a Coteaux de Saumur Cuvée Moise, a sapid, sweet chenin tasting of minerals and sultanas.

Domaine Saint-Nicolas ☆

85470 Brem-sur-Mer; 02.51.33.13.04; www.domaine-saint-nicolas.com

Wine: Fiefs Vendéens. $ to $$

Thierry Michon converted his domaine to biodynamics and has been producing strikingly pure, surprisingly delicious (and ambitious) wines from vines facing the Atlantic Ocean. Everything is highly recommended, from Les Clous and Les Haut des Clous, two mellow, mineral whites, to Gammes en May, a juicy light red, to the more complex, structured, and even more succulent reds Jacques, Le Poiré, Plante Gaté, and Reflets.

St.-Nicolas de Bourgueil

A western Touraine AC producing juicy, medium-bodied cabernet franc–based reds and rosés. The wine is essentially the same as Bourgueil, though reputedly (but not necessarily) lighter.

BEST RECENT VINTAGES: 2005, (2004, where yields were controlled), 2003, 2002. Best vintages of the recent past: 1997, 1996 (but only for very top).

PRICES: $ to $$

PRODUCERS: YANNICK AMIRAULT ☆ ◆ Clos des Quarterons: Thierry Amirault (not to be confused with Yannick) makes good, bistro-ready reds. Look for the Vieilles Vignes bottling ◆ Lydie & Max Cognard-Taluau: this good family winery consistently produces some of the best St.-Nicolas. Look for the Cuvée Les Malgagnes, always my favorite from this house ◆ Dom de la Cotelleraie: Gérard Vallée, whose first harvest was 2000, has quickly placed himself among the top producers of the appellation, particularly with cuvées Les Perruches, L'Envol, and Le Vau Jaumier ↑ ◆ Frédéric Mabileau: it would be difficult to find a more seductive cabernet franc than Mabileau's silky Les Coutures. The more tannic Les Rouillières, also recommended, needs a bit of cellaring (there are many Mabileaus in this AC with wines worth trying, including Jacques & Vincent, Jean-Claude, Jean-François, Jean-Paul, and Laurent) ◆ TALUAU & FOLTZENLOGEL.

St.-Pourçain-sur-Sioule

A small AC in central France with light, fragrant whites made from chardonnay, sauvignon blanc, and a local grape called tressallier, and light, sassy reds and rosés made from gamay and pinot noir. Drink the youngest available.

PRICES: $

PRODUCERS: Dom de Bellevue: a reliable source of good St.-Pourçain, particularly their Grande Réserve bottlings in both red and white ◆ Famille Laurent: another good family domaine with two chardonnay-based wines,

Prestige and an oak-aged bottling ◆ François Ray: a fixture on the local wine scene, the Ray family produces very pleasant versions of the AC ◆ VIGNERONS DE SAINT-POURÇAIN.

Sancerre

An important eastern Loire AC for whites, reds, and rosés. The whites, made from pure sauvignon blanc, are invigorating and fragrant (often to the point of pungency) and have created the model for sauvignon the world over. They are generally dry, though some producers (COTAT, for example) make off-dry wines from very ripe grapes.

Most vintners make at least two types of white, with increasing attention to soil type, notably Kimmeridgean marl (called *terres blanches*), the same soil that gives Chablis its distinctive character; compact chalk (*caillottes*); and soils with significant outcroppings of silex. Many of these *terroir*-specific wines use the name of the vineyard, particularly when it concerns a *lieu-dit*. The best and most famous of the *lieux-dits* include: Chemarin, Chêne Marchand, and La Poussie (in the charming village of Bué); Les Bouffants, Le Cul de Beaujeu, and Les Monts Damnés (in the even more charming village of Chavignol); Clos du Roy and Côte de Champtin (in Champtin); Le Paradis in Sancerre; and La Perrière in Verdigny.

GRAPES: Reds and rosés are made from pinot noir. The reds have improved significantly over the past decade. The best can give non-Côte d'Or Burgundies a run for the money. The rosés, when taken seriously, are delightful.

BEST RECENT VINTAGES: 2005, (2004, for those who kept yields low), (2003, if you like your Sancerres fat), 2002.
PRICES: $ to $$$

PRODUCERS: GÉRARD & THIBAUT BOULAY ☆ ◆ HENRI BOURGEOIS ☆ ◆ Roger Champault & Fils: skip the 2003s in favor of the delightful 2002s, both the grapefruit-mineral Les Pierris and the broader, higher-pitched Clos du Roy. The reds are light and appealing ◆ Dom Daniel Chotard: very pleasant Sancerres, particularly the special cuvées, like the grapefruit- and fig-accented Marcel Henri in white and the inviting Le Champ de l'Archer in red. There's also a fragrant rosé ◆ François Cotat: Sancerres unlike any other—except those of cousin PASCAL. Both work the same slopes in Chavignol, Monts Damnés, Grandes Côtes, and Cul de Beaujeu and follow similar practices in vineyard and cellar. These ample, complex, mineral, lime-and-linden-blossom Sancerres are highly sought after, age well, and often have some residual sugar ☆ ◆ PASCAL COTAT ◆ FRANÇOIS CROCHET ↑ ◆ LUCIEN CROCHET ☆ ◆ Dom Vincent Delaporte: stylish Sancerres in three colors for sleek brasseries ◆ André Dezat & Fils (Les Celliers St.-Romble): endearing family winery with charming Sancerres that have been served at the table of the Queen of England, which shows good royal taste, at least in things vinous ◆ PASCAL JOLIVET ◆ Dom Laporte: see HENRI BOURGEOIS ◆ ALPHONSE MELLOT ☆ ◆ Dom Millet: Franck Millet makes a pleasant red and two good cuvées of white, a juicy entry-level Sancerre and the ampler, more mineral L'Insolite ◆ DOM HENRY NATTER ◆ DOM HENRY PELLÉ ☆ ◆ DOM VINCENT PINARD ☆ ◆ Pierre Prieur/Dom de St. Pierre: a highly respected (and recommended) family domaine. Try the oak-aged red Maréchal Prieur ◆ Bernard Reverdy: super Sancerre rosés. Pair with prosciutto and melon. Yum! ◆ Hippolyte Reverdy: a good family domaine with particularly successful 2003s (there are many Reverdys in Sancerre; other Reverdys whose Sancerres merit sampling are Daniel; Jean; Pascal & Nicolas, especially the Vieilles Vignes; and Bailly-Reverdy ◆ Jean-Max Roger: reliable Sancerre-area *négociant*, a safe bet ◆ DOM VACHERON ☆ ◆ Dom André Vatan: lively, mainstream whites, particularly the cuvée Saint François.

Sansonnière: See FERME DE LA SANSONNIÈRE.

Saumur

A region and an umbrella AC forming a crescent south of the Loire essentially in the Maine et Loire department. It has the same grape varieties as Anjou, with whites based on chenin blanc and reds and rosés on cabernet franc. The region's most important wines are Saumur-Champigny and sparkling wine, either Saumur made by the *méthode traditionnelle* (*mousseux*) or CRÉMANT DE LOIRE. COTEAUX DE SAUMUR, a sweet white, has more in common with VOUVRAY than with COTEAUX DU LAYON. Saumur rouge is the simpler cousin of SAUMUR-CHAMPIGNY; Saumur blanc is the dry chenin made throughout the region, even by producers whose reds are within the more limited Saumur-Champigny zone. Cabernet de Saumur is an off-dry to sweet rosé, in the style of Cabernet d'Anjou.

BEST RECENT VINTAGES: 2005, (2004, where yields were controlled), 2003, 2002.
PRICES: $ to $$$

PRODUCERS OF SAUMUR BLANC AND SAUMUR ROUGE: Cave de Vignerons de Saumur-St.-Cyr-en-Bourg: see SAUMUR-CHAMPIGNY ◆ DOM DES CHAMPS FLEURIS ↑ ◆ CLOS ROUGEARD ☆ ◆ DOM DU COLLIER ↑ ◆ Ch Fouquet: see FILLIATREAU ◆ DOM GUIBERTEAU ↑ ◆ DOM LAVIGNE ◆ RENÉ NOËL LEGRAND ◆ Dom de Nerleux: see SAUMUR-CHAMPIGNY ◆ DOM DES ROCHES NEUVES ◆ DOM DE SAINT-JUST ◆ Ch de Targé: see SAUMUR-CHAMPIGNY (in white, try barrel-aged Les Fresnettes) ◆ Dom Saint-Vincent: see SAUMUR-CHAMPIGNY (in white, try La Papareille) ◆ CH LA TOUR GRISE ◆ CH DE VILLENEUVE ☆.

Saumur-Champigny

An AC for reds based on cabernet franc from nine communes forming a lumpy triangle between Saumur, Montsoreau, and St.-Cyr-en-Bourg. As in Chinon, which Saumur-Champigny resembles, there are two general styles: juicy, lively, and easy-drinking, with vibrant fruit; and a more serious style that has all the attributes of the first but is more complex and more structured. This, in good vintages, can age for five to eight years, longer in great years and from top producers.

BEST RECENT VINTAGES: 2005, (2004, where yields were controlled), 2003, 2002. Best vintages of the recent past: 1997, 1996, 1995, 1990, 1989.
PRICES: $ to $$$

PRODUCERS: Cave des Vignerons de Saumur-St.-Cyr-en-Bourg: very good cooperative with reliably good Champigny. Look, in particular, for those labeled *lieu-dit* ◆ DOM LES CHAMPS FLEURIS ↑ ◆ CLOS ROUGEARD ☆ ◆ Yves Drouineau: worthwhile domaine, try Les Beaumiers ◆ PAUL FILLIATREAU ☆ ◆ LANGLOIS-CHÂTEAU ◆ DOM LAVIGNE ◆ RENÉ NOËL LEGRAND ◆ Dom de Nerleux: a reliable domaine, especially Clos des Chatains and Les Loups Noirs ◆ Dom le Petit St.-Vincent: Dominique Joseph is a conscientious vigneron; look for Pelo ◆ DOM DES ROCHES NEUVES ◆ DOM DE SAINT-JUST ◆ Dom St.-Vincent: Patrick Vadé makes above-average Champigny, particularly his cuvées La Chataigneraie and Les Adrialys ◆ Ch de Targé/Édouard Pisany-Ferry: winemaking seems to have improved at this well-known estate; the Champignys last tasted were juicier and less blunt than in the past ◆ CH DE VILLENEUVE ☆.

Saumur–*méthode traditionnelle* (also *mousseux* or brut)

An AC for sparkling wine produced by the Champagne method throughout Saumur and into parts of Anjou. Whites are based on chenin blanc, cabernet, côt, grolleau, pineau d'Aunis, and pinot noir (there's a maximum of 60 percent red grapes for whites), with the possible addition of chardonnay or sauvignon blanc (up to 20 percent). Rosés are made from cabernet, côt, grolleau, gamay, pineau d'Aunis, and pinot noir. Most are nonvintage.

PRICES: $$($)

PRODUCERS: BOUVET-LADUBAY ◆ DOM DE BRIZE ◆ DOM DES CHAMPS FLEURIS ↑ ◆ Gratien & Meyer: large, well-distributed producer, the best is Cuvée Flamme ◆ Dom de Nerleux: see SAUMUR-CHAMPIGNY ◆ CH LA TOUR GRISE.

Domaine Sauvète ↑

41400 Monthou-sur-Cher; 02.54.71.48.68; domaine-sauvete@wanadoo.fr
Wine: Touraine. $($)
Organic, old-fashioned in the best sense of the word, Jérôme Sauvète makes lipsmackingly delicious country reds—Les Gravouilles (gamay), Antea (côt), and the old-vines Privilège, based on côt and cabernet—and a range of sauvignon blancs, of which my clear favorite is Oneiros, a low-yields, old-vines bottling that's full of flavor and character.

Savennières

An AC for cerebral, very mineral, potentially regal, age-worthy whites made from chenin blanc in a pocket of land west of Angers on the north bank of the Loire. The wines are generally dry, sometimes off-dry, and in great vintages, there is usually a small percentage of *moelleux*. There are two recognized *crus*, COULÉE DE SERRANT and ROCHE-AUX-MOINES.

BEST RECENT VINTAGES: 2005, (2004, where yields were controlled), 2003, 2002. Best vintages of the recent past: 1997, 1996, 1995, 1990, 1989.
PRICES: $$ to $$$($)

PRODUCERS: DOM DES BAUMARD ☆ ◆ DOM DE LA BERGERIE ↑ ◆ Clos de Coulaine: Claude Papin of Pierre-Bise had taken charge of this domaine but has told me that he is transferring his efforts to Chamboureau. To follow ◆ DOM DU CLOSEL ◆ COULÉE DE SERRANT ☆ ◆ CH D'ÉPIRÉ ◆ DOMAINE DES FORGES ☆ ◆ DOM LAUREAU DU CLOS FRÉMUR ↑ ◆ DOM ÉRIC MORGAT ↑ ◆ Ch de la Mulonnière: see DOM GUY SAGET ◆ VINCENT OGEREAU ☆ ◆ Ch de Plaisance: see CHAUME ◆ CH SOUCHERIE ☆.

Silice de Quincy ☆

36260 St.-Lizaigne; 02.54.04.04.48; fax: 02.54.04.07.35
Wines: Touraine and Quincy. $$ to $$$
Jacques Sallé, a wine writer and editor, set out to make elegant Quincy—and succeeded. Sallé follows biodynamic principles, keeps yields low, ferments his wines in new or newish barrels, and ages them on their fine lees. The wines are excellent, with picture-perfect Loire balance. Depending on the market, Silice de Quincy can be very expensive; in which case, opt for Sallé's Sauvignon de Silice, in Touraine AC.

Château Soucherie ☆

49750 Beaulieu-sur-Layon; 02.41.78.31.18; chateausoucherie@yahoo.fr
Wines: Anjou range, including Coteaux du Layon, Chaume, and Savennières. $ to $$$
Although Pierre-Yves Tijou and his sons do a fine job with the entire Anjou range, they excel with chenin blanc. The Savennières Les Perrières is superb; the Chaume is a knockout; and the many cuvées of Layon (the Vieilles Vignes, Latour, and Les Mouchis, for example) are as scrumptious as they are regal.

Domaine de la Taille aux Loups (Jacky Blot) ☆

37270 Montlouis-sur-Loire; 02.47.45.11.11; la-taille-aux-loups@wanadoo.fr
Wines: Montlouis, Vouvray, and Bourgueil. $$ to $$$
Blot is proving to be one of Touraine's most energetic vintners. He earned his spurs in Montlouis at the Domaine de la Taille aux Loups, where he continues to produce numerous delectable, barrel-fermented cuvées of chenin blanc—from

a delightful non-dosed *pétillant,* to intriguing dry and off-dry cuvées (including Les Dix Arpents and Rémus), to succulent sweet wines (such as Cuvée des Loups, Romulus, and Romulus Plus). He crossed the river to make equally successful Vouvrays, including the well-positioned Clos de Venise and Clos de la Bretonnière. In 2002 he purchased 14 hectares of hillside vines in Bourgueil, now Domaine de la Butte, from which he makes four fragrant, delicious Bourgueils: the early-drinking Le Pied de la Butte, the near-term-drinking Perrières, Le Haut de la Butte, and the age-worthy Mi-Pente.

Taluau et Foltzenlogel

37140 St.-Nicolas de Bourgueil; 02.47.97.78.79; fax: 02.47.97.95.60

Wines: St.-Nicolas de Bourgueil and Bourgueil. $ to $$

The leading producer of St.-Nicolas de Bourgueil, Joël Taluau has taken a stance against oak; only one of his wines ages in barrel. He makes a very juicy, tasty unoaked Vieilles Vignes and does a good job with other bottlings as well. These include Jeunes Vignes, Vau Jaumier, and Insoumise, part of which ages in new oak.

Touraine

A region and umbrella AC in central Loire, extending west to the borders of Saumur and east to Sologne. The most famous wines include Bourgueil, Chinon, Montlouis, St.-Nicolas de Bourgueil, and Vouvray.

Touraine AC spans the entire region and covers a broad range of wines: dry, off-dry, and sweet whites; reds and rosés; and sparkling wines made by the Champagne method (called *méthode traditionelle*). The whites are made from chenin blanc, sauvignon blanc, arbois, and chardonnay. The reds and rosés come from gamay, cabernet franc, and sauvignon, côt, pinot noir, pinot gris (for rosés), pinot meunier, pineau d'Aunis, and grolleau. Quality varies greatly. Most are flavorful country wines with lively acid and vibrant fruit. The very best can—and do—grace any table, including some at the finest restaurants in France.

BEST RECENT VINTAGES: 2005, (2004, for those who kept yields low), 2003, 2002.

PRICES: $ to $$($)

PRODUCERS: Dom d'Artois: see DOM GUY SAGET ◆ Michel Augé: characterful, idiosyncratic natural wines, sometimes scrumptious, sometimes works in progress ◆ Dom Jacky Augis: see VALENÇAY ◆ PAUL BUISSE ◆ CAILLOUX DU PARADIS ◆ Dom de la Charmoise: see DOM HENRY MARIONNET ☆ ◆ Clos de la Briderie: see CH GAILLARD ☆ ◆ CLOS ROCHE BLANCHE ☆ ◆ CLOS DU TUE-BOEUF (PUZELAT BROTHERS) ◆ CONFRÉRIE DES VIGNERONS DE OISLY ET THÉSÉE ◆ DOM DES CORBILLIÈRES ☆ ◆ Dom Joël Delaunay: very good Touraine AC, particularly L'Antique des Cabotières, an impressive red based on cabernet franc and côt ◆ Famille Durand: see TOURAINE-AMBOISE ◆ Dom Dutertre: see TOURAINE-AMBOISE ◆ Xavier Frissant: see TOURAINE-AMBOISE ◆ CH GAILLARD ☆ ◆ Dom de la Gabillière: see TOURAINE-AMBOISE ◆ DOM DE LA GARELLIÈRE ☆ ◆ DOM HENRY MARIONNET ☆ ◆ Dom Jacky Marteau: tasty Touraine wines include an exemplary gamay and a juicy red blend of côt and cabernet called Cuvée Harmonie ◆ Jean-Pierre Perdriau: see TOURAINE–AZAY-LE-RIDEAU ◆ Ch du Petit Thouars: Since Stéphane Filliatreau took over the winemaking there has been an overall improvement in the wines. Filliatreau keeps a portion to sell himself: try the Cuvée Panatela and the more elegant Lancero ◆ Pascal Pibaleau: see TOURAINE–AZAY-LE-RIDEAU ◆ Ch de la Presle (Jean-Marie Penet): a reliable source for very tasty Touraines, from the grapefruit-mineral sauvignon blancs to the gulpable gamays and stew-friendly cabernets ◆ DOM RICARD ↑ ◆ DOM SAUVÈTE ↑ ◆ VIGNOBLES DE BOIS VAUDONS ↑ ◆ Many producers in specific Touraine regions (for example, Montlouis, Bourgueil, and particularly Touraine hyphenates) also make Touraine AC.

Touraine-Amboise

A small AC in and around the historic town of Amboise (and its Renaissance château). A fraction are light whites made from chenin blanc; most are easy-drinking country reds and rosés made from cabernet franc, gamay, and côt. Often a producer's top red is a blend of the three grapes called François 1er. Most also make wines under the Touraine AC.

BEST VINTAGES: 2005, 2004, 2003, 2002.
PRICES: $ to $$

PRODUCERS: Jacques Bonnigal: a reliable family domaine in the shadow of Mick Jagger's château ◆ Famille Durand: the Durands make the type of characterfully charming wines I love finding in wine bars, from their feisty sauvignon blancs, to the warm, minty François 1ers, to their kirsch-accented côts ◆ Dom Dutertre: one of the largest family domaines in Touraine produces fragrant rosés, convincing chenins (particularly the Vieilles Vignes cuvée) and a supple François 1er ◆ Xavier Frissant: a good, conscientious producer with a solid range of Touraines and a particularly successful Cuvée Renaissance, a red blend similar to François 1er. The 2002, a blend of cabernet franc and côt with a touch of cabernet sauvignon, was a mighty tasty, sophisticated, and ambitious country red. And a steal at $ ◆ Dom de la Gabillière: wine made by the students of the Lycée Viticole d'Amboise from the school's own vines. Look for the barrel-aged chenin called Cuvée Expression and Authenticot, pure côt ◆ DOM DE LA GRANGE TIPHAINE ↑.

Touraine–Azay-le-Rideau

A small AC in the countryside surrounding the charming town and the beautiful château of Azay-le-Rideau. Half of the production is white wine—dry, off-dry, or *moelleux*—made from chenin blanc; half is rosé made from gamay, grolleau (60 percent minimum), côt, and cabernet. The chenins are still fairly rustic, though potentially steely, mineral, and fine-boned; the gamays can be delightful. Producers also make Touraine AC.

BEST RECENT VINTAGES: See TOURAINE.
PRICES: $

PRODUCERS: Thierry Besard: Besard can make very nice Touraine cabernet and, when he makes a Vieilles Vignes chenin from rigorously selected grapes, it reveals the potential of this AC ◆ Jean-Pierre Perdriau: tall, dark, ruggedly handsome, and generous, Perdriau's best wines often resemble their creator ◆ Pascal Pibaleau: consistently one of the best producers in the AC, making full, clean, sapid whites and rosés ◆ Franck Verronneau: above-average wines from a well-trained young winemaker.

Touraine-Mesland

A small AC southwest of the historic town (and château) of Blois. Whites are made from chenin blanc; reds and rosés, from gamay, cabernet, and côt. Reds predominate and are usually blends of the three grapes. The wines, similar to those from Amboise, are amiable country reds and, occasionally, a good bit more. Producers also make Touraine AC. For vintages, see TOURAINE. Prices: $($). Producers: Dom d'Artois: see GUY SAGET ◆ Clos de la Briderie: see CHÂTEAU GAILLARD ☆ ◆ CHÂTEAU GAILLARD ☆.

Touraine–Noble Joué

A tiny appellation on the outskirts of Tours for potentially delightful rosés made from pinot noir, pinot gris, and pinot meunier. Producers here also make Touraine AC. Drink the youngest available. Prices: $. Producers: The two best are Rousseau Frères and Jean-Jacques Sard.

Château la Tour Grise

49260 Le Puy Nôtre Dame; 02.41.38.82.42; philippe.gourdon@latourgrise.com

Wines: Saumur, Coteaux de Saumur, and Anjou. $ to $$

Since Philippe Gourdon converted his domaine to biodynamics there has been a massive improvement in the wines, now among the purest, tastiest, and most interesting in the Puy Nôtre Dame area. Les Amandiers (tender, easy to like) and Les Fontenelles (vivacious and apple-scented), both white, and his juicy Anjou rouge Cuvée Bleu are particularly recommended.

La Tour Saint Martin

18340 Croises; 02.48.25.02.95; tour.saint.martin@wanadoo.fr

Wines: Menetou-Salon and Valençay. $ to $$

Albin and Bertrand Minchin produce generous, slightly New World sauvignon blancs (both the unoaked Morogues and the barrel-fermented Honorine) and appealing oaked and unoaked reds.

Château de Tracy ☆

58150 Tracy-sur-Loire; 03.86.26.15.12; tracy@wanadoo.fr

Wine: Pouilly-Fumé. $$

There has been substantial improvement in the wines from this beautiful property. The lightly rustic 2002 was a punchy sauvignon with gripping mineral-lime-grapefruit flavors; the 2003 may well be the best wine Tracy has ever made.

Domaine Vacheron ☆

18300 Sancerre; 02.48.54.0993; vacheron.sa@wanadoo.fr

Wine: Sancerre. $$

This wonderful family domaine—one of the few wineries left in the town of Sancerre—is justly appreciated for its reds as well as its whites. (The rosés are pretty good too!) Particularly noteworthy are the beautifully mineral Les Romains (white) and the vibrantly fruity Belle Dame (red).

Valençay

Recently promoted to AC, the same grapes are used in Valençay as in Touraine for similar, if somewhat sharper, reds, whites, and rosés. Fié, a mutation of sauvignon blanc, is the most unusual grape in the local mix. (Valençay is also the name of the town, its château, and a local goat cheese.) Producers also make Touraine AC. Drink the youngest available.

PRICES: $($)

PRODUCERS: Dom Augis: a good family domaine. Try the pure côt ◆ Le Clos Delorme: a promising domaine, owned by Albane and Bertrand Minchin of the very good LA TOUR SAINT MARTIN in Menetou-Salon ◆ Jacky Preys: wines of variable quality, popular in Paris wine bars. Try the Fié.

Domaine Vigneau-Chevreau

37210 Chançay; 02.47.52.93.22; contact@vigneau-chevreau.com

Wine: Vouvray. $ to $$

Jean-Michel Vigneau is a delightful man who makes distinctive, personalized Vouvrays that can be raw in lean years but are always honest, flavorful, and worthwhile. Vigneau has recently converted the domaine to biodynamics and has gotten the right to work the Clos de Rougemont vineyard on the grounds of the historic Abbey of Marmoutier just outside Tours. Vigneau also makes a number of different cuvées according to the vintage; two regulars are Clos Baglin and Château Gaillard. Older vintages are also available and definitely worth trying.

Vignerons de Saint-Pourçain

03500 St.-Pourçain-sur-Sioule; 04.70.45.42.82; udv.stpourçain@wanadoo.fr
Wine: St.-Pourçain. $

A good cooperative and an appropriate ambassador for the wines of St.-Pourçain. Ficelle, their knock-back gamay, is always a quaffing pleasure. More serious cuvées include the Réserve Spéciale red and white (the latter is based on the rare tressallier grape), Cuvée Printanière, a floral white, and Domaine de la Croix d'Or, amiable in both white and red.

Les Vignes de l'Ange Vin: See ANGE VIN.

Vignoble de l'Arbre Blanc: See ARBRE BLANC.

Vignobles de Bois Vaudons ↑

41400 St.-Julien de Chedon; 02.54.32.14.23; merieau2@wanadoo.fr
Wine: Touraine. $($)

Jean-François Merieau's domaine is one of the current favorites of up-to-the-minute Paris wine bars, and a wine bar is the best place to discover his quirky, characterful, often delectable wines. His cuvées are numerous and always interesting, starting with three very good sauvignon blancs. I give a slight edge to L'Arpent des Vaudons, which is aged on its lees and has an enticingly fresh, mineral character, though the barrel-fermented old-vines Coeur de Roche does grab your attention. Reflêts d'Été, his pineau d'Aunis–based rosé, is my kind of summer wine. Le Bois Jacou, a gamay, is a lipsmackingly delicious light red. Of his cabernet, côt, and blends thereof, my favorites are Les Cent Visages, a dark, bold country red, and another pure côt, Gueule de Bois (which means "hangover"). Then there's his low-yield, wild-yeast, unfiltered Boa line, which is his real entry into the realm of wacko wines, particularly the Tu le Boa, an off-dry, unfiltered sauvignon blanc that spent more than four years in barrel, developed a fino-sherry-like film, and bears more than a slight resemblance to Tio Pepe. Working with Vincent Carême (Domaine de la Haute Borne) he has begun making a very fresh, mineral, tender Vouvray.

Château de Villeneuve ☆

49400 Souzay-Champigny; 02.41.51.14.04; fax: 02.41.50.58.24
Wines: Saumur-Champigny and Saumur blanc. $ to $$$

Jean-Pierre Chevallier, a Bordeaux-trained enologist, is one of the most talented and dedicated winemakers in the Loire, and his wines are among the very best. His two whites and three reds are all ardently recommended, particularly the top-of-the-line barrel-fermented Saumur blanc, Les Cormiers (mellow, complex, wonderful with haute cuisine), and the rich, elegant Champignys, Vieilles Vignes and Grand Clos.

Vin de Pays

The Loire is one of the country's major producers of Vin de Pays, 95 percent of it sold under the vast regional appellation Vin de Pays du Jardin de la France, which covers thirteen departments from the Loire-Atlantique and the Vendée to the Loiret and Nièvre. Others take the name of a specific department, for example Vin de Pays du Cher, Vin de Pays de Vendée, de Vienne, or de Puy-de-Dôme (in Auvergne). Still others bear the name of one of the following zones: Vin de Pays Coteaux Charitois, in the Nièvre, around La Charité-sur-Loire south of Pouilly; Vin de Pays des Coteaux du Cher et de l'Arnon, on the banks of the Cher and Arnon rivers; Vin de Pays Marches de Bretagne, southeast of Nantes, overlapping Muscadet de Sèvre et Maine; Vin de Pays de Retz, south of the Loire estuary; and Vin de Pays d'Urfé, in the Loire Department. All are subject to specific rules. Wines that don't fit any rules are sold as Vin de Table.

Producers use a Vin de Pays (or Table) designation generally for one of the following reasons: their land doesn't lie within an AC or VDQS; they want to make wine in ways not countenanced by the law—either because of the choice of grape varieties, the method of production, or a sum of all of the parts that results in a wine that other vignerons in a given region find atypical.

Depending on the reason a producer has used the Vin de Pays or Vin de Table designation, the wine may be made to be drunk immediately (DYA) or should be cellared. It may be cheap as chips or one of the most expensive wines in the Loire. Of the multitude of producers making Vin de Pays or Vin de Table, the ones listed below have all been recommended elsewhere in this chapter.

PRODUCERS: AMPELIDAE ($$) ◆ LES VIGNES DE L'ANGE VIN ($$) ↑ ◆ Donatien Bahuaud (DYA/$) ◆ Dom de la Barbinière ($) ◆ DOM LE BRISEAU ($$) ↑ ◆ PHILIPPE CADY (DYA/$) ☆ ◆ CAILLOUX DU PARADIS ($$) ◆ CLOS DE TUE-BOEUF ($/$$) ◆ BRUNO CORMERAIS (DYA/$) ◆ DOM DE L'ÉCU ($/$$) ☆ ◆ CH GAILLARD (DYA/$) ☆ ◆ Dom des Griottes ($/$$) ◆ DOM LES HAUTES NOËLLES (DYA/$) ◆ DOM LAME-DELISLE-BOUCARD ($/$) ◆ Lapandéry: see CÔTE ROANNAISE ◆ DOM DE MONTGILET ($$) ☆ ◆ CH DE LA RAGOTIÈRE ($$) ☆ ◆ DOMAINE DES SABLONNETTES ($/$$) ↑.

Vin de Thouarsais

A tiny VDQS near Saumur producing light whites based on chenin blanc and reds and rosés from cabernet franc and gamay. Drink the youngest available. $ One of the few growers who bottles his own wine is François Gigon in Oiron.

Vouvray

One of the greatest ACs of the Loire and a benchmark for wines made from chenin blanc the world over. Vouvray's vines begin just beyond the city of Tours and stretch east along the banks of the Loire. Vouvray makes an encyclopedic range of whites from chenin blanc, all of which tend to be less alcoholic than chenins from Anjou. The most representative style is an off-dry white, locally referred to as *sec-tendre,* but Vouvray may also be bone-dry, demi-sec (half-sweet), *moelleux* (sweet), or *liquoreux* (syrupy-sweet). The rich sweetness comes from botrytized, sun-shriveled, and/or overripe grapes. Sparkling wines are a significant part of Vouvray production (particularly in weak vintages) and come in two basic styles: *méthode traditionelle* (made like Champagne) and *pétillant,* a slightly sparkling or half-sparkling wine that has less fizz but more flavor than *méthode traditionelle.* The wines are great agers, particularly the sweeter versions of the still wines, which can become breathtakingly complex.

BEST RECENT VINTAGES: 2005, (2004, for dry wines where yields were controlled), 2003, 2002. Best vintages of the recent past: 1997, 1996, 1995, 1990, 1989. Legendary vintages: 1959, 1947, 1945, 1921.
PRICES: $ to $$$$

PRODUCERS: Allias Père & Fils: a meticulous family winery and a recent convert to organic viticulture. At its best, this domaine can make absolutely perfect Vouvray, including excellent *pétillant* ◆ DOM DES AUBUISIÈRES ☆ ◆ Marc Brédif: owned by Pouilly-Fumé's DE LADOUCETTE, the Brédif Vouvrays are always discreet and well above average. Their *méthode traditionelle* brut is among the best in that category ◆ Dom Georges Brunet: good Vouvrays in all styles, including the admirable *pétillant,* which spends two years on its lees before being disgorged, and a *méthode traditionelle* brut *réserve* that spends fifty-four months on its lees, a path more of the Loire's sparkling-wine producers should follow ◆ Dom Le Capitaine: the Le Capitaine brothers have beautifully situated vineyards on a hillside overlooking the Loire. In its richness, freshness and complexity, the 2003 cuvée Marie Geoffroy, a *liquoreux,* expresses the superiority of the site ◆ Cave des Producteurs de Vouvray La Vallée Coquette: a worthy cooperative whose Réserve des Producteurs and *lieu-dit* wines (part of the ALLIANCE LOIRE program) are recommended ◆ CATHERINE & DIDIER CHAMPALOU ☆ ◆ Clos Baudoin: see FRANÇOIS CHIDAINE ☆ ◆ DOM DU CLOS NAUDIN (PHILIPPE FOREAU) ☆ ◆ Régis Cruchet: a conscientious vintner who makes honest, pure Vouvrays ◆ Dom de la Fontainerie (Dhoye-Deruet): gorgeous, nuanced, eco-friendly Vouvrays emerge from Catherine Dhoye-Deruet's cellars, above all, those from the great vineyard Coteaux les Brûlées ◆ CH GAUDRELLE ☆ ◆ DOM DE LA HAUTE BORNE ↑ ◆ HUET ☆ ◆ LEMAIRE-FOURNIER ↑ ◆ THIERRY NÉRISSON ↑ ◆ Dom des Orfeuilles: Bernard Hérivault's floral, crystal-clear Vouvrays display a thrilling mineral undertow that seems a delicious expression of his particular *terroir* in the commune of Reugny ◆ FRANÇOIS PINON ☆ ◆ Alain Robert: Robert keeps a low profile but his wines speak for him. When the results of blind tastings are revealed, I often find that I've singled out one or more of his characterful Vouvrays ◆ DOM VIGNEAU-CHEVREAU.

Château Yvonne ☆

49730 Parnay; tel/fax: 02.41.67.41.29; chateau.yvonne@wanadoo.fr

Wines: Saumur blanc and Saumur-Champigny. $$($)

Most known for its stylish whites, this small domaine, owned by a French-Swiss publisher, is a popular fixture on up-to-the-minute Paris wine lists. Viticulture is eco-friendly; yields are extremely low; wines are made using indigenous yeast and new oak barrels. Neither whites nor reds are filtered. The Saumur blanc is rather Burgundian; Chenin gets a bit lost. Saumur-Champigny, which accounts for a mere 10 percent of Yvonne's production, is fine-grained, fresh, and elegant. All the wines need time to digest their oak.

LOIRE CRIB SHEET

MUST TRYS

Philippe Alliet: Chinon, particularly Coteaux du Noiré
Domaine de Bellivière: Jasnières, particularly Élixir de Tuf or Discours de Tuf
Domaine du Clos Naudin (Philippe Foreau): Vouvray
Coulée de Serrant
Didier Dagueneau: Pouilly-Fumé, particularly Silex or Pur Sang
Huet: Vouvray, especially Clos du Bourg
Domaine de Juchepie: Coteaux du Layon
Domaine de Noiré: Chinon
Château Pierre-Bise: Quarts de Chaume, Layon, and Savennières
Château de Villeneuve: Saumur-Champigny Grand Clos and Saumur blanc Les Cormiers

MUST TRYS # 2

If you doubt there's such a thing as serious Muscadet, if you doubt that it can age, charm, delight, provoke thought and admiration, and accompany food other than oysters, try at least two of the following:

Domaine de l'Écu: especially Expression Granite
Domaine la Haute Févrie: especially the Excellence bottling
Domaines Landron: especially Fief de Breil
Domaine Luneau-Papin: especially Le L d'Or

BEST BUYS

Cave des Vignerons de Saumur-St.-Cyr-en-Bourg: Saumur-Champigny
Catherine & Didier Champalou: Vouvray
Clos Roche Blanche: Touraine
Confrérie des Vignerons de Oisly et Thésée: Touraine
Serge Dagueneau & Filles: Pouilly Fumé and Pouilly-sur-Loire
Domaine de la Garrelière: Touraine
Domaine les Grandes Vignes: Anjou and Bonnezeaux
Lapandery: Vin de Pays d'Urfé pinot noir
François Pinon: Vouvray
Domaine Ricard: Touraine

SAFE HOUSES

Domaine des Aubuisières: Vouvray
Domaine Bernard Baudry: Chinon
Domaine des Baumard: Savennières and Quarts-de-Chaume
Henri Bourgeois: Sancerre and Pouilly-Fumé
François Chidaine: Montlouis and Vouvray
Couly-Dutheil: Chinon
Paul Filliatreau: Saumur-Champigny
Domaine Henry Marionnet: Touraine
Alphonse Mellot: Sancerre
Domaine Richou: Anjou and Coteaux de l'Aubance

ALSACE
BORDEAUX
BURGUNDY
CHAMPAGNE
JURA AND SAVOIE
LANGUEDOC-ROUSSILLON
LOIRE

PROVENCE AND CORSICA

RHÔNE
SOUTHWEST

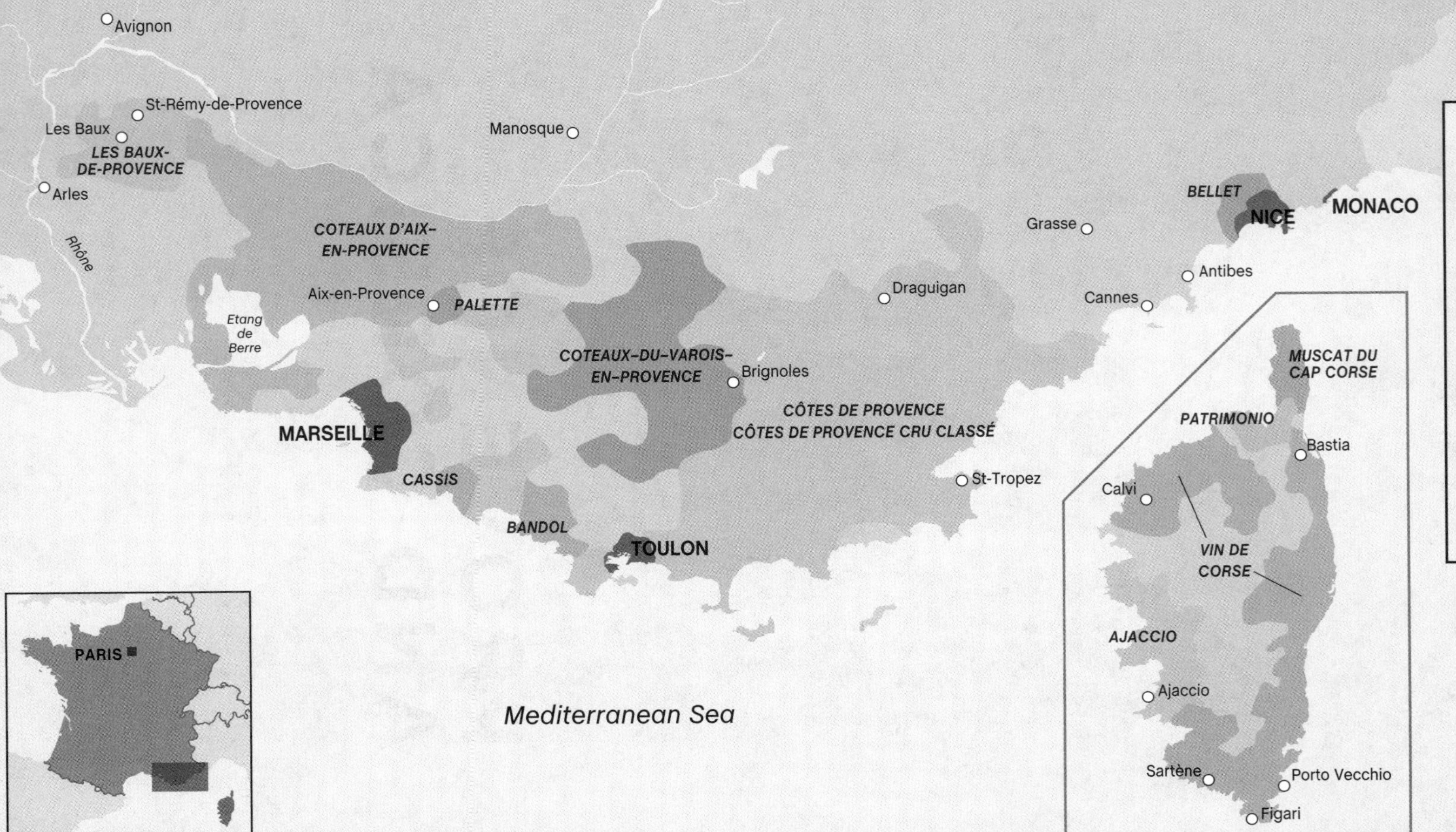
THE PROVENCE AND CORSICA REGIONS
Avignon
St-Rémy-de-Provence
Les Baux
LES BAUX-
DE-PROVENCE
Arles
Rhône
Manosque
COTEAUX D'AIX-
EN-PROVENCE
Aix-en-Provence
PALETTE
Etang
de
Berre
MARSEILLE
CASSIS
BANDOL
TOULON
COTEAUX-DU-VAROIS-
EN-PROVENCE
Brignoles
CÔTES DE PROVENCE
CÔTES DE PROVENCE CRU CLASSÉ
Draguigan
St-Tropez
Grasse
Cannes
Antibes
BELLET
NICE
MONACO
MUSCAT DU
CAP CORSE
PATRIMONIO
Bastia
Calvi
VIN DE
CORSE
AJACCIO
Ajaccio
Sartène
Porto Vecchio
Figari
Mediterranean Sea
PARIS

Of all the French regions lumped together for administrative, editorial, or other purposes, few have less in common than Provence and Corsica. Why, then, combine them in one chapter? Because you, dear reader, are likely to find them joined at the hip on restaurant wine lists and on shop shelves. To treat them one by one would result in a cruelly distant alphabetical separation that would mostly serve to inconvenience the time-pressed shopper. Therefore, I'll keep them in one chapter. I'll consider them separately: Provence first, then Corsica.

Beginning where the Rhône ACs leave off, the wines of Provence might be considered the wines of the Riviera and its backlands. The large region runs from Les Baux de Provence and the outskirts of Marseille in the west to Nice in the east. The tail wags the dog here: Provence's most famous appellations—Bandol, Bellet, Palette, and Cassis—are relatively small; some are microscopic. Not surprisingly, they are all situated on the coast itself. The most important ACs volume-wise are the Côtes de Provence and Coteaux d'Aix-en-Provence, which, along with Les Baux and the Coteaux du Varois-en-Provence, account for 95 percent of the wine produced in the region. More than 70 percent is rosé; 24 percent is red; the balance is white.

Corsica, or the Île de Beauté, is a mountain in the sea. Its altitude explains the stimulating freshness of the white wines, which have none of the heaviness you might expect from vines growing on a sunstruck island. Corse or Vin de Corse—red, white, and rosé—accounts for 75 percent of Corsica's production of appellation wines. Vin de Corse can be produced anywhere but in Patrimonio. Five subregions may attach their name to that of Corse or Vin de Corse: Calvi, Coteaux du Cap Corse, Figari, Porto-Vecchio, and Sartène. Additionally, there are three independent ACs: Ajaccio, Patrimonio, and Muscat du Cap Corse for Vin Doux Naturel (fortified sweet wine).

GRAPES: In Provence the range is enormous. Most reds and rosés are made from cinsault, grenache, mourvèdre, syrah, and a rare local grape called tibouren, thought to have been brought to France by the Greeks. Depending on the AC, cabernet sauvignon, carignan, a local grape called calitor (or pecoui-touar), counoise, braquet, terret, and fuella (folle noire) may be added. Whites are chiefly clairette, sémillon, ugni blanc, and rolle (vermentino). Chardonnay, muscat, marsanne, colombard, and picpoul may also be included. Many of Provence's ACs permit a percentage of white grapes to be used in the making of reds and rosés.

Corsica's principal white grapes are vermentino, locally called malvoisie, and muscat for the AC Muscat du Cap Corse. Additional white grapes include the local bianco gentile and ugni blanc. Reds and rosés may include up to 20 percent vermentino. The primary red grapes include nielluccio (Tuscany's sangiovese) and sciacarello, along with grenache, carignan, cinsault, mourvèdre, syrah, and barbarossa.

STYLES OF WINE: In Provence the variety is huge, with quality constantly progressing. Rosés range from pure plonk, to sunny quaffs, to serious wines worthy of attentive sipping. Reds start life sturdy, vigorous, and sometimes hard; with age, the best can become suave and warm and have flavors reminiscent of black olives and such Provençal herbs as thyme, rosemary, and bay leaf. (I find most of the reds, particularly the young ones, benefit from being in a carafe for an hour or so before serving; they also benefit from being served slightly chilled but not cold.) Whites, generally, are more vinous than varietal; they're strong and full and marry beautifully with the bold, salty, fishy specialties of the Riviera.

At their best, Corsica's dry whites are potent, invigorating, and vinous. The sweet wines all have muscat's heady perfumes, and the best also balance freshness and lushness. The red wines are rather bland, although they will undoubtedly improve, particularly in the hands of some of the dynamic vintners listed here. After all, some of France's most exquisite charcuterie and toothsome sheep's-milk cheeses come from Corsica. Can great reds be far behind?

BEST RECENT VINTAGES: 2005, 2004, (for 2003, as elsewhere, atypical heat resulted in quite a few unusually alcoholic, heavy wines, often lacking acidity), 2001.

PRICES: $ to $$$: I find many Provençal wines too expensive. There are very few that, if purchased in France, are worth $$$ a bottle. It is, however, part of the pleasure of wine to drink the product of a particular *terroir* when visiting that *terroir.*

Domaine Aghje Vecchie ↑

20230 Canale-di-Verde; 06.03.78.09.96; jerome.gerard@attglobal.net

Wine: Vin de Corse. $ to $$

Florence Guidicelli created her domaine in 2000. Thoughtful and very professional, she keeps yields low, harvests by hand, and refused to bottle any of her 2002s because, owing to the rainfall, the quality wasn't up to her standards. (She sold the wine to *négociants.*) Her reds, based on nielluccio, are lightly tannic and very promising; her rosé is vinous, strong, and food-friendly. My favorite is her Vecchio vermentino, a ripe, stony white, with accents of citrus zest and smoke—nice.

Ajaccio

A small AC on the southwestern coast of Corsica. The local red grape sciacarello flourishes here. Producers: CLOS D'ALZETO ♦ CLOS CAPITORO.

Domaine d'Alzipratu

20214 Zilia; 04.95.62.75.47; fax: 04.95.60.32.16

Wine: Vin de Corse–Calvi. $ to $$

Pierre Acquaviva's white Calvi Cuvée Fiumeseccu is vinous, fresh, and tasty; the nicely structured red has pleasant fruit, and the rosé would be ideal with Corsica's charcuterie and pungent sheep's-milk cheese.

Antoine Arena ☆

20253 Patrimonio; 04.95.37.08.27; fax: 04.95.37.01.14
Wine: Patrimonio. $$($)
If you taste only one Corsican wine, let it be a white from Arena—either the Patrimonio Carco, a fragrant, big white, or the oak-aged bianco gentile, a strictly local grape, that Arena fashions into a wine with a tangible presence. The reds, both Carco and Grotto di Sole, are supple, with ripe, sweet fruit. The rosé is big and dry, and the fresh, perfumed Muscat du Cap Corse, a Vin Doux Naturel, would make a lovely aperitif.

Bandol

A small but important AC centered on the eponymous Riviera seaport west of Toulon, Bandol is rightly reputed for its potent, age-worthy reds of stature. It also produces ample, structured rosés, and whites. Reds are primarily mourvèdre, blended usually with grenache and cinsault; syrah and carignan may also be used. White grapes include bourboulenc, clairette, ugni blanc, and sauvignon blanc.

BEST RECENT VINTAGES: 2005, 2004, (2003), 2001, 1998, 1996, 1995.
PRICES: $ to $$$

PRODUCERS: La Bastide Blanche: a recent convert to biodynamics, this domaine makes dark, chewy, promising reds ◆ Dom de la Bégude: Guillaume Tari, the former owner of Bordeaux's CH GISCOURS, makes restrained, silky Bandols, leaner than many (which is not necessarily a criticism); they're also organic ◆ Jean-Pierre Gaussen: invariably interesting reds, so concentrated, dense, and fragrant they border on the Port-like ◆ DOM DU GROS'NORÉ ☆ ◆ Dom Lafran-Veyrolles: straightforward, crowd-pleasing Bandols ◆ Moulin des Costes: this property along with Ch Rouvière are the jewels in the crown of the dynamic Bunan family, whose broad range of styles runs from the easy-drinking, two-dimensional to the heroic (Charriage, for example) ◆ CH DE PIBARNON ☆ ◆ Ch Pradeux: tannic, potent, rock-solid Bandols that demand cellaring for ten years ◆ La Roque: the Bandol co-op makes fragrant, approachable wines at reasonable prices ◆ CH SAINTE ANNE ◆ Ch Salettes: silky, elegant Bandols in all three colors ◆ Dom Sorin: fragrant, stylish Bandols for upscale bistros ◆ Dom la Suffren: this promising domaine recently began bottling its own wine rather than selling to the cooperative. To follow ◆ DOM TEMPIER ☆ ◆ DOM DE TERREBRUNE ◆ DOM DE LA TOUR DU BON ◆ Ch Vannières: blue-ribbon Bandols with plenty of succulent fruit and lots of structure.

Les Baux de Provence

A tiny AC for reds (80 percent) and rosés at the hilly western edge of the Coteaux d'Aix-en-Provence AC (whites made within the Baux zone are still considered AC Coteaux d'Aix-en-Provence). The reds are based on grenache, mourvèdre, and syrah, with the possible addition of cinsault, counoise, and cabernet sauvignon. Rosés are made principally from cinsault.

BEST RECENT VINTAGES: See COTEAUX D'AIX-EN-PROVENCE.
PRICES: $$ to $$$

PRODUCERS: DOM HAUVETTE ◆ MAS DE GOURGONNIER ◆ DOM MILAN ↑ ◆ CH ROMANIN.

Domaine des Béates

13410 Lambesc; 04.42.57.07.58; www.domaine-des-beates.com
Wine: Coteaux d'Aix-en-Provence. $ to $$$
A solid address in the Aix area, the domaine specializes in reds, from the spicy, fruit-packed Les Béatines to the oak-aged, old-vines Terra d'Or, a bold,

balanced blend of cabernet, grenache, and syrah, which needs a couple of years of cellaring before drinking. The whites and rosés are also very good.

Bellet

A minuscule AC above Nice, where most of these wines are drunk, Bellet is primarily known for pleasant dry whites based on bourboulenc, clairette, rolle (vermentino), chardonnay, muscat, and ugni blanc, but there are also rosés and reds based on the local grape braquet (Italy's brachetto) and fuella (folle noire). Most are sold on the spot. Generally made to be drunk immediately. High prices ($$) reflect the location. Producers: Ch de Bellet ◆ Clos St. Vincent ◆ Max Gilli.

Château Calisanne

13680 Lançon-de-Provence; 04.90.42.63.03; www.calissanne.fr
Wine: Coteaux d'Aix-en-Provence. $ to $$
A large estate with worthwhile wines, starting with the bistro-ready Cuvée Prestige in both red and white. The Clos Victoire bottling is a step up; the barrel-fermented white (chiefly clairette) is fresh, balanced, and satisfying; the red, a blend of syrah and cabernet, is succulent and inviting.

Château la Calisse ☆

83670 Pontevès; 04.94.77.24.71; www.chateau-la-calisse.fr
Wine: Coteaux Varois-en-Provence. $ to $$$
Patricia Ortelli, the owner and winemaker, is as meticulous as she is determined. She produces three grades of wine, all of them well made. The top of her range is the ambitious Cuvée Étoiles. I'd pair the taut, flavorful rosé with *biryani*. The stylish, breezy white is a wine you could bring anywhere; and the red is intense and concentrated, almost a liqueur of black currant.

Cassis

A tiny AC to the east of Marseilles, Cassis principally (80 percent) produces white (mostly clairette, ugni blanc, and marsanne), although some reds and rosés (chiefly mourvèdre, grenache, and cinsault) are made there. Most of its wine is sold and drunk on the spot. Generally made to be drunk immediately. (Note: Cassis AC is not related to the black-currant liqueur made in Burgundy and used for Kirs.) Prices: $ to $$. Producers: Dom du Bagnol: above average and reasonably priced ◆ Clos d'Albizzi: character-filled whites ◆ Clos Ste.-Magdeleine: the best-known Cassis producer, with full, vinous whites.

Clos d'Alzeto

20151 Sari-d'Orcino; 04.95.52.24.67; www.closdalzeto.com
Wine: Ajaccio. $ to $$
Some particularities: Pascal Albertini's vines are at the western limit of the appellation and are also the highest. He's among the few who use the local red grape sciacarello, blended or not, with nielluccio and grenache. The results are warm and easy-drinking, and, as in the case of the Cuvée Prestige, oaky.

Clos Canarelli ☆

20114 Figari; 04.95.71.07.55; y.canarelli@terre-net.fr
Wines: Vins de Corse-Figari. $$ to $$$
Yves Canarelli, who practices organic viticulture and keeps yields low, has some nice tricks up his sleeve: he'll be releasing wine made from ancient, prephylloxera vines in the near future and currently he, alone with Antoine Arena, uses the local grape bianco gentile. Vinified in old barrels, with a bit of residual sugar, it's a very good off-dry white. His barrel-aged vermentino is fresh, balanced, and delicious, as is his rosé made from sciacarello. The red, chiefly nielluccio with some syrah, is spicy and inviting.

Clos Capitoro

20166 Porticcio; 04.95.25.19.61; www.clos-capitoro.com
Wine: Ajaccio. $ to $$
Jacques Bianchetti directs a large, historic domaine, making pleasant, sciacarello-based reds and rosés. The vermentino-based white, Cuvée Louis Bianchetti, is focused and creamy with flavors of oak and ripe fruit. It ages fairly well (for drinking within five years) but I prefer it young and feisty.

Clos Landry

20260 Calvi; 04.95.65.04.25; closlandry@wanadoo.fr
Wine: Vin de Corse–Calvi. $ to $$
Fabien and Kathy Paolini excel in producing delectable rosés *(vin gris)*. Their reds, while less distinctive, are ripe and hearty.

Clos Nicrosi

20247 Rogliano; 04.95.35.41.17; fax: 04.95.35.47.94
Wine: Muscat du Cap Corse. $($)
I've tasted only Clos Nicrosi's muscat Vin Doux Naturel and a strong, concentrated white, but each makes me want to follow this domaine.

Clos Petra Rossa

20220 Île Rousse; 04.95.61.53.92; fax: 04.95.61.53.62
Wine: Vin de Corse–Calvi. $
François Fancisci, who practices organic viticulture, is someone to follow. His muscat Vin Doux Naturel is balanced and refined. His red U Monticellu is fresh and promising.

Corse or Vin de Corse

An umbrella AC accounting for 75 percent of the island's Appellation Contrôlée wine. It applies to reds, whites, and rosés. Five subzones may attach their name to that of Corse or Vin de Corse. They are Calvi, Coteaux du Cap Corse, Figari, Porto-Vecchio, and Sartène.

Coteaux d'Aix-en-Provence

An AC centered on Aix-en-Provence. Bordered on the north by the Durance River and on the south by the Mediterranean, it spreads east to Les Baux. Nearly 70 percent of the wine is rosé; reds account for nearly 30 percent, the tiny remainder is white. The wines resemble those made in the Côtes de Provence AC. Reds and rosés are made from grenache with the possible addition of cabernet sauvignon, carignan, syrah, cinsault, counoise, and mourvèdre. White grapes include bourboulenc, rolle (vermentino), clairette, and grenache blanc, with the possible addition of ugni blanc, sauvignon blanc, and sémillon.

BEST RECENT VINTAGES: 2005, 2004, (2003).

PRODUCERS: Ch Bas: while not perfect, the wines from this domaine are ambitious and worthwhile, particularly the top-of-the-line Cuvée du Temple, in which the white suffers by being a tinge too oaky but the red needs only to be poured into a carafe a good hour before serving to release its fragrance and flavor ◆ DOM DES BÉATES ◆ Ch de Beaupré: good enough wines on several levels. The least expensive white is tight and fresh. The Collection du Château bottling, at twice the price, is ampler and riper but too oaky. Still, the white's food-friendly; the red Château, dominated by cabernet sauvignon, merely needs finishing school in a carafe ◆ Ch Calavon: the Grande Cuvée red, which ages in new oak, is smooth and fairly elegant, impressive ◆ CH CALISANNE ◆ Ch de Fonscolombe: here's a focused, appetizing, refreshing rosé, a hefty blend of grenache and syrah; the lightly oaked red isn't bad either ◆ Ch Pigoudet: the Grande Réserve red, aged in new oak, is juicy, appetizing, and reasonably priced ◆ CH ROMANIN.

Coteaux du Varois-en-Provence

A small Var AC centered around the provincial town of Brignoles, Coteaux Varois-en-Provence's primary production (70 percent) is rosé. Of the rest, the reds are based on cinsault, grenache, mourvèdre, and syrah and the whites are chiefly clairette, grenache blanc, rolle, sémillon, and ugni blanc. Best recent vintages: 2005, (2004), (2003). Prices: $ to $$$. Producers: CH LA CALISSE ☆ ◆ DOM DU DEFFENDS ☆.

Côtes de Provence and Côtes de Provence Cru Classé

A large AC with a southern boundary stretching along the Riviera's gold coast. The zone then billows to the north as far as Draguignan, Seillans, and Lorgues. Rosés account for the lion's share of the production, with reds a distant second, followed by a relatively small quantity of white. Styles, quality, and prices vary greatly.

In 1955 Cru Classé status was created for a limited number of domaines—fourteen today. There is, however, no discernable difference in quality between the classified estates and those without the classification. Qualitative differences, at this point, seem more allied with the producer than with the classification. For the record, the fourteen Cru Classés are Château de Brégançon, Clos Cibonne, Château du Galoupet, Domaine du Jas d'Escalns, Château de Mauvanne, Château Minuty, Clos Mireille, Domaine de Rimauresq, Château Roubine, Château Ste.-Marguerite, Château de St.-Martin, Château St.-Maur, Château Ste.-Roseline, and Château de Selle.

PRINCIPAL GRAPES: For reds and rosés, cinsault, grenache, mourvèdre, syrah, tibouren, which may be blended with cabernet sauvignon, calitor (pecoui-touar), and carignan. For whites, clairette, sémillon, ugni blanc, and rolle (vermentino).

BEST RECENT VINTAGES: 2005, 2004, (2003).
PRICES: $ to $$($)

PRODUCERS: CC stands for Cru Classé. Ch de Brégançon (CC): the taut, appealing rosé and the tannic, syrah-cabernet Cuvée Prestige are worth trying although they're a bit pricey ◆ Clos Cibonne (CC): footnote lovers, listen up—the rare local grape tibouren gets a starring role here, making the reds and rosés good options to taste by the glass ◆ Dom de la Courtade: a domaine located on the island of Porquerolles, which is probably the best place to taste their wines ◆ Dom du Dragon: owned by a Belgian wallpaper magnate, this domaine turns out a full, vinous, dry rosé Grande Cuvée, a lovely red quaffer Hautes Vignes, and a stylish, oak-aged red Cuvée St.-Michel ◆ CH DU GALOUPET (CC) ◆ DOM GAVOTY ◆ Dom du Jas d'Esclans (CC): pleasant organic wines, particularly the textured, oaky Cuvée du Loup in both white and red ◆ CH MINUTY (CC) ◆ DOM OTT (CC) ◆ DOM DES PLANES ◆ DOM RABIEGA ☆ ◆ Dom du Revaou: tasty, pure organic wines, particularly the rosé and the pungent white ◆ DOM RICHEAUME ◆ RIMAURESQ (CC) ☆ ◆ CH DE ROQUEFORT ☆ ◆ DOM SAINT ANDRÉ DE FIGUIÈRE ◆ CH SAINTE ROSELINE (CC).

Domaine Culombu

20260 Lumio; 04.95.60.68.70; culumbu.suzzani@wanadoo.fr
Wine: Vin de Corse–Calvi. $ to $$
Étienne Suzzoni, the owner, makes big, refreshing whites; tight, vinous rosés; and chewy reds.

Domaine du Deffends ☆

83470 St.-Maximin-la-Sainte-Baume; 04.94.78.03.91; www.deffends.com
Wine: Coteaux Varois-en-Provence. $ to $$($)

The first Varois wine I tasted (to my knowledge) came from this domaine—a fine introduction. The top red, Clos de la Truffière, is a sophisticated blend of syrah and cabernet sauvignon. It's intelligent, pure, and focused. Clos du Bécassier, a simpler red, would be perfect in a wine bar, with a plate of charcuterie.

Château du Galoupet

83250 La Londe-les-Maures; 04.94.66.40.07; galoupet@club-internet.fr
Wine: Côtes de Provence Cru Classé. $ to $$

Facing the sea and the Hyères Islands, this domaine makes wines that surely sell like hotcakes on the Riviera—they range from the thick, tooth-staining red (needs to spend time in a carafe before drinking), to Tibur, an agreeable rosé based on the local grape tibouren, to the full, mellow white.

Domaine Gavoty

83340 Cabasse; 04.94.69.72.39; domaine.gavoty@wanadoo.fr
Wine: Côtes de Provence. $ to $$

Rosé accounts for 70 percent of Gavoty's production, and it's very, very good—particularly the taut Cuvée Clarendon. The Clarendon red is just fine but I prefer the fresh, ample white, which with several years of bottle age would nicely accompany a loudly flavored fish dish.

Domaine Gentile

20217 St.-Florent; 04.95.37.01.54; domaine.gentile@wanadoo.fr
Wines: Patrimonio and Muscat du Cap Corse. $ to $$($)

Domaine Gentile's spicy red Grande Expression asks to be served with Corsican game—or any hearty, winter stew. The perfumed Muscat du Cap Corse, with its appetizing hints of orange zests, can be brought anywhere. (I'd drink it as an aperitif; others might drink it with dessert.)

Domaine Giudicelli

20200 Bastia; tel/fax: 04.95.35.62.31; muriel.giudicelli@wanadoo.fr
Wine: Patrimonio. $ to $$

The aperitif muscats are lovely here—with whiffs of mint and apricot. Domaine Giudicelli also produces nice rosés and respectable reds.

Domaine du Gros'Noré ☆

83740 La Cadière d'Azur; 04.94.90.08.50; www.gros-nore.com
Wine: Bandol. $$($)

Domaine du Gros'Noré's Alain Pascal makes full-bodied, dark reds that are smooth and balanced and seem to have swallowed the southern sun. His rosés are full, firm, and strong, great partners for Provençal recipes.

Domaine Hauvette

13210 St.-Rémy-de-Provence; 04.90.92.03.90; fax: 04.90.92.08.91
Wines: Les Baux de Provence and Coteaux d'Aix-en-Provence. $$($)

A popular family domaine run according to organic principles. I have a soft spot for the Cuvée Améthyste, based on the unpopular cinsault grape. It's a real Provençal red, structured and spicy, with a whiff of the wild.

Domaine Leccia ☆

20232 Poggio-d'Oletta; 04.95.37.11.35; domaine.leccia@wanadoo.fr
Wine: Patrimonio. $ to $$($)

A reliably good family domaine, Domaine Leccia produces taut, dark rosés and generous, sturdy reds, particularly the Petra Bianca, pure nielluccio from the domaine's best parcels. Its whites are strong and creamy, and the muscat Vin Doux Naturel is fresh and balanced.

Domaine Maestracci

20225 Feliceto; 04.95.61.72.11; clos.reginu@wanadoo.fr
Wines: Vins de Corse; Calvi. $ to $$$
Owner Michel Raoust's simplest white, Clos Reginu, is a lemon-lime-scented quaffer. The more serious E Prove line starts with a strong, vinous white, perfect for keenly flavored food, and includes an equally strong rosé *(vin gris)* and a medium-bodied, user-friendly red.

Mas de Gourgonnier

13890 Mouries; 04.90.4.50.45; fax: 04.90.47.51.36
Wines: Les Baux de Provence. $$ to $$$
Situated in the hottest valley of the Baux area, this domaine makes very appealing wines that immediately struck me as being "new-old fashioned," something of a conservator (or revitalizer) of a beloved, outmoded style. The top of the line is the Réserve du Mas, and there is also a bottling produced exclusively for the market in the United States. The reds, unfiltered and aged in big, old barrels, are fragrant and structured, with spice and Provençal herb flavors.

Domaines Milan ↑

13210 St.-Rémy-de-Provence; 04.90.92.12.52; fax: 04.90.92.33.51
Wines: Les Baux de Provence, Vin de Pays Bouches de Rhône. $$($)
Henri Milan practices organic viticulture at his two Baux domaines, La Tuilière Vieille and Clos Milan. He doesn't filter his reds and he bottles his whites without sulfur. The grenache-dominated Clos Milan is the most elegant and *terroir*-driven of his reds. The barrel-fermented Tuilières Vieilles white was so rich you hardly sensed the oak and was fresh as a waterfall. Ma Terre is the name given to a wine in which Milan blends the eleven different types of grapes he cultivates. It's relatively light and lean but charming.

Château Minuty

83580 Gassin; 04.94.56.12.09; fax: 04.94.56.18.38
Wine: Côtes de Provence Cru Classé. $$($)
A winery located near St.-Tropez might be expected to let proximity do all the work. But the wines from this domaine seem ambitious and intelligent. The Prestige reds are structured and richly fruity. Carafe before serving. The Prestige white is bracing, oaky, and tight; several years of bottle age should flesh things out nicely.

Domaine Mouresse

83550 Vidauban; 04.94.73.12.38; fax: 04.94.73.57.04
Wine: Côtes de Provence. $ to $$
Sophie and Patrick Horst run an eco-friendly domaine, avoiding insecticides and chemical fertilizers, harvesting by hand, and using wild yeasts. They seem to be improvising as they go but the wines come out just fine. I particularly liked their pale, dry rosé Grande Cuvée, which aged on its lees, and their oak-aged red Grande Cuvée Vieilles Vignes, a silky blend of cabernet and syrah.

Muscat du Cap Corse

A small AC in same zone as Patrimonio that produces Vin Doux Naturel (fortified sweet wine) made from muscat à petits grains. Best recent vintages: 2005, 2004. Prices: $$ to $$$. Producers: ANTOINE ARENA ☆ ◆ DOM GENTILE ◆ DOM GIUDICELLI ◆ ORENGA DE GAFFORY ◆ DOM PIERETTI.

Orenga de Gaffory

20253 Patrimonio; 04.95.37.45.00; orenga.de.gaffory@wanadoo.fr
Wine: Patrimonio. $ to $$
Henri Orenga de Gaffory's wines are well represented on local lists. The white Cuvée Félice is pleasant; the muscat Vin Doux Naturel is improving but can be heavy.

Domaine Ott (Château de Selle)

83460 Taradeau; 04.94.47.57.57; chateaudeselle@domaines-ott.com
Wine: Côtes de Provence Cru Classé. $$ to $$$
The major Champagne house Roederer bought 66 percent of the shares of the Ott estates. Though the Ott family remains associated with the domaines, I hope Roederer brings its habitual level of quality to its Provençal acquisitions. I've always found the extremely well distributed Ott wines dilute and expensive. They are still very pricey, but the 2004 rosé Coeur de Grain was fragrant, focused, and well made.

Palette

A minuscule AC outside Aix-en-Provence known for whites (chiefly clairette, colombard, ugni blanc, picpoul, and muscat), reds, and rosés (mainly mourvèdre, grenache, cinsault, and syrah). Palette's wines are potentially, though not always, quite fine—for a price. Best recent vintages: 2005, (2004). Prices: $$($). Producers: The largest and best-known producer is Château Simone whose white is taut and appetizing.

Patrimonio

This small AC, at the base of the fingerlike crook at the northeast tip of the island, reputedly makes Corsica's best wines. Nielluccio is used for reds; vermentino and bianco gentile for whites. The AC Muscat du Cap Corse is situated in the same zone. Producers: ANTOINE ARENA ☆ ◆ DOM GENTILE ◆ DOM GIUDICELLI ◆ DOM LECCIA ☆ ◆ ORENGA DE GAFFORY ◆ DOM PIERETTI ◆ DOM SANTA-MARIA.

Domaine Pero Longo

20100 Sartène; tel/fax: 04.95.77.10.74
Wine: Vin de Corse–Sartène. $
Pierre Richarme is the only Corsican vintner I know of who practices biodynamics. His 2004 white is strong, fresh, and focused; the red Tradition is a supple, easy wine with flavors of crushed berries; the Réserve red is more concentrated, oaky, and slightly tannic. This is another domaine to follow.

Château de Pibarnon ☆

83740 La Cadière-d'Azur; 04.94.90.12.73; www.pibarnon.fr
Wine: Bandol. $$ to $$$
One of the undisputed leaders of the AC, Château de Pibarnon produces an appetizing white; a full, taut rosé; and deep, vibrant reds made almost entirely from mourvèdre. Young, they taste of dried red fruit, mint, and Provençal herbs. With age, they are so comforting they bring out your inner couch potato.

Domaine Pieretti

20228 Luri; tel/fax: 04.95.35.01.03
Wine: Vin de Corse and Muscat de Cap Corse. $ to $$
A source for nice Muscat de Cap Corse, fresh, vermentino-based whites, a novel sweet cuvée red Rappu, and a dry old-vines red that is among the best on the island.

Domaine des Planes

83520 Roquebrune-sur-Argens; 04.98.11.49.00; www.dom-planes.com

Wine: Côtes de Provence. $ to $$

Two interesting rosés lead Domaine des Planes's pack. The first, based on tibouren, is supple and pleasant. Less unusual but more substantial is the textured Cuvée Admirable. Sémillon and rolle, fermented in new oak, produce the Cuvée Élégance, a suave, streamlined white. The mouvèdre-based red is fragrant and well balanced—a relaxed restaurant red with enough oomph to cut through fatty foods.

Domaine Rabiega ☆

83000 Draguignan; 04.94.68.44.22; fax: 04.94.47.17.72

Wines: Côtes de Provence and Vin du Pays du Var. $ to $$

Owned by the Swedish drinks monopoly Vin & Spirit, this domaine produces a number of different products. Bottles labeled Rabiega are purchased wines. Of these, I particularly liked the fennel-scented white, a Vin de Pays du Var, and the fresh, easy-drinking rosé. The stars, however, are the three wines labeled Clos d'Ière. Cuvée I, chiefly syrah, is smooth and polished. Cuvée II, a blend of grenache and carignan, is suave and spicy. III is an oak-aged white blend of chardonnay, sauvignon blanc, and viognier; fresh and luscious, it's delicious young but can age. The reds, particularly Cuvée I, need up to nine years in bottle.

Domaine Renucci

20225 Feliceto; tel/fax: 04.95.61.71.08

Wine: Vin de Corse. $ to $$

Domaine Renucci's Cuvée Vignola white is strong and invigorating. Its rosé is full and fragrant. Its red is structured and appetizing.

Domaine Richeaume

13114 Puyloubier; 04.42.66.31.27; fax: 04.42.66.30.59

Wine: Côtes de Provence. $ to $$$

Run according to organic principles, this domaine produces admirable, forthright wines, both red and white. Their top cuvée of red is Columelle. The wine I tasted seemed flawed. Other critics, however, have had happier experiences with different bottles of the same cuvée. I would retry without hesitating.

Rimauresq ☆

83790 Pignans; 04.94.48.80.45; www.rimauresq.fr

Wine: Côtes de Provence Cru Classé. $ to $$$

The standard bottlings are very good, but spring for the ambitious R line. The label on R red says to carafe before drinking. It's wise to heed the advice. The wine is serious and concentrated; with aeration, it becomes fragrant, with lovely mingled aromas and lipsmacking flavors. The white, a selection of old-vines rolle, aged on its lees, is deep, complex, and layered with flavors of minerals and exotic fruit. Simply wonderful.

Château Romanin

13210 St.-Rémy-de-Provence; 04.90.92.45.87; contact@romanin.com

Wines: Les Baux de Provence, Coteaux d'Aix-en-Provence, and Vin du Pays Bouches du Rhône. $$($)

Run according to biodynamic principles, this domaine produces concentrated, very pure whites based on rolle; a pleasant, chiefly counoise rosé; and an ever-evolving number of reds. Jean de Troubadour, from a parcel outside the AC, is an ample, easy blend of syrah and grenache. Chapelle de Romanin, a slightly more serious quaffer, is within the Baux AC. The top-of-the-line is Coeur Tertius, an ambitious, nuanced selection of the domaine's best grapes. At twice the price of the domaine's most representative wine (called simply Château Romanin), however, I think I'd go for the latter. A delectable blend of grenache, cabernet sauvignon, syrah, and mourvèdre, it's structured, fresh, specific, and both food- and user-friendly.

Château de Roquefort ☆

13830 Roquefort-la-Bedoule; 04.42.73.20.84; fax: 04.42.73.11.19

Wine: Côtes de Provence. $ to $$$

Raimond de Villeneuve's biodynamically inspired domaine sits on a high hill behind Bandol and Cassis. His wines are unique and seem very much in the hypernatural style, starting with Les Genêts, a *terroir*-driven, structured white with tangible presence. In reds, Les Mûres is lipsmackingly juicy, a delight; Rubrum Obscurum ex Veteribus Vitibus is made from old vines, as its name indicates (if you speak Latin), specifically grenache, carignan, and mourvèdre. It's pure and deliciously thought-provoking.

Domaine Saint André de Figuière

83250 La Londe-les-Maures; 04.94.00.44.70; www.figuiere-provence.com

Wine: Côtes de Provence. $ to $$$

Expect pleasant, mealtime reds (both the Cuvée Réserve and the Vieilles Vignes) and slightly more serious whites—vinous, ample, invigorating.

Château Sainte Anne

83330 St.-Anne-d'Évenos; 04.94.90.35.40; fax: 04.94.90.34.20

Wine: Bandol. $ to $$($)

Françoise Dutheil de la Rochère's eco-friendly wines are pure and authentic. The whites border on viscous, with scents of pineapple and hazelnut. The reds, despite the occasional prickle (not unusual in rich, hypernatural reds), are spicy, with blueberry and black olive flavors. They age with grace. It's worth noting that the top-of-the-line Cuvée Collection needs several years' more cellaring than the silky, reassuring basic bottling. Either that, or pour it in a carafe and pair it with wild boar.

Château Sainte Roseline

83450 Les Arcs-sur-Argens; 04.94.99.50.30; www.sainte-roseline.com

Wine: Côtes de Provence Cru Classé. $ to $$$

This very large estate has an equally large *négociant* arm, a tourist attraction (a twelfth-century abbey), specially designed and patented bottles, and an array of technically correct wines that simply don't correspond to styles I like, for example the Cuvée Prieuré red (chiefly syrah with cabernet sauvignon), which is squarely in the tannic, oaky, fruit-bomb camp. There is, however, an audience for this approach.

Château de Saint Martin

83460 Taradeau; 04.94.99.76.76; chateaudesaintmartin@wanadoo.fr

Wine: Côtes de Provence Cru Classé. $ to $$($)

This large domaine offers several different bottlings of red, white, and rosé, among them a Grande Réserve and the richer Cuvée Comtesse Vieilles Vignes. I prefer the whites and rosés in each. The flavorful, structured rosés would be great with spicy food; the textured whites might accompany salty, anchovy-spiked Provençal staples like tapenade.

Domaine Santa-Maria

20232 Oletta; 04.95.39.03.51; fax: 04.95.39.07.42

Wine: Patrimonio. $ to $$

Look to Domaine Santa-Maria for invigorating whites made to sip with seafood, lively reds for barbecues, and a very sweet muscat that gives a bang for the buck.

Domaine Sant'Armettu

20113 Olmeto; 04.95.76.05.18; santarmettu@wanadoo.fr

Wine: Vin de Corse–Sartène. $

A source for pleasant whites and reds to drink on the spot.

Domaine Tempier ☆

83330 Le Plan du Castellet; 04.94.98.70.21; fax: 04.94.90.21.65

Wine: Bandol. $$ to $$$

What nice wines to come home to! Venerable Bandol classics, Tempier's whites are vinous and strong and call out for Provençal food. The rosés are nearly unbeatable. And the reds—of which there are numerous versions—seem to glow with an inner force of warmth, generosity, and resolute character. Favorites include two single parcels: La Migoua, in which mourvèdre is refined by being blended with a number of other grapes, including the dulcet presence of grenache; and La Tourtine, a yummy, site-specific red with the mingled flavors of Provençal herbs.

Domaine de Terrebrune

83190 Ollioules; 04.94.74.01.30; fax: 04.94.88.47.51

Wine: Bandol. $$ to $$$

This eco-friendly domaine produces very good Bandols, including a floral rosé and two kinds of red, each distinctive. In the late fall of 2005 the basic bottling of 2001 was rich and very dry, its sweetly ripe fruit blending with flavors of Provençal herbs. The 1998 Réserve was solid and smooth, still full of sap and vigor, but in its prime, with flavors of dried fruit and sandalwood.

Domaine de la Tour du Bon

83330 Le Brûlat-du-Castellet; 04.98.03.66.22; tourdubon@wanadoo.fr

Wine: Bandol. $$ to $$$

The wines from this domaine seem ambitious, even idealistic, but works in progress. The emphatically concentrated top red St. Férreol had impressive mourvèdre fruit but I couldn't drink a lot of it. The basic bottling is easier to approach, though it, too, is potent. Go for a glass at a wine bar and enjoy the forthright herb, game, black olive, and blackberry flavors.

Domaine de Trévallon ☆

13103 St.-Étienne-du-Grès; 04.90.49.06.00; www.trevallon.com

Wine: Vin de Pays des Bouches du Rhône. $$($)

Eloi Dürrbach, a 1980s pioneer and iconoclast, makes some of the best wine in the Baux region. But to preserve his liberty, Dürrbach sells it as Vin de Pays. Blends of cabernet sauvignon and syrah, the reds are impressive, deliciously scented with Provençal herbs and black olives, and say "Rhône" unequivocally. The barrel-fermented white, a blend of roussanne and marsanne, with a touch of chardonnay, is a mellow pleasure.

Vin de Pays

In Provence you'll find a multitude of appellations in a vast zone. Some take the names of their departments, for example Bouches du Rhône or Var; others, of small localities, such as Argens. Most of the production is red, though there is quite a bit of rosé as well. In addition to traditional Rhône varietals, the wines are made from such popular grapes as chardonnay, sauvignon blanc, cabernet sauvignon, and merlot. Generally made to be drunk immediately. Prices: $ to $$. Corsican wines use the name Vin de Pays de l'Île de Beauté: These are mainly given over to such fashionable grape varieties as chardonnay and merlot. Producer: DOM AGHJE VECCHIE.

PROVENCE AND CORSICA CRIB SHEET

FOR PROVENÇAL ROSÉS

Domaine Gavoty: Côtes de Provence
Domaine du Gros'Noré: Bandol
Château Minuty: Côtes de Provence Cru Classé, especially Cuvée de l'Oratoire
Domaine Mouresse: Côtes de Provence
Château de Pibarnon: Bandol
Domaine des Planes: Côtes de Provence, especially the Cuvée Admirable
Château Saint Martin: Côtes de Provence Cru Classé
Domaine Tempier: Bandol

MUST TRYS

Antoine Arena: Patrimonio (Corsica), especially the dry whites
Domaines Milan: Les Baux de Provence, Le Clos Milan
Château de Pibarnon: Bandol
Château de Roquefort: Côtes de Provence
Domaine de Trévallon: Vin de Pays des Bouches du Rhône (Provence)
Rimauresq : Côtes de Provence Cru Classé, especially the R line
Domaine Tempier: Bandol

SMART BUYS

Château de Beaupré: Coteaux d'Aix-en-Provence
Château Calavon: Coteaux d'Aix-en-Provence
Domaine Culombu: Vin de Corse–Calvi, especially the whites and rosés
Domaine du Dragon: Côtes de Provence
Château Pigoudet: Coteaux d'Aix-en-Provence
Domaine Renucci: Vin de Corse, especially Cuvée Vignola
Domaine de la Tour du Bon: Bandol

SAFE HOUSES

Domaine des Béates: Coteaux d'Aix-en-Provence
Château la Calisse: Coteaux Varois en Provence
Domaine du Deffends: Varois en Provence
Domaine du Gros'Noré: Bandol
Domaine Leccia: Patrimonio (Corsica)
Domaine Rabiega: Côtes de Provence, the Clos d'Ière label

ALSACE
BORDEAUX
BURGUNDY
CHAMPAGNE
JURA AND SAVOIE
LANGUEDOC-ROUSSILLON
LOIRE
PROVENCE AND CORSICA
RHÔNE
SOUTHWEST

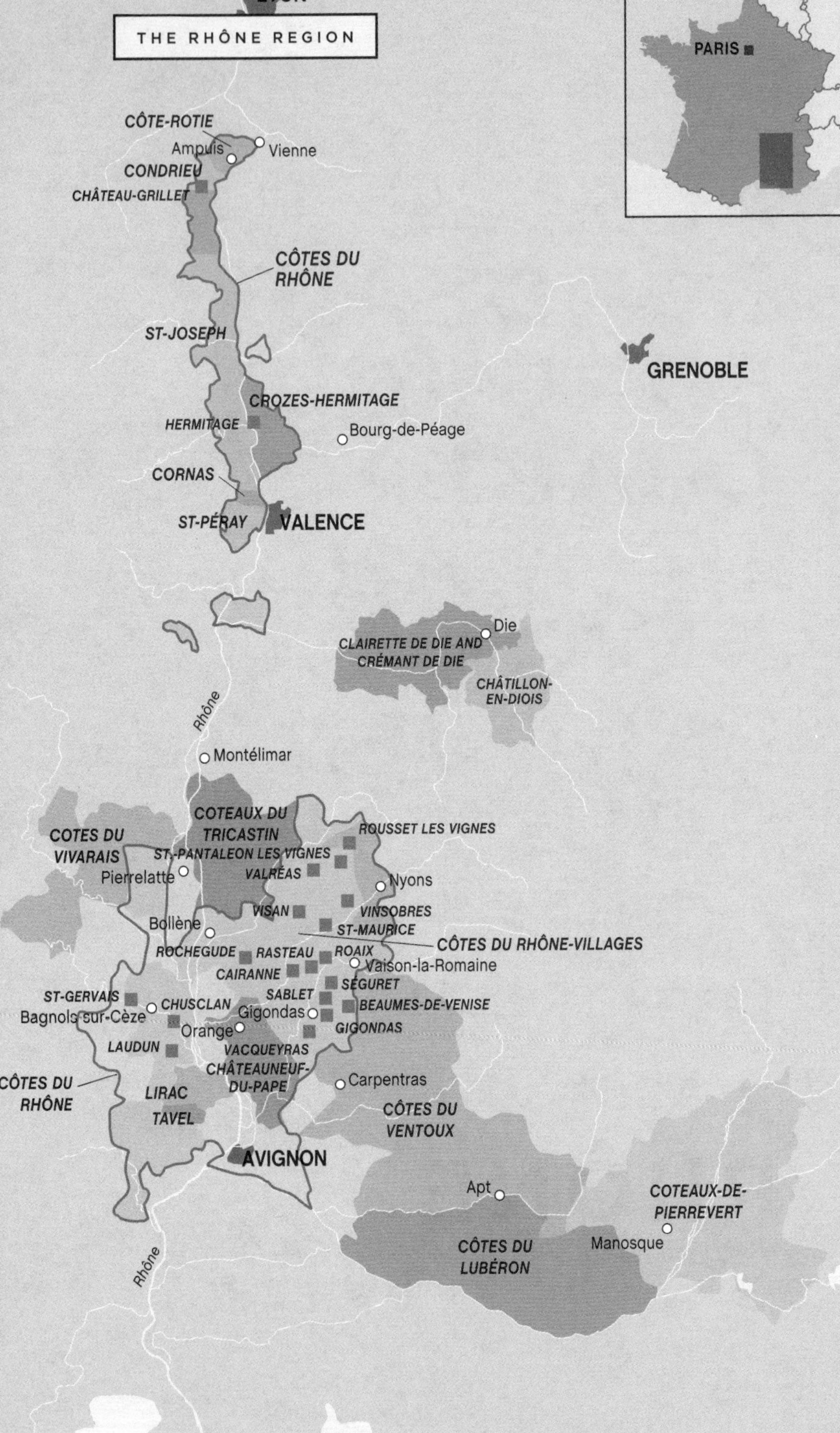

THE RHÔNE REGION
LYON
PARIS
CÔTE-ROTIE
Ampuis
Vienne
CONDRIEU
CHÂTEAU-GRILLET
CÔTES DU RHÔNE
ST-JOSEPH
GRENOBLE
CROZES-HERMITAGE
HERMITAGE
Bourg-de-Péage
CORNAS
ST-PÉRAY
VALENCE
Die
CLAIRETTE DE DIE AND CRÉMANT DE DIE
CHÂTILLON-EN-DIOIS
Rhône
Montélimar
COTEAUX DU TRICASTIN
ROUSSET LES VIGNES
COTES DU VIVARAIS
ST.-PANTALEON LES VIGNES
VALRÉAS
Pierrelatte
Nyons
VISAN
VINSOBRES
Bollène
ST-MAURICE
CÔTES DU RHÔNE-VILLAGES
ROCHEGUDE
RASTEAU
ROAIX
Vaison-la-Romaine
CAIRANNE
SÉGURET
ST-GERVAIS
CHUSCLAN
SABLET
Bagnols-sur-Cèze
Gigondas
BEAUMES-DE-VENISE
Orange
GIGONDAS
LAUDUN
VACQUEYRAS
CHÂTEAUNEUF-DU-PAPE
CÔTES DU RHÔNE
Carpentras
LIRAC
TAVEL
CÔTES DU VENTOUX
AVIGNON
Apt
COTEAUX-DE-PIERREVERT
CÔTES DU LUBÉRON
Manosque
Rhône

Beginning south of Lyon and continuing south, along the banks of the river, to Avignon and beyond, the vineyards of the Rhône valley are among the most extensive in France. There are two key viticultural zones: the north, from the town of Vienne to Valence, and the south, beginning below the town of Montélimar and continuing to Avignon. The north—the home of the ACs Hermitage, Crozes-Hermitage, Côte-Rôtie, Cornas, Condrieu, Château-Grillet, St.-Joseph, and St.-Péray—seems like a bridge between Burgundy and the wines of Provence. Its best vineyards are impossibly steep hills bordering the river, and its best wines are elegant, racy, and detailed. The south—the home of Châteauneuf-du-Pape, Gigondas, Vacqueyras, and scores of Côtes du Rhône-Villages—is the gateway to Provence, a series of small villages, their squares lined with linden trees, rugged fields of wild lavender and thyme, and vineyards strewn with rocks the size of footballs. Its wines are more sun-kissed, spicier, and forthright. The mistral blows throughout, a wind so strong it is said to drive people mad, so strong that it can, and does, prevent you from opening your car door.

There are also a number of satellite appellations sprawling a bit beyond the valley: to the west, the various appellations of the Ardèche; to the south, the Côtes du Ventoux, the Coteaux du Tricastin, and the Côtes du Lubéron; and to the east, Clairette de Die and Châtillon-en-Diois. (Although the Costières de Nîmes AC is often listed with the wines of the Rhône, in this book it is found in the Languedoc-Roussillon chapter.) Additionally, the Rhône is the source of two noteworthy Vin Doux Naturel (VDN): Rasteau, from the Côtes du Rhône village of the same name, and Muscat de Beaumes-de-Venise.

GRAPES: In the north, syrah is the sole red grape; the whites are viognier, marsanne, and roussanne. In the south, grenache (both blanc and noir) predominates. As the wines are almost always blends, it is joined by syrah, mourvèdre, cinsault, clairette, bourboulenc, roussanne, and more. Muscat, however, is the sole grape in the AC Muscat de Beaumes-de-Venise. (Less familiar grapes are mentioned, where used, in the specific entries for those ACs.)

STYLES OF WINE: Although there is a wide range of styles—starting with the distinct differences between wines from the north and those from the south—Rhône wines all share richness in alcohol and big, bold flavors. They are not shy. The whites, with the exception of those based on viognier and muscat, are vinous and, depending on the blend, creamy and mineral. The best age well. Viognier and muscat are exceptionally perfumed. Reds from the north feel cooler and more focused than those from the south. Southern reds seem broader and are generally spicier, cozier, and more down-home, though the finest, as with some Châteauneuf-du-Papes, have more than a whiff of the regal about them.

The best age well: ten years and counting for a good northern red; up to twelve years (for my palate) for all but the most structured Châteauneufs.

BEST VINTAGES: The year 2005 is expected to be excellent; and 2004 is very promising throughout the Rhône. In 2003 the wines range from heavy and jammy to super; they will probably evolve more quickly than wines from more classic years, so drink them in the near term. As for 2002, rain in the north and disastrous floods in the south resulted in some decent to very good wines in the former and generally disappointing wines in the latter. The 2001 vintage was excellent in the north but more variable in south, although essentially a first-rate year for Châteauneuf and good southern producers. The year 2000 was good but quick to evolve, though wines from the most serious producers seem to be real stayers. As for 1999, it was a great vintage for both Châteauneuf and Côte-Rôtie; 1998 was greater in the south (where the wines are keepers) than in the north but generally a very good year. Except for the top producers, 1997 was a weak year. In 1996 the north was better than south, especially Hermitage. And 1995 was an excellent vintage, particularly for grenache, so look at—and drink up—Châteauneuf and Gigondas. Best vintages of the recent past: 1989, 1990.

PRICES: Once again, with such variety prices vary from $ to well above the $$$$ mark.

Domaine Thierry Allemand ☆

07130 Cornas; tel/fax: 04.75.81.06.50

Wines: Cornas. $$$($)

Gifted and demanding, Thierry Allemand turns out masterly, fine-grained, deep Cornas from his tiny property. He normally makes three or four cuvées, including Reynard from old vines. In the differently difficult vintages of 2002 and 2003, however, he made only one cuvée: the 2002 is fresh, focused, and specific with smooth black cherry fruit; the 2003, is fleshy, structured, delicious, and real though it does have a Napa-esque opulence. In general, these are nuanced, regal Cornas that could convert those who think of the wine as stoic and impenetrable.

L'Anglore ↑

30126 Tavel; tel/fax: 04.66.33.08.46

Wines: Tavel, Côtes du Rhône, and Vin de Table. $ to $$

Eric Pfifferling is one of those irrepressible spirits who can't help fiddling with his wines. The viticulture is organic and Pfifferling's range is delightfully surprising. His unfiltered Tavel rosés are truly appetizing, potent, and riveting. There are numerous cuvées of red Côtes du Rhône, all worth tasting, like the lean, mineral, ultrapure Cuvée des Travers and the Cuvée de la Pierre Chaude, a smooth blend of grenache and cinsault. Simultaneously strong and light, it would be great with Moroccan food. Among his various Vins de Table there's a fizzy, off-dry chasselas called Cuvée des Caprices and a pure grenache, Terre de l'Ambre, that strikes a tasty balance between red and rosé.

Domaine des Aphillanthes ↑

84850 Travaillan; tel/fax: 04.90.37.25.99

Wines: Côtes du Rhône. $ to $$

Created in 1999, this biodynamically run domaine turns out impressive southern Rhônes. I could have drunk several bottles of the fresh, delicious, beautifully balanced Rhône-Villages Cuvée des Galets on the spot. The 2001 Villages Vieilles Vignes, while a bit gamey and tannic, was better than many Châteauneuf-du-Papes.

Ardèche: The name of a department on the right bank of the Rhône, Ardèche is home to several well-known ACs—Condrieu, Cornas, St.-Joseph, St.-Péray, and generic Côtes du Rhône—as well as three unsung and/or newly minted appellations: Côtes du Vivarais AC, Vin de Pays des Coteaux de l'Ardèche, as well as Côtes du Rhône and, just to complicate matters by splitting appellational hairs, Côtes du Rhône-Villages–Côte Ardèche. The wines are produced in the rude mountainous regions west and southwest of Montélimar. Whites, reds, and rosés are all made, but the current emphasis is on reds based on syrah. I think this is a mistake and would put my money on viognier-based whites, generally sold as Vin de Pays. The best of the reds are cool mountain wines, their relatively high alcohol levels concealed by their freshness. They're fine for wine bars. The viogniers, however, show real promise. The most accomplished of them verge on world-class. There is also a red made from the rare grape chatus. Roughly 80 percent of the wine is made by twenty-five cooperatives, which have grouped together under the name Vignerons Ardéchois. Most is sold to tourists. Recommended producers are listed under the various appellations.

Gilles Azzoni/Le Raisin & l'Ange ↑

07170 St.-Maurice d'Ibie; 04.75.94.70.10

Wines: Côtes du Vivarais, Vin de Pays de l'Ardèche. $ to $$

Another young, impassioned, organic crusader, Azzoni generally succeeds in making hypernatural wines that charm and delight. I'm most impressed by his whites—all of which are Vin de Pays and all of which contain a good percentage of viognier. They're perfumed, balanced, fresh, flavorful, and with a bit of roussanne in the mix, mineral and creamy. L'Hommage, a red Vin de Table, is a soft, pure, cool blend of merlot and grenache. Fable, a red Côtes du Vivarais made with syrah and cabernet sauvignon, is fragrant and juicy, a characterful quaffer.

Château de Beaucastel ☆

84350 Courthézon; 04.90.70.41.00; www.beaucastel.com

Wines: Châteauneuf-du-Pape, Côtes du Rhône. $$ to $$$$

One of *the* great Rhône houses, this large property is run fastidiously by François and Jean-Pierre Perrin. In addition to pioneering organic viticulture in the region, the Perrins have a controversial approach to just about every aspect of making Châteauneuf-du-Pape. Not everyone agrees with the methods, though few would argue that this is one of the must-trys of the Rhône, perhaps even of all of France. The full thirteen permissible grape varieties enter into the red blend, including muscardin and vaccarèse. The wines are good agers. Always deep, pure, full of character, and complex, they are specific, spicy, and meaty, evolving toward flavors of leather, sandalwood, and coffee with age. Detractors fault bottle variation—which, I fear, may be one of the prices to pay for hypernaturalness (in this, they are far from alone). However, the white Châteauneuf, made from pure, old-vines Roussanne, is always sumptuous. It is simply a great wine. Across the road from the Châteauneuf vineyards, the Perrins produce a reliably tasty Côtes du Rhône called Cru de Coudoulet. See also PERRIN & FILS.

Beaumes-de-Venise

A small AC for red wines based chiefly on grenache and syrah. Six miles north of Carpentras, Beaumes-de-Venise was, until recently, a designated Côtes du Rhône-Villages. It is more famous for another wine, Muscat de Beaumes-de-Venise.

BEST RECENT VINTAGES: 2005, 2004, 2003, 2001.
PRICES: $ to $$$

PRODUCERS: Arnoux & Fils/Le Vieux Clocher: simple but pleasant ◆ Dom de Beaumalric: small family domaine with supple, discreet wines ◆ Dom de Cassan: a good family domaine making balanced, tasty AC reds and Côtes du Rhône whites ◆ DOM DE DURBAN ◆ Dom de Fenouillet: see MUSCAT DE BEAUMES-DE-VENISE ◆ Dom de la Ferme St.-Martin: see CÔTES DU VENTOUX ◆ Vignerons de Beaumes-de-Venise: look for the Cuvée Terres du Trias.

Domaine de Beaurenard

84231 Châteauneuf-du-Pape; 04.90.83.71.79; www.beaurenard.fr
Wines: Châteauneuf-du-Pape, Rasteau. $$ to $$$
An enterprising family with vines in Châteauneuf-du-Pape and Rasteau, the Coulons also run a wine museum on the road between the two appellations. The traditional Châteauneuf bottling is stylish and ample; the top-of-the-line Boisrenard is based on low-yielding old vines. Rich but light on its feet, the red is meaty and structured, with good flavors of black cherry and oak and a note recalling *eau-de-vie de prune*; the white is rich and vinous, with flavors of preserved lemons. The Rasteau is soft, suave, and ready and waiting. Their Rasteau Vin Doux Naturel is among the best in that AC.

Domaine Bois de Boursan

84230 Châteauneuf-du-Pape; 04.90.83.51.73; fax: 04.90.83.52.77
Wine: Châteauneuf-du-Pape. $$
A source of unfiltered reds that are full of character and cry out for aging. The traditional Châteauneuf starts off life fragrant and chewy and evolves toward sweet spices, game, and sandalwood. The Cuvée des Félix is even more demanding. The 2001 is a case in point: when first opened, it was fluid and friendly, fresh, with light notes of game, black olives, and sandalwood and a solid sense of place. Recorked, half-full, and left for a month, its spiciness was accentuated, it was extremely dry, the embodiment of a red made on mistral-swept stones.

Henri Bonneau/Réserve des Célestins

84230 Châteauneuf-du-Pape; 04.90.78.13.81
Wine: Châteauneuf-du-Pape. Prices unknown
Many, many things have been said about Henri Bonneau: that he's a right-wing eccentric, that he won't allow visitors, that his various cuvées inspire reverence—if you can ever find a single bottle of any one of them. Well, I found one—a 1994—on the wine list of Chez Ramulaud in Paris. I loved it. It was still fresh, had good balance, a hint of old wood, and sweet spices. I heard some not-so-complimentary out-of-school tales of how Bonneau vinifies and accepted the general verdict that this was a very good example of a 1950s-style Châteauneuf-du-Pape.

Domaine Christophe Bonnefond ☆

69420 Ampuis; 04.74.56.12.30; gaec.bonnefond@terre-net.fr
Wines: Côte-Rôtie and Condrieu. $$$ to $$$$
From a small parcel, Bonnefond makes a discreet, racy Condrieu. He's got a larger piece of Côte-Rôtie from which he makes several delicious cuvées. The traditional bottling in 2002 was well made but didn't transcend the vintage. The Les Rochains cuvée, aged in new oak, however, did outclass the vintage: oaky but elegant, it's very pretty. Bonnefond made three successful, pedigreed cuvées in 2003. I found the Côte Rozier to be the freshest and most elegant

and Les Rochains the deepest, most massive, and most concentrated—though still fresh and elegant.

Domaine Bosquet des Papes

84232 Châteauneuf-du-Pape Cedex; 04.90.83.72.33; fax: 04.90.83.50.52
Wine: Châteauneuf-du-Pape. $$ to $$$
The Boirons make classic (in the good sense of the word) Châteauneufs that age well. There are several cuvées, starting with a truffle, fruit, and sandalwood-scented traditional bottling; then À la Gloire de Mon Grand-Père, made from a single parcel of old grenache vines. It's dulcet and textured, a tribute to both *grand-père* and grenache. Chante le Merle Vieilles Vignes is the densest and darkest, a very rich, very dry Rhône with deep flavors of black cherry and sweet spices.

Domaine Brusset ☆

84290 Cairanne; 04.90.30.82.16; fax: 04.90.30.73.31
Wines: Gigondas, Cairanne, Côtes du Rhône, and Côtes du Ventoux. $ to $$$
This is a substantial, sensible, and conscientious family domaine, with a wide range of wines in four appellations. Their Côtes du Ventoux Boudale is a feisty, fruity red. The Côtes du Rhône Laurent Brusset, incisively marked by its 20 percent syrah, is deeply rich, fruity, and delicious, as is the lipsmacking, sappy Cairanne red Coteaux des Travers. Moving up the ladder, there's the unfiltered, partially barrel-aged Cairanne Vendange Chabrille, an excellent, deep, fresh red; and the new-oak-aged Gigondas Les Hauts de Montmirail, lush, suave, balanced, three-dimensional, and yummy. There are good rosés and whites, particularly the oak-aged Cairanne blanc, with its blend of oak and viognier flavors. And in exceptional vintages, like 2000, there's Cuvée Hommage à André Brusset, a red Cairanne made from very old vines from selected parcels. It's strong, discreet, smooth, and balanced, a wine with gravitas.

Cairanne

One of the most dynamic designated Côtes du Rhône-Villages, for red, white, and rosé. Reds predominate. Grenache is the main red grape, with syrah and mourvèdre in supporting roles. In fairness, Cairanne merits its own AC. See Côtes du Rhône for vintages and prices.

PRODUCERS: Dom d'Aeria: especially cuvée Prestige ◆ Dom des Amadieu: particularly cuvées Vielle Vignes and Vitalis ◆ Dom Berthet-Rayne: attractively rustic general bottling and oak-aged Prestige Castel Mireio ◆ Dom Boisson: particularly L'Exigence from their oldest vines ◆ DOM BRUSSET ☆ ◆ Cave de Cairanne: notably the old-vines cuvée Les Salyens ◆ Dom Galuval: a newcomer, who started with the 2004 harvest, is making some succulent reds and whites, particularly the syrah-dominated Grand Coeur ↑ ◆ DOM LES GRANDS BOIS ◆ Dom de l'Oratoire Saint Martin: look for the unfined, unfiltered red and barrel-fermented white Cuvée Haut Coustias from one of Cairanne's best *terroirs;* also recommended are the cuvées Réserve des Seigneurs and Prestige ◆ DOM RABASSE-CHARAVIN ☆ ◆ DOM MARCEL RICHAUD ☆ ◆ ÉRIC TEXIER ☆ ◆ LES VINS DE VIENNE ☆.

Cave de Rasteau

84110 Rasteau; 04.90.10.90.10; www.rasteau.com
Wines: Rasteau and Côtes du Rhône. $ to $$($)
This good cooperative accounts for 50 percent of Rasteau's production. Their Côtes du Rhône blanc Les Viguiers is vinous, lightly mineral, and food friendly. R de Rasteau is a jolly, bright cherry-flavored bistro red; Rasteau Prestige is slightly beefier and more complex; Les Hauts du Village is a dark fruit- and black-olive flavored Rasteau. The Cave's Vins Doux Naturels include a ruby Port-like Signature, a mellow tawny, the older the better.

Cave de Tain

26601 Tain l'Hermitage Cedex; 04.75.08.20.87; www.cave-tain-hermitage.com
Wines: Hermitage, Crozes-Hermitage, Cornas, St.-Joseph, St.-Péray, and Vins de Pays. $ to $$$

This reliable and progressive cooperative, founded in 1933, has nearly four hundred members and controls more than 1,000 hectares of vines, with prime holdings in Hermitage AC. Its simplest wines, Vin de Pays des Collines Rhodaniennes, include the pleasant Cépage Marsanne in white and the impressive Pure Syrah in red. The latter comes from their best parcels in Crozes-Hermitage and St.-Joseph and ages in new American oak. It's cool, fresh, and balanced, with discreet but firm syrah fruit. Favorites among their other wines are the Crozes-Hermitage blanc, a very good, well-priced, fresh and rich marsanne; the nicely structured, juicy Crozes-Hermitage rouge Les Hauts du Fief, pure syrah from selected parcels; the mellow, refined Hermitage blanc, another pure marsanne; and the classic Hermitage rouge and, a distinct step up, Gambert de Loche, named for the founder of the cave who bequeathed this parcel of vines to the cave.

Domaine du Cayron

84190 Gigondas; 04.90.65.87.46; fax: 04.90.65.88.81
Wine: Gigondas. $$

Captivating and deliciously old-fashioned, these Gigondas, neither fined nor filtered, are smooth, supple, and spicy. They age beautifully: a 1990, drunk in 2006, had plenty of sap left but displayed a beautiful weave of dried cherries, old wood, sweet spices, and ash, all accented by black olive and sandalwood. Pure pleasure.

Chapoutier ☆

26601 Tain l'Hermitage Cedex; 04.75.08.28.65; www.chapoutier.com
Wines: Hermitage and almost every other Rhône AC. $ to $$$$

When Michel Chapoutier succeeded his father in the late 1980s he transformed what had been a venerable but frequently disappointing grower-*négociant* house into one of the most exciting domaines in the Rhône. Not only did he convert his sizable holdings to biodynamics, he improved the quality of the wines dramatically. While everything from Coteaux du Tricastin to Cornas is recommended, the tastiest, if most expensive, bets are the domaine's deluxe cuvées. The St.-Joseph Les Granits is one of the best representatives of that AC, as is the Côte-Rôtie La Mordorée. Chapoutier owns a hunk of Hermitage—which he prefers to call Ermitage—and produces a number of stunning cuvées from the vineyard, including L'Ermite, Le Pavillon in red, Le Méal in red and white, and the lush, oaky De l'Orée in white.

Domaine Didier Charavin

84110 Rasteau; 04.90.46.15.63; earllesbuisserons@terre-et.fr
Wines: Rasteau and Côtes du Rhône. $ to $$

Solid producer of Côtes du Rhône and Rasteau–Côtes du Rhône-Villages. The best cuvée is Les Parpaiouns, a focused blend of grenache and syrah, which is probably what many people want when they think of Rhône red. Charavin also produces appealing Vin Doux Naturel—both a fresh, fluid red, and a mild, balanced *rancio*.

Domaine de la Charbonnière ☆

84230 Châteauneuf-du-Pape; 04.90.83.74.59; fax: 04.90.83.53.46
Wines: Châteauneuf-du-Pape and Vacqueyras. $$ to $$$($)

Michel Maret's wines could be ambassadors for the Rhône. His Vacqueyras is a hearty red, with ash and spice flavors, a perfect winter stew wine. His white Châteauneuf-du-Pape is tight, fresh, vinous, and mineral. You don't perceive the alcohol no matter how rich the vintage. There are four red Châteauneuf bottlings, starting with a warm, spicy, somewhat rough-hewn (though not rustic) version accented with mild oak and ash flavors. Les Hautes Brusquières, a blend of syrah and grenache, bridges classic and modern styles. Warm and inviting, it has vibrant crushed cherry fruit blended with oak and spices—very tasty. I have a soft spot for the Mourre des Perdrix bottling. It seems the most old-fashioned: very dry, spicy, structured, racy, and specific. It's also the most austere. The Old Vines cuvée, practically pure grenache from eighty-plus-year-old vines mixed with a dash of mourvèdre, is a forthright, hair-on-the-chest red, a real crowd-pleaser, the biggest fans of which are rugby addicts. All three cuvées age in large and small barrels, and all reds may be bottled unfiltered depending on the wishes of the client. (This means that the bottlings, imported into the United States by Kermit Lynch, will be unfiltered.)

Château-Grillet

Legendary 3-hectare AC for distinctive white wine made from Viognier. Vintages: Try whatever is available. Prices: $$$ to $$$$. The AC consists of a single domaine: CHÂTEAU GRILLET ☆.

Châteauneuf-du-Pape

Important AC, situated on the left bank of the Rhône, starting just above Avignon. About 10 percent of the production is white, the rest red. Thirteen grape varieties are permitted. In practice, whites are based on bourboulenc, clairette, grenache, and roussanne; reds, on grenache, syrah, mourvèdre, cinsault, counoise, muscardin, and terret. The best whites are strong, vinous, and mineral, with backbones of steel. The reds may start off life juicy and succulent. They'll close up and slowly evolve toward flavors of ash, sandalwood, sweet spices, and leather. Those truest to their *terroir* are always big, very dry wines, the image of their very particular landscape—hillsides of mistral-battered vines growing between sun-bleached stones the size of large loaves of country bread.

BEST RECENT VINTAGES: 2005, 2004, (2003), 2001, 1999, 1998, 1995, 1990.
PRICES: $$ to $$$($)

PRODUCERS: Dom Pierre André: my introduction to this domaine was a truly seductive 2003; velvety, structured, and fragrant, it's a wine that makes me want to know more about this house ◆ Dom Paul Autard: if opened before their fifth birthday these very dry, very Rhône wines are best carafed before drinking; look, in particular, for the Cuvée la Côte Ronde, an oaky, ripe blend of grenache and syrah ◆ La Bastide St.-Dominique: the traditional bottling is so calm and easy-drinking you don't perceive its ample alcohol; the cuvée Secrets de Pignan Vieilles Vignes gives an agreeably old-fashioned impression, with its flavors of spice, fruit, sandalwood, and the sensation of old wood ◆ CH DE BEAUCASTEL ☆ ◆ DOM DE BEAURENARD ◆ DOM BOIS DE BOURSAN ◆ DOM BOSQUET DES PAPES ◆ Dom la Boutinière: an unusual but attractive Châteauneuf, with lots of good mineral and fruit flavors ◆ DOM DE LA CHARBONNIÈRE ☆ ◆ Les Clefs d'Or/Dom Jean Deydier: smooth, cool, easy-drinking Châteauneufs with no rough edges ◆ CLOS DU CAILLOU ☆ ◆ CLOS DES PAPES ☆ ◆ DOM DE CRISTIA ◆ Dom Duclaux: Jérôme Quoit has several properties in the AC, including Dom du Vieux Lazaret; the reds are so-so but the whites are creamy, mineral, and three-dimensional ◆ Château de la Font du Loup: the Cuvée des Fondateurs, chiefly grenache, is concentrated, lipsmacking, deep, and specific ◆ DOM FONT DE MICHELLE ◆ CH FORTIA ◆ CH LA GARDINE ☆ ◆ Dom Giraud: try the multifaceted cuvée Les Gallimardes for its appealing leather, spice, and oak flavors ◆ DOM GRAND VENEUR ☆ ◆ DOM DE LA JANASSE ☆ ◆ DOM LAFOND-ROC-ÉPINE ◆ DOM DE MARCOUX ☆ ◆ CH MONT-REDON ◆ Mas de Boislauzon: no destemming, no filtration, somewhat rustic Châteauneufs that are chewy but full of character; see also CÔTES DU RHÔNE listing ◆ Dom Monpertuis: see CH VALCOMBE ◆ Dom du Mourre du Tendre: solid, layered Châteauneuf, atypical but very interesting ◆ CHÂTEAU LA NERTHE ☆ ◆ Ogier-Cave des Papes: once-venerable house currently being resuscitated; look for Clos de l'Oratoire des Papes, especially Les Chorégies, which is full of personality ◆ DOM DU PEGAU ◆ CH RAYAS ☆ ◆ Dom de la Roncière: the well-balanced cuvée Flor de Ronce, very lightly chilled, would make a fine bistro bottle ◆ Dom de la Roquette: see DOM DU VIEUX

TÉLÉGRAPHE ☆ ◆ Roger Sabon: very appealing Châteauneufs, including a 2003 Les Olivets, a silky, elegant red with fig, cherry, and provençal herb flavors ◆ CH SAINT-ROCH ☆ ◆ Dom des Saumades: smooth, fluid white Châteauneufs; pleasant reds, both for near-term drinking ◆ DOM DE LA SOLITUDE ☆ ◆ DOM LA SOUMADE ☆ ◆ TARDIEU-LAURENT ☆ ◆ DOM PIERRE USSEGLIO ◆ Dom Vieille Julienne: personalized, handcrafted wines include lean, pure, mineral Châteauneufs; rugged, spicy, specific Côtes du Rhônes, and fresh, herby red blends (which include cabernet sauvignon) under the Vin de Pays da la Principauté d'Orange moniker ◆ Dom du Vieux Donjon: age-necessary (ten years is a good start), honest-to-god, three-plus-dimensional Châteauneufs, with evolving flavors of dried fruit, spices, tar, and leather ◆ Dom du Vieux Lazaret: see Dom Duclaux in this listing ◆ DOM DU VIEUX TÉLÉGRAPHE ☆ ◆ DOM DE VILLENEUVE ☆ ◆ LES VINS DE VIENNE ☆.

Châtillon-en-Diois

Minuscule northern Rhône AC for light, gamay-based reds and chardonnay-aligoté-based whites. Drink the youngest available. Prices: $. Producers: Cave de Die-Jaillance ◆ Didier Cornillon.

Domaine Jean-Louis Chave ☆

07300 Mauves; 04.75.08.24.63; fax: 04.75.07.14.21

Wine: Hermitage. $$$$

It is impossible to overestimate the magnificence of the Chave Hermitages. The whites are elegant, fresh, structured, potent, and age beautifully. Superb in their youth, with ten years of cellaring, they are works of art. Exhaling light notes of honey and ginger, they are sublime blends of power and finesse, absolutely made for haute cuisine. Or meditation. The reds are no less remarkable, with vibrant black cherry and mineral flavors, tons of pedigree, and the silkiest of tannins. Pure gorgeousness. And, for more modest budgets or more casual contexts, get the fragrant, seductive St.-Joseph red and drink it while its fruit is still in the first flush of its succulent youth.

Yann Chave ↑

26600 Mercurol; 04.75.07.42.11; fax: 04.75.07.47.34

Wines: Hermitage and Crozes-Hermitage. $$ to $$$

Yann Chave took over from father Bernard in 1996, built new cellars, banished industrial fertilizers and other vine treatments, and in general, rejuvenated the domaine. Both the white and the red Crozes are tasty, succulent, and food-friendly. The Hermitage is downright seductive and tempts you to drink it immediately.

Chusclan

Tiny designated Côtes du Rhône-Villages AC for red and rosé. Vintages: 2005, 2004, 2003, 2001. Prices: $ to $$$. Producers: Dom Clavel, especially cuvée Étienne ◆ CH SIGNAC ☆.

Domaine de la Citadelle

84560 Ménerbes; 04.90.72.41.58; www.domaine-citadelle.com

Wines: Côtes du Lubéron, Vin de Pays de Vaucluse. $ to $$$

One of the most well-known Lubéron producers, this eco-friendly domaine makes appealing wines in all price ranges. In a rare instance of luck, I prefer their cheapest red, Le Chataignier. I've even ordered it by the case as my house quaff.

Clairette de Die and Crémant de Die

Northern Rhône ACs for dry or semisweet sparkling wines. Muscat and clairette for the dry ones; exclusively clairette for the semisweet. Drink the youngest available. Prices: $ to $$. Producers: Carod ◆ Jacques Faure ◆ Jean-Claude Raspail.

Domaine Auguste Clape ☆

07130 Cornas; 04.75.40.33.64; fax: 04.75.81.01.98

Wines: Cornas, St.-Péray, Côtes du Rhône, Vin de Pays. $$ to $$$$

Among wine lovers, the name Clape has become synonymous with Cornas. Deservedly so. But, wait. The domaine, now run by three generations of Clape fellows, also makes superb whites and some toothsome, laid-back reds. The white Côtes du Rhône is big, vinous, mineral, and pretty terrific; the St.-Péray is even more mineral, layered, with a creamy texture and a sense of grandeur. There's a pure syrah Vin de Pays called—appropriately—Vin des Amis; by rights, it should be drunk in an ebullient atmosphere. The red Côtes du Rhône is nuanced and seductive, both elegant and sunny, a total pleasure. Back to Cornas. The young-vines cuvée, called Renaissance, is potent, tasty, and begins to be authoritative. The key cuvée, simply called Cornas, is a silk-velvet blend of lush, exotic fruit. Powerful and majestic, it evolves toward spices and mint with a texture as comforting as a down pillow. A great game wine.

Louis Clerc

38121 Chonas l'Amballan; 04.74.56.31.64; fax: 04.74.56.51.20

Wines: Condrieu and Côte-Rôtie. $$ to $$$

Quirky, personalized, handcrafted versions of Condrieu and Côte-Rôtie. Not the most elegant but never anonymous.

Clos du Caillou ☆

84350 Courthézon; 04.90.70.73.05; fax: 04.90.70.76.47

Wines: Châteauneuf-du-Pape and Côtes du Rhône. $$ to $$$($)

Stars all over my notebook for every wine tasted. Even the simplest Côtes du Rhône—red or white—is delectable, specific, thoroughly admirable. Move up a notch to the Côtes du Rhône Bouquet de Garrigues and you'll find it fresh, smooth, and spicy. In very good vintages, like 2004, there's a pure grenache Côtes du Rhône-Villages that could make you dance with pleasure, a veritable candidate for the grenache hall of fame. The Châteauneuf blanc is complex, oaky, and big; a wine to take on southern flavors like aioli and bouillabaisse with its piquant rouille. The basic cuvée of red is fragrant, sumptuous, and concentrated. It's almost impossible to resist drinking it too young. Les Quartz, the deluxe bottling, comes across like a cult-wine cum *vin de garage*—super fragrant, deeply saturated, layered, profound, structured, and dangerously succulent.

Clos du Joncuas

84190 Gigondas; 04.90.65.86.86

Wines: Gigondas, Séguret, and Vacqueyras. $$

Biodynamically farmed Gigondas with sap and vigor, plenty of stuffing, specificity, and flavors of black cherries and provençal herbs. The cuvée Esprit de Grenache is particularly impressive. The domaine also produces a sparkling wine by the *méthode traditionelle* and has offshoots in Vacqueyras (Dom la Font de Papier) and in Séguret (Dom la Garancière).

Clos des Papes ☆

84230 Châteauneuf-du-Pape; 04.90.83.70.13; www.clos-des-papes.com

Wine: Châteauneuf-du-Pape. $$$

The Avrils make characterful Châteauneufs in both colors. They use all six white grapes for the blanc, a rich, vinous, food-friendly, and forceful wine. All seven permitted red grapes go into the rouge, though grenache makes up more than half the blend. Structured and spicy, their wines are the embodiment of southern Rhône.

Domaine Clusel Roch ☆

69420 Ampuis; 04.74.56.15.95; cluseroc@terre-net.fr

Wines: Côte-Rôtie and Condrieu. $$$

A minuscule domaine with excellent wines, Clusel Roch finessed 2002 with a thin but elegant Côte-Rôtie. In 2003, the first Côte-Rôtie, which includes some viognier in the blend, was focused, fresh, deep, and graceful. The cuvée Grandes Places, pure syrah from a single vineyard, is surely one of the stars of that atypical vintage. It's superb. Ditto the 2004, which, much like the Condrieu of the same year, is pure, racy, and eloquent.

Condrieu

A tiny but important northern Rhône AC for white wines made exclusively from viognier. Seductive and heady, the wines are highly perfumed, ample, and rich. Most are best drunk "on the fruit" but some can age. Recently a number of producers have been making special cuvées of late-harvest wines.

BEST RECENT VINTAGES: 2005, 2004, 2003, 2001.
PRICES: $$ to $$$($)

PRODUCERS: Cave de Chante Perdrix: focused, fresh, discreet Condrieus and, in special years like 2004, a succulent, riveting cuvée Grains Dorés ◆ Dom Chèze: flavorful, fruit-driven Condrieus ◆ LOUIS CLERC ◆ DOM YVES CUILLERON ☆ ◆ DELAS ◆ DOM PHILIPPE FAURY ◆ DOM PIERRE GAILLARD ☆ ◆ DOM GANGLOFF ☆ ◆ DOM JEAN-MICHEL GERIN ☆ ◆ E. GUIGAL ☆ ◆ PAUL JABOULET AINÉ ◆ DOM DU MONTEILLET ↑ ◆ DOM ROBERT NIERO ☆ ◆ Alain Paret: some very special barrel-fermented (in new oak) Condrieus—the focused and mineral Les Ceps du Nébadon and the ample, excellent Lys de Volan; Paret also makes Vin de Pays d'Oc ↑ ◆ ANDRÉ PERRET ◆ ÉRIC TEXIER ☆ ◆ DOM GEORGES VERNAY ☆ ◆ DOM FRANÇOIS VILLARD ☆ ◆ LES VINS DE VIENNE ☆.

Jean-Luc Colombo

07130 Cornas; 04.75.84.17.10; www.vinsjlcolombo.com

Wines: Cornas and many Rhône ACs. $ to $$$$

Grower-*négociant* Jean-Luc Colombo is one of the movers and shakers of the Rhône, putting together groups of winemakers for traveling road shows and turning out respectably good wine himself in a wide range of Rhône appellations. His simple Côtes du Rhône blanc Les Figuières is clean, fresh, and vinous; the white Hermitage Le Rouet is big, strong, oaky, and mineral, a real presence. In reds, his Cairanne La Pavillon des Courtisanes is a friendly bistro red; his St.-Joseph Les Lauves is scented and smooth; and at the top of the line, his Cornas Les Ruchets is dark, oaky, and stylish, with no jagged edges.

Cornas

A tiny northern Rhône AC in the form of an amphitheater facing Valence, Cornas is a source of potent, striding, age-worthy (and age-necessary) reds made from syrah.

BEST RECENT VINTAGES: 2005, 2004, (2003), (2002), 2001, 2000, 1999, 1996, 1990.
PRICES: $$ to $$$($)

PRODUCERS: DOM THIERRY ALLEMAND ☆ ◆ Dom Balthazar: small, four-year-old domaine, the vineyards of which were previously worked by Noël Verset; watch for succulent, structured, fresh Cornas ↑ ◆ Dom du Biguet/Cave Jean-Louis & Françoise Thiers: fluid, well-made Cornas, though the 2003, while rich and juicy, was a bit too hot and gamy ◆ CAVE DE TAIN ◆ Dom Stéphane Chabaud: a domaine worth trying; both the normal and the reserve bottlings were lush but brawny in

2003 (not surprising) ◆ DOM AUGUSTE CLAPE ☆ ◆ JEAN-LUC COLOMBO ◆ Dom du Coulet: biodynamic viticulture and hypernatural Cornas; tasty, mineral, and true, the cuvée Les Billes Noires would make a great wine-bar discovery ◆ DOM COURBIS ◆ DELAS ◆ Dumien-Serrette: a bit lean in 2002, a tad hot in 2003, the cuvée Patou Vieilles Vignes would make a worthy wine-bar discovery ◆ LA FERME DES SEPT LUNES ↑ ◆ PAUL JABOULET AINÉ ◆ Marcel Juge: fragrant, spicy, slightly rustic versions of the AC that go down very easily; look for Cuvée Coteaux ◆ ROBERT MICHEL ☆ ◆ DOM VINCENT PARIS ☆ ◆ DOM JEAN-MICHEL STEPHAN ◆ DOM DU TUNNEL ↑ ◆ LES VINS DE VIENNE ☆ ◆ DOM VOGE ◆. Note that many Cornas producers also make St.-Péray AC.

Domaine de Corps de Loup

69420 Tupin et Semons; tel/fax: 04.74.56.84.64; daubree.martin@free.fr

Wine: Côte-Rôtie. $$($)

Lucette and Martin Daubrée produce three generous cuvées of Côte-Rôtie on their promising domaine. The first bottling, blended with viognier, is succulent and kirschy. The second, pure syrah, is thicker and more velvety, with chocolate accents. The top cuvée, Paradis, is supple, deep, and dark, with satisfying complexity. They expect to add Condrieu to their lineup.

Costières de Nîmes: See the Languedoc-Roussillon chapter.

Côte-Rôtie

A small but extremely important northern Rhône AC for red wines made from syrah, to which some producers add a percentage of the white grape viognier. The vines grow on slopes so steep, they're practically vertical. The wines are elegant, detailed, and majestic.

BEST RECENT VINTAGES: 2005, 2004, 2003, (2002), 2001, 2000, 1997, 1996. Prices: $$$ to $$$$

PRODUCERS: Dom Barge: specific, meaty wines; the best is the nicely fresh, graceful, yet robust Cuvée du Plessy; worth trying, as are Barge's Condrieus ◆ Guy Bernard: not regal, perhaps, but delicious? absolutely; the Côte-Rôties are unfined and unfiltered and are rich with black cherry, herb, and mellow oak flavors ◆ DOM CHRISTOPHE BONNEFOND ☆ ◆ Burgaud: unfined, unfiltered, serious, firmly structured wines, though a bit thick and gamy in 2003 ◆ CHAPOUTIER ☆ ◆ LOUIS CLERC ◆ DOM CLUSEL-ROCH ☆ ◆ DOM DE CORPS DE LOUP ◆ DOM YVES CUILLERON ☆ ◆ DOM PHILIPPE FAURY ◆ DOM PIERRE GAILLARD ☆ ◆ DOM GANGLOFF ☆ ◆ DOM JEAN-MICHEL GERIN ☆ ◆ E. GUIGAL ☆ ◆ PAUL JABOULET AINÉ ◆ DOM JAMET ☆ ◆ DOM JASMIN ☆ ◆ DOM DU MONTEILLET ↑ ◆ DOM ROBERT NIERO ☆ ◆ DOM OGIER ◆ DOM JEAN-MICHEL STEPHAN ◆ DOM GEORGES VERNAY ☆ ◆ Vidal-Fleury: now in the Guigal stable, the wines are obviously well made, full, and richly fruity, though they lack the splendor and dignity of the Côte-Rôties under Guigal's name ◆ DOM FRANÇOIS VILLARD ☆ ◆ LES VINS DE VIENNE ☆.

Coteaux-de-Pierrevert

A tiny satellite AC around Manosque, the source for for light reds, whites, and rosés. Most are consumed locally. Drink the youngest available. Prices: $.

Coteaux du Tricastin

A satellite AC on the left bank of the Rhône, facing the Coteaux du Vivarais. Produces reds, whites, and rosés made from the usual southern Rhône mix. Vintages: 2005, 2004, 2003. Prices: $ to $$. Producers: Ch des Estubiers: owned and run by CHAPOUTIER ◆ DOM SAINT LUC.

Côtes du Lubéron

The southernmost Rhône AC (on the north and south slopes of the Lubéron range) for reds, whites (including late harvest), and rosés made from the usual mix of southern Rhône grapes.

BEST RECENT VINTAGES: 2005, 2004, 2003.
PRICES: $ to $$

PRODUCERS: DOM DE LA CITADELLE ◆ Ch des Tourettes: see GUFFENS-HEYNEN ◆ Ch Val Joanis: especially the Réserve Les Griottes ◆ Verget du Sud: see GUFFENS-HEYNEN.

Côtes du Rhône and Côtes du Rhône-Villages

There are three ACs here: the vast, simple Côtes du Rhône, the more restricted Côtes du Rhône-Villages, and the still more restricted Côtes du Rhône-Villages, preceded by the name of a specific village. Each of the designated villages has a separate entry here. They are: Cairanne, Chusclan, Laudun, Rasteau, Roaix, Rochegude, Rousset les Vignes, Sablet, St.-Gervais, St.-Maurice, St.-Pantaléon-les-Vignes, Séguret, Valréas, Visan. In 2005 and 2006 Signargues, Plan de Dieu, Puyméras, and Massif d'Uchaux were added to the Côtes du Rhône-Villages roster. Despite the legal distinctions, the wines are more alike than they are different; variations, to date, have more to do with the producer than the individual village. (Vinsobres and the red wines from Beaumes-de-Venise were formerly in this third category of AC but were recently bounced up a level and are now permitted to use their names alone on labels, without specifying Côtes du Rhône. Personally, I feel Cairanne and Rasteau merit equal promotion and can't understand why this has not yet been done.)

Unless otherwise specified, the wines may be white, rosé, or red. Reds are generally made from grenache, syrah, cinsault, and mourvèdre. For whites, it's grenache, bourboulenc, clairette, marsanne, roussanne, and viognier. Occasionally, other, more obscure grapes are used in both reds and whites. Côtes du Rhône and Côtes du Rhône-Villages should be drunk within five years.

BEST RECENT VINTAGES: 2005, 2004, 2003, 2001.
PRICES: $ to $$$

PRODUCERS: Those listed here make simple Côtes du Rhône and Côtes du-Rhône-Villages. Wines from named villages are listed in the entry for that village. ◆ Dom des Amouriers: see VACQUEYRAS ◆ Dom d'Andezon: see LES VIGNERONS D'ESTÉZARGUES ◆ L'ANGLORE ↑ ◆ APHILLANTES ↑ ◆ Dom des Bacchantes: see LES VIGNERONS D'ESTÉZARGUES ◆ DOM BRUSSET ☆ ◆ CAVE DE RASTEAU ◆ DOM AUGUSTE CLAPE ☆ ◆ JEAN-LUC COLOMBO ◆ Dom Coulange: the best wines from this Ardéchois producer are the Côtes du Rhône red cuvées mistral (chiefly grenache) and Rochelette (mainly syrah) ◆ Dom de Couron: the Côtes du Rhône-Villages red from this Ardèche producer would be pleasant to try in a wine bar ◆ Dom Cros de la Mure: rich, nicely structured Côtes du Rhône-Villages reds ◆ Cru de Coudelet: see CH DE BEAUCASTEL ◆ Dom de l'Échevin: see DOM LA FLORANE ◆ DOM LA FAVETTE ↑ ◆ DOM LA FLORANE ◆ Fond du Vent: see DOM FONT DE MICHELLE ◆ Ch de Fonsalette: see CH RAYAS ☆ ◆ Dom les Genestas: see LES VIGNERONS D'ESTÉZARGUES ◆ DOM GRAMENON ☆ ◆ DOM DES GRANDS DEVERS ↑ ◆ DOM GRAND VENEUR ☆ ◆ Les Grands Vignes: see LES VIGNERONS D'ESTÉZARGUES ◆ Dom Grès St. Vincent: see LES VIGNERONS D'ESTÉZARGUES ◆ E. GUIGAL ◆ DOM DE LA JANASSE ☆ ◆ DOM LAFOND ROC-ÉPINE ◆ PATRICK LESEC SÉLECTIONS ☆ ◆ Mas de Boislauzon: producers of both Châteauneuf and Côtes du Rhône, both interesting, but I prefer the latter, particularly in the 2004 vintage ◆ MAS DE LIBIAN ↑ ◆ Dom la Millière: the truly nice cuvée Les Champauvins, from a parcel bordering Châteauneuf, is more Châteauneuf than Millière's wines from within that prestigious AC ◆ Dom de la Montagnette: see LES VIGNERONS D'ESTÉZARGUES ◆ Dom de Montfaucon: the tastiest wines from this domaine are the mellow white Comtesse Madelaine and the classic red Baron Louis ◆ CH

MONT-REDON ◆ DOM NÔTRE DAME DE COUSIGNAC ◆ Dom de Perillière: see LES VIGNERONS D'ESTÉZARGUES ◆ DOM PERRIN & FILS ☆ ◆ Dom Roger Perrin: Perrin's Châteauneufs are just so-so but his Côtes du Rhône are very appealing, particularly the Cuvée Laura, a white based on viognier, and the red Cuvée Prestige Vieilles Vignes ◆ Dom de Pierredon: see LES VIGNERONS D'ESTÉZARGUES ◆ DOM RABASSE-CHARAVIN ☆ ◆ DOM LA REMEJEANNE ◆ Dom de la Renjarde: toothsome, bistro Côtes du Rhône-Villages with rich berry flavors ◆ DOM MARCEL RICHAUD ☆ ◆ DOM ROCHE BUISSIÈRE ↑ ◆ DOM ROUGE GARANCE ↑ ◆ Dom Saint Laurent: this eco-friendly domaine does a much nicer job with its red Côtes de Rhône (particularly L'Aubespin and La Tamardière) than it does with its Châteauneuf ◆ Ch St.-Jean: solid, bistro Côtes du Rhône-Villages ◆ DOM SAINT LUC ◆ Dom Santa Duc: good producer of a range of Côtes du Rhône and Côtes du Rhône-Villages; look, in particular, for the floral, fresh Sablet blanc and the Côtes du Rhône Les 4 Terres, a smooth, kirschy and orange peel–accented red ◆ CH SIMIAN ◆ Dom Saladin: an Ardéchois domaine to follow as two talented, dedicated daughters (who have done stints in Argentina, Chile, and California) take control; look for the cuvées Haut Brissan and Chaveyron 1422 ↑ ◆ CH SIGNAC ☆ ◆ DOM DE LA SOLITUDE ☆ ◆ ÉRIC TEXIER ☆ ◆ Ch des Tours: see CH RAYAS ☆ ◆ Dom Trapadis: see RASTEAU ◆ DOM DES TREILLES ◆ CH DU TRIGNON ◆ Dom Vieille Julienne: see CHATEAUNEUF-DU-PAPE ◆ Les Vignerons des Coteaux d'Avignon: the cuvée selected by importer Kermit Lynch is lively, user-friendly, and agreeably old-fashioned, perfect for a cozy, animated bistro ◆ LES VIGNERONS D'ESTÉZARGUES ☆ ◆ LES VINS DE VIENNE ☆ ◆ DOM VIRET ☆.

Côtes du Ventoux

A large AC spread throughout the Vaucluse department between Vaison-la-Romaine and Apt. The most dynamic of the Rhône satellites, the AC has more than doubled the percentage of estate bottling within the past five or six years. There's lots of room for improvement. It produces mostly reds, but some whites and rosés, all made from the usual southern Rhône mix.

BEST RECENT VINTAGES: 2005, 2004, 2003.
PRICES: $ to $$

PRODUCERS: Most of the best are those whose main activity is in more prestigious ACs. ◆ Dom des Anges: promising young domaine with ambitious Anglophone owners; try the wine-bar-ready red L'Archange ↑ ◆ DOM BRUSSET ☆ ◆ Dom de la Ferme Saint Martin: look for the organic, unfiltered, very tasty red, Clos des Estaillades ◆ Ch Talaud: best is the grenache-syrah blend called Cuvée Antoine ◆ Dom Terres de Solence: organic wines; look for the red cuvées Les Trois Pères and Cippus, and the white, Léonides ◆ CH VALCOMBE ◆ Dom le Van: the top cuvée, Alizarine, makes a good, organic, wine-bar red.

Côtes du Vivarais

Recent, and improving, AC west of Montélimar, near the gorges of Ardèche, a source of whites based on grenache, clairette, and marsanne, and reds based on syrah and grenache.

BEST RECENT VINTAGES: 2005, 2004, 2003.
PRICES: $ to $$

PRODUCERS: Note that producers here may also make Côtes du Rhône and Vin de Pays de l'Ardèche. ◆ GILLES AZZONI ↑ ◆ Dom de Belvezet: the old-vines red is a firm, cool mountain wine ◆ DOM LA FAVETTE ↑ ◆ DOM NÔTRE DAME DE COUSIGNAC ◆ Dom de Vigier: the Cuvée Romain recalls a minor Côtes du Rhône; much better is the domaine's Vin de Pays-Ardèche Cuvée Mathilde, a late-harvest viognier that would make a very pleasant aperitif.

Domaine Courbis

07130 Châteaubourg; 04.75.81.81.60; domaine-courbis@wanadoo.fr
Wines: Cornas, St.-Joseph, and Vin de Pays de l'Ardèche $$ to $$$
Laurent and Dominique Courbis are the most recent generation to run this family domaine with roots reaching back to the sixteenth century. They produce pleasant St.-Joseph, both white and red, but the focus is on Cornas, of which there are three cuvées. Champelrose is a juicy, characterful quaffer; Les Eygots is more concentrated and packs the power of the AC; even more potent is the velvety La Sabarotte. Rich, mineral, deep, and austere, it should age in good vintages like 2001 and, in years like 2002, it should be carafed and enjoyed for its lipsmacking succulence.

Domaine le Couroulu

84190 Vacqueyras; 04.90.65.84.83; fax: 04.90.65.81.25
Wines: Vacqueyras, Côtes du Rhône, and Vin de Pays. $ to $$
A solid, eco-friendly family domaine with a pleasant syrah-merlot Vin de Pays de Vaucluse; a vinous, fresh Cuvée Laura in Vacqueyras blanc, and two very good cuvées of red: the traditional cuvée is so succulent you could drink it from barrel; the old-vines bottling is structured, silky, and spicy with juicy cherry and cherry pit flavors.

Domaine de Cristia ↑

84350 Courthézon; 04.90.70.24.09; domainecristia@hotmail.com
Wines: Châteauneuf-du-Pape. $$ to $$$
Baptiste and Dominique Grangeon started bottling their own wine in 1999 and the prospects are mighty promising. Of the several bottlings of Châteauneuf, there is a bright, focused, black-cherry accented Cuvée Regulière; a smooth, velvety, ambitious cuvée based on old-vines grenache; and the succulent, ambitious Renaissance, the most concentrated and tannic of the lot.

Crozes-Hermitage

The largest of the northern Rhône ACs, generally making easy-going, full-bodied, reasonably priced whites (marsanne and roussanne) and reds (syrah) for drinking within five or six years, though some producers make truly ambitious cuvées well worth cellaring.

BEST RECENT VINTAGES: 2005, (2004), 2003.
PRICES: $($) to $$$.

PRODUCERS: CAVE DE TAIN ◆ CHAPOUTIER ☆ ◆ YANN CHAVE ↑ ◆ Dom du Colombier: pleasant whites; in reds, try the Cuvée Gaby; the domaine also makes Hermitage, but it's a work in progress ◆ Dom Combier: appetizing, sturdy reds and whites ◆ DARD & HIBO ◆ Emmanuel Darnaud: several juicy cuvées of red Crozes; look for La Guiraude, as sumptuous as any *vin de garage* and well worth a star ◆ DELAS ◆ DOM DES ENTREFAUX ↑ ◆ DOM GRAILLOT ☆ ◆ PAUL JABOULET AINÉ ◆ DOM DES REMIZIÈRES ◆ Gilles Robin: soft, vinous whites; in reds, look for the deeply fruity, oak-aged Cuvée Albéric Bouvet ◆ ÉRIC TEXIER ☆.

Domaine Yves Cuilleron ☆

42410 Chavanay; 04.74.87.02.37; ycuiller@terre-net.fr
Wines: Condrieu, Côte-Rôtie, and St.-Joseph. $$ to $$$($)
One thing's for certain with Cuilleron's wines: you won't be bored. Of his numerous cuvées of Condrieu, Les Chaillets and La Petite Côte are thrillingly mineral and appetizing, simultaneously riveting and easy to approach. I haven't gotten a handle on the Vertige bottling, at least not the 2002, which at times has come across oaky and lightly vegetal and at others like an aperitif made of distilled apricots. Eguets is Cuilleron's late-harvest bottling. Extremely sweet, perfumed, floral, and creamy, it's an unusual and exciting expression

of Condrieu. His truly tasty Côte-Rôtie Bassenon and the even finer Terres Sombres are fresh, focused, specific, and succulent. Both scrumptious and serious. (See also LES VINS DE VIENNE.)

Dard & Ribo

26600 Mercurol; 04.75.07.40.00; fax: 04.75.07.71.02
Wines: Crozes-Hermitage and St.-Joseph. $$ to $$$
Hypernatural stalwarts, Dard and Ribo make several cuvées of strong, vinous, mouthfilling Crozes-Hermitage whites; a juicy, drink-me-up Crozes red called C'est le Printemps, and red Crozes and St.-Joseph bottlings that are rich, fresh, and succulent. All great wine-bar discoveries.

Delas

07300 St.-Jean-de-Muzols; 04.75.08.60.30; www.delas.com
Wines: Hermitage, Condrieu, and other Rhône ACs. $$ to $$$$
Reliable grower-*négociant* house making soft-spoken versions of the ACs. There are many cuvées. All have something to say. Most impressive, and expensive, are the Hermitage Les Bessards and Côte-Rôtie La Landonne. Less expensive and very much worth trying are the Hermitage Marquise de la Tourette, Cornas Chante-Perdrix, and Condrieu Clos-Boucher, as well as the special bottlings in St.-Joseph, Crozes-Hermitage, and Vacqueyras.

Duché d'Uzès

A VDQS created in 2006 for Rhône-style reds, whites, and rosés from the Gard department. Formerly Vin de Pays.

Domaine de Durban

84190 Beaumes-de-Venise; 04.90.62.94.26; fax: 04.90.65.01.85
Wines: Beaumes-de-Venise, Muscat Beaumes-de-Venise, and others. $$ to $$$
Owned by the Leydier family, this sizable domaine is a good bet for fragrant, user-friendly, unfiltered reds, from the Vin de Table, which includes a percentage of the grape marselan (a cross of grenache and cabernet sauvignon) to the deeper Cuvée Prestige, a lovely food wine. But the star here is the Muscat Beaumes-de-Venise, the hands-down best in the AC.

Domaine des Entrefaux ↑

26600 Chanos-Curson; 04.75.07.33.38; fax: 04.75.07.35.27
Wine: Crozes-Hermitage. $$
A serious, young, eco-friendly domaine making a half-dozen cuvées of Crozes, among them a creamy, barrel-aged white Coteau des Pends; a juicy generic red that should be enjoyed in the full vibrancy of its syrah fruit and a flowery red Les Champs Fourné, also demanding to be drunk young. The ambitious Les Mâchonnieres, a tannic, barrel-aged red, with lovely mineral, cherry pit, and black cherry flavors, can age a good five years.

Domaine des Escaravailles

84110 Rasteau; 04.90.46.14.20; fax: 04.90.46.11.45
Wines: Côtes du Rhône designated Rasteau Vin Doux Naturel and Côtes du Rhône-Villages Rasteau and Roaix. $ to $$($)
Sizable family domaine with parcels in various Côtes du Rhône villages. Heritage 1924 (pure, unfiltered grenache from vines planted in 1924) is serious and emphatically Rhône with its accents of ash and provençal herbs. The Côtes du Rhône Antimagnes is a robust, hearty red; and the Côtes du Rhône Ventabren could be an ambassador for the generic Rhône AC. The Roaix Les Hautes Granges, chiefly syrah, is rich, oaky, and tasty; the Rasteau Cuvée la Ponce is equally satisfying—rich, smooth, and balanced. The fruity and strong Vin Doux Naturel comes across like a good ruby Port.

Domaine des Espiers
84190 Vacqueyras; 04.90.65.81.16; fax: 04.90.65.81.16
Wines: Gigondas and Côtes du Rhône. $ to $$$
Two enticing cuvées of Gigondas, both juicy, flavorful, and elegant—although the deluxe Sélection Blaches is, indeed, superior—very fine, very promising, excellent work here.

Estézargues: See LES VIGNERONS D'ESTÉZARGUES.

Domaine Philippe Faury
42410 Chavanay; 04.74.87.26.00; p.faury@42.sideral.fr
Wines: Condrieu, Côte-Rôtie, and St.-Joseph. $$ to $$$$
Faury's St.-Josephs are plump, juicy bistro reds that go down extremely easily; the Côte-Rôties, with about 20 percent viognier, are succulent and balanced, with lovely fruit. There are three worthy cuvées of Condrieu, the two most interesting being the Cuvée La Berne, an old-vines bottling that's supple, perfumed, and mineral, and the very alluring Cuvée Brumaire, a late-harvest wine made, in 2003, from botrytized grapes.

Domaine la Favette ↑
07700 St.-Just d'Ardèche; 04.75.04.61.14; domainelafavette@cario.fr
Wines: Côtes du Rhône, Côtes du Vivarais, and Vin de Pays Coteaux de l'Ardèche et de Cèze. $ to $$
This is one of a handful of domaines that will put the wines from the Ardèche on the map. In 1999, after studying enology, Philippe Fauré joined his father on the family property, which, in addition to vines in four appellations, includes orchards and a campground. Most of the vines are in the Côtes du Rhône AC and 95 percent of those are turned into a simple, smooth grenache/syrah blend. A distinct step up is the cuvée Roche-Sauve. Based on old carignan vines, it's suave, textured, and mouthwatering, with an appetizing austerity—a cool, very pure mountain red with plenty of character. Fauré vinified his first whites in 2003, all of them Vin de Pays and all of them absolutely delicious. Exubérance is pure viognier and Élégance blends roussanne, viognier, chardonnay, and sauvignon blanc. No oak in these whites. They're airy, perfumed, and cool, lovely food wines.

La Ferme des Sept Lunes ↑
07340 Bogy; tel/fax: 04.75.34.86.37; jean.delobre@wanadoo.fr
Wines: St.-Joseph and Vin de Pays de l'Ardèche. $ to $$($)
Young Jean Delobre left the local co-op and began making his own wine in 2001. Viticulture is organic and filtration is not systematic. A light, burnished gold, his white St.-Joseph is big, ripe, and mouthwatering, with pineapple accents; his reds, particularly the barrel-aged, unfiltered Pleine Lune, are serious and rich, with dark black olive and cassis flavors. Full of character, they recall Cornas. Delobre's Vin de Pays, pure, low-yielding syrah, is pungent, well made, and wine-bar-ready. I just wish he'd plant viognier on this land instead.

Domaine la Florane/Domaine l'Échevin
84820 Visan; tel/fax: 04.90.41.90.72; www.domainelaflorane.com
Wines: Côtes du Rhône-Villages St.-Maurice, Visan. $ to $$
Florane is the domaine in Visan; l'Échevin is in St. Maurice. The wines from each property are well made and offer good value for the dollar. From Échevin comes a strong, tender white, vinified and aged in used Yquem barrels, and two fruit-driven reds, including the top-of-the-line Guillaume de Rouville, a pungent, cassis- and black olive–flavored blend dominated by syrah. Florane's top wine is Terre Pourpre, a tasty oak-aged blend of grenache and syrah from a single vineyard.

Domaine Font de Michelle

84370 Bedarrides; 04.90.33.00.22; www.font-de-michelle.com
Wines: Châteauneuf-du-Pape and Côtes du Rhône. $$ to $$$
Jean and Michel Gonnet produce reliably good, professional, organic wines on their sizable estate, which combines Châteauneuf-du-Pape (Font de Michelle) and Côtes du Rhône (Font du Vent). In Châteauneuf there are two cuvées in both red and white. The initial bottling of each is nicely made, solid, and reasonably priced; the deluxe Cuvée Étienne Gonnet is a distinct step up. The barrel-aged white, chiefly roussanne, has depth and resonance; the red is structured, concentrated, and sappy. The red is worth cellaring until at least 2008. At Font du Vent the Gonnets produce three cuvées of very good Rhône red—Les Promesses, a cheery quaffer based on young vines; the fresh, juicy Nôtre Passion, a Villages AC; and the barrel-aged Confidentia, a suave, syrah-dominated blend with flavors of black cherry, spice, ash, and Provençal herbs, perfect for a bistro.

Château Fortia

84230 Châteauneuf-du-Pape; 04.90.83.72.25; fortia@terre-net.fr
Wine: Châteauneuf-du-Pape. $$ to $$$
Historic Châteauneuf domaine returning to fine form after a weak patch. The silky, perfumed Cuvée du Baron is only slightly better, and slightly more expensive, than the standard bottling.

Domaine Pierre Gaillard ☆

42520 Malleval; 04.74.87.13.10; vinsp.gaillard@wanadoo.fr
Wines: Condrieu, Côte-Rôtie, and St.-Joseph. $$ to $$$
Pierre Gaillard makes exciting, delicious wines in all three appellations. His St.-Joseph, in both white and red, is better than more prestigious ACs from less devoted, less artistic growers. Both cuvées of Côte-Rôtie are excellent, with lush, concentrated fruit and real freshness. Rose Pourpre, made from grapes from La Landonne, is a beauty, smooth and rich but never heavy, with a fine sense of place. His standard Condrieu is deep, perfumed, and mineral. Fleur d'Automne, a late-harvest bottling, is soft, rich, and blossomy. Jeanne-Élise, a *vin de paille* in which the harvested grapes are laid out to dry until December, is surprisingly fresh, very rich, layered with flavors of peach and dried fruit, a super aperitif or wine to serve with blue cheese. Gaillard has extended his reach into the Roussillon (see DOM MADELOC). And he is partners with Yves Cuilleron and François Villard in LES VINS DE VIENNE.

Domaine Gangloff ☆

69420 Condrieu; 04.74.59.57.04; ygangloff@wanadoo.fr
Wines: Condrieu and Côte-Rôtie. $$ to $$$
Yves Gangloff, another northern Rhône artist-vintner, makes dense, fragrant, focused, and extremely mineral Condrieu. His Côte-Rotie, deep and concentrated, is ravishing.

Château de la Gardine ☆

BP 35, 84231 Châteauneuf-du-Pape Cedex; 04.90.83.73.20; www.gardine.com
Wine: Châteauneuf-du-Pape. $$$ to $$$$
This large family domaine is a sure bet for very good, stylish Châteauneuf. The traditional white is strong, mineral, and racy. The Cuvée des Générations Marie Léoncie is chiefly roussanne fermented and aged in new oak barrels. Mellow, powerful, and pellucid, it has a salty mineral tang. I'd love it with bouillabaisse or simply with Maine lobster. The entry-level red is clear, bright, specific, and fairly elegant, with seductive dark fruit. The Cuvée des Générations Gaston Philippe, made from old vines and aged in new oak, is extremely deep, rich, and lush. It needs age—ten years at least—to reveal its specificity but it's so tasty, it may never get to live that long. And the Cuvée Immortelle is even more intense, rich and profound. (See also CH SAINT-ROCH.)

Domaine la Garrigue

84190 Vacqueyras; 04.90.65.84.60; www.domaine-la-garrigue.fr

Wines: Vacqueyras and Côtes du Rhône. $$

A large property making good, unfined, unfiltered versions of the AC. The several cuvées of red, including Hostellerie and Romaine, are appetizing, spicy, and quite dry. (Vinified with their stems, the reds can seem woody, though they have not aged in barrel.)

Domaine Jean-Michel Gerin ☆

69420 Ampuis; 04.74.56.16.56; gerin.jm@wanadoo.fr

Wines: Côte-Rôtie and Condrieu. $$$

Three cuvées of excellent, unfined, unfiltered Côte-Rôtie. The first, Champin le Seigneur, has 10 percent viognier in the blend. Very mineral, with jewel-like fruit, it's a real success in off-vintages like 2002 and comes across like the Côte d'Or in the Rhône in fine vintages, such as 2001, when it's coolly elegant, long, and downright aristocratic. The single-vineyard cuvées, pure syrah, are the deep, detailed, pillowy La Landonne and emphatically *terroir*-driven Les Grandes Places. I loved all of them more in 2001, 2002, and 2004 than in 2003. The only Condrieu I've tasted was the very mineral 2004 while it was still fermenting. To follow.

Gigondas

A charming southern Rhône AC for reds (mostly) and rosés. Grenache is the main grape with, again, syrah and mourvèdre assisting. The wines are full-hearted, warm, and at their best, can rival Châteauneuf-du-Pape. Great for near- to mid-term drinking and possibly excellent value.

BEST RECENT VINTAGES: 2005, 2004, (2003), 2001, 1999.
PRICES: $$ to $$$

PRODUCERS: Dom la Bouissière: honorable and tasty in off vintages (like 2002), the wines are ripe and silky with hints of black olive and Provençal herbs in good years; particularly succulent is the darker, deeper cuvée La Font de Tonin ◆ DOM BRUSSET ☆ ◆ DOM DU CAYRON ◆ CLOS DU JONCUAS ◆ DOM DES ESPIERS ◆ Dom les Goubert: *caveat lector*—it took a full month before the 2000 Cuvée Florence, which I'd opened, tasted, and recorked half-full, to progress from opaque tar and game flavors and become supple and silky, with still plenty of flesh on its bones ◆ Dom du Grapillon d'Or: aged in big, old barrels, the Gigondas from this domaine are ashy, chewy, and agreeably old-fashioned ◆ DOM MONTIRIUS ☆ ◆ Ch de Montmirail: nicely old-fashioned too, the pungent Cuvée de Beauchamp blends flavors of ripe fruit, ash, and Provençal herbs ◆ DOM LES PALLIÈRES ◆ Dom de Piaugier: pleasant Côtes du Rhônes ◆ Dom Santa Duc: good Côtes du Rhône producer with delicious, fragrant, barrel-aged Gigondas; both the traditional cuvée and the ampler, more complex Prestige de Haute Garrigues are highly recommended ☆ ◆ CH DU TRIGNON.

Domaine Graillot ☆

26600 Pont de l'Isère; 04.75.84.67.52; graillot.alain@wanadoo.fr

Wine: Crozes-Hermitage. $$ to $$$

More, rather than less, organic, Alain Graillot's wines are a sure bet on a wine list as well as some of the best representatives of his AC. He makes a small amount of drink-me-up white from marsanne and roussanne, and in very good vintages, two cuvées of red, a supple, ripe standard bottling, and La Guiraude, a cellar-worthy syrah with exotic fruit flavors.

Domaine Gramenon ☆

26770 Montbrison-sur-Lez; 04.75.53.57.08; fax: 04.75.53.68.92
Wines: Vinsobres and Côtes du Rhône. $$ to $$$
Michèle Aubéry-Laurent succeeds with the risky hypernatural approach without falling into any of its traps. She makes fresh, focused whites and rosés and a juicy, gulpable syrah called Poignée de Raisins (a handful of grapes). Then comes an ever-increasing number of toothsome cuvées. Sierra du Sud is a pure syrah Côtes du Rhône, as concentrated as it is fresh and succulent. Les Hauts de Gramenon, a Vinsobres, has notes of cocoa powder along with lush fruit and quite a bit of gravitas. La Sagesse, a pure grenache Côtes du Rhône, is fine grained, lightly oaky, and very mouthwatering. The deluxe cuvée À Pascal S is very good, but I prefer the Ceps Centennaire la Mémé, a serious, drop-dead-delicious grenache that transports me to the best vineyards of Collioure. Cuvée Sibardises is a blockbuster made in 2003 for the owner of Caves Auge in Paris, where Gramenon and many other hypernaturalists sell their wines.

Domaine Grand Veneur/Vignobles Alain Jaume & Fils ☆

84100 Orange; 04.90.34.68.70; www.domaine-grand-veneur.com
Wines: Châteauneuf-du-Pape, Lirac (Clos de Sixte), Vacqueyras, and Côtes du Rhône. $$ to $$$
One of my favorite discoveries of 2005, this multitasking family domaine is now run (brilliantly) by Christophe Jaume. You simply can't go wrong here—whatever the AC, whatever the cuvée, whatever the vintage. The two white Châteauneufs are both excellent. La Fontaine ferments and ages in oak and is definitely a wine for a three-star meal. The standard red is stylish, succulent, and lipsmackingly delicious. Les Origines is more elegant and there's more new oak, but it's equally lush and delectable. Jaume's irresistible Vacqueyras are sapid, cool reds with insinuating cherry and cherry pit flavors. His Lirac rosé is both strong and tender; the red, mouthwatering and specific. There's a fresh, vinous white Côtes du Rhône blend and a pure viognier, so graceful and nuanced it's better than many Condrieus.

Domaine les Grands Bois

84290 St.-Cecile-les-Vignes; 04.90.30.81.86; www.grands-bois.com
Wines: Cairanne and Côtes du Rhône. $ to $$
This very good family domaine makes a range of reasonably, even charitably priced wines. The reds, all varying blends of grenache, syrah, carignan, and often mourvèdre, are unfiltered and all based on low yields. All are recommended. My favorites are both Cairannes: the 100 percent barrel-aged Cuvée Éloise and the partially oak-aged Cuvée Mireille, which, even in 2002, was concentrated and delicious.

Domaine des Grands Devers ↑

84600 Valréas; 04.90.35.15.98; www.grandsdevers.com
Wines: Valréas, Visan, and Côtes du Rhône. $ to $$
These promising newcomers are not new to wine but to the Rhône. They're four Bouchard brothers, formerly from the eponymous house in Burgundy, who created this Rhône domaine in 1999. The wines do need some polish, some rounding off of jagged edges, but they're made from good raw materials. My favorite thus far is the Côte du Rhône La Syranne, a rich, tasty, pure syrah.

Château Grillet ☆

42410 Verin; 04.74.59.51.56; fax: 04.78.92.96.10
Wine: Château-Grillet. $$$($)
One of France's smallest ACs and most legendary wines, Château Grillet has belonged to the Canet family since the nineteenth century. The wine is fragrant, mellow, and mineral when young, with floral and apricot accents. In other words, rather like a Condrieu. But unlike most, if not all, Condrieus, it must be cellared. Then it will reveal its majesty. Look for a 1989 or 1990.

Domaine Bernard Gripa

07300 Mauves; 04.75.08.14.96; fax: 04.75.07.06.81
Wines: St.-Joseph and St.-Péray. $$
This eco-friendly family domaine makes a solid red St.-Joseph and impressive whites in both St.-Péray and St.-Joseph. There are two cuvées of each, all recommended for their tight focus and appetizing blend of fruit and minerals. The deluxe cuvée in St.-Péray is the barrel-fermented, old-vines Les Figuiers; in St.-Joseph, it's the pure, old-vines Le Berceau.

Guffens-Heynen/Verget du Sud/Château des Tourettes ☆

71960 Vergisson; 03.85.51.66.00; jmggestion@aol.com
Wines: Vin de Pays de Vaucluse or Lubéron. $ to $$
Jean-Marie Guffens, who proved to anyone who was paying attention that Mâcon could make wines as exquisite as those from Burgundy's Côte d'Or, has extended his reach to the Vaucluse and the Lubéron. As in Burgundy, the wines are eco-friendly and can be topped with corks or screw caps. There are two lines: those labeled Verget du Sud are wines that fit the young vines' drink-me-up profile; Château des Tourettes applies to the top-of-the-line wines, with the further distinction of Plâteau de l'Aigle for the very best whites and Endes for the reds. If Guffens gets his way, the Verget du Sud line will sell in the United States for less than $8. What treats lie in store there! A lipsmackingly fresh and fruity blend of grenache and syrah, for example, or a smooth, creamy, mineral white blend. For just a bit more money, there are delicacies like a late-harvested, old-vines roussanne and a fantastically succulent red blend, both under the Château des Tourettes label. To single out just two of the top wines, there is the 2003 chardonnay Plâteau de l'Aigle, a Côte d'Or ringer; and the 2004 Endes 56—pure grenache, planted in 1956—a silky, long, oak-accented joy of a wine.

E. Guigal/Château d'Ampuis ☆

69420 Ampuis; 04.74.56.10.22; www.guigal.com
Wines: Côte-Rôtie, Condrieu, and all Rhône ACs. $$ to $$$$
This is the family—Étienne, Marcel, and now Philippe—that quietly, painstakingly, brought Côte-Rôtie to a worldwide fine-wine audience and, in the process, created one of the foremost family wineries in France. The Guigals themselves have a small though ever-expanding domaine. They are also *négociants,* buying grapes from throughout the Rhône valley. The wines that come from their own grapes are among the best wines in the world; the *négociant* wines range from good to splendid and are usually good value for the dollar. (Guigal's own wines are expensive but worth saving up for.) As there are too many wines to describe, I'll stick to some favorites from Guigal's own property: Condrieu La Doriane is fresh and focused, both mineral and subtly perfumed and about as elegant as you could wish; the Côte-Rôtie Brune et Blonde, in the *négociant* line, is a big-boned, irreproachable red; the version from Château d'Ampuis is oaky, simultaneously cool and brawny, and very delicious. Then come the devastating single vineyards: La Mouline is Côte-Rôtie at its most ravishing, a detailed red with notes of truffles and black cherry and a monumental future. La Turque, also fresh and elegant, is meatier, more tannic. And La Landonne is a brooding, dark aristocrat, austere in its youth. The Guigals are now making outstanding Hermitage and St.-Joseph from vines they recently purchased from well-established vintners.

Hermitage

A tiny AC consisting of a vast monolithic wall of vines producing long-lived, commanding, inimitable whites (marsanne and roussane) and reds (syrah).

BEST RECENT VINTAGES: 2005, 2004, 2003, 2001, 2000, 1996, 1990.
PRICES: $$$ to $$$$

PRODUCERS: CAVE DE TAIN ◆ CHAPOUTIER ☆ ◆ DOM JEAN-LOUIS CHAVE ☆ ◆ YANN CHAVE ↑ ◆ JEAN-LUC COLOMBO ◆ DELAS ◆ DOM DES ENTREFAUX ↑ ◆ PAUL JABOULET AINÉ ◆ DOM DES REMIZIÈRES ◆ Dom Marc Sorrel: very good, not extravagantly priced wines, in both colors; top cuvées are Le Gréal in red and Les Rocoules in white, also Crozes-Hermitage.

Paul Jaboulet Aîné

26600 La Roche de Glun; 04.75.84.68.93; www.jaboulet.com
Wines: Hermitage and all Rhônes. $ to $$$$
This venerable Rhône grower-*négociant* house was recently sold to Jean-Jacques Frey of Château la Lagune in Bordeaux and formerly of Champagne Ayala. The jewels in this particular crown were, and are likely to remain, Hermitage rouge La Chapelle and Hermitage blanc Le Chevalier de Stérimberg.

Domaine Jamet ☆

69420 Ampuis; 04.74.56.12.57; fax: 04.74.56.02.15
Wine: Côte-Rôtie. $$$
The Jamets make only one cuvée of Côte-Rôtie. It's pure syrah and it's a beauty—deep, focused, sensual, and full of gorgeous fruit with accents of black olive and Provençal herbs.

Domaine de la Janasse ☆

84350 Courthézon; 04.90.70.86.29; www.lajanasse.com
Wines: Châteauneuf-du-Pape, Côtes du Rhône, and Vin de Pays. $ to $$$
Good eco-friendly family domaine with a strong, vinous, serious white Châteauneuf and several cuvées of unfiltered red. The simplest bottling is deeply berried and mineral. The Vieilles Vignes is warm and charming but doesn't reveal all quickly. The Cuvée Chaupin, made from more than eighty-year-old grenache, is pure and concentrated, with sweet, sweet fruit, intense cherry flavors, and accents of mint and oak. The Côtes du Rhône Les Garrigues, which is 100 percent grenache, offers many of the same pleasures on a lighter scale.

Domaine Jasmin ☆

69420 Ampuis; 04.74.56.16.04; fax: 04.74.56.01.78
Wine: Côte-Rôtie. $$$($)
A small domaine making a single cuvée of elegant, viognier-accented Côte-Rôtie. The wines are very mineral and pedigreed with a silky texture and a youthful austerity that recalls the Burgundies of Hubert de Montille. The relatively light-bodied 2002 is the one to drink now; subtle and beautifully knit, it's all of a piece and as fresh as if a river ran through it.

Domaine Jaume

26110 Vinsobres; 04.75.27.61.01; www.domaine-jaume.com
Wines: Vinsobres and Côtes du Rhône. $$
Not to be confused with the Jaumes of DOM GRAND VENEUR, this family domaine makes strong, fragrant whites in the Côtes du Rhône and creamier, oaked versions in Vinsobres. There are several cuvées of pleasant, easy-drinking reds, the best being the vibrantly juicy unoaked Vinsobres and the Vinsobres Clos des Échalas, a new-oak-aged blend of grenache and mourvèdre. Stylish and modern, it's a crowd-pleaser with character.

Domaine du Joncier

30126 Tavel; 04.66.50.27.70; domainedujoncier@free.fr
Wine: Lirac. $$
Interesting, organic, somewhat hypernatural Liracs, from a strong, taut rosé to ripe, unfiltered reds, including the cuvée Les Muses, a potent but not brutish blend full of crushed berry flavors. Le Maudit, sold as either a Vin de Pays or a Vin de Table, is a barrel-fermented blend of overripe marsanne, roussanne, and bourboulenc. Vinous and very strong, it could handle dishes with keen, piercing flavors, like garlic and anchovies.

Domaine Lafond Roc-Épine

30126 Tavel; 04.66.50.24.59; lafond@roc-epine.com
Wines: Châteauneuf-du-Pape, Tavel, Lirac, and Côtes du Rhône. $$ to $$$
This good-size family domaine makes wines to fit a broad spectrum of sun-drenched meals. The firm, dry Tavel is your archetypal Midi rosé. The Lirac

blanc is a fresh, fragrant blend of roussanne and viognier. The basic Lirac rouge is forthright and juicy. The cuvée La Ferme Romaine ups the ante with some new oak aging. It's soigné and ripe, with good balance. The Châteauneufs are alluring, toothsome, and three-dimensional. Drink the Liracs first.

Laudun

Small Côtes du Rhône-Villages AC for red, white, and rosé wines.

BEST RECENT VINTAGES: 2005, 2004, 2003, 2001.
PRICES: $ to $$$

PRODUCERS: Cave des Vignerons de Saint Victor la Coste: especially the Cuvée Santus Victor la Costa ◆ Cave des Vignerons de Tresques ◆ Dom Pélaquié: particularly Cuvée Prestige, an oak-aged white ◆ Dom de Serre-Biau: notably the Cuvée les Cadinières ◆ Les Vignerons des 4 Chemins: reliable co-op.

Patrick Lesec Sélections ☆

BP 62001, 30702 Uzès Cedex; 04.66.37.67.20; lesec.patrick@wanadoo.fr
Wines: Most Rhônes. $ to $$$
Lesec, a new-wave *négociant,* unearths excellent cuvées of wine from good producers that he then matures, bottles, and sells—at very attractive prices. You really can't do better, price- and quality-wise, than his 2004 Côtes du Rhône-Villages Les Tendrelles, with its solid cherry fruit and good structure, selling for the equivalent of $5 in French hypermarkets.

Lirac

A southern Rhône AC for reds, rosés, and whites. Next to Tavel, many producers make wines in both ACs.

BEST RECENT VINTAGES: 2005, 2004, 2003, 2001.
PRICES: $ to $$$

PRODUCERS: Clos de Sixte: see DOM GRAND VENEUR ☆ ◆ Ch le Devoy Martine: Circius, a chunky red, is worth trying by the glass ◆ DOM DU JONCIER ◆ DOM LAFOND ROC-ÉPINE ◆ Dom Maby: La Fermade red would make a nice wine-bar quaff ◆ CH MONT-REDON ◆ DOM DE LA MORDORÉE ☆ ◆ DOM SAINT-ROCH ☆.

Domaine de Marcoux ☆

BP 31. 84231 Châteauneuf-du-Pape; 04.90.34.67.43; domaine-marcoux@wanadoo.fr
Wine: Châteauneuf-du-Pape. $$$
Biodynamically farmed vines and very real wines. The young whites are floral and vinous; with ten-plus years of age, they develop appetizing notes of herbal tea. The traditional red is marked by sweet spices, cherry, and cherry pit flavors; the Vieilles Vignes bottling, pure grenache, is a real mouthful, concentrated, rich, and full of character.

Mas de Libian ↑

07700 St.-Marcel d'Ardèche; 04.75.04.66.22; h.thibon@wanadoo.fr.
Wines: Côtes du Rhône and Vin de Pays de l'Ardèche. $
This serious, ambitious Ardèche domaine makes a creamy, amiable Côtes du Rhône white, a lightly oaked blend of clairette and viognier, and an even better pure viognier Vin de Pays. The clutch of reds starts with a Vin de Pays Vin de Pétanque, a charming light red that serves as the domaine's rosé. There are two or three different but all very agreeable Côtes du Rhônes, for casual

lunches and wine-bar snacks, and La Calade, a dark, chewy, mourvèdre-based cuvée. Finally, there's the very good Khayyam, their most subtle and supple red.

Domaine du Mazel ↑

07400 Val Vignères; 04.75.52.54.21; fax: 04.75.52.51.02
Wine: Vin de Pays de l'Ardèche. $
Gérard Oustric makes ambitious, endearing, hypernatural wines, not always perfect but uniformly interesting and sometimes provocative. Favorites include Cuvée Raoul, a Vin de Table, a very cute and tasty carignan that drinks like a lipsmacking serious rosé; the Cuvée Larmande, a very pure, slightly austere syrah; and the Cuvée St. Philippe, a lean, slightly oaky syrah with scents of cocoa powder.

Robert Michel ☆

07130 Cornas; 04.75.40.38.70; fax: 04.75.40.58.57
Wine: Cornas. $$$
I think Michel's were the first Cornas I ever tasted, too many years ago. I still love his wines. There's the Cuvée des Coteaux, the excellent 2003 of which was already complex in 2005, with leather evident under the succulent fruit. The 2003 La Geynale, from vines planted in 1910, was downright majestic. Through the flavors of crushed raspberries and blueberries you felt the power of the land. The much lighter 2002 Geynale could be drunk now, with both pleasure and interest.

Domaine la Monardière

84190 Vacqueyras; 04.90.65.87.20; monardiere@wanadoo.fr
Wine: Vacqueyras. $ to $$
A large and improving domaine, with attractive whites fermented in new oak barrels, and three solid cuvées of red: Les Calades to serve chilled and drink on the attractive fruit; the slightly richer Réserve des 2 Monardes, to age for a year or two; and the ambitious, unfined, unfiltered Vieilles Vignes, a succulent red with plenty of oomph.

Domaine du Monteillet/Vignobles Montez ↑

42140 Chavanay; 04.74.87.24.57; stephane.montez@worldonline.fr
Wines: Condrieu, Côte-Rôtie, and St.-Joseph. $$ to $$$$
Young Stéphane Montez, who has worked in California and Australia, is turning out exciting and very promising wines on his small parcels of Condrieu and Côte-Rôtie. In Condrieu, there's the excellent cuvée Les Grandes Chailles, an airy blend of minerals, ripe apricots, and blossoms and a rather bizarre cuvée La Mobilette, which spent two years in new oak and is, surprise surprise, extremely oaky. La Grande Place is a sensual expression of Côte-Rôtie. Fortis, aged in new oak, seems more fruit-driven but delicious all the same. Montez has a bit more land in St.-Joseph, from which he makes the less expensive, earlier-drinking, but very delicious cuvée La Cabride blanc.

Domaine Montirius ☆

84260 Sarrians; 04.90.65.38.28; www.Montirius.com
Wines: Gigondas, Vacqueyras, Côtes du Rhône, and Vin de Pays de Vaucluse. $$ to $$$
Christine and Eric Saurel run a large domaine adhering to biodynamic principles—and then some. Every single step of the winemaking process is the result of reflection. Wild yeasts, no wood, no fining or filtering, and lots of other details that result in successful hypernatural wines. A few favorites: the supple, fluid Vacqueyras blanc; the simply delectable Côtes du Rhône rouge; and the cool and succulent traditional cuvée of Vacqueyras rouge. The Clos Montirius, a grenache and syrah blend from a parcel in Vacqueyras, is sapid, succulent, concentrated, and addictively appetizing. With four years of aging, this red gets pretty serious.

Château Mont-Redon

BP 10-84231 Châteauneuf-du-Pape Cedex; 04.90.83.72.75; châteaumontredon@wanadoo.fr
Wines: Châteauneuf-du-Pape, Lirac, and Côtes du Rhône. $ to $$$
Having worked in vineyards around the world—including those of Joseph Phelps in California—the latest generation of the Abeille-Fabre family has brought a burst of new energy to this large, traditional family domaine. The wines aren't blockbusters but are very professional, good representatives of their respective ACs, and quite attractively priced. The Châteauneuf blanc is penetrating, textured, and vinous, a good, strong food white. The reds are fragrant, mingled, and well mannered. They're classic and spicy, with clear fruit, good balance, and not an aggressive bone in their bodies. The Côtes du Rhônes, in both colors, are supple and savory. The Liracs are distinctly superior. The white, partially barrel fermented, presents an appetizing integration of oak and fruit; the very classic red is what most people think of when they want a good, hearty Côtes du Rhône-Villages.

Domaine de Montvac

84190 Vacqueyras; 04.90.65.85.51; dusserre@domaine-de-montvac.com
Wine: Vacqueyras. $$
There's good work here, although the wines, whether the basic bottlings or the cuvée Variation, come across as somewhat raw; and the whites, in particular, are rather oaky. The rich Cuvée Vincila, made only in good years, is based on old vines and is very good and a clear step up.

Domaine de la Mordorée ☆

30126 Tavel; 04.66.55.00.75; www.domaine-mordoree.com
Wines: Lirac and Tavel. $$
The Delormes own and run a good-size, seriously eco-friendly, and idealistic domaine with very good wines to show for their labors. La Dame Rousse is a Tavel that should win friends and influence people in favor of the tastiness and usefulness of firm, taut rosés. And the Lirac Reine des Bois in both colors is simply delicious.

Domaine du Moulin

26110 Vinsobres; 04.75.27.65.59; denis.vinson@wanadoo.fr
Wines: Vinsobres and Côtes du Rhône. $ to $$
Nice Côtes du Rhônes, both red and white—a bright, pretty, perfumed Vinsobres blanc, flaunting its viognier; a juicy, winsome Vinsobres red, perfect for bistros; and a warm Vinsobre rouge Cuvée Charles Joseph Vieilles Vignes with velvety texture and real personality.

Muscat de Beaumes-de-Venise

An AC with highly perfumed, very sweet fortified wine (Vin Doux Naturel) made from muscat in the same area as Beaumes-de-Venise AC. Drink the youngest available. Prices: $$. Producers: DOM DE DURBAN ☆ ◆ Dom de Fenouillet: formerly members of the local cooperative, the eco-friendly Soards make red Beaumes de Venise that are full of character and fragrant, truly lovely versions of its special Vin Doux Naturel ↑ ◆ Dom de la Pigeade: good, fresh, precise, and textured; worth trying ↑.

Château la Nerthe ☆

84230 Châteauneuf-du-Pape; 04.90.83.70.11; fax: 04.90.83.79.69
Wine: Châteauneuf-du-Pape. $$$ to $$$$
Large, first-rate Châteauneuf property with two cuvées of both red and white, the very good traditional and the excellent Clos de Beauvenir in white and, in red, Cuvée des Cadettes, an oaky, stylish wine accommodating New World tastes and Old World *terroir*.

Domaine Robert Niero ☆

69420 Condrieu; 04.74.59.84.38; fax: 04.74.56.62.70

Wines: Condrieu and Côte-Rôtie. $$$ to $$$$

From a banker turned vintner, two lovely cuvées of Condrieu—a fresh, tight, fruit-driven version and the Cuvée de Chery, pure power, pedigree, and elegance. The Côte-Rôtie, with 5 percent viognier, is not massive but razor sharp and seductive, with exotic fragrances and a long and lovely finish.

Domaine Nôtre Dame de Cousignac

07700 Bourg St.-Andéol; 04.75.54.61.41; raphael.pommier@libertysurf.fr

Wines: Côtes du Rhône, Côtes du Vivarais, and Vin de Table. $ to $$

The seventh generation of Pommiers working the cold mountain vineyards of the Ardèche—and doing a good job of it. They make fresh, pleasant whites under both the Côtes du Rhône and the Vivarais ACs, as well as a tart little wine-bar red. There's also the Ardesc Vin de Table, an unfiltered red blend of grenache, carignan, and syrah, either oaked (the Léon Pommier bottling) or unoaked. The oak does add a certain something, but I prefer the gracious suppleness of the unoaked.

Domaine Ogier

69420 Ampuis; 04.74.56.10.75; sogier@club-internet.fr

Wine: Côte-Rôtie. $$$

Michel Ogier succeeded his father in 1997. He makes several worthwhile (and evolving) cuvées of Côte-Rôtie, all pure syrah. The traditional bottling, mostly from Côte Blonde, is velvety and appetizing; Les Embruns is sapid, beefier, and somewhat minty, with an austerity that argues in favor of cellaring for at least five years; La Belle Hélène is very concentrated, rich, and serious, something of a diamond in the rough.

Domaine les Pallières

84190 Gigondas; 04.90.33.00.31; www.brunier.fr

Wine: Gigondas. $$($)

Frédéric and Daniel Brunier (see DOM DU VIEUX TÉLÉGRAPHE), in collaboration with their American importer, Kermit Lynch, have taken over this important Gigondas property. The wine seems to thumb its nose at the sleek and the stylish, preferring to evoke an old-fashioned, refined sort of rusticity. When the sweet cherry fruit with its mild oak seasoning evolves toward soft-textured spices, black olives, Provençal herbs, and leather, it's one of the few current French reds I can think of that I'd be tempted to pair with a tomato sauce.

Domaine Vincent Paris ☆

07130 Cornas; 04.75.40.13.04; vinparis@wanadoo.fr

Wines: Cornas and Vin de Pays. $$$($)

Eco-friendly Vincent Paris names his cuvées of Cornas after the gradient of the slope. Thus, Cornas Granit 30, from young vines, is extremely pure and mineral; Granit 60, from old vines, is so *terroir*-driven you can almost taste the incline. Both cuvées succeed in the very different vintages of 2002 and 2003, the latter, of course, being much richer and more powerful. The 2004 promises to be excellent. Paris also makes a merlot Vin de Pays de l'Ardèche. It's interesting and tasty, but I much prefer his Cornas.

Domaine du Pegau

84230 Châteauneuf-du-Pape; 04.90.83.56.61; www.pegau.com

Wines: Châteauneuf-du-Pape. $$ to $$$

Laurence Féraud makes meaty, spicy, unfiltered Châteauneufs. They caress the palate and have a lovely old-fashioned feel.

André Perret

42410 Chavanay; 04.74.87.24.74; www.andreperret.com

Wines: Condrieu and St.-Joseph. $$ to $$$

There are good, reasonably priced St.-Josephs, both red and white, but Condrieu is the star here. There are three cuvées—a floral but solid traditional bottling; the tender, mineral, nicely focused Clos Chanson; and the racy, deep, very mineral De Chery.

Domaine Perrin & Fils ☆

84100 Orange; 04.90.11.12.04; www.domainesperrin.com
Wines: Gigondas, Vacqueyras, Vinsobres, Cairanne, and Rasteau Côtes du Rhône-Villages. $ to $$($)
The boys from CH DE BEAUCASTEL created this domaine in the 1990s, though the label dates from 2001. Farming organically, as at Beaucastel, they produce the gamut of southern Rhône wines—at quite reasonable prices. Favorites include a Côtes du Rhône Réserve blanc and rouge, each one a junior Châteauneuf; and a Vacqueyras so adamantly mouthwatering, it's not only irresistible, it's better than many Châteauneufs. This domaine also encompasses the popular Côtes du Ventoux La Vieille Ferme.

Domaine Rabasse-Charavin ☆

84290 Cairanne; 04.90.30.70.05; couturier.corinne@wanadoo.fr
Wines: Cairanne, Rasteau, Côtes du Rhône, and Vin de Pays. $ to $$
Longtime favorite Corinne Couturier is indefatigable. She manages a huge domaine, making wines in many appellations, without ever missing a step or making a bad wine. The reds are unfiltered. And all are characteristic of their respective ACs as well as satisfying and user-friendly. Favorites include a focused, lipsmacking Cairanne blanc Corinne Couturier "Cuvée d'Estevenas" made from pure roussanne, and a similarly named cuvée in red, a super-ripe, kirsch and mineral Cairanne. (Note: Rabasse-Charavin is in small print on these last two labels.)

Rasteau and Rasteau–Côtes du Rhône-Villages

Two very distinct but closely related ACs. The latter is one of the designated Côtes du Rhône-Villages. Like its confrères, it applies to reds, whites, and rosés made from the usual southern Rhône mix but with heavy reliance on grenache. Rasteau on the other hand is a Vin Doux Naturel (fortified wine). Rich and sweet, it is based almost exclusively on grenache and may be red, white, or *dorée* (*rancio*), meaning that it has aged and has taken on oxidative colors and aromas. It accounts for no more than 3 percent of production. Rasteau-Côtes du Rhône-Villages should be drunk before its tenth birthday; the Vin Doux Naturel may age indefinitely.

PRICES: $ to $$$

PRODUCERS: Dom Beau Mistral: attractive oak-aged whites; and a delicious, deep gold Rasteau Vin Doux Naturel *dorée* (*rancio*) that would make a lovely aperitif or an even better partner for a cheese course ◆ DOM DE BEAURENARD ◆ CAVE DE RASTEAU ◆ DOM DIDIER CHARAVIN ◆ Dom des Coteaux des Travers: vinified in oak barrels, Robert Charavin's cuvée Marine, a blend of viognier, marsanne, and roussanne, is a seductive white with beguiling flavors of apricots and minerals; his Vin Doux Naturel is amiably fruity and lightly tannic ◆ DOM DES ESCARAVAILLES ◆ Dom de la Girardière: juicy, uncomplicated Rhône reds—lovely lunch wines ◆ Dom les Girasols: Paul Joyet makes a rough-hewn, singular but quickly evolving red and a punchy, rustic, highly alcoholic Vin Doux Naturel *rancio* ◆ Dom Gourt de Mautens: Jérôme Bressy's reds are rich, ripe, almost cult-like, and very ambitious ◆ DOM PERRIN & FILS ☆ ◆ DOM RABASSE-CHARAVIN ☆ ◆ Dom Santa Duc: see GIGONDAS listing ◆ DOM LA SOUMADE ☆ ◆ DOM DU TRAPADIS ◆ CH DU TRIGNON.

Château Rayas ☆

84230 Châteauneuf-du-Pape; 04.90.83.73.09; fax: 04.90.83.51.17
Wine: Châteauneuf-du-Pape. $$$$
Old vines and a great vineyard site combine to make this legendary house owned by the Reynaud family one of the best producers in the AC, though the wines might surprise those expecting hefty, tooth-staining reds. Made from pure grenache, these are lightly colored, stone- and Provençal herb–threaded

Châteauneufs with the creamy, dulcet texture particular to the grape variety. Despite their pale-rose-ish color, they are firm, decisive and long-lived. And they may be the only red wines I'd pair with Moroccan tagines. The normal bottling is the richest; there's a second wine, Pignan, which is fresher, lighter, and truly captivating. The white Châteauneuf, a blend of grenache and clairette, is more mainstream—creamy, mineral, toothsome, and a delicious food wine. The Reynauds also make similarly styled—though less grand—wines in the Côtes du Rhône at Ch Fonsalette and Ch des Tours and a Vin de Pays de Vaucluse called Domaine des Tours. The best of these is Ch des Tours Vacqueyras, a creamy, spicy, cherry-accented red.

Domaine la Réméjeanne

30200 Sabran; 04.66.89.44.51; fax: 04.66.89.64.22
Wine: Côtes du Rhône. $$
Popular Côtes du Rhône domaine in which each cuvée is named after a plant or a shrub or some natural force or other. My favorites are the red and the white Églantiers bottlings, both of which seem to come from older vines and are subtly marked by oak.

Domaine des Rémizières

26600 Tain l'Hermitage; 04.75.07.44.28; desmeure-philippe@wanadoo.fr
Wines: Hermitage and Crozes-Hermitage. $$ to $$$
The Cuvée Émilie corresponds to the top-of-the-line Hermitage—a structured, mineral, oaky white and a velvety, pleasantly specific red. In certain vintages, there's an additional red, L'Essentiel, which, in 2003, was rich and tasty. Most of the domaine's production is in Crozes-Hermitage. The Cuvée Christophe is the bottling to look for here, in both red and white. It's ambitious and reasonably priced.

Domaine Marcel Richaud ☆

84290 Cairanne; 04.90.30.85.25; marcel-richaud@wanadoo.fr
Wines: Cairanne and Côtes du Rhône. $ to $$($)
One of the most influential of the current generation of Rhône producers, Marcel Richaud, as modest as he is fun-loving and generous, brought the wines into the modern era. They may verge on the hypernatural—eco-friendly, wild yeasts, no fining, no filtration, little or no sulfur, no chaptalization, no acidification—but the wines are uniformly succulent, juicy, vibrant, and ultradelicious. You can't go wrong here. The white Cairanne is assertive and appetizing. L'Ebrescade corresponds to a single-vineyard Cairanne, equal parts grenache, syrah, and mourvèdre. It's smooth and rich and alluring, with great freshness and dimension. The deep, fleshy Estrambordes ages in barrel. All are great food wines. Les Garrigues, a simpler Cairanne, has such delicious fruit allied with black pepper and thyme accents that it makes you want to have lunch on the spot—*un petit lapin à la moutarde, par example.*

Roaix

Minuscule designated Côtes du Rhône-Villages AC for reds, whites, and rosés. Vintages: 2005, 2004, 2003, 2001. Prices: $ to $$$. Producer: DOM DES ESCARAVAILLES.

Domaine Roche Buissière ↑

84110 Faucon; 04.90.46.49.14; rochebuissiere@wanadoo.fr
Wines: Côtes du Rhône and Vin de Pays. $ to $$
Pierre, Antoine, and Laurence Joly started bottling their organic wine in 1999. With wild yeasts, no fining, and no filtration, the wines are basically hypernatural. They're not perfect but they're vibrant and tasty and headed in the right direction. Les Claux is a rich, fresh, juicy red Côtes du Rhône; ditto for Gaia, which gets some barrel age. Abracadabra, chiefly grenache, is perfumed and truly succulent. Their Vin de Pays Coteaux des Baronnies is rustic but satisfying.

Rochegude

Tiny designated Côtes du Rhône-Villages AC for reds, whites, and rosés. Versions from the local co-op will give you an adequate idea. Vintages: 2005, 2004, 2003, 2001. Prices: $ to $$$.

Domaine Romaneaux-Destezet ↑

07410 Arlebosc; tel/fax: 04.75.08.57.20; souhaut.herve@wanadoo.fr

Wine: Vin de Pays de l'Ardèche. $$ to $$$

Hervé Souhaut, firmly in the hypernatural camp, has the right the use the St.-Joseph AC for many of his wines, but he would rather save himself the bureaucratic aggravation and so opts for Vin de Pays instead. La Souteronne, an old-vines gamay (yes!), more mineral than varietal, has great mountain freshness. Syrah has all those attributes plus tremendous juiciness. Sainte Épine, named for its *lieu-dit* within St.-Joseph, has deliciously exotic syrah fruit and lovely freshness. All are great wine-bar wines and then some.

Domaine Rouge Garance ↑

30210 St.-Hilaire d'Ozilhan; 04.66.37.06.92; rougegarance@wanadoo

Wine: Côtes du Rhône-Villages. $ to $$

The actor Jean-Louis Trintignant co-owns the property but has entrusted its management to two dedicated vintners. The wines are not quite ready for prime time but are very promising and steadily improving. Favorites thus far include the mellow Côtes du Rhône-Villages Garance, made from old carignan and grenache vines; the unfiltered Côtes du Rhône-Villages Rouge Garance, a solid blend of syrah, grenache and mourvèdre; and Les Saint Pierre, a *barrique*-aged syrah.

Rousset-les-Vignes

Thimble-size designated Côtes du Rhône-Village for reds, whites, and rosés. Best recent vintages: 2005, 2004, 2003, 2001. Prices: $ to $$$. Producers: Domaine la Bouvade (especially the oak-aged cuvée of red) ◆ Château Suzeau: spicy, flavorful reds ◆ Cave de Saint Pantaléon les Vignes: particularly the Cuvée des Seigneurs Alrics.

Sablet

Small designated Côtes du Rhône-Village for reds, whites, and rosés. There are roughly ten independent producers, including: Dom des Pasquiers: solid, tasty, nicely structured wines ◆ Dom de Piaugier: try the fragrant, characterful Cuvée Montmartel ◆ Dom Santa Duc: see CÔTES DU RHÔNE and GIGONDAS listings ◆ CH DU TRIGNON ◆ Dom de Verquière: nice wine-bar quaffs.

St.-Gervais

Minuscule designated Côtes du Rhône-Villages for reds, whites, and rosés.

BEST RECENT VINTAGES: 2005, 2004, 2003, 2001.
PRICES: $ to $$$

PRODUCERS: Cave de Saint Gervais: especially Réserve de Cruzeau, a smooth, supple syrah at a reasonable price ◆ Domaine Clavel: look for the very good oak-aged, syrah-dominated cuvée ◆ Dom de Sainte-Anne: top local producer ☆ ◆ ÉRIC TEXIER ☆.

St.-Joseph

A northern Rhône AC on steep slopes facing the Alps, known for medium-bodied peppery reds (syrah) and vinous whites (marsanne and roussanne) to drink (generally) in the near term. This AC is very popular in the *bouchons* of Lyon.

BEST RECENT VINTAGES: 2005, 2004, 2003, 2000.
PRICES: $$ to $$$($)

PRODUCERS: CAVE DE TAIN ◆ CHAPOUTIER ☆ ◆ Dom Chèze: the Cuvée des Anges (red) is a pleasant wine-bar quaff ◆ JEAN-LUC COLOMBO ◆ DOM COURBIS ◆ Dom Coursodon: improving family domaine with several cuvées of red and white; all are worth trying but especially the deep, rich La Sensonne, Le Paradis St. Pierre, and L'Olivaie ☆ ◆ DARD & RIBO ◆ DELAS ◆ DOM PHILIPPE FAURY ◆ LA FERME DES SEPT LUNES ↑ ◆ PIERRE GAILLARD ☆ ◆ Pierre Gonon: well-structured, mineral whites; juicy, lipsmacking reds with an occasional hint of gaminess ◆ DOM BERNARD GRIPA ◆ ANDRÉ PERRET ◆ ÉRIC TEXIER ☆ ◆ DOM FRANÇOIS VILLARD ☆ ◆ LES VINS DE VIENNE ☆.

Domaine Saint Luc

26790 La Baume de Transit; 04.75.98.11.51; www.dom-saint-luc.com
Wines: Côtes du Rhônes-Villages and Coteaux du Tricastin. $ to $$
Very nice, easy-drinking reds. From the gracious, silky Coteaux du Tricastin to the ripe, lipsmacking Côtes du Rhône Clos Chanteduc, these are perfect, user-friendly wines for bistro or casual at-home meals.

St.-Maurice

Small designated Côtes du Rhône-Villages for reds, whites, and rosés. Vintages: 2005, 2004, 2003, 2001. Prices: $ to $$$. Producers: Cave de St.-Maurice, especially the pure viognier Cuvée St.-Maurice ◆ Dom l'Échevin (see DOM LA FLORANE) ◆ DOM VIRET ☆.

St.-Pantaléon-les-Vignes

Vest-pocket designated Côtes du Rhône-Village for red, white, and rosé wines. Vintages: 2005, 2004, 2003, 2001. Prices: $ to $$$. Producers: Cave de Saint Pantaléon les Vignes, particularly the cuvée Préstige and Goutillonage ◆ Dom Gigondan: especially cuvée Réserve.

St.-Péray

A minuscule AC facing the town of Valence, on the right bank of the Rhône, producing still and sparkling (*méthode traditionelle)* whites based on marsanne and roussanne.

BEST RECENT VINTAGES: 2005, 2004, 2003.
PRICES: $ to $$$.

PRODUCERS: Dom du Biguet: fresh and easy-drinking pure marsanne, both still and sparkling ◆ Dom Stéphane Chabaud: by-the-glass options—a pleasant sparkling wine of pure marsanne and an ample, still wine blending marsanne and roussanne ◆ CAVE DU TAIN ◆ DOM AUGUSTE CLAPE ☆ ◆ DOM BERNARD GRIPA ◆ DOM DU TUNNEL ↑ ◆ LES VINS DE VIENNE ☆ ◆ DOM VOGE.

Château Saint-Roch ☆

BP 17, 30150 Roquemaure; 04.66.82.82.59; www.chateau-saint-roch.com
Wines: Châteauneuf-du-Pape and Lirac. $$ to $$$
The Brunel brothers of CH DE LA GARDINE have taken over this good-size domaine and have been turning out a range of admirable wines. There are numerous cuvées and all are recommended, including the simple, flavorful Lirac

blanc with a cork that looks like lipstick and the barrel-fermented Cuvée Confidentielle, based on clairette. It's a strong, concentrated but subtle and self-assured white that drinks like a junior Châteauneuf-du-Pape. In reds, the classic Lirac is inviting in every respect, a perfect bistro red. The barrel-aged Cuvée Confidentielle, one third each of grenache, syrah, and mourvèdre, is subtler, deeper, and more structured, with deep fruit flavors. The vineyard from which it comes borders on Châteauneuf, and the wine tastes as if it belongs in that AC.

Domaine le Sang des Cailloux ☆

84260 Sarrians; 04.90.65.88.64; le-sang-des-cailloux@wanadoo.fr

Wine: Vacqueyras. $$ to $$$

Eco-friendly Serge Férigoule makes generous, structured Vacqueyras, year in, year out. Indeed, he seems to have escaped all the potential pitfalls of the very different 2002 and 2003 vintages. Everything is recommended. Favorites include Un Sang Blanc, an absolutely yummy, original, honest white with just the right amount of oak. Reds are neither fined nor filtered. The Cuvée Doucinello, primarily grenache, is as dulcet as it is mouthwatering; Cuvée Azalais, also based on grenache, is deep, cool, succulent, and tender. Cuvée Lopy, a grenache-syrah blend, is oakier but promises to be delectable with about five years of cellaring. And the surprisingly silky Cuvée Vieilles Vignes could only have drawn its blood from local stones.

Séguret

A small but well-known (for its charming site) designated Côtes du Rhône-Village, a source of red, rosé, and white wines.

BEST RECENT VINTAGES: 2005, 2004, 2003, 2001.
PRICES: $ to $$$

PRODUCERS: Dom de Cabasse: especially the smooth, classic Cuvée Casa Bassa ◆ Ch la Courançonne: look for the rich, plummy Cuvée la Fiole du Chevalier d'Ébenne ◆ Dom Jean David: organic wines, look for cuvées Les Levants and Les Couchants ◆ Dom la Garancière: see CLOS DU JONCUAS ◆ ÉRIC TEXIER ☆.

Château de la Selve

07120 Grospierres; 04.75.93.02.55; www.chateau-de-la-selve.fr

Wine: Vin de Pays de l'Ardèche. $$

This good-size serious young domaine practices organic viticulture and makes a range of very promising wines. My favorite is the bracing viognier-sauvignon blanc blend but the reds, which are unfiltered, are worth following, particularly the lightly minty Palissaire, a blend of merlot, cabernet sauvignon, and grenache.

Château Signac ☆

30200 Bagnols-sur-Céze; 04.66.89.58.47; châteausignac@wanadoo.fr

Wine: Côtes du Rhône-Villages. $ to $$

Serious and seriously delicious Côtes du Rhône-Villages reds, especially the cuvées Terra Amata, a powerful though suave blend of dark red fruit and spice; and the soigné Chusclan Combe d'Enfer, made from old grenache and syrah vines and rich with flavors of black cherry and black olive.

Château Simian

84420 Piolenc; 04.90.29.50.67; fax: 04.90.29.62.33

Wines: Châteauneuf-du-Pape, Côtes du Rhône, and Vin de Pays de la Principauté d'Orange. $ to $$$

I like the whites here better than the reds, both Châteauneuf and Côtes du Rhône. Font Simian, the Vin de Pays, is a very light red, of interest because of the unusual mix of grapes—tempranillo, merlot, caladoc, plus the usual Rhône suspects.

Domaine de la Solitude ☆
BP 21, 84321 Châteauneuf-du-Pape Cedex; 04.90.83.71.45; fax: 04.90.83.51.34
Wines: Châteauneuf-du-Pape and Côtes du Rhône. $$ to $$$($)
The wines from the Lançons' large property, which produces 300,000 bottles of Côtes du Rhône and 150,000 bottles of Châteauneuf-du-Pape annually, have improved dramatically since 2000. The Côtes du Rhônes of both colors are just fine but their raison d'être appears to be to provide a support for the excellent Châteauneufs. Whites make up 20 percent of the latter; all age in barrel and the roussanne always ferments in barrel. Jodie Foster drank the standard bottling of the white in the movie *The Panic Room* while taking a bath. A good choice. It's racy and elegant. The Cuvée Barbarini, almost pure roussanne vinified in new oak, is even better and even more elegant. There is no press wine in the red Châteauneufs, and all age in newish barrels. The traditional cuvée has rich berry and cherry pit flavors, with layers of lush fruit on a stony, mineral base. The unfiltered Cuvée Barberini is sensual and fragrant, mingling flavors of cherry, spice, black olives, and minerals. In great vintages, the Lançons also make a Réserve Secret. An intense, concentrated red based primarily on grenache, it is as lush and impressive as any garage-cult wine. A note on serving: I drank the 2000 in 2004 with the owner. It had been carafed for at least an hour. He liked drinking it at that stage. Me too.

Domaine la Soumade ☆
84110 Rasteau; 04.90.46.13.63; fax: 04.90.46.18.36
Wines: Côtes du Rhône-Villages–Rasteau and Vin Doux Naturel. $$ to $$$
André Romero may be the sole Rhône producer to work with the brilliant Bordeaux-located consultant Stéphane Derononcourt. He's also the only vintner I know of who sent cases of his wine to NYC firemen after 9/11. Sentiments aside, his reds, particularly the cuvées Prestige and Fleur de Confiance, are deep, concentrated, and beautifully focused, with a finely integrated oak. His several cuvées of Vin Doux Naturel are first-rate but demand cellaring. The 2000 Ambré, which spent thee years in barrel, will be gorgeous in about twenty years, when the rich, cashew-accented raw material digests all that oak. Romero recently acquired a property in Châteauneuf-du-Pape; 2005 was the first vintage. The wine, 90 percent grenache, is seductive, with intense black cherry flavors, accented by Provençal herbs.

Domaine Jean-Michel Stephan
69420 Tupin-Semons; 04.74.56.62.66; fax: 04.74.56.62.66
Wine: Côte-Rôtie. $$ to $$$($)
Unfiltered, hypernatural Côte-Rôties. You either love them or you accept that these wines don't always escape the pitfalls of that risky approach to vinification. My favorite was a pure, lean, and mineral 2002 Coteau de Tupin.

Tardieu-Laurent ☆
84160 Loumarin; 04.90.68.80.25; fax: 04.90.68.22.65
Wines: Many Rhône ACs. $$ to $$$$
New-wave *négociants* with reliably high-quality wines from Cornas and Côte-Rôtie to Châteauneuf-du-Pape. A Cuvée Spéciale of Châteauneuf, for example, was smooth, suave, and inviting, with an appetizing mingling of black cherry fruit, black olives, spices, and thyme.

Tavel
A southern Rhône AC on the right bank of the river known for big, dry rosés with a distinctly southern tang. Drink the youngest available.

PRICES: $ to $$

PRODUCERS: L'ANGLORE ↑ ◆ Ch d'Aqueria: the best-known Tavel producer; competent, commercial wines ◆ DOM DU JONCIER ◆ DOM LAFOND ROC-ÉPINE ◆ Dom Maby: the La Forcadière bottling is strong, mineral, and firm—very nice ◆ DOM DE LA MORDORÉE ☆ ◆ Ch de Trinquevedel: lovely, fresh, structured, lipsmacking Tavel.

Éric Texier ☆

69380 Charnay; 04.72.54.4593; www.eric-texier.com

Wines: Everything Rhône. $ to $$$$

Éric Texier is sui generis. I'm not sure I understand his setup even after having met and tasted with him twice and checked out his web site. He seems to vinify for a lot of other people—throughout the Rhône and in the Mâconnais—and to keep some wine to sell under his own label. He also seems to have his own vines, which may include those in Brézeme, an obscure vineyard area about 10 miles south of Valence. Here are some Rhône highlights: O Pale, with less than 8 percent alcohol and 75 grams of residual sugar; it's a one-off, labeled "juice of partly fermented grapes"; Condrieu Janrode, a lightly off-dry, both tight and tender, Ostertag-style wine, with a long finish; a perfumed, mineral Côtes du Rhône from pure viognier; a textured, appetizing Côtes du Rhône Brézeme from pure roussanne; and an oaky, racy Châteauneuf-du-Pape blanc. In reds: scrumptious, seductive Côtes du Rhône old-vines Brézeme; a super fresh Côtes du Rhône Brézeme Domaine de Pervault located near Côte-Rôtie, unique in that it's a red but as perfumed as any Condrieu; a silky, concentrated, lightly oaked, quite elegant St.-Joseph; a ripe, very well made Chusclan with flavors of cherries and cherry pits; and a juicy Châteauneuf with gravitas.

Domaine du Trapadis

84110 Rasteau; 04.90.46.11.20; durand.helen@wanadoo.fr

Wines: Rasteau and Côtes du Rhône

An eco-friendly domaine run by intelligent, young Helen Durand. Look for the Rasteau Les Adres which comes from three parcels of very old grenache vines. It's a serious, balanced, generic red. There's also an ambitious, unfiltered, hand-bottled white, nearly pure grenache and aged in barriques; several noteworthy Vin Doux Naturels; a very sweet, cherry-accented Rasteau; and La Ponchonniere, a Vin de Table made from pure late harvest grenache that would be great with aged sheep's milk cheese.

Domaine des Treilles

26770 Montbrizon; 04.75.53.51.69; fax: 04.75.53.68.01

Wines: Valréas and Côtes du Rhône. $

Patrice Méry is another member of the hypernatural club, using organic, wild yeasts, no destemming, and little or no sulfur. What's more, his wines are extremely inexpensive. I think they're best drunk young. The 2005s should be delicious. In 2004, the Côtes du Rhône white was perfumed, with an appetizingly nubbly texture; the red was juicy and lipsmacking; the Valréas was focused, succulent and mouthwatering.

Château du Trignon

84190 Gigondas; 04.90.46.90.27; trignon@chateau-du-trignon.com

Wines: Gigondas, Sablet, and Rasteau. $$ to $$$

A good-size domaine with dark, juicy wines. The Gigondas is by far the fleshiest, but all the wines are in the same family style—fluid, supple, succulent—despite the occasional accent on spices and bacon in, say, the Gigondas, and raspberries and cherry pits in the Rasteau.

Domaine du Tunnel ↑

07130 St.-Péray; 04.75.80.04.66; fax: 04.75.80.06.50

Wines: Cornas, St.-Péray, St.-Joseph. $$ to $$$

Stéphane Robert created his small domaine in 1994. He's definitely someone to watch. His St.-Péray, fragrant, a barrel-aged blend of marsanne and roussanne, is mellow, ample and structured. His Cornas is rich, silky, and elegant. Truly delicious.

Domaine Pierre Usseglio

84230 Châteauneuf-du-Pape; 04.90.83.72.98; domaine-usseglio@wanadoo.fr
Wine: Châteauneuf-du-Pape. $$ to $$$
Recent improvement at this classic family property. The standard bottling is rich, with good structure and warm, serious fruit. The cuvée Mon Aïeul, nearly pure grenache, is very deep and very saturated, a big wine with an engagingly rustic texture.

Vacqueyras

A dynamic southern Rhône AC (until recently a designated Côtes du Rhône-Villages) for reds, whites, and rosés.

BEST RECENT VINTAGES: 2005, 2004, 2003, 2001.
PRICES: $ to $$$

PRODUCERS: Dom les Amouriers: look for cuvées Signature and Les Genestes ◆ CLOS DU JONCUAS/La Font de Papier ◆ Dom le Colombier: fresh, gracious whites; silky, supple, nonoaked reds to drink slightly chilled (including the old-vines cuvée); and an oaky Cuvée G to let age for a couple of years ◆ DOM LE COUROULU ◆ DOM LA GARRIGUE ◆ DOM GRAND VENEUR ☆ ◆ DOM LA MONARDIÈRE ◆ DOM MONTIRIUS ☆ ◆ DOM DE MONTVAC ◆ DOM PERRIN & FILS ☆ ◆ DOMAINE LE SANG DES CAILLOUX ☆ ◆ LES VINS DE VIENNE ☆.

Château Valcombe/Domaine Montpertuis/Vignobles Paul Jeune

84232 Châteauneuf-du-Pape; 04.90.83.73.87
Wines: Côtes du Ventoux and many others. $ to $$$
Here's another one-man band who, with vineyards in the Languedoc, Provence, the Ventoux, and Châteauneuf, seems to make more wine than an average cooperative, including pretty decent Counoise and Alicante in a bag-in-box format. Airlines, take note. His Châteauneuf Vieilles Vignes, under the Montpertuis label, is an ingratiating red with flavors of Montmorency cherries and cherry pits. You can drink it young. He's got innumerable cuvées of AC Côtes du Ventoux, and all have something to say. Signature blanc is appley, fresh, and appetizing; the red is light and easy-drinking. Les Griottes is an appealing, early-drinking blend of syrah and grenache. The partially barrel-fermented Les Genevrières blanc, primarily grenache with a bit of roussane, is full, rich, textured, and surefooted; the red version, predominantly grenache and carignan with a bit of oak age, is succulent and flavorful, with notes of Montmorency cherries and white ash. La Sereine blanc, a partially barrel-fermented blend of grenache and roussanne, is a hefty, consequential white, a good meal companion; the red version, almost pure syrah, is rich and lipsmacking but meant to be drunk young, despite the vigneron's recommendation to cellar for ten years.

Valréas

A fair-size designated Côtes du Rhône-Village (a former papal enclave) for red, white, and rosé wines.

BEST RECENT VINTAGES: 2005, 2004, 2003, 2001.
PRICES: $ to $$$

PRODUCERS: Cave la Gaillarde: the co-op accounts for 80 percent of production; try the Cuvée des Hespérides ◆ DOM DES GRANDS DEVERS ↑ ◆ Dom de la Prévosse: nice local whites and reds, as well as cuvées from Chusclan ◆ DOM DES TREILLES.

Domaine Georges Vernay ☆

69420 Condrieu; 04.74.56.81.81; www.georges-vernay.fr
Wines: Condrieu and Côte-Rôtie. $$$ to $$$$
Reliably superb family domaine. The Condrieus—Les Chaillées de l'Enfer, the Coteau de Vernon, and Les Terrasses de l'Empire—are racy, exotic, and fragrant, with great lift, focus, and freshness. In Côte-Rôtie, La Blonde du Seigneur is elegant, harmonious, and nuanced. As for the silky Maison Rouge, which spends two years in barrel, well, if Dom Pérignon said he was tasting stars, with this Côte-Rôtie, I was tasting rubies, spiced rubies.

Domaine du Vieux Télégraphe ☆

84370 Bédarrides; 04.90.33.00.31; www.vieuxtelegraphe.com
Wines: Châteauneuf-du-Pape and others. $$$
Frédéric and Daniel Brunier run a model family domaine with wines that could be ambassadors for their AC. The statuesque white is fresh, ripe, mineral, and lipsmackingly tasty. The red has a nose so seductively fragrant you want to dive into it. It has an effortless elegance, real stature. The Bruniers make a second wine from Vieux Télégraphe called Vieux Mas des Papes. They also have another, smaller property called Domaine de la Roquette, the wines of which are similarly made and as heartily recommended. They make a plump, affable Vin de Pays de Vaucluse called Le Pigeoulet des Brunier and delicious Gigondas at DOM LES PALLIÈRES.

Les Vignerons d'Estézargues ☆

30390 Estézargues; 04.66.57.03.64; les.vignerons.estezargues@wanadoo.fr
Wines: Côtes du Rhône and others. $ to $$
An unusual, dynamic, eco-friendly cooperative consisting of typically eight to ten domaines. As most of the wines are estate bottled, here are the names, at last count: Les Grandes Vignes (using grapes from all members), Dom de Pierredon, Dom de la Montagnette, Dom les Genestas (in the Signargues, a new *cru* in the Côtes du Rhône-Villages AC), Dom les Bacchantes, Dom Grès St. Vincent, Dom d'Andézon, Dom de Périllère. Most are either Côtes du Rhône or Côtes du Rhône-Villages, although there is some Vin de Pays and some Costières de Nîmes; the wines are made with wild yeasts, are vinified without sulfur, and are neither fined nor filtered. Not surprisingly, there is a wide variety of choice here but all is of high quality. I've tasted the entire range in both the 2003 and 2004 vintages, and there isn't a bottle I wouldn't enjoy drinking, from the gulpable Dom des Bacchantes red, to the oak-aged syrah from Dom d'Andézon, to the concentrated, very mineral Côtes du Rhône-Villages from Dom de Périllère. And then there's another group bottling, La Granacha, which consists of the best, oldest, and lowest-yielding grenache vines. It's a rich "light" red made with wild yeasts, no sulfur, and so on, and would be a super wine-bar discovery. Additionally, each domaine has original labels for each bottling—every single one of them more endearing than the Mouton artist labels.

Domaine François Villard ☆

42410 St.-Michel-sur-Rhône; 04.74.56.83.60; vinsvillard@aol.com
Wines: Côte-Rôtie, Condrieu, St.-Joseph, and Vin de Pays. $ to $$$
Amiable, elfin François Villard makes mouthwatering St.-Joseph, but you quickly want to pass on to the very serious stuff: Condrieu and Côte-Rôtie. There are three cuvées of Condrieu, each a single vineyard—Le Grand Vallon, Les Terrasses du Palat, and Deponcins. Each is so racy, so *terroir*-driven, focused, and limpid as to be downright thrilling. You can't get enough of them. In Côte-Rôtie, La Brocarde, with 15 percent viognier, is sinuous and seductive; Le Gallet Blanc is greatly detailed, racy, and potent. Can't get enough of them either.

Domaine de Villeneuve ☆

84100 Orange; 04.90.34.57.55; fax: 04.90.51.61.22
Wine: Châteauneuf-du-Pape. $$$($)
Two fascinating, serious, biodynamic cuvées of Châteauneuf-du-Pape, starting with a fragrant, structured Vieilles Vignes, interweaving flavors of black cherry, licorice, ash, and oak, and the darkly voluptuous, garage-cult-style Les Bienaimés, which called to mind Ellington and Strayhorn's *Satin Doll,* a sleek beauty with ash dripping from her cigarette holder.

Vin de Pays

Inevitably, in a region this large, there exist a multitude of Vins de Pays, some of them taking the names of their departments, others some other geographically inspired name, like the Principauté d'Orange and the Collines Rhodanniennes. In terms of recommending producers, the most important for our purposes are the Vins de Pays des Coteaux de l'Ardèche and the Vins de Pays de Pays de Vaucluse. Details follow. In general, drink the youngest available. Prices: $ to $$.

COTEAUX DE L'ARDÈCHE PRODUCERS: Production is dominated by a half-dozen co-ops. There are roughly a dozen independent producers—many of which also use the ACs Côtes du Vivarais and/or Côtes du Rhône. Two items worth noting: The local grape châtus, which seems unique to this region, makes bland red wines. And many producers also make Cartagène, an aperitif along the lines of Pineau de Charente. ◆ Dom de Belvezet: see CÔTES DU VIVARAIS ◆ Dom de Brechon: look for the pure syrah ◆ Cave Co-op la Cévenole: look for châtus Monnaie d'Or, a smooth, inoffensive red ◆ Cave des Rosiers: châtus and several types of Cartagène ◆ Dom du Couron: see CÔTES DU RHÔNE ◆ DOM LA FAVETTE ↑ ◆ Maison Louis Latour: good, inexpensive whites based on chardonnay and viognier ◆ DOM DU MAZEL ↑ ◆ DOM NÔTRE DAME DE COUSIGNAC ◆ CH DE LA SELVE ◆ Dom de Vigier: see CÔTES DU VIVARAIS.

VAUCLUSE PRODUCERS: Dom les Amouriers (though the pure syrah Hautes Terrasses cuvée is a bit expensive at $30, it's pretty impressive: see also VACQUEYRAS ◆ GUFFENS-HEYNEN ☆ ◆ DOM LA MONARDIÈRE ◆ DOM MONTIRIUS ☆.

Les Vins de Vienne ☆

38200 Seyssuel; 04.74.85.04.52; www.vinsdevienne.com
Wines: Diverse Rhône ACs. $$ to $$$($)
The northern Rhône's redoubtable gang of three—Yves Cuilleron, Pierre Gaillard, and François Villard (all of whom are separately listed)—teamed up to plant vines in Seyssuel, an ancient vineyard region at the northern limits of the Rhône valley abandoned after phylloxera. They hope to get AC status for the zone but, for now, the wines from this property are labeled Vin de Pays des Collines Rhodaniennes. The white, Taburnum, based on barrel-fermented viognier, is cool and truly lovely, with mineral and apricot flavors. The red, Sotanum, is barrel-aged syrah, very pure, steely, very cool and concentrated, a total pleasure. The threesome has also created a *négociant* line for wines throughout the Rhône. For northern Rhône ACs, the three buy grapes in northern Rhône ACs and make the wines themselves. Condrieu ferments in barrel. The basic bottling is mineral with light exotic fruit flavors. La Chambée is creamy, structured, fragrant, and extremely long and ample. Always a discovery. The St.-Péray Les Bialères is mouthwatering, vinous, and perfumed. Reds are not filtered. The Côte-Rôtie Les Essartailles is succulent, inviting, and racy. The Cornas Les Barcillants is silky and seductive, surprisingly gentle for the AC. The St.-Joseph L'Arzelle is concentrated and limpid; a far from simple wine, it satisfies the mind and the palate. In southern Rhône ACs the team buys the wines and then ages them. The Cairanne La Perpendaille is a smooth, fresh, spicy red, despite the evident oak; the Visan La Tine is oaky, concentrated, and ambitious; and the Vacqueyras La Sillotte, similarly oaky, is sapid and pure.

Vinsobres

Oxymoronic name for a southern Rhône AC, promoted from a designated Côtes du Rhône-Village in 2005/2006.

BEST RECENT VINTAGES: 2005, 2004, 2003, 2001.
PRICES: $ to $$$

PRODUCERS: Dom Chaume Arnaud: the cuvée La Cadène is a chewy red that gives a bang for the buck ◆ Dom du Coriançon: look for Les Hauts de Côte ◆ Domaine de Deurre: good white, best red is Cuvée Jean Marie Valeyer ◆ DOM GRAMENON ☆ ◆ DOMAINE JAUME ◆ DOM DU MOULIN ◆ La Vinsobraise: look for the Cuvée Sélection des Terroirs.

Domaine Viret ☆

26110 St.-Maurice-sur-Eygues; 04.75.27.62.77; www.domaine-viret.com
Wines: Côtes du Rhône-Villages St.-Maurice, Côtes du Rhône, and Vin de Table. $$ to $$$$
Ever heard of Cosmoculture? Yet another variation on the theme of extreme organic winemaking, it's based on principles apparently known to the Incas. Long story short, Philippe Viret, the proselytizing young enologist/vigneron who practices this red and white art, sums it up as "acupuncture for vines." One of the sole producers of wine from the micro Côtes du Rhône subzone of St.-Maurice, Viret produces an unknowable number of cuvées: each one owes its life to "inspiration." In keeping with hypernaturalism, no "enological correctives" are used (that is, cultured yeasts, chaptalization, acidification, filtration, and so on). Not surprisingly, the wines are not perfect, but they are invariably interesting and provocative. The bottlings you are most likely to encounter start with the viognier-dominated, barrel-fermented La Coudée d'Or, a rich, perfumed white with a solid mineral core and a tender finish. There are also the mineral-driven Énergie, a supple, very tasty red expressly destined for wine bars; Émergence, a grenache and old-vines syrah-based red, is deeply mineral with light tannins; Renaissance, a stony, very pure wine with flavors of cooked fruit; and the partially barrel-aged Maréotis, a fascinating, tannic, richly fruity (almost Porty, though completely dry) red, which comes from the southernmost parcels of vines. Les Colonnades, based on one-hundred-year-old grenache vines, aged only in cement tanks (for three years) to preserve the pure fruit quality, is a marvel of well-knit flavors of fruit, licorice, black olives, and black pepper. Very special, indeed.

Visan

A medium-size designated Côtes du Rhône-Village, producing white, red, and rosé wines.

BEST RECENT VINTAGES: 2005, 2004, 2003, 2001.
PRICES: $ to $$$

PRODUCERS: DOM LA FLORANE ◆ Dom de la Fourmente: local wines worth looking for, especially oak-aged red ◆ DOM DES GRANDS DEVERS ↑ ◆ LES VINS DE VIENNE ☆.

Domaine Voge

07130 Cornas; 04.75.40.32.04; fax: 04.75.81.06.02
Wines: Cornas and St.-Péray. $$ to $$$
Several interesting cuvées of St.-Péray of which my favorite is the discreet, vinous, lightly oaked Fleur de Crussol, a really tasty, mineral white. The Cornas Les Chailles is juicy, fresh, and pure. The Vieilles Vignes is more austere but deeper, with succulence and complexity clearly in the wings.

RHÔNE CRIB SHEET

MUST TRYS

Château de Beaucastel: Châteauneuf-du-Pape
Domaine Jean-Louis Chave: Hermitage
Domaine Auguste Clape: Cornas
Domaine Clusel-Roch: Condrieu and Côte-Rôtie
Domaine Yves Cuilleron: Condrieu and Côte-Rôtie
Domaine Gangloff: Condrieu and Côte-Rôtie
Domaine Jean-Michel Gerin: Condrieu and Côte-Rôtie
E. Guigal/Château d'Ampuis: Côte-Rôtie la Mouline
Domaine du Vieux Télégraphe: Châteauneuf-du-Pape
Domaine François Villard: Condrieu and Côte-Rôtie

SMART BUYS

L'Anglore: Tavel and Côtes du Rhône
Domaine la Favette: Côtes du Rhône and Côtes du Vivarais
Guffens-Heynen/Verget du Sud: Vin de Pays
Patrick Lesec Sélections: various
Domaine de la Mordorée: Tavel and Lirac
Domaine Perrin & Fils: various southern Rhônes
Domaine Rabasse-Charavin: Cairanne, Rasteau, and others
Château Signac: Côtes du Rhône
Domaine la Soumade: Rasteau
Les Vignerons d'Estézargues: various Côtes du Rhône

SAFE HOUSES

Domaine Brusset: Côtes du Rhône, Cairanne, Gigondas
Chapoutier: especially northern Rhône ACs
Domaine de la Charbonnière: Châteauneuf-du-Pape and Vacqueyras
Clos du Caillou: Châteauneuf-du-Pape and Côtes du Rhône
Château de la Gardine: Châteauneuf-du-Pape
Domaine Gramenon: Vinsobres and Côtes du Rhône
Domaine Grand Veneur, including Clos Sixte: Châteauneuf-du-Pape, Vacqueyras, Lirac, and Côtes du Rhône
Domaine de Marcoux: Châteauneuf-du-Pape
Domaine Marcel Richaud: Cairanne and Côtes du Rhône
Domaine de la Solitude: Châteauneuf-du-Pape
Domaine Georges Vernay: Côte-Rôtie and Condrieu

ALSACE
BORDEAUX
BURGUNDY
CHAMPAGNE
JURA AND SAVOIE
LANGUEDOC-ROUSSILLON
LOIRE
PROVENCE AND CORSICA
RHÔNE

SOUTHWEST

THE SOUTHWEST REGION

BERGERAC
THE MONTRAVELS
ROSETTE
Bergerac
PÉCHARMANT
Dordogne
BORDEAUX
SAUSSIGNAC
MONBAZILLAC
CÔTES DE DURAS
ENTRAYGUES–LE FEL
MARCILLAC
ESTAING
CÔTES DU MARMANDAIS
CAHORS
Lot
Villeneuve-sur-Lot
COTEAUX DU QUERCY
Agen
BUZET
Aveyron
CÔTES DU BRULHOIS
Montauban
LAVILLEDIEU
Albi
GAILLAC
Mont-de-Marsan
CÔTES DE GASCOGNE
CÔTES DU FRONTONNAIS
Adour
Dax
TURSAN
CÔTES DE ST-MONT
Auch
TOULOUSE
MADIRAN
Biarritz
Bayonne
PACHERENC
DU VIC-BILH
PARIS
BÉARN
Pau
JURANÇON,
JURANÇON SEC
Tarbes
IROULÉGUY

The Southwest encompasses a sparse patchwork of diverse appellations scattered between Bordeaux in the north and France's Atlantic border with Spain to the south. The common threads are few, although one can organize the disparate appellations—ACs, VDQSs, and Vins de Pays—into three distinct subzones.

To the north, Bergerac (or the Bergeracois) dangles like a tail from the eastern limits of Bordeaux and includes the ACs Monbazillac, Saussignac, Montravel, and Pécharmant. Moving inland, toward the foothills of the Massif Central, the key ACs are Cahors and Gaillac. The southern bloc, situated near the foothills of the Pyrenees, encompasses Jurançon, Madiran, and Irouléguy. But there's much more and a staggering diversity of wine, ranging from breathtaking crus to some utterly forgettable brews.

GRAPES: There are many. Indeed, part of the challenge of the Southwest is that there is a mind-boggling collection of obscure grapes that figure in the wines on a regular basis, therefore: The principal white grapes are sémillon, sauvignon blanc, muscadelle, gros manseng, and petit manseng. The principal reds are the cabernets, merlot, malbec (côt), and tannat. Ancillary grapes (often completely unknown): for whites, courbu, ondenc, len de l'el (loin de l'oeil), mauzac, arrufiac, baroque, and camaralet; and for reds, fer (fer servadou, also known as braucol or pinenc), abouriou, négrette, and merille.

STYLES OF WINE: These are as diverse as the grape varieties. More than anywhere else in France, however, the Southwest has the blackest of red wines; it also has more than its fair share of great sweet wines. And it's a terrific and untapped source for the cheap and cheerful reds and whites.

VINTAGES: The year 2005 promises to be excellent throughout the region. For those who controlled yields, 2004 was a good year—overall the wines were fresher and fruitier than in 2003; dry whites fared better than reds, and the *liquoreux* fared best of all. The exceptional heat and exceptionally low yields of 2003 affected the Southwest as it did other regions. There are some excellent *liquoreux* but, in general, the wines are atypical and will probably evolve quickly. That said, many are delicious, and 2003 is considered a very good, if not great vintage. Though often dismissed, 2002 provides quite nice near-term drinking. And 2001 was a great vintage, particularly for *liquoreux*.

PRICES: Start at $ for easy-drinking whites and reds and work up to $$$$ for sensational *liquoreux*.

Domaine de l'Ancienne Cure ☆

24560 Colombier; 05.53.58.27.90; ancienne-cure@wanadoo.fr

Wines: Bergerac, Pécharmant, and Monbazillac. $ to $$$($)

Christian Roch acts as a *négociant* in the Pécharmant AC. He makes good selections there, but I prefer his best bottlings from Bergerac and Monbazillac. The cuvée L'Extase is his top-of-the-line in Monbazillac and in both Bergerac sec (white) and rouge. All three are excellent, but the red surprises (or not) by its striking resemblance to a really good Bordeaux satellite.

Domaine Arretxea ☆

64220 Irouléguy; tel/fax: 05.59.37.33.67; arretxea@free.fr

Wine: Irouléguy. $$

Michel and Thérèse Riouspeyrous run a model—and organic—winery. Their Hegoxuri is a pungent, flavorful white, and their two reds (Cuvée Haitza is the top-of-the-line) are dark as ink, with deep black-cherry flavors and hints of resin and tar. They may not be for everyone, but they are emphatically arresting.

Château d'Aydie ☆

64330 Aydie; 05.59.04.03.96; pierre.laplace@wanadoo.fr

Wines: Madiran and Pacherenc du Vic-Bilh. $ to $$

If you want to fall in love with Madiran, here's the place to start. The three Laplace brothers run a wonderful, eco-friendly domaine and, good vintage or bad, turn out exemplary wines. The top Madiran, Château d'Aydie, is chiefly tannat, which the Laplaces have managed to tame by keeping yields low, picking very ripe, and aging the wine for two years in large oak barrels. It's a dark, fragrant, downright soulful red, with flavors of black cherries, sweet spices, and oak and should appeal to fans of mountain zinfandels. The simpler reds include Ode d'Aydie and Le Fruit, sort of a nouveau Madiran, all charming, up-front fruit. The domaine also makes good Pacherencs—both dry and sweet—the best being the barrel-fermented sweet version made solely from petit manseng. Burnished gold, it presents a lovely melding of oak and dried fruit with fine acid support.

Béarn

A tiny AC between Biarritz and Pau, for reds and rosés, chiefly from the cabernets, fer servadou, and tannat, and a small amount of whites, mainly from the mansengs, courbu, sauvignon blanc, and the local grapes raffiat and camarelet de Lasseube. The name Bellocq may be attached to Béarn for quaffing wines from a microscopic subzone. Drink the youngest available. Prices: $. Producers: Dom Lapeyre ◆ CAVE DE CROUSEILLES.

Château Bélingard

24240 Pomport; 05.53.58.28.03; www.chateaubelingard.com

Wines: Bergerac and Monbazillac. $ to $$

An important domaine with ambitious wines, its Bergerac red Alliance, aged in American oak, is mellow, serious, and structured. Ortus, the top cuvée of Côtes de Bergerac rouge, is rich, ripe, and concentrated, with abundant oak. The Monbazillac Cuvée Blanche de Bosredon is harvested grape by grape and is rich and honeyed.

Château Bellevue la Forêt

31620 Fronton; 05.34.27.91.91; www.chateaubellevuelaforet.com

Wines: Fronton. $

One of the best producers—as well as the largest private producer—in the AC, Patrick Germain makes solid, juicy, easy-drinking reds and rosés. The spiciest and most structured red is Optimum, a blend of négrette, syrah, and cabernet sauvignon.

Domaine Belmont ☆

46250 Goujounac; 05.65.36.68.51; www.domaine-belmont.com

Wine: Vin de Pays du Lot. $$

Christian Belmon, an architect, just happened to build the cellars of Stéphane Derenoncourt, one of France's leading wine consultants. Derenoncourt, in turn, instructs Belmon on winemaking. The results are delectable. Belmon's vines lie outside the Cahors AC, so he's not hemmed in by legalities. There's a charming chardonnay and several delectable cuvées of red, all based on different percentages of cabernet franc and syrah. Rich, fresh, and succulent, they have a whiff of the New World about them, although there's no doubt that they're French.

Bergerac

The largest region in the Southwest, the Bergeracois arguably should be included as part of Bordeaux: it begins immediately to the east of several of Bordeaux's satellite regions, and its wines, for the most part, are based on the same grape varieties and are similar in style. But the Bergeracois is habitually joined with the other regions of the Southwest. Bergerac itself is a town (primarily associated with Cyrano de B.) and an umbrella AC for dry whites, reds, and rosés. Its subzones are distinct ACs in more strictly delimited areas. The wines of each represent a step up in quality over those of the Bergerac AC (although the Bergeracs of a really good vintner can rival the wines from the subzones), but the smaller ACs are often needlessly confusing. Never mind, they boil down to the following. For reds: Côtes de Bergerac rouge, PÉCHARMANT, and MONTRAVEL rouge. For dry whites: MONTRAVEL. For sweet (*moelleux*) whites: Côtes de Bergerac blanc, Côtes de Montravel, Haut-Montravel, and ROSETTE. For very sweet (*liquoreux*) whites: MONBAZILLAC and SAUSSIGNAC.

GRAPES: Whites are based on muscadelle, sauvignon blanc, and sémillon. Reds and rosés are made from cabernet franc, cabernet sauvignon, merlot, and malbec.

STYLES OF WINE: Medium-bodied and quite fruity, the dry whites from Bergerac have a unique freshness, as if a cool breeze rushes through them. The supersweet (*liquoreux*) whites—notably those from Monbazillac and even more notably from Saussignac—can be extraordinary, true discoveries. The reds, particularly those from Montravel and Côtes de Bergerac, most closely resemble Bordeaux, while those from Pécharmant take on a slightly more southern tang.

BEST RECENT VINTAGES: The year 2005 is expected to be a super vintage. While 2004 is a great year for whites, it's only fair for reds. The 2003 vintage is as overstated here as elsewhere, atypical but tasty. Many of the whites have Alsace-like perfumes and some of the reds, particularly at the cheaper end, can be jammy. They'll probably evolve quickly. (Within the region 2003 is considered a very good to great vintage.) And 2001 was a great year, particularly for sweet whites, as were 1997 and 1995.

PRICES: $ to $$$

PRODUCERS: Most make Bergerac and/or Côtes de Bergerac, which you'll find here, and wine from one of the smaller ACs, which are covered separately. DOM DE L'ANCIENNE CURE ☆ ◆ Ch la Barde les Tendoux: the hypermarket Leclerc seems to have the monopoly on this delicious, unfiltered Côtes de Bergerac rouge; it's worth the detour ◆ CH BÉLINGARD ◆ Belles Filles: a fluid, easy-drinking Bergerac red with a kiss of oak ◆ CH DU BLOY ☆ ◆ Dom les Brandeaux: the wine of interest here is Le Nectar des Brandeaux, a citrus zest- and honey-flavored sweet white with good focus ◆ Ch le Cléret: a promising domaine with wines that seem works in progress but are worth following; best for now is the Côtes de Bergerac Cuvée Cornélia, an attractive, plum- and cherry-flavored red ◆ Clos de Joncal: the barrel-aged Mirage de Joncal, a kirsch-scented red, and the mellow, oaky dry white are wines to look for here ◆ CLOS DES VERDOTS ☆ ◆ CLOS D'YVIGNE ↑ ◆ Ch le Chabrier: good organic domaine with promising, barrel-aged red Côtes de Bergerac Gros Caillou and very reasonably priced, fresh, floral Bergerac sec dominated by sauvignon blanc ◆ Ch le Clou: Manuel Killias, who practices organic viticulture, turns out fragrant, silky reds in Bergerac and Côtes de Bergerac, especially the Cuvée Cassiopée Vieilles Vignes ◆ CH LA COLLINE ☆ ◆ Court les Muts: herbaceous, barrel-fermented Bergerac secs; pleasant, semisweet Côtes de Bergerac blanc; and easy-drinking reds ◆ Ch des Eyssards: oak masks the fruit in the Bergerac sec Prestige but it's still a nice white; the reds are ambitious. The merlot-based cuvée Adagio, a smoky, rich wine aged primarily in new oak barrels, is particularly recommended ◆ Ch de Fayolle: the domaine belongs to England's Ringwood Brewery, but the wines might convert some beer drinkers to the vinous camp, for example the fragrant Bergerac sec, largely sémillon, and the oaky, structured red called Sang de Sanglier ◆ Ch les Hauts de Caillevel: Ébène, made only in good vintages, is an ample Côtes de Bergerac rouge, somewhat stylish but also specific; Les Terres Chaudes is less expensive, an easy, supple red; ◆ Dom du Haut-Montlong: makes a fresh, discreet Bergerac sec with appetizing texture. Les Vents des Anges, Côtes de Bergerac with 90 percent merlot, is a bit too oaky but worth following ◆ CH DE LA JAUBERTIE ☆ ◆ Ch Jonc Blanc: Blanches Pierres is a good Bergerac rouge, a bit jammy in 2003, not surprising for the vintage; the barrel-aged Cuvée Automnale is a bit richer and more serious ◆ Ch de la Mallevieille: nice, if thick reds; textured dry whites with notes of ginger and tropical fruit ◆ Ch les Marnières: the cuvée La Côte Fleurie, 95 percent merlot, is velvety and ambitious, worth following ◆ CH MASBUREL ◆ Ch Masmontet: a fragrant little red at an appealing price ◆ Ch les Merles: the reserve bottling Lajonie is a bit austere but appealing ◆ CH LES MIAUDOUX ◆ CH MONASTIER LA TOUR ↑ ◆ Ch la Moulière: I like the clean, bracing, apricot and white currant Bergerac sec and particularly like its consumer-friendly price ◆ CH MOULIN CARESSE ☆ ◆ Moulin des Dames: see CH TOUR DES GENDRES ☆ ◆ CH PANISSEAU ◆ Ch le Payral: an eco-friendly domaine making textured, perfumed Bergerac sec and a red Terres Rouges with pretty, black cherry fruit, good freshness, and structure. Nice wine. Saussignac, too ◆ Ch Marie Plaisance: delightful Bergerac sec at bargain prices from a producer who also makes wine in Saussignac, Bordeaux, and Bordeaux Supérieur ◆ CH RICHARD ↑ ◆ Ch la Robertie: the red is impressive, rich, and concentrated ◆ Ch le Tap: the barrel-aged Cuvée Grande Chêne (Côtes de Bergerac) is an honest, sturdy red that needs a carafe and would go well with casual meals like meat loaf and pizza ◆ Ch Thénac: look for the new-oak-aged Côtes de Bergerac rouge Fleur de Périgord, a silky red with mint and fruit flavors ◆ CH THEULET ◆ CH TOUR DES GENDRES ☆ ◆ Ch Tour de Grangemont: my favorite wine here is the charitably priced Bergerac sec, a sophisticated, grapefruit-scented, invigorating white ◆ Ch Tourmentine: the domaine does a decent job with all the styles of wine in the Bergerac–Côtes de Bergerac ACs, as well as a nice job with Saussignac, but perhaps its most impressive wine is an inexpensive, nonfiltered red Bergerac selected by consultant Éric Verdier called Quentin de la Tourmantine; it's tasty and has a very good ratio of price to quality ◆ Ch Trolliet-Lafite: the cuvée Estelle Touzet is a fragrant, serious Côtes de Bergerac rouge, well worth trying ◆ Les Vérdots: see CLOS DES VERDOTS ◆ Vignerons de Sigoules: Légende is the name of the merlot aged in new oak from this good co-op. It's mellow, rich, and civilized.

Domaine Berthoumieu

32400 Viella; 05.62.69.74.05; barre.didier@wanadoo.fr

Wines: Madiran and Pacherenc du Vic-Bilh. $$

The Madiran Tradition is a creditable version of the AC, but the cuvée Charles de Batz is a real step up. Almost Bordelais in structure, it's 90 percent old-vines tannat, aged in new and nearly new oak barrels. It's something of a blockbuster, but once in a carafe and served with boldly flavored food it would calm down nicely. The domaine makes an appealing sweet Pacherenc, but I prefer the dry version. A blend of both the mansengs and courbu, aged in oak, it's a strong and tasty food wine.

Château du Bloy ☆

24230 Bonneville; 05.53.22.47.87; chateau.du.bloy@wanadoo.fr

Wines: Bergerac and Montravel. $ to $$

Some very alluring wines come out of this eco-friendly domaine, recently created by two Parisians. The barrel-fermented dry white Le Bloy is limpid, elegant, and mineral. Another white, the *terroir*-driven Lilia—no oak here—is even lovelier, with notes of poached pear and apricot, thrilling texture, freshness, and minerality. The unfined, unfiltered red, also elegant, is structured and fragrant, a Bordeaux ringer.

Domaine Bru-Baché ☆

64360 Monein; 05.59.21.36.34; domaine.bru-bache@wanadoo.fr

Wine: Jurançon. $$ to $$$

Claude Loustalot turns out exemplary Jurançons. The dry versions are rich and savory and would complement just about any dish you'd serve with white wine. The sweet versions—Quintessence and the even lusher Éminence—are nectar, incredible weaves of dried fruit such as apricots that seem to have been steeped in honey, accented with herbs like thyme, and balanced by superb freshness. Simply excellent.

Alain Brumont/Château Montus–Château Bouscassé ☆

32400 Maumusson-Laguian; 05.62.69.74.67; www.brumontalain.com

Wines: Madiran, Pacherenc du Vic-Bilh, and Vin de Pays Côtes de Gascogne. $$ to $$$$

Few people are as driven as Alain Brumont. In his cellars, every beam, every wrought-iron banister is handcrafted by a local artisan. No, it's not a trophy winery. It's just one manifestation of Brumont's obsession with perfection. His "take no prisoners" mentality partly explains how he put Madiran and Pacherenc du Vic-Bilh on the map; and it is surely part of the reason his business is now on shaky financial footing. An optimist hopes that Brumont resolves his fiscal woes. Difficult as he can be to deal with, he's too important to the region and his wines are too good to wish him anything but success.

Brumont has two properties, Montus and Bouscassé. Roughly speaking, Montus is the prestige property, but the wines from Bouscassé are anything but shabby. (Favorites here include the dry Pacherenc and the Madiran Vieilles Vignes.) Indeed, all his wines have something to say, including the Vin de Pays Les Menhirs, a toothstaining blend of tannat and merlot. My very favorites, however, come from Montus, ranging from the eye-opening Pacherenc sec based on petit courbu (who knew this grape could make such a riveting wine?); to the Madiran Cuvée Prestige, a plum–prune–black cherry–packed red you can literally sink your teeth into; to the single vineyard La Tyre; and finally to the sweet, new-oak-aged Pacherenc Brumaire, which is fresh and succulent and layered.

Buzet

An AC west of the town of Agen, whites based on sauvignon blanc, sémillon, and muscadelle and reds and rosés made from the cabernets, côt, and merlot. Most of the wines taste like minor (or very minor) Bordeaux. Best recent vintages: 2005, 2003, 2002, and 2001. Prices: $($). Producers: Dom du Pech: pleasant quaffing wines include the cuvée La Badinerie ◆ Les Vignerons de Buzet: an OK co-op.

Cahors

An important Southwest AC located on both banks of the river Lot around the town of Cahors. The wines, exclusively red, are made chiefly from malbec with the possible addition of merlot or tannat. Dark and dense, they are habitually known as "the black wines of Cahors." Though I find Madiran and Irouléguy a blacker shade of red, the wines from Cahors can be rough and chewy in their youth. There is a trend to make them juicy and quaffable young—and a much better trend to make them richer, riper, and more refined.

BEST RECENT VINTAGES: 2005, (2004), (2003), 2001, and 2000. Best vintages of the recent past: 1988, 1989, 1990, 1995, and 1998.
PRICES: $ to $$$$

PRODUCERS: Dom des Bateliers: the cuvée "classique"—malbec flavored with merlot and tannat—is slightly rustic, with tart wild-berry flavors and hints of tobacco. The cuvée Terroir et Tradition, pure old-vines malbec aged in new oak, is fragrant, spicy, and smooth with seductive cherry-pit flavors ◆ Ch la Caminade: makes three grades of first-rate Cahors, including a juicy, user-friendly bottling at $ ☆ ◆ Ch de Cayrou: an eco-friendly domaine with engagingly old-fashioned wines ◆ CH DU CÈDRE ☆ ◆ Ch de Chambert: of the numerous different bottlings, my favorites are the Ch de Chambert, a muscular, chewy red, and Orphée, pure malbec from selected parcels. It's a juicy, spice-scented Cahors that would nicely accompany hare stewed in red wine ◆ Clos la Coutale: truly tasty, easy-drinking, three-dimensional reds with friendly prices ◆ CLOS TRIGUEDINA ◆ Dom du Colombier: cheap and cheerful reds ◆ Dom Cosse Maisonneuve: Catherine Maisonneuve and Matthieu Cosse run their young domaine according to biodynamic principles. The results are impressive—each of the four bottlings is recommended. Le P'tit Sid, a midrange bottling, is rich, generous, and easy-drinking. Not hard on the wallet either ◆ Ch Lagrezette: thoroughly modern Cahors at this property owned by Alain-Dominique Perrin, who runs luxury goods companies like Cartier. Michel Rolland consults. The top three cuvées are Ch Lagrezette (blended with a bit of merlot and tannat); Dame d'Honneur, minus the tannat; and Pigeonnier, pure malbec at its ripest, most intense, and probably most expensive ($$$$) ◆ Ch Lamartine: a well-situated domaine making several levels of good reds. Look for the top-of-the-line Expression. Made from pure old-vines malbec and aged in new oak, it's structured and succulent, a truly handsome red.

Domaine Cauhapé ☆

64360 Monein; 05.59.21.33.02; www.cauhape.com
Wine: Jurançon. $$($)
Henri IV may have declared Jurançon his favorite wine. Henri Ramonteau makes you understand why. His Jurançons are exquisite: the dry Sève d'Automne is an explosion of freshness and lemon, lime, and grapefruit. Noblesse du Temps is chiseled in its honeyed precision, appetizing and gorgeous. Quintessence du Petit Manseng, weaves an elegant tapestry of honey, mint, pineapple, oak, and more. And the finely etched Symphonie de Novembre, both unctuous and crystalline, is a sheer delight. One glass leads immediately to another.

Domaine de Causse Marines

81140 Vieux; 05.63.33.98.30; causse-marines@infonie.fr
Wine: Gaillac. $ to $$
When he is not rehearsing an Ionesco play, Patrice Lescarret is making wines that venture far into wacko land yet still come out tasty. The most mainstream may be his nicely concentrated dry white blend of len de l'el, muscadelle, mauzac, and muscat. Zacmau is his firm, tight, pure mauzac. Peyrouzelles, fer with syrah and duras, and Rasdu, pure duras, are OK but less interesting than La Causse, a seductive blend of syrah and fer with accents of tar, bark, and herbal tea. His sweet wines are based on ever-changing percentages of mauzac and ondenc. The most docile is the pleasant Folie Douce. Lescarret ups the ante with Folies Pures, Graal, and Délire d'Automne, based on grapes so ripe and sweet the wines have trouble fermenting—some are as low as 5 percent alcohol. What's left is almost marmalade, extremely complex syrups with precise flavors of licorice, herbs, honey, and dried fruit.

Cave de Crouseilles

64350 Crouseilles; 05.59.68.10.93; fax: 05.59.68.14.33
Wines: Madiran and Pacherenc du Vic-Bilh. $ to $$$
Now associated with the PRODUCTEURS PLAIMONT, this very good small co-op gets better and better. There's a wide range of wines and a wide range of prices, starting with the Folie du Roi, a hand-harvested, oak-aged blend of tannat and the cabernets, an easy-drinking bistro red for less than $10. At the top end is Château de Crouseilles Premium. A blend of the best grapes from the best parcels, it's rich and ripe and as perfumed as an eau-de-vie of cherries. Among the various Pacherencs, Prélude à l'Hivernal is the last to be harvested—in December. It's a well-balanced sweet white lightly accented with oak.

Château du Cèdre ☆

46700 Vire-sur-Lot; 05.65.36.53.87; chateauducedre@wanadoo.fr
Wine: Cahors. $$ to $$$($)
Frankly, I've never tasted Pascal Verhaeghe's most expensive wine, the Cahors Grand Cru ($$$$), but I'm more than happy with the Le Cèdre bottling. Pure malbec, it's deeply colored and deeply satisfying, with intense berry fruit and impressive structure. Its baby brother, Prestige, is lighter but still a meaty "black" wine. Both are fragrant, delicious, and robust.

Chapelle Lenclos

32400 Maumusson Laguian; 05.62.69.78.11; fax: 05.62.69.75.87
Wines: Madiran and Pacherenc du Vic-Bilh. $$($)
Patrick Ducournau, the owner of this domaine as well as Domaine Mouréou, is the pioneering enologist who developed a method of refining wines before they are bottled that has now spread worldwide under the name micro-oxygenation. Such is the demand for his counsel that he has asked his cousins, the Laplace family of CH D'AYDIE, to take responsibility for his wine properties. I prefer the wines from Chapelle Lenclos to those of Domaine Mouréou (though the latter have the advantage of being less expensive) and the Madirans (slightly more "modern" than those from d'Aydie) and the Pacherencs are both heartily recommended.

Clos Lapeyre ☆

64110 Jurançon; 05.59.21.50.80; jean-bernard.larrieu@wanadoo.fr
Wine: Jurançon. $$ to $$$
Jean-Bernard Larrieu, a conscientious vintner who practices organic viticulture, makes two good cuvées of Jurançon sec, of which the Vieilles Vignes (Vitatge Vielh in Occitane) is a clear step up, richer, suppler, and with more character than the entry level wine. His standard bottling of Jurançon *doux* is discreet, lightly honeyed, and classic. La Magendia, made from his best petit manseng, is even better—more concentrated, with lively acidity. My favorite is a wine Larrieu doesn't make every year. It's Vent Balaguer, a supersweet wine made from shriveled petit manseng grapes, so lush and unctuous the flavors of new oak are completely masked.

Clos Triguedina

46700 Vire-sur-Lot; 05.65.21.30.81; triguedina@laposte.net
Wine: Cahors. $$ to $$$
One of the classic addresses of Cahors, Clos Triguedina produces several different bottlings (as well as a number of white Vins de Pays) starting with a manly, age-worthy classic cuvée. The pure malbec Prince Probus is quite rich and very heavily oaked. It demands a carafe. The latest entry is Black Wine, an effort to reproduce the legendary Cahors of the past. For this, malbec grapes are dried until shriveled. The resulting wine has a certain sweetness and suppleness that makes it more approachable than the Probus bottling.

Clos Uroulat ☆

64360 Monein; 05.59.21.46.19; charleshours@wanadoo.fr

Wine: Jurançon. $$

Charles Hours, a jovial bear of a man (coincidentally his name is a homonym for the word for bear in French, which is *ours*) is one of the most popular vintners in France—beloved by his colleagues in the wine world for his sincerity, generosity, and integrity. The wines resemble the man. Cuvée Marie is a steely but full "take me anywhere, I'll go with any dish" dry Jurançon. Clos Uroulat is the luscious sweet version. Fermented in barrel, it is a velvet blend of exotic fruit such as ripe mangoes with subdued oak accents.

Clos des Verdots ☆

24560 Conne-de-Labarde; 05.53.58.34.31; fourtout@terre-net.fr

Wines: Bergerac, Côtes de Bergerac, and Monbazillac. $ to $$$

David Fourtout's wines could be ambassadors for their ACs. Everything here is recommended. The basic Bergerac sec is svelte, long, and apple-scented. The Vieilles Vignes sec ferments in barrel and is fresh, rich, structured, and serious. The red Bergerac, neither fined nor filtered, is rich, balanced, soigné—downright worldly. And Fourtout's Monbazillac L'Excellence, as honeyed, voluptuous, and structured as any Sauternes, is sublime.

Clos d'Yvigne ↑

24240 Gageac et Rouillac; 05.53.22.94.40; patricia.atkinson@wanadoo.fr

Wines: Côtes de Bergerac and Saussignac. $$ to $$$

Patricia Atkinson, an English writer, took over this property in 1991. She makes scrumptious, barrel-fermented Saussignac (almost pure sémillon), captivating, barrel-fermented Bergerac sec, and a very promising red Le Petit Prince, an oak-aged Côtes de Bergerac based primarily on merlot.

Château la Colline ☆

24240 Thénac; 05.53.61.87.87; www.la-colline.com

Wines: Bergerac and Côtes de Bergerac. $ to $$($)

Charles Martin, a Welsh iconoclast who made wine in South Africa before moving to France, fashions excellent Côtes de Bergerac *moelleux*, but I prefer his dry wines. He often changes his cuvées. For now, he's got two lines of wine: Côté Sud for drink-me-up wines; Côté Ouest for more serious wines. Both lines are exemplary. In the Côté Sud line, I love his rosé Pink. It's cabernet sauvignon made by pressing the red grapes on the dried skin of his sauvignon blanc grapes. The results are both thirst-quenching and singular. The white is crisp, crunchy, and extremely professional; the red could take on any New World quaffer. In the Côté Ouest line, the dry white, chiefly sémillon, is focused and fresh, excellent; the red is structured with good balance, perfect for near-term drinking. Carminé, his top red, is mostly merlot from his best parcels, which Martin ferments in 500-liter barrels. Rich and concentrated, it's wonderfully fragrant and deep. It should see a carafe before being served.

Coteaux du Quercy

A tiny VDQS north of Toulouse, between the ACs Gaillac and Cahors, for reds and rosés made from cabernet franc, tannat, côt, gamay, and merlot. Best recent vintages: 2005, 2002, and 2001. Prices: $. Producers: Two decent co-ops (Vignerons de Quercy and Cave des Trois Moulins) ♦ Dom de Lacoste (part of the local winemaking school).

Côtes du Brulhois

A mini VDQS bordering Buzet, Côtes de Brulhois makes uncomplicated reds and rosés from the cabernets, merlot, tannat, côt, and fer servadou. There are five producers including the co-op. Drink the youngest available. Prices: $.

Côtes de Duras

Immediately south of the Bergeracois, the AC Côtes de Duras is known principally for dry and sweet whites made from sauvignon blanc, sémillon, ugni blanc, ondenc, and muscadelle. Reds and rosés are based on the cabernets, côt, and merlot. Drink the youngest available. Prices: $. Producers: Dom des Allegrets ◆ Dom de Durand (organic) ◆ Dom du Grand Mayne ◆ Ch Haut-Lavigne.

Côtes de Millau

A miniature VDQS in the Aveyron for reds made from gamay, syrah, duras, fer servadou, and cabernet sauvignon and whites made from mauzac and chenin. There are seven producers, including the cooperative Les Vignerons des Gorges du Tarn. Meant to be drunk immediately. Prices: $.

Côtes du Marmandais

Located between Bergerac and Agen, the Côtes du Marmandais produces whites based on sauvignon, sémillon, muscadelle, and ugni blanc; and reds and rosés from abouriou, the cabernets, fer servadou, merlot, and syrah. Best recent vintages: 2005, 2003, 2001, and 2000. Prices: $ to $$($). Two co-ops make more than 90 percent of the wine. Producers: DOM ÉLIAN DA ROS ☆ ◆ Lasolle: Stéphanie Roussel runs an eco-friendly domaine. Her rich, ripe, oak-aged reds are neither fined nor filtered. They are not perfect, but their many assets say that this is a domaine well worth following ↑.

Côtes de St.-Mont

Abutting Madiran to the north, the reds and rosés from Côtes de St.-Mont are made from tannat, fer servadou (locally called pinenc), and the cabernets; whites are made from arrufiac, courbu, and the mansengs. There are five producers including the excellent co-op: PRODUCTEURS PLAIMONT.

Domaine Élian da Ros ☆

47250 Cocumont; 05.53.20.75.22; fax: 05.53.94.79.29

Wine: Côtes du Marmandais. $$ to $$$

Young Élian da Ros is a star. Having earned his spurs working with the great Léonard Humbrecht in Alsace (see ZIND-HUMBRECHT), he brings an enlightened approach to winemaking to his obscure AC. Chante Coucou consists of merlot blended with cabernet sauvignon, malbec, and abouriou. It is first-rate, a perfect red for the new bistro gourmands like Chez Michel in Paris. Clos Baquey, merlot, both cabernets, and abouriou, all from a single parcel, is very deep, intense, and nuanced. There's lots of oak but it's entirely digested by the richness of the fruit. Excellent. (Neither red is fined or filtered.) Sua Sponte is an interesting white in the hypernatural vein. This domaine is worth following.

Entraygues–Le Fel

A microscopic VDQS north of AC Marcillac for whites based on chenin and mauzac and reds based on the cabernets, fer servadou, and gamay. Drink the youngest available. Prices: $. There are six producers.

Domaine d'Escausses

81150 St.-Croix; 05.63.56.80.52; www.escausses.com

Wine: Gaillac. $($)

This intelligently run family domaine offers a range of reasonably priced Gaillac, including three pleasant, subtly oaked, dry whites (Ingénue, the mellow

L'Oubli, and the fresh and structured La Vigne Mythique, pure mauzac); three tasty reds (La Vigne Blanche, the fragrant, ambitious La Croix Petite, and La Vigne Mythique, pure fer servadou); and a couple of admirable sweet whites, La Vigne Galante and Vendanges Dorées.

Estaing

A microscopic VDQS for whites and reds that are very similar to those of the nearby Entraygues. The smallest co-op in France (with twelve producers) accounts for 70 percent of the wine made here. Drink the youngest availalble. Prices: $.

Domaine Etxegaraya ☆

64430 St- Etienne de Baigorry; tel/fax: 05.59.37.23.76
Wine: Irouléguy. $ to $$
Marianne and Joseph Hillau make very civilized, relatively restrained Irouléguy. The rich, dark, almost elegant Cuvée Lehengoa would be a good choice in a Michelin-starred restaurant serving Basque specialties.

Floc de Gascogne

An AC for *vin de liqueur* made in the Armagnac region from fresh, unfermented grape juice blended with Armagnac. Sweet and high in alcohol, Floc is generally served as an aperitif. Prices: $($). Producers: Dom des Cassagnoles (see VIN DE PAYS CÔTES DE GASCOGNE); DOM DU TARIQUET.

Fronton (or Côtes du Frontonnais)

An AC situated on the northern outskirts of Toulouse for extremely juicy, casual reds and rosés made chiefly from négrette, cabernet sauvignon, gamay, and syrah. Drink the youngest available. Prices: $. Producers: CH BELLEVUE LA FORÊT ◆ Ch Bouissel: agreeable and easy-drinking ◆ Cave de Fronton: especially Comte de Negret Excellence ◆ Ch Plaisance: makes above-average versions of Fronton ◆ DOM LE ROC ☆.

Gaillac

A good-size AC in the deep Southwest, Gaillac has a long history of winemaking. Today it fascinates because of the numerous obscure grapes that continue to be cultivated there, such as the apple-scented mauzac, the robust duras, fer, len de l'el (also loin de l'oeil), and ondenc. More widely known grapes are also planted—sauvignon, muscadelle, syrah, and so on—and the INAO has byzantine laws about which may be used and to what extent. These seem to be largely ignored. The region also produces an encyclopedic range of wines, with sturdy reds heading the list. I find the most appealing wines to be the whites with just a tickle of bubbles (Gaillac *perlé*), the semisweet sparkling wines *(méthode gaillacoise)*, and the fully sweet whites from the region's traditional grapes. Drink the youngest available, although the sweet whites from great vintages like 2001 are delicious right now.

PRICES: $ to $$($)

PRODUCERS: DOM DE CAUSSE MARINES ◆ Cave de Técou: a good co-op with a pleasant Gaillac *perlé* and several nice versions of sweet Gaillac, among them Confidences, and my favorite, Fascination, a fresh blend of muscadelle and len de l'el ◆ Dom la Croix des Marchands: the lightly tingling blanc *perlé* is vivacious and very easy to drink ◆ DOM D'ESCAUSSES ◆ Dom de Labarthe: the *méthode gaillacoise*, a naturally sweet sparkling wine, is as fresh and pleasant as a spring Sunday in the park. Grains d'Or, made from len de l'el grapes that shriveled on the vine, would make a satisfying aperitif. The reds are a touch rustic but appealing, if you're in the mood ◆ Ch Palvie: under the same direction as Dom la Croix des Marchands, this property offers two grades of wine—the basic wines are lean, dry, spicy reds and pleasant sweet whites. Les Secrets du Ch Palvie is a real step up, with a chewy, new-oak aged, old-vines red and, in great vintages like 2001, an impressive, extremely sweet blend of muscadelle and len de l'el, with flavors of honey, peach, and white currants ◆ ROBERT PLAGEOLES & FILS ☆ ◆ DOM DE LA RAMAYE ↑ ◆ DOM ROTIER ◆ Dom des Terrisses: the fer servadou and syrah-based reds recall austere hybrids from New York's Finger Lakes; the dry and sweet whites—mauzac with or without len de l'el—are tasty curiosities to try on the spot ◆ Dom des Très Cantous: see ROBERT PLAGEOLES.

Domaine de Grand Jaure

24100 Lembras; 05.53.57.35.65; domaine.du.grand.jaure@wanadoo.fr
Wine: Pécharmant. $$

Low yields and careful vinification result in a plummy, balanced, easy-drinking red and a more ambitious, oakier cuvée Mémoire with even deeper plummy-cherry pit flavors. Keep an eye on this domaine.

Château Grande Maison ↑

24240 Monbazillac; 05.53.58.26.17; thierry.despres@free.fr
Wines: Monbazillac and Bergerac. $$ to $$$

Thierry Despres, who practices organic viticulture, is one of these ACs' up-and-coming stars. His Bergerac sec is fragrant and tender with flavors of tropical fruit. His Tête de Cuvée presents an elegant integration of fruit and oak. His Monbazillac Château is suave, honeyed, and specific; Monstres is superb, with beautiful balance and the texture of velvet.

Domaine du Have ☆

32370 St.-Christie d'Armagnac; 06.03.89.31.02
Wine: Vin de Pays Côtes de Gascogne. $($)

Has the jug-wine grape colombard ever had it so good? Unlikely. Maybe it takes idealistic Parisians like the Lassignordies who harvest the grapes by hand and ferment and age them in new barrels—under the guidance of a student of Michel Rolland. They come up with a wine that is much more serious than it needs to be. That's the case with their creamy, mellow white, a really nice food wine. Bravo.

Irouléguy

A tiny AC located south of Bayonne, on France's border with Spain for full-bodied whites based on courbu and the mansengs and rugged, nearly black, age-worthy reds and ample rosés from tannat and the cabernets. (For more on the style of tannat-based wines, see MADIRAN.)

BEST RECENT VINTAGES: 2005, 2004, 2003, 2002, and 2000.
PRICES: $ to $$

PRODUCERS: Dom Ameztia Etzaldea: a good small domaine with structured, tasty wines ◆ DOM ARRETXEA ☆ ◆ Étienne Brana: firm, vinous rosés and a relatively light and smooth red called Axeria ◆ DOM ETXEGARAYA ☆ ◆ Herri Mina: strong, vinous, food-friendly whites ◆ Dom Mourguy: 2003 was the first vintage for this ambitious domaine. To follow ◆ Les Vignerons du Pays Basque: a good co-op with nearly a dozen different bottlings, of which my favorites are the chewy Omenaldi (a good red for barbecues); the Dom de Mignaberry, another strong, sturdy red; and two flavorful whites, Anderena and the oak-aged Xuri d'Ansa.

Château de la Jaubertie ☆

24560 Colombier; 05.53.58.32.11; jaubertie@wanadoo.fr

Wine: Bergerac. $ to $$($)

Hugh Ryman produces a pungent, rich, and stylish Bergerac sec. His cuvée Mirabelle—made in both white and red—is excellent and ambitious. The white is a subtle blend of apple, mineral, and oak flavors. The red is plush, with lovely fruit and garage-style concentration and a whiff of the New World.

Jurançon and Jurançon sec

A small but important AC near the town of Pau in the foothills of the Pyrenees, the AC applies to dry and sweet whites made chiefly from gros and petit manseng, although courbu may be used in dry wines. These are incisive and vinous, riveting wines that nicely accompany just about any dish that calls for a dry white. The sweet whites are made from overripe grapes that have shriveled on the vine. They are golden and luscious, balanced by an appetizing freshness. Wonderful as aperitifs, sweet Jurançons may also be drunk with cheese and with plain or fruit-based desserts. The dry whites should be drunk young (any vintage from the turn of the century) and will cost $ to $$; the sweets may be drunk young or old—good older vintages include 1990, 1995, and 1997—and cost $$ to $$$.

PRODUCERS: DOM BRU-BACHÉ ☆ ◆ DOM CAUHAPÉ ☆ ◆ CLOS LAPEYRE ☆ ◆ CLOS UROULAT ☆ ◆ Didier Dagueneau: the controversial vintner who makes fabulous Pouilly-Fumé (where he is more fully described) recently bought a vineyard in Jurançon. I haven't yet had the pleasure of tasting its wine, but can't imagine Didier making a less than excellent wine, thus the star ☆ ◆ Ch Jolys: a large family domaine with a good Cuvée Jean ◆ Dom Latapy: tart but promising dry whites and sweet whites that are less unctuous than many but more adaptable to food. Look for the barrel-fermented Passion ◆ Dom de Souch: if you saw the film *Mondovino* you undoubtedly remember the charming widow, Yvonne Hégoburu, who lavished her vines with TLC. The results are as enchanting as expected, especially Cuvée de Marie Kattalin Hégoburu ☆ ◆ Clos Thou: good, punchy dry whites; pleasant sweet whites, particularly Cuvée Julie and Suprême de Thou.

Lavilledieu

A diminutive VDQS north of the Fronton AC, Lavilledieu reds and rosés are similar to those of Fronton. There are three producers including the co-op. Drink the youngest available. Prices: $.

Madiran

An important Southwest AC located due west of Toulouse for virile reds made chiefly from tannat, which makes the blackest of black wine with Force 10 tannins. The challenge of Madiran is to tame the wild tannat. Other grape varieties—the cabernets and fer servadou (locally called pinenc)—as well as different methods of aging, soften it. Still, it's not a wine for everyone. But Madiran bursts with character and could never be mistaken for a high-tech-driven beverage wine that could come from anywhere. To best enjoy it, carafe the the wine at least two hours before serving.

BEST RECENT VINTAGES: 2005, (2004), (2003), and 2001.
PRICES: $$ to $$$

PRODUCERS: CH D'AYDIE ☆ ◆ DOM BERTHOUMIEU ◆ ALAIN BRUMONT/CH MONTUS AND BOUSCASSÉ ☆ ◆ CAVE DE CROUSEILLES ◆ CHAPELLE LENCLOS ◆ Clos Baste: this relatively young domaine makes Madiran that could put hair on your chest, it's so packed with black fruit, new oak, and tannins; the top cuvées are the cranberry-scented L'Esprit and Tête de Cuvée (pure tannat), a deep, meaty wine that blankets the tongue ◆ Dom du Crampilh: the domaine's heavy soils—good for farming—manifest themselves in the wines, which are well made but big and brawny, particularly the old-vines, pure tannat bottling. The cheaper bottling L'Originel is good value ◆ Dom Damiens: the Cuvée St.-Jean is a dense, truffley red that could take on the bulls of Pamplona ◆ Ch Labranche-Laffont: Christine Dupuy makes dark kirsch- and prune-scented Madirans with notes of oak, tar, and toast. The Vieilles Vignes cuvée, part of which comes from prephylloxera vines, is a bit more refined but definitely in the family style ◆ Ch Laffitte-Teston: with several years of bottle age, the well-made cuvée Vieilles Vignes evolves into a flavorful red with an engaging whiff of rusticity ◆ DOM DE MAOURIES ◆ Ch Montus-Ch Bouscassé (see ALAIN BRUMONT) ☆ ◆ PRODUCTEURS PLAIMONT ☆.

Marcillac

A tiny AC outside of Rodez in the Aveyron, Marcillac's wines are almost purely fer servadou (locally called mansoi). Drink the youngest available. Prices: $. There are twelve producers including the (OK) co-op. Producers: Dom du Cros, especially cuvée Lo Sang de Pais ◆ Dom Terres d'Angles cuvée Vieilles Vignes.

Domaine de Maouries

32400 Labarthète; 05.62.69.63.84; domaine-maouries@32.sideral.fr
Wine: Madiran. $$
Pampered vines, from a vineyard that is also home to wild orchids, and TLC for the harvested grapes (they're destemmed by hand, for example, and then fermented in small, new oak barrels) result in Les Orchis de Pyren, a statuesque, complex, and fragrant red made from pure tannat. Richer and denser—although a tad less refined—another pure tannat, Cailloux de Pyren, is a blanket of crushed blackberries.

Château Masburel

33220 Ste.-Foy la Grande; 05.53.24.77.73; www.chateau-masburel.com
Wines: Côtes de Bergerac and Montravel. $$
Look for two lovely, oak-aged Côtes de Bergerac, Lady Masburel and the more complex, more elegant Château Masburel, and a serious, barrel-fermented Montravel that's appetizingly tender and mellow.

Château les Miaudoux

24240 Saussignac; 05.53.27.92.31; www.chateaulesmiaudoux.com
Wines: Bergerac and Saussignac. $ to $$
Another domaine converting to organic viticulture, Miaudoux makes very good Saussignac and ambitious reds, particularly the silky L'Inspiration des Miaudoux, which is dominated by merlot.

Domaine de Mirail

32700 Lectoure; 05.62.68.82.52; fax: 05.62.68.53.96
Wine: Vin de Pays Côtes de Gascogne. $ to $$($)
Charles Hochman is another vintner making a silk purse out of colombard with his Cuvée Singulière, a syrupy-sweet white fermented in new oak barrels. Excellent work but a bit pricey. I'd opt for the energetic little dry colombard and for Les Mirlandes, a smooth, easy-drinking blend of merlot and cabernet sauvignon.

Château Monestier la Tour ↑

24240 Monestier; 05.53.24.18.43; www.chateaumonestierlatour.com
Wines: Bergerac and Côtes de Bergerac. $$
Philip de Haseth-Möller has the good sense to consult with Bordeaux's Stéphane Derenoncourt. His wines are admirable and improving. The simplest, a Bergerac red, was a bit chewy and tannic but the white was textured, ripe, and rather deep. The top-of-the-line Cuvée Emily, a Côtes de Bergerac rouge, based on old vines and aged in new oak barrels, had lovely focus, structure, and dark, concentrated fruit. There was depth here, too. Definitely a domaine to follow.

Monbazillac

Perhaps the most celebrated of the Bergeracois ACs, Monbazillac is located south of the town of Bergerac and the Dordogne. The AC applies to very sweet (*liquoreux*) whites made from the botrytized grapes (harvested by successive passes through the vineyard) of muscadelle, sauvignon, and sémillon.

BEST RECENT VINTAGES: 2005, 2003, 2001, 1997, 1995, and 1990. Older mythic vintages: 1982, 1975, 1967, and 1966.
PRICES: $$($)

PRODUCERS: DOM DE L'ANCIENNE CURE ☆ ◆ CH BÉLINGARD ◆ CLOS DES VERDOTS ☆ ◆ Ch le Clou: an organic domaine with ambitious, apple- and spice-scented Monbazillac ◆ CH GRANDE MAISON ↑ ◆ Ch Haut-Bernasse: nicely balanced Monbazillac with rich flavors of dried apricots and golden raisins ◆ Dom du Haut-Montlong: the cuvée Font Romaine is less nuanced and dynamic than others but is tasty for all that ◆ Ch du Haut Pezaud: Christine Borgers created her domaine in 1999. She's worth following, as evidenced by two Monbazillacs—a light, pineapple- and honey-accented bottling and the cuvée Révélation. Vinified in new oak, it has sumptuous flavors of apricots steeped in honey and manages to remain fresh and bracing ↑ ◆ Ch les Marnières: could use a bit more concentration and substance but worth following ◆ Ch Monbazillac: the local co-op makes a good version of the AC, appetizing, light, and tasty ◆ Ch Montdoyen: fresh, pleasant, honeyed Monbazillac ◆ Ch la Robertie: the excellent cuvée Vendanges de Brumaire is focused, soigné, honeyed, and complex ◆ CH THEULET ◆ Ch Tillac: it's not massive, but the Monbazillac is nicely focused and well balanced ◆ Vieux Touron: a very tasty Monbazillac with flavors of oak, ginger, and orange peel.

The Montravels

Spreading along the right bank of the Dordogne, Montravel AC is an extension of the St.-Émilion vineyard area. The AC Montravel applies to reds and dry whites. The reds, made from merlot, the cabernets, and malbec, often reveal their proximity to Bordeaux: a taster would be hard put to distinguish a good red Montravel from a good Right Bank satellite. White Montravel is made from muscadelle, sauvignon blanc, and sémillon. Haut-Montravel and Côtes de Montravel blanc are whites made from the same grapes but are *liquoreux* and *moelleux*, respectively.

BEST RECENT VINTAGES: See BERGERAC.
PRICES: $ to $$

PRODUCERS: CH DU BLOY ☆ ◆ Ch le Bondieu: Didier Feytout turns out ambitious, tasty wines but some seem like works in progress, for example Les Portes, which seemed to lack structure but which was so interesting it made you want to follow the progress of the domaine, as did Calabre, a mellow, attractive white with good texture and exotic fruit flavors ◆ Ch Fayolle-Luzac: chiefly muscadelle, the white is fragrant and very reasonably priced ◆ Dom Grimardy: the oak-aged white is easygoing; Révélation de Grimardy, an attractive oak-aged red, chiefly merlot, it's fragrant, focused, and a step up ◆ Ch Haut-Mayne: ripe, floral, mineral sauvignon-based white at give-away prices ◆ Ch Laulerie: there's a lively domaine white, but the cuvée to look for is Comtesse Ségur in both a barrel-fermented, mellow, and ripe white and a red with inviting fruit, good focus, and balance ◆ Ch de la Mallevieille: floral, perfumed dry whites with good balance ◆ CH MASBUREL ◆ Ch Masmontet: a pleasant, late-harvested Côtes de Bergerac, with appealing freshness; and a lively white Bergerac sec, both specific and balanced ◆ CH MOULIN CARESSE ☆ ◆ Ch Puy Servain: the dry white is a bit too oaky, but the Haut-Montravel Terremont is fresh, balanced, and clean with appetizing notes of honey and herbal tea ◆ Ch le Raz: pleasant whites, particularly the cuvée Grande Chêne and the more ambitious, admirable Haut-Montravel Cuvée Pierres Blanches. Spicy and oaky, the red Les

Filles is a good wine for pizza with sweet sausage ◆ Ch Roque Peyre: amiable whites include a ripe, tangy sec at $ and a fragrant, textured, oak-aged version with exotic fruit notes; the merlot-based red needs time in a carafe, but it's firm and gratifying.

Château Moulin Caresse ☆

24230 St.-Antoine-de-Breuilh; 05.53.27.55.58; moulin.caresse@wanadoo.fr

Wines: Bergerac and Montravel. $ to $$

If proof is needed that the Bergeracois is really part of Bordeaux, try Jean-François Deffarge's Montravel rouge Grande Cuvée Cent pour 100. An unfiltered blend based on merlot and malbec, it is elegant, concentrated, and very delicious. The white Montravel Cent pour 100 is equally impressive, vinous, tight, mineral, and riveting. The textured, perfumed Premières Vendanges, another Montravel white, would go beautifully with shellfish. From the Bergerac AC there's an oak-aged cuvée Magie d'Automne in both white and red; the white is subtle and simultaneously tender and invigorating; the red is fresh, fragrant, and spicy.

Pacherenc du Vic-Bilh

A tiny AC in the same zone as the Madiran AC for dry and sweet whites made chiefly from petit and gros manseng and courbu with the possible addition of arrufiac, sauvignon blanc, and sémillon. The wines resemble those from Jurançon: dry, they are vinous, full, and food-friendly; sweet, they are luscious and honeyed.

BEST RECENT VINTAGES: 2005, 2004, 2003, and 2001.
PRICES: $$

PRODUCERS (most make both Madiran and Pacherenc): CH D'AYDIE ☆ ◆ DOM BERTHOUMIEU ◆ ALAIN BRUMONT/CH MONTUS AND BOUSCASSÉ ☆ ◆ CAVE DE CROUSEILLES ◆ CHAPELLE LENCLOS ◆ Dom du Crampilh: a Pacherenc for those who love oak ◆ Ch Laffitte-Teston: very good Pacherenc with depth and structure and a pleasant mingling of oak and honey flavors ◆ Dom Sergent: a lively, three-dimensional wine with appetizing flavors of oak and honey, a very good aperitif.

Château de Panisseau

24240 Thénac; 05.53.58.40.03; panisseau@ifrance.com

Wines: Bergerac and Côtes de Bergerac. $ to $$($)

A reliable family domaine with two good Bergerac secs, the Cuvée Nymphéa, a mellow but lively white, and the richer, more serious, barrel-aged Divin, made from old-vines sémillon, sauvignon blanc, and muscadelle. There are also two good reds, the lightly jammy Côtes de Bergerac Cuvée Tradition and Baccarat; neither fined nor filtered, the latter is a plush red based chiefly on merlot.

Pécharmant

A small AC consisting of south-facing slopes north of the town of Bergerac on the right bank of the Dordogne. The AC is for reds made from the cabernets, malbec, and merlot, which must be blends of at least three of these grapes. My impression is that the standard Pécharmant is warmer and spicier than the Bergeracois reds, although the most ambitious are very elegant.

BEST RECENT VINTAGES: see BERGERAC.
PRICES: $ to $$($)

PRODUCERS: DOM DE L'ANCIENNE CURE ☆ ◆ Ch Champarel: spicy, smooth, and ingratiating, with character and specificity ◆ Les Chemins de l'Orient: the handcrafted cuvée Nouria is a fragrant, well-upholstered red that needs several years of bottle age ◆ Ch les Farcies du Pech: spicy, smooth, easy-drinking reds at reasonable prices ◆ DOM DE GRANDE JAURE ◆ Dom Puy de Grave: aged in new oak barrels, this is a silky, spicy, interesting red that invites you to drink it ◆ Ch Terre Vieille: this fragrant though tannic, thick, barrel-aged red (mostly merlot) needs a carafe ◆ Ch le Tilleraie: pleasant, textured red, a blend of all four grapes ◆ CH DE TIREGAND.

Robert Plageoles & Fils ☆

81140 Cahuzac-sur-Vère; 05.63.33.90.40; robert-bernard.plageoles@wanadoo.fr

Wine: Gaillac. $ to $$$

The Plageoles put Gaillac—and its local grapes—on the map. Drink their Mauzac Natur, a light, sparkling white, the minute it comes on the market and you'll swear it's the freshest thing you've ever tasted. Their Mauzac Vert is a zingy, stony-edged white with more than a scent of Granny Smith apples. And their range of sweet wines includes a plush Muscadelle *doux* with ripe apricot aromas and two pure ondencs, the first a mildly sweet white with appetizing fruit and herbal tea notes, the second, Vin d'Autan, simultaneously syrupy and buoyant. All three sweet wines would make for excellent by-the-glass discoveries.

Producteurs Plaimont ☆

32400 St.-Mont; 05.62.69.62.87; www.plaimont.com

Wines: Madiran, Côtes de St.-Mont, and Vin de Pays Côtes de Gascogne. $ to $$

This outstanding co-op should give lessons: How to Insist on Wine Quality Every Step of the Way 101. The co-op makes so many wines—some blends, some from specific properties—that describing them all could fill an entire book. Perhaps it's best known for its least expensive wines, Colombelle, simple, juicy reds and whites with flagrant fruit. At less than $6, they deserve praise. But the price-to-quality ratio holds through the entire range. Here are a couple of favorites: for just a dollar or two more than Colombelle there's the more interesting Labriole, a bracing white. Move up another step and there's Les Vignes Retrouvées, an ample, textured blend of gros manseng, arrufiac, and courbu. Then comes Le Faîte, a mellow blend of local grapes fermented in new oak; the red version of Le Faîte is an ambitious wine with plush fruit. And finally, two excellent wines that should see a carafe before drinking, the Madirans Arte Bénédicte and Plénitude.

Domaine de la Ramaye ↑

81600 Gaillac; 05.63.57.06.64; fax: 05.63.57.35.54

Wines: Gaillac and Vin de Pays Côtes du Tarn. $$ to $$$

Michel Issally produces a range of ambitious, hypernatural wines that are always fascinating but sometimes come across like works in progress. I'd love to find every one of them served by the glass. La Combe d'Aves, a blend of duras and braucol (fer), is an extremely dark, totally honest red. Les Sousbois de Rayssac is a very sweet, honeyed, and appley white with a touch of caramel. The mead—like La Quintessence, made from mauzac harvested grape by grape, is extremely sweet and concentrated, with layers of flavor. Le Vin de l'Oubli, another mauzac, ages for six years in barrel and comes across like a very strong fino sherry, loaded with toffee and nut flavors. La Grande Terre, a real vinous footnote, is made from prunellard, a nearly extinct grape, and is tasty but as potent as a knockout punch.

Château Richard ↑

24240 Monestier; 05.53.58.49.13; www.chateaurichard.com

Wines: Bergerac and Saussignac. $ to $$($)

A geologist by training, Richard Doughty runs his domaine according to organic principles, uses wild yeasts, and neither fines nor filters his red wines. The barrel-aged Bergerac red Cuvée Osée exhibited the softness I associate with hypernatural wines; it was good—worth discovering, it had something to say but wasn't lipsmacking. His Saussignacs, on the other hand, are decidedly scrumptious—particularly the Cuvée Noble, which was fresh as a waterfall, suave, with luscious flavors of honey and dried fruit.

Domaine le Roc ☆

31620 Fronton; 05.61.82.93.90; fax: 05.61.82.72.38

Wine: Fronton. $

Frédéric Ribes may be the best winemaker in Fronton. His rosés are strong and decisive. His reds are succulent, balanced, and satisfying. His top cuvée is Don Quichotte, a gratifying blend of négrette and syrah. If you're looking for an easygoing red with a sense of place and value for the dollar, your search is over.

Rosette

An infinitesimal AC in the hills northwest of Bergerac, for demi-sec and *moelleux* whites based on sauvignon blanc, muscadelle, and sémillon. The only producer I know is Dom de Coutancie. Try on the spot.

Domaine Rotier

81600 Cadalen; 05.63.41.75.14; rotier@terre-net.fr

Wines: Gaillac. $ to $$

A solid Gaillac property with a couple of inexpensive, tasty reds (Gravels and Renaissance), a lively dry white to drink well iced, and several sweet wines, among them Renaissance, which in most vintages makes a nice aperitif; in 2001 it was so lovely it could compete with wines from far more prestigious appellations.

Saussignac

A small AC west of Monbazillac known for potentially dazzling, unctuously sweet (*liquoreux*) whites based on sauvignon blanc, sémillon, and muscadelle. The grapes must be hand-harvested by successive passes through the vineyard. At their best, they are sensational.

BEST RECENT VINTAGES: 2005, 2003, 2001, and 1997.
PRICES: $$ to $$$

PRODUCERS: Ch le Chabrier: a good family domaine run on organic principles making lovely Saussignacs, particularly the barrel-fermented Cuvée Éléna, a focused wine with fine balance ◆ CLOS D'YVIGNE ↑ ◆ Ch Court les Muts: A very nice domaine with very nice, chiefly sémillon, barrel-fermented wine. It's lovely, fresh, with honey and white currant flavors; drink the 1995 now ◆ Ch des Eyssards: less syrupy than many, the Cuvée Flavie is nevertheless an appealing, pineapple- and herbal tea–scented wine ◆ CH LES MIAUDOUX ◆ Ch le Payral: an eco-friendly domaine with a gracious Cuvée Marie-Jeanne, full of apple and honey flavors ◆ CH RICHARD ↑ ◆ CH TOUR DES GENDRES ☆ ◆ Ch Tourmentine: here's a reasonably priced, fresh, aromatic, barrel-fermented sémillon with accents of orange peel and honey ◆ Vignerons de Sigoules: a good co-op with an admirable special bottling Vendanges d'Autrefois, a refreshing sweet wine with flavors of honey and grapefruit.

Domaine du Tariquet

32800 Eauze; 05.62.09.87.82; www.tariquet.com

Wine: Vin de Pays Côtes de Gascogne. $ to $$

Yves Grassa continues to make a good deal of Armagnac, but he truly pioneered the production of fresh, commercial table wines in the region. There are numerous cuvées—some varietal (sauvignon blanc, chardonnay), some blends, some oaked, some not—and all are very professional, clean, balanced, inexpensive, and perfectly suited to a market looking for this kind of beverage wine. He produces good Floc de Gascogne and another aperitif option, a sweet white made from petit manseng fermented in new barrels, called Dernières Grives.

Château Theulet

24240 Monbazillac; 05.53.57.30.43; alardetfils@wanadoo.fr

Wines: Bergerac, Côtes de Bergerac, and Monbazillac. $ to $$$

The good reds made by this family domaine are upstaged by the barrel-fermented whites, among them a supple, perfumed Bergerac sec with flavors of ripe, exotic fruit and a fresh Monbazillac Cuvée Antoine with notes of ginger, peach, and apricot.

Château de Tiregand

24100 Bergerac; 05.53.23.21.08; chateautiregand@club-internet.fr

Wine: Pécharmant. $$

Owned by the Saint-Exupéry family, the domaine makes a pretty, bistro red and a more polished, hand-harvested and oak-aged cuvée Grand Millésime, which needs at least three years of bottle age.

Château Tour des Gendres ☆

24240 Ribagnac; 05.53.57.12.43; fammilledeconti@wanadoo.fr

Wines: Bergerac, Côtes de Bergerac, and Saussignac. $ to $$$

Luc de Conti, one of the fathers of the quality revolution in Bergerac, makes some drop-dead-delicious (and organic) wine. There's an inexpensive range that's just fine for everyday drinking and there are the special cuvées, all aged in new or newish barrels. Gloire de Mon Père is a fragrant and plush red, full of charm. Moulin des Dames is a silky, appetizing red. Anthologia is de Conti's garage wine. Not made every year, it's the ultimate "hands-on" wine. The grapes are dropped into special oak barrels one by one, *terroir* by *terroir*, and then subjected to a gentle vinification devised by de Conti—superb. The white Moulin des Dames is rich and fresh and age-worthy. And Clos de la Mémé, a Saussignac, is a glimmering burnished gold, a velvet weave of honey, dried fruit, and roasted nuts. It's exquisite.

Tursan

A tiny VDQS for reds and rosés made primarily from tannat, the cabernets, and fer servadou, and whites based on the local grape baroque as well as the mansengs and sauvignon blanc. There are three producers, including the co-op Les Vignerons Landais, whose whites, particularly Esprit and Impératrices, are good little café quaffs. The most famous producer is the three-Michelin-star chef Michel Guérard, whose whites from the Château Bachen are firm and tasty. Most are $ but Château Bachen's most ambitious wine, Baron de Bachen, is $$. Drink the youngest available.

Vin de Pays

As in other large, diverse regions, there are numerous Vins de Pays in the Southwest. Among them: Côtes du Condomois; Comte Tolosan: Dom Ribonnet's wines as well as the Cave de Rabasten's easy-drinking *vins de soif* can be sampled in and around Toulouse; Côtes de Gascogne (see below); Côtes du Tarn: ROBERT PLAGEOLES & FILS and Dom Vigne Lourac; du Lot: DOM BELMONT ☆.

Vin de Pays Côtes de Gascogne

An important Vin de Pays covering the Armagnac zone. As sales of Armagnac slumped, growers began making table wines from their brandy grapes, chiefly ugni blanc and colombard. They also replanted with more popular grapes: chardonnay, sauvignon blanc, the mansengs, making dry, off-dry, and sweet whites. There are reds and rosés, but the whites are by far the most successful—generally fresh and frisky and very reasonably priced. Drink the youngest available. Prices: $.

PRODUCERS: Dom d'Arton: Les Hauts d'Arton, a blend of colombard and sauvignon blanc, goes down easily. The oak-aged Victoire is ripe and flavorful. Les Deux Cèdres nicely blends petit and gros manseng to make a pleasant sweet white ◆ Dom des Cassagnoles: fresh, clean, eminently drinkable whites, particularly the textured Réserve Sélection made from gros manseng ☆ ◆ DOM DU HAVE ☆ ◆ Dom de Maubet: the off-dry white, based on gros manseng, would make a nice opener for a simple meal ◆ Dom de Pellehaut: Harmonie de Gascogne is a crisp, squeaky-clean white ◆ Les Terrasses de Rubens: the syrupy-sweet, hand-harvested, barrel-aged petit manseng would make a tasty aperitif ◆ DOM DE MIRAIL ◆ DOM DU TARIQUET ◆ Dom d'Uby: my preferred wine from this house is the fresh blend of sauvignon blanc and colombard; the others aren't bad either.

SOUTHWEST CRIB SHEET

MUST TRYS

Domaine Belmont: Vin de Pays du Lot
Domaine Bru-Baché: Jurançon
Alain Brumont/Château Bouscassé: Madiran and Pacherenc du Vic-Bilh
Domaine Cauhapé: Jurançon
Château du Cèdre: Cahors
Clos des Verdots: Bergerac, including Monbazillac
Clos d'Yvigne: Saussignac
Domaine Élian da Ros: Côtes du Marmandais
Château Grande Maison: Monbazillac and Bergerac
Château Moulin Caresse: Bergerac and Montravel

SMART BUYS

Château la Barde les Tendoux: Bergerac
Château Bellevue la Forêt: Fronton
Domaine des Cassagnoles: Vin de Pays Côtes de Gascogne
Clos la Coutale: Cahors
Château Haut-Mayne: Montravel
Domaine du Have: Vin de Pays Côtes de Gascogne
Producteurs Plaimont: Madiran, Côtes de St.-Mont, and Vin de Pays Côtes de Gascogne
Domaine le Roc: Fronton
Domaine Rotier: Gaillac for simple wines
Domaine du Tariquet: Vin de Pays Côtes de Gascogne

SAFE HOUSES

Domaine de l'Ancienne Cure: Bergerac, Pécharmant, and Monbazillac
Domaine Arretxea: Irouléguy
Château d'Aydie: Madiran and Pacherenc du Vic-Bilh
Château du Bloy: Bergerac and Montravel
Clos Uroulat: Jurançon
Château la Colline: Bergerac and Côtes de Bergerac
Domaine d'Escausses: Gaillac
Domaine Etxegaraya: Irouléguy
Robert Plageoles & Fils: Gaillac
Château Tour des Gendres: Bergerac, Côtes de Bergerac, and Saussignac

EIGHT GOOD PARIS WINE SHOPS

Caves Augé
116 Bd Haussmann, 8ème Arr; 01.45.22.16.97; fax: 01.44.70.08.80
Closed: All day Sunday and Monday morning
Vest-pocket wine shop, jam-packed with wines—many of them hypernatural.

Lafayette Gourmet
48 Blvd Haussmann, 9ème Arr; 01.42.82.34.56
Closed: Sunday
The fancy foods department of the Galeries Lafayette department store. An excellent selection of wines is located in an alcove cum shop in the midst of a dazzlingly broad and dangerously tempting array of food.

Lavinia
3–5 Blvd de la Madeleine, 1èr Arr; 01.42.97.20.27; fax: 01.42.97.54.50
Closed: Sunday
Europe's largest wine and spirits shop in a mammoth, loft-like setting. The top floor houses a restaurant, wine bar, and book and wine accessories boutique.

Legrand Filles & Fils
1, rue de la Banque, 2ème Arr; 01.42.60.07.12; fax: 01.42.61.25.51
Closed: Sunday
Excellent shop in charming passage. Snacks available at lunchtime.

Caves Miard
9, rue des Quatres-Vents, 6ème Arr; tel/fax: 01.43.54.99.30
Closed: Sunday and Monday
Former turn-of-the-century cheese shop now transformed into a charming wine shop–wine bar favoring biodynamic wines.

Les Papilles
30, rue Gay-Lussac, 5ème Arr; 01.43.25.20.79; fax: 01.43.25.24.35
Closed: Sunday
A shop within a restaurant. There's one set menu a day, but it's a good one. You pick your wine from the shelves—a selection of some five hundred different wines—and pay a corkage fee. You can also buy to take away.

Caves Taillevent
199 rue du Faubourg-Saint-Honoré, 8 ème Arr; 01.45.61.14.09; fax: 01.45.61.19.68
Closed: All day Sunday and Monday morning
The wine shop annex of the Michelin 3-star restaurant. Great selection.

Le Verre Volé
67, rue de Lancry, 10ème Arr; 01.40.40.07.11
Open: Daily
Located on the trendy Canal St. Martin, a wine bar and shop featuring organic, biodynamic, and hypernatural wines.

ORDERING OR BUYING WINE IN FRANCE

My attempt to give an idea of French pronunciation is very crude. These are just the broad lines. I'm leaving out aspects like the general nasality that affects pronunciation of many words. Further, don't try to pronounce the guttural French "r"—ten to one you won't succeed, and should you succeed, your victory will be counterproductive as you will have deprived a French person of one of the easiest ways to mock American accents. Finally, resist the urge to get the clerk or waitperson's attention by saying "Excusez-moi." Instead, say, "S'il vous plait."

WHAT

wine — *vin* (van pronounced as in vanilla)
white — *blanc* (blahnk or blonk)
red — *rouge* (rooj)

HOW MUCH

glass — *verre* (vair)
two glasses — *deux verres* (de vair)
bottle — *bouteille* (boo tay)
half bottle — *demi-bouteille* (demi—as in the actress Demi Moore—and boo tay; actually, just saying demi will suffice)
pitcher — *pichet* (pee shay)
small pitcher of 25 cl — *un quart* (ahn car)

LISTS AND BOARDS

wine list — *carte de vin* (cart duh van)
blackboard — *ardoise* (ar dwaz)

WHAT REFINED

light and fruity — *leger et fruite* (lay zhay ay fwee tay)
hearty, full-bodied — *corsé* (core say)
synonyms for full-bodied — *charnu* (shar noo) and *riche* (reesh)
ample — *ample* (ahm pluh)
supple — *souple* (sooo pluh)
elegant — *élégant* (ell ay gahnt)
sweet — *moelleux* (mwah le)
half-sweet — *demi sec* (demi sek)
very sweet — *doux* (doo)
oaky — *boisé* (bwa zay)
expensive — *cher* (cher—as in Sonny and Cher)
not too — *pas trop* (pa tro—pronounce as in grow)

ORDERING

I'd like — *je voudrais* (zhe vooo dray)
We'd like — *nous voudrions* (new voo dree onz)

CONVERSION TABLES

Hectares to Acres

- 1 hectare = 2.47 acres

Hectoliters to Gallons, Cases, and Tons

- 1 hectoliter (100 liters) equals roughly 26.4 gallons or 11 cases (of 12 bottles of 75 centiliter capacity) of wine
- 10 hectoliters a hectare (hl/ha) equals roughly 264 gallons a hectare (roughly 100 gallons an acre), about 40 cases an acre
- One ton of grapes an acre equals roughly 15 hl/ha
- One ton of grapes equals about 60 cases of wine
- 35 hl/ha equals a bit over 140 cases an acre
- 3 tons an acre equals 180 cases an acre

Temperatures

10ºC = 50ºF
15ºC = 59ºF
20ºC = 68ºF
25ºC = 77ºF
30ºC = 86ºF
35ºC = 95ºF

GRAPE VARIETIES

The following are the major—and not so major—grape varieties used in making French wine. Additional varieties, generally obscure grapes specific to a particular region or appellation, will be described in the chapter that covers that area.

ABOURIOU: A minor red grape used in the Southwest, notably in the Côtes du Marmandais.

ALIGOTÉ: Burgundy's secondary white grape. The wine made from it is usually quite sharp; it's traditionally mixed with crème de cassis to make the cocktail called Kir.

ALTESSE: The white grape responsible for some of Savoie's best wines.

ARRUFIAC: A minor white grape used, mostly for blending, in the Southwest.

BOURBOULENC: A key white grape used, mostly in blends, in the Languedoc-Roussillon, Provence, and the Rhône.

CABERNET FRANC: The principle red grape of the central-west Loire (Bourgueil, Chinon, Saumur-Champigny, and so on), where it is often called Breton, cabernet franc is also an important blending grape in the Bordelais, particularly in St.-Émilion where it is known as bouchet. It enters into blends in the Southwest and in the Languedoc-Roussillon.

CABERNET SAUVIGNON: A noble red grape of Bordeaux, particularly in the Médoc, making tannic, structured, age-worthy wines. It is also cultivated in the Languedoc-Roussillon, in the Southwest, and in parts of Provence.

CARIGNAN: A red wine grape generally used for blending in the Languedoc-Roussillon, Provence, and the Rhône. Some maverick vintners are turning out very convincing pure versions of carignan.

CARMENÈRE: A nearly extinct red grape used in Bordeaux blends.

CÉSAR: A local and rare red grape used in Irancy in the Auxerrois region of Burgundy.

CHARDONNAY: This noble white grape is planted almost everywhere (Bordeaux is a notable exception) but is at its finest in Burgundy and Champagne. It is capable of making splendid, nuanced, age-worthy whites and heartbreakingly fine Champagne, as well as agreeable quaffers.

CHASSELAS: A secondary white grape grown in the Loire, as the base of Pouilly-sur-Loire, in Alsace, and in Savoie.

CHENIN BLANC: A potentially noble white grape cultivated in the Southwest and the Languedoc-Roussillon (principally Limoux) but mostly associated with the Loire, where it is made into a complete range of wines from sparkling to dry, off-dry, semisweet, *moelleux, doux,* and *liquoreux,* many of them breathtaking in their majesty.

CINSAULT: Sometimes spelled cinsaut, this is a red grape used principally for blending in the Rhône, Provence, Languedoc-Roussillon, and Corsica.

CLAIRETTE: A white grape, typically part of the blends of the Languedoc-Roussillon, Provence, and the Rhône.

COLOMBARD: A ho-hum white grape used in the Southwest, where a couple of vintners do a fine job with it, and the Bordelais.

CÔT: See malbec.

COUNOISE: A red grape mostly used for blending in the Rhône and Provence.

COURBU: An interesting white grape used in Southwest wines.

FER: Also referred to as fer servadou, braucol, and pinenc, this is a red grape used in the Southwest, usually, but not always, for blending.

FIÉ: a pink mutation of sauvignon blanc, also called sauvignon rosé, planted in Touraine (the Loire) and in northern Burgundy.

FOLLE BLANCHE: Also known as gros plant, this high-acid white grape is cultivated in the Loire. It is more felicitously used to make brandy.

GAMAY: A vibrantly fruity, popular red grape most commonly associated with Beaujolais but also cultivated with great success in the Loire. In addition it is used as a blending grape in the Southwest and both in blends and on its own in Savoie.

GEWÜRZTRAMINER: A key Alsace white grape, gewürztraminer is spicy and easily identifiable, with aromas recalling lychee and roses.

GRENACHE BLANC, GRIS, AND NOIR: Widely planted, grenache is a hot-climate grape found mainly in the Rhône, Languedoc-Roussillon, Provence, and Corsica. Grenache blanc and gris are used to make white wines; gris and noir are used for rosés; and noir is used to make reds. Grenache is often blended, but there is a trend, particularly in parts of the Languedoc-Roussillon, to bottle it on its own. Fortified wines, such as Banyuls, Maury, and Rivesaltes, are also made from grenache.

GROLLEAU: Also known as groslot, grolleau is a minor red and rosé grape used in the Loire, where it is generally blended, although it can make interesting light reds and taut rosés on its own.

GROS MANSENG: See manseng.

JACQUÈRE: A light white grape used in Savoie.

KLEVENER: white grape grown in—and the specialty of—Heiligenstein in Alsace.

KLEVNER: white grape grown in Alsace, believed to be part of the pinot family.

LEN DE L'EL: Also known as loin de l'oeil and many other orthographic variations, this is a white grape used in the Southwest, generally for blending.

LLADONER PELUT: A red grape of Catalan origin used in the Languedoc-Roussillon.

MACCABEU: A white grape used in Languedoc-Roussillon, generally for blending. Also spelled macabeu.

MALBEC: Also known as côt, malbec is a strongly colored and flavored red grape mostly associated with Cahors in the Southwest and the Loire but also used in Bordeaux blends.

MANSENG: Both petit and gros manseng are white grapes cultivated in the Southwest, particularly in Jurançon and Pacherenc du Vic-Bilh, and used for dry and sweet wines. Petit manseng is superior and has the potential to become a world player.

MARSANNE: An important white grape used either on its own or in blends in the Rhône, Provence, and Languedoc-Roussillon.

MAUZAC: A white grape closely associated with the apple-scented wines from Gaillac but cultivated throughout the Southwest and in Limoux in the Languedoc-Roussillon.

MELON DE BOURGOGNE: Also known as muscadet, melon de bourgogne is a white grape that makes fresh, light wines that are mineral rather than varietal. It's now grown almost exclusively in the Loire, though it is also used in simple Burgundy blends.

MERLOT: A widely planted, user-friendly red grape, merlot is capable of making plush, fragrant wines. Mostly associated with Bordeaux—particularly with the Right Bank, especially Pomerol and St.-Émilion—it's also cultivated throughout the Southwest and increasingly planted in the Languedoc-Roussillon (and anywhere else local French politics will permit).

MONDEUSE: A red grape used in Savoie.

MOURVÈDRE: A broodingly dark red grape used in the Rhône, Provence, Corsica, and Languedoc-Roussillon. Generally mourvèdre is blended with other grapes; it speaks most eloquently in Bandol.

MUSCADELLE: An aromatic white grape used mostly for blending (generally in small quantities) in Bordeaux, the Southwest, and Languedoc-Roussillon.

MUSCAT: A highly perfumed white grape, of which there are many varieties. Muscat blanc à petits grains is the best and is used in Alsace, Corsica, Languedoc-Roussillon, Provence, and the Rhône for everything from dry, to sweet (often fortified), to sparkling wines. Other varieties include muscat d'Alexandrie and muscat ottonel.

NÉGRETTE: A minor red grape used in the Fiefs Vendéens in the Loire and in Fronton in the Southwest.

NIELLUCCIO: Tuscany's sangiovese, the red grape nielluccio is used in Corsica.

ONDENC: A white grape, ondenc is used in the Southwest for both dry and sweet wines.

PETIT MANSENG: See manseng.

PETIT VERDOT: A fragrant red grape, petit verdot is used in Bordeaux blends, generally in small quantities.

PICPOUL: Sometimes spelled piquepoul, this is a white grape that makes light, easy-drinking whites in Languedoc-Roussillon. It's also grown in Provence and the Rhône.

PINEAU D'AUNIS: A red grape used in the Loire to make peppery light reds and rosés; pineau d'aunis is often blended.

PINOT BLANC: A light, somewhat bland white cousin of pinot noir, pinot blanc is used in Alsace and Burgundy.

PINOT GRIS: An interesting grape used to make textured whites in Alsace, the Loire, and Jura. In Alsace wines made from pinot gris were traditionally called Tokay. As this is now prohibited by European law, in order to avoid confusion with Hungary's Tokaj, it is gradually being phased out. Current Alsace labels often read "Tokay-Pinot Gris."

PINOT MEUNIER: A light red grape used in Champagne and the Loire.

PINOT NOIR: A noble red grape capable of making heart-stoppingly delicate, nuanced wines in Burgundy and Champagne, as well as fragrant, seductive wines in Alsace, the Loire, Jura, and Savoie.

POULSARD: Also known as ploussard, this grape makes light but character-filled reds and rosés in the Jura and Savoie.

RIESLING: A noble white grape of Alsace, where the wines it makes can be of breathtaking complexity.

ROLLE: See vermentino.

ROMORANTIN: An interesting white grape grown exclusively in Cour-Cheverny and parts of Touraine in the Loire.

ROUSSANNE: A fine white grape grown in the Rhône, Languedoc-Roussillon, and Savoie.

SAUVIGNON BLANC: A pungent and easily identifiable white grape, sauvignon blanc is sometimes called blanc fumé. It is most associated with the Loire and Bordeaux but is also grown in Burgundy (St.-Bris), Provence, the Languedoc, and the Southwest.

SAVAGNIN: Jura's fascinating white grape.

SCIACCARELLO: A red grape used in Corsica.

SÉMILLON: A textured white grape, key to Bordeaux's dry and sweet whites. Sémillon is equally important in the Southwest, specifically in the Bergeracois.

SYLVANER: A part of the array of white grapes in Alsace. Sylvaner is often bland but potentially charming.

SYRAH: A noble red grape of the Rhône, Provence, Corsica, and Languedoc-Roussillon, syrah is either blended or bottled on its own.

TANNAT: A red grape with gale-force tannins used in Madiran and Irouléguy as well as in other Southwest regions.

TERRET: A white grape used in Provence and the Rhône, principally for blending.

TIBOUREN: A minor red grape used in Provence.

TRESSALLIER: A light, sharp white grape grown in St.-Pourçain in the Loire.

TROUSSEAU: A red grape used in the Jura.

UGNI BLANC: A workhorse white grape, ugni blanc is generally used for blending, principally in the Rhône, Provence, the Southwest, and Corsica.

VERMENTINO: Also known as rolle, vermentino is a characterful white grape used in Languedoc-Roussillon, Provence, and Corsica (where it's called malvoisie).

VIOGNIER: A seductively aromatic white grape mainly cultivated in the Rhône, viognier is increasingly being used in the Languedoc-Roussillon as well.

GLOSSARY

I have tried to avoid technical words in this book where possible, using instead words from everyday life, but some wine jargon is inescapable. Definitions for technical terms are given here, followed by two sections—the first covering my own personal wine terminology (some of which has seeped into this book) and another decoding some "winespeak."

AC: An abbreviation for Appellation d'Origine Contrôlée, AC is a designation for wine that comes from a geographically limited zone and has been made according to legal specifications, including which grape varieties are used and the permitted yield, ripeness, and alcohol levels. With rare exceptions (for example, muscadet), an AC is named after a place. This may cover an entire region, such as Alsace, or be as small a specific vineyard, such as Château-Grillet.

ASSEMBLAGE: The blending of a number of wines (from the same or different grapes, depending upon the appellation) to produce a finished wine or wines.

BAN DE VENDANGE: The authorized date for the start of harvest.

BARRELS: Wooden containers in which wines are fermented and/or aged. The best barrels are made from oak. Both the size of the barrel and the number of times it has been used influence the impact it will have on the wine. Large and/or old barrels will have little effect other than to provide a porous atmosphere that will soften the wine by facilitating limited oxidation. The smaller and newer the barrel, the greater its influence, not only because of the amount of contact with air the wine receives but also because the barrel contributes flavor (vanilla, toast, or oak, for example) and tannins. Barrel age is sometimes indicated on the label, often with the words *vieilli en fûts de chêne.*

Some barrel terminology:

> ***BARRIQUE:*** a Bordeaux barrel holding 225 liters.
>
> ***DEMI-MUID:*** a barrel of 300- to 600-liter capacity.
>
> ***FOUDRE:*** a large wood cask that can hold 200 to 300 hectoliters.
>
> ***PIÈCE:*** a Burgundy barrel with a 228-liter capacity.

BIODYNAMICS: A philosophy of viticulture as set forth by Austrian philosopher Rudolph Steiner. Homeopathic vine treatments are used in place of chemicals. Planting, pruning, and other vineyard operations are scheduled according to the positions of the planets.

BLANC DE BLANCS: A white wine made of white grapes.

BLANC DE NOIRS: A white or a pale pink wine made from red grapes that have been immediately pressed off—or separated from—their skins and vinified like a white wine.

BLEEDING: The drawing off of juice from a vat of red grapes. It is one method used to make rosé wines as well as a technique some vintners use to make their reds more concentrated.

BOTRYTIS CINEREA: The name of a mold that under certain conditions causes grapes to shrivel, resulting in a concentration of sugar and acid. The wines made from these grapes, notably Sauternes, are characterized by aromas and flavors of honey and often a dense, almost syrupy richness. *Botrytis cinerea* is also called noble rot (*pourriture noble*).

BRASSAGE: The stirring up of the lees of a white wine as it ages (presumably on its lees).

BRUT: The term *brut* applies to dry sparkling wine that has a sugar content of .8 to 1.5 percent and to an unfinished wine that is taken from a tank or barrel for sampling, as in *brut de cuve,* a *cuve* being a tank.

CARAFE: (a) a beaker, with or without a stopper, into which a wine is poured; (b) a method of aerating wine by pouring it into a carafe. I have used the word *carafe* as a verb instead of the related term *decant.* The latter is more closely associated with the service of old wine in which the aim is to ensure that only clear wine enters the decanter, leaving the sediment behind in the bottle. When I speak of pouring a wine into a carafe, however, I am generally talking about young wines. Although there is no agreement on the subject, I think most young wines benefit from aeration. In other words: let it breathe, let it breathe.

CARBONIC MACERATION: A method of fermentation in which bunches of whole grapes are put into a tank filled with CO_2. Fermentation starts within the individual berries. This method, which produces supple, early-drinking, very aromatic wines, is primarily used with gamay, particularly in Beaujolais.

CÉPAGE: Grape variety.

CHAI: A winery building; an aboveground cellar.

CHAPTALIZATION: The process of adding sugar to grape juice either before or during fermentation in order to raise the degree of alcohol of the finished wine.

CHÂTEAU: The translation is "castle," and sometimes the winery does, indeed, have one. But this is not necessary. Generally a château is a winery, especially in Bordeaux.

CLASSIFIED GROWTH: See *cru classé.*

CLIMAT: Primarily associated with Burgundy, the term *climat* refers to a specific vineyard or part of that vineyard.

CLONE: A plant reproduced asexually, retaining the genetic makeup of its ancestor. A number of clones may exist for a given grape variety; one may be a high yielder, another may resist rot, a third ripen earlier, and so forth.

CLOS: A walled (or otherwise enclosed) vineyard.

COOPERATIVE: An association of wine growers in which the members bring either all or part of their production to a common cellar and share its winemaking facilities, winemakers, labs, and other costs.

CRÉMANT: Literally, "creaming," *crémant* is a sparkling wine generally with creamier, less forceful bubbles than Champagne.

CRU: *Cru* translates as "growth." The term is applied to a vineyard or a specific area of production, generally one of superior quality.

CRU CLASSÉ: A classified growth. For more details see the individual chapters, including Alsace, Bordeaux, and Burgundy.

CULT WINE: See garage wine.

CUVAISON: Refers to the making of red wine—specifically, the practice of fermenting the grape juice with the grape solids (skins, pips, and so forth) in order to extract color, tannins, and aroma. Generally, the longer the *cuvaison* (or vatting), the deeper the color of the wine and the more tannic it will be.

CUVE: Tank.

CUVÉE: Derived from the word *cuve,* cuvée usually applies to a specific blend or lot of wine, for example a reserve wine or a single vineyard or a young- or old-vines bottling.

DÉBOURBAGE: In white wine production, *débourage* is the practice of allowing the *bourbes* (solid matter such as pits, stems, seeds, and bits of pulp and skin) to settle out of the grape juice before fermentation begins.

DEPARTMENT: One of ninety-five French administrative units, a department is smaller than a state but larger than a county. It has no precise equivalent in the United States.

DISGORGING: Part of the process of making Champagne. See *méthode traditionelle.*

DOSAGE: see *Méthode Traditionelle.*

DOUX: A *vin doux* is an extremely sweet wine.

FERMENTATION: The process of transforming sugar into alcohol and turning grapes into wine.

FILTRATION: The process of clarifying a wine before bottling to remove yeast cells and other matter, usually by passing the wine through filter pads or diatomaceous earth (*kieselguhr*).

FINING: A method of clarifying wine by adding any of a number of coagulants or clays (egg whites, isinglass, gelatin, bentonite). As these substances settle to the bottom of the tank or barrel, they draw impurities with them, leaving the wine clear.

FINISH: The flavors and sensations left in the mouth after the wine has been swallowed. Fine wines will have long, complex finishes (length is a closely related concept here). Simple wines may appear to have no finish whatsoever. It's "Hi. Good-bye."

GARAGE WINE: A number of people have taken credit for coining this term but, although its authorship remains disputed, its meaning is clear. Originally, it described vintners—generally on the Right Bank of Bordeaux—who had such tiny operations they could (and often did) make their wines in a garage (see Château de Valandraud). The wines in question were as pampered as those from the most famous houses in Bordeaux and were able to command similar prices. Currently the term applies to any wine produced by a winemaker—a *garagiste*—who makes a very expensive, select, hands-on wine. These are generally based on extremely low yields, from the producer's best and oldest vines, and the ripest grapes. The wine is treated with the gentlest of TLC and aged in the most expensive new barrels. Such wines are also referred to as cult wines.

GOÛT DE TERROIR: See *terroir.*

GRIS: A *vin gris* is a pale rosé; like a *blanc de noirs,* it is made by a direct pressing of red grapes.

HECTARE: 2.47 acres.

HECTOLITER: 100 liters or 26.4 gallons. One hectoliter produces eleven cases of wine.

INAO: The Institut National des Appellations d'Origine, frequently referred to as the INAO, is the government agency responsible for determining and regulating French appellations of origin, including AC and VDQS wines.

LEES: The deposits thrown off by a young wine, the lees, which are remnants of yeast cells, settle on the bottom of the tank or barrel.

LIEU-DIT: Literally place-name, *lieu-dit* is the time-honored way of referring to a particular parcel, which may or may not be a vineyard. It has no legal force.

LIQUOREUX: A very lush sweet wine.

MACERATION: See *cuvaison.*

MALOLACTIC FERMENTATION: The transformation of sharp malic acid (think apples) into creamier lactic acid (think milk), which normally occurs after alcoholic fermentation and which results in a less acidic wine.

MÉTHODE TRADITIONELLE: Formerly referred to as the *méthode champenoise,* this is a technique for making sparkling wine following the model of Champagne. A still wine is bottled with the addition of yeast and sugar. It undergoes a second fermentation or *prise de mousse,* during which carbonic dioxide is produced and trapped in the wine, begetting the bubbles. Using a process called riddling, the sediment produced by this second fermentation is directed to the neck of the bottle, where it will rest against the cork. Over a period of time the bottle is tilted and twisted on a specially designed A-frame rack called a *pupitre* until finally it is upside down. Disgorging is the name for the process by which the sediment is removed. To top up the bottle, producers add a syrup called a *liqueur de tirage.* The percentage of sugar in this syrup is called dosage.

MILLÉSIME: Vintage.

MOELLEUX: A term referring to sweet wines, such as those from the Loire, *moelleux* literally means "marrowy"—a wine with marrow. It can, and often is, applied to dry wines, particularly those that have aged *sur lie.*

MOUSSEUX: Sparkling wine.

MUST: Unfermented grape juice.

NÉGOCIANT: A wholesale wine merchant. The term generally refers to someone who buys grapes and/or finished wine, then ages or blends it before bottling the wine under his own label.

NOBLE ROT: See *Botrytis cinerea.*

PASSERILLÉ: A term describing raisined or shriveled grapes with sugars that have been concentrated as a result of the loss of water.

PERLANT: Describes an ever-so-slightly sparkling wine.

PÉTILLANT: A slightly sparkling wine (see Vouvray).

PHYLLOXERA: A vine louse transported from America that, between 1860 and 1890, ravaged the vineyards of France.

POURRITURE NOBLE: Noble rot. See *Botrytis cinerea.*

PRESSE: In the production of red wine the term *vin de presse,* or press wine, refers to the wine pressed from the grape solids after the major part of the wine has been drawn off (devatted). Usually quite tannic, press wine may be blended into an *assemblage* or kept apart.

PRISE DE MOUSSE: See *méthode traditionelle.*

RACKING: The siphoning of young wine from one tank (or barrel) to another in order to separate it from its lees.

RACY: A translation of the French *racé,* which basically means pedigreed, aristocratic, blue-blooded. A wine that is racy shows its superior breeding.

RESIDUAL SUGAR: The sugar left in wine after fermentation has ended or been stopped.

SEC: Dry. In Champagne, however, wines that are labeled *sec* have up to 25 grams of residual sugar per liter and so are sweeter than those labeled *brut.*

SÉLECTION DE GRAINS NOBLES: European law permits vintners to label any *vin liquoreux* as Grains Nobles. In France, some vineyard regions, such as Alsace and parts of the Loire, have adopted more stringent standards. Grapes must have the potential to achieve a level of 17.5 degrees of alcohol when picked—or possess a natural richness of 298 grams of sugar per liter. Sélection de Grains Nobles is often abbreviated as SGN or GN.

SKIN CONTACT: A method of obtaining richer flavors and texture in white wines by leaving the grapes in contact with their skins for anywhere from several hours to several days before pressing them off their skins for fermentation. (Red wines are made by fermenting the grapes with their skins.)

SULFUR: Sulfur is used in the vineyard to combat various fungi, pests, and maladies. In the cellar it cleans barrels, prevents oxidation, stuns indigenous yeasts, and arrests the fermentation of sweet wines. It is also added at bottling as a preservative. Wines with too much sulfur often smell and taste reduced—unexpressive except for a vaguely dirty aroma—until they are sufficiently aerated. Decanting is advised. See the discussion of the trend to make wines without sulfur in "Extreme Wines: The Wines of Redemption" in the Introduction.

SUR LIE: The practice of allowing a wine to rest on its lees, or dead yeast cells, as it ages. The lees sink to the bottom of the wine after alcoholic fermentation. They create amino acids that combine with polysaccharides and, despite the chemical sound, add flavor, fleshiness, and a wonderful, rich marrowy texture. By preventing oxidation, aging *sur lie* preserves a wine's breezy vitality and somehow seems to underscore the expression of *terroir.* While associated primarily with muscadet, aging *sur lie* is a method increasingly used by vintners throughout France.

TANNIN: A substance found in grape skins and stems, as well as in oak barrels, that imparts flavor and structure to a wine. It is also an antioxidant and helps the wine age. Tannic wines often taste astringent when young—think of strong tea or underripe walnuts—but become softer and rounder as the tannin precipitates when the wines age, forming part of a red wine's sediment.

TERROIR: The concept of *terroir* unites the specifics of a vineyard site, encompassing its soils, subsoils, exposure, and the opening of the countryside. When a wine expresses the specific aspects of its unique place of origin, it has a *goût de terroir.* This is a stamp of identity and an aspect of complexity. Depending upon its intensity, such a wine may be said to be *terroir*-driven.

THERMOREGULATED: Temperature controlled.

TRI: In winemaking, *tri* has two uses. A *tri* is a labor-intensive method of harvesting by successive passes through the vineyard to pick selected bunches, or grapes, at each pass, rather than harvesting all the grapes at once. And it is also the sorting of grapes once they have arrived at the winery, to discard those that have been affected by rot. The table on which this second *tri* occurs is a *table de tri,* or sorting table.

VDQS: An abbreviation for Vin Délimité de Qualité Supérieure, this is a rank for wines between that of AC and Vin de Pays. VDQS wine is produced within a designated zone according to laws regarding production that are similar to those governing an AC. Most VDQS wines have applied for promotion to AC.

VENDANGE: A harvest; a *vendange tardive* is a late harvest.

VIEILLES VIGNES: Literally "old vines," the term *vieilles vignes* has no official definition. It is abbreviated as VV.

VIGNERON: A wine grower or winemaker. When a woman, a vigneronne.

VIN DOUX NATUREL: Vin Doux Naturel, or VDN, is a fortified wine. Its fermentation is stopped by the addition of eau-de-vie or brandy, thus leaving residual sugar. Banyuls and Rivesaltes are both examples of Vin Doux Naturel.

VIN D'HONNEUR: The wine served to kick off a ceremony, for example a wedding or local fair.

VIN DE MÉDITATION: A term commonly used to describe a wine that is so fine and so complex, you don't want to pair it with food. You want to drink it all by itself and ruminate about it. It provokes thoughts that generally begin something like "To think that a cluster of grapes made this."

VIN DE PAYS: Loosely translated as "country wine," Vin de Pays is a rank beneath VDQS, and generally covers broad regions such as Vin de Pays d'Oc or Jardin de la France. It's an increasingly important category, as the rules governing it are less strict than those for AC wines and, perhaps more important, the name of the grape can be featured on the label.

VIN DE TABLE: Literally, "table wine," the term *vin de table* is generally used to describe wines not subject to any regulations.

VQPRD: Vins de Qualité Produits dans une Région Déterminée is the European Economic Community term for wines of a quality greater than that of table wine. In France, this means all AC and VDQS wines.

VINIFICATION: The process of turning grapes into wine, starting when the grapes reach the winery and ending with the bottling of the wine.

VITICULTURE: The practice and methods of grape growing.

YIELD: The amount of grapes harvested within a given vineyard area.

YEAST: The agent that provokes fermentation, yeasts can either be indigenous (wild) or created in laboratories.

SOME PERSONAL WINE TERMINOLOGY

ECO-FRIENDLY: I have generally used *eco-friendly* to indicate that the winemaker tries to respect nature and avoid using chemical treatments, and so the wine is more or less organic. A related term, widely used in France these days, is *lutte raisonnée,* which means "reasoned battle." In practice, it means as organic as the vintner in question finds it convenient to be.

HYPERNATURAL: This is an expression I came up with to describe a growing trend in viticulture and winemaking that seems to regard with suspicion any procedure that came after the Industrial Revolution. See the discussion "Extreme Wines: The Wines of Redemption" in the Introduction.

SPECIFICITY: This is a term I often use when a wine seems clearly to come from a particular place. Specificity is related to, but not entirely synonymous with, *terroir.* For example, a tasty, light red from Touraine-Amboise in the Loire might not have anything so blue-chip or blueblood as the influence of *terroir* but may very well speak of a certain time and place—it's specific. I mean this as a compliment.

WACKO WINES: Usually made by hypernatural practitioners, "wacko" wines are wines that are the results of "what if" ruminations. They push the envelope. Sometimes they are delicious as well as intriguing. Sometimes they represent ideas that should never have been put into practice. They are always interesting. Try them by the glass. (For more, see the discussion in "Extreme Wines: The Wines of Redemption" in the Introduction.)

WINESPEAK: ON AROMAS AND FLAVORS

The aromas and flavors of wine fall into nine or ten recognized groups. These have been classified by enologists, for example Émile Peynaud in his *Goût du Vin*. The groups include fairly easy associative leaps into categories like flowers (violets and roses); fruits (berries, apples, lemons, and figs); vegetables (bell peppers and green beans); and spices (cinnamon, clove, and pepper). There are also less-familiar comparative categories such as animal (visceral aromas and tastes like musk, and game); balsam (pine, cedar, eucalyptus, and mint); wood (vanilla and coconut); roasted scents (toast, coffee, crème brûlée, and leather); chemical/fermentation (yeasts, hard candy); and off-odors (rotten egg, garlic, and onion).

Some words or associations will be more meaningful than others to a given taster. Here are several descriptions I often use, some of which may seem strange or off-putting.

HERBS AND QUININE: I adore the nuances of quinine and herbal tea (*tisane* in French) and such medicinal herbs as chamomile, linden blossom (*tilleul*), and verbena (*verveine*) in wine (and in other beverages, like Schweppes Bitter Lemon and Campari). They are slightly bitter but extremely appetizing.

LACY: the French often use the word *dentelles*—lace—to describe a delicate, ethereal, very fine wine.

PITS: Many fruity red wines have a flavor reminiscent of cherry pits. While you may never have tasted cherry pits, this flavor is quite focused and succulent—mixing the flavor of the cherry with that of bitter almond. You may recognize the taste from cherry eaux-de-vie or liqueurs, since cherry pits are often macerated with the pulp in the production of fruit brandies.

PEE: Ever since I began tasting wine seriously I have felt that many sauvignon blancs had an aroma of cat's pee. As revolting as this sounds, it is not a disagreeable scent in a wine. It's a pungent vegetal aroma with a bit of something feral in it. If you've ever had a close relationship with a cat, you'll probably agree that the image is apt.

PETROL: Sounds unappetizing, too, but this aroma—and flavor—is typical in many fine rieslings (from Germany and Alsace) as well as Loire chenin blancs and sauvignon blancs.

INDEX

C

D

E

F

G

H

I

J

K

L

N

O

P

T

U

V